Poetry
for Students

Poetry for Students

Presenting Analysis, Context and Criticism on
Commonly Studied Poetry

Volume 4

Mary K. Ruby, Editor

David Kelly, College of Lake County, Advisor
Jan Mordenski, Mercy High School, Advisor

Foreword by David Kelly, College of Lake County

GALE

DETROIT · LONDON

Poetry for Students

Staff

Series Editor: Mary Ruby.

Contributing Editors: Margaret Haerens and Lynn Koch.

Managing Editor: Drew Kalasky.

Research: Victoria B. Cariappa, *Research Team Manager.* Andy Malonis, *Research Specialist.* Julia C. Daniel, Tamara C. Nott, Tracie A. Richardson, and Cheryl L. Warnock, *Research Associates.* Jeffrey Daniels, *Research Assistant.*

Permissions: Susan M. Trosky, *Permissions Manager.* Kimberly F. Smilay, *Permissions Specialist.* Kelly Quin, *Permissions Assistant.*

Production: Mary Beth Trimper, *Production Director.* Evi Seoud, *Assistant Production Manager.* Shanna Heilveil, *Production Assistant.*

Graphic Services: Randy Bassett, *Image Database Supervisor.* Robert Duncan and Michael Logusz, *Imaging Specialists.* Pamela A. Reed, *Photography Coordinator.* Gary Leach, *Macintosh Artist.*

Product Design: Cynthia Baldwin, *Product Design Manager.* Cover Design: Michelle DiMercurio, *Art Director.* Page Design: Pamela A. E. Galbreath, *Senior Art Director.*

Copyright Notice

National Advisory Board

Dale Allender: Teacher, West High School, Iowa City, Iowa.

Dana Gioia: Poet and critic. His books include *The Gods of Winter* and *Can Poetry Matter?* He currently resides in Santa Rosa, CA.

Carol Jago: Teacher, Santa Monica High School, Santa Monica, CA. Member of the California Reading and Literature Project at University of California, Los Angeles.

Bonnie J. Newcomer: English teacher, Beloit Junior-Senior High School, Beloit, Kansas. Editor of KATE UpDate, for the Kansas Association of Teachers of English. Ph.D. candidate in information science, Emporia State University, Kansas.

Katherine Nyberg: English teacher. Coordinator of the language arts department of Farmington Public Schools, Farmington, Michigan.

Nancy Rosenberger: Former English teacher and chair of English department at Conestoga High School, Berwyn, Pennsylvania.

Dorothea M. Susag: English teacher, Simms High School, Simms, Montana. Former president of the Montana Association of Teachers of English Language Arts. Member of the National Council of Teachers of English.

Table of Contents

Guest Foreword
"Just a Few Lines on a Page"
by David J. Kelly x

Introduction .xii

Literary Chronology xv

Acknowledgments xx

Contributors .xxii

Ah, Are You Digging on My Grave?
(by Thomas Hardy) 1
    Author Biography 2
    Poem Text .2
    Poem Summary 3
    Themes 4
    Style 6
    Historical Context 6
    Critical Overview 8
    Criticism .8

As I Walked Out One Evening
(by W.H. Auden) 14
    Author Biography 14
    Poem Text 15
    Poem Summary 16
    Themes .18
    Style 19
    Historical Context 19
    Critical Overview 20
    Criticism 21

Concord Hymn
(by Ralph Waldo Emerson) 29
  Author Biography 29
  Poem Text 30
  Poem Summary 30
  Themes 32
  Style 33
  Historical Context 33
  Critical Overview 35
  Criticism 36

The Death of the Hired Man
(by Robert Frost) 41
  Author Biography 42
  Poem Text 42
  Poem Summary 44
  Themes 46
  Style 47
  Historical Context 47
  Critical Overview 49
  Criticism 49

Hawk Roosting (by Ted Hughes) 53
  Author Biography 53
  Poem Text 55
  Poem Summary 55
  Themes 56
  Style 57
  Historical Context 58
  Critical Overview 59
  Criticism 60

The Highwayman (by Alfred Noyes) 65
  Author Biography 66
  Poem Text 66
  Poem Summary 68
  Themes 71
  Style 72
  Historical Context 73
  Critical Overview 74
  Criticism 74

Hunger in New York City
(by Simon Ortiz) 78
  Author Biography 79
  Poem Text 79
  Poem Summary 79
  Themes 81
  Style 82
  Historical Context 82
  Critical Overview 83
  Criticism 84

Oysters (by Anne Sexton) 90
  Author Biography 91
  Poem Text 91
  Poem Summary 91
  Themes 93
  Style 94
  Historical Context 94
  Critical Overview 95
  Criticism 96

Psalm 23 (in King James Bible) 102
  Poem Text 103
  Poem Summary 103
  Themes 104
  Style 105
  Historical Context 105
  Critical Overview 107
  Criticism 107

Richard Cory (by E. A. Robinson) 115
  Author Biography 115
  Poem Text 116
  Poem Summary 117
  Themes 118
  Style 119
  Historical Context 119
  Critical Overview 121
  Criticism 121

The Rime of the Ancient Mariner
(by Samuel Taylor Coleridge) 125
  Author Biography 126
  Poem Text 127
  Poem Summary 132
  Themes 141
  Style 144
  Historical Context 145
  Critical Overview 146
  Criticism 147

Shine, Perishing Republic
(by Robinson Jeffers) 160
  Author Biography 160
  Poem Text 161
  Poem Summary 162
  Themes 163
  Style 164
  Historical Context 165
  Critical Overview 165
  Criticism 166

Sir Patrick Spens (Anonymous) 176
  Poem Text 177
  Poem Summary 177

Themes 179
Style .180
Historical Context 180
Critical Overview 182
Criticism 182

Sonnet 30 (by William Shakespeare) 191
Author Biography 191
Poem Text 192
Poem Summary 193
Themes 194
Style .195
Historical Context 195
Critical Overview 197
Criticism 197

Strong Men, Riding Horses
(by Gwendolyn Brooks) 207
Author Biography 208
Poem Text 209
Poem Summary 209
Themes 211
Style .212
Historical Context 212
Critical Overview 213
Criticism 214

Tears, Idle Tears
(by Alfred, Lord Tennyson) 219
Author Biography 220
Poem Text 220
Poem Summary 220
Themes 222
Style .223
Historical Context 223
Critical Overview 225
Criticism 225

This Is My Letter to the World
(by Emily Dickson) 232
Author Biography 232
Poem Text 233
Poem Summary 233
Themes 234
Style .235

Historical Context 235
Critical Overview 237
Criticism 237

Toads (by Philip Larkin) 242
Author Biography 242
Poem Text 244
Poem Summary 244
Themes 246
Style .247
Historical Context 247
Critical Overview 248
Criticism 248

The Tropics in New York
(by Claude McKay) 254
Author Biography 254
Poem Text 255
Poem Summary 255
Themes 256
Style .256
Historical Context 257
Critical Overview 258
Criticism 258

When I Was One-and-Twenty
(by A. E. Housman) 266
Author Biography 266
Poem Text 268
Poem Summary 268
Themes 269
Style .270
Historical Context 271
Critical Overview 272
Criticism 273

Glossary of Literary Terms 277

Cumulative Author/Title Index 297

*Cumulative Nationality/Ethnicity
Index* 301

Subject/Theme Index 303

Just a Few Lines on a Page

I have often thought that poets have the easiest job in the world. A poem, after all, is just a few lines on a page, usually not even extending margin to margin—how long would that take to write, about five minutes? Maybe ten at the most, if you wanted it to rhyme or have a repeating meter. Why, I could start in the morning and produce a book of poetry by dinnertime. But we all know that it isn't that easy. Anyone can come up with enough words, but the poet's job is about writing the *right* ones. The right words will change lives, making people see the world somewhat differently than they saw it just a few minutes earlier. The right words can make a reader who relies on the dictionary for meanings take a greater responsibility for his or her own personal understanding. A poem that is put on the page correctly can bear any amount of analysis, probing, defining, explaining, and interrogating, and something about it will still feel new the next time you read it.

It would be fine with me if I could talk about poetry without using the word "magical," because that word is overused these days to imply "a really good time," often with a certain sweetness about it, and a lot of poetry is neither of these. But if you stop and think about magic—whether it brings to mind sorcery, witchcraft, or bunnies pulled from top hats—it always seems to involve stretching reality to produce a result greater than the sum of its parts and pulling unexpected results out of thin air. This book provides ample cases where a few simple words conjure up whole worlds. We do not ac-

tually travel to different times and different cultures, but the poems get into our minds, they find what little we know about the places they are talking about, and then they make that little bit blossom into a bouquet of someone else's life. Poets make us think we are following simple, specific events, but then they leave ideas in our heads that cannot be found on the printed page. Abracadabra.

Sometimes when you finish a poem it doesn't feel as if it has left any supernatural effect on you, like it did not have any more to say beyond the actual words that it used. This happens to everybody, but most often to inexperienced readers: regardless of what is often said about young people's infinite capacity to be amazed, you have to understand what usually does happen, and what could have happened instead, if you are going to be moved by what someone has accomplished. In those cases in which you finish a poem with a "So what?" attitude, the information provided in *Poetry for Students* comes in handy. Readers can feel assured that the poems included here actually are potent magic, not just because a few (or a hundred or ten thousand) professors of literature say they are: they're significant because they can withstand close inspection and still amaze the very same people who have just finished taking them apart and seeing how they work. Turn them inside out, and they will still be able to come alive, again and again. *Poetry for Students* gives readers of any age good practice in feeling the ways poems relate to both the reality of the time and place the poet lived in and the reality of our emotions. Practice is just another word for being a student. The information given here helps you understand the way to read poetry; what to look for, what to expect.

With all of this in mind, I really don't think I would actually like to have a poet's job at all. There are too many skills involved, including precision, honesty, taste, courage, linguistics, passion, compassion, and the ability to keep all sorts of people entertained at once. And that is just what they do with one hand, while the other hand pulls some sort of trick that most of us will never fully understand. I can't even pack all that I need for a weekend into one suitcase, so what would be my chances of stuffing so much life into a few lines? With all that *Poetry for Students* tells us about each poem, I am impressed that any poet can finish three or four poems a year. Read the inside stories of these poems, and you won't be able to approach any poem in the same way you did before.

David J. Kelly
College of Lake County

Introduction

Purpose of the Book

The purpose of *Poetry for Students* (*PfS*) is to provide readers with a guide to understanding, enjoying, and studying poems by giving them easy access to information about the work. Part of Gale's "For Students" Literature line, *PfS* is specifically designed to meet the curricular needs of high school and undergraduate college students and their teachers, as well as the interests of general readers and researchers considering specific poems. While each volume contains entries on "classic" poems frequently studied in classrooms, there are also entries containing hard-to-find information on contemporary poems, including works by multicultural, international, and women poets.

The information covered in each entry includes an introduction to the poem and the poem's author; the actual poem text; a poem summary, to help readers unravel and understand the meaning of the poem; analysis of important themes in the poem; and an explanation of important literary techniques and movements as they are demonstrated in the poem.

In addition to this material, which helps the readers analyze the poem itself, students are also provided with important information on the literary and historical background informing each work. This includes a historical context essay, a box comparing the time or place the poem was written to modern Western culture, a critical overview essay, and excerpts from critical essays on the poem, when available. A unique feature of *PfS* is a specially commissioned overview essay on each poem by an academic expert, targeted toward the student reader.

To further aid the student in studying and enjoying each poem, information on media adaptations is provided when available, as well as reading suggestions for works of fiction and nonfiction on similar themes and topics. Classroom aids include ideas for research papers and lists of critical sources that provide additional material on the poem.

Selection Criteria

The titles for each volume of *PfS* were selected by surveying numerous sources on teaching literature and analyzing course curricula for various school districts. Some of the sources surveyed included: literature anthologies; *Reading Lists for College-Bound Students: The Books Most Recommended by America's Top Colleges;* textbooks on teaching the poem; a College Board survey of poems commonly studied in high schools; and a National Council of Teachers of English (NCTE) survey of poems commonly studied in high schools.

Input was also solicited from our expert advisory board, as well as educators from various areas. From these discussions, it was determined that each volume should have a mix of "classic" poems (those works commonly taught in literature classes) and contemporary poems for which information is often hard to find. Because of the interest in expanding the canon of literature, an emphasis was also placed on including works by international, multicultural, and women authors. Our advisory board members—current high school and college teachers—helped pare down the list for each volume. If a work was not selected for the present volume, it was often noted as a possibility for a future volume. As always, the editor welcomes suggestions for titles to be included in future volumes.

How Each Entry Is Organized

Each entry, or chapter, in *PfS* focuses on one poem. Each entry heading lists the full name of the poem, the author's name, and the date of the poem's publication. The following elements are contained in each entry:

- **Introduction:** a brief overview of the poem which provides information about its first appearance, its literary standing, any controversies surrounding the work, and major conflicts or themes within the work.

- **Author Biography:** this section includes basic facts about the poet's life, and focuses on events and times in the author's life that inspired the poem in question.

- **Poem Text:** when permission has been granted, the poem is reprinted, allowing for quick reference when reading the explication of the following section. Line numbers, in increments of five, are also included as an aid for readers.

- **Poem Summary:** a description of the major events in the poem, with interpretation of how these events help articulate the poem's themes. Summaries are broken down with subheads that indicate the lines being discussed.

- **Themes:** a thorough overview of how the major topics, themes, and issues are addressed within the poem. Each theme discussed appears in a separate subhead and is easily accessed through the boldface entries in the Subject/ Theme Index.

- **Style:** this section addresses important style elements of the poem, such as form, meter, and rhyme scheme; important literary devices used, such as imagery, foreshadowing, and symbolism; and, if applicable, genres to which the work might have belonged, such as Gothicism or Romanticism. Literary terms are explained within the entry, but can also be found in the Glossary.

- **Historical and Cultural Context:** This section outlines the social, political, and cultural climate *in which the author lived and the poem was created.* This section may include descriptions of related historical events, pertinent aspects of daily life in the culture, and the artistic and literary sensibilities of the time in which the work was written. If the poem is a historical work, information regarding the time in which the poem is set is also included. Each section is broken down with helpful subheads. (Works written after the late 1970s may not have this section.)

- **Critical Overview:** this section provides background on the critical reputation of the poem, including bannings or any other public controversies surrounding the work. For older works, this section includes a history of how poem was first received and how perceptions of it may have changed over the years; for more recent poems, direct quotes from early reviews may also be included.

- **Sources:** an alphabetical list of critical material quoted in the entry, with full bibliographical information.

- **For Further Study:** an alphabetical list of other critical sources which may prove useful for the student. Includes full bibliographical information and a brief annotation.

- **Criticism:** at least one essay commissioned by *PfS* which specifically deals with the poem and is written specifically for the student audience, as well as excerpts from previously published criticism on the work, when available.

In addition, most entries contains the following highlighted sections, set separately from the main text:

- **Media Adaptations:** a list of audio recordings as well as any film or television adaptations of the poem, including source information.

- **Compare and Contrast Box:** an "at-a-glance" comparison of the cultural and historical differences between the author's time and culture and late twentieth-century Western culture. This box includes pertinent parallels between the major scientific, political, and cultural movements of the time or place the poem was written, the time or place the poem was set (if a historical work), and modern Western culture. Works written after the mid-1970s may not have this box.

- **What Do I Read Next?:** a list of works that might complement the featured poem or serve as a contrast to it. This includes works by the same author and others, works of fiction and nonfiction, and works from various genres, cultures, and eras.

- **Study Questions:** a list of potential study questions or research topics dealing with the poem. This section includes questions related to other disciplines the student may be studying, such as American history, world history, science, math, government, business, geography, economics, psychology, etc.

Other Features

PfS includes a foreword by David J. Kelly, an instructor and cofounder of the creative writing periodical of Oakton Community College. This essay provides a straightforward, unpretentious explanation of why poetry should be marveled at and how *Poetry for Students* can help teachers show students how to enrich their own reading experiences.

A Cumulative Author/Title Index lists the authors and titles covered in each volume of the *PfS* series.

A Cumulative Nationality/Ethnicity Index breaks down the authors and titles covered in each volume of the *PfS* series by nationality and ethnicity.

A Subject/Theme Index, specific to each volume, provides easy reference for users who may be studying a particular subject or theme rather than a single work. Significant subjects from events to broad themes are included, and the entries pointing to the specific theme discussions in each entry are indicated in **boldface**.

Illustrations are included with entries when available, including photos of the author and other graphics related to the poem.

Citing Poetry for Students

When writing papers, students who quote directly from any volume of *Poetry for Students* may use the following general forms. These examples are based on MLA style; teachers may request that students adhere to a different style, so the following examples may be adapted as needed.

When citing text from *PfS* that is not attributed to a particular author (i.e., the Themes, Style, Historical Context sections, etc.), the following format should be used in the bibliography section:

"Angle of Geese." *Poetry for Students.* Eds. Marie Napierkowski and Mary Ruby. Vol. 1. Detroit: Gale, 1997. 8–9.

When quoting the specially commissioned essay from *PfS* (usually the first piece under the "Criticism" subhead), the following format should be used:

Velie, Alan. Essay on "Angle of Geese."*Poetry for Students.* Eds. Marie Napierkowski and Mary Ruby. Vol. 1. Detroit: Gale, 1997. 8–9.

When quoting a journal or newspaper essay that is reprinted in a volume of *PfS,* the following form may be used:

Luscher, Robert M. "An Emersonian Context of Dickinson's 'The Soul Selects Her Own Society.'" *ESQ: A Journal of American Renaissance* 30, No. 2 (Second Quarterl, 1984), 111–16; excerpted and reprinted in *Poetry for Students,* Vol. 2, eds. Marie Napierkowski and Mary Ruby (Detroit: Gale, 1997), pp. 120–34.

When quoting material reprinted from a book that appears in a volume of *PfS,* the following form may be used:

Mootry, Maria K. "'Tell It Slant': Disguise and Discovery as Revisionist Poetic Discourse in 'The Bean Eaters,'" in *A Life Distilled: Gwendolyn Brroks, Her Poetry and Fiction,* edited by Maria K. Mootry and Gary Smith (University of Illinois Press, 1987, 177–80; excerpted and reprinted in *Poetry for Students,* Vol. 1, Eds. Marie Napierkowski and Mary Ruby (Detroit: Gale, 1997), pp. 59–61.

We Welcome Your Suggestions

The editors of *Poetry for Students* welcome your comments and ideas. Readers who wish to suggest poems to appear in future volumes, or who have other suggestions, are cordially invited to contact the editor. You may write to the editor at:

Editor, *Poetry for Students*
Gale Research
27500 Drake Rd.
Farmington Hills, MI 48331–3535

Literary Chronology

ca. 970 B.C: Psalm 23 is believed to have been written at this time.

ca. 700: *Beowulf* is composed at about this time.

1300–1699: Humanism as a philosophical view of the world is prevalent in this period.

1300–1699: The Renaissance begins in the 14th century and continues for the next 300 years.

1558–1603: The Elizabethan Age begins with the coronation in 1558 of Elizabeth I as Queen of England and continues until her death in 1603. Elizabethan literature is recognized as some of the finest in the English language.

1564: William Shakespeare is born in Stratford-upon-Avon.

1575–1799: The literary style known as Baroque arises in the late 16th century and remains influential until the early 18th century.

1600–1625: The Tribe of Ben, followers of Ben Jonson, were active in the early part of the 17th century.

1600–1799: The Enlightenment period in European social and cultural history begins in the 17th century and continues into the 18th century.

1600–1650: Metaphysical poetry becomes a prominent style of verse in the first half of the 17th century.

1603–1625: The Jacobean Age begins with the coronation in 1603 of James I of England and continues until his death in 1625.

1609: William Shakespeare's "Sonnet 30" is published in his collection *Shake-speare's Sonnets*.

1611: An English translation of Psalm 23 is published in the King James version of the Bible.

1616: William Shakespeare dies in Stratford and is buried in the chancel of Trinity Church.

1625–1649: The Cavalier Poets, a group of writers that includes Robert Herrick, Richard Lovelace, and John Suckling, are active during the reign of Charles I of England (1625–1649).

1660–1688: The Restoration Period begins when Charles II regains the throne of England, and it continues through the reign of his successor, James II (1685–1688). Restoration literature includes the first well-developed English-language works in several forms of writing that would become widespread in the modern world, including the novel, biography, and travel literature.

1675–1799: Neoclassicism as the prevailing approach to literature begins late in the 17th century and continues through much of the 18th century.

1700–1799: The English Augustan Age (the name is borrowed from a brilliant period of literary creativity in ancient Rome) flourishes throughout much of the 18th century.

1700–1725: The Scottish Enlightenment, a period of great literary and philosophical activity, occurs in the early part of the 18th century.

1740s–1775: Pre-Romanticism, a transitional literary movement between Neoclassicism and Romanticism, takes place in the middle part of the 18th century.

1740s–1750s: The Graveyard School, referring to poetry that focuses on death and grieving, emerges as a significant genre in the middle of the 18th century.

1750–1899: The Welsh Literary Renaissance, an effort to revive interest in Welsh language and literature, begins in the middle of the 18th century and continues into the following century.

1765: The anonymous ballad "Sir Patrick Spens" is published in *Reliques of Ancient English Poetry*, edited by Thomas Percy.

1772: Samuel Taylor Coleridge is born in the village of Ottery Saint Mary, Devonshire, England.

1775–1850: Romanticism as a literary movement arises in the latter part of the 18th century and continues until the middle of the 19th century.

1798: Samuel Taylor Coleridge's "The Rime of the Ancient Mariner" is published in the collection *Lyrical Ballads*, a collaboration with William Wordsworth.

1800–1899: The Gaelic Revival, a renewal of interest in Irish literature and language, takes place throughout much of the 19th century.

1803: Ralph Waldo Emerson is born in Boston, Massachusetts.

1809–1865: The Knickerbocker School, a group of American writers determined to establish New York as a literary center, flourishes between 1809 and 1865.

1809: Alfred, Lord Tennyson is born in Somersby, Lincolnshire, England.

1817: Samuel Taylor Coleridge's poem "Rime of the Ancient Mariner" is published in his collection *Sibylline Leaves*, revised and with a marginal gloss.

1830s–1860s: The flowering of American literature known as the American Renaissance begins in the 1830s and continues through the Civil War period.

1830–1855: Transcendentalism, an American philosophical and literary movement, is at its height during this period.

1830: Emily Dickinson is born in Amherst, Massachusetts.

1834: Samuel Taylor Coleridge dies from complications stemming from his opium addiction.

1837–1901: The Victorian Age begins with the coronation of Victoria as Queen of England, and continues until her death in 1901. Victorian literature is recognized for its magnificent achievements in a variety of genre s.

1840: Thomas Hardy is born in Higher Bockhampton, Dorset, England.

1847: Ralph Waldo Emerson's poem "Concord Hymn" is published in his collection *Poems*.

1847: Alfred, Lord Tennyson's poem "Tears, Idle Tears" is published as part of his long poem *The Princess: A Medley*.

1848–1858: The Pre-Raphaelites, an influential group of English painters, forms in 1848 and remains together for about ten years, during which time it has a significant impact on literature as well as the visual arts.

1850: The poets of the so-called Spasmodic School are active in the 1850s.

1850: Alfred, Lord Tennyson is named Poet Laureate of England.

1859: A. E. Housman is born in Fockbury, Worcestershire, England.

ca. 1862: Emily Dickinson's poem "This Is My Letter to the World" is believed to be written at this time.

1869: Edward Arlington Robinson is born in Head Tide, Maine.

1874: Robert Frost is born in San Francisco, California.

1875–1899: Aestheticism becomes a significant artistic and literary philosophy in the latter part of the 19th century.

1875–1899: Decadence becomes an important poetic force late in the 19th century.

1875–1925: Expressionism is a significant artistic and literary influence through the late 19th century and the early 20th century.

1875–1925: The Irish Literary Renaissance begins late in the 19th century and continues for the next several decades.

1875–1925: The Symbolist Movement flourishes in the closing decades of the 19th century and the opening years of the 20th century.

1875–1950: Realism as an approach to literature gains importance in the 19th century and remains influential well into the 20th century.

1880: Alfred Noyes is born in Wolverhampton, England, on September 16.

1882: Ralph Waldo Emerson dies in Concord, Massachusetts.

1886: Emily Dickinson dies.

1887: Robinson Jeffers is born in Pittsburgh, Pennsylvania.

1889: Claude McKay is born in Sunny Ville, Jamaica.

1890–1899: The decade of the 1890s, noted for the mood of weariness and pessimism in its art and literature, is known as the Fin de Siècle ("end of the century") period.

1890: Emily Dickinson's poem "This Is My Letter to the World" is published posthumously, in the collection *Poems by Emily Dickinson*.

1892: Alfred, Lord Tennyson dies in southeast England and is buried in Poet's Corner in Westminister Abbey.

1896: A. E. Housman's poem "When I Was One-and-Twenty" is published in his collection, *A Shropshire Lad*.

1897: Edward Arlington Robinson's poem "Richard Cory" is published in his collection *The Children of the Night*.

1900–1999: The philosophy of Existentialism and the literature it inspires are highly influential throughout much of the 20th century.

1900–1950: Modernism remains a dominant literary force from the early part to the middle years of the 20th century.

1904: Alfred Noyes writes his poem "The Highwayman".

1907–ca. 1930: The Bloomsbury Group, a circle of English writers and artists, gathers regularly in the period from 1907 to around 1930.

1907: W. H. Auden is born in York, England.

1907: Alfred Noyes's poem "The Highwayman" is published in *Forty Singing Seamen and Other Poems*.

1910s–1920s: Georgian poetry becomes a popular style of lyric verse during the reign of King George V of England.

1910s–1930s: New Humanism, a philosophy of literature, is influential for several decades, beginning around 1910.

1912–1925: The Chicago Literary Renaissance, a time of great literary activity, takes place from about 1912 to 1925.

1912–1922: Imagism as a philosophy of poetry is defined in 1912 and remains influential for the next decade.

1913: Thomas Hardy's poem "Ah, Are You Digging on My Grave?" is published in his collection *Satires of Circumstance: Lyrics and Reveries with Miscellaneous Pieces*.

1914: Robert Frost's poem "The Death of the Hired Man" is published in his collection *North of Boston* .

1917: Gwendolyn Brooks is born in Topeka, Kansas.

ca. 1919–ca. 1960: The Scottish Renaissance in literature begins around 1919 and continues for about forty years.

1920: The Harlem Renaissance, a flowering of African American literary activity, takes place.

1920s–1930s: The label Lost Generation is applied to a generation of American writers working in the decades following World War I.

1920s–1930s: The Montreal Group, a circle of Canadian poets interested in dealing with complex metaphysical issues, begins in the late 1920s and flourishes for the next decade.

1920s–1970s: New Criticism as a philosophy of literature arises in the 1920s and continues to be a significant approach to writing for over fifty years.

1920s–1960s: Surrealism, an artistic and literary technique, arises in the 1920s and remains influential for the next half century.

1922: Philip Larkin born in Coventry, Warkwickshire, England, on August 9

1922: Edward Arlington Robinson is awarded the Pulitzer Prize for his *Collected Poems*.

1922: Claude McKay's poem "The Tropics in New York" is published in *Harlem Shadows: The Poems of Claude McKay*.

1924: Robert Frost is awarded the Pulitzer Prize in poetry for his collection *New Hampshire*.

1925: Edward Arlington Robinson is awarded the Pulitzer Prize in poetry for his *The Man Who Died Twice*.

1925: Robinson Jeffers's poem "Shine, Perishing Republic" is published in his collection *Roan Stallion, Tamar, and Other Poems*.

1928: Upon his death, Thomas Hardy is given a public funeral and his ashes are buried in Poet's Corner of Westminster Abbey, London.

1928: Anne Sexton is born in Newton, Massachusetts.

1928: Edward Arlington Robinson is awarded the Pulitzer Prize for poetry for his collection *Tristram*.

1930s–1965: Negritude emerges as a literary movement in the 1930s and continues until the early 1960s.

1930s–1970s: The New York Intellectuals, a group of literary critics, are active from the 1930s to the 1970s.

1930: Ted Hughes is born in Mytholomroyd, Yorkshire, England, on August 17.

1931: Robert Frost is awarded the Pulitzer Prize in poetry for his *Collected Poems.*

1935–1943: The Works Progress Administration (WPA) Federal Writers' Project provides federally funded jobs for unemployed writers during the Great Depression.

1935: Edward Arlington Robinson dies of cancer.

1936: A. E. Housman dies.

1937: Robert Frost is awarded the Pulitzer Prize in poetry for his collection *A Further Range.*

1940: The New Apocalypse Movement, founded by J. F. Hendry and Henry Treece, takes place in England in the 1940s.

1940s: Postmodernism, referring to the various philosophies and practices of literature that challenge the dominance of Modernism, begins in the 1940s.

1940: W. H. Auden's poem "As I Walked Out One Evening" is published in the collection *In Another Time.*

1941: Simon Ortiz is born at the Pueblo of Acoma in New Mexico.

1943: Robert Frost is awarded the Pulitzer Prize in poetry for his collection *A Witness Tree.*

1948: W. H. Auden is awarded the Pulitzer Prize in poetry for his collection *The Age of Anxiety.*

1948: Claude McKay dies of heart failure in Chicago on May 22 and is buried in New York City.

1950: The so-called Beat Movement writers begin publishing their work in the 1950s.

1950: The Black Mountain Poets, emphasizing the creative process, become an influential force in American literature in the 1950s.

1950–1975: Structuralism emerges as an important movement in literary criticism in the middle of the 20th century.

1950: Gwendolyn Brooks is awarded the Pulitzer Prize in poetry for her collection *Annie Allen.*

1955: Philip Larkin's poem "Toads" is published in his collection *The Less Deceived.*

1958–1959: Robert Frost serves as Consultant in Poetry to the Library of Congress.

1958: Alfred Noyes dies on June 23.

1960s–1970s: The Black Aesthetic Movement, also known as the Black Arts Movement, takes place from the 1960s into the 1970s.

1960s–1999: Poststructuralism arises as a theory of literary criticism in the 1960s.

1960: Gwendolyn Brooks's poem "Strong Men, Riding Horses" is published in her collection *The Bean Eaters* .

1960: Ted Hughes's poem "Hawk Roosting" is published in his collection *Lupercal.*

1962: Robinson Jeffers dies in Carmel, California.

1963: Robert Frost dies in Boston.

1967: Anne Sexton is awarded the Pulitzer Prize for poetry for her collection *Live or Die.*

1970s–1999: New Historicism, a school of literary analysis, originates in the 1970s.

1972: Anne Sexton's poem "Oysters" is published in her collection *The Book of Folly.*

1973: W. H. Auden dies while on a trip to Vienna, and is subsequently buried in Poet's Corner of Westminster Abbey.

1974: Anne Sexton dies of carbon monoxide poisoning.

1976: Simon Ortiz's poem "Hunger in New York City" is published in his collection *Going for the Rain.*

1984: Ted Hughes is named Poet Laureate of England.

1985–1986: Gwendolyn Brooks serves as Poet Laureate for the United States.

1985: Philip Larkin dies soon after an operation for throat cancer.

1996: *United States of Poetry*, a soundtrack mingling spoken word poetry of writers from Allen Ginsberg to Ai with music samples and "found poetry," premieres on PBS.

1996: Jorie Graham is awarded the Pulitzer Prize in poetry for the collection *The Dream of the Unified Field.*

1997: Lisel Mueller is awarded the Pulitzer Prize in poetry for her collection *Alive Together: New and Selected Poems*.

1997: Robert Pinsky serves as Poet Laureate of the United States.

1998: Ted Hughes's collection of verse *Birthday Letters* is published; the poems address his past marriage to poet Sylvia Plath.

1998: Charles Wright is awarded the Pulitzer Prize in poetry for his collection *Black Zodiac*.

Acknowledgments

The editors wish to thank the copyright holders of the excerpted criticism included in this volume and the permissions managers of many book and magazine publishing companies for assisting us in securing reproduction rights. We are also grateful to the staffs of the Detroit Public Library, the Library of Congress, the University of Detroit Mercy Library, Wayne State University Purdy/ Kresge Library Complex, and the University of Michigan Libraries for making their resources available to us. Following is a list of the copyright holders who have granted us permission to reproduce material in this volume of **PFS**. Every effort has been made to trace copyright, but if omissions have been made, please let us know.

COPYRIGHTED EXCERPTS IN *PFS*, VOLUME 4, WERE REPRODUCED FROM THE FOLLOWING PERIODICALS:

CLA Journal, v. XXXIV, September, 1990. Copyright (c) 1990 by The College Language Association. Used by permission of The College Language Association.—*The Journal of Religious Thought* , v, 52, Summer/Fall, 1995. Reproduced by permission.—*Modern Language Quarterly*, v. 38, March, 1977. (c) 1977 University of Washington. Reproduced by permission of Duke University Press.—*Southern Folklore Quarterly*, v. 44, 1980. Reproduced by permission of The University Press of Kentucky.—*Victorian Poetry* , v. 30, Autumn-Winter, 1992 for "Temporal Topographies: Tennyson's Tears" by J. Hillis Miller. Reproduced by permission of the author.

COPYRIGHTED EXCERPTS IN *PFS,* VOLUME 4, WERE REPRODUCED FROM THE FOLLOWING BOOKS:

Auden, W. H. From "As I Walked out One Evening" in **W. H. Auden: Collected Poems by W. H. Auden**. Edited by Edward Mendelson. Random House, 1940. Copyright 1940 and renewed 1968 by W. H. Auden. Reproduced by permission of Random House, Inc. In the British Commonwealth by Faber & Faber Limited.—Highet, Gilbert. From "An American Poet" in *People, Places and Books* . Oxford University Press, 1953. All rights reserved. Reproduced by permission of Oxford University Press, Inc.—Hughes, Ted. From "Hawk Roosting" in *Lupercal*. Faber and Faber, 1960. Reproduced by permission.—Jeffers, Robinson. From "Shine, Perishing Republic" in *Selected Poems*. By Robinson Jeffers. Vintage Books, 1965. Copyright 1925 and renewed 1953 by Robinson Jeffers. Reproduced by permission of Random House, Inc.—Juhasz, Suzanne. From "Seeking the Exit or the Home: Poetry and Salvation in the Center of Anne Sexton" in *Shakespeare's Sisters: Feminist Essays on Women Poets.* Edited by Sandra M. Gilbert and Susan Gubar. Indiana University Press, 1979. Copyright (c) 1979 by Sandra M. Gilbert and Susan Gubar. All rights reserved. Reproduced by permission.—Krieger, Murray. *From A Window to Criticism: Shakespeare's Sonnets and Modern Poetics*. Princeton University Press, 1964. Copyright (c) 1964, renewed 1992 by Princeton University Press. Reproduced by permission of Princeton University Press.—Marcus, Mordecai. From *The Poems of Robert Frost*. G. K. Hall & Co., 1991. Copyright 1991 by Mordecai Marcus. All rights reserved. Reproduced by permission of G. K. Hall & Co., an imprint of Simon & Schuster Macmillan.—Ortiz, Simon. For "Hunger in New York City" in *Going For the Rain: Poems*. Harper & Row, 1976. Reproduced by permission of the author.—Sexton, Anne. For "Oysters" in *The Book of Folly*. Houghton Mifflin Company, 1972. Copyright (c) 1972 by Anne Sexton. Reproduced by permission of Sterling Lord Literistic, Inc.

PHOTOGRAPHS AND ILLUSTRATIONS APPEARING IN *PFS*, VOLUME 4, WERE RECEIVED FROM THE FOLLOWING SOURCES:

Auden, W. H., photograph. Corbis-Bettmann. Reproduced by permission.—Brooks, Gwendolyn, photograph. AP/Wide World Photos, Inc. Reproduced by permission.—Coleridge, Samuel Taylor, photograph. The Library of Congress.—Dickinson, Emily, photograph of a painting. The Library of Congress.—Emerson, Ralph Waldo, engraving by S.A. Choff c1878. The Library of Congress.—From an illustration for Samuel Taylor Coleridge's "The Rime of the Ancient Mariner" illustrated by Gustave Dore. Dover Publications, 1970. Copyright (c) 1970 by Dover Publications, Inc. All rights reserved. Reproduced by permission of the publisher.—From an illustration for Samuel Taylor Coleridge's "The Rime of the Ancient Mariner" illustrated by Gustave Dore. Dover Publications, 1970. Copyright (c) 1970 by Dover Publications, Inc. All rights reserved. Reproduced by permission of the publisher.—From an illustration for Samuel Taylor Coleridge's "The Rime of the Ancient Mariner" illustrated by Gustave Dore. Dover Publications, 1970. Copyright (c) 1970 by Dover Publications, Inc. All rights reserved. Reproduced by permission of the publisher.—From an illustration for Samuel Taylor Coleridge's "The Rime of the Ancient Mariner" illustrated by Gustave Dore. Dover Publications, 1970. Copyright (c) 1970 by Dover Publications, Inc. All rights reserved. Reproduced by permission of the publisher.—Frost, Robert (hands resting on thighs, pen in left breast pocket), photograph. The Library of Congress.—Hardy, Thomas, photograph. Corbis-Bettmann. Reproduced by permission. Housman, A. E., photograph. Archive Photos, Inc. Reproduced by permission.—Hughes, Ted, photograph. AP/Wide World Photos. Reproduced by permission.—Jeffers, Robinson, photograph. The Library of Congress.—Larkin, Philip (seated in chair), painting by Humphrey Ocean. National Portrait Gallery, London. Reproduced by permission.—McKay, Claude, photograph. The Library of Congress.—Noyes, Alfred, photograph. The Library of Congress.—Ortiz, Simon J., photograph by Nancy Crampton. (c) Nancy Crampton. Reproduced by permission.—Robinson, Edwin Arlington, photograph. AP/Wide World Photos. Reproduced by permission.—Sexton, Anne, photograph. AP/Wide World Photos. Reproduced by permission.—Shakespeare, William photograph of a illustration. Archive Photos, Inc. Reproduced by permission.—Tennyson, Alfred, Lord, photograph of illustration. The Library of Congress.

Contributors

Gerald E. Brennan: Gerald E. Brennan lives in Arcata, California, where he is completing a book about William Burroughs's *Naked Lunch*. He is the former editor of the bowling journal *Hare Lip*. Entries on *"Ah, Are You Digging on My Grave?"; The Highwayman; Psalm 23; The Rime of the Ancient Mariner;* and *Sir Patrick Spens*.

Brent Goodman: Brent Goodman is currently working as a business and freelance writer in Madison, Wisconsin. He earned an MFA in creative writing from Purdue University and has taught undergraduate and high school poetry workshops. Goodman is the former poetry editor of *Sycamore Review* and has had poems published in *Poetry, Passages North, Green Mountain Review,* and *Puerto del Sol*. Entries on *As I Walked Out One Evening; The Death of the Hired Man; Hawk Roosting; Hunger in New York City, Oysters; Shine, Perishing Republic; Sonnet 30; Strong Men, Riding Horses; This Is My Letter to the World; Toads;* and *The Tropics in New York*.

Jhan Hochman: Jhan Hochman is a writer and instructor at Portland Community College in Portland, Oregon. He is the author of *Green Cultural Studies: Nature in Film, Novel and Theory,* 1998. Original essays on *"Ah, Are You Digging on My Grave?"; The Death of the Hired Man; Hawk Roosting; Psalm 23; The Rime of the Ancient Mariner; Sir Patrick Spens; Sonnet 30; Toads;* and *When I Was One-and-Twenty*.

Jeannine Johnson: Jeannine Johnson is a writer who has taught at Yale University. Original essay on *As I Walked Out One Evening*.

David Kelly: David Kelly is a writer and instructor at Oakton Community College, in Des Plaines, Illinois. He is the cofounder of a creative writing periodical at Oakton Community College and has a novel in progress. Entries on *Concord Hymn; Richard Cory; Tears, Idle Tears* and *When I Was One-and-Twenty*. Original essays on *"Ah, Are You Digging on My Grave?"; Richard Cory;* and *The Tropics in New York*.

Carolyn Meyer: Carolyn Meyer holds a Ph.D. in Irish and British Literature from McMaster University and has taught modern and contemporary literature at the University of Toronto and Mt. Allison University. Her articles on contemporary Irish poetry include "Orthodoxy, Independence, and Influence in Seamus Heaney's *Station Island*," reprinted in *Critical Essays on Seamus Heaney,* edited by Robert F. Garratt, G.K. Hall, 1995. She is the coeditor of *Separate Islands: Contemporary Irish and British Poetry,* 1990. Original essay on *Sir Patrick Spens*.

Bruce Meyer: Bruce Meyer is director of the creative writing program at the University of Toronto's School of Continuing Studies. He is the author of 14 books, including the poetry collections *The Open Room, Radio Silence,* and *The*

Presence. Orginal essays on *As I Walked Out One Evening, Sonnet 30,* and *Toads.*

Marisa Anne Pagnattaro: Marisa Anne Pagnattaro is a writer and teaching assistant at the University of Georgia in Athens. She is the book review editor and editorial board member of the *Georgia Bar Journal.* Pagnattaro is currently writing a dissertation on women, justice, and American literature. Original essay on *Strong Men, Riding Horses.*

Sean K. Robisch: Sean K. Robisch teaches composition and literature at Purdue University and holds a Ph.D. in American literature. His fiction has appeared in *Hopewell Review* and *Puerto del Sol.* He lives in Indiana with his wife, fiction writer Patricia Henley. Original essays on *Hawk Roosting; Hunger in New York City;* and *Shine, Perishing Republic.*

David J. Rothman: David J. Rothman is executive director of the Robinson Jeffers Association; executive director of the Western Slope Summer Music Festival; and Headmaster of Crested Butte Academy, a private secondary school in Crested Butte, Colorado, where he lives with his wife and family. He is the author of several books of poetry and coauthor with Steven Powers and his father, Stanley Rothman, of *Hollywood's America: Social and Political Themes in Motion Pictures.* His poetry, essays, and journalism have appeared in hundreds of journals and books. Original essay on *Shine, Perishing Republic.*

Chris Semansky: Chris Semansky holds a Ph.D. in English from Stony Brook University and teaches writing and literature at Portland Community College in Portland, Oregon. His collection of poems *Death, But at a Good Price* received the Nicholas Roerich Poetry Prize for 1991 and was published by Story Line Press and the Nicholas Roerich Museum. Semansky's most recent collection, *Blindsided,* has been published by 26 Books of Portland, Oregon. Original essays on *Concord Hymn; The Highwayman; Hunger in New York City; Oysters; Strong Men, Riding Horses; Tears, Idle Tears; This Is My Letter to the World;* and *The Tropics in New York.*

Aidan Wasley: Aidan Wasley is a writer and instructor at Yale University in New Haven, Connecticut. Original essay on *As I Walked Out One Evening.*

Ah, Are You Digging on My Grave?

Thomas Hardy
1913

"Ah, Are You Digging On My Grave?" was first published in the *Saturday Review* on September 27, 1913, then in Thomas Hardy's 1914 collection, *Satires of Circumstance: Lyrics and Reveries with Miscellaneous Pieces.* The poem reflects Hardy's interest in death and events beyond everyday reality, but these subjects are presented humorously, with a strong dose of irony and satire. This treatment is somewhat unusual for Hardy, who also produced a number of more serious poems concerning death. In "Ah, Are You Digging On My Grave?" a deceased woman carries on a dialogue with an individual who is disturbing her grave site. The identity of this figure, the "digger" of the woman's grave, is unknown through the first half of the poem. As the woman attempts to guess who the digger is, she reveals her desire to be remembered by various figures she was acquainted with when she was alive. In a series of ironic turns, the responses of the digger show that the woman's acquaintances—a "loved one," family relatives, and a despised enemy—have all forsaken her memory. Finally, it is revealed that the digger is the woman's dog, but the canine, too, is unconcerned with his former mistress and is digging only so it can bury a bone. Though the poem contains a humorous tone, the picture Hardy paints is bleak; the dead are almost completely eliminated from the memory of the living and do not enjoy any form of contentment. This somber outlook is typical of Hardy's verse, which often presented a skeptical and negative view of the human condition.

Thomas Hardy

Author Biography

Hardy was born in 1840 and raised in the region of Dorsetshire, England, the basis for the Wessex countryside that would later appear in his fiction and poetry. He attended a local school until he was sixteen, when his mother paid a substantial amount of money for him to be apprenticed to an architect in Dorchester. In 1862 he moved to London, where he worked as an architect, remaining there for a period of five years. Between 1865 and 1867 Hardy wrote many poems, none of which were published. In 1867 he returned to Dorchester and, while continuing to work in architecture, began to write novels in his spare time. Hardy became convinced that if he was to make a living writing, he would have to do so as a novelist. Drawing on the way of life he absorbed in Dorsetshire as a youth and the wide range of English writers with which he was familiar, Hardy spent nearly thirty years as a novelist before devoting himself to poetry. In 1874 Hardy married Emma Lavinia Gifford, who would become the subject of many of his poems. They spent several years in happiness until the 1880s, when marital troubles began to shake the closeness of their union.

Hardy's first book of verse was published in 1898, when he was fifty-eight years old and had achieved a large degree of success as a novelist. Although his verse was not nearly as successful as his novels, Hardy continued to focus on his poetry and published seven more books of verse before his death, developing his confidence and technical competence. With the composition of *The Dynasts: A Drama of the Napoleonic Wars* (1904-08), an epic historical drama written in verse, Hardy was hailed as a major poet. He was praised as a master of his craft, and his writing was admired for its great emotional force and technical skill. Hardy continued to write until just before his death in 1928. Despite his wish to be buried with his family, influential sentiment for his burial in Poet's Corner of Westminster Abbey instigated a severe compromise: the removal of his heart, which was buried in Dorchester, and the cremation of his body, which was interred in the Abbey.

Poem Text

"Ah, are you digging on my grave
    My loved one?—planting rue?"
—"No; yesterday he went to wed
One of the brightest wealth has bred.
'It cannot hurt her now,' he said,   5
    'That I should not be true'."

"Then who is digging on my grave?
    My nearest dearest kin?"
—"Ah, no; they sit and think, 'What use!
What good will planting flowers produce?   10
No tendance of her mound can loose
    Her spirit from Death's gin'."

"But someone digs upon my grave?
    My enemy?—prodding sly?"
—"Nay; when she heard you had passed the Gate   15
That shuts on all flesh soon or late,
She thought you no more worth her hate,
    And cares not where you lie."

"Then, who is digging on my grave?
    Say—since I have not guessed!"   20
—"O it is I, my mistress dear,
Your little dog, who still lives near,
And much I hope my movements here
    Have not disturbed your rest?"

"Ah, yes! *You* dig upon my grave …   25
    Why flashed it not on me
That one true heart was left behind!
What feeling do we ever find
To equal among human kind
    A dog's fidelity!"   30

"Mistress, I dug upon your grave
    To bury a bone, in case
I should be hungry near this spot
When passing on my daily trot.
I am sorry, but I quite forgot   35
    It was your resting place."

Poem Summary

Lines 1-2:

These first two lines of the poem present a certain mystery to the reader. Who is asking this question? Is it indeed a person in the grave, or is it a person imagining an experience that might happen after they die? This mystery helps to draw the reader into the poem, though we will soon understand that the speaker is indeed a woman who is dead and buried. Hardy will continue to make use of an anonymous voice in the poem, however, when he introduces the second character in the work.

These lines also suggest some underlying elements that can help us to better understand the situation. The reference to the "rue" being planted by the woman's loved one seems an important detail. The word rue has two essential meanings and both can be applied to the poem. First, rue means sorrow or regret, so the woman might be indicating that her loved one is experiencing these emotions. Initially, the speaker seems to feel that her death has caused sorrow for the loved one and that she remains strong in his memory. In this sense, he would be "planting rue" by mourning her death. In the following lines, however, we learn he is not full of sorrow, so if she has this idea, it proves to be a mistake. Rue is also the name of a shrub having bitter, strongly scented leaves. This definition of rue seems to hint at the true nature of the relationship between the woman and the loved one. The bitter plant contrasts with the beautiful flowers that are often placed on graves, and this contrast becomes stronger when we remember that flowers are a traditional symbol of love and purity. In other words, the speaker doesn't imagine the man offering a remembrance of beauty and affection, just one of bitterness.

Lines 3-4:

In these lines, the speaker's first question is answered by the "digger" of her grave, though the digger's identity is unknown at this point in the poem. The anonymous speaker becomes an important factor in the poem, urging the reader to push on and discover who is talking to the woman. What's made clear in this first stanza is that this voice does not belong to the loved one that the woman thought she was addressing. This is indicated by the use of the third-person "he" to refer to the man. The voice explains that the woman's loved one—perhaps a husband or lover—has married another woman. What's more, he has married a very wealthy mate and appears to be doing quite well without the woman in the grave.

Lines 5-6:

Here, the digger quotes the words of the loved one, and the man states that his recent marriage will have no effect upon the deceased woman. With this, the poet completes the first of several ironic passages that continue throughout the poem. In all of these, the woman in the grave wants to believe that others are thinking of her following her death. In reality, however, she has been largely forgotten. Hardy uses these ironic reversals to create a somewhat humorous tone, and this type of unexpected switch is often used to make people laugh. In this poem, Hardy's writing becomes a kind of "black humor" because it centers on death—a grim event that is not usually associated with merriment. This effect is intensified because the humor of the poem reveals a sad message: the dead woman is forgotten and eternally lonely.

Lines 7-8:

This stanza again begins with a variation of the refrain, "Who is digging on my grave?" The "Then" moves the poem forward as it enables the narrator to discount the lover and move toward other possibilities. She chooses members of her family and imagines that they are remembering her by caring for her grave.

Lines 9-12:

Again, the voice answers the woman, telling her that her relatives are not the ones she hears digging. Instead, they think that it's pointless to tend her grave, as no amount of care will raise her from the dead.

Lines 13-14:

Again there is the variation of the refrain "Are You Digging On My Grave?" but this time it is not as definitive. The speaker is more hesitant, as if she doubts herself. She also seems to be more desperate to find someone who remembers her. Since her loved one and her relatives have forsaken her memory, she imagines that the digging is being done by a woman she disliked in her life, perhaps a rival. While there was ill feeling between the two, it seems that the buried woman finds some solace in the idea that her enemy is still concerned enough with her presence to cause some kind of harm to her grave.

Lines 15-16:

The reference to passing "the Gate" is another term for the woman's death. Hardy's use of the phrase seems to allude to the idea of the pearly gates that theoretically mark the entrance to heaven. He does not present a glorified picture of this passageway, however, as is typically the case with such an image. Instead, "the Gate / ... shuts on all flesh," a phrase that suggests death is like a trap, not a place where one receives heavenly rewards. This image reinforces the one in line 12, where the unknown speaker made reference to "Death's gin"—gin meaning a type of snare or trap that is used to catch animals.

Lines 17-18:

Here, the unknown voice presents one of the most direct, and most chilling, statements of the poem's central idea: the deceased woman has been forgotten by the living and does not concern them at all.

Lines 19-20:

In this stanza, the woman finally gives up her game of trying to guess who is digging on the grave and asks a direct question of the unknown voice.

Lines 21-24:

Here, the identity of the unknown speaker is revealed. This is a key turning point in the poem. Until now, the reader has been involved in the mystery of who might be speaking to the woman, and this puzzle has been one of the elements that has kept the reader caught up in the developing narrative. Now that this mystery has been solved, the poet must find a new way to hold the reader's interest. He does this in two ways. First, he uses the unexpected and humorous twist of having a dog be the individual who is speaking. Second, he creates another ironic set-up in the following stanzas to once again show that the woman has little importance in the living world.

Lines 25-30:

The fifth stanza is given over completely to the woman who talks of the dog's loyalty. This is the woman's longest stretch of unbroken commentary in the poem, and it serves to build up the reader's expectations for the ironic conclusion in the final paragraph. In a sense, this final situation is exactly same as the ones that have preceded it: the woman's explanation for the digging shows that she wants her former acquaintances to remember her and be touched by her death; the reality is the opposite—they have little concern for her now that she is gone. By lengthening the woman's explanation in this paragraph, as well as the dog's subsequent reply, Hardy gives more zing

to this last incident and brings the poem toward its conclusion.

Lines 31-34:

In the final stanza, Hardy takes the poem to its highest level of satire as the dog indicates that the bone is a more important than his former mistress. The mention of the bone also suggests the way in which those in the living world now view the woman; she is simply a pile of bones buried in the ground and no longer has importance to those she used to know.

Lines 35-36:

With the final lines, Hardy drives home his central point: the woman has been forgotten by those she once knew.

Themes

The Human Condition

Despite its not-so-subtle humor, Thomas Hardy's "Ah, Are You Digging On My Grave?" paints a bleak picture of human nature. Human feelings, according to the poem, are utterly transient. Death means not only the end of physical existence, but extinction in the hearts of the living as well. The tone of the poem is set immediately in the first line. In typical Hardy fashion, it is spoken by a dead woman, who is awakened in her grave by the sound of someone scratching at the dirt above. Which of the people she knew in life could be visiting her grave site? Is it her lover, her family, her enemy? One by one her illusions are shattered. None of them seem to care for her anymore. Even her dog, who is digging there, chose the spot by chance, not because his former mistress was buried there.

The poem's bitterness goes even deeper. The voice at the grave relates, with brutal honesty, how the woman's loved—and hated—ones have *willfully* excluded her from their affections and thoughts. Her loved one got married the day before to another woman, and "one of the brightest wealth," at that. Her family refuses to tend her grave. The dead woman has even lost the "affection" of her old foe who believes a dead woman is "no more worth her hate." By the time the poem reaches this point, Hardy's lack of faith in human nature is complete. No ties bind. He suggests that everyone can expect the same fate. The dog's carefree lack of fidelity is the final blow. Any hope the woman might have had to live on in the memory of the living is dashed.

Sentimentality

The narrative of "Ah, Are You Digging On My Grave?" presents a pessimistic view of human nature. But this viewpoint is undercut to a large degree by other elements in the poem—structure and language—that Hardy uses as an ironic commentary on the sentimentality of the Victorian era. The woman draws our compassion and our ridicule, and this sets up a tug of war between high feeling and ridicule. In the end, ridicule wins out. The authenticity of the noble "emotions" is thrown into doubt. By the time the poem concludes, the dead woman's sensibility has been exposed as a cliche and Hardy's readers are forced to confront their own feelings in the same light.

The structure of "Ah, Are You Digging On My Grave?" is a familiar one, although not one commonly associated with poetry: the joke. A situation is established and briefly developed, then the punch line turns everything on its head. In Hardy's bitter joke, a dead woman has high-flown expectations of the living: her loved one will remain forever faithful to her; her family will continue to look after her exactly as they did in life; and even her enemy's hatred will not wane. The poem's punch line deflates her hopes and reveals them as vain and ridiculous.

Hardy sets up his joke carefully, with a poet's attention to the language he uses. The atmosphere is set in the first two lines. A sigh from the grave seems to signal a profound meditation on mortality and love. The phrasing of the two lines is almost self-consciously "poetic." Such language is maintained throughout the first three stanzas. Expressions like "planting rue," "Death's gin," "the Gate that shuts on all flesh" portray feeling that is heightened, more sensitive and authentic than everyday, run-of-the-mill emotion. They awaken a sense of tragedy and compassion in the reader. But Hardy is merely setting us up for the punch line.

The tone of the poem's language begins to change in the fourth stanza. One hardly notices it, so great is the reader's surprise that it was a "little dog" that was poeticizing all along. The first seeds of doubt have been planted; this poem may not be exactly what it at first seemed. The dead woman recognizes the dog's voice and utters the article of faith she feels most deeply: a dog's love outshines anything human. As she speaks the poem slides

Topics for Further Study

- Lytton Strachey noted that if Hardy had ended his poem after the fifth stanza it would have had a very different effect on its readers. Imagine the poem ended after the third stanza or after the fifth stanza. Discuss what different effects each would have had. How would those poems have been different from and similar to the actual poem?

- Although the poem is ultimately humorous, the humor is black. Do you agree with Hardy's view of the human condition? Give reasons to support your answer.

- Describe the reactions you felt as you read the poem for the first time. What emotions did you feel towards the various characters? Towards the author?

- The first three stanzas suggest that the living have betrayed the dead woman? Have they? Explain.

swiftly from tragedy into bathos. Her mannered speech shows how cliched her hopes are. It climaxes in the rhetorical question that concludes the stanza. It is as cloying and hackneyed as a greeting card, so much so that one is shocked to encounter it in a work by a poet of Hardy's stature.

But when the dog replies, the reader realizes that Hardy is up to something else. The "poetry" and sentimentality have vanished. The dog's voice is as ordinary and plainspoken as that of the Hardy's Wessex country folk. He deflates her last hope so offhandedly and without pretense that its effect is brutal. This brutality counterbalances the sentimentality, turns it on its head and shows it to be ridiculous. At the same time the dead woman's expectations about her lover, her family and enemy are portrayed as products of the same ridiculous sentimental outlook.

Hardy's use of contrasting language does two things: it portrays the feelings of the dead woman and, at the same time, evokes feelings in readers.

We feel compassion in the first three stanzas. We feel critical of the living characters. We are drawn to share her feelings, largely because of the way Hardy describes them in the first half of the poem. Once he has evoked them in us, however, he turns on them and shows them to be false and artificial. If they are false in the dead woman, they are false in us as well. He is not really criticizing the dead after all. Dead people have no hopes and dreams. They are dead, a fact that all the living people recognize. "It cannot hurt her now," her lover says. He does not wish to hurt her. "What good will planting flowers produce?" her family wonders, since they will not bring her back to life. We, the living, are the ones with expectations of how the living will remember us after we have died. Hardy forces us to look at those expectations and ask ourselves how realistic they are.

Style

"Ah, Are You Digging on My Grave?" is composed of six stanzas each containing six lines. The first line of each stanza is a variation of the question "Are you digging on my grave?" The repetition of this line gives continuity to the poem and provides a refrain that is similar to the repeated phrases that are used in songs. After this initial refrain, the final words in Lines 2 and 6 rhyme with one another, while the Lines 3, 4, and 5 also contain end rhymes. Hardy also employs a fairly regular pattern of syllables in the lines of each stanza. Though there are occasional variations, the first, third, fourth, and fifth lines in each stanza usually contain eight syllables, while the second and sixth lines usually contain six syllables. This regular pattern helps to create the lyrical sound of the poem—a musical rhythm that makes the poem sound much like a song when read aloud. The design of the first three stanzas of the poem are also identical in how the dialogue between the two speakers is presented; the first two lines of these stanzas consist of a question asked by the woman buried in the grave, while the remaining lines consist of a reply to the question. Quotation marks are used to signify the beginning and end of each speaker's words. The last two stanzas of the poem vary this structure—each stanza being devoted to a single speaker—but the dialogue between the two characters remains the central organizational element throughout the poem.

Historical Context

When Hardy wrote "Ah, Are You Digging on My Grave?" a revolution of values was underway in the world that would shake the foundations of almost every area of life; it was a change that would influence artists and intellectuals, leaders and common man alike. The change affected how the world was perceived and how man perceived himself.

Queen Victoria died in 1900, but the attitudes and mores that characterized the period of her reign lingered a decade after. For many historians the start of the Great War signaled the close of the Victorian Age. A gentility of manners and a code of morals that is seen in retrospect as prudish and straitlaced marked the period. Hardy had challenged many of these attitudes in his novels, in which he depicted the struggles of individuals against the intolerant, hypocritical society in which they lived. The books treated controversial issues such as adultery and sexuality outside marriage with candor. Public reaction to the open treatment of topics that Victorians considered fundamentally private was hostile, and it ultimately drove Hardy to abandon novel writing completely in favor of poetry.

In the same year that Hardy's *Satires of Circumstance* was published, the *The Rite of Spring,* a ballet by Igor Stravinsky and Vaslav Nijinsky was premiered in Paris. Stravinsky's music broke radically with the norms of composition of the previous four centuries. Rhythm, instead of harmony and melody, was uppermost. It was marked by abrupt changes in tempo and dynamics; it was not music that could be easily hummed. Nijinsky's choreography replaced the graceful movement of classical ballet with jerky, awkward steps that simulated the primitive rituals of the distant past that the ballet portrayed. It was so strange and different than earlier dance that when it was performed for the first time a riot broke out in the theater. *The Rite of Spring* initiated an era of experimentation. Arnold Schoenberg would reject harmony entirely, jazz would be absorbed, and classical balance and form of music of previous centuries would not return for decades.

A similar revolution occurred in painting. Art had moved rapidly from pure representation through Impressionism, a genre focused on light and perception and featuring experiments in color by artists like Cezanne and Matisse. In 1907 Pablo Picasso painted the *Les Demoiselles d'Avignon,* the first work of a movement that came to be known

Compare
&
Contrast

- **1913:** Life expectancy in advanced nations is just over 50.

  Today: Life expectancy is 76 and scientists predict that over the next 25 to 50 years, U.S. life expectancy will increase by 10 to 15 years. Experimenters, using techniques of genetic engineering, claim to have extended the life of cells in the laboratory indefinitely and believe the techniques can be used to extend human life as well.

- **1913:** Henry Ford sets up the world's first assembly line at his factory in Highland Park, Michigan. His daily wage of $5 is more than double the prevailing rate for manual labor and thousands of workers come to Detroit seeking employment.

  Today: More and more assembly work in factories is performed by robots. Unskilled factory jobs decrease, and wages fall as well.

- **1913:** The Sixteenth Amendment is ratified, introducing the first federal income tax in the United States. Rates range from one percent for the lowest income brackets to as high as seven percent for the highest brackets. Less than one percent of the population was subject to the income tax.

  Today: Since 1993 there have been five tax brackets, 15 percent, 28 percent, 31 percent, 36 percent, and 39.6 percent.

- **1913:** Emily Davison, English suffragette, runs out onto the track at the English Derby as a demonstration for women's voting rights and is trampled to death by one of the horses. Her death focuses the attention of thousands on the English suffragette cause.

  Today: Widespread inequality still exists for women. For example, women continue to earn lower wages than male counterparts in the same job.

---

as Cubism. Cubism cut the last ties that bound painting to reproducing the real world. Picasso (and other painters after him) reduced their subjects to geometrical shapes, as seem from different points of view. They were rearranged on the canvas in a sort of kaleidoscopic view. Those three-dimensional forms, shattered and reduced to two dimensions on canvas, reflected the fragmentation of man's view of the universe that was taking place. *Les Demoiselles d'Avignon* was such a radical break that it was not exhibited until twenty years after it was painted.

As Hardy was writing "Ah, Are You Digging On My Grave?" another revolution was underway in the arts, one whose impact was not yet foreseen. Movies were just beginning to establish themselves as popular entertainment. Edwin S. Porter's *Great Train Robbery,* released in 1903, had revealed the enormous story-telling possibilities of the new medium. Over the next ten years, movie houses sprang up everywhere in Europe and the United

States. While literature was becoming more difficult and less accessible to mass audiences, film engaged them easily with its pace, visual style, and realism. Movies would eventually give way to radio, television, and recordings, media that ultimately displaced reading for many as a pastime.

The arts were also influenced by the revolutionary view of the human mind that was being developed by Sigmund Freud early in the twentieth century. Freud's psychoanalytic picture of humans was very different from that which had dominated the Christian era. For nearly two thousand years man had been seen as a free being. Humans might act from selfish or noble reasons, but they freely and consciously *chose* all their actions. Freud maintained that many of the mind's mechanisms were *not* conscious. Past events left their mark on the mind in the form of repressed desires and fantasies which affected our behavior even when we were not aware of them. Freud's view also cast doubt on the degree to which humans were ultimately responsible for their actions as well, a debate that continues today. Freud's view that sexuality lay at the root of human behavior and had its origins in childhood and infancy also scandalized turn-of-the-century society. Freud's ideas continued to have an impact on all areas of the arts until late in the twentieth century.

Critical Overview

Producing poetry from the mid-1890s until his death in 1928, Hardy has been viewed as a transitional poet who combined features of traditional verse with more experimental elements. He made use of established poetic devices such as regular forms, meter, and rhyme, but critics have also been interested in the rough, common language and unpolished verse that he frequently employed in his poems. Lytton Strachey, writing in *New Statesman* in 1914, referred to the "clumsy" nature of Hardy's verse, but found it to be a positive characteristic. "He fumbles," Strachey wrote of Hardy, "but it is that very fumbling that brings him so near ourselves." For Strachey, Hardy's "ugly and cumbrous expressions" successfully present "the quiet voice of a modern man or woman." This common language is evident in "Ah, Are You Digging on My Grave?," especially in the use of utterances such as "ah" and in the repeated use of dashes to indicate the hesitations that are often present in everyday conversation. In fact, the poem's extended use of spoken dialogue is another way that Hardy emphasizes unpolished discourse.

Critic P. E. Mitchell in "Music and Hardy's Poetry" finds that the poet's work incorporates many elements from English folk music, especially in regard to the irregular rhythms that are found in the songs. "In his poetry, [Hardy] brings the unadorned and rugged qualities of folk song back to life," Mitchell writes. "Ah, Are You Digging on My Grave?" has some of these qualities. Its regular refrain and uniform construction give it a musical sound, but Hardy occasionally varies the rhythm by adding extra syllables to certain lines. The poem's subject matter also seems in keeping with the style of folk songs, as death and a person's experiences in the afterlife are frequently referred to in traditional ballads. In drawing on folk music, Mitchell believes that Hardy hoped to invoke "an ideal social existence to be held up against the modern world" and that this ideal life was taken from "the unsophisticated rural past of England." In other words, the poet used elements of folk songs in order to remind readers of the simpler way of life that once existed in the English countryside; he believed this rural lifestyle was better than the hectic existence of modern times.

Criticism

Jhan Hochman

Jhan Hochman is a writer and instructor at Portland Community College in Portland, Oregon. In the following essay, Hochman explores various stylistic aspects of "Ah, Are You Digging on My Grave?" including its use of satire.

Thomas Hardy's "Ah, Are You Digging on My Grave?" (1913) is a dramatic and satiric dialogue between the dead and living. A buried woman asks the same question—the title of the poem—three times, first of her lover whom she mistakenly thinks is planting rue (a kind of flower symbolizing sorrow) near her gravestone, then of a member of her family, and lastly, of her enemy whom she thinks is at the burial site not to plant flowers but to desecrate the grave. After being told each time by the digger that her guesses are wrong, the buried woman gives up and asks who it is that *is* digging on her grave. Her interlocutor, the woman is finally told, is her little dog still living somewhere in proximity to where she is buried.

The buried woman is relieved and happy until her dog tells her he did not know that it was her grave on which he was digging and that he is there only to bury a bone, not because he misses the woman. This is a poem of surprising outcomes, both for the woman and the dog.

In "Ah, Are You Digging on My Grave?" Hardy not only surprises the reader as to content, but also form. His technique, maintains Florence Hardy in *The Life of Thomas Hardy 1840-1928,* involves a consistent employment of "cunning irregularity" applicable to what he once learned as an architect and what he later applied to his poetry. Hardy's interest is in "the principle of spontaneity, found in mouldings, tracery, and such like— resulting in the 'unforeseen' (as it has been called) character of his metres and stanzas, that of stress rather than of syllable, poetic texture rather than poetic veneer; the latter kind of thing, under the name of 'constructed ornament,' being what he … had been taught to avoid as the plague."

This statement certainly applies to "Ah, Are You Digging on My Grave?" which has regular stanzas of six lines and, generally, a consistent number of syllables per line—eight—except for the second and last lines of each stanza which usually have six syllables. The rhyme scheme is also regular: abcccb. Yet meter and accent are irregular, with accents falling on different syllables throughout the poem as can be heard if one reads the first lines of each stanza together and then the second lines, and so on. This is the poem's cunning irregularity—that of rhythm—and an instance of a poet who knows "the art of concealing art."

"Ah, Are You Digging on My Grave?" is a satire, a word once thought to be derived from *satyr,* a creature half-animal, half-human, that appeared in the chorus of Greek drama. Now, however, it is believed to be derived from the Latin word *satira,* meaning medley or hodgepodge, the term being applied to early conversational pieces on a variety of subjects. However, it is the present definition of satire that applies to "Are You Digging?"; this definition indicates a verse or prose form in which prevailing vices or follies are held up to ridicule. Sometimes the word is used interchangeably with *lampoon* which applies to the ridicule of persons, situations, or institutions. With our definitions clear, what then is the "prevailing vice or folly held up to ridicule" in Hardy's poem? It is Western idealism or sentimentalism associated with continual devotion to the dead. The buried woman imagines she is missed by those who were close to her, or is still hated by her former enemy. She is mistaken. The living, while remembering her, have moved on to other preoccupations.

Depending on the genre of story in which the dead appear as characters, they are most often wise or horrific. In Shakespeare's *Hamlet,* for example, the dead King speaks to his son Hamlet of dastardly deeds and hatched plots of which only the dead King and the murderers have knowledge. In Bram Stoker's *Dracula,* the dead bleed the living to create more dead, who are not forever dead (as is the more pedestrian notion), but instead, forever alive. But the dead woman of Hardy's poem is neither wise nor terrifying. She is, like a living character would be, unable to see due to her permanent enclosure. She is, however, able to hear and speak a very normal, conversational, and misguided speech like the living.

This combination of factors renders the woman, despite the fact that she is dead, a non-threatening and sentimental presence/absence; per-

What Do I Read Next?

- Poem XXVII of A. E. Housman's *A Shropshire Lad* was not only one of Hardy's favorites, it was also the model and starting point for "Ah, Are You Digging on My Grave?" The "Poems of 1912-1913" written in memory of his recently deceased wife stand in stark contrast to the irony in "Ah, Are You Digging on My Grave?" and have been called some of the most beautiful love poems in the English language.

- Lytton Strachey's book *Eminent Victorians* revolutionized the art of biography. In it Strachey casts an ironical eye on some of the icons of Victorian England.

- *The Guns of August* by Barbara Tuchman chronicles the unstable political situation in Europe that led directly to the outbreak of the First World War.

---

haps this sentimentalism accounts for her living on in death, since hope, even when sentimental, is thought to keep one "alive." In a phrase, it can be said—playing with the double meaning of dumb—that the buried woman is and is not dumb. In many traditional narratives of death, dead souls are thought to have learned from death. That this woman foolishly thinks she is devotedly remembered even as she lies in her grave, then, is surprising.

In this poem there is not only a dead woman but a talking dog. The dead are able to speak, so why not animals? The significance is that beings usually thought dead or unconscious are brought to life, or in the case of the dog, made to be what humans consider more fully alive. But is this wholly true? On one hand the dog *is* made to appear more fully alive with the "gift" of speech, but on the other, the dog is voided of what dogs are usually thought to have, something that often makes them really "alive" for humans: loyalty. While making the life of the dog more human by having the dog speak, Hardy also renders the dog a more living example of "dogginess": the dog has his own life

After coming to the end of 'Ah, Are You Digging on My Grave?' the reader realizes that the title would have been more accurate—even if less interesting—if called, 'Oh. No One Is Digging on My Grave.'"

apart from human concerns. He is too busy burying bones to worry about loyalty.

The dog is, in addition, rendered painfully honest—he does not lie to spare the corpse the hurt of not being remembered. This makes the dog seem more like an animal since humans, it is usually thought, are the creatures who lie (variously called an asset or defect), while animals, it is also thought, cannot help but be honest. Yet at the same time, Hardy makes the dog more of what is "supposedly" conceived of as human because he—like the lover, family member, and enemy—has moved on with his life. While some might call selfishness or self-involvement a trait of animals, the trait is not usually applied to what is generally believed to be the most loyal and human of pets, the dog.

Finally, there is one last surprising development regarding the dog. Though dogs are rarely thought to exhibit such behavior, the buried woman sentimentally believes that the dog tries to reach her beneath the ground. Because the woman seems so much to want to be missed, she makes a further, perhaps even bigger error in judgment after asking the main question—after all this is a dog, not some lovesick or vengeful human. All in all, the dog's behavior is so rich and the woman's behavior so simple-minded—even if also rather surprising in the context of that most romantic of mediums, poetry—that readers understand that Hardy's satire is aimed at the behavior of the woman. The dog's behavior, while made complex by Hardy, is not ridiculed as much as it is made surprising and humorous.

In his *The Pattern of Hardy Poetry*, Samuel Hynes calls Hardy's poems, of which there are over

900, "antinomial." What Hynes means is that Hardy does not, at least in his poems, present the classic elements of a syllogism: a thesis and an antithesis reconciled by a synthesis. Instead, Hardy more often presents a dramatic conflict without reconciliation. In "Ah, Are You Digging on My Grave?" thesis and antithesis are represented by the buried woman and living dog, respectively. No final statement reconciles the woman to those who have not remembered her. Rather than Hardy so obviously presenting *his* view of remembrance of the dead, he presents a particular view. As there is nothing for the buried woman to do but accept the antithetical statements presented by the dog, there is little for the reader to do but accept that the living do, with time, abandon the dead.

Of course, the reader might also deny such human behavior, or at least denounce this subject, as one unfit for poetry, a medium more often thought to contain the best of what people think it means to be human (and less of what people think it means to be animal). For Hardy, however, this latter behavior by the reader would be missing the point. As he explained in his *Apology* (*Late Lyrics and Earlier*), Hardy composed his poems with "obstinate questionings" and "blank misgivings" in order to take a full look at the *worst* of human foibles and behavior. He suggests that this is not pessimism, but optimism under conditions of undeviating honesty.

Finally accepting the worst in Hardy's poem—that the living come to forget the dead—makes readers understand the poem's title as ironic. After coming to the end of "Ah, Are You Digging on My Grave?" the reader realizes that the title would have been more accurate—even if less interesting—if called "Oh. No One Is Digging on My Grave."

Source: Jhan Hochman, in an essay for *Poetry for Students*, Gale, 1998.

David Kelly

David Kelly is a writer and instructor at Oakton Community College in Des Plaines, Illinois. In the following essay, Kelly delves into Hardy's personal life to explore the motivation—whether ominous, humorous, or even kind—behind "Ah, Are You Digging on My Grave?"

"Ah, Are You Digging on My Grave?" is frequently chosen to represent Hardy's poetry in anthologies for students, but scholars often pass it by, giving at best an embarrassed commentary on the language or pointing to its possible pedigree (the poems that may have inspired it). It is easy to see why beginning poetry readers would like this piece: unlike much of the poetry that is studied in schools, which is often chosen for study precisely because it is hard to understand—and therefore deserves some effort or concentration—, the Hardy poem seems to rely on no symbolism or "deep hidden meaning," so the casual reader feels comfortable with understanding it after just one reading. Also, it doesn't hurt the poem's popularity that it is written in fairly common language. Modern American readers might find its tone a little stiff, but it is certainly more comfortable than works using complex phraseologies or archaic language of the "thou" or "whilst" variety. It is just as easy to understand why literary critics might not consider this poem worth their time, since its message—that a dead woman anxious to find out who has remembered her finds out that no one has—presents critics with no intellectual challenge. Critics also tend to shudder when they see that a poem has played out as a joke, as this one is, with the humiliating revelation at the end that the dead woman had no graveside visitor, just her dog, and that even the dog was just at her grave by coincidence. Edgar Allan Poe's stories face the same dilemma of being popular with normal people but dismissed as "lightweight" by critics. The thinking here seems to be that a writer who as shaped her or his work to be amusing must surely have neglected its literary content. Whether or not this is true is not as important as knowing that it is believed to be true, and so humor frightens critics away.

The mistake made by both the poem's fans and those who dismiss it lightly is that they assume the whole story is on the page, and there is nothing more to it. In most cases, a poem should be forced to stand by itself, instead of relying on how its subject coincides with facts from the author's life. In this case, however, the piece is ten times more interesting than just its words because its first publication was in September of 1913.

Why is this significant? Because Hardy's first wife, whom he had been married to for nearly forty years, the last thirty of them unhappily, died in November of 1912. By April of 1913 Hardy had already proposed marriage to a good friend of hers, who he would marry the next year. The implications are more chilling than most dark comedies would dare attempt: it is one thing to believe that the author invented a pathetic character, a dead woman so unloved that her friends abandon her and her husband remarries quickly, and quite another thing to believe that the pathetic creature is a person from the author's real life, that the callous hus-

> " ... [I]t is one thing to believe that the author invented a pathetic character, a dead woman so unloved that her friends abandon her and her husband remarries quickly, and quite another thing to believe that the pathetic creature is a person from the author's real life...."

band is the poet himself. Even dark humor, as this poem clearly traffics in, requires some lack of sympathy for the person who takes a pie in the face or falls off the scaffold, or is abandoned by her dog. Once the suspicion has been raised that Hardy would shamelessly play such a dirty trick on his dead wife Emma, the focus of attention shifts from the subject of the joke to the teller.

In life, maybe she deserved this scorn. Accounts of Hardy's marriage linger on the dark side of the spectrum, hovering somewhere between "cold" and "hate-filled." They met at St. Juliot, Cornwall, in 1870, when Hardy was working as an architect and was involved of the restoration of the rectory there. In his essay in *The Genius of Thomas Hardy*, Geoffrey Grigson describes Emma's father as "a failed solicitor, an impoverished idler, given to drink." So Hardy's future father-in-law certainly had very little to be proud of and no reason, other than family history, to think he was better than Hardy, but that did not keep him from writing a note before their marriage in 1874 calling the poet a "low-born churl who has presumption to marry into my family." That unearned snobbishness carried over to Emma after her marriage. At first, she seemed to have been grateful to be settling down: she was thirty (Hardy was 34) and not very good looking, and her social prospects were unpromising. She went into marriage happily, and at the beginning, at least, things went well between Thomas Hardy and Emma Lavinia Gifford Hardy.

Maybe jealousy had something to do with it. Hardy was a writer when he met Emma and he had published a few minor works, but, as noted, he wasn't successful enough to quit his day job. Nothing could have predicted the success that he was to become. His first major novel, *Far From The Maddening Crowd,* was published the year of their wedding, and the proceeds helped finance a honeymoon in France. Still, her own ego must have ached as his fame grew with the subsequent publication of such classics as *The Return of the Native, The Mayor of Casterbridge, Tess of the D'Urbervilles,* and *Jude the Obscure.* In her book *Thomas Hardy's Women and Men: The Defeat of Nature,* concerning the writer's treatment of gender, Anne Z. Mickelson reported that "Like Zelda Fitzgerald, another woman living in the shadow of her husband's fame, Emma tried her hand at various things and then turned to writing—with the same lack of encouragement and success that Zelda experienced."

Maybe he disgusted her. Emma, apart from being such a snob that she would not let Hardy's parents into their house, was a deeply religious person. Hardy offended her, and much of the reading public, by discussing matters of sexuality in his novels—not as graphically as we hear them discussed today on the average comedy program on television, but strongly enough to raise protests and force the author to speak out in his own defense. In 1890 he published an essay titled "Candour in English Literature," an intellectual piece explaining his reasons for talking frankly and openly, stating that suppression caused, among other things, "the catastrophes based on sexual relations." This theme would appear throughout his fiction. His next and last novel, 1895's *Jude the Obscure,* was about bad marriages, and was more concerned with sexuality than any of his previous books. Emma was so scandalized that she went to London and tried, unsuccessfully, to block its publication.

From 1895 to the end of his life in 1928, Hardy's literary output concentrated mainly on poetry, with miscellaneous essays and short stories being published along the way. He always considered himself a poet, even while his novels were praised the world over and their sales were keeping him financially comfortable. With the literary reputation Hardy had established, it didn't matter whether his poems were critically successful, which was what allowed him to continue his poetic efforts. Even in his novels, Hardy's use of language had always been an awkward mix of the common and the elevated, and isolated in poems, his flaws became magnified. In an essay about Hardy's use of English in *Thomas Hardy: The Writer and His Background,* Norman Page included a quote from T. S. Eliot that captures the feelings of most literary critics and may tell us something about the type of man Hardy was: "he was indifferent even to the prescripts of good writing; he wrote sometimes overpoweringly well, but always very carelessly; at times his style touched sublimity without ever having passed through the stage of being good." This sounds like the sort of man who could publish a poem about a dead woman after his wife's death without seeing how the two might seem to be related. As noted before, he was a dedicated poet, and critics agree that the abuse he took for using "common" language probably just marked him as ahead of his time, but there is no consensus about whether we would know him today if he wrote poetry alone.

Hardy's poetry took a turn with Emma's death in 1912. Biographers and historians note that, just as his works during the late decades of their forty-year marriage reflected couples with little in common, living distantly from each other even when they were in the same house, his poetry started reflecting good things when she died. "One forgets all the recent years and differences," he wrote to a friend (as noted in Timothy Hands's book *Thomas Hardy*), "and the mind goes back to the early times when each was much to each other—in her case and mine, intensely much." This is the relationship between the Hardys that literary critics like to remember: cool, aloof, estranged yet consistently so for decades, and tragically only revived too late, after her death—the poet awash in nostalgia and regret. To quote Grigson again: "Hardy once more loved and longed for his young wife, as he had first known her, in a total of 116 poems, about an eighth of the poems he ever wrote." "Ah, Are You Digging on My Grave?" would have to be an incredible piece of absentmindedness if this "renewed love" theory is to be taken seriously.

We have Hardy's inspiration for this piece. Poem XXVII of A. E. Housman's *A Shropshire Lad* was one of Hardy's favorites: starting with the line "Is my team ploughing?" it is structured as a question and answer series between a recently deceased man and his best friend, ending with a strong sexual suggestion ("I cheer a dead man's sweetheart, Never ask me whose"). In *The Poems of Thomas Hardy: A Critical Introduction,* Kenneth Marsden points to a poem by German poet Heinrich Heine called *"Ich stand in dunkeln Traumen"* that both

Housman and Hardy would have read and that he thinks was the basis for both their works. Maybe, just maybe, Hardy looked upon "Ah, Are You Digging on My Grave?" as an intellectual exercise, oblivious to the strong similarity between his late wife, Emma, and the abandoned woman of the poem. Or maybe he was joking about callousness, an indication that he felt so secure in his love for Emma that he did not believe anyone would seriously think she lay abandoned in her grave.

Clearly, Hardy was not the type of man to worry much about the public's perception of him, or he would have stuck to his successful career in novel writing and he might not have published the massive volume of poetry that nobody loved more than he loved himself. Given the overwhelming tenderness that he showed toward Emma after her death, it is unlikely that he would have published a poem openly slandering her, with nothing to gain but spite. The most probable answer is that he felt she would have understood this poem and its inferences, that it was something like a private joke between them, much as this seems uncommonly tender for the distant couple that the world saw them as for years.

Source: David Kelly, in an essay for *Poetry for Students,* Gale, 1998.

Sources

Brooks, Jean, *Thomas Hardy: The Poetic Structure,* Ithaca, NY: Cornell University Press, 1971.

Brown, Joanna Cullen, *A Journey into Thomas Hardy's Poetry,* London: Allison & Busby, 1989.

Cox, R. G., *Thomas Hardy: The Critical Heritage,* New York: Barnes and Noble, 1970.

Grigson, Geoffry, "The Poems," *The Genius of Thomas Hardy,* edited by Margaret Drabble, New York: Alfred A. Knopf, 1976, pp. 80-93.

Hands, Timothy, *Thomas Hardy,* New York: St. Martin's Press, 1995.

Hynes, Samuel, *The Pattern of Hardy Poetry,* Chapel Hill: University of North Carolina Press, 1961.

Marsden, Kenneth, *The Poems of Thomas Hardy: A Critical Introduction,* New York: Oxford University Press, 1969.

Mickelson, Anne Z., *Thomas Hardy's Women and Men: The Defeat of Nature,* Metuchen, NJ: The Scarecrow Press, Inc., 1976.

Mitchell, P. E., "Music and Hardy's Poetry," in *English Literature in Transition: 1880-1920,* Vol. 30, No. 3, 1987, pp. 308-21.

Orel, Harold, in *Critical Essays on Thomas Hardy's Poetry,* G.K. Hall, 1995.

Page, Norman, "Hardy and the English Language" in *Thomas Hardy: The Writer and His Background,* New York: St. Martin's Press, 1980.

Strachey, Lytton, "Mr. Hardy's New Poems," in *New Statesman,* 1914.

For Further Study

Bailey, J.O., *The Poetry of Thomas Hardy: A Handbook and Commentary,* Chapel Hill, NC: University of North Carolina Press, 1970.
    A reference book whose entries briefly discuss the origins and themes of the thousand or so poems Hardy wrote in his lifetime.

Brennecke, Ernst, Jr., *Thomas Hardy's Universe,* New York: Haskell House, 1966.
    Brennecke's discussion of Hardy's poem focuses on its "cynical and bitter lack of faith in human nature."

Brooks, Jean, *Thomas Hardy: The Poetic Structure,* Ithaca, NY: Cornell University Press, 1971
    Brooks compares the question/answer structure of in "Ah, Are You Digging on My Grave?" with other Hardy poems.

Zietlow, Paul, *Moments of Vision: The Poetry of Thomas Hardy,* Cambridge: Harvard University Press, 1974.
    Approaches Hardy's "Ah, Are You Digging On My Grave?" as a "grim joke."

As I Walked Out One Evening

W. H. Auden

1940

W. H. Auden is considered one of the most important English poets of the twentieth century. He is noted for his strong lyrical voice, technical craftsmanship, and sharp intelligence. Auden quickly gained a reputation as a talented poet while still a young man (publishing his first book at only 26), and was considered by many during his lifetime to be a spokesperson for a whole generation of writers.

First published in the collection *Another Time* (1940), "As I Walked Out One Evening" describes an allegorical conversation between Love and Time as they discuss the power of love to conquer eternity. The speaker, walking down to the river one evening, overhears two lovers pledging their undying devotion to each other. Just as their promises reach the peak of melodrama, the clocks around the city begin to chime, interrupting the two. The speaker imagines this interruption as the clock's way of reminding us we are mortal creatures, unable to transcend Time. In that chiming he hears a voice which scolds the lovers and their "crooked hearts."

Author Biography

Auden was born in 1907 and was raised in northern England, the son of a doctor and a nurse. He received his primary education at St. Edmund's School in Surrey and Gresham's School in Kent.

Auden's early interest in science and engineering earned him a scholarship to Oxford University; however, his interest in poetry led him to switch his field of study to English. While at Oxford, Auden became familiar with modernist poetry, particularly that of T. S. Eliot, and he became a central member of a group of writers that included Stephen Spender, C. Day Lewis, and Louis MacNeice, a collective variously labeled the "Oxford Group" or the "Auden Generation." In 1928 Auden's first book, *Poems,* was privately printed by Spender. During the same year, Eliot accepted Auden's verse play *Paid on Both Sides: A Charade* for publication in his magazine *Criterion.* After graduating from Oxford Auden lived for over a year in Berlin before returning to England to become a teacher. During the 1930s Auden traveled to Spain and China, became involved in political causes, and wrote prolifically. In this period he composed *The Orators: An English Study* (1932), an experimental satire that mixes poetry and prose; three plays in collaboration with Christopher Isherwood; two travel books—one of which was written with Louis MacNeice; and the poetry collection *Look, Stranger!* (1936; published in the United States as *On This Island*). Auden left England in 1939 and became a citizen of the United States. His first book as an emigrant, *Another Time* (1940), contains some of his best-known poems, among them " September 1, 1939," and " Musée des Beaux Arts." His 1945 volume *The Collected Poetry,* in which he revised, retitled, or excluded many of his earlier poems, helped solidify his reputation as a major poet. Throughout his career Auden won numerous honors and awards, including the Pulitzer Prize for *The Age of Anxiety: A Baroque Eclogue* (1947) and the National Book Award for *The Shield of Achilles* (1955). In his later years, Auden continued to teach, to deliver lectures, and to edit and review books. He wrote several more volumes of poetry, including *City without Walls and Many Other Poems* (1969), *Epistle to a Godson and Other Poems* (1972), and the posthumously published *Thank You, Fog: Last Poems* (1974). He died while on a trip to Vienna in 1973. He is buried in Poet's Corner of Westminster Abbey.

W. H. Auden

Poem Text

As I walked out one evening,
    Walking down Bristol Street,
The crowds upon the pavement
    Were fields of harvest wheat.

And down by the brimming river   5
    I hear a lover sing
Under and arch of the railway:
    "Love has no ending.

"I'll love you, dear, I'll love you
    Till China and Africa meet,   10
And the river jumps over the mountain
    And the salmon sing in the street.

"I'll love you till the ocean
    Is folded and hung up to dry
And the seven stars go squawking   15
    Like geese about the sky.

"The years shall run like rabbits,
    For in my arms I hold
The Flower of the ages
    And the first love of the world."   20

But all the clocks in the city
    Began to whirr and chime:
"O let not Time deceive you
    You cannot conquer Time.

"In the burrows of the Nightmare   25
    Where Justice naked is,
Time watches from the shadow
    And coughs when you would kiss.

"In headaches and in worry
    Vaguely life leaks away,   30
And time will have his fancy
    To-morrow or to-day.

"Into many a green valley
    Drifts the appalling snow

Time breaks the threaded dances   35
  And the diver's brilliant bow.

"O plunge your hands in water
  Plunge them up to the wrist;
Stare, stare in the basin
  And wonder what you've missed."   40

"The glacier knocks in the cupboard,
  The desert sighs in the bed,
And the crack in the tea-cup opens
  A lane to the land of the dead.

"Where the beggars raffle the banknotes   45
  And the Giant is enchanting to Jack,
And the Lily-white Boy is a Roarer
  And Jill goes down on her back."

"O look, look in the mirror,
  O look in your distress;   50
Life remains a blessing
  Although you cannot bless.

"O stand, stand at the window
  As the tears scald and start;
You shall love your crooked neighbor   55
  With your crooked heart."

It was late, late in the evening
  The lovers they were gone;
The clocks had ceased their chiming,
  And the deep river ran on.   60

Poem Summary

Lines: 1-4

This first stanza establishes a setting and a pace for the walk we are about to begin with the speaker. Auden introduces the time of day ("one evening") and specific location ("Bristol Street"), which we might guess is in the city of Bristol, just west of London, England. Bristol Street is crowded this time of day, and the people moving together reminds the speaker of "fields of harvest wheat." As we walk down the crowded street with the speaker we begin to feel the pace of his stride echoed in the rhythm of each line.

Notice too that Auden describes the wheat in terms of time, or when it is to be harvested. Fall, the harvest season, is often used in art as a metaphor for old age because it is the last stage of the life cycle, with the plants past bloom and fruit and cold winter coming. Here the speaker sees the crowd and thinks of the fields in the fall, the golden wheat, and our journey to our "winter" years.

Lines: 5-8

After passing through the crowd, the speaker arrives at a "brimming river" where he hears two lovers talking under "an arch of the railway." The poem becomes a dialogue which will extend for the rest of the stanzas, and here the scenery seems to reflect the mood of the lovers: the water in the river rises on its banks, the arch they stand under resembles a huge door to a cathedral or the gates of heaven. The two perhaps believe their love will keep them together forever, since "Love has no ending."

Lines: 9-16

The speaker eavesdrops on the lovers, and for the next several lines listens to their promises of eternal devotion. Their words seem almost absurd, like when they place their love on a geologic time scale. They conclude that their love will survive as long as it would take for China and Africa to slide together in continental drift, or for a river to find its course over a mountain. The "seven stars" in line 15 are probably the constellation Pleiades, known in mythology to be the seven sisters.

Lines: 17-19

In these lines the lover makes perhaps the most grandiose claim; he asserts that the years will pass as fast as "rabbits" because he holds the "flower of the ages" in his hand, as if their love were so apart from time he could pluck all of history like a flower and offer it to her. Perhaps like many lovers, they are convinced their love is "the first love of the world." This image is the last of several which imply that love can conquer time and keep the two together for eternity. But these lines also mark the end of the lover's dialogue, which is cut short by the tolling of the city bells.

Lines: 20-24

Just as the lovers reach their most exaggerated claims of devotion, "all the clocks in the city / began to whirr and chime." The speaker imagines in the tolling bells another voice, perhaps responding to the youthful promises of the lovers. Line 22 begins a dialogue which will extend for the next eight stanzas; Auden gives the clocks human voices in a poetic device called "allegory." Using allegory, a poet treats more abstract concepts like "time" and "justice" as if they were characters in a play, their names capitalized appropriately. In this way the clocks are able to speak for Time, warning the lovers "O let not Time deceive you, / You cannot conquer Time." No matter how much they may love each other, it is not going to save them from the their own mortality.

Lines: 25-32

The description of Time in these lines is compared to something that hides in the "burrows of the nightmare," watching the lovers from the shadows and waiting for them to kiss just so it can interrupt with a cough. Whereas the dialogue of the lovers is filled with statements of eternal hope, the clocks quickly remind the two that Time is always there, lurking, clearing its throat like an impatient conductor waiting for the last few passengers to get aboard the dark train. We are not going to live forever, Time reminds us, because the day we are born is the first day counting down to our death, because "In headaches and in worry / Vaguely life leaks away." Time's "fancy" in line 31 may be death itself, which could arrive at any moment, even "tomorrow or today." This horrible, raw truth may be the naked Justice mentioned a few lines previous, the mortal rules we must all follow.

Lines: 33-40

Echoing the image of "harvest wheat" at the beginning of the poem, this stanza returns to the cycle of the seasons, the green valley of youth giving way to winter and its "appalling" snow that covers the ground. "Appalling" means "terrible," but also literally means "to make pale." The snow makes the hills white, "white" like the color of an old man's hair or the pale faces of the sick and dying. The clocks seem to scold the arrogance of the lovers, telling them that not only is it impossible to conquer time, but rather Time itself "breaks the threaded dances / and the diver's brilliant bow."

Following the image of a diver's descent from cliff to water, Time's instructions for the lovers to "plunge your hands in water, / Plunge them in up to the wrist" may be a symbolic act of cleansing, similar to the ritual of baptism or the washing of a body before its burial. While their hands are submerged, Time commands the lovers to look at themselves in the mirrored surface of the water and "wonder what you've missed." The lovers up until now had only been looking forward; here Time reminds them to look back and take inventory of their short lives.

Lines: 41-48

The tone shifts in the next two stanzas, taking on almost fairy-tale or nursery-rhyme qualities. The images become more fanciful and absurd, such as a glacier knocking in a cupboard and a desert sighing in a bed. Even the crack starting in the teacup widens until we can see the road we are walking down in life for what it is: "A lane to the land of

Media Adaptations

- *Tell Me the Truth About Love* is an audio cassette of Auden reading his own work.

- Auden is included on the audio cassette *The Caedman Treasury of Modern Poets Reading Their Own Poetry.*

the dead." The tone shift to a more childlike voice (while still describing the morbid reality we face) gives these lines an even spookier effect, the soundtrack and the scene not quite right for each other, leaving us feeling uneasy. Time goes on for another stanza in this nursery-rhyme voice, invoking images from "Jack and the Beanstalk" and "Jack and Jill." Unlike their moral and innocent counterparts, the characters in these stanzas are a bit more perverse, the giant "enchanting to Jack" and Jill—seduced—who "goes down on her back."

Lines: 49-52

Bringing us back to the water's reflection, Time commands the lovers again to "look in the mirror," to look inside themselves and realize who they really are. What does Time want them to see? Perhaps their status as "fallen" creatures expelled from the garden of eternal beauty and life. According to Judeo-Christian mythology, man was expelled from Eden for his sins and willingness to be corrupted. As a result, we are mortals who are given a short time to walk on the earth, no longer in control of time but prisoner to it, as "Life remains a blessing / Although [we] cannot bless."

Lines: 53-56

The mirror of the previous stanza gives way to a window in line 53, as if the reflective surface faded and the lovers now stare through clear glass. Realizing their mortal fate, their "tears scald and start," blurring their vision. The corruption introduced in lines 45-48 seems to resurface in this stanza. These lines seem to trace Judeo-Christian mythology which cites our own sin and corruption as the reason for our mortal lives; in other words,

Adam and Eve had the chance to live in a garden of eternal love, but were seduced by Satan and forced to leave.

Lines: 57-60

After eight stanzas of allegorical dialogue where Time scolds the lovers for their arrogance, these last four lines return the reader to the dramatic situation of the poem—the two lovers near the river. Just as sudden as they had started, the bells stop their chiming, and we realize the whole imagined dialogue may have only spanned the time it took for the clock tower to toll 8, 9, or 10 times.

The dramatic situation of the poem may be as simple as this: the speaker walks down to the river and hears the lovers singing; the city clocks chime the hour and interrupt the lovers. But in that brief chiming, the speaker hears the underlying meaning of the moment. No matter what the lovers may promise each other, the clock is ticking, and their time on this earth is measured out in hours, days, months and years.

Before the speaker realizes how far his mind had drifted, "the lovers they were gone," perhaps final proof of their impermanence. Even for the speaker it is "late, late in the evening" by the end of the poem. But like the cycle of seasons we pass through, Time will continue as we come and go, just as the river brimming nearby will continue to flow, carving its path forever deeper toward the ocean.

Themes

Time

"As I Walked Out One Evening" is a conversation between a lover and the clocks that interrupt his claims of eternal devotion. No matter what promises the lover makes— "Till China and Africa meet, / And the river jumps over the mountain / And the salmon sing in the street"—Time will be watching from the shadows, ready to remind them (as they are about to kiss) that another hour has passed. The lovers realize that they are one hour closer to their mortal fate. This poem uses allegory to provide a voice for Time, and Time uses that voice to scold the young lovers for their foolish hopefulness. The message Time conveys to the lovers is clear: "In headaches and in worry / Vaguely life leaks away." Our stay on this planet is metered out, hour by hour, day by day, and like

the hourglass sand pouring out since birth, "the desert sighs in the bed."

Set as a backdrop to this dialogue between mortality and eternity is the "brimming, ... deep river" where the speaker stops and overhears the lovers. Rivers are often used as metaphors for Time because they flow seemingly forever, from horizon to horizon, and we are too small in perspective to be able to see either a source or a destination. We can walk up to the bank and put a foot in the cold water, but the whole river keeps flowing past us. The chimes of the clock tower remind us of Time passing.

Cycle of Life

Underlying the theme of Time is the cycle of life, or seasons revolving like a smaller gear turning a larger wheel. The speaker may already be thinking about the passing seasons of his own life when the crowds on the pavement remind him of "harvest wheat." Auden describes the wheat in terms of time: fall, the harvest season, is often used in art as a comparison, or metaphor, for old age. It is the last stage of the life cycle—the plants past bloom and fruit, the cold winter imminent. Here the speaker sees the crowd and thinks of the fields in autumn, the golden wheat, and is perhaps reminded of the cycle we all pass through in heading toward our "winter" years. Even the young lovers will grow pale with old age, just as "into many a green valley / Drifts the appalling snow."

Death

Auden portrays Time allegorically in almost sinister terms, inhabiting the "burrows of nightmare" and watching the lovers from the shadows. It waits until they are just about to seal their love with a kiss before it coughs its objection. The same church bells that chime the hour also toll for the dead, and on this night near the river both bells have the same tenor.

The bells serve as a scheduled reminder that "the crack in the teacup opens / A lane to the land of the dead." The speaker, walking along the river down Bristol Street, may have found himself suddenly further down that lane than expected, finding himself located somewhere between the lovers and "all the clocks in the city." Standing there at in the midst of the chiming bells, he loses track of time, hearing an entire song in response to the lover's singing. He suddenly realizes how much time has passed: "It was late, late in the evening, / The lovers they were gone."

Style

W. H. Auden is highly regarded for his formally crafted and musical lines. "As I Walked Out One Evening" is constructed using four-line stanzas called quatrains, the second and fourth lines locking rhymes to create on overall poetic form known as "common measure." Emily Dickinson also used this form on a regular basis, and its origins are old. Each line holds three stressed syllables which echo the speaker's footsteps toward the river, and as we walk down the crowded street with the speaker, we begin to feel the pacing of his stride in the rhythm of each line.

Each pattern of accents in a line is called a "foot," and in this poem's lines we feel the alternating feet stepping forward: "the **crowds** up**on** the **pave**ment / were **fields** of **Har**vest **wheat.**" The "ta-**dum** ta-**dum**" unstressed and stressed metric foot is called an iamb. Iambic meter is probably the most familiar to our ears, used commonly by William Shakespeare, Robert Frost, John Milton and many rap artists writing today.

Historical Context

The years immediately surrounding the publication of "As I Walked Out One Evening" influenced Auden on many levels. In the late 1930s, he left England and moved to America. His departure and subsequent application for United States citizenship left many British critics feeling betrayed. Many believed Auden possessed a universal voice that was deeply in touch with their own hopes, fears, and resentments. His move to America on the eve of World War II marked the dominating influence of American political power and culture.

Auden traveled to America in January, 1939, with fellow poet and friend Christopher Isherwood aboard the French liner the *Champlain* (which would later be sunk by naval mines near Bordeaux during World War II). The two settled quickly into the New York literary scene, attending readings and parties in Greenwich Village.

It was at one of these parties that the poet met 18-year-old Chester Kallman. The two began having tea together regularly at Auden's apartment, and by the beginning of June, Auden was convinced he was deeply in love. He wrote his brother: "It's really happened at last after all these years. Mr. Right has come into my life. This time, my

Topics for Further Study

- Write a poem from the point of view of a speaker who walks into the school cafeteria only to overhear the beginning of a conversation the next table over. Craft the dialogue into formal quatrains, like Auden's style. Use only three stressed syllables per line. The poem does not have to rhyme. Halfway through the poem, the cafeteria bell should ring, and the speaker will imagine what the clocks might be saying to the room of eating students. Finish the poem in dialogue, keeping the tight structure. Compare results and discuss.

- What do you think Auden is referring to when he writes "Life remains a blessing / Although you cannot bless?" What about "You shall love your crooked neighbour / with your crooked heart?" How would you describe the speaker's impression of the lovers?

- How do you feel the poem would change if the speaker responded to the lover's conversation rather than using the clocktower speak allegorically about Time? Do you think the speaker agrees more with the argument for Love or for Time? Discuss your answers using examples from the poem.

dear, I really believe it's marriage." He told another friend around the same time that he was "mad with happiness." He would later explain to an interviewer he never really had loved anyone before, and that "[Chester] became so much part of my life that I keep forgetting that he is a separate person. I have also discovered what I never knew before, the dread of being abandoned and left alone."

This love affair may have been on Auden's mind as he wrote "As I Walked Out One Evening." There was a sense of doom on a national scale as well, and as Auden and Kallman returned from their honeymoon, the war in Europe exploded. Hitler invaded Poland on September 1st, 1939, and that night Auden composed a poem. One of his most famous, it is a farewell to his generation's

Compare & Contrast

- **1940:** Karl Pabst introduces the Jeep, a light-weight, 4-wheel drive, off-road vehicle. The United States military would purchase more than 649,000 over the next five years during World War II.

  1998: Jeeps are available from American Motors, popular as all-terrain vehicles as well as for city driving.

- **1940:** Germany invades Belgium, the Netherlands, Luxembourg, Norway, Denmark and Romania, extending its control across Europe. America provides weapons to England, but hesitates joining the war against Germany.

  1945: Defeated, Germany is divided into four sections to be partitioned by England, Russia, and the United States.

  1949: Communist leaders divide Germany in half, constructing a wall through the center of Berlin. East Germany would become communist while the West stays democratic.

  1989: With the decline of communist power in Russia, East Germany removes the Berlin wall and unites a city that had been divided for forty years.

  1998: Germany is growing to become a major power in the European Economic Community.

- **1940:** The Olympics in Tokyo and Helsinki are canceled due to the war.

  1944: Officials decide not to schedule the Olympics in London again because of the war.

  1998: Olympic officials ask that the United States postpone any possible military actions against Iraq in honor of the Olympic treaty. The conflict is avoided for the time being, and the winter Olympics take place as scheduled in Nagano, Japan.

"clever hopes." The 1930s in England had been known as the "Age of Auden," but in 1939 he deliberately distanced himself from the man he was the decade earlier.

Auden made the transition from British subject to American citizen, from liberal progressive to Orthodox Episcopalian. And perhaps most important, like the person singing under the railroad arch in the poem, he was in love for the first time. But unfortunately, this love did not last: Kallman had been unfaithful, and a year after the poems were published, the two parted, sending Auden into a rage which would leave him weeping and cynical.

Critical Overview

W. H. Auden is often categorized with the modernist poets or with a group of "left-wing" British poets, including Stephen Spender, Louis MacNeice, and Cecil Day-Lewis. As tempted as critics are to place Auden within a tradition, many agree he is unique because of his well-crafted, evocative poetry that effectively captured the political and cultural mood of the day.

The poems collected in *Another Time,* a volume including "As I Walked Out One Evening" are the first works Auden completed in America after moving from England in 1939. The publication of the collection marked a transition for Auden. As Richard Johnson asserts in *The Directory of Literary Biography,* "the poems mark one of the balance points of Auden's career, where lyrical gift, formal discipline, and ethical impulse come together, with considerable vitality, and in an idiom almost unique in modern poetry."

The editors of *The Norton Anthology of Modern Poetry* characterize Auden's early work as being preoccupied with "impending doom, of our general complicity in seemingly individual evil conduct." This is perhaps evident in such lines as "the crack in the tea-cup opens / A lane to the land of the dead" and "You shall love your crooked neighbor / With your crooked heart." The editors also point out his fondness for "invoking large forces—mountains, floods, glaciers, deserts—as symbols of human needs or defects." Auden invokes three of these in "As I Walked Out One Evening," almost in precise order, including the "brimming river," a glacier that "knocks in the cupboard" and a "desert [sighing] in the bed."

Criticism

Jeannine Johnson

Jeannine Johnson is a freelance writer who has taught at Yale University. In the following essay Johnson explains how Auden's ballad addresses the ideas of both the authenticity and durability of love.

W. H. Auden's poem "As I Walked Out One Evening" has the rhythm and sound of a chant or song. In fact, the poem was first published in 1938 under the title "Song." The poem as a whole is a song, and so are its two main statements. The poem begins and ends with the poet's voice, and in between are the voice of a singing lover and a chorus of chiming clocks. The second song is a response to the first, as the clocks contradict the lover's claim to the timelessness of his passion. All of this is contained in the poet's melody about his stroll through London and through life.

The poem is composed in ballad meter, a form that nineteenth-century American poet Emily Dickinson often used. A ballad is a kind of song, and thus a poem written in ballad meter has some of the qualities of music. A poem in ballad meter contains quatrains, or groups of four lines together. In each of the quatrains, the last word of the second and fourth lines rhyme: for example, in the first stanza "Street" rhymes with "wheat." These rhymes create a pattern that, as the poem progresses, our ears come to expect. In choosing the ballad form, Auden differs from many other twentieth-century poets who have preferred to write without rhyming their verses. One effect of the rhyme in Auden's poem is to create the informal feeling of a folksong. But this is not a simplistic piece, as the poet shows by making several clever rhymes such as "sing" and "ending" and "wrist" and "missed" and by incorporating inexact rhymes (called "near rhymes" or "slant rhymes") such as "hold" and "world" and "is" and "kiss."

What Do I Read Next?

- The editor to first publish Auden's poetry is the poet T. S. Eliot. His work, including *The Waste Land,* is considered central to the Modernist poetry movement.

- Best known for his award-winning poetry, Auden's critical and travel prose is also available in *The Complete Works of W. H. Auden: Prose and Travel Books in Prose and Verse, Volume I.*

- For a brief critical overview of virtually every poem Auden published, read John Fuller's 1970 book *A Reader's Guide to W. H. Auden.*

- Another Auden poem from the same collection *Another Time* is "Musee des Beaux Arts," included in *Poetry For Students,* Vol. 1.

A regular syllable count reinforces the rhyming pattern. In traditional ballad form, the first and third lines contain seven or eight syllables, while the second and fourth lines contain six. There are always three accented beats in each of the four lines. For instance, in the first line of the poem the words "I" and "out" and the first syllable of "evening" should be read with more emphasis than the other syllables in the line. Auden varies the number of syllables in "As I Walked out One Evening," but the second and fourth lines are usually shorter than the first and third, and he always assigns three strong stresses to a line.

The title of the poem tells us that the time is evening which, as its name suggests, is a period when day and night are evenly balanced. This is important because the poem tries to balance two different ideas expressed by the two songs. The poet indirectly invites us to compare, or weigh against each other, the conflicting philosophies of the lover and the clocks. On the one hand, the lover argues that at least one part of human life—love—is eternal and eternally youthful. On the other hand, the clocks contend that all of life is subject to time and decay. Though the poet does not want to deny the lover's idealism, he ultimately gives more credit to the clocks' pragmatic attitude.

The poet recalls walking among crowds of Londoners in the early evening. He hears someone singing from below a railroad bridge, "Love has no ending." Although the poet is among lots of other people, he is somewhat isolated. He does not see the singer, and he seems to be the only one to hear the song. We might imagine, then, that the poet is listening to his own thoughts rather than receiving ideas from outside sources.

In any case, the lover's song continues as he makes exaggerated promises to his beloved: "I'll love you till the ocean / Is folded and hung up to dry / And the seven stars go squawking / Like geese about the sky." The singer claims that his affection will last until the end of the world and even until the end of the universe. These are conventional boasts that most of us have heard before. By putting these familiar words in the mouth of the lover, Auden may be indicating that the lover's feeling is universal and therefore important.

Conversely, though, the lover's common phrases may suggest that, despite his protests, his love is not unique and is therefore insignificant. There is some indirect evidence for this idea. The "seven stars" refer to a group of bright stars called the Pleiades, or seven sisters, in the constellation Taurus. According to ancient Greek myth, the hunter Orion was in love with these sisters, although they did not return his love. Orion pursued them for a long time but was never successful in capturing any of them. Eventually Zeus, the king of the Greek gods, took pity on the sisters and installed them in the heavens as stars. This story is about selfish and unrequited passion. Its presence here may imply that the lover in the poem does not possess a true or real love.

More important than the question of love's authenticity is the question of its durability. After the lover sings that his feeling has existed from the beginning of time and will last until its end, all the city clocks respond with a song of their own: "O let not Time deceive you, / You cannot conquer time." Since the purpose of clocks is to measure minutes and hours, it is not surprising that they speak of the monotony and authority of time. The clocks' song is more mechanical and regular than the lover's. They "whirr and chime" and argue that time is more powerful than anything human, even love. "Time watches from the shadow / And coughs when you would kiss." Time is a stealthy and inescapable force that can disrupt joyful moments and can replace a kiss—which brings people together—with a cough—which drives people apart.

The clocks maintain that time is so strong because, for each of us, our lifespan is finite. Such limits make our daily choices difficult, create regret, and render life burdensome. As the timepieces tell it, "In headaches and in worry / Vaguely life leaks away."

The clocks continue, and we see that time not only presents minor anxieties and small agonies such as headaches, but it also brings larger hazards: "The glacier knocks in the cupboard, / The desert sighs in the bed, / And the crack in the tea-cup opens / A lane to the land of the dead." A cupboard, bed, and tea-cup are all objects found in the home. Normally this is a familiar and safe place, but immense powers from the natural world threaten us even here. Death, the greatest danger of all, also lingers in this domestic place. The cracked tea-cup is proof that things wear out as time passes, and it is symbolic of the human condition. We, too, deteriorate and steadily approach death because time is almighty.

Auden personifies the clocks by allowing them to speak. In reality, of course, these machines do not have the capacity for human language. The clocks' argument, like the lover's, may well be taking place inside the poet's head. The poet is thinking about, or reflecting on, the nature of human life, and in the clocks' song there are several references to vision and to literal reflections. In one of these the timepieces urge, "O look, look in the mirror, / O look in your distress; / Life remains a blessing / Although you cannot bless." Here, the mirror reflects an image of sadness, yet the negative tone of this and preceding stanzas is qualified somewhat by the statement that "Life remains a blessing." Nevertheless, the clocks make it clear that we are unable to appreciate life's pleasures, and they give one final order: "You shall love your crooked neighbour / With your crooked heart." According to the clocks, we love only partially, and incorrectly at that.

The clocks' long narration undercuts the lover's optimism and certainty. Auden gives the clocks three times as many stanzas as the lover in which to state their ideas about life, love, and time. This imbalance, coupled with the fact that the timekeepers get the last word in the debate, seems to show that their philosophy is the dominant one. But in fact the clocks do not get the last word in the poem. In the final stanza, the poet is finished quoting them, and he returns to speak in his own voice. Many hours have elapsed since the beginning of the poem. The crowds are gone, and so are the lover and his beloved. The clocks have fallen silent, and, the poem concludes, "the deep river ran on." This last line may be hopeful: it might indicate that the cycle recorded in the poem will repeat itself and that lovers and other idealists will again sing of their hopes and passions, despite the dire pronouncements of clocks and other realists. Conversely, this final line may be pessimistic: the river seems to be symbolic of time's relentless forward motion. The river, like the "appalling snow," the glacier, and the desert, appears to have little concern for the human world and is unaffected by our pleasures and sorrows. Regardless of our fate, nature and time will march on.

The poet seems to advance the clocks' message over the lover's. He cannot deny that love is diminished by the difficulties and limitations of life. However, perhaps one aspect of human life— poetry—will also move ahead endlessly. The ballad form in which this poem is written may, in theory, continually renew itself. The poet's consistent rhymed quatrains mimic the regular ticks of a clock, but the poem's chimes are under human control. "As I Walked Out One Evening" and other individual poems must end, but poetry as an art and as a representative of human achievement has the potential to live on.

Source: Jeannine Johnson, in an essay for *Poetry for Students,* Gale, 1998.

Bruce Meyer

Bruce Meyer is the director of the creative writing program at the University of Toronto. He has taught at several Canadian universities and is the author of three collections of poetry. In the following essay, Meyer discusses how Auden uses the ballad form to present a poem about the struggle for love in modern society.

In the "Prologue" to *The Canterbury Tales,* Geoffrey Chaucer hangs an brooch around the neck of his Prioress, and the jewel is inscribed with the Latin phrase *Amor vincit omnia,* or "love conquers all." Countless generations of poets have returned to this same theme to address the issue of the power of love. In *The Sonnets* Shakespeare points out that the great enemies of love and the poetic ideal are time and the world, neither of which have any bearing on or regard for beauty. Indeed the great subject of love poetry is, by contradiction, struggle, and the need to hold back the world, as in Andrew Marvell's "To His Coy Mistress," in which the poet laments, "Had we but world enough and time." W. H. Auden's love ballad "As I Walked Out One

Evening" takes up the cause of love in the face of a perverse and degenerate modern world that is just as time-bound and corrupting, if not more so, as the worlds known by Shakespeare, Marvell, and the great love poets of the past. The lover's promise "Love has no ending" in line 8 is a universal pledge of constancy that others have taken up, such as Philip Larkin in the closing lines of "Arundel Tomb" ("What will survive of us is love"). The lines that follow in Auden's ballad, "I'll love you, dear, I'll love you / Till China and Africa meet" remind the reader of the pledge Robert Burns made in his beautiful song, "My Love Is Like a Red, Red Rose:" "Till all the seas gang dry my dear / And rocks melt with the sun / And I will love thee still my dear / Though sands of time should run." But Auden locates his love pledge in the midst of a conundrum. The modern world and all its perversions stand in direct contradiction to the beauty, innocence, and simplicity of the lover's pledge. The solitary persona of "As I Walked Out One Evening" must make his way in a world that despises love and denigrates the eternal with the brute force of the temporal.

The poem, which takes the ballad form, is in keeping with the eighteenth–century English tradition of "the progress piece," in which a journey is described and various landmarks are pointed out along the way. For Auden, however, the journey is an evening stroll on a night in the middle of the twentieth century, and the landmarks are, at best, bathetic reminders of how far the contemporary world has drifted from the poetic ideals laid down by the traditions of poetic literature. Along the way, on a casual evening walk "down Bristol Street," the persona encounters crowds (who bear a vague resemblance to the crowds pouring over London Bridge in T. S. Eliot's "The Waste Land"), clocks (the great poetic symbol of entropy, pressure, and decay), and a tawdry allusion to nursery rhyme characters such as Jack and the Beanstalk and Jack and Jill, who have been reduced to street prostitutes. More than being a walk or "progress piece" through the streets of a typical modern city, "As I Walked Out One Evening" is a journey through the experiential, an account of a progress not to a destination but to the realization that in the flow of time the only redeeming human value is the pledge of love between two people.

What is curious about Auden's choice of poetic form is that the ballad traditionally focuses narratively on a dramatic episode. The chief episode in "As I Walked Out One Evening" is not just the love pledge that the persona overhears on his stroll,

... 'As I Walked Out One Evening' is a journey through the experiential, an account of a progress not to a destination but to the realization that in the flow of time the only redeeming human value is the pledge of love between two people."

but the realization that the only saving grace for the world is love—"You shall love your crooked neighbour / With your crooked heart"—and that the entire scope of humanity is in some way corrupt. What redeems the world, however, is that even those who are corrupt are still capable of love, and that love must start somewhere. The declaration "O look, look in the mirror, / O look in your distress; / Life remains a blessing / Although you cannot bless" suggests that love is contingent upon the capacity of the individual to commit themselves to an act of spiritual generosity. If the world is loveless, Auden appears to say, it is because we lack the courage of commitment. This message, couched in the ballad form with its short, four–foot lines and its simple yet effective abab rhyme, is meant to strike a chord. The notion of the ballad form is that its enticing meter and its inviting yet direct narrative are meant to be remembered—hence its popularity and recurring appeal. As a "populist" poetic form, the ballad is meant to be memorized and recited or sung and to function as a vehicle for messages that are meant to have broad and lasting appeal. One is reminded of "Lord Randal," "Sir Patrick Spens" and "Barbara Allan" as examples of how the ballad form can be put to effective use. Auden's point in choosing the ballad form is that the message of love, even in the face of temporal challenges, must be heard and spread. As if by necessity, Auden is not only declaring the virtue of love, but also the seemingly endless difficulties that love encounters as a bond between willing and generous human beings.

Auden was aware of the musical aspects inherent in "As I Walked Out One Evening." John Fuller reminds us that Auden saw the poem as "a pastiche of folksong" in the tradition of Burns and A. E. Housman. Fuller also points out that the first two stanzas contain images of "fullness and fruition" when Auden compares the "crowds upon the pavement" to "fields of harvest wheat" and tells us that the river is "brimming." But these Arcadian suggestions aside, the moment of pledge is located not in a golden vale or some suitably bucolic location, but under a railway arch, a bathetic venue that locates the action of the poem in the undeniably modern setting of the grimy, industrial modern world. Even the snow, Fuller mentions, is "appalling snow." This is not the world of the ideal, but the world that seeks out a fading vision of the innocent and the true.

As in many of his other poems from the late 1930s, such as "The Unknown Citizen" and "Musee des Beaux Arts," Auden juxtaposes the extemporal and the poetic with the daily realities of life in an industrial society. The beloved, who is addressed by the overheard lover in stanza 5, is heralded as "The Flower of the Ages, / And the first love of the world," high praise even for the most remarkable of beloveds. What Auden is doing is locating the moment of the pledge beyond the temporal world in a realm that is still populated by the beloveds of the "Song of Solomon"—the realm of the ideal. Stanza 6 answers this directly with a statement on the nature of the world: "But all the clocks in the city / Began to whirr and chime: / 'O let not Time deceive you, / You cannot conquer Time." The capitalization on Time serves to personify the concept as a functioning villain in the little drama of love against the world. "Time," says Auden, inhabits "the burrows of the Nightmare / Where Justice naked is," as if all the universal truths are in peril for their safety.

True to the conventions of love poetry, into which Auden has deftly fit his ballad, the world is an unpleasant, if not dangerous place in which things fall apart and entropy runs riot over beauty and human values no matter how determined they may be. In terms of Auden's political message, that the human race must be warned against its enemies, the "glacier in the cupboard" and that "desert" in the "bed" are symptoms of a much larger problem in the world that can only be corrected through small acts of personal commitment and declaration. The world, Auden seems to suggest, is worth saving if only we have the moral courage to find the strength within ourselves to pursue virtue rather than perversion. The answer lies "in the mirror," and ultimately in ourselves. The poem affirms the capacity of the individual to love, which is a positive note of reinforcement and which links "As I Walked Out One Evening" to Auden's other poems of the period—poems that constantly remind us of our capacity to reform the world through small acts of dedication.

Even love, however, can run riot. The oversexed behaviour of the perverse incarnations of the archetypally innocent Jack and Jill is paralleled by the parodic treatment of the language of love in stanzas 4 and 5 in which the lover declares his undying love "Till China and Africa meet" and "the salmon sing in the street." The overused language of love, its hyperbole and its stretched conceits (spread far thinner than any conceit dreamed of in the love poems of a John Donne or an Elizabeth Barrett Browning) becomes totally absurd by the time the reader reaches stanza 6. Here the lover, in a fit of pledge-craft, promises to love his beloved until "the ocean / Is folded and hung up to dry / And the seven stars go squawking / Like geese about the sky." Comic as these "forced images" may be, they serve to underscore the poem with a dark subtext—that the language of love is something that must not only be expressed, but must also be mediated and creatively controlled. The distance between the pledge maker of "As I Walked Out One Evening" and Andrew Marvell in "To His Coy Mistress" is enormous, and Auden appears to suggest—rather playfully—that love itself has become something of an absurd cliché. There is also a strong suggestion on Auden's part that poetry itself is suffering from abuse at the hands of amateurs. One of the answers to the ills of the contemporary world may be to restore meaning and power to language and dignity to the art of poetry; this was Auden's personal mission as a poet. But however absurd the language of love may become in the hands of modern amateurs, love is still a human necessity and one that must be pursued as both a natural instinct and as a saving grace.

In the final stanza of the poem, the threat of time appears to have become absented. "The clocks have ceased their chiming, / And the river deep ran on." The river image picks up as a functioning timepiece where the clocks leave off. Archetypally, rivers imply time, death and inevitability. The strange use of the word "deep" as an adjective in the final line is reminiscent of the use of "deep" in Genesis 1 where The Bible an-nounces that before the act of divine creation set the universe in order "There was darkness upon the face of the deep." This association of "deep" with chaos and disorder is Auden's final warning of the ballad. The river that was "brimming" at the start of the poem when the action was located in "evening," is now coursing darkly through a chaotic night in which "the lovers" are "gone" and only the persona of the poem remains to bear witness to the emptiness that has overtaken the once lively civic scene he encountered on his casual stroll. The implication seems to be that without love, there is nothing, and that the alternative to love, human presence, human activity, and human observation is a dark, isolating, and horrible experience bereft of all activity except witness. As a note of warning that we must love each other at all costs, Auden seems to be sounding a grim, almost post-Christian note that there is no alternative to love, regardless of how badly that love is expressed. Any contact, any attempt to reach beyond the hedonism of the "Lily-white Boy" or "Jack" and "Jill" is a welcome respite from the complete isolation that marks the poem's ending. Auden reinforces his sense of warning in the opening line of the final stanza with the phrase "It was late, late in the evening," as if Time itself has finally vanquished the lovers, their hopes, and the truths contained in those hopes. Read as either a sad poem of isolation and detached, loveless observation, or as a signal to readers not only of the possibilities of commitment but of the necessities of love, "As I Walked Out One Evening" reminds us of the passions, the frailties and the dignities to which love inspires us—if only as sojourners who stroll out for an evening to mingle with the crowds and by chance discover beauty in foolish absurdity and possibilities for life in a world and nature set against our best aspirations.

Source: Bruce Meyer, in an essay for *Poetry for Students*, Gale, 1998.

Aidan Wasley

Aidan Wasley is a writer and instructor at Yale University. In the following essay, Wasley points out how Auden's perception about the power of poetry—its ability to outlast love, death, and time—is expressed in "As I Walked Out One Evening."

W. H. Auden's poem "As I Walked Out One Evening" is, as Auden himself described it, a "pastiche of folksong." That is, it incorporates a number of features of traditional forms of oral poetry, particularly those of the folk ballad. Customarily, ballads are short–verse narratives, characterized by strong rhymes and heavy metrical patterns, which make them easy to memorize and to recite, and attest to their origins as popular song. Ballads often express the drama of their subject—usually love, death, or some significant public event—through dialogue or the voice of an unnamed narrator who speaks as a kind of generalized representative of collective sentiment. We can find all of these qualities in Auden's poem, which recounts a surreal debate between a rapturous lover and an array of admonitory clocks on the nature of love, death, and time. The nameless speaker of the poem, whose observations in the first and last stanzas frame the debate, seems to stand outside of the world of the argument, even outside of time, despite his apparently specific locale, "out one evening / Walking down Bristol Street." The speaker's perspective is a distanced, ironic one, which offers commentary on, but not engagement with, the things he sees and hears. His is the voice of the detached, omniscient observer, like that of the artist or poet who articulates or describes events around him, but does not participate in them.

The question of poetry's engagement and involvement with the world was an extremely important one for Auden. Throughout his early poetic career, many of Auden's poems had addressed the issue of the relation between poetry and politics, a theme whose urgency was underscored by the catastrophic political events that were sweeping Europe during the 1930s. In a well-known poem called "Spain," written seven months before this one, Auden had exhorted his readers to join in the fight against Fascism in the Spanish Civil War (Auden himself enlisted as an ambulance driver during that conflict). Auden was widely known as the leader of a group of highly political young poets who endorsed socialist ideals, writing poems in the service of public awareness and a belief that poetry could help make a difference in what Auden, in "Spain," called "the struggle." In this poem, though, written after Auden's somewhat disillusioned return to England from Spain, we can perhaps see the poet, in the figure of the dispassionate, analytical spectator, stepping back from the notion that a poet's words can help stop wars or convince people to live justly. Auden's changing sense of poetry's role in the world would reach its most famous expression just over a year later in his elegy for Yeats (written following Auden's emigration to the United States, on the eve of World War II), which asserts "Poetry makes nothing happen." In recognition that poetry could neither help

ensure the defeat of the Spanish Fascists, nor prevent the calamity that was about to engulf all of Europe, Auden tried to redefine poetry's relationship to the world outside it. While poetry cannot precipitate social change or public action, he decided, it could be a form of action in itself. It is, he claims in the Yeats elegy, "a way of happening, a mouth." Poetry, says Auden, is what "survives," and it is this survival in the face of the world's assaults—its capacity to speak even after those who wrote it or those it recorded have been swept away—that gives poetry a kind of power over death and time. This is a theme we will see addressed in "As I Walked Out One Evening."

The first two stanzas of the poem set the stage for the debate between the lover and the clocks and introduce images and ideas that will recur throughout the poem. The scene it describes is a distinctly modern and urban one, with its "streets," "pavements," "crowds," and "railways." This both recalls the "Unreal City" of T. S. Eliot's *The Waste Land* (Auden was heavily influenced by Eliot) and announces that though the poet may be employing the ancient rural folk-ballad form, he is appropriating it for his own nontraditional purposes. The speaker's account of what he sees and hears on his walk subtly prefigure the poem's concern with the themes of death and time. The crowds are "fields of harvest wheat" ready to be cut down by time's scythe; the river is "brimming," connoting eyes filling with tears; and the lover—whose place "under an arch of the railway" implies a less lofty romantic encounter than his song would suggest—sings a song of constant, eternal love beneath a modern symbol of transit and transience. The lover's song in the third, fourth, and fifth stanzas, with its colorful claims of originality and unending devotion, closely echoes in form and imagery a very famous love song by eighteenth-century Scottish Romantic poet Robert Burns titled "A Red, Red Rose" that addresses the poet's lover in similarly florid terms (and a Scots accent):

O My Love's like a red, red rose,
    That's newly sprung in June;
O My Love's like the melody
    That's sweetly played in tune.

As fair thou art, my bonnie lass,
    So deep in love am I;
And I will love thee still, my dear,
    Till all the seas gang dry,

Till all the seas gang dry, my dear,
    And rocks melt with the sun:
O I will love thee still, my dear,
    While the sands of life shall run.

Auden's lover makes comparable protestations, insisting that his love will also endure longer than the mountains, oceans, stars, even time itself. The subtle irony here is that the very claims the lover is making for the uniqueness and permanence of his love are the same claims that have been made by countless lovers and poets before him. His assertion of his own originality is itself a poetic cliche. His identification with a particular kind of Romantic poetry also suggests that one of the secondary debates this poem is enacting is that between Romanticism, personified by the lover, and Modernism, figured in the answering clocks.

The clocks, which "whirr and chime" like a tolling bell in response to the lover's song, signal the lover's naivete in his belief that any love can be eternal. "O let not Time deceive you, / You cannot conquer Time," chime the clocks as they ring the hours that mark the lover's inescapable march toward death. In a series of grim and often obscure images and utterances—which evoke a certain mode of Modernist poetic anxiety and difficulty and place the clocks in the position of the modern anti-Romantic poet—the clocks reject the lover's claims, arguing that Time destroys love, just as it destroys life:

> "In headaches and in worry
>   Vaguely life leaks away,
> And Time will have his fancy
>   To-morrow or to-day.

> "Into many a green valley
>   Drifts the appalling snow;
> Time breaks the threaded dances
>   And the diver's brilliant bow.

The valley's summer green yields to winter's snows ("appall" literally means "to grow pale"), as even the most vigorous artist or athlete must eventually be covered over by a funeral "pall." The seasonal motif explicitly connects the themes of time and death, as does this poem's most well-known stanza:

> "The glacier knocks in the cupboard,
>   The desert sighs in the bed,
> And the crack in the tea-cup opens
>   A lane to the land of the dead.

Here death is figured in the "glacier" and the "desert," two huge natural and impersonal forces that overwhelm the landscape in a slow, inexorable, and all-engulfing progress. The domestic scene of the "cupboard" and "bed" is invaded by these devouring presences, as death comes calling even to the tidiest household. The "crack in the tea-cup" is the fault line of death, waiting at any moment to swallow us up. And if love is doomed in life, it is

> *The clocks address the lover—and the reader—in a sequence of stanzas that trace a progression of awareness and appreciation of love's fragile power in a world of death and time."*

entirely meaningless in "the land of the dead." There, all the comforting rules governing our affections are without significance, and the eternal verities expressed in the lover's song amount to little more than twisted nursery rhymes. In death, "the first love of the world" and "Jill go[ing] down on her back" add up to the same thing.

The clocks are not entirely cynical, however. They believe in love, though they know it cannot endure. In fact, they argue, it is precisely love's ephemerality and unreliability that makes it precious. The clocks address the lover—and the reader—in a sequence of stanzas that trace a progression of awareness and appreciation of love's fragile power in a world of death and time. In stanza ten, the clocks imagine the lover's inevitably doomed search for eternal love tempting him to suicide, as he stares into the basin into which the blood from his slit wrists would seep. The image of the basin also hints at an allusion to the Greek oracles, who used bowls mounted on tripods to conjure their prophetic visions. Thus the lover's faith in transcendant love is likened to a foolish faith in oracles, a belief in a visionary truth that exists outside of man's earthly experience.

By stanza thirteen, the prospective lover has progressed from suicidal despair to simple "distress," and from the basin to the mirror, where he looks not toward some mystical conception of love, but into himself. It is through love of himself that he will learn that "Life remains a blessing / Although you cannot bless." That is, he will discover that his earlier conception of timeless love is false and that it is the capacity for earthly love—however fleeting—that makes life a "blessing." The final phase of the lover's education brings him in the penultimate stanza from the mirror to the window, where his vision of his fellow man inspires in him the awareness that self-love is not sufficient and that "You shall love your crooked neighbour / With your crooked heart." Human love may be be faulty and "crooked," the clocks tell us, but it is all that we have. As Auden put it in another poem written around this time, "We must love one another or die" ("September 1, 1939").

The poem ends where it began, with the voice of the nameless observer:

> It was late, late in the evening.
>   The lovers they were gone;
> The clocks had ceased their chiming
>   And the deep river ran on.

The voices of the lover and the clocks have fallen silent. The debate has subsided, the crowds have disappeared. Time has conquered even the clocks themselves. All that remains is the voice of the poet, singing on late into the night, in tune with the river. It is the poet's voice that "survives" while all else has passed away.

In its presentation of the debate between the lover and the clocks, mediated by the narrator's commentary, the poem offers an array of different perspectives on the same subject, namely the place of love in a world where all men die. But while the clocks seem to have the upper hand in the argument, the poem doesn't take sides. It allows the reader to inhabit opposing perspectives and engage the debate for him or herself. We see the value in the lover's touching idealism while at the same time we acknowledge the clocks' clear-eyed view of human frailty. We must choose for ourselves which perspective is the true one and then, when we have finished reading the poem, act accordingly in our own lives. Reading this poem is thus, in a sense, a kind of rehearsal for life, just as Auden hoped it would be. While poems may indeed "make nothing happen," if we listen attentively to the choices the poem offers us, they can at least be "a way of happening."

Source: Aidan Wasley, in an essay for *Poetry for Students,* Gale, 1998.

Sources

Ellman, Richard, ed., *The Norton Anthology of Modern Poetry,* W. W. Norton, 1988, pp. 732-34.

Johnson, Richard, "W. H. Auden," in *The Dictionary of Literary Biography,* Volume 20: *British Poets, 1914-1945,* edited by Donald E. Stanford, Gale Research, 1983, pp. 19-49.

For Further Study

Frederick Buell, *W. H. Auden As a Social Poet,* Cornell University Press, 1973.
    Provides a general critical overview of Auden's work.

Humphrey Carpenter, *Auden: A Biography,* Houghton Mifflin Co., 1981.
    Offers some interesting insight into the personal and political events surrounding the publication of this poem.

Richard Hoggert, *Auden: An Introductory Essay,* Chatto & Windus, 1951.
    This highly enthusiastic essay both celebrates Auden's work and offers insight into the type of reviews his work received.

Concord Hymn

Ralph Waldo Emerson
1847

Also known as the "Concord Ode," "Concord Hymn" was one of Ralph Waldo Emerson's earliest published poems, appearing in 1847 when he was in his mid-thirties. Prior to that time, he had been known primarily as a lecturer and naturalist. This is probably Emerson's single best-known piece and has been memorized by many a school-age child. A battlefield monument that commemorates the initial battle of the American Revolutionary War and those who fought in it, the poem also celebrates the merging of the spirit of political liberty and the wonder of natural splendor that is quintessentially American.

As the subtitle—"Sung at the Completion of the Battle Monument, July 4, 1837"—suggests, this poem was written for a single public occasion. It was also apparently meant to be sung, not simply recited. The tune, if there ever was one, has been lost. The use of the word "hymn" suggests that it was a celebratory piece, composed especially for a communal event. Perhaps Emerson is consciously elevating his poem to the public sphere, to distinguish it from a work of more personal expression. This poem makes a fine companion piece to Henry Wadsworth Longfellow's poem "Paul Revere's Ride," another great work about the American Revolution.

Author Biography

Emerson was born in Boston in 1803. He was the son of Ruth Haskins Emerson and William Emer-

Ralph Waldo Emerson

the theory of Transcendentalism, which holds that humanity and nature are in essence the same and are merely different manifestations of the divine spirit. Transcendentalism has been one of the most influential ideas in American literary history. Emerson's first book, *Nature,* an important statement of his Transcendentalist views, was published in 1836. The succeeding decade was the most productive period in Emerson's career, in which he continued to deliver lectures while publishing collections of his philosophical essays and poetry as well as serving as editor of the *Dial,* a publication of the Transcendentalist Movement. During the 1850s and 1860s Emerson was an outspoken opponent of slavery and actively campaigned for abolition. By the end of the 1860s, however, his memory began to fail, and he gradually slipped into senility. He died at home in Concord in 1882.

son, a Unitarian minister who died when his son was eight. Emerson attended Boston Public Latin School and then enrolled in Harvard College at the age of fourteen. After graduation he briefly tried teaching but soon returned to Harvard to attend divinity school. He was ordained a minister in 1829. That same year he married Ellen Tucker, who died of tuberculosis only a year and a half later. Experiencing doubts about Christianity and the validity of organized religion, Emerson resigned his ministry in 1832. He spent the next several months traveling in Europe. While visiting a Paris botanical exhibition, Emerson had a vision of the intimate connection between humans and nature, and he resolved to be a naturalist. In Great Britain he met several of his literary idols, including Samuel Taylor Coleridge, William Wordsworth, and Thomas Carlyle, who became a lifelong friend. Upon returning to the United States in 1833, Emerson began a career as a public lecturer, speaking on various topics, including science, biography, literature, and travel. Emerson married Lydia Jackson in 1835 and settled in Concord, Massachusetts, where, except for regular trips in America and abroad, he resided for the rest of his life. In Concord, he became the center of a discussion group called the Transcendentalist Club, which met to discuss religious and philosophical issues. Emerson and the other members of the group developed

Poem Text

Sung at the Completion of the Battle Monument, July 4, 1837

By the rude bridge that arched the flood,
    Their flag to April's breeze unfurled,
Here once the embattled farmers stood
    And fired the shot heard round the world.

The foe long since in silence slept;   5
    Alike the conqueror silent sleeps;
And Time the ruined bridge has swept
    Down the dark stream which seaward creeps.

On this green bank, by this soft stream,
    We set to-day a votive stone;   10
That memory may their deed redeem,
    When, like our sires, our sons are gone.

Spirit, that made those heroes dare
    To die, and leave their children free,
Bid Time and Nature gently spare   15
    The shaft we raise to them and thee.

Poem Summary

Line 1:

"Rude" here means "crude." While the flood was not a literal flood, this is the beginning of water imagery used in the poem; the actual stream is an implied metaphor for the river of time that is also a theme in the poem. Emerson may be thinking also of the "flood" of freedom that swept over the new nation.

Lines 2-3:

According to the British law at the time, it was illegal to display the colonial flag referred to here. So unfurling it in the breeze, in the face of advancing British troops, was a defiant and courageous act. Note, too, that Emerson continues the imagery of both time and nature with "April's breeze." Not only did the Battle of Concord take place on April 19th, 1775, but April is the beginning of spring, the season of rebirth. Thus, this bridge could be considered the birthplace of the war that resulted in the colonies gaining their freedom.

Line 4:

We are so familiar with this phrase, and it has been reused in so many contexts since it was written, it may be difficult for us to imagine what it was like to have heard it for the first time. In our television age, when CNN shows us battles as they are happening, a shot can quite literally be heard around the world. Not so in Emerson's time, or when the Battle of Concord actually occurred. The American Revolution was the first successful rebellion by a citizenry against a colonial power; it was an inspiration to many revolutionary movements to come and continues to be so today. So the image of "the shot heard round the world" is quite powerful and appropriate, emphasizing that the battle did more than just defeat these specific soldiers—it marked the dawning of a new age in world history.

Lines 5-6:

The alliteration of "silence slept" is echoed a line later by "silent sleeps." The first phrase, referring to the invading British troops, is in the past tense, emphasizing that they are gone forever. The second phrase is in the present tense, reminding the reader (and any future potential foes) that the spirit of the victorious embattled farmers is still alive and breathing, ready to awaken at a moment's notice.

Lines 7-8:

The bridge itself, just like the men who fought there, has been washed down the river of time. This is not just an image from Emerson's mind; the original bridge had indeed been replaced. Emerson manages to use this actual fact symbolically, integrating the truth into the theme of the poem rather than inventing another image himself.

Line 9:

It is a simple "green bank" and "soft stream," the kind of place about which Emerson might have

Media Adaptations

- *The Spiritual Light of Emerson,* an audio cassette read by Richard Kiley, is available from Audio Literature.

- *Emerson Poetry* read by Archibald MacLeish was released on both audio cassette and phonographic record in 1971 by Caedmon.

- A record titled *Ralph Waldo Emerson: American Philosopher* was released by Listening Library in 1960.

- Folkways Records released *Ralph Waldo Emerson: A Selection from the Essays, the Poetry and the Journals* in 1963.

- An audio cassette titled *Nature and Spirit: Henry David Thoreau and Ralph Waldo Emerson* was released by Audio Partners Inc., in 1992.

written a nature poem. The place itself does not have the physical majesty of the fields of Agincourt or Waterloo, the sites of two famous British victories (Agincourt was the site of Henry V's victory over France in 1415; Waterloo was the site of Napoleon's ultimate defeat in 1815), yet it still echoes with the enormity of the colonist's accomplishment.

Lines 10-12:

"Votive" means dedicated in fulfillment of a vow or pledge, or symbolizing a wish. In this case, the wish is that the stone will remind the generations to come of what transpired here. In addition, the term might remind us of a "votive candle," as if to say that this is a living shrine, and the stone commemorates the flame of freedom that still burns.

Lines 13-14:

Emerson addresses himself not just to God, but to the Spirit that gave a collection of farmers and merchants the strength to stand on the bridge and face down the British army, the most formidable military power of the time.

Lines 15-16:

The monument is not only to the memory of the departed men, but to their spirit of liberty and the other inalienable rights they believed they were endowed with by their creator. Emerson here recalls the ruined bridge that time has swept away, as described in line 7, and asks that the monument be spared a similar fate. It is important to remember, too, that while the colonists won the Battle of Concord—they drove the British back to Boston, a retreat that cost the invaders two hundred casualties—Emerson barely mentions that fact. Throughout the poem, he is more interested in acknowledging the deeper meaning of what the colonists achieved on the bridge than in celebrating a military victory.

Themes

Permanence

Much is made in this poem about the effects of the passage of time. In the first stanza, this theme is only slightly alluded to: in the crude bridge that has withstood the flood; the crude army of farmers that stood up against the troops that tried to bring them down; and in the fact that it mentions April, which is the month when dormant plants all over the northern hemisphere come to life. The second stanza makes change the dominant theme of the poem. It tells readers that not only is the foe gone, but also that the conqueror is gone, and even the bridge that they fought over has been torn apart in time. This idea is picked up again at the end of the next stanza, which contains the reminder that not only will the present generation but also the generations to follow it will eventually die out. After drawing readers' attention to the ravages of time, Emerson focuses readers' attention to the fact that the monument being dedicated is made up of stone, which, according to the laws of physics, could be expected to last much longer than either human lives or a wooden bridge. He asks the unspecified Spirit to watch over the monument and to keep Time and Nature from harming it. The poem is therefore not as noble in its praise or reverence for the dead as it might seem at first glance. Freedom and courage are presented as vulnerable things that might be lost in history if they are not recorded for future generations on a stone, and the stone itself is shown to be a fragile thing in the greater universal measurement of time. Only the Spirit, larger than Time or Nature, is presented as being truly permanent, tying the events of the Revolutionary War with the dedication ceremony and on into the future.

Patriotism

This poem itself, although written for a patriotic occasion, is conspicuous in its lack of enthusiasm. It does not portray the Americans as the bearers of all things virtuous or the British as the instruments of evil. The only mentions of the confrontation at Concord during the Revolution are colorlessly descriptive, calling the Americans "the embattled farmers" and "the conqueror," and explaining that the monument is being erected to remember "their deed" without giving details about what that deed might be. It is not until the fourth stanza that the poem becomes so biased as to praise the dead militiamen as heroes who died for the freedom of their children. The poem does not argue this point or try to prove it, but only takes their heroism for granted. The subject of "Concord Hymn" is not really the acts of the dead soldiers themselves, but the monument that has been erected to them, and in that sense it is more a reflection on patriotism than on heroism, a distinction that is too often ignored. As presented here, the monument is patriotic, because a country is defined by the way it remembers people after their sacrifices are long gone. More than any one human life or generation of individuals, or any functional object such as a bridge, the stone monument would appeal to Emerson's philosophic nature as a sign of the way that ideas are eternal. It may be the philosopher in Emerson that kept him from speaking strongly for or against any particular nation, making him focus on abstract concepts and objects of nature instead. His brief mention of heroism and freedom, combined with the sense of nationalism that is always bound to battle monuments, however, gives this poem a sublime but powerful sense of patriotism that is appropriate for its intended use.

Nature

The imagery that Emerson uses in this poem directs the reader's attention—again and again—to the natural setting that surrounds the battle monument. Most of these references are to the river, so that the story that Emerson does not tell directly can be found by paying attention to the river's actions. The first stanza, for instance, introduces the Battle of Concord with only a few details (embattled farmers and a shot), but it gives the prominent opening line to the image of a bridge being assaulted by a flood, which evokes the battle just as well as statistics about troops and weapons would. The second stanza, concerning the idea that all of the people involved in the conflict were dead by then, tells readers that the bridge was also gone, "swept / Down the dark stream which seaward creeps." This might seem to imply a sinister fate for the war heroes, being dragged away in creepy darkness, except that the sea seems more impartial and fair than it does frightening, just as the deaths of both "foe" and "conqueror" show death to be impartial. At the time of the monument's dedication, Emerson calls the river "this soft stream": it is no longer viewed as hectic and dangerous, just as life is no longer hectic and dangerous to those who take the time to sit back and reflect. This is more than a case of a poet using nature to convey coded messages about life: Emerson is linking human affairs to the motion of nature, implying that we can understand the course of our history by watching how nature behaves.

Style

"Concord Hymn" is tightly constructed of sixteen lines, four stanzas of four lines apiece, with (usually) eight syllables to each line. The lines also end in alternating rhymes, as we can see in the first four lines: "flood" on line 1 rhymes with "stood" on line 3; while lines 2 and 4 end with the rhyming of "unfurled" and "world." This regularity creates a musical order, which helps the reader enter into the poem in the same way one might enjoy a popular song. Our ears begin to anticipate what will come next. This musicality is also important given that Emerson notes in his subtitle that the poem was "sung" at its first performance.

Another device that Emerson employs here is alliteration, particularly with the "s" sound. Notice "silence slept," "silence sleeps," and "soft stream." In addition to these obvious uses where one word immediately follows another, look at line 12:

When, like our sires, our sons are gone.

Both "sires" and "sons" begin and end with "s," and their similar sound emphasizes the connection between past and future generations, which in turn is a major element in the theme of time in the poem. While the word "fathers" would have had the same literal meaning as "sires," it would not have provided the thematic emphasis, and also would have added an extra syllable to the line.

Topics for Further Study

- Write a "hymn" to some news event that you would not want future generations to forget. Follow the poetic structure of Emerson's poem.

- Research the "Intolerable Acts" passed by Britain in March of 1774 to punish the colony of Massachusetts for defying British policies. Form teams to debate the fairness of such actions, using modern-day political situations as examples.

- This poem was written more than fifty years after the "shot heard round the world." How is this fact shown in the poetic strategies Emerson uses?

Historical Context

April 19, 1775

Emerson's claim that American farmers "fired the shot heard round the world" has become the version of history familiar to most students throughout the nineteenth and twentieth centuries. The phrase has been repeated in history textbooks and Revolutionary War memorials until it has become a part of the nation's identity, but historians have never been able to prove which side actually fired that famous first shot. Whether it was the last blow struck in oppression or the first blow in freedom, the significance to world history would be the same: it marked the start of the first fight against the colonial system, a system that has often been fought since and still shows itself today, though mostly just as pale tradition. The Battle of Concord, which the monument in the poem honors, began after a grueling night of preparation on both sides. The drama began on the night of April 18th, in Boston, where the British military headquarters in the colonies was located. For several years resentment had been building, with the British passing increasingly restrictive laws and the colonists becoming more bold in their disobedience. On April 18th, the Sons of Liberty, a network of spies

Compare & Contrast

- **1775:** American consumers protested Britain's treatment of the Colonies by refusing to buy British products and buying American goods instead; imports from Britain fell by 95 percent.

  1837: Due to reckless government investments in the country's expansion to the West, the United States fell into a period of economic depression, forcing the collapse of many businesses. Great Britain also entered into a depression, partially as a result of bad investments in American businesses.

  Today: The International Monetary Fund acts to contain economic crises before one country's problems can spread to others.

- **1775:** The first Abolitionist Society in America, dedicated to abolishing slavery, was founded in Pennsylvania.

  1837: Debates between supporters of slavery and supporters of freedom were dangerously violent so often that Congress enacted a "gag law" to suppress public discussion of the subject.

  1863: In the middle of the Civil War, President Abraham Lincoln declared freedom for all slaves in the United States with the Emancipation Proclamation.

  Today: Equal treatment for all people in the country continues to be a goal, as government policies seek to cancel traditional oppression.

- **1775:** Paul Revere and William Dawes rode on horseback from what is now downtown Boston to Concord, to deliver the message about the approaching British troops. Riding at top speed but stopping at every farmhouse to sound the alarm, the twenty-mile trip took all night.

  1837: The first patent was issued for an electronic telegraph, and Samuel F. B. Morse developed the system of telegraphic code that is used to this day.

  1876: Alexander Graham Bell received a patent for the first telephone.

  1895: Guglielmo Marconi invented the first radio.

  1928: The first television receiver for the home, working on the same basic principles that television uses today, was demonstrated in New York.

  Today: The Internet is increasingly a source of up-to-the-minute news, although there is no way to assure the truth of what is posted there.

---

for the colonists, found out about a planned British military maneuver to attack the American underground, take away their weapons, and arrest Revolutionary leaders John Hancock and Samuel Adams. Paul Revere and William Dawes were chosen to ride from Boston to Concord to warn inhabitants there—and in all of the villages in between—about the coming invasion. (Henry Wadsworth Longfellow's 1863 poem "Paul Revere's Ride" has made a simplified version of this warning familiar to generations of school children.) At Lexington, where they stopped to report the news to Hancock, they were joined by a third rider, Dr. Samuel Prescott; when Dawes and Revere were temporarily held by British soldiers, Prescott escaped and took the alarm to Concord.

At the North Bridge over the Concord River, the tired and cold British troops, who had been marching all night from Boston, met a small company of militiamen, who had been waiting for them with loaded rifles. American observers later said that the British commander gave the order to fire, but British participants said that they had been under orders to wait; when the shooting did begin, the casualties were overwhelmingly on the American side, with eight dead and nine wounded, while only a few minor injuries were suffered by British troops. It was after the initial conflict, though, that the British were dealt the first losses of the war. They marched back to Boston in rank, out in the open, in their red uniforms, and from the sides of the road crowds jeered them as they approached. As end of the line passed, the militiamen, who did not have the strong military training that the British troops had, fired at them from behind trees, stones, and walls, picking off British soldiers one at a time. By the end of the day, the British had lost 65 men, 15 of them officers. Both sides felt they had been attacked, and the Revolutionary War was officially declared.

July 4, 1837

The patriotic subject of this poem is fitting for the dedication of a war monument during a Fourth of July celebration, but it is not the sort of theme that is usually associated with Ralph Waldo Emerson, whose strongly expressed ideas seldom dwelled on the glories of war. During his lifetime and in the time since, Emerson has best been known as a leading supporter of the American philosophical movement called Transcendentalism. Religious in the way that it speculated on the nature of God (referred to by Emerson as the "Oversoul"), Transcendentalism placed more emphasis on nature and reason than on the rules of behavior upon which many religions rely. The movement was the natural outgrowth of the Romantic movement that swept through Europe and America in the late eighteenth century. Romanticists looked to nature in itself as a source of knowledge for man, while Transcendentalists viewed nature as a way to come to know the Oversoul, which, like God, was seen as the life force that runs through all things in the universe. Like the militia that fought at Concord, both movements were seen as groups of rebels, casting aside tradition. In the case of Transcendentalism, the rebellion was against the strict religious practices of the Puritans, whose views had dominated the American way of thought ever since the country was settled. The Puritans had been strict in their rules about human behavior: if they had not been, they might not have found it necessary or acceptable to leave Europe, come to an undeveloped land, and wrest it from the native inhabitants. Transcendentalists believed that society was not the standard that determined how humans related with the eternal, but that studying nature was better than studying books for understanding the universe. Famous Transcendentalists included Emerson, Bronson Alcott, Margaret Fuller and Henry David Thoreau, whose 1854 book *Walden,* about his life away from society in

a shack in the woods, is an American literary classic. In some ways, it is strange that Emerson—who was known as an essayist, lecturer, and a leader of this philosophic movement, but who was not to publish a book of poetry until ten years later—would be chosen to present a poem for this monument's dedication. On the other hand, the Transcendentalists' emphasis on independence and self-reliance was every bit as much a part of the American character then as it was when the Revolutionaries first stood up against the army of their rulers.

Critical Overview

Matthew Arnold, a British poet and critic, was not a fan of Emerson's poetry, considering it too indirect and lacking in energy and passion. In an 1884 essay later published in his "*Discourses on America,*" however, Arnold did single out "Concord Hymn" for praise, even if it was somewhat backhanded: "Such good work as the noble lines on the Concord Monument is the exception," Arnold wrote, meaning the poem is superior to Emerson's other work. Interestingly, while Arnold went to great lengths to criticize Emerson's poetry, in the final analysis he did consider him a man of superior importance and "a friend and aider of those who would live in the spirit." Along with Benjamin Franklin, Arnold considered Emerson the most original and "infinitely important" American writer. Another critic, George Arms, has described the language of "Concord Hymn" as "disappointing in its decadent poetic flatness," but also noted the effective evolution of the piece, beginning as it does with a description of the physical battle and ending by celebrating the non-destructive and "tranquil aspects of time."

In an 1880 essay, Walt Whitman declared that he did not find Emerson a great poet in his use of language or his choice of subjects and themes, and he also found Emerson's verse cold and artificial. Whitman even went so far as to say that "it has been doubtful to me if Emerson really knows or feels what Poetry is." Whitman did consider Emerson's spirit to be "exactly what America needs," however, because Emerson urged the still-young nation to sever itself from its ties to European colonialism and to create itself anew.

Writing in 1897, John Jay Chapman considered the first two lines to be "worthy of some mythical Greek" poet, but then found the rest of the verse to be "crude ... lame and unmusical," a criticism he applied to all of Emerson's poetry. Chapman maintained that some passages "hurt the reader and unfit him to proceed." However, he still considered Emerson a "colossus," towering over not only American literature but the entire culture.

Poet Robert Frost considered Emerson to be one of the four greatest Americans of all time (along with George Washington, Thomas Jefferson, and Abraham Lincoln). Frost had particularly high praise for "Concord Hymn": "If Emerson had left us nothing else, he would be remembered for the monument at Concord that he glorified with lines surpassing any other ever written about soldiers." Frost also emphasized that these words are not merely printed on a page but are carved in stone at the actual spot of the bridge they celebrate. Perhaps Emerson the Transcendentalist would have appreciated the stature, and the possible irony, of having his words immortalized while surrounded by Nature's glory. Interestingly, Emerson's grave is also in Concord, Massachusetts, and it too is marked by a rough stone.

Criticism

Chris Semansky

Chris Semansky teaches writing and literature at Portland Community College in Portland, Oregon, and he is a frequent contributor of poems and essays to literary journals. In the following essay, Semansky provides historical information concerning the Battle of Concord.

Emerson's "Concord Hymn" was an occasional poem sung to the tune of "Old Hundred" at the dedication of the battle monument in Concord, Massachusetts on July 4, 1837. The poem evokes the heroism of American Revoultionary War soldiers while at the same time encouraging Americans not to forget the ideals for which those soldiers died. After originally being printed as a broadside and distributed at the ceremony, the poem was frequently reprinted in newspapers. It became so popular that it was even memorized by schoolchildren. Indeed, the line "The shot heard round the world" (which signifies the first shot of the battle) has become part of the American vernacular.

Fought on April 19, 1775, the the Battle of Concord was the second engagement of the American Revolutionary War, following the initial out-

break of hostilities in Lexington earlier that same day. Both skirmishes took place in what is now the state of Massachusetts, and combined casualty numbers show that the British lost 272 men and the Americans 95.

The conflict was precipitated by that news that American colonists had gathered large quantities of ammunition and military stores at Concord. British General Thomas Gage ordered approximately 700 soldiers under the command of Lieutenant Colonel Francis Smith to destroy or capture the supplies. The colonists had warning of the impending attack, however. Although popular lore tells of Paul Revere receiving the signal of "One, if by land, and two, if by sea" and alerting the minutemen (American armed civilians who pledged to be ready to fight on a minute's notice), others, including William Dawes and Samuel Prescott, were also purveyors of that critical information. The readied colonists ambushed the British in Lexington, arousing excitement throughout the countryside but causing no serious impediment to the advancing force.

At 7:30 in the morning, the minutemen took position on one side of the Old North Bridge and stubbornly resisted the advancing troops for a time before retreating. After seeing the smoke from the fire the British had set to destroy their supplies, however, the Americans stormed back. Led by Major John Buttrick, the Americans charged the British, who fell back and began retreating toward Boston. The colonists chased the British all the way to Charlestown, on Boston Harbor. The victory raised American morale and inspired confidence that they could indeed pull off a successful armed resistance against the British Empire.

This is the backdrop to Emerson's poem, whose images tell us about the young nation that was formed from this battle. The "rude bridge" of the first stanza of "Concord Hymn" refers to the Old North Bridge over the Concord River in Concord, Massachusetts. Emerson personifies the bridge, calling it "rude," because rather than acting as a means of traveling safely over an obstacle, the bridge became a literal killing ground. "Their flag to April's breeze" refers to the colonial soldiers' flag blowing in the wind of April, the month of the battle. The flag was of utmost importance to soldiers of the era; if the flagbearer fell in battle, another soldier rushed to keep the vaunted banner from touching the ground. By calling the American troops "embattled farmers," Emerson emphasizes the fact that, unlike their counterparts, the

What Do I Read Next?

- In the early 1830s French author Alexis de Tocqueville visited the United States, interviewing citizens and politicians, and examining the government of this relatively new country. His two-part *Democracy in America,* first published in 1835 and 1840 and in constant publication since, has become a standard handbook for understanding the nation in Emerson's time up through today.

- The late Carlos Baker was one of the most respected literary biographers of his generation. Just before his death in 1995, he was working on *Emerson among the Eccentrics,* which not only gives a portrait of Emerson and of the lives of his contemporaries, including those who were involved in the Transcendentalist movement with him, but also such giants of American literature as Hawthorne (his college roommate) and Melville.

- Henry David Thoreau's name is often linked with Emerson's: the two were close friends and were the most articulate and prolific of the New England Transcendentalists. Thoreau lived in Emerson's house for two years before moving to a crude hut on the shores of Walden Pond to prove that man can live alone with nature and be self-reliant. The book that Thoreau wrote about his experience, *Walden, or, Life in the Woods,* is as insightful to students today as it was when it was written in 1854.

- Many biographies of Emerson deal with his writings and the times in which he lived. Robert D. Richardson published *Emerson: The Mind On Fire* in 1995. This is a very human biography of the poet as a real person, covering his loves, his relationship with his family, his inspirations and ordinary day-to-day affairs such as shopping and finances.

- Part of the story of the Battle of Concord was covered later in poetry by Henry Wadsworth Longfellow, who wrote "Paul Revere's Ride" in 1863. Longfellow's poem is similar to Emerson's in that it gives a reverent version of a part of American history that had already been mythologized as the heroic birth of the country, but Longfellow takes more liberties with the truth in order to tell a dramatic story. This poem can be found in *The Complete Works of Henry Wadsworth Longfellow,* which has been in print since its first appearance in 1893.

Americans were not professional soldiers. The phrase "embattled farmers" also puts forth an image of the Americans as largely self-reliant, self-taught men who depended almost exclusively on their courage and strength of conviction to defeat the better trained and equipped British troops in freeing themselves from tyrranical rule. This type of representation, which inspires admiration and empathy on the part of the audience, is necessary for a poem whose function is to commemorate. The success of "Concord Hymn" then, is directly rooted in Emerson's own (persuasive) representation of an American identity.

The second stanza of "Concord Hymn" refers to the powerful British empire (the "foe") long af-ter the battle, and the United States ("the conquerer"), sleeping. Time has passed since the fight occurred, and Emerson suggests that people have forgotten the struggle. "The dark stream which seaward creeps" is an image that suggests the phenomenon of forgetting. It is this memory loss, Emerson implies, that Americans must now fight. Though primarily a poem written to commemorate an historical event, "Concord Hymn" nonetheless embodies Emerson's own convictions about experience and the role of the poet. A staunch advocate of looking inward for universal truths, Emerson believed that a "true" poet is representative. As someone who had suffered through the early deaths of his father, his young wife, two brothers, and his first son, Emerson knew grief deeply. Urging Americans not to forget the Revolutionary War dead, then, was also a way he used to keep the memory of those he loved alive. That Emerson's father was himself a preacher in Concord during the Revolutionary War makes the poem all the more poignant.

In the third stanza Emerson describes the bank of the river as "green" and the stream as "soft." These descriptions stand in contrast to the "ruined" bridge and "creeping" stream of the preceding stanza, because now the victors (Americans) are in the process of remembering. Indeed, the "votive stone" Emerson mentions is in fact carved with the first stanza of "Concord Hymn." Emerson accomplished quite literally, then, what critic Donald Stauffer claimed, in *A Short History of American Poetry,* he sought: "a union of nature and spirit through the medium of language, which, if it was succcessful, would equate the word with the object and result in a truly symbolic poem." This stone commemorates the brave action of the Americans, while the inscribed poem helps Americans to remember what the stone on which it is carved memorializes.

The fourth stanza is a plea to Spirit (for Emerson, a kind of nondenominational God) that made the men brave to preserve the tribute that Emerson and other Americans raised to the dead soldiers. Only if "Time and Nature" spare the monument, Emerson suggests, will humanity remember the dead and the cause for which the soldiers fought. Pleas and invocations are common features of hymns, which historically have denoted songs that celebrate God or express religious sentiment and have been sung at services or ceremonies. However, Emerson used the form to celebrate the human spirit which, for Emerson, was itself divine and to praise the lives of those who died to make America what it is.

The significance of "Concord Hymn" resides in the fact that it commemorates the beginning of the American Revolution and that for a period in American history it became a means by which Americans learned about the Revolution itself as well as the identity of a young nation. Critic Jean Ferguson said that Emerson's aim as a writer was less to originate a tradition than to produce active readers, who would then refashion themselves and their culture." "Concord Hymn's" sustained popularity suggests that he has done just that.

Source: Chris Semansky, in an essay for *Poetry for Students,* Gale, 1998.

George Santayana

In the following excerpt, Santayana praises Emerson for his transcendent and independent thought, his love of nature, and his adherence to "natural law."

The New England on which Emerson opened his eyes was a singular country. It manifested in an acute form something not yet quite extinct in America—the phenomenon of an old soul in a new body.

The inevitable simplicity of the new life was a part of its virtue, and its accidental isolation seemed a symbol of divine election and the harbinger of a new era of righteousness.

But no such pleasing reflections could remove the anomaly of an old soul in a young body, an anomaly much too violent to last. The dogmas which Calvinism had chosen for interpretation were the most sombre and disquieting in the Christian system, those which marked most clearly a broken life and a faith rising out of profound despair. But what profound despair or what broken life could exist in young America to give meaning and truth to those spectral traditions? People who looked and thought for themselves, people who yearned for that deeper sincerity which comes from shaking off verbal habits and making belief a direct expression of instinct and perception, challenged at last their ancestral dream, threw off its incubus, rubbed their eyes, as it were, in the morning light, and sprang into the world of nature.

In no man was this awakening more complete than in Emerson. No one greeted it with greater joy or recognized more quickly his inward affinity to nature rather than to the artificial moral world in which he had been reared. The scales dropped of themselves from his eyes and left his vision as pure and clear as if no sophistications had ever existed in the world. The instinct which took him at one leap into the bosom of reality, and brought him face to face with unbiased experience, is the greatest evidence of his genius, or perhaps we should say, of his simplicity; for he shed the incrustations of time, not by a long and mighty effort of reflection, not by a laborious sympathetic progress through all human illusions; but rather by a native immunity and a repulsion on his part. Other people's troubles could not adhere to him; he remained like a grain of sand, clean and whole in any environment. This simplicity clarified and disinfected the world for him as only the ripest wisdom could disinfect or clarify it for other men....

The love of nature was Emerson's strongest passion; no other influence swayed him so often, stirred him so deeply, or made him so truly a poet. If he regarded any moral or political problem with sympathetic or steady attention, he immediately stated it in terms of some natural analogy and escaped its importunity and finality by imagining what nature, in such a conflict, would pass to next. What seems mysticism in his moral philosophy and baffles the reader who is looking for a moral solution, is nothing but this rooted habit of inattention to what is not natural law, natural progression, natural metamorphosis....

Emerson's love of nature was honest and unserved; it was founded on nature's irresistible charm, grace, power, infinity. It was sincere adoration, self-surrendering devotion; it was not qualified or taken back by any subsumption of nature under human categories, as if after all she were nothing but her children's instrument, illusion or toy. "Dearest nature," as he calls her, remained for him always a mother, a fountain not only of inspiration but of life. The spiritual principle he discovered in her was her own spirit, which man, being a bubble in her stream, might well breathe in for a moment and joyfully share; but it was she that the more deeply inspired. She was the mistress and sibyl, he the pupil, the trembling interpreter of her oracles. Firmly, even arrogantly, as Emerson could assert his spiritual freedom in the face of men and human traditions, in nature's presence he had no transcendental conceit. For this reason his poetry about nature, though fanciful as such poetry may well be, remains always receptive, always studied from life and free from sentimental impertinence....

All men of letters in the 19th century have been inclined to love and describe nature; but this somewhat novel theme has entered an imagination filled already with other matters, preoccupied, perhaps, with political or religious revolutions. A moral and human substratum, a national and personal idiosyncrasy, has existed in every case and has furnished a background for the new vision of nature; and it makes a great difference in a poet whether behind the naturalist in him there lies, for instance, a theologian, a statesman, or an artist. In Emerson what lay behind the naturalist was in a measure a political thinker, a moralist interested in institutions and manners, a democrat and a Puritan; but chiefly what lay there was a mystic, a moralist athirst for some superhuman and absolute good. The effect of this situation upon his poetry is what remains for us to consider.

> *Nothing in all Emerson's writings is more eloquent and popular than some bits of his patriotic verse."*

Nothing in all Emerson's writings is more eloquent and popular than some bits of his patriotic verse. There are not only the Concord and Boston hymns, but sparks of the same fire shoot out in other places; for Emerson could not have written so well upon occasion, I may almost say to order, if he had not been full already of the enthusiasm which that occasion demanded. Art or a merely sympathetic imagination never dictated a line to this Puritan bard, who if he was perfectly bland was also absolutely unyielding and self-directed. No force affected him save those which made him up. Freedom, in its various expressions, was his profoundest ideal, and if there was anything which he valued more than the power to push on to what might lie before, it was the power to escape what lay behind. A sense of potentiality and a sense of riddance are, as he might have said, the two poles of liberty. In America both poles were highly magnetic, for here, more than elsewhere, old things had been thrown off and new things were to be expected. Potentiality, cosmic liberty, nature perpetually transforming and recovering her energy, formed his loftiest theme; but the sense of riddance in escaping kings, churches, cities, and eventually self and even humanity, was the nearer and if possible the livelier emotion.

The verses which he devoted to memories of the Revolutionary War and to the agitation against slavery, though brief, are the most thrilling and profound which those themes have yet inspired. Everybody knows of the "embattled farmers" who "fired the shot heard round the world." Perhaps less present to the younger generation are his stirring lines, in which he denounced slavery and dreamt of the negro's future....

And while the master was thus bitterly challenged, the slave was idealized....

We need not ask whether verses like these have a place in literature: it is certain that they have a place in American history and put vividly before us the passions of a momentous hour.

But Emerson's love of freedom did not need crying abuses to kindle it to flame; it was a speculative love that attached him to whatever was simple, untrammelled, idyllic in any time or sphere.

[W]hat shall we see in Emerson's poetic achievement? Briefly this: his verses put together in a more pungent and concentrated form his guiding ideas. They are filled with high thought, enthusiasm, terseness; they contain snatches of lyric beauty.

Source: George Santayana, "Emerson's Poems Proclaim the Divinity of Nature, With Freedom as His Profoundest Ideal," in *George Santayana's America: Essays on Literature and Culture,* collected and with an introduction by James Ballowe, University of Illinois Press, 1967, pp. 85–95.

Sources

Arnold, Matthew, "Emerson," in *Macmillan's Magazine,* Vol. 50, No. 295, May, 1884, reprinted in his *Discourses in America,* The Macmillan Company, 1924, pp. 138-208.

Birnbaum, Louis, *Red Dawn at Lexington,* Boston: Houghton Mifflin Co., 1986.

Chapman, John Jay, "Emerson, Sixty Years After," in the *Atlantic Monthly,* Vol. 79, January-February, 1897, reprinted as "Emerson" in his *Emerson: And Other Essays,* Charles Scribner's Sons, 1898, pp. 3-108.

Emerson, Ralph Waldo, *The Journals of Ralph Waldo Emerson,* abridged, edited and with an introduction by Robert N. Linscott, New York: The Modern Library, 1969.

Frost, Robert, "On Emerson," in *Daedalus: Journal of the American Academy of Arts and Sciences,* (copyright 1959 by the American Academy of Arts and Sciences, Cambridge, MA), Vol. 88, No. 4, Fall, 1959, reprinted in *Emerson: A Collection of Critical Essays,* edited by Milton R. Kovitz and Stephen E. Whicher, Prentice-Hall, Inc., 1962, pp. 12-17.

Gross, Robert, *The Minutemen and Their World,* Hill & Wang, 1976.

Lauter, Paul, ed., *The Heath Anthology of American Literature,* NY: Houghton Mifflin, 1998.

McAleer, John, *Ralph Waldo Emerson: Days of Encounter,* Boston: Little Brown and Co., 1984.

Stauffer, Donald Barlow, *A Short History of American Poetry,* E.P. Dutton & Co., 1974.

Whitman, Walt, "Emerson's Books, (the Shadows of Them)," in *The Literary World,* Vol. XI, No. 11, May 22, 1880, pp. 177-78.

For Further Study

Duncan, Jeffery L., *The Power and Form of Emerson's Thought,* Charlottesville: The University of Virginia Press, 1973.

Emerson is one of America's earliest and best thinkers, and it is likely that his ideas on social duty and on the place of the individual in society and the universe will be studied for as long as the country exists. In this book, Duncan attempts, for the most part successfully, to explain a system that ties all of Emerson's writings throughout his lifetime together into one coherent system.

Gross, Robert A., *The Minutemen and Their World,* New York: Hill and Wang, 1976.

The information in this book has been covered extensively in other places, but Gross has a good sense of what the times were like, and he conveys the information in a lively, interesting manner.

Howe, Irving, *The American Wilderness: Culture and Politics in the Age of Emerson,* Cambridge, Massachusetts: Harvard University Press, 1986.

Howe, one of the finest literary critics our country has produced, looks at how all of American society has been influenced by Emerson's thought. In the three essays collected in this book, all scrupulously detailed with footnotes, he traces a form of intellectualism that appears to have started with Emerson and continues through this day.

Miles, Josephine, *Ralph Waldo Emerson,* Minneapolis: The University of Minnesota Press, 1964.

Like all of the pamphlets in this University of Minnesota series, this is a short book (under fifty pages), but it does an excellent job of encapsulating the life and works of this very complex American thinker, covering the high points of his career.

Stokesbury, James L., *A Short History of the American Revolution,* New York: William Morrow and Company, Inc., 1991.

The Revolution has been the source of countless books and classes each year, but this book covers the basics that readers of "Concord Hymn" should know in order to gain the poem's full effect. An historian might find Stokesbury to be shallow and lacking in insight, but for the casual reader, there is plenty in this book to think about.

The Death of the Hired Man

First published in Robert Frost's collection *North of Boston* in 1914, "The Death of the Hired Man" is a moderately long, dramatic dialogue that occurs between a farmer, Warren, and his wife, Mary. The "hired man" of the title is Silas, who wants to work for Warren during the winter but is unreliable during other seasons when farm work is more plentiful. Warren has grown impatient with Silas, but Mary urges him to "be kind," since she believes Silas has returned to die. This debate between Mary and Warren represents the ambivalence often felt between two conflicting desires, here the desire to be charitable toward others and the desire not to be taken advantage of. For whatever reason, Silas is unable to ask his own family for assistance. Eventually, Warren agrees to speak with Silas, but he returns to Mary quickly, informing her that Silas is dead. Like many of Frost's poems, "The Death of the Hired Man" occurs in a rural setting, and the characters' concerns are those of people who live in a rural environment. Unlike many of Frost's other more well-known poems, however, this one does not conclude with a sudden insight on the part of the speaker; rather, because the poem is not a lyric but a narrative that tells a story, the interest here lies in the drama of the situation. Through the presence of substantial dialogue, this poem easily illustrates Frost's theory that poetry can be most effective when it relies on ordinary language.

Robert Frost

1914

Robert Frost

Author Biography

Born in San Francisco, Frost was eleven years old when his father died, and his family relocated to Lawrence, Massachusetts, where his paternal grandparents lived. In 1892, Frost graduated from Lawrence High School and shared valedictorian honors with Elinor White, whom he married three years later. After graduation, Frost briefly attended Dartmouth College, taught at grammar schools, worked at a mill, and served as a newspaper reporter. He published a chapbook of poems at his own expense and contributed the poem "The Birds Do Thus" to the *Independent,* a New York magazine. In 1897 Frost entered Harvard University as a special student, but left before completing degree requirements because of a bout with tuberculosis and the birth of his second child. Three years later the Frosts' eldest child died, an event which led to marital discord and which, some critics believe, Frost later addressed in his poem "Home Burial."

In 1912, having been unable to interest American publishers in his poems, Frost moved his family to a farm in Buckinghamshire, England, where he wrote prolifically, attempting to perfect his distinct poetic voice. During this time, he met such literary figures as Ezra Pound, an American expatriate poet and champion of innovative literary approaches, and Edward Thomas, a young English poet associated with the Georgian poetry movement then popular in Great Britain. Frost soon published his first book of poetry, *A Boy's Will* (1913), which received appreciative reviews. Following the success of the book, Frost relocated to Gloucestershire, England, and directed publication of a second collection, *North of Boston* (1914). This volume contains several of his most frequently anthologized pieces, including "Mending Wall," "The Death of the Hired Man," and "After Apple-Picking." Shortly after *North of Boston* was published in Great Britain, the Frost family returned to the United States, settling in Franconia, New Hampshire. The American editions of Frost's first two volumes won critical acclaim upon publication in the United States, and in 1917 Frost began his affiliations with several American universities as a professor of literature and poet-in-residence. Frost continued to write prolifically over the years and received numerous literary awards as well as honors from the United States government and American universities. He recited his work at the inauguration of President John F. Kennedy in 1961 and represented the United States on several official missions. Though he received great popular acclaim, his critical reputation waned during the latter part of his career. His final three collections received less enthusiastic reviews, yet contain several pieces acknowledged as among his greatest achievements. He died in Boston in 1963.

Poem Text

Mary sat musing on the lamp-flame at the table
Waiting for Warren. When she heard his step,
She ran on tip-toe down the darkened passage
To meet him in the doorway with the news
And put him on his guard. "Silas is back."   5
She pushed him outward with her through the door
And shut it after her. "Be kind," she said.
She took the market things from Warren's arms
And set them on the porch, then drew him down
To sit beside her on the wooden steps.   10

"When was I ever anything but kind to him?
But I'll not have the fellow back," he said.
"I told him so last haying didn't I?
'If he left then,' I said, 'that ended it.'
What good is he? Who else will harbor him   15
At his age for the little he can do?
What help he is there's no depending on.
Off he goes always when I need him most.
'He thinks he ought to earn a little pay,
Enough at least to buy tobacco with,   20
So he won't have to beg and be beholden.'

'All right,' I say, 'I can't afford to pay
Any fixed wages, though I wish I could.'
'Some one else can.' 'Then some one else will
      have to.'
I shouldn't mind his bettering himself   25
If that was what it was. You can be certain,
When he begins like that, there's some one at him
Trying to coax him off with pocket-money,—
In haying time, when any help is scarce.
In winter he comes back to us. I'm done."   30

"Sh! not so loud: he'll hear you," Mary said.

"I want him to: he'll have to soon or late."

"He's worn out. He's asleep beside the stove.
When I came up from Rowe's I found him here,
Huddled against the barn-door fast asleep,   35
A miserable sight, and frightening, too—
You needn't smile—I didn't recognize him—
I wasn't looking for him—and he's changed.
Wait till you see."

      "Where did you say he'd been?"   40

"He didn't say. I dragged him to the house,
And gave him tea and tried to make him smoke.
I tried to make him talk about his travels.
Nothing would do: he just kept nodding off."

"What did he say? Did he say anything?"   45

"But little."

      "Anything? Mary, confess
He said he'd come to ditch the meadow for me."

"Warren!"

      "But did he? I just want to know."   50

"Of course he did. What would you have him say?
Surely you wouldn't grudge the poor old man
Some humble way to save his self-respect.
He added, if you really care to know,
He meant to clear the upper pasture, too.   55
That sounds like something you have heard before?
Warren, I wish you could have heard the way
He jumbled everything. I stopped to look
Two or three times—he made me feel so queer—
To see if he was talking in his sleep.   60
He ran on Harold Wilson—you remember—
The boy you had in haying four years since.
He's finished school, and teaching in his college.
Silas declares you'll have to get him back.
He says they two will make a team for work: 65
Between them they will lay this farm as smooth!
The way he mixed that in with other things.
He thinks young Wilson a likely lad, though daft
On education—you know how they fought
All through July under the blazing sun,   70
Silas up on the cart to build the load,
Harold along beside to pitch it on."

"Yes, I took care to keep well out of earshot."

"Well, those days trouble Silas like a dream.
You wouldn't think they would. How some things   75
      linger!

Harold's young college boy's assurance piqued
      him.
After so many years he still keeps finding
Good arguments he sees he might have used.
I sympathize. I know just how it feels
To think of the right thing to say too late.   80
Harold's associated in his mind with Latin.
He asked me what I thought of Harold's saying
He studied Latin like the violin
Because he liked it—that an argument!
He said he couldn't make the boy believe   85
He could find water with a hazel prong—
Which showed how much good school had ever
      done him.
He wanted to go over that. But most of all
He thinks if he could have another chance
To teach him how to build a load of hay—"   90

"I know, that's Silas' one accomplishment.
He bundles every forkful in its place,
And tags and numbers it for future reference,
So he can find and easily dislodge it
In the unloading. Silas does that well.   95
He takes it out in bunches like big birds' nests.
You never see him standing on the hay
He's trying to lift, straining to lift himself."

"He thinks if he could teach him that, he'd be
Some good perhaps to some one in the world.   100
He hates to see a boy the fool of books.
Poor Silas, so concerned for other folk,
And nothing to look backward to with pride,
And nothing to look forward to with hope,
So now and never any different."   105

Part of a moon was falling down the west,
Dragging the whole sky with it to the hills.
Its light poured softly in her lap. She saw
And spread her apron to it. She put out her hand
Among the harp-like morning-glory strings,   110
Taut with the dew from garden bed to eaves,
As if she played unheard the tenderness
That wrought on him beside her in the night.
"Warren," she said, "he has come home to die:
You needn't be afraid he'll leave you this time."   115

"Home," he mocked gently.

      "Yes, what else but home?
It all depends on what you mean by home.
Of course he's nothing to us, any more
Than was the hound that came a stranger to us   120
Out of the woods, worn out upon the trail."

"Home is the place where, when you have to go
      there,
They have to take you in."

      "I should have called it
Something you somehow haven't to deserve."   125

Warren leaned out and took a step or two,
Picked up a little stick, and brought it back
And broke it in his hand and tossed it by.
"Silas has better claim on us, you think,
Than on his brother? Thirteen little miles   130
As the road winds would bring him to his door.

Silas has walked that far no doubt today.
Why didn't he go there? His brother's rich,
A somebody—director in the bank."

"He never told us that."   135

   "We know it though."

"I think his brother ought to help, of course.
I'll see to that if there is need. He ought of right
To take him in, and might be willing to—
He may be better than appearances.   140
But have some pity on Silas. Do you think
If he'd had any pride in claiming kin
Or anything he looked for from his brother,
He'd keep so still about him all this time?"

"I wonder what's between them."   145

   "I can tell you.
Silas is what he is—we wouldn't mind him—
But just the kind that kinsfolk can't abide.
He never did a thing so very bad.
He don't know why he isn't quite as good   150
As any one. He won't be made ashamed
To please his brother, worthless though he is."

"I can't think Si ever hurt any one."

"No, but he hurt my heart the way he lay
And rolled his old head on that sharp-edged   155
         chair-back.
He wouldn't let me put him on the lounge.
You must go in and see what you can do.
I made the bed up for him there tonight.
You'll be surprised at him—how much he's
         broken.
His working days are done; I'm sure of it."   160

"I'd not be in a hurry to say that."

"I haven't been. Go, look, see for yourself.
But, Warren, please remember how it is:
He's come to help you ditch the meadow.
He has a plan. You mustn't laugh at him.   165
He may not speak of it, and then he may.
I'll sit and see if that small sailing cloud
Will hit or miss the moon."

   It hit the moon.
Then there were three there, making a dim row,   170
The moon, the little silver cloud, and she.

Warren returned—too soon, it seemed to her,
Slipped to her side, caught up her hand and waited.

"Warren," she questioned.

   "Dead," was all he answered.   175

Poem Summary

Lines 1-10:

This opening stanza functions as an introduction to the situation, presenting the attitudes of the two main characters as well as broaching the major conflict. We are told that "Silas is back," though we

don't yet know who Silas is, and we gather that Warren will be upset with this information, though Mary is more patient. The rhythm of the opening line is unusual compared to most lines in the poem because the accent or stress occurs on the first syllable of the first metrical foot, because "lamp-flame" is a spondee with both syllables stressed, and because the line contains thirteen syllables rather than the usual ten. Frost is also able to vary the rhythm of this stanza by including two short emphatic sentences among the longer ones: "Silas is back" and "Be kind, she said." Note also the alliteration, or repetition of initial consonant sounds, in "Mary sat musing" and "Waiting for Warren. When."

Lines 11-30:

In this section, Warren presents his interpretation of the past events, referring in a flashback to his experience with Silas. He distinguishes between being kind to Silas and hiring him to work on the farm. Apparently, Silas has left and returned repeatedly, until last haying season when Warren ordered him not to return if he was going to leave. One indication that this act has occurred repeatedly is Warren's use of present tense verbs; if this had happened only once, Warren would have said that Silas "came back" rather than that he "comes back." "Haying season" would be the time when all of the farmers in the area would need extra help. Some of them would be willing to pay wages rather than simply room and board or a portion of the crop, but Warren is apparently not financially able to do so. Warren indicates that Silas does not use the cash to "better himself" but perhaps wastes it.

Lines 31-46:

In this section, the differences between the attitudes of Warren and Mary become clear. Warren is frustrated because of his past experience while Mary is compassionate because she has observed Silas's current condition. She describes him with words that could describe an animal rather than a human being: "huddled," "miserable," "frightening." And he'd placed himself "against the barn door" rather than the door to the house. Although Mary attempted to care for him physically, Silas seemed to be too exhausted to receive her care. The fact that he was unable to wake up to drink tea or smoke foreshadows the end of the poem, when he will be permanently unable to wake up. The break between lines 39 and 40 indicates that the speaker is changing from Mary to Warren, but that Mary's line needs to be filled out metrically with Warren's—together the lines consist of ten syllables.

Lines 47-73:

At the beginning of this section, Warren's tone is sarcastic. He speculates that Silas has "come to ditch the meadow" as he's promised to do in the past, but Warren knows Silas is incapable of the task. Even after Mary provides more detail about her conversation with Silas, Warren remains unsympathetic. Mary, though, recognizes that Silas makes promises he can't keep to protect his dignity; he promises to work because he doesn't want to beg. Yet Mary also recognizes how ill Silas is through his conversation; he's nearly incoherent. In this section, Frost continues to use colloquial idioms rather than formal vocabulary to emphasize the oral nature of the poem: Silas "ran on Harold Wilson" and describes him as a "likely lad."

Lines 74-90:

This section begins with a simile: Silas's past troubles him "like a dream"; his memory is like a nightmare. This simile is particularly appropriate because of Silas's inability to stay awake during his conversation with Mary and because by the end of the poem he will drift from sleep to death. The younger boy is represented by Latin and a violin, much more cultural and formal types of knowledge than Silas's folk knowledge, how to "find water with a hazel prong." The conflict between Silas and Harold Wilson also relates to Silas's dignity and feelings of self-worth. His solution is to teach Harold "how to build a load of hay," knowledge Harold probably won't use but knowledge that gives value to Silas's life.

Lines 91-105:

In these two stanzas, the argument continues between Warren and Mary. Warren relies on a simile to explain Silas's inept methods: he forks hay "in bunches like big birds' nests." This type of simile would be natural to Warren, who lives in the country and would have observed such birds' nests. Mary seems to share Silas's attitude that formal education is somewhat useless, for she refers to Harold as a "fool of books." She believes that if Silas can transmit his knowledge to someone else, he will not believe he has lived in vain.

Lines 106-113:

In this section, the tone shifts substantially, becoming much more lyrical. For the first time, attention shifts away from the characters to the setting. The description becomes somewhat peaceful, as the moon is personified, that is, given the characteristics of a living being. Mary—not Warren—

Media Adaptations

- A 1958 interview with the poet is available on video cassette from Zenger.

- Mystic Fire Video released a videocassette titled *Robert Frost* as volume 3 of their "Voices and Visions" series.

- You can see interviews with the poet as well as hear him reading on the video *Robert Frost,* which is part of the "Poetry America Series" released by AIMS Media.

- An audio cassette titled "Robert Frost Reads the Poems of Robert Frost" is available from Decca press.

receives the quiet light and seems to be more aware of the beauty of their surroundings. She notices that the stems of the morning glories resemble the strings of a harp, a simile that is extended when Mary touches them "As if she played unheard." Frost is using these details in order to emphasize Mary's character; as a gentle person, she interprets her surroundings with gentleness.

Lines 114-125:

The dialogue in this section reveals the crux of Mary's disagreement with Warren. They debate the meaning of "home" with Warren providing a cynical and calloused definition: "when you have to go there, / they have to take you in." His attitude is exceptionally practical, while Mary's is more emotional.

Lines 126-153:

At the beginning of this section, Warren's action reinforces the difference between him and Mary. While Mary had earlier treated the plants gently, Warren breaks a stick and tosses it aside. Their conversation here provides some additional background material regarding Silas. He has a brother who is quite successful by conventional standards but with whom Silas does not get along. Warren and Mary know this as people in small towns tend to know about each other's lives, not because Silas has himself revealed anything. Warren understands relationships as if they are contracts—Silas should go to his brother because he has a "better claim" on a blood relative. Mary agrees that his brother has an obligation, but she argues that Silas's dignity has greater value.

Lines 154-168:

Here Mary continues to urge Warren to treat Silas with sympathy. She speculates that he's too weak to recover enough to do any work, though she does not want to make Silas feel useless. She concludes her statement with a whimsical statement that she'll watch a cloud sail past or hit the moon. These lines recall the earlier reference to the moon, when Mary noticed and captured the light in her apron.

Lines 169-175:

In this section, the abrupt nature of Silas's death is conveyed by the structure of the lines. The cloud "hit the moon," and the tone shifts briefly from whimsy to aggression. At this point, the natural elements of the moon and cloud become characters with a status equal to Mary's. When Warren returns, his attitude is somewhat more compassionate; he responds gently to Mary even if he could not have to Silas. Then he needs only one word, "Dead," to convey the event. Although he seems very matter-of-fact, he does not add any of the sarcastic comments that characterized his speech earlier. One interpretation of this direct statement, "Dead, was all he answered," is that at the end of human life, no interpretation is necessary or possible. Because of this abrupt ending, the poem acquires a much darker significance—Warren is given the last word, and Silas's life seems to have been without meaning.

Themes

Duty and Responsibility

"The Death of the Hired Man" uses an extended dialogue between Mary and Warren to explore questions of duty and responsibility. The poem opens with Mary "musing on the lamp-flame at the table / Waiting for Warren." She does not seem to have anything else to do but to wait for her husband and stare at candle; or alternatively, she has forsaken her other duties to wait for him. This opening image prompts questions about her role in the relationship. She does not even wait a moment (after hearing his step) to tell him the news, running "on tip toe down the darkened passage." After she shuttles him out the door back onto the porch, she instinctively takes "the market things from Warren's arms / And set[s] them on the porch." This first silent exchange between the two implies a strong sense of duty she may feel toward her husband Warren. But as soon as they begin speaking, we learn her sense of responsibility is to kindness more than to some sort of marital obedience. Her first two sentences are a quick "Silas is back" and a plea for Warren to "Be kind."

During the last haying season, Silas quit his job and left Warren and Mary to make up his work. Warren, wanting to keep his promise not to hire Silas back, does not feel much responsibility for an old farm hand he cannot depend on: "What good is he? Who else will harbor him / At his age for the little he can do?" Any duty he owed to Silas was severed when Silas walked off the job—that is, if Silas was just an employee who came on a few seasons ago. Is Silas really "nothing" to them, as Warren would insist, "any more / Than was the hound that came as stranger?" We learn as the conversation develops that Silas has been working for them for a long time, long enough to be incorporated into the family. Mary is perhaps more in touch with this sense of family duty at the beginning of the poem, though Warren begins to rethink his attitude toward Silas. When Mary tells him Silas is not doing well, that she found him "huddled against the barn-door fast asleep," Warren grows more concerned, asking "Where did you say he'd been?"

Silas claims to still feel a duty toward the farm when he tells Mary "he meant to clear the upper pasture" and "ditch the meadow." He has returned with a plan for the work, deciding it would be a good idea if they hired his old coworker, Harold Wilson, back too. Silas may also feel like family to the couple, as they had given him food, shelter, and respect for so many years. He asks for available work, though it is soon clear he has actually come to the house to spend his last days. With this realization, the issues of work and family responsibilities become larger issues, including the duty we have to guard human dignity and responsibility to strangers. Warren, echoing Cain in Genesis (demanding "Am I my brother's keeper?"), asks Mary why Silas did not go to his own brother's house to die; it should be his responsibility to tend to the dying Silas. The brother is a prosperous "director in the bank," so he would have no problems paying the bills. "I think his brother ought to help, of course," he rationalizes to Mary, "He ought of right / To take him in."

Although Warren finally agrees to go in and see Silas for himself, having reconsidered his distanced stance, Mary still feels responsible for the man's dignity and self-respect. She is not going to tolerate any of Warren's possible harsh words, begging "But Warren, please remember how it is: / He's come to help you ditch the meadow. / He has a plan. You mustn't laugh at him." Mary does not want to disrespect Silas. Silas wants to come "home" and work and die in peace; Warren does not believe it is his duty to offer his house to the man who walked off the job in the middle of haying season.

The simple question seems to be "What is 'home'?" Once again Frost reminds us it is a matter of responsibility: either home is "the place where, when you have to go there, / They have to take you in," as Warren asserts, or vise versa, as compassionate Mary corrects him, "I should have called it / Something you somehow haven't to deserve."

Style

In part because much of this poem is dialogue, the stanzas are not arranged regularly. Through most of the poem, the stanzas function like prose paragraphs, with a stanza break occurring with each new speaker. When the speaker shifts in the middle of a line, the opening line of the new stanza is appropriately indented to indicate that the opening line also completes the closing line of the previous stanza. Frost does this to maintain metrical regularity.

Much—but not all—of this poem is written in blank verse. This means that the meter of the lines is iambic pentameter, but there is no rhyme. Iambic means that each metrical foot contains one unstressed syllable followed by one stressed syllable, and pentameter means that there are five metrical feet in each line. In iambic pentameter each line will contain a total of ten syllables. One way to tell that this poem is not written entirely in iambic pentameter is to notice the number of lines that contain more than ten syllables. A line that varies from the established pattern is called a variant line. A poem that contains so much dialogue can be written in iambic pentameter in part because the English language is almost naturally stressed as iambic.

To understand this more easily, a diagram will help. Read line 21, found in the second stanza:

Enough at least to buy tobacco with

Topics for Further Study

- Why do you think Warren has a more difficult time sympathizing with Silas? Why does Mary understand him so well?

- Warren makes several conclusions about what "home" means. Do you agree with Warren when he says "Home is the place where, when you have to go there, they have to take you in"? Or do you agree with Mary that home is "something you somehow haven't to deserve." Who do you agree with? What is your definition of "home?"

- Write a narrative poem that features a conversation between two people discussing a person not present in the room. Using only dialogue, develop a life—including biographical details and personality traits—for the absent person which is real for the reader.

When the stresses are recorded, the iambic pentameter becomes clear:

Enough / at **least** / to **buy** / to**bac** / co **with.**

Historical Context

World War I

Frost's collection *North of Boston* was published on the eve of World War I, which was the first war to use submarines, aerial bombings and chemical warfare. It began in Europe, where the battles between ethnic groups in the Balkan nations at the end of the nineteenth century led to a balance of power between two rival military alliances: the triple alliance of Germany, Austria-Hungary, and Italy, and the triple entente of Great Britain, France, and Russia. Most of the smaller countries were affiliated with one of these or the other. On June 28, 1914, Austrian Archduke Franz Ferdinand was assassinated by a Serbian. When the Austrian government blamed Serbia, obligations to existing treaties pulled most of the nations into war, one at a time.

Compare *&* Contrast

- **1914:** World War I begins less than a month after the assassination of the heir to the Austrian throne in Sarajevo, Bosnia. The war quickly spreads to Europe, Russia, and even Japan and will last most of the decade. America enters the war in 1917, though European losses are already reaching catastrophic figures.

  Today: The region that made up the former Yugoslavia, which includes Serbia, Kosovo, Croatia, and Bosnia-Herzegovina, remains unstable after recent civil war and continued skirmishes between Serbs and other ethnic and religious groups.

- **1914:** The German military creates two new weapons that will forever change the face of modern warfare. In August German pilots conduct the very first air raid on Paris, dropping small bombs on the city from low–flying biplanes. In April of the same year German ground troops attack French soldiers in Ypres with the first chemical weapons. The greenish-yellow clouds of chlorine gas, though only

deadly at high exposure, blister the skin and delicate lung tissue of anyone within range of its contact.

Today: The Gulf War against Iraq in 1991 brought air warfare and chemical weapons back to the front of American consciousness. United States military "smart bombs" and "Cruise missiles" destroy targets located miles inside enemy territory with chilling accuracy. American troops, still in the region as of 1998, prepare to counter Iraq's threats to use chemical and biological weapons. United Nations Security Council inspectors work to ensure that stockpile is methodically located and destroyed.

- **1914:** Only two years after White Star Line passenger vessel SS *Titanic* sinks, the company launches a sister ship, the SS *Britanic.*

  1998: American fascination with the tragic sinking sweeps the nation as the movie *Titanic* becomes the top-selling feature film of all time, earning numerous Oscars and millions in gross sales.

Originally, Americans were reluctant to become involved; after all, President Woodrow Wilson was reelected in 1916 with the campaign slogan "He Kept Us Out Of War." In early 1917, though, Germany started using submarines against ships travelling to Great Britain, and the United States, which had warned against such action, was drawn into participating. When peace was declared in 1918, 32 nations had been involved in the fighting, with 37 million casualties and ten million civilian deaths.

The veterans who returned to the United States in 1918 were angry and disillusioned, having participated in destruction on a greater scale than the world had ever known. Of the one million Americans drafted and sent overseas, many came from small rural towns. They may never have gone beyond the county limits, much less traveled to Europe and killed people, if not for the war; the returning veterans brought back stories of their

experiences, cracking the shell that secluded farm towns from the outside world.

American Literature

In the 1910s, American writers began to look inward to create a distinctive American style, separate from European literature. Many regional writers, such as midwestern authors Willa Cather, Sherwood Anderson, Carl Sandburg, and Theodore Dreiser gained popularity and influenced younger authors such as Ernest Hemingway and John Dos Passos. These writers were determined to reflect the realities of everyday life, in both urban and rural settings. Many of the decade's most important works were placed in rural settings, such as Sherwood Anderson's *Winesburg, Ohio* (1919) and Willa Cather's *O Pioneers!* (1913).

American poets strived to break free from established traditions and create new, innovative forms. Frost's first book, *A Boy's Will,* was published to critical acclaim in May, 1913. One of his first major reviews was authored by Ezra Pound, an integral figure in Modern poetry. Although the book was praised for its technical craftsmanship, it was his next volume, *North of Boston,* that would show his true innovation and lasting contribution to American poetry. Frost invented a poetic language rich in dialogue between realistic people, crafting his lines around structures he called "sentence sounds." This technique would become Frost's first major contribution to American poetry.

Critical Overview

Although most critics consider "The Death of the Hired Man" to be memorable, they disagree about its overall success. In his book *A World More Attractive: A View of Modern Literature and Politics,* Irving Howe considers Frost's lyric poems to be generally more successful than his more dramatic ones but acknowledges that these dramatic monologues and dialogues represent a significant aspect of Frost's work. About poems like "The Death of the Hired Man," he says, they "are not contemptible but neither are they first-rate. They lack the urge to move past easy facilities that characterizes major writing. They depend too much on stock sentiments, ... " Similarly, W.W. Robson, writing in *The Southern Review,* describes this poem as accomplished but not great: "This is one of Frost's best known and finest poems, and no better illustration could be given of the poignancy he can achieve in spare allusive dialogue. Yet something forbids us to call 'The Death of the Hired Man' great poetry, ... " Because he classifies this among Frost's best works but declines to call it "great," Robson seems to be saying that, compared to some other poets, Frost wrote very little great poetry.

On the other hand, A. Zverev, in a collection titled *20th Century American Literature: A Soviet View,* reaches a much more positive conclusion about this poem, which he calls "one of Frost's most brilliant," and about Frost's work in general. Part of the success of "The Death of the Hired Man," according to Zverev, lies in the fact that it provides "the fullest treatment of Frost's major themes." In part because he is so enthusiastic about this poem, Zverev declares that, "Frost's realism and sincere democratic impulses made him the greatest American poet of the 20th century."

Criticism

Jhan Hochman

Jhan Hochman is a writer and instructor at Portland Community College in Portland, Oregon. In the following essay, Hochman examines the possible motivations behind the actions and dialogue of the characters in "The Death of the Hired Man."

Robert Frost said that "all truth is a dialogue, that the big thing is conflicting goods, not good and evil." One of the finest examples of Frost's assertion is the poem "The Death of the Hired Man," included in his second book of poetry, *North of Boston* (1914). The two conflicting goods in this poem are represented by Mary and Warren, a farm couple who must decide what to do about a chronically undependable hired hand named Silas. Silas returns to Mary and Warren's farm after a period of absence, maintaining that he wants to work. As Mary tells Warren, it is plain to her that after having seen and talked to Silas, he is too worn out to do any work. It seems, instead, that Silas has come back to the farm not to work but to die. In choosing the farm, Silas has chosen well, since both Mary and Warren are depicted as kind, reasonable people.

"The Death of the Hired Man" is an extended dispute between wife and husband. Some commentators interpret the dialogue as one between justice (Warren) and mercy (Mary); it might also be construed as a dialogue between a Judaic or male love of principle first and individuals second (Warren), and a Christian or female love of the individual first and principle second (Mary). Warren's position is based on a principle of exchange. Since Warren feels Silas did not keep up his end of the bargain, Warren believes he owes Silas nothing. Mary, on the other hand, placates Warren in the tradition of principle based on need—that those who can must take care of those who cannot, regardless of whether they deserve it. Warren gradually acquiesces to Mary's entreaties and agrees to keep Silas on at the farm. When Warren goes to check on Silas, Silas is dead.

Because the farm hand died only a short time after returning to the farm, some critics believe that Silas knew he was too sick to work. For the sake of the poem, it is important to realize that Silas did not tell Mary and Warren just how sick he was. If he had told the truth about his impending death, it would have been easy for Mary and Warren to forgive him and take him in. The question of forgiveness would have hardly been worth the debate, and for Frost, that is the heart of the poem.

What Do I Read Next?

- Another New England poet many critics called the "new Frost" is Robert Francis. His well-crafted nature poems, gathered in *Robert Francis: Collected Poems 1936-1976* nicely compliment any reading of Robert Frost.

- One of Frost's favorite books was *Walden* by Henry David Thoreau. He was said to have read the book many times during his life, and was influenced by Thoreau's in-depth discussion of ecological philosophies and communing with nature.

- In order to get a larger sense of just how influential Robert Frost was to American poetry, read George Montiero's *Robert Frost and the New England Renaissance,* published in 1988.

As befits a subject conveyed in dialogue, "The Death of Hired Man" is written in blank verse, or usually unrhymed iambic pentameter (five pairs of unaccented and accented beats per line). Frost's poem, however, deviates widely from both iambic and pentameter forms, inviting an even greater feel of conversation and of free verse (verse without rhyme or regular meter). He professed that he did not like the free-verse form, disparagingly referring to it as playing tennis without a net. Frost strived to write verse that sounded like conversation, and as a result, free verse often overpowered his intent to write regular iambic pentameter.

"The Death of the Hired Man" is a type of poem called an "eclogue," a pastoral poem usually in dialogue form. Use of this form can be traced to Theocritus (c.308-c.240 B.C.), up to Virgil (70-19 B.C.), to John Gay (1685-1732) and to William Wordsworth (1770-1850). Wordsworth's *Lyrical Ballads* influenced Frost with such statements as, "The principal object then, which I proposed to myself in these poems was to choose incidents and situations from common life…. Low and rustic life was generally chosen, because in that condition of life our elementary feelings co-exist in a state of greater simplicity …." And, as did Wordsworth in

such long narrative poems as *The Ruined Cottage* (written in 1797-98) and *Michael* (written in 1800), Frost takes his time with "The Death of a Hired Man" so as to let the argument and context unfold slowly as a rural conversation might.

The slow unfolding of "The Death of a Hired Man" is crucial not only to the pace of rural conversation, but also to the kind of suspense that is an important ingredient of the poem. The title lets readers know immediately that somewhere in this poem Silas will die, though when is uncertain. While Mary pleads and reasons with Warren, readers are likely to anticipate Silas's inevitable death. Like an Alfred Hitchcock film where characters casually argue or converse while the threat of death or its discovery is imminent, Frost gives away the focus of the poem. This "giving away" is not like that of Greek plays, whose original audiences were likely to know not only the ending, but the story they were watching, enabling them to focus on the particular version or retelling. Frost's title, then, does not undercut suspense, as it might seem by giving away the death, but creates it.

Furthermore, Frost's relaxed pacing places the discovery of Silas's corpse at the end of the poem, a time when the death can have no impact on the conversation. Had Silas been dead at the beginning or in the middle of the poem, Mary and Warren's moral dilemma would have been undermined. Still, there is less of a predicament for Mary since, like the reader who has seen the poem's title before its reading, Mary has seen the sad state Silas is in before her conversation with Warren. Her superior knowledge is likely to place the reader more on her side, even as Warren's side of the story must also be taken into consideration.

There are two conflicts in this poem. One of these conflicts is concerned with gender. The fact that critics have associated Mary with mercy can be attributed to Mary being female. Yet while Mary's gender might indeed make her more sympathetic to Silas's plight, it is probably even more important that Mary has already seen Silas and has evaluated his poor condition, whereas Warren has not. Had Warren seen Silas, it is unlikely Warren would have turned Silas away. He, too, would have had mercy on the dying man. That Mary has seen Silas and has therefore, as the expression goes, "seen the light" about Silas's condition is reinforced by images of Mary "musing on the lamp flame" at the beginning of the poem and trapping moonlight (the light of love) in her apron when the poem makes a significant turn (known as a *peripeteia*) on Mary's decision to tell Warren that Silas has not come back to work but to die. Mary not only shows tenderness toward Silas (perhaps the lamp flame) but toward Warren (the moonlight).

The other conflict is about class. Silas's being uneducated is set beside Harold's education. Silas cannot understand how Harold could study Latin because he liked it, and then criticizes Harold for not believing that Silas could find water with a divining rod ("hazel prong"). Silas's use of the hazel prong relates to his apparently long history of being a bit loose with the truth. There is also the contrast between Silas's brother, who is rich, and Silas who refuses to ask his brother for anything. These stories position Silas as an uneducated, itinerant farm worker, yet a man who refuses to beg, who can "build a load of hay," and who thinks he could have taught Harold "not to be the fool of books." With his pride and prevarication, Silas is made a complicated figure, someone who evokes neither simple pity or simple scorn (depending on one's view of the poor). This depiction of Silas prevents Warren, Mary, and readers from merely pitying an abject man. Thus the decision to take Silas becomes a greater challenge. Even Mary is not totally certain she wants to take Silas in since she agrees to visit Silas's brother before she and Warren agree to take him in for an extended time.

While Silas and Mary are focal points for this poem, perhaps no character is as interesting as Warren, for he is the only character who changes. While Mary is always tender and Silas proud and deceptive, Warren changes from being resolute to being kindly uncertain. After Mary gathers moonlight and plays upon the morning glories strung from ground to roof, and redefines home as something one should not have to deserve (in other words, something that is everyone's right), Mary is able accept Silas's return. To show Warren beaten by superior logic and mercy, Frost has Warren commit a bit of violence against a little stick on the ground—he snaps it, indicating his anger at being made to buckle. With this gesture there is little need for Warren to speak, as is also true for Warren's final gesture—Warren holding on to Mary's hand when he tells her Silas is dead.

Warren's reticence casts him as a mere stereotype of the silent male, or more specifically, the typical rural male. But Warren is no mere stereotype. He listens to Mary and is able to change, even making tactile contact with her at the end. If most readers are likely to identify or agree with Mary, the most important readers for this poem are those

identifying with Warren. After all, nothing is as difficult for an artwork as changing those who come into contact with it. Perhaps after "The Death of a Hired Man" the definition of home will not be the lesser good that Warren called "the place where they have to take you in," but the greater good Mary calls "something you somehow haven't to deserve."

Source: Jhan Hochman, in an essay for *Poetry for Students,* Gale, 1998.

Mordecai Marcus

In the following excerpt, Marcus summarizes the critical reception of Frost's North of Boston *and analyzes the narratives of the two speakers in "The Death of the Hired Man."*

Frost's second book, *North of Boston,* was published by David Nutt in London in 1914 and by Henry Holt in New York later the same year. Several of the poems seem to have been written during Frost's first year in England, though some are probably revisions of draft material brought from America. The striking changes in style and Frost's invention of a novel blank-verse narrative form represent highly self-conscious efforts partly based on his keen attention to common human speech. The book's initial favorable reception in England and America was stronger than that given *A Boy's Will;* many reviewers recognized the novelty of Frost's blank-verse narratives, with their dialogue that combined convincing conversational idiom with traditional meters. The poet was also praised for his penetrating observations on human nature and a strong regional sense, though he later objected to being considered a local colorist. A few reviewers and some later critics, however, were so puzzled by the experimental element in his meters that they could not recognize them as blank verse, and some critics thought that Frost should turn his gifts to prose fiction. As the years passed, the reputation of the book and many of its poems continued to rise, and some critics think the volume remains his best. In 1948 W. G. O'Donnell argued that the book represented a tremendous advance over *A Boy's Will,* which he saw as uncertain in voice, excessively old-fashioned in diction, and often close to sentimentality. *North of Boston,* on the other hand, he found to be Frost's most enduring accomplishment because of its striking portrait of New England life and wonderfully honest representation of isolation and fractured human relationships.

Among its poems still considered masterpieces are "Mending Wall," "Home Burial," "A Servant to Servants," and "The Wood-Pile," while the frequently anthologized "The Death of the Hired Man" and "The Black Cottage" are rated only a little behind those....

The readily accessible and popular "The Death of the Hired Man" ... treats conflicts between individuality and social values, as manifested in the exchanges between Warren and Mary and acted out by their disloyal former hired man, Silas. As farm husband and wife debate whether to take Silas back, they examine his plight and claims, his strengths and weaknesses, and reveal their own feelings by gestures as well as words. Their talk focuses on how Silas's disloyalty is a failure to fulfill obligations, which leaves open the question of their obligations to him. The characters and values of Mary and Warren are contrasted in the foreground, while their reminiscences sketch the character and history of the decent but weak Silas. Mary's handling of Warren shows a wise, tender, and firm attitude toward both her husband and Silas. Her principles are mercy and love, whereas Warren, bordering on harshness, appeals to justice, law, and mutual responsibility. Silas's plight is greater than theirs, his attempts to preserve self-respect having divided him between loyalty to longtime employers and self-delusion about his own value and deserts.

Silas's obligation to them is halfway between the formal and the informal, and Warren feels betrayed by Silas's not respecting what Warren has done for him. A truly formal obligation is represented by Silas's rich brother, but Silas is too aware of his own weaknesses to ask for family help, though with his adopted family he can save his pride, for he knows they value his abilities and care about him. Silas's conflicts between self-rejection and inflated pride are shown in the background by his verbal fights with Harold Wilson, the former college student turned teacher. Mary understands the mutual respect between them, which was partly soured by Silas's defensive pity for Harold's bookishness and lack of practical wisdom. Mary's report on Silas's weak condition and wandering attention contrasts to Warren's self-righteous rehearsal of Silas's flaws and his own grim determination to tell Silas that his disloyalty keeps him unwelcome.

Mary's physical gestures suggest openness and control, whereas Warren's show him working out aggression. Warren does, however, show admiration and possibly forgiveness for Silas when he recalls his farm skills, especially in haying. The conflict between Mary and Warren is delicately balanced in

their famous alternative definitions of home. Warren's calling it the place "Where, when you have to go there, / They have to take you in" appeals to formal, almost legal, responsibility. Rather than contradict his view, Mary's reply qualifies it subtly. For her, home is "Something you somehow haven't to deserve," meaning not an obligation fulfilled but rather a source of generosity or mercy. This thoughtful exchange leads Warren's and Mary's tones to merge, her tenderness admitting more criticism and his harshness softening but then veering back toward practicality as he goes to confront the already dead Silas, perhaps with some acceptance. Mary's last speech and the description of the cloud striking the moon provide gentle foreboding, and the couple's final handclasp, initiated by Warren, implies a bond of love including Silas.

Source: Mordecai Marcus, "North of Boston (1914)," in *The Poems of Robert Frost: An Explication,* G. K. Hall and Co., 1991, pp. 41–44.

Sources

Brower, Reuben A., *The Poetry of Robert Frost: Constellations of Intention,* Oxford University Press, 1963.

Doyle, John Robert, *The Poetry of Robert Frost: An Analysis,* Witwatersrand University Press, 1962.

Frost, Robert, *Robert Frost: Poetry and Prose,* edited by Edward Connery Lathem and Lawrance Thompson, Holt Rinehart and Winston, 1972.

Howe, Irving, "Robert Frost: A Momentary Stay," in *A World More Attractive: A View of Modern Literature and Politics,* Horizon Press, 1963, pp. 144-57.

Marcus, Mordecai, *The Poems of Robert Frost: An Explication,* G. K. Hall, 1994.

Pritchard, William H., *Robert Frost: A Literary Life Reconsidered,* University of Massachusetts Press, 1984.

Robson, W.W., "The Achievement of Robert Frost," in *The Southern Review,* Vol. 2, Autumn, 1966, pp. 735-61.

Zverev, A., "A Lover's Quarrel with the World: Robert Frost," *20th Century American Literature: A Soviet View,* Progress Publishers, 1976, pp. 241-60.

For Further Study

Cramer, Jeffrey, *Robert Frost Among His Poems,* McFarland & Co., 1996.
    Provides background information on almost every poem in Frost's canon.

Cox, James, ed., *Robert Frost: A Collection of Critical Essays,* Prentice-Hall, 1962.
    In this lengthy volume, Cox assembles a diverse range of essays on the life and work of Robert Frost.

Hawk Roosting

Ted Hughes
1960

"Hawk Roosting" is from Ted Hughes's second book, *Lupercal*, published in 1960. It is one of the earliest poems in which Hughes used animals to imply the nature of man and to spark thought about just how much of man's behavior is instinctual, as opposed to how much of man is ruled by his divine, or God-like, side. The hawk, who is the first-person speaker of this poem, speaks entirely of instinctual actions, giving examples of actions that are natural to hawks but repugnant to creatures of conscience: "my manners are tearing off heads," he says, and "the one path of my flight is direct / Through the bones of the living." The stark lack of emotion in this voice, along with the intelligence of the word choices and the pride the hawk feels for itself, have led some readers to believe that the author's intention in writing this poem was to glorify violence, or at least to make violent behavior acceptable. Hughes answered this charge directly in a 1971 interview. "Actually what I had in mind was that in this hawk Nature is thinking. Simply Nature. It's not so simple because maybe Nature is no longer so simple." Whether or not the poem expresses approval of the behavior that its speaker describes is debatable; a strong argument may be presented for each viewpoint.

Author Biography

On August 17, 1930, Hughes was born in Mytholomroyd, a town located in the West Riding

Ted Hughes

district of Yorkshire; he was the third child of William Henry and Edith Farrar Hughes. Mytholomroyd is situated in a valley deep within the Pennine Mountains beneath a large cliff, and later in his life Hughes depicted the scene in his writings and related his experiences exploring the surrounding moors and hunting small game with his brother. When Hughes was seven years old, his family moved to Mexborough, a town in South Yorkshire, where he began attending school and was encouraged by his teachers to write poetry. Hughes was awarded a scholarship to Cambridge University in 1948, but he opted to serve in the Royal Air Force (RAF) before pursuing higher education. He served two years as a ground wireless mechanic at a remote RAF radio station, where, by his own admission, he spent most of his time reading Shakespeare. In 1951 Hughes began his studies in English literature at Cambridge's Pembroke College, which he continued for two years before spending his third and final year at Cambridge engaged in the study of archaeology and anthropology. After leaving college, Hughes resided in London and Cambridge, where he held a variety of jobs, including stints as a rose gardener, schoolteacher, and zoo attendant. During this period, Hughes cultivated a number of friendships with literary figures of the time and published several poems in literary periodicals. In 1956 he met American poet Sylvia Plath, and after a courtship that lasted only four months, the two were married on June 16. Plath introduced Hughes to contemporary American poetry and encouraged him to submit his manuscript for *The Hawk in the Rain* to an American literary contest. Hughes's manuscript was selected out of 287 entries by the judges, noted authors W. H. Auden, Stephen Spender, and Marianne Moore, and was published in both the United States and England in 1957.

From 1957 until 1959 Hughes and Plath lived in the United States, where they both became college instructors—Hughes at the University of Massachusetts and Plath at her alma mater, Smith College—before deciding against academic careers. The couple returned to England in December, 1959, and in April, 1960 their daughter Frieda was born in London. In January, 1962 the couple's son Nicholas Farrar was born in a small mid-Devon village, where the couple resided in a cottage. Although reportedly the Hugheses' marriage was rewarding in many ways, there were difficulties, and they ultimately separated and planned to divorce. Plath returned to live in London, where she committed suicide in February, 1963. Hughes was devastated, and wrote little poetry during the three years following Plath's death. Hughes carefully edited and promoted his late wife's poetry and journals, and is primarily responsible for the success of Plath's posthumously published works. During the late 1960s, Hughes again began to write prolifically, and published several works of poetry and prose before the close of the decade. In March, 1969, Hughes's companion, Assia Gutman, killed herself, taking her young daughter with her; Hughes's sorrow over this loss and the earlier loss of Plath is reflected in his works. Hughes married his second wife, Carol Orchard, in 1970 and took up residence on a farm in Devon, where he began raising sheep and cattle. Throughout the 1970s and 1980s, Hughes continued to publish poetry, prose, drama, literary criticism, and works for children, as well as editing the works of Plath and other writers. Hughes's works have garnered numerous awards throughout his career; he received the Guinness Poetry Awards first prize in 1958, a Guggenheim fellowship in 1959, the Somerset Maugham Award in 1960, the Premio Internazionale Taormina in 1973, and the Queen's Medal for Poetry in 1974. In addition to these awards, Hughes had conferred upon him the Order of the British Empire in 1977, and in 1984 he was named Great Britain's Poet Laureate.

Poem Text

I sit in the top of the wood, my eyes closed.
Inaction, no falsifying dream
Between my hooked head and hooked feet:
Or in sleep rehearse perfect kills and eat.

The convenience of the high trees!   5
The air's buoyancy and the sun's ray
Are of advantage to me;
And the earth's face upward for my inspection.

My feet are locked upon the rough bark.
It took the whole of Creation   10
To produce my foot, my each feather:
Now I hold Creation in my foot

Or fly up, and revolve it all slowly—
I kill where I please because it is all mine.
There is no sophistry in my body: 15
My manners are tearing off heads—

The allotment of death.
For the one path of my flight is direct
Through the bones of the living.
No arguments assert my right: 20

The sun is behind me.
Nothing has changed since I began.
My eye has permitted no change.
I am going to keep things like this.

Poem Summary

Lines 1-4:

"The wood" in line 1 refers to a forest, as in the American expression "the woods." Seated in a treetop, the hawk is able to look down on the world like a king. Hughes establishes the hawk's personality in the first line, though, by describing it as having its eyes closed: the hawk is impressed with neither the vastness of the world nor with itself for being above the world. This hawk has no "falsifying dreams" about anything being better or worse than it really is. In line 3, the imagery, or physical symbol of the bird being "hooked" at top and bottom not only reminds the reader of the physical appearance of the bird, but also emphasizes the sharp parts of the bird that are used for attacking and killing. In addition, the use of "feet" instead of "claws" creates a link in the reader's mind between the hawk's life and human existence; this sort of connection is called personification.

The hawk's claim in line 2 that it has no falsifying dreams is contradicted by its statement in line 4 that it rehearses "perfect" kills in his sleep. Critics have pointed out that, although this hawk is supposed to be an impersonal killing machine, it

has too much self-consciousness for us to consider it to be motivated by instinct alone. The hawk has an opinion about what would be perfection in killing, which shows that it is not outside of the sphere of morality, despite its claim to the contrary.

Lines 5-8:

In its tone, this stanza displays a sense of self-importance that matches the hawk's physical position above the world. The words "convenience," "buoyancy," "advantage," and "inspection" are all examples of elevated, sophisticated diction. Spoken by the hawk, these words indicate that it is a very intelligent bird. This use of language implies that the hawk is mentally as well as physically superior. In line 8, the hawk uses the word "face" to give human qualities to the earth, and it says not only that it can see the earth's face but that it is there "for my inspection," as if the earth awaits the hawk's inspection.

Lines 9-12:

"Creation," because it is capitalized, refers not just to all that exists, but to God, since references to God or pronouns that stand for God are usually capitalized. The understanding of God here is less specific than the images usually accepted by major religions. In the third stanza, there are three mentions of the hawk's feet. The first is a somewhat simple one, linking the hawk to its natural habitat, which is portrayed as a difficult one through the use of the word "rough." In the second mention, the hawk asserts that it is not just part of the world, but the end of, the reason for all that exists. In line 12, the hawk takes this self-important view even further, implying that since it exists as the summation of all that is, it is superior even to God. According to such reasoning, God and other beings are not recognized as having any more will or desire than the tree's bark has. The hawk sees others as creatures performing their specific functions, just as it performs its function when it kills. Presumably, in this worldview, the hawk's victims understand that it has no purpose but to kill them.

Lines 13-16:

"Sophistry" is reasoning that is clever and seems to be well-founded, but in actuality is hollow and false. When the hawk says in line 15, "There is no sophistry in my body," it is indicating that the body does not reason badly because it does not reason at all; it acts. In this way, the poem

Media Adaptations

- Ted Hughes, who has a strong and rhythmic reading voice, is a pleasure to listen to. He has recorded many of his poems on audio cassette, including the recently released *The Thought Fox & Other Poems,* available from Faber & Faber.

seems to express the idea that any amount of reasoning will have some falseness to it and that the only way to avoid falseness is to avoid reasoning. The author has responded to criticisms that "Hawk Roosting" seems to approve of cruelty by saying that he only wanted the hawk to show what "Nature is thinking." If nature's thoughts are direct and without reason (such as "I see the mouse, I kill the mouse"), then this poem could be seen as a record of responses to physical stimuli. However, the hawk has ideas about the ways of the world ("I kill where I please because it is all mine") that seem to come from the exact sort of sophistry that the hawk denies. Similarly, line 16 uses language that is intentionally harsh ("tearing off their heads," rather than a more impartially descriptive phrase like "removing heads," which would match the diction of stanza 2). The hawk appears quite conscious of the fact that its actions are vicious, and almost seems to enjoy it.

Lines 17-20:

Each stanza of this poem begins with a direct, declarative statement that is brought to a stop at the end of the first line with punctuation. Lines such as these are called "end-stopped lines." An end-stopped line that brings the flow of the poem to a halt just as the stanza is beginning gives the speaker's tone a cold sharpness, as if the speaker is stating conditions and making demands rather than having a conversation with the reader. In line 17 this technique is used to make the hawk's position on killing seem absolute and undisputable. As with the earlier reference to "the whole of Creation" (line 10), this stanza makes absolute statements such as "the one path," "direct," "through" (as op-

posed to "into"), and "No arguments" to convey the hawk's unhesitating certainty.

In line 20 the hawk says that the rights it is entitled to are not the product of any arguments, implying that it has undeniable rights and that these rights are more important than anything, including God. This echoes the claim made in lines 18 and 19. Both lines emphasize a division between rationality and nature (referred to here as Creation), implying that man, as a rational creature, is separate and distinct from the natural world and from God.

Lines 21-24:

In lines 1, 5, 9, and 21 this poem intermittently establishes a setting for the hawk who is speaking. The image in line 21 is especially notable because it does not emphasize the hawk's viewpoint but specifically tells us about something, the sun, that is out of the range of the hawk's vision. For the reader who is imagining a hawk on a tree branch, this detail helps to paint a picture, but given the hawk's self-centered attitude throughout the poem, that it would mention something it does not see is unusual. To some extent, the perspective in this stanza is not just the hawk's, but an objective point of view that is spoken through the hawk's "I." This is seen in the difference between lines 22 and 23: line 22 is an impartial statement, and line 23 expresses the same basic idea, but through the hawk's all-encompassing ego. In making these two statements, one a passive observation and the other an aggressive claim, this poem draws attention to the different degrees of animal mentality that it offers. The final line is pure arrogance, extending the hawk's previous claims about being the center of all that came before and all that currently exists to include all that will come to be.

Themes

Death

The hawk is a cunning and silent death from above, a bird of prey often portrayed as the noble killer who perches on top of the food chain. The poem begins with the regal image of the hawk sitting "on top of the wood ... and the earth's face upward for my inspection." The theme of death in "Hawk Roosting" may be closely tied to its images of creation, as many religions also believe our lives on this earth are temporary. The hawk's speaking tone, with its elevated diction bordering on arrogance, combined with the bird's physical position overlooking the whole of its world, seem to place it firmly in control of life or death. Even the "Creation" which produced its claws and "each feather" now becomes its prey, gripped firmly in its talons.

While the subject of death is often weighted with grief and remorse, the hawk is emotionless in its discussion, referring to it as an "allotment," as if it were to be rationed out. There is no room for remorse in that small skull, since the bird's path toward survival "is direct / through the bones of the living."

Violence and Cruelty

Students first encountering Ted Hughes's work in the *Norton Anthology of Modern Poetry* are greeted with the following introduction: "Ted Hughes works within a subject-matter of violence, and his acknowledged talent in this area has evoked uneasy admiration." While "Hawk Roosting" does portray images of violence, as in the line "My manners are tearing off heads," this theme is balanced by a sort of nonchalant tone that diffuses the cruelty normally associated such a harsh act.

Some critics have called the hawk's ability to kill without remorse and speak of her killing with such casual ease proof the bird is symbolically a fascist, citing lines like "I kill where I please because it is all mine." Ted Hughes denies this, instead saying he intended the bird to represent "Nature thinking. Simply Nature." Hughes may have put himself (and the hawk) in the line of criticism by crafting the voice of the poem in first person. By making the bird the narrator, the reader feels as though he or she is listening to another person talking, and judges what is said accordingly.

Perhaps a central theme of "Hawk Roosting" is that violence and cruelty are really a matter of perspective: while to humans any harmful act upon another person is cruel, in nature there are laws of survival which can not or should not be judged in human terms.

Natural Law

When Hughes himself defended the hawk against accusations of cruelty and of even being a fascist, he said he rather intended the bird to represent "Simply Nature." Perhaps this means the poem's theme shows that while a human act of violence against another human can be judged as wrong, nature has its own set of laws. Hughes has said that we are too "corrupted" by Christian morality and judgment to be able to see nature. The hawk

Topics for Further Study

- Write a poem from the point of view of an animal that might be the hawk's prey. Would the prey have the same perspective on "Natural Law" as the hawk? Would it use the same sort of language? Compare poems and discuss your answers.

- Compare Hughes's portrayal of a hawk with Robinson Jeffers's poem "Hurt Hawks," included in the 3rd volume of *Poetry for Students*. In your opinion, in what ways do both authors use the bird of prey to comment on our relationship with nature and other humans? Do you feel one poet's portrayal is more accurate than the other? How so?

- How does the fact that the hawk is aware of itself, referring to itself in first person, influence how you feel about what it says? Would you be more or less likely to accept its claims if the poem were written in the third person? Discuss your answers.

doesn't kill out of anger, evil or greed, but out of pure survival, a need for "perfect kills and eat." The sense that the bird's actions follow a "Law" which should not be questioned are reinforced by lines that repeatedly refer to "legal" phrases, such as "my inspection," "sophistry" and "No arguments assert my right." Instead the hawk follows a natural law that has been in place for so long it will remain long after humans have left the earth. As the poem begins with "inaction," so it ends "nothing has changed since I began. / My eye has permitted no change. / I am going to keep things like this."

Style

This poem has no strict pattern to its rhythm or its rhyme scheme, thus it is considered an open form poem. However, the poem does make use of structural devices and repetition in other ways to make its point.

The most obvious structural pattern in "Hawk Roosting" is that there are four lines to each stanza, or cluster of lines. The lengths of the lines within each stanza are different, so the number of words in each stanza varies. Nevertheless, there is a visual consistency as the eye skims down the page. This degree of order corresponds to the poem's subject matter by giving the piece an overall design, just as the speaker of the poem implies in stanza 3 that Creation has an overall design. A poem with a more rigid structure—for example, uniform rhythm in each line, or a regular rhyme scheme—would contradict the hawk's sense of being accountable to no one.

There are rhymes at the ends of the third and fourth lines in the first stanza and again in the first and third lines in the second. The fact that these are in the beginning of the poem, and that the poem never rhymes again, may indicate that the author intended his readers to think at first that this poem was more traditional in sentiment and structure than it really is in order to make the hawk's coldness more shocking. Throughout the poem there are internal rhymes, or rhyming words placed near each other but not at the ends of lines, such as "flight" and "right" in stanza 5. Many of these rhymes use assonance, in which the vowel sounds of the two words are alike, even though the end sounds of the words are not. Some examples of these are "sleep" and "eat" in stanza 1; "ray" and "face" in stanza 2; "took" and "foot" in stanza 3; and "began" and "am" in stanza 6. Such repetition of sounds allows the author to give a musical quality to the poem without adopting a rigid structure.

Historical Context

At the time "Hawk Roosting" was published in 1960, Ted Hughes was a fairly young poet. At only thirty years old, he was barely four years into his troubled marriage with fellow poet Sylvia Plath, a marriage that would end only three years later in bitter arguments, separation, and Plath's tragic suicide. Some critics point first to Hughes's biography to explain the nature of his often violent or cruel subject matter. While his relationship with the clinically depressed Sylvia Plath may account for the emotional tragedy that infuses his work, Hughes often contended that the natural world sustains it-self on a different set of terms. Natural law is not to be judged on a scale of violence, but survival. As a boy Hughes regularly caught and tended wild animals around his home in Yorkshire, England. Perhaps this is why he "thinks of poems as a sort of animal [that] have a vivid life of their own, outside mine."

In order to get a better context of Hughes's work in 1960, it is important to note the poetic modes of the 1950s. With the publication of his first book, *The Hawk in the Rain,* in 1957, his work illustrated a strong move away from the popular poetic styles of the time. The stereotypical poem of the day was mostly domestic, mildly ironic, polite and understated. In contrast, Hughes hit the scene with almost Shakespearean language to explore themes that were more elemental and mythical. His bold and unflinching look at the natural world turned many heads, and younger poets began to follow his new path. Since then many poets have followed his lead into less self-conscious styles. Critics point out that from his earliest work to present, he has virtually ignored the social structures known as "manners," choosing instead to take on the root of man's relationship with man and the other living creatures which inhabit this planet.

In the years immediately preceding the publication of his second book, *Lupercal,* Ted Hughes and his wife lived in the United States. They both taught at universities for a short while, but quickly choose to dedicate their time to living frugally and writing. It was a period of great prosperity, hope, energy and power in the United States, and it was still possible to live nominally on meager earnings in order to pursue artistic careers. Both poets finished books during that time, Hughes his second, and Plath her first, *The Colossus.*

In December, 1959, they returned to England, where they planned to settle permanently, moving into a small village. Their daughter Frieda was born in 1960. Unfortunately the happy times did not last for long. Within a few years and the birth of a second child, Nicholas, the two complex and talented personalities began to clash. Hughes began falling in love with another woman, and when Plath discovered the attachment, the marriage collapsed. They separated, and in February, 1963, Sylvia Plath committed suicide in London. Hughes, overcome by guilt, would not publish another book after *Lupercal* until 1957, dedicating his time wholly to editing and bringing Plath's work to posthumous publication.

Compare & Contrast

- **1960:** America's relationship with Cuba quickly deteriorates after Fidel Castro signs an agreement at Havana on February 13th with Soviet first deputy premier Anastas Mikoyan. The paper strongly ties the neighboring island to Communist Russia both politically and militarily. Tensions caused by both American and Russian threats of nuclear action over the tiny country later come to a head in a naval standoff known as "The Cuban Missile Crisis."

   1998: Although Cuba is one of only a very small handful of Communist countries remaining, the relationship between Castro, still in power, and the American government, continues to get stronger. Castro shows a sign of goodwill by allowing the visit of Pope John Paul II, and American business investors pressure Washington to ease sanctions on Cuba so they may invest in the market there.

- **1960:** The first commercial lasers are introduced by Hughes Laboratory in Malibu, California.

   The laser, an acronymn that stands for "light amplification by stimulated emission of radiation," provides thousands of watts of energy in a single, consistent beam of light. They will be used for industrial metalwork cutting and welding.

   1998: Lasers are widely used in a variety of diverse applications, from corrective eye and dental surgery to military targeting and "smart bombs." Scientists and science-fiction writers alike imagine lasers as being the eventual first line of defense against any stray asteroids heading toward Earth.

- **1960:** Domino's Pizza opens in Detroit. Local entrepreneur Thomas Monaghan, 23, borrows $500 to buy his first pizza parlor.

   1998: Having grown to become a multi-million dollar business with thousands of franchises nationwide, Domino's has pioneered pizza delivery as we know it with "30 minutes or less" door-to-door service guarantees and its distinctive blue, red and white logos.

Critical Overview

"Hawk Roosting" received its greatest amount of critical attention after it was republished in Hughes's *Selected Poems: 1957-1967.* By then, the poem was more than thirteen years old, and critics could study it as part of the overall pattern of Hughes's work. Critics are sharply divided over the effectiveness of "Hawk Roosting." Peter Meinke wrote a generally favorable review of Hughes's work in *The New Republic:* "[A]s a description of his own inner landscape, which we all touch on somewhere, Hughes' poems are completely compelling, but as a description of reality they suffer 'tunnel vision' ..." Calvin Bedient wrote in *The New York Times* a month earlier (January 1974): "At his worst, [Hughes's] poems say 'TAKE THAT!' He seems to boast that he can swallow more gore and nothingness than anyone else on the block ..." But criticisms such as these blame the author for narrowness and bleakness, which Hughes could easily defend as his intention. Worse yet is Marjorie Perloff's charge that " 'Hawk Roosting' ... has no meaningful reference to any conceivable situation." She explains this by pointing out a weak link in Hughes's poetry, that "in Hughes' poetic universe, the relation of the individual to the hostile, amoral violence that surrounds him remains obscure." Even worse than accusations of meaninglessness, though, are the critics who see "Hawk Roosting" as being pro-fascist. Although Hughes denied this claim, critic Robert Stuart responded that, because of a "lack of any note of self-awareness," there is hardly any way to understand the murderous hawk except as a fascist. The little written about the poem's technical and verbal skill is generally favorable, but many commentators do not accept the poem's neutral moral stance as being characteristic of good poetry.

Criticism

Jhan Hochman

Jhan Hochman is a writer and instructor at Portland Community College in Portland, Oregon. In the following essay, Hochman discusses Hughes's portrayal of the hawk in "Hawk Roosting."

Few poems match the unruffled violence, the omnipotence-at-rest of Ted Hughes's "Hawk Roosting." From his second collection of poems entitled *Lupercal* (1960), "Hawk Roosting" is just one of many poetic meditations on the violence of, or surrounding, animals.

The poem's six quatrains (four-line stanzas) of free verse (poetry mostly devoid of rhyme and meter) are written from the point of view of a hawk. In "Hawk Roosting," Hughes attempts the impossible: to think like a hawk. His close-eyed hawk rests at the top of a tree, meditatively contemplating perfect kills made possible by the perfection of her body, a kind of flying, killing machine devoid of feeling, morals, and rationalization. Some critics accuse Hughes's project of thinking like a hawk to be doomed, from the outset, to failure, a failure issuing from just another example of human ignorance or arrogance, or both. Why *this* accusation? Because critics have claimed that neither Hughes nor anyone else should have the audacity to believe they can understand the thought patterns of a being of another species (let alone an individual of the same species). And conversely, Hughes should not have deluded himself that persons can ever stop being who they are to the point that they can successfully imagine another.

Should Hughes have attempted this poem from the view of a hawk, knowing that he would never really get it right? Should a project be undertaken if it can't be fully realized? Maybe, if we are to apply this question to such projects as roads and bridges. But whether it pertains to the realms of sympathy, empathy, and identification in terms of other individuals might just be another story.

To attempt to answer this question about the value of a human being thinking like a hawk or a non-human animal, at least one of several preliminary questions had better be asked: Is the hawk just one instance of nature or a representative of nature? The same question might also be asked this way: Is this "just a hawk," or is this nature, itself, speaking through a hawk? Or finally, another version of the same question: Does the hawk speak for

itself or for all of nature? If Hughes, himself, is allowed to answer this question, it seems that one would have to conclude that in the poem, nature is speaking through the hawk: "That bird is accused of being a fascist … the symbol of some horrible genocidal dictator. Actually what I had in mind was that in this hawk, Nature is thinking. Simply Nature."

But putting aside until later the issue as to whether the hawk is a fascist, it might be argued that Hughes did not carefully weigh his words. But let him be taken at his word—one hawk as a representative of not only all hawks, but of nature. If readers were prone to assert that thinking like a hawk was already folly or arrogance, then what can be said of Hughes attempting to penetrate the very "mind of nature," not far different from penetrating the "mind of God." Is Hughes's body of animal poems, then, an attempt to write a bible of nature, the book of a world without God, a world based upon violence, a nature "red in tooth and claw?" If so, Hughes is assuredly even more arrogant than his roosting hawk. The trouble here is that assuming Hughes is merely arrogant stifles a discussion of a poem which seems to warrant more than quick dismissal or scorn.

Let us not take Hughes at his word. At least not yet, since Hughes could have meant only that his hawk as "Nature thinking" was just *one* example of nature thinking, not what nature would say if it were speaking through a vegetarian animal, say deer or rabbits. If this is the case, then Hughes attempted something less grandiose than understanding the "mind of nature." Keeping in perspective that Hughes is still subject to the criticism that it is hubristic folly to think/speak as a hawk, or any animal for that matter, the hawk rendered as merely one voice in nature makes nature only partially, not wholly, violent. Since nothing in "Hawk Roosting" mentions the hawk as a representative of all nature, and since nature is as full of predators as of prey, it seems wiser to come down on the side of the poem being about a hawk, a hawk that is no more than a representative of hawks in general, and with caution, of carnivorous predators in general.

Another question can now be asked: Is the hawk an evil fascist, and therefore, are hawks and predators therefore evil? Hughes has already said his hawk is not a fascist, a word synonymous with dictators like Hitler and Mussolini. Hughes has also said the following: "The laws of the Creation are the only literally rational things, and we don't yet know what they are. The nearest we can come to rational thinking is to stand respectfully, hat in hand before this Creation exceedingly alert for a new word." This statement contends nature is deserving of respect and awe. Is "Hawk Roosting," then, an example of "respectful standing"? Here, as always, the last word should be the poem's—and the poem is completely silent as to whether this hawk deserves our respect or disgust. There is no other creature in this poem that might judge the hawk. And the poet seems about as absent as he can be from a piece he himself penned. Without any obvious manifestations of judgment, how then are readers to judge?

But perhaps this is precisely the point—we are not to stand in judgment of this hawk, or of predators in general. We are, first and foremost, to accept the bird on her own terms, to acknowledge her perfection in eye and feather, beak and claw, her absolute efficiency in distributing her allotment of death, her utter lack of need to rationalize or philosophize her killings. And not only the hawk's own perfection, but we must also acknowledge how other parts of nature collaborate with the hawk to enable her killing: the sun's light, the air's buoyancy, the height of the trees, and the earth turned up to her inspection. And not only do the forces and elements of nature enable her, but all of creation has made this hawk the way she is.

If all the above were not enough evidence that this hawk is neither evil nor a symbol of human evil, there is one last reason that Hughes's hawk deserves admiration, not condemnation. The hawk's nature and philosophy is inherent, bestowed at birth by the laws of creation. So the hawk's reasoning is true and invulnerable to the muddled and confused mental processes that affect humans. One might go even further to say that all argument and reasoning apart from that of creation's is false argument, or *sophistry*. If this is the point of "Hawk Roosting," then not only is the hawk a superior creature, but human beings are inferior since they, by outer force or inner need, or both, use mouth and mind to argue the merits of their actions. Such a scenario casts humanity as fallen from a nature that has not fallen from God, a nature on a par with Godliness.

One last question must now be posed: In spite of a decision that the hawk is depicted as awesome, not awful, is "Hawk Roosting" still a display of arrogance? In other words, is it presumptuous to believe that one can understand and duplicate the mental state of a hawk, or, for that matter, any animal? Unfortunately there is no way to assert one

What Do I Read Next?

- Another British poet contemporary to Hughes who also shares a strong American popularity is Thom Gunn. The two poets have poems anthologized in a collection edited by Alan Bold, *Thom Gunn and Ted Hughes*.

- For his similar, unflinching poetic voice and approach toward man's relationship with nature, many critics mention Robinson Jeffers in studies of Hughes's work. His has numerous editions of selected poems, and is also included in Volume 3 of *Poetry for Students*.

- Ted Hughes spent much of his time editing and publishing the posthumous poems of Sylvia Plath, his wife who committed suicide in 1963. You can read her poem "The Mirror" in Volume 1 of *Poetry for Students*, or check out her most famous and widely reprinted volume, *Ariel*.

- When Hughes took the position of Britain's Poet Laureate in 1984, he was not the first choice. Philip Larkin, who turned down the high profile poetic spotlight and thus made way for Hughes, is widely published in England and America. His *Collected Poems* is available at bookstores, and his poem "Toads" is included in this volume.

way or another whether Hughes has been successful in his attempt to think and speak like another. Thus it is difficult to determine if the poem is arrogant.

If anything, it might be supposed that the enterprise of thinking like another is fraught with obstacles and risks. While the path of obstacle and risk is sometimes better avoided, sometimes it is better confronted. "Hawk Roosting" is likely the occasion for the need of fight, not flight. Rather than a gesture of arrogance—Hughes having the audacity to think he can speak like a hawk—might it not be more prudent to praise Hughes for having accomplished the opposite of arrogance, for having made an attempt to imagine what a hawk feels? Is this not instead the height of empathy, to walk inside another's shoes?

If this seems at all agreeable, then another question will inevitably arise: Did Hughes depict a hawk successfully, or has he fallen into the trap of anthropomorphism, depicting an animal with human attributes? While this question should be difficult to answer confidently, it can easily be said that Hughes succeeded in doing something interesting and provocative; that is, he acknowledged the killing that is so much a part of a hawk's life without depicting the hawk as evil. In this way, Hughes has undermined the reductionist connection between violence and evil, a connection probably unnecessary when examining the nature of hawks, and perhaps only slightly necessary when examining the culture of humans.

Source: Jhan Hochman, in an essay for *Poetry for Students,* Gale, 1998.

Sean Robisch

Sean Robisch teaches composition and literature at Purdue University and holds a Ph.D. in American Literature. His fiction has appeared in Hopewell Review *and* Puerto del Sol. *In the following essay, Robisch discusses the importance of Nature in Hughes's work.*

In response to the accusation that his poem "Hawk Roosting" celebrated violence, Ted Hughes responded, "Actually, what I had in mind was that in this hawk Nature is thinking. Simply Nature. It's not so simple maybe because Nature is no longer so simple." In this quote we find the essence of both the poem and of Hughes's philosophy behind many of his writings about animals and the non-human world. His thinking is much like Robinson Jeffers, whose "inhumanism" examined how other species, climatic conditions, and ecological systems seemed to challenge human beings' ideas about being supreme over nature. But Hughes's approach, particularly in "Hawk Roosting" and other poems like it, departs from Jeffers's in a very important way. Hughes uses Nature, with the capital "N," as an abstract and mythological figure to invest his observations with symbolic value, while Jeffers used observation and the nonhuman world to critique the way humans use myth. Hughes may be a little less cynical, but also a little more romantic and less realistic than Jeffers, because the creatures of his poems are designed to connect us less to what is not human than to what is ancient and human—to the world of myth.

In 1960, after moving from Great Britain to teach at the University of Massachusetts, Hughes wrote *Lupercal,* the book in which "Hawk Roosting" appears. He began the project in Boston and finished it while travelling throughout the United States with his wife, writer Sylvia Plath. *Lupercal* was only Hughes's second volume of poetry, the first being *The Hawk in the Rain,* which had won several British prizes and brought him much attention. Hughes would go on to write a great many poems about birds, even an entire collection called *Crow,* probably his most celebrated work. He also wrote about wolves and other animals in his poetry and in children's books, often focussing on predators and the nature of the hunting animal, especially as it connected with the mythic rituals of cultures from all over the planet. This is important to remember when reading "Hawk Roosting," because it fits into a book that Hughes designed according to an ancient Roman ritual.

The ritual was called the "Lupercalia," which loosely refers to the wolf, and it was carried out as a rebirth or Spring rite, both to bring fertility to the land and to keep the wolves away from the new lambs. This Roman ceremony inspired the structure of *Lupercal,* which runs according to the various rules and components of the Lupercalia and in which we find "Hawk Roosting." The poem itself was inspired by a project that Hughes had started earlier and abandoned, a long poem about England that carried the river as a repeated image; Hughes would use this in a later work rather than retain it in "Hawk Roosting." The poem is both part of what Hughes considered a kind of "buried life" in England, that of experiencing the natural world, and a similarly buried life of humanity, that of the ancient animal myths.

Although Hughes hoped to show "Nature thinking," he also said that every poem "is both a violation of the facts it uses and a violation of what we feel about the facts." This means—according to Hughes—that fact, while important to some kinds of observation and reportage on the natural world, are not what govern the poet. He immediately acts on this impulse to challenge fact as the gauge of Nature thinking by writing the poem in the hawk's thoughts. Its "voice" is presented in the first person, as a soliloquy or monologue. We are to suspend disbelief and accept, for the moment, that this is truly the hawk thinking. From this perspective, we learn that the hawk is pure and true to itself (it dreams "no falsifying dream"). Therefore, the dream it does have just two lines later, in which during sleep it may "rehearse perfect kills and eat" must be accurate and honest. What the hawk thinks and what the poet tells us it thinks are, in other words, the *facts*. We may at any time during the poem remember that these are actually the poet's words being placed in the hawk's mind. So if we stop imagining and simply trusting that the hawk is thinking this poem, we are aware of the poet's speculation, his guessing at the hawk's mind, which is commonly called "anthropomorphism." Anthropomorphism means giving human thought or action to a nonhuman animal. It differs from personification in that it involves giving human qualities (rather than simply "life") to that which is not human. For instance, we might anthropomorphize God by imagining a man with a white beard living in the clouds. In this poem, the hawk imagines itself as a kind of god, and we are invited to imagine along with it.

If we come across a line that seems too unlike a hawk, we may have to look at the poem from another perspective in order to appreciate it. For instance, let's say we come to the word "sophistry," which means the use of rhetoric that is plausible but flawed and usually self-important or posturing. We might question how a hawk conceives of such a notion, and therefore change our perspective to looking at what the poet is doing with the hawk, rather than at the hawk itself. In such complicated moments, we begin to encounter one of the frictions created by anthropomorphism, and by the ancient influences of myth, which is the question, "When do the facts matter and when do they not?"

And that is perhaps what Hughes wants us to ask. We never learn, for instance, the hawk's sex. We call animals "it" when we are in doubt, and the animal becomes a kind of object, though one invested in the natural world in a way that humans are not. For Hughes, that connection of the hawk to its world extends beyond anthropomorphism. Here he uses a technique called "theriomorphism," which means the attribution of divinity to an animal. We get this term from the Latin (incidentally, the language of the Roman Lupercalia). "Therio" means the "great, good beast," or the perfect and divine form of the animal. And thus we are returned to the ancient mythic traditions. For example, critic Keith Sagar shows us that a line from the book of Job (41:11), "Whatsoever is under the whole heaven is mine," is very much like the hawk's line, "I kill where I please because it is all mine." The hawk claims to "hold Creation," and that "It took the whole of Creation / To produce my foot." This

> *We may see in 'Hawk Roosting' a kind of quest for consciousness— the poet speculating about the thoughts of a hawk in order to learn something about what humans think of Nature."*

divinity in the animal is what Hughes implies as Nature capitalized, and the hawk as its representative, that is capable of thinking such grandiose thoughts.

Hughes's approach, therefore, tells us in "Hawk Roosting" that if the hawk is divine, and Nature is thinking, then Nature must be pretty cold and unforgiving. "My manners are tearing off heads," says the hawk. It claims to fly "Through the bones of the living." This view of the divine and natural as being hard and frightful is what prompted some critics to say that Hughes "celebrated violence." His answers about Nature thinking and about the violation of facts are so complex partly because he is trying to juggle his interest in nature with his respect for and fear of its power. Therefore the poem is important to understand as mythic rather than "accurate," and as violent though hardly celebratory. In fact, we are not necessarily seeing a hawk at all, but something like the mask of a hawk. By reading the poem, we are part of a ritual the poet is performing on the page, so that the hawk teaches us something about ourselves. When it sits with its back to the sun, declaring that "Nothing has changed since I began," it speaks like the Egyptian god Horus, the hawk with the powerful, all-seeing eye. This reminds us about the power of myth in poetry and about the role that poetry has in forming our mythologies. In this way, Hughes is acting very much like the Romantic poets of the nineteenth century just as much as a poet of the 1960s.

As Leonard Scigaj has explained, during the time when Ted Hughes wrote "Hawk Roosting," formalism and the New Criticism were still being practiced by many poets. Formalism meant that the poem's meter, rhyme, and structure were important and had to be held together consistently and properly for the poem to "work." New Criticism said that the text on the page was all that was important, and that from a close reading of the forms at work in a poem, a reader could understand all that was necessary about its meaning. Hughes's first book conformed to these ideas about standard form, but *Lupercal* began to depart from them. Hughes found in his own work and in the work of his contemporaries that the inner life—the human spirit—could be articulated through poetry, and that history, ritual, and religious practice were powerful forces in poems. He often expressed this through animal figures, just as societies have done for thousands of years, and eventually his experimentation and subsequent success would earn him the title of Poet Laureate of England.

So we may see in "Hawk Roosting" a kind of quest for consciousness—the poet speculating about the thoughts of a hawk in order to learn something about what we humans think of Nature. We often think only of beauty in nature—the awe at viewing the Grand Canyon or of a great storm far away. Critic Craig Robinson reminds us "that awe includes horror." The canyon may be dangerous, and the storm might soon approach. The will to live, the role of the predator, and the barriers that exist between humans and animals are all a part of life. Even as Hughes gives us an imaginary hawk thinking of itself as a god and asserting its "right," that same hawk's arrogant assumption that it will "keep things like this" will prove to be, in time, a violation of the facts. Perhaps then, if a hawk is incapable of thinking such thoughts, we could just as easily picture ourselves perched "in the top of the wood," giving human qualities to hawks, and godlike qualities to humans.

Source: Sean Robisch, in an essay for *Poetry for Students,* Gale, 1998.

Sources

Bedient, Calvin, *New York Times Book Review,* January 13, 1974, pp. 3-4.

Gifford, Terry, and Neil Robert, *Ted Hughes: A Critical Study,* Faber and Faber, 1981.

Hughes, Ted, *Lupercal,* London: Faber & Faber, 1960.

Hughes, Ted, *New Selected Poems 1957-1994,* Faber and Faber, 1995.

Meinke, Peter, *The New Republic,* February 16, 1974, p. 32.

Perloff, Marjorie, *The Washington Post Book Review,* February 10, 1974, pp. 1-2.

Robinson, Craig, *Ted Hughes As Shepherd of Being,* NY: St. Martin's, 1989.

Sagar, Keith, *The Art of Ted Hughes,* London: Cambridge University Press, 1978.

Sagar, Keith, ed., *The Achievement of Ted Hughes,* Athens: University of Georgia Press, 1983.

Scigaj, Leonard M., *The Poetry of Ted Hughes: Form and Imagination,* University of Iowa Press, 1986.

Stuart, Robert, "Ted Hughes," *British Poetry Since 1970: A Critical Survey,* Carcanet Press, 1980, pp. 75-84.

West, Thomas, *Ted Hughes,* Methuen, 1985.

For Further Study

Bently, Paul, *Ted Hughes: Studies in 20th Century Literature,* Longman Publishing Group, 1990.
   Collects critical essays which place Hughes in the context of a larger scope of writers.

Sagar, Keith, ed., *The Challenge of Ted Hughes,* St. Martin's Press, 1994.
   A collection of critical essays providing commentary on Hughes's work since 1970.

Scigaj, Leonard, ed., *Critical Essays on Ted Hughes,* G.K. Hall Press, 1992.
   A variety of critical essays, grouped by theme.

The Highwayman

Alfred Noyes
1907

According to his own report, Alfred Noyes wrote "The Highwayman" over a two-day period in 1904 when he was 24 years old. (The poem was published in 1907 in the collection *Forty Singing Seamen and Other Poems*.) "The Highwayman" is a romantic ballad, which means that it is a narrative poem that celebrates passion and adventure. Set in the England of King George III, the poem tells the story of a highwayman, or robber, who has fallen in love with Bess, an innkeeper's beautiful daughter. The lovers are betrayed by a jealous stablehand, and soldiers attempt to trap the highwayman by taking Bess hostage. In an oddly sadistic scene, the soldiers tie Bess up with a gun pointing into her chest, and then wait in ambush for the highwayman. When Bess hears the highwayman approaching, she warns him by shooting herself; he hears the gunshot and escapes. The soldiers pursue him, however, and he, too, is killed. The poem is notable for the way in which it reverses our expectations concerning light and dark imagery. Ordinarily, we think of the clarity of daylight in positive terms. In "The Highwayman," however, Noyes associates the daylight with the destructive powers of mankind, and he identifies the nighttime with the mysterious forces of nature.

Although Noyes wrote "The Highwayman" at the beginning of the Modernist period, the poem seems more characteristic of the Victorian period. The poem is notable for its logical narrative structure and its vivid, highly detailed descriptions—elements the Modernists tended to avoid. Noyes,

Alfred Noyes

however, considered himself a traditionalist and rejected the poetic innovations of the Modernists. Deeply religious, Noyes also disapproved of the explicit violence and sexuality that was sometimes evident in his contemporaries' work. "The Highwayman," then, represents something of an anomaly in Noyes's career, for it derives much of its narrative tension and excitement not only from its bloody conclusion, but from its sexually charged atmosphere.

Author Biography

Noyes was born in Wolverhampton, England, on September 16, 1880. His father Alfred was a grocer who later became a teacher. His mother Amelia Adams Rawley Noyes developed a nervous disorder that left her an invalid following the birth of the last of her three sons. Despite this, Noyes always maintained that his childhood was a happy one. He attended school in Wales and later attended Oxford University, leaving without earning a degree. Noyes was considered the most popular poet of his time, with much of the appeal of his early poetry stemming from his optimistic and patriotic worldview. His first collection of poetry, *The Loom*

of Years, was published in 1902. In 1904 Noyes wrote "The Highwayman," one of his most popular poems, in two days. In 1907, he married Garnett Daniels, an American, and together they sometimes resided in the United States.

During World War I, Noyes turned his interest to writing fiction, particularly fiction with paranormal and psychic themes. He was named a Commander of the Order of the British Empire in 1918, in part for his work as a reporter for the International News Service during the war. Noyes served as Murray Professor of Literature at Princeton University from 1914 until 1923 (except for his stint as a reporter during the war). Among his students were F. Scott Fitzgerald, Edmund Wilson, and John Peale Bishop. His wife died in 1926, and the following year he married Mary Angela Mayne Weld-Blundell. In addition to Mary's daughter by her first marriage, Agnes, the couple had three children together—Henry, Veronica, and Margaret. Noyes's already considerable interest in religion grew, and during the 1930s he came to believe, like the Romantic poets, that nature is a parable directing the individual toward spiritual truth. In 1942 Noyes lost his eyesight to glaucoma, which limited his literary activity to compiling and revising his poems for inclusion in volumes of collected works. Noyes died on June 23, 1958.

Poem Text

Part One

I

The wind was a torrent of darkness among the
     gusty trees,
The moon was a ghostly galleon tossed upon
     cloudy seas,
The road was a ribbon of moonlight over the
     purple moor,
And the highwayman came riding—
     Riding—riding—   5
The highwayman came riding, up to the old inn-
     door.

II

He'd a French cocked-hat on his forehead, a bunch
     of lace at his chin,
A coat of the claret velvet, and breeches of brown
     doe-skin;
They fitted with never a wrinkle: his boots were up
     to the thigh!
And he rode with a jewelled twinkle,   10
     His pistol butts a-twinkle,
His rapier hilt a-twinkle, under the jewelled sky.

III

Over the cobbles he clattered and clashed in the
    dark inn-yard,
And he tapped with his whip on the shutters, but
    all was locked and barred;
He whistled a tune to the window, and who should   15
    be waiting there
But the landlord's black-eyed daughter,
    Bess, the landlord's daughter,
Plaiting a dark red love-knot into her long black
    hair.

IV

And dark in the dark old inn-yard a stable-wicket
    creaked
Where Tim the ostler listened; his face was white   20
    and peaked;
His eyes were hollows of madness, his hair like
    mouldy hay,
But he loved the landlord's daughter,
    The landlord's red-lipped daughter,
Dumb as a dog he listened, and he heard the robber
    say—

V

"One kiss, my bonny sweetheart, I'm after a prize   25
    to-night,
But I shall be back with the yellow gold before the
    morning light;
Yet, if they press me sharply, and harry me
    through the day,
Then look for me by moonlight,
    Watch for me by moonlight,
I'll come to thee by moonlight, though hell should   30
    bar the way."

VI

He rose upright in the stirrups; he scarce could
    reach her hand,
But she loosened her hair i' the casement! His face
    burnt like a brand
As the black cascade of perfume came tumbling
    over his breast;
And he kissed its waves in the moonlight,
    (Oh, sweet black waves in the moonlight!)   35
Then he tugged at his rein in the moonlight, and
    galloped away to the West.

Part Two
I

He did not come in the dawning; he did not come
    at noon;
And out o' the tawny sunset, before the rise o' the
    moon,
When the road was a gipsy's ribbon, looping the
    purple moor,
A red-coat troop came marching—   40
    Marching—marching—
King George's men came marching, up to the old
    inn-door.

II

They said no word to the landlord, they drank his
    ale instead,
But they gagged his daughter and bound her to the
    foot of her narrow bed;
Two of than knelt at her casement, with muskets at   45
    their side!
There was death at every window;
    And hell at one dark window;
For Bess could see, through her casement, the road
    that *he* would ride.

III

They had tied her up to attention, with many a
    sniggering jest;
They had bound a musket beside her, with the   50
    barrel beneath her breast!
"Now keep good watch!" and they kissed her.
    She heard the dead man say—
Look for me by moonlight;
    Watch for me by moonlight;
I'll come to thee by moonlight, though hell should   55
    bar the way!

IV

She twisted her hands behind her; but all the knots
    held good!
She writhed her hands till her fingers were wet
    with sweat or blood!
They stretched and strained in the darkness, and
    the hours crawled by like years,
Till, now, on the stroke of midnight,
    Cold, on the stroke of midnight.   60
The tip of one finger touched it! The trigger at
    least was hers!

V

The tip of one finger touched it; she strove no
    more for the rest!
Up, she stood up to attention with the barrel
    beneath her breast,
She would not risk their hearing; she would not
    strive again;
For the road lay bare in the moonlight;   65
    Blank and bare in the moonlight;
And the blood of her veins in the moonlight
    throbbed to her love's refrain.

VI

Tlot-tlot; tlot-tlot! Had they heard it? The horse-
    hoofs ringing clear;
Tlot-tlot, tlot-tlot, in the distance? Were they deaf
    that they did not hear?
Down the ribbon of moonlight, over the brow of   70
    the hill,
The highwayman came riding,
    Riding, riding!
The red-coats looked to their priming! She stood
    up, straight and still!

VII

Tlot-tlot, in the frosty silence! *Tlot-tlot*, in the
    echoing night!
Nearer he came and nearer! Her face was like a   75
    light!
Her eyes grew wide for a moment; she drew one
    last deep breath,
Then her finger moved in the moonlight,
    Her musket shattered the moonlight,
Shattered her breast in the moonlight and warned
    him—with her death.

VIII

He turned; he spurred to the Westward; he did not   80
    know who stood
Bowed, with her head o'er the musket, drenched
    with her own red blood!
Not till the dawn he heard it, and slowly blanched
    to hear
How Bess, the landlord's daughter,
    The landlord's black-eyed daughter,
Had watched for her love in the moonlight, and   85
    died in the darkness there.

IX

Back, he spurred like a madman, shrieking a curse
    to the sky,
With the white road smoking behind him and his
    rapier brandished high!
Blood-red were his spurs i' the golden noon; wine-
    red was his velvet coat;
When they shot him down on the highway,
    Down like a dog on the highway,   90
And he lay in his blood on the highway, with the
    bunch of lace at his throat.

X

*And still of a winter's night, they say, when the
    wind is in the trees,*
*When the moon is a ghostly galleon tossed upon
    cloudy seas,*
*When the road is a ribbon of moonlight over the
    purple moor,*
A highwayman comes riding—   95
    Riding—riding—
*A highwayman comes riding, up to the old inn-
    door.*

XI

*Over the cobbles he clatters and clangs in the dark
    inn-yard;*
*And he taps with his whip on the shutters, but all is
    locked and barred;*
He whistles a tune to the window, and who should   100
    be waiting there
    But the landlord's black-eyed daughter,
Bess, the landlord's daughter,
*Plaiting a dark red love-knot into her long black
    hair.*

Poem Summary

Lines 1-6:

The first stanza establishes the stormy tone that
will pervade the entire poem. On its most basic
level, the stanza describes a windy night and the
highwayman's approach on horseback. But in describing the violent wind, Noyes uses images that
we might just as easily associate with stormy waters: "a torrent of darkness" and "cloudy seas." By
attributing sea-like characteristics to the wind,
Noyes magnifies its intensity. He also creates a
world that seems oddly unsettled: not only is the
ocean confused with the wind, but even the moon
itself seems unstable—it is "tossed" about in the
sky. It is from this wildly disordered nighttime
world that the highwayman first emerges. That is,
from the start, we associate the highwayman with
the chaotic and mysterious forces of nature.

Lines 7-12:

Noyes devotes an entire stanza to describing
the highwayman's clothing. We can gather from
these lines that the highwayman is a sexy, fash-
ionable dresser. Although Noyes draws our attention to the highwayman's weapons, they appear
more decorative than functional: his pistols and
sword (which are really the tools of his trade!)
"twinkle." Note that the word "twinkle" (which
rhymes with "wrinkle" in the middle of the third
line) is repeated three times. With his sparkling
weapons, the highwayman himself seems almost
like one of the stars in the "jewelled sky."

Lines 13-18:

In the third stanza, the highwayman arrives at
the inn. The repetition of the hard "c" and "k"
sounds in the first line mimics the sound of the
horse's hooves on the cobblestones; this repetition
of stressed consonants is called alliteration. The
third stanza also offers an excellent example of narrative compression: that is, Noyes manages to convey a lot of information in a very few lines. Not
only does Noyes inform us that Bess opens the window to the highwayman, but through careful diction he suggests that Bess and the highwayman are
already lovers. Bess is "waiting" for the highwayman, which implies that she had expected his arrival, and she is braiding a "love-knot," or token of
love, into her hair. Noyes makes careful use of color
in these lines: with her sensual black eyes and long
black hair, Bess—like the highwayman—is also
identified with the night. Moreover, both the highwayman and Bess wear a dark red article of cloth-

ing (the highwayman's jacket is "claret" velvet): this color effectively foreshadows the bloody end to which they will each come.

Lines 19-24:

The fourth stanza introduces Tim, a jealous stablehand who is spying on Bess and the highwayman. Noyes repeats the word "dark" twice in the first line; we are no longer aware of the moonlight that illumined the first three stanzas. Oddly, the only mention of light in this stanza is Tim's sickly white face. Noyes has reversed our normal expectations: usually, we associate the dark with evil and the light with good; here, however, the light seems dangerous and forbidding.

Lines 25-30:

Still underneath her window, the highwayman tells Bess about the robbery he plans to commit later that night (a conversation that Tim the ostler overhears). Noyes continues to establish the highwayman as a creature of the night: not only does the highwayman intend to return to Bess before daybreak, but his greatest concern is being pursued "through the day." Notice the recurrence of the phrase "by moonlight" in the last three lines of the stanza. The first two instances occur in the two trimeter lines; the third occurs in the first half of the final hexameter line. By echoing the same three-stressed phrase three times, Noyes creates a climactic effect. This climactic build prepares us for the dramatic stanza which follows.

Lines 31-36:

This stanza concludes the first part of the poem. In it, the highwayman bids farewell to Bess and rides off to the west of England—probably toward Wales (where Noyes himself grew up). The description of their farewell is at once highly sensual and sexually charged. As Bess's long hair spills over the highwayman's face, we are told that it "burnt like a brand." A brand is a tool used to burn an identifying mark in the flesh, and we have a sense here that, in parting, the two lovers have become permanently identified with each other. Notice, too, the recurrence of the water imagery that appeared in the first stanza. Bess's hair is described as a "cascade," or waterfall, and as having "waves." By reinvoking this water imagery, Noyes links Bess to the stormy, windy night. At the end of Part One, then, Noyes has not only portrayed the passionate bond between the highwayman and Bess, but he has also associated both the lovers with the chaotic and dark night.

Media Adaptations

- Three poems by Noyes, "Sherwood," his poem about Robin Hood; "The Barrel-Organ," which was perhaps his best-known poem in his lifetime; and "Epilogue," from *The Flower of Old Japan;* were included in Louis Untermeyer's 1920 anthology *Modern British Poetry*. The collection is available on-line at http://www.columbia.edu/acis/bartleby/mbp/58.html.

- Phil Ochs set "The Highwayman" to music and recorded it on his 1965 album, *I Ain't Marching Anymore*. The album has been re-released by Hannibal.

Lines 37-42:

The narrative resumes at sunset the following day; almost a full day has passed, but the highwayman has not yet returned. Instead, a whole troop of British soldiers appear, warned, no doubt, by Tim. Note the many ways in which this stanza echoes the very first stanza of the poem: the second lines of both stanzas mention the moon; the third lines describe the "road" as a "ribbon" on the "purple moor"; in the fourth, fifth, and sixth lines, a present participle verb, separated by dashes, is repeated four times ("riding" in the first stanza and "marching" here); and both stanzas conclude with the "old inn-door" being approached. The first stanza heralded the appearance of the highwayman. Given the way this stanza so closely echoes the first, we expect him to reappear. It is all the more disquieting, then, when in his place the red-coats appear.

Lines 43-48:

This stanza is extraordinarily violent. It begins with a violation of the landlord himself: the soldiers barge into the inn and take his ale. More important, the red-coats gag and tie up Bess—an action that is deliberately suggestive of sexual violence. Note the difference between the highwayman's and the soldiers' treatment of Bess. We would expect the soldiers (the representatives of the King) to be orderly and law-abiding and the highwayman (a criminal) to be cruel and uncaring. Exactly the opposite is true. Again we see Noyes reversing our expectations.

Lines 49-54:

The images of sexual violence and abuse become even more pronounced as the soldiers mock and then kiss Bess. They "tie her up to attention" with a gun pointed to her chest—a grotesque parody of a soldier. This stanza is remarkable for its sadistic overtones: given Noyes's otherwise conservative attitudes toward the portrayal of sexuality and violence, one wonders why he would have written such a cruel scene. At best, we can say that the soldiers' behavior serves as a useful contrast to the highwayman's. Their repulsiveness makes us appreciate even more the purity of the highwayman's love for Bess. (Note that in the third line the highwayman is described as "dead," even though he has not yet been killed. For a moment, we see the situation through Bess's eyes: to her, the highwayman's death is so inevitable that she already thinks of him as dead.)

Lines 56-61:

Having recognized that the highwayman will certainly be killed if he reaches the inn, Bess attempts to warn him. She strains against the rope until she is able to reach the trigger. In describing this scene, Noyes uses a series of discordant, grating rhymes: "good" and "blood"; "midnight" and "it"; "years" and "hers." "Good" and "blood" are called eye rhymes; the others are called off rhymes. All create a sense that something is, in fact, slightly "off" or wrong—no accident, considering the terribly wrong act of suicide that Bess is about to commit.

Lines 62-67:

The first line of this stanza echoes the last line of the previous stanza, reminding us that Bess only needs to be able to reach the trigger in order to kill herself. In the second line, we are told that Bess "stood up to attention," an odd echo of line 49, which described the soldiers' mocking treatment of her. In this context, however, the sense of the phrase is transformed: rather than being demeaned, Bess grows in nobility as she prepares to sacrifice herself for her lover. The reference to "blood" in the last line of the stanza warns us that Bess's own blood will soon be spilled. This line also reminds us of the permanent bond between the two lovers:

we are told the pulse of the blood in Bess's veins "throbs" to the same beat as her lover's "refrain." It is not until the following stanza, however, that we are told what the highwayman's "refrain" is.

Lines 68-73:

We are now told that the "refrain" is actually the sound of the highwayman's horses' hoofs (and in fact, the rhythm of a fast heartbeat can feel like the beat of horses' hoofs). For the second time in the poem, we hear the highwayman approaching the inn. Noyes again uses the same formula that he used in the first stanza to describe the highwayman's approach: the third line repeats the image of a "ribbon of moonlight"; and the fourth and fifth lines repeat the word "riding" three times. But here Noyes makes a notable change. In the first stanza, the word "riding" also appears in the final line: it signals the highwayman's arrival at the inn door. In this stanza, Noyes substitutes the word "priming" for "riding." This unexpected substitution drives home the idea that instead of arriving at the inn-door, the highwayman will meet the "primed" muskets of the soldiers.

Lines 74-79:

Just as the highwayman is about to be shot, Bess pulls the trigger and kills herself. Note, however, that the gun "shatters" not only Bess's chest, but the "moonlight" itself. Because both Bess and the highwayman are so closely identified with the moonlight, Bess's death seems to disrupt the entire night world. Note, moreover, the caesura, or break, in the last line of the stanza. Just as the moonlight has become shattered, or broken, the rhythm of the line itself has been shattered.

Lines 80-85:

The highwayman hears the gunshot and escapes, not realizing that Bess has killed herself. Notably, he does not learn the truth until the next morning—and daylight. Bess, he is told, "died in the darkness." Her death signals an end to the mysterious and sensual nighttime world she and her lover had inhabited. Bess's death thrusts the poem into the glaring light of day; Noyes's diction underscores the unpleasant nature of the "whiteness" associated with the daylight hours. When the highwayman learns of Bess's death, for instance, he "blanches," or turns white, with dread.

Lines 86-91:

The imagery of this stanza reminds us that we are now indeed in the ugly daylight world dominated by the soldiers: no longer a "ribbon of moon-light," the road is "white" and "smoking." If the highwayman had governed the nighttime world, he is clearly out of his element in the daylight. With no trouble, the soldiers pursue and shoot him: he dies in the very "highway" he had once ruled. He has been reduced from the mysterious "highway *man*" to a "*dog* on the highway."

Lines 92-103:

The final two stanzas repeat, almost word for word, the first and third stanzas of the poem. After the bloody carnage of Part Two, these lines take on added dimension. On one level, they bring us full circle to the beginning of the poem, reminding us of the pure love that Bess and the highwayman once shared. On another level, the repetition of these lines suggests that despite the carnage, the bond between the two lovers is so strong that even death cannot destroy it. In spirit—and in our imaginations—the renegade highwayman will forever be riding up the inn-door, where Bess will forever be there to welcome him. One is left to wonder then, where the victory lies: With the cruel and ugly powers of the day? Or with the mysterious forces of the night?

Themes

Love and Passion

Above all else, "The Highwayman" is a poem that celebrates the passionate love of its two central characters. The poem's subject is revealed in the third stanza, when the highwayman first arrives at Bess's window. Although it is the middle of the night and the inn is "locked and barred," Bess has eagerly anticipated his arrival by tying a "dark red love-knot" in her hair. (The color red, which is associated with intense passion, recurs throughout the poem: in Bess's red lips, the highwayman's red coat, and the color of their blood.) The scene at Bess's window is charged with images of sensual love—the moonlight, Bess's perfumed hair, and the highwayman's face which "burn[s] like a brand." The fact that the two lovers can barely touch—"he scarce could reach her hand"—simply intensifies the feeling of passion. The highwayman can only kiss the "sweet black cascade of perfume" that is Bess's hair. Their brief but romantic encounter builds up anticipation for their next meeting. Before leaving her, the highwayman makes a fateful promise that reveals the depth of his love and fore-

shadows his final sacrifice: "I'll come to thee by moonlight," he tells her, "though hell should bar the way."

The first part of "The Highwayman" introduces the notion of romantic love, but the high drama of the second part manifests it. Held prisoner by soldiers, Bess is used to lay a trap for the highwayman and is forced to watch as they prepare to murder him. She strains against her bonds, oblivious to the pain, "till her fingers were wet with sweat or blood." As the highwayman approaches, her finger pulls the trigger of the rifle bound against her. Its report warns the highwayman but kills Bess.

Bess's action expresses the epitome of the nineteenth-century Romantics' concept of a love so intense and unselfish that one is willing to die for another. The Romantics believed that love had a religious, almost mystical quality. In this context, passion took the place of grace, and the loved one took the place of God. In the Middle Ages, it was believed a saint transfigured by God's grace would take on a holy glow. Just before she kills herself, Bess is transfigured by love: "Her face was like a light." After her death, Bess is "drenched with her own red blood," which symbolizes Bess's passion for the highwayman.

The highwayman loves Bess just as passionately. After hearing of her death, he makes good on his promise to return. The highwayman too is overwhelmed by his love, and like Bess's final moments, his have religious overtones. But the highwayman is no calm saint; rather he seems possessed by the devil—"spurred like a madman, shrieking a curse." Riding back to Bess, expressing his anguish with violence, he brandishes his weapon for the first time. He disregards his own safety as he rushes back; his reckless and violent ride seems as much a suicide as when Bess pulled the musket trigger. He dies on the highway "like a dog": his love, like Bess's, is sealed in his own blood.

The Romantics, however, believed that a passionate, true love conquered all. Because their love is so strong and genuine, death is not able to separate Bess and her highwayman. On the contrary, it unites them forever. The power of their love has made them immortal, and on dark and stormy nights their love is renewed at the inn. As the poem ends, Bess is eternally plaiting a love-knot in her hair for the highwayman.

The Outlaw

The outlaw held an important place in the Romantic imagination. The Romantics maintained

Topics for Further Study

- Write a scene in which the highwayman is robbing some victims at gunpoint. Is he as charming as when we see him in this poem, or is he ruthless when he works? Does he rob for personal gain or political principle? Are the people he robs terrified or charmed?

- What do you think Tim the ostler, mentioned in stanza 3, has to do with this situation? Why does Noyes mention him? What do you think happened to him when the poem was over.

---

that the rules and norms of bourgeois society—such as money lust and the denial of feelings—made it impossible to experience life to the fullest. Far from being a criminal, the outlaw had the courage to flaunt society's rules. As a result, he won deeper insight into the world and himself, and he had more genuine emotional experience than ordinary people. In general, the outlaw lived a more worthwhile life.

Both the highwayman and Bess are outlaws in this tradition. The highwayman is literally an outlaw who prowls the roads robbing travelers. But the poem hints that his actions are more adventure than crime. The gold he will bring Bess is not booty, it is his "prize," or his reward for meeting a challenge successfully. In the first stanza of the poem he is associated with the moon, which is depicted as a "galleon," or the vessel in which pirates travel. He dresses like an outsider as well, wearing, for instance, "a French cocked-hat" rather than an English one.

Bess and the highwayman are outsiders in other ways as well. They meet in the dead of night when, according to tradition, normal daytime rules are suspended. Their love is a secret one, hidden from daytime view. At least, they think it is; but in fact, Tim the ostler knows about them. Tim views the highwayman and Bess with the prejudice, suspicion, and disapproval of the middle-class world. With jealousy, as well, for he lusts after Bess, but

is too cowardly to approach her. The unhealthiness of Tim's feelings is reflected in his physical appearance, which is in stark contrast to the gallant and debonair impression the highwayman makes. Tim is pale, sickly, degenerate, and "his eyes were hollows of madness." What's more, he is "dumb as a dog." He cannot comprehend the life or emotions of Bess and the highwayman although he is directly confronted with them.

The highwayman is associated with the night, but also with goodness and purity of feeling. His weapons are not threatening, they merely "twinkle" at his sides. He does not use them—at least not until after Bess's death. The highwayman's essential goodness is thrown into sharp relief by the sadistic soldiers who barge into the inn, drink without paying, and take Bess hostage. The highwayman is content merely to breath the perfume from Bess's hair because he loves her. In contrast, the soldiers mistreat her; they bind her to her bed with a musket tied beneath her bosom. After they bind and gag her, they commit a symbolic rape by forcing their kisses upon her. Most horribly, she is forced to watch as they prepare to murder her lover. The soldiers are supposed to enforce and uphold the law. Their immoral behavior shows just how meaningless their daytime laws really are. Noyes implies that it is no crime to oppose these men, but rather, it is honorable to live outside the law in such a world.

Style

"The Highwayman" is composed of six-line stanzas that rhyme in an *aabccb* pattern. Notice, however, that the "c" rhymes actually repeat the same word: "twinkle" and "twinkle," for instance, in the second stanza. In fact, one of the most noteworthy features of this poem is its use of repetition. Throughout the poem, Noyes reinvokes key words, phrases, and images: the word "moonlight," for example, appears nineteen times in the poem. Noyes also echoes individual sounds by using alliteration and assonance in literally every stanza. These different forms of repetition intensify the poem's dramatic impact.

The poem is written in hexameters, which means that each line has six stressed syllables. If we scan, or identify the stresses in the first line of the poem, for instance, it appears as follows:

The **wind** was a **tor**rent of **dark**ness **a**mong the **gus**ty **trees**.

Try reading the line aloud. Its fast and heavily pulsing rhythm contributes to the poem's energy.

Note, however, that the fourth and fifth lines (the "c" rhymed lines) generally each have only three stresses, a form of meter called trimeter. Look, for instance, at the two trimeter lines from the second stanza:

> And he **rode** with a **jewe**lled **twink**le
> His **pistol butts** a-**twink**le.

For purposes of scansion, we might simply regard these two trimeter, or three-stressed lines, as one hexameter, or six-stressed line. Doing so, however, would ignore the dramatic effect of the trimeters. Because the two trimeter lines are, in fact, so short—and because they repeat each other—they must be read very quickly. In fact, if you read them aloud, you will notice that it is easy to become breathless. This sense of breathlessness adds to the excitement and passion of the poem.

Historical Context

In 1907, when "The Highwayman" was first published, a period of profound transition was taking place throughout English society; this included the areas of politics, international relations, economics, literature, and ultimately in the self-image of the English. The most notable event during this period of transition was the death of Queen Victoria, who had reigned over Britain for more than 62 years, in January of 1901. Her death symbolized the end of the pastoral Britain that existed before the onset of the Industrial Revolution and heralded a new century rife with uncertainty.

Queen Victoria had been stabilizing force in European politics as well; she was the matriarch of many European royal families through the marriages of her children and grandchildren. In that role, she linked isolationist-minded Britain with the continent. In particular, she had kept relations with Britain's main European rival, Germany, from becoming too tense.

During the last quarter of the nineteenth century, Germany's development of strong steel, coal, machine-building, and railroad industries challenged Britain's century-long predominance in industry. Even more critically, Germany had begun an accelerated ship-building program designed to create a German Navy equal to England's. These developments made the English uneasy. They sensed both an economic threat to their dominant position in the world and a military threat to their security. Although the Germans claimed their navy would pose no threat to the British, this failed to settle their uneasiness, because a strong navy could be used to pursue German colonial interests abroad.

Although the British Empire encompassed some 11 million square miles of territory on every continent, it was showing early signs of disintegration in the first decade of the century. Britain had fought an unpopular and controversial colonial war against Boer settlers in South Africa between 1899 and 1902. Even though Britain won the war, the Transvaal and Orange Free State (now regions of South Africa) were each granted self-government shortly after the victory. This foreshadowed Britain's losses of other parts of the Empire later in the twentieth century.

In 1902 England signed the Anglo-Japanese Alliance with Japan. It was significant in that it was the first time a European nation had recognized a non-European nation as diplomatically equal. Historians consider it one of the most important diplomatic agreements of modern times. It thrust Japan out of its long isolation and onto the world stage. The Alliance provided that Japan would attempt to suppress Russian invasions of China and Korea. Two years later the Russo-Japanese War broke out; in 1905 Japan emerged victorious. That a European nation, even one in Russia's decrepit condition, could be defeated by an Asian country was completely unexpected. By the end of the 1920s, Japan had strengthened its military and laid plans for an empire of its own in the Pacific. Interestingly, a year after the treaty was signed, Noyes published his collection *The Flower of Old Japan.*

In 1900 English poetry was felt to be on the ebb. During the 1800s poetry had enjoyed a level of popularity in England unmatched before or since. But the poets who were responsible for much of that popularity were gone: Alfred Lord Tennyson and Robert Browning were dead, and other poets, including A. C. Swinburne and George Meredith, were past their primes. No new writers of their genre had risen to take their place and a successor was eagerly awaited. When Alfred Noyes published his first books of poetry between 1902 and 1905, he was eagerly hailed at the next great English poet who would take the tradition over into the twentieth century. His work was firmly rooted in nineteenth-century poetic aesthetics however, and by the middle of the next decade, he was overtaken by modernist poets such as T. S. Eliot and Ezra Pound.

Compare & Contrast

- **1907:** Great Britain permits self-rule in the Orange Free State in South Africa leading to the institutionalization of Apartheid.

  Today: Apartheid has ended, but whites and blacks in South Africa continue to deal with its legacy as the controversial Truth and Reconciliation Committee investigates atrocities committed by the former government.

- **1907:** The United States enters a brief economic depression and the Panic of 1907 hits. Under the leadership of financier J. P. Morgan, the quick infusion of millions of dollars into the economy saves it from more serious problems.

  Today: A serious recession in Pacific Rim nations, including Japan, Korea, Indonesia, and Singapore, destabilizes local governments and threatens to spread to the rest of the world.

- **1907:** Busses and taxicabs are introduced in New York City.

  Today: Despite warnings about pollution and global warming, most Americans still own and drive a private automobile.

- **1907:** President Theodore Roosevelt creates approximately 16 million acres of federal forest land. The forests are supposed to remain untouched by lumber interests.

  Today: More than 377,000 miles of logging roads—eight times the length of the national highway system—have been cut into national forests so the timber industry can harvest trees.

- **1907:** Nearly 1.29 million immigrants are admitted to the United States, an all-time high.

  Today: About 915,900 immigrants entered the country in 1996, despite pressure from various groups to place tighter governmental restrictions on entry requirements.

Critical Overview

In 1906, *The Bookman* described Noyes's poetry as having "music, colour, and sparkle." In many ways, this response characterizes later critical reactions to "The Highwayman." Through the years, critics have appreciated the poem's compelling narrative and its metrical energy. In his book on Alfred Noyes, Walter Jerrold praises the poem for its "popular appeal" and its "dramatic intensity." Jerrold goes on to call the poem "a fine rendering of something finely done." Patrick Braybrooke, in *Some Victorian and Georgian Catholics: Their Art and Outlook*, also praises the poem for its popular appeal. He notes that the verse itself recreates the feel of someone riding. He characterizes the poem, moreover, "as an absolute model of careful and skilled romanticism." Braybrooke does qualify his praise, however, commenting that it would be inaccurate "to observe that Noyes is a poet who can transcend beauty and produce poetry of a 'terrific nature.'" Instead, Braybrooke commends Noyes for "know[ing] the limits of his craft" and for having "a tremendous sense ... of the romantic."

Criticism

Chris Semansky

Chris Semansky teaches writing and literature at Portland Community College in Portland, Oregon, and is a frequent contributor of poems and essays to literary journals. In the following essay, Semansky delineates the reasons for the popularity of "The Highwayman," pointing to Noyes's use of suspense, physical description, and imagery.

Alfred Noyes's poem "The Highwayman" is called a ballad, an old English form that tells a story. As such, it is also an example of a narrative poem. Narratives have characters, events, settings, and a point-of-view from which the narrative, or story, is told. Though Noyes, an English professor at Princeton, wrote criticism and novels as well as poetry, it was "The Highwayman," and its punchy style, rocking rhythms, and fast-paced action which won him the most acclaim.

Unlike modern poetry which is often dense and opaque and requires a degree in literature to understand, "The Highwayman" is accessible because it tells a suspenseful story about colorful characters in simple, straightforward language. Children, as well as adults, enjoy the poem, which adds to its popularity.

"The Highwayman" is composed of fifteen stanzas. If we think of the poem as a film, we might shoot fifteen scenes to tell the story. A skeleton of such a script might look like this:

I: Night. Wind howling. Storm-tossed trees. In the distance we see a man on a horse ferociously galloping toward an old stone inn.

II: Close up: Camera pans the man's body from toe to head, focusing on his boots, pants, sword and guns, finally resting on his "fancy" hat, jauntily cocked on his head and a bunch of lace at his chin.

III: After riding around the inn yard and finding all doors locked, he taps on a window with his whip, and whistles. The audience understands that this is something that he has done before. A raven-haired young woman opens her shutters. She is braiding her long hair.

IV: Cut to a shot of a wild-eyed man with dirty-blonde hair leaning against the gate in the horse stable. His head is cocked to the side, so that we understand he is eavesdropping.

V: Cut to a close up of the highwayman, in his horse in front of the window. He asks the dark-haired woman for a kiss and promises to return before morning.

VI: Middle shot. Highwayman rises in his stirrups and leans over to kiss the woman, who is leaning into him. Long passionate kiss. Hold shot for fifteen seconds. Kiss finished. Man settles back into his horse, looking longingly into his lover's eyes. Suddenly, he turns and gallops away.

VII: Dusk. A troop of English army men dressed in their red coats approaches the inn on the same road that the highwayman approached from in scene I. Camera pans to their legs, focusing on their rhythmic, almost hypnotic lock-step marching.

VIII: Troops enter the inn. They ignore the landlord but drink his beer. They gag and bind his daughter to her bed and two of them kneel in front of her window, guns at their sides. We see, from Bess's point of view, the road that her lover will come in on.

IX: Middle shot. Bess is now standing at the window, a musket tied to her body, its barrel just below her breast, her hands tied in front of her. A British

What Do I Read Next?

- Noyes wrote poetry rooted in the traditions of the past and was extremely hostile to the modernist poets. His harsh criticism of their work can be found in his book *Some Aspects of Modern Poetry.*

- Noyes was often compared as a poet to Rudyard Kipling, who celebrated the British Empire in his poems and stories. *The Phantom 'Rickshaw, and Other Tales* contains stories of the fantastic and supernatural, often set in exotic lands.

- Just before Noyes celebrated the outlaw in "The Highwayman," Thorstein Veblen published *A Theory of the Leisure Class,* a sarcastic, highly readable critique of middle-class consumer society.

- Noyes was seen as the heir to Poet Laureate Alfred Lord Tennyson. Tennyson's *Idylls of the King,* a verse treatment of the story of King Arthur, offers a different viewpoint on love than Noyes's. The forbidden love of Lancelot and Queen Guinevere leads to the fall of Camelot.

- *A Modern Utopia* by H.G. Wells was published two years before Noyes's poem. Rather than turning back to the romantic past in the face of rapid change, Wells looked forward to the improvements science, technology, and socialism would bring in the future.

soldier taunts her. Close up to her eyes. Flashback of scene V in which her lover promises to return.

X: Close up to Bess's hands, torn and bloody now from her struggle to untie herself. Light fades into darkness signalling the passage of time. Finally, she manages to touch the gun's trigger.

XI: Night. Close up of Bess's face. She is gazing out the window, straining to hear the approach of her lover before the British do.

XII: Middle shot. We see Bess's expression as she hears the clopping of her lover's horse in the distance. The British troops, stationed in front of Bess and looking out the window, are preparing their muskets for use.

XIII: Shot of the highwayman's approach. His face is full of anticipation. Shot of Bess's eyes, full of apprehension. She tries to scream, but is gagged, and all that comes out is a muffled sob. Cut to her hand, her finger on the trigger. Cut to the moon. We hear the horse's steps, then we hear a shot.

XIV: Cut to the highwayman, who hears the shot, then stops and turns his horse around, galloping again into the west. Cut to shot of the highwayman in town, speaking to someone. He is being told that the shot he heard the night before was Bess trying to warn him by killing herself.

XV: Shot of the highwayman galloping toward the inn, screaming in a rage, waving his sword in the air. Then a volley of shots from the British troops. Slow motion shot of highwayman falling from his horse, blood pouring from his wounds. Last shot of highwayman's body on the road. Camera pans over his body, settling on the bunch of lace at his throat.

In narratives, whether they be films or ballads, we learn about the characters by how they appear, act, and what they say. Characterization—literally, the process of building the character—allows writers to show readers what is happening without telling them everything about the characters. Readers have to infer motivation of the characters and make connections among them based on what they have been shown. For example, Noyes "tells" us about the highwayman by "showing" us how he dresses:

> He'd a French cocked-hat on his forehead, a bunch of lace at his chin,
> A coat of the claret velvet, and breeches of brown doe-skin;
> They fitted with never a wrinkle; his boots were up to the thigh!
> And he rode with a jewelled twinkle,
> His pistol butts a-twinkle,
> His rapier hilt a-twinkle, under the jewelled sky.

From this description we can imagine the highwayman as very well-dressed, almost fastidiously so. With his unwrinkled doe-skin pants and a patch of lace below his chin, the highwayman is presented as a dandy. But unlike the stereotypical dandy, often depicted as effeminate and intellectual, this dandy is a thief, a mischievous thief who rides with a "jewelled twinkle." His actions also underscore his roguish nature. With all of the seducer's charm, he whistles a tune and taps on the shutters with his whip when "all was locked and barred" at the innyard. After promising Bess he would return by morning with the "yellow gold," he wins a kiss from her. He might be a thief and a seducer, but he is also a gentleman. "I'll come to thee by moonlight," he tells her, "though hell should bar the way."

The highwayman is a version of the mythic anti-hero; like Zorro or Robin Hood, he is a people's hero. Though we are not told who he is stealing from, we can infer from the way his enemy, the British Army, is depicted, that it is probably someone who deserves it. In stark opposition to the gentlemanly behavior of the highwayman, the redcoats ignore the landlord and proceed to bind and gag his daughter, "with many a sniggering jest" and hold her as bait.

Representing the institutionalized power of the state in diabolical terms is nothing new in folktales. The "little people" have always been at the mercy of the rich and the powerful. The highwayman, as a good "bad guy" who opposes the state, is also what is known as a "stock character," that is, a character type that occurs repeatedly in a given literary genre. Think of the way that Germans have been represented in espionage films of the last forty years. Invariably, they are the enemy, and they are monocle-wearing, humorless, sadistic, and ambitious. All of the characters in "The Highwayman" are stock characters, not only the highwayman himself, but Bess, the redcoats, and Tim the stable hand, the idiot man-child, from whose point of view we learn about the highwayman's plans.

Noyes's physical descriptions and concrete imagery also contribute heavily to this poem's appeal because they help readers to visualize the story. For example, when the highwayman is leaning into the window to kiss Bess, we are told that "his face burnt like a brand / As the black cascade of perfume came tumbling over his breast." Brands are the marks put on animals with a hot iron to signify ownership. By comparing the rush of blood into the highwayman's face to a brand, Noyes not only vividly presents the highwayman's sexual excitement, but he also suggests that the highwayman has been branded by the love of the woman. Hence, he belongs to her. We know from this point in the poem that the highwayman is not merely a seducer, but that he will keep his promise to return.

His use of descriptors is also similar to his use of characters. Adjectives such as "blood-red" and "wine-red" are stock descriptors; one might even call them cliches. Noyes, however, uses them in a self-conscious way to position his ballad in the tradition of folk stories which make use of these very same adjectives.

Finally, Noyes's poem is successful because it is full of suspense. As readers we cannot wait to find out what happens to the highwayman and his lover. Will he rescue her, or will he perish trying to? That both the highwayman and Bess die in the end does not make the story less satisfying, for it also confirms what we know to be true—love does not conquer all, and bad guys win too.

Source: Chris Semansky, in an essay for *Poetry for Students,* Gale, 1998.

Sources

"The Bookman Gallery: Alfred Noyes," in *The Bookman,* Vol. 30, No. 180, September 1906, pp. 199-200.

Braybrooke, Patrick, "Alfred Noyes: Poet and Romantic," in his *Some Victorian and Georgian Catholics: Their Art and Outlook,* Burns Oates & Washbourne Ltd., 1932, pp. 171-202, reprinted by Books for Libraries Press, Inc., 1966; distributed by Arno Press, Inc.

Davison, Edward Lewis, *Some Modern Poets and other Critical Essays,* Freeport, NY: Books for Libraries, 1968.

Kernahan, Coulson, *Six Famous Living Poets,* Freeport, NY: Books for Libraries, 1968.

For Further Study

Brenner, Rica, *Ten Modern Poets,* Freeport, NY: Books for Libraries, 1968.
    A readable overview of Noyes's poetic output up to 1930.

Jerrold, Walter, in his *Alfred Noyes,* Harold Shaylor, 1930, 251 p.
    A highly appreciative consideration of Noyes's work—in particular his longer, historical poems—that calles the poet the heir to Tennyson and Browning.

Saul, G. B., "Yeats, Noyes and Day Lewis," in *Notes and Queries,* No. 195, 1950.
    A comparison of three poets who dealt explicitly with religious material in their works.

Hunger in New York City

Simon Ortiz

1976

"Hunger in New York City" was first published in 1976 in Simon Ortiz's collection *Going for the Rain* and is also included in the 1991 book *Woven Stone: A 3-in-1 Volume of Poetry and Prose,* which collects all of the poet's published poetry to that time. "Hunger in New York City" contrasts the America exemplified by New York City to what Ortiz calls "the real America," which is "the Native America of indigenous people and the indigenous principle they represent." In fact, while one of the purposes of Ortiz's work is to define "Native America," another is to call for its survival. "Hunger in New York City" is a variation on this theme, as it tells the story of how dehumanizing city life can be in its separation from "mother earth." Indeed, Ortiz has said that "[a]s a writer, I've tried to consider most importantly my life as a Native American who is absolutely related to the land and all that that means culturally, politically, personally."

Basic to Ortiz's work as a writer are the Native-American oral storytelling tradition and the ritual of prayer. This poem tells the story of engaging fully with a hunger that takes on the magnitude of a symbolic opponent and ends with a prayer to "Bless me." The alienation of the individual in the city that this hunger represents is not, however, a solely Native-American experience. But it is perhaps possible for the rest of us to understand through the Native-American experience of the land as mother how to heal the wound of alienation.

Author Biography

Ortiz was born in 1941 at the Pueblo of Acoma, near Albuquerque, New Mexico, the son of Joe L. Ortiz and Mamie Toribio Ortiz. He attended Grants High School in Grants, New Mexico, and then worked briefly in the uranium mines and processing plants of the Grants Ambrosia Lake area. Ortiz then attended Fort Lewis College, where he became interested in drama and English studies. A leader of the Indian Student Organization, Ortiz became involved in issues of fair treatment for native peoples. He enlisted in the U.S. Army in 1963, after which he attended the University of New Mexico at Albuquerque. He received a Master's of Fine Art degree from the University of Iowa in 1969. He then taught writing and American Indian literature at various colleges and universities, including San Diego State University, the Institute of American Arts in Santa Fe, and the University of New Mexico. In December, 1981 he married Marlene Foster, and they had three children, Raho, Rainy, and Sara, but divorced in 1984. Since 1982 Ortiz has been the consulting editor of the Pueblo of Acoma Press, and in 1989 he became First Lieutenant Governor for Acoma Pueblo in New Mexico.

Simon J. Ortiz

Poem Text

Hunger crawls into you
from somewhere out of your muscles
or the concrete or the land
or the wind pushing you.

It comes to you, asking   5
for food, words, wisdom, young memories
of places you ate at, drank cold spring water,
or held somebody's hand,
or home of the gentle, slow dances,
the songs, the strong gods, the world   10
you know.

That is, hunger searches you out.
It always asks you,
How are you, son? Where are you?
Have you eaten well?   15
Have you done what you as a person
of our people is supposed to do?

And the concrete of this city,
the oily wind, the blazing windows,
the shrieks of automation cannot,   20
truly cannot, answer for that hunger
although I have hungered,
truthfully and honestly, for them
to feed myself with.

So I sang to myself quietly: 25
I am feeding myself
with the humble presence
of all around me;
I am feeding myself
with your soul, my mother earth;   30
make me cool and humble.
Bless me.

Poem Summary

Lines 1-2:

The poem begins with the disturbing image of hunger as a creature that can "crawl into you." But although it seems to be presented in line 1 as something external, in line 2 we understand that it is actually crawling from somewhere "out of your muscles." Thus, this hunger is not located in your spirit or your soul, or even your mind. It comes to you through the tension in your muscles.

Lines 3-4:

The final two lines of the stanza offer alternatives through the use of the word "or." In effect, this hunger must come from somewhere before crawling into you out of your own muscles. The images presented are, first, of the "concrete" of the city itself, but perhaps, it is offered, this hunger

Media Adaptations

- An audio recording titled *American Indian Myths and Legends* featuring Richard Erdoes, Alfanzo Ortiz, and Jill Momaday was released by Sunset Productions in 1991.

- In 1992 Fulcrum Publishers released an audio recording titled *Keepers of the Animals: Native American Stories.*

comes from the thought of the land beneath the "concrete" of the city. Or perhaps it is in the wind forced against you through the "concrete" of the buildings. Your muscles tense against any of these things; this is how the hunger enters you—through your physical response to the city.

Line 5:

Once hunger has access to you, and you have identified it, it begins to demand things. The poet personifies hunger in this stanza, giving it the power to ask.

Lines 6-11:

At first these demands seem reasonable, and small enough, but then the memories hunger feeds on become more specific. In line 8 the hunger places such emphasis on holding somebody's hand that it seems to want not just the memory of human contact but human contact itself. And then it wants to go home where the real human contact of the Native-American world can be made through its ritual dances and songs and gods who listen: "the world you know." In short, in New York City the speaker of this poem is an alien.

Lines 12-17:

By creating the desire for "the world you know" hunger "searches you out." And once it has you, it asks you the kinds of questions family asks. Again, at first these seem simple enough and easy to answer. But in line 15 the simple question calls up the power of hunger expanded full force in line 16. This time hunger takes you further into the

world you know than you care to travel: into your own responsibility to that world.

Lines 18-20:

The guilt that follows from trying to answer that question pushes the persona of the poem back from his memories and his desire for his home, back into "the concrete of this city."

The images of the next lines are physically distressing, assaults on human senses, expressed through the adjectives "oily" and "blazing," and the noun "shrieks." These images recall, and build on, the poem's beginning physical images of the muscles in response to the concrete and the wind in lines 3 and 4.

Finally the word "cannot" appears at the end of line 20. While the meaning is not yet fully disclosed, it is clear that there is nothing that the concrete and wind and windows and shrieks can do for the persona.

Lines 21-22:

In fact, the repetition of "cannot" with the addition of "truly" speaks with certainty that the city is not the answer to the hunger the speaker has felt inside himself. Indeed the repetition of "cannot," begun in lines 20-21, takes force in lines 21-22 with the repetition of "hunger." This creates a chant and invests the lines with the quality of prayer.

Up to this point the persona has been speaking objectively, using the second-person pronoun "you." This has allowed him to speak about himself, as well as to speak about experiences that a reader might participate in. Finally, however, the persona accepts his experience as belonging completely to himself. "[A]lthough I have hungered" expresses the beginning of this self-knowledge.

Lines 23-24:

It is the position of the persona that he has made every possible effort to feed his hunger with things he could find in the city.

Lines 25-32:

The speaker begins to feed himself, not his hunger, softly with song in a ritual reminder of the living presence of things that surround him. As a result the almost angry images of the "wind" and "shrieks" in the preceding stanza are understood to be at least as much in him as in the city. His singing calms this angry response to the city and reminds him that the soul of "mother earth," if not her presence, surrounds him. He concludes the poem, which has become a prayer, with the plea to be blessed by her.

Themes

Identity

The Native-American speaker in "Hunger in New York City" describes his search for identity in terms of hunger, or a physical need for sustenance. At first this "hunger" seems to be creeping in from the outside, from the "concrete or the land." But as the poem continues into the third stanza, his longing asks questions of the speaker: "How are you? Where are you?" The voice of this longing may remind us of our parents.

Identity is such a huge topic it is almost impossible to grasp. "Have you eaten well?" the voice asks the Native-American speaker, starting with the easy questions. But quickly the Native American living in New York City must confront a larger issue. "Have you done what you as a person / of our people is supposed to do?" The scope of his search suddenly broadens over two cultures and into his people's past.

Custom and Tradition

In the middle of this poem lies a haunting question: "Have you done what you as a person / of our people is supposed to do?" Although "Hunger in New York" makes no specific mention of the poet's ethnicity or Native-American roots, there is an underlying theme of custom and tradition that informs the work as the speaker tries to find his way around the unfamiliar New York landscape.

Unable to answer clearly these questions of heritage, the speaker explains that he has been looking in all the wrong places: "the oily wind, the blazing windows, / the shrieks of automation cannot, / truly cannot, answer for that hunger." If there are no fulfilling answers for the speaker in this new land and culture, where can he find something to feed his spirit? The answer comes from his past and his people's past. Unsatisfied with the barriers city life places between man and the natural world, the speaker returns to the "humble presence" of his heritage in the last stanza, hoping that the traditions of his fathers will help feed his hunger for identity.

Nature and Its Meaning

The speaker finds a cure for his hunger in the final stanza. "I am feeding myself," he declares,

Topics for Further Study

- Write a poem in the voice of someone praying to Mother Nature. Think of each element—water, wind, earth and fire—as a spirit which can either create or destroy and ask for a specific blessing from each, shaping your poem into four distinct sections.

- Do you think mankind's drive to "conquer the elements" by building modern cities is helping us progress as human beings, or is it distancing us from nature to the point of harming both man and the environment? Use recent news stories to discuss and support your answer(s).

- Have you ever lived on or visited an Indian reservation? Are you or any of your friends Native American? What kind of impression do you have about the Native-American sense of tradition, nature, and the spiritual world? Discuss your answers. Are these impressions accurate?

"with the humble presence of all around me; I am feeding myself with your soul, my mother earth." A Native American living in the city, after too many years of concrete and "oily wind" separating him from the natural world, the speaker returns again to the source of all living things. The indigenous people of North America have a profound relationship with the earth, regarding its many plants and creatures as much more than "natural resources" to take and use. The balance between man and nature requires a spiritual respect; a humble, grateful attitude which returns as much as it receives. Just as concrete pours over concrete and layers of smog coat office windows, years of disrespect for the Earth have accumulated until the speaker is haunted with an indescribable empty feeling. What the persona learns is that under these urban layers still lives the natural spirit which can give his life meaning, which has been giving his people's lives meaning for centuries. The speaker ends the poem by asking mother earth for peace of mind and spirit: "make me cool and humble. / Bless Me."

Style

"Hunger in New York City" is a poem in five stanzas, ranging from the four-line first stanza to the eight-line final stanza. There is quite a variation in line length, from the closing line of two words, to the longest line (7), with nine words. Thus, the poem does not follow any traditional form or consistent layout. Instead, it is the story that is being told that seems to shape the poem. In the first stanza, "hunger" is introduced as an external force. The second explores the reasons for this relationship with hunger. Hunger in the third stanza becomes nagging, asking pointed questions, merging itself with guilt. The fourth stanza explains why the questions hunger asks cannot find answers in the city. The final stanza presents a response to hunger, if not the answers to its questions.

Structurally, the first lines of each stanza signal the stages of development of the story. Stanza 1: Initially, "Hunger crawls into you" in a particular way. Stanza 2: Once inside, it "comes to you, asking … " for things. Stanza 3: "That is" indicates a digression in which the storyteller-poet presents an explanation of "asking" that ultimately results in specific questions. Stanza 4: The conjunction "And" provides a connection of the story with "the city." Stanza 5: The adverb "So" signals the conclusion of the story.

The speaker initally directs the story in the poem to the reader, but also allows it to spring from his own personal experience. This is achieved by his use of the second-person pronoun "you." At the end of fourth stanza, however, the "you" shifts to the first-person "I" as the persona places himself fully in his experience of "hunger."

Historical Context

The year Simon Ortiz published "Hunger in New York City," 1976, marked almost the transition point between the end of the idealist 1960s and the beginning of the conservative 1980s. It was during this year author Tom Wolfe coined the term *The "Me" Generation,* an expression describing the decade's slide toward selfishness and self-absorption. "Hunger in New York City" expressed one man's feelings of emptiness and need to reconnect with the natural world.

Some historians describe the 1970s as the "non-decade" due to its lack of distinctive symbols or trends. Unlike the environmental, peace, and civil rights movements of the 1960s, or the conservative, evangelical "Reagan years" of the decade to follow, the 1970s seem bland. In 1976, the most popular icon was the smiley face; the yellow sun with blank eyes and glazed smile stared out from bumper stickers, jacket patches, billboards, and toilet seats, yet no one really knew what it meant. Looking back, some critics call it the perfect symbol of a nation without meaning, an expression of the era. It is this national sense of unfulfillment, of a spiritual absence, which perhaps Ortiz felt as a hunger creeping into the city.

Americans of the time thought that progress was synonymous with development; in other words, the better you are at conquering the elements, the more advanced a people you were. One of the goals of the Vietnam War, which ended only a few years before 1976, was to build a capitalist nation in the face of a communist threat. America declared itself the model of government and stated that other "underdeveloped" nations should shape themselves after its democracy.

This attitude is evident from our country's earliest years, when settlers thought of the Native-American peoples as "savages" and cut down forests to build houses for shelter against the elements. By 1976, millions of Americans lived in cities of concrete and glass, while the Native Americans who survived the European colonization mostly lived on remote reservations. Those younger Indians who chose to move to the city, like Ortiz, often felt a profound sense of spiritual loss, disconnected from the land and their history.

The trend toward industrialism has covered the natural world with concrete, poured toxins in the water, and littered the sky with office buildings. It was in 1976 that the National Academy of Science first reported that gasses from spray cans can cause damage to the atmosphere's ozone layer, a fact generations to come will have to deal with in terms of global warming and an increase in environmental disasters. While scientists continued to discover evidence of how man's drive to conquer the elements in the name of progress was in fact harming our children, more and more Native-American people expressed a deeper, spiritual connection to the earth as their generations of tradition had taught them. Their tradition stresses a balance between man and nature which respects the cycles of growth and destruction which we are a part of, not apart from.

Compare & Contrast

- **1976:** A United Nations Security Council resolution calls for a total withdrawal of Israeli troops from Arab lands occupied since a retaliatory offensive in 1967. The United States veto blocks the pullout and denies the formation of an independent Palestinian State.

  1993: After decades of fighting, Israeli Prime Minister Rabin and PLO leader Yasir Arafat meet in Washington, D.C. to sign an agreement to end Israeli settlement of the West Bank and other occupied territories.

  1998: The PLO continues its series of terrorist attacks, and Israeli withdrawal from the territories remains incomplete. Many fear the chance for peace in the region may be replaced by more fighting.

- **1976:** Advancements in technology allow a new generation of fax machines to cut transmission time from six minutes per page down to three.

  1998: Most computers come supplied from the factory with virtual fax programs which allow users to transmit the document on their screen to another person's fax machine in less than a minute. E-Mail provides an almost instantaneous transmission to anywhere in the world and increasingly replaces fax machines in both home and the workplace.

- **1976:** Soft drink sales in the United States, namely Coke and Pepsi products, edge past milk after millions of dollars are poured into their advertising.

  1998: Unable to persuade Americans to buy milk on the merits of health and well-balanced nutrition, the National Dairy Council sponsors its own multi-million dollar magazine and billboard ad campaign to gain back its share of the market. The advertisements, which feature celebrities holding a glass of milk and wearing a distinctive milk "mustache," ask the simple and catchy question "Got Milk?"

Critical Overview

Many literary and cultural critics value the work of Ortiz because they feel it serves as a representation of Native–American culture. These scholars feel that the work of Native Americans and other cultural minorities has been underrepresented in American society and the prominence of poets like Ortiz helps to correct this situation.

There are other critics who prize the work of Native–American writers as the true voice of America. These scholars argue that the literature of tribal peoples is more authentic to the spirit of the Americas than are works produced by individuals of non-native ancestry, such as European settlers and their descendants. According to Willard Gingerich, however, this is a mistake. He argues that the "American sensibility" belongs to a wide variety of writers including those of both European and Native-American ancestry. While Gingerich concedes that there is a current literary vogue for minority writers, he also acknowledges that, for writers like Ortiz, the struggle to achieve a position in the American literary tradition has created tremendous vitality in their work. The critic notes that being poor or oppressed or speaking Spanish does not ensure good poetry, but that "the felt distance [minority writers] travel to arrive at full sensibility of themselves and their contexts is greater [than that of non-minorities] and generates therefore a finer tension of meaning, phrase, and allusion in their writing."

While Harold Jaffe praises Ortiz as among "the strongest" of current American Indian writers, including N. Scott Momaday and Leslie Marmon Silko, he maintains that "their writings are frequently more problematic than those of their forbears." He notes the poetry of Ortiz, particularly, as having "apparently simple, yet elusive, syntax" which at times "seems fractionally off, as if the English were adapted from another language."

> " *... Ortiz opts for a direct, unadorned style that has more in common with speech than writing.* "

Gingerich, who says that Ortiz is an "Indian" poet in the same way as Gerard Manley Hopkins is a "Catholic" poet, seems content to accept the poet's unusual use of language. He maintains that while the images a writer brings to the literary tradition may be specific to a cultural or ethnic tradition, it is "the spirit of the language itself" that enlivens these values. Because of this, the critic feels that a reader of Ortiz's poetry understands something about life itself, and not only something about Native–American life.

Geary Hobson insists that Ortiz's work needs to be read for "his contribution as a remarkably incisive critic of contemporary society, both in the Indian as well as the non-Indian world." Hobson feels that this critical ability is acutely expressed in "Hunger In New York City," a poem that speaks eloquently of "felt distance" in its characterization of hunger as symbol of the relationship between the individual and the city.

Criticism

Jhan Hochman

Jhan Hochman is a writer and instructor at Portland Community College in Portland, Oregon. In the following essay, Hochman provides an overview of "Hunger in New York City" and analyzes what "hunger" means to Ortiz as a Native American.

In "Hunger in New York City," Simon Ortiz writes of hunger as a gnawing, aggressive, omnipresent need that will never be satisfied because it cannot be satisfied. For Ortiz, hunger is not merely the biological desire for food to nourish the body, though it is that as well; it is, more than anything else, a voice that is always there, asking him to justify himself, his life, and the choices he has made.

The speaker describes hunger's paradoxical nature in the first stanza when he writes that "Hunger crawls into you / from somewhere out of your muscles." It is paradoxical because it is at once something that wants to get into the body and yet is already a part of it. By saying that it "crawls" Ortiz underscores how insidious hunger can be, how subtle. His inability to physically locate hunger or provide any definitive description of it also emphasizes its elusive character.

Hunger asks for things, both concrete and abstract, in the second stanza. This asking positions hunger as a kind of vampire or parasite, working from the outside in, desiring of its "victim" information (blood) about the victim's life, his memories, his emotions. It comes to you, asking for food, words, and wisdom. It asks about young memories of places you ate at, drank cold spring water, or held somebody's hand. The stuff of memories is the stuff of life, but what does hunger want with this information, and why is it so demanding? And why does hunger's tone change in the third stanza and become more parental, more solicitous?

We can answer these questions if we consider the speaker's hunger to be a voice, not outside of himself, but inside his own head. This voice wants to know what the speaker has made of his life. He has internalized the voice of a parent or parents because it is parents who ask questions such as "How are you, son? Where are you? / Have you eaten well?" But this voice is not the voice of the speaker's biological parents; it is the voice, rather, of parental responsibility. When hunger asks "Have you done what you as a person / of our people is supposed to do?" we begin to understand hunger as a concern with, and a driving need to fulfill, the desires of a group of people, in this case Native Americans.

Significantly, this voice haunts the speaker while he is in New York City, an international symbol of urban culture. As a Native American, Ortiz has written about his people's ties to the land and the destructive and alienating effects that Western culture, particularly city culture, has had on their traditions and identity. These effects are evidenced in the images he chooses to represent New York City: "the concrete of this city, / the oily wind, the blazing windows, / the shrieks of automation." Ortiz has not, however, flatly rejected the city. Like members of many cultures who have had their land and way of life ripped from them by the "progressive" forces of industrialized Western capitalism, Ortiz has grown to depend on the very thing oppressing him in order to survive: "… I have hungered, / truthfully and honestly, for them / to feed myself with." Ortiz reaffirms this is his prose, saying, "Just as it claimed land and sovereignty, American society and culture can claim your soul."

How, then, does Ortiz deal with this situation? How does he answer this hunger, this voice hounding him, asking him to account for himself? He prays. "So I sang to myself quietly: I am feeding myself with the humble presence of all around me; I am feeding myself with your soul, my mother earth; make me cool and humble. Bless me." In this last stanza, Ortiz learns how to deal with his hunger. He does this not by taking his sustenance from the city but by finding it within himself. He feeds himself "with the humble presence / of all around me."

In his introduction to *Woven Stone,* a collection of his poetry, Ortiz writes that reality is living in the here and now. "Being present with and for ourselves, being responsible to ourselves and, consequently, for our role in social struggles and changes in the Americas is a major part of this. Too often we have, as victims of colonialism, longed for the past nostalgically and whimsically, although there is appropriate importance in what elders say about remembering the past. And too often we look abstractly at a romanticized future that is past."

Underscoring the resolution of the speaker's conflict between the past and the present, between his desires and responsibilities, is the poem's shift from the second person to the first in the fourth stanza. This shift emphasizes the relation between tribal ("you") and individual ("I") identity, and the speaker's realization that only by calling on his "true parent" (mother earth) can he achieve satisfaction from his hunger.

It is the earth and his people's relation to it that Ortiz needs to reclaim. Memory plays a major role in Native-American poetry in general, and in Ortiz's in particular. Memory allows traditions to survive. Ortiz writes, "I have often heard Native American elders repeat 'We must always remember,' referring to grandmothers and grandfathers, heritage, and the past with a sense of something more than memory or remembering at stake. It is knowing present place and time, being present in the here and now essentially, just as past generations knew place and time whether they were Acoma, Lakota, or Mayan people. Continuance, in this sense, is life itself."

What Do I Read Next?

- Simon Ortiz is also an editor of *Speaking for the Generations: Native Writers on Writing.* The anthology points out it is impossible to discuss Native-American art without also discussing Native-American sovereignty.

- In *The People Shall Continue,* Ortiz teams up with photographer Sharol Graves to present an epic story of the Native-American people, written in the rhythms of traditional oral narrative.

- For a comprehensive collection of Native-American songs, prayers, myths, photos, and literature which captures the traditions, beliefs, and history of Native-American people, read *American Indian Voices* by Karen Harvey.

- Contemporary Native-American writers are introducing bold new voices to the fiction scene as well as poetry. For a good sampling of their work, read *The Lightning Within: An Anthology of Contemporary American Indian Fiction.*

The simplicity of Ortiz's poetic language helps him locate himself and his people in the here and now. Rather than the dense, ironic, emotionally distant style of so much modern and contemporary poetry, Ortiz opts for a direct, unadorned style that has more in common with speech than writing. Ortiz explains this, maintaining his simplicity is a response to an oppressive "reality that's so powerful you can't expect it to recognize you. Especially if you are a people who has been historically subjected to the meanest, cruelest treatment by social and economic forces backed up by military power."

Corruption and oppression must be fought with honesty, not language games. A major part of becoming healthy and positive, Ortiz says, "has to do with the consciousness we have of our selves, the language we use (not necessarily only native languages but the consciousness of our true selves at the core of whatever language we use, including English), and our responsible care for and relationships we have with our communities and communal lands. This is the way as Native Americans we will come into being as who we are within the reality of what we face."

If this is a poem about one Native American's response to the untenable situation of having to survive in a city and a country which has been and continues to be hostile to his very existence, how are non-indigenous peoples to read this poem? While some readers might admit to or recognize their own complicity in the oppression of others, this complicity continues to exist by the very fact of our continued silence, our reluctance to enact change. This tradition of complicity is born of ignorance, not of remembering. Unlike that of Native American peoples—in which history frequently is passed through the oral tradition—mainstream American society has depended on history books and the stories told in movies and on television for their versions of the past.

Not surprisingly, these stories, more often than not, have favored the victors and demonized the vanquished. "Hunger in New York City" might be viewed as both an expression of an oppressed people's response to their treatment and, implicitly, as a reproach to those responsible for their situation. It has the possibility of creating in readers a hunger similar to the one described in Ortiz's poem, a hunger born of responsibility to others.

Source: Jhan Hochman, in an essay for *Poetry for Students,* Gale, 1998.

Sean Robisch

Sean Robisch teaches composition and literature at Purdue University and holds a Ph.D. in American Literature. His fiction has appeared in Hopewell Review *and* Puerto del Sol. *In the following essay, Robisch explores the role of history in Ortiz's poetry.*

Simon Ortiz has been an important influence on what we think of as "American" literature since his first collection of poetry, *Going for the Rain,* appeared in 1976. He writes with what Willard Gingerich has called, in the *Southwestern Review,* a "clairvoyant sophistication that sees the continual rebirth of spirit in all materialism."

Ortiz's work first appeared during what has been called the Native American Renaissance, the beginning of which may be during the year between the founding of the American Indian Movement (AIM) in 1968 and N. Scott Momaday's receipt of the Pulitzer Prize for *House Made of Dawn* in 1969. Among the many reasons that Native American (or

American Indian) literature has been important to the course of literature in general is that it has challenged, strengthened, and resurrected stories of national and individual identity—of what it means to live in the United States and what it means to "be American."

During the time when the British colonists were still trying to build a new England, a rebellion took place in the Southwest that preceded the more famous colonial revolution of the late 1700s. Many Pueblos joined with the Navajo and the Apache and rose up against the Spanish occupation of their land; they succeeded in securing their freedom until 1692. Later, during the 1840s, a new occupation would take place, this time by primarily Anglo-Saxon pioneers settling the land and trying to build a new nation, rather than merely a new England. During these times, people living in such places as the Acoma Pueblo were fighting to maintain their language, traditions, and beliefs as the land was being invaded.

We may be able to see why these times would be important to Simon Ortiz's work, not only because he is Acoma, speaks the language, and knows the history, but because he is a reader and a believer in the transformative power of language. In *World Literature Today,* Robert Berner has written that Ortiz is at his best "when he adapts the traditional poetic utterances of Indian people to poems of his own which are simultaneously personal and traditional." Many poets have used the past in their work, but for Ortiz, events of the present may be directly linked to, even understood in terms of, the course of history in America.

Ortiz grew up during the 1950s and 1960s, when uranium mining was a major industry on Pueblo lands (he worked for a uranium company after high school) and long after the United States had been established as a single nation in the opinion of most of its population. But that establishment was still being conducted, often through many of the same harsh methods used one hundred years prior. During Ortiz's own childhood, schools had been designed to separate Acoma and other Pueblo children from their families and to prevent them from speaking their languages. A government program was begun that gave American Indians a one-way ticket to a big city in order to look for a job and move into the dominant culture.

The color barrier was still obviously advertised: all over the country there were segregated bathrooms, water fountains, and buses. And because to be "colored" often meant merely "dark-skinned," not only African American, the frictions of culture and race were complex for those people whose families had lived on the North American continent for many centuries before the establishment of the United States, Canada, even Mexico. This is why the conditions of history are so important to Ortiz's work; they have never stopped affecting the way we think today about culture, race, and—most importantly to Simon Ortiz—language.

He has said, "What I do as a writer, teacher, and storyteller is to demystify language." This means he wants to make sentences and poetic figures accessible and practical, to correct the idea that poetry is something only for certain people and not for all of us. He became a writer in part to answer some of the big questions: "What is loneliness?" "What is love?" And, in light of "Hunger in New York City," we could add the question: "What is hunger?"

Used to address such questions, writing becomes a way for us to remember, to build upon those things others have said, so that as we learn more, remember more, we may come closer to some answers. *Going for the Rain,* the book in which "Hunger in New York City" appears, is about a journey that takes place on many different levels of experience, including the preservation of memory through writing poems. In the course of his journey, the poet asks several of the big questions, and provides us some material by which we might consider them ourselves.

The book is divided into four parts, an important number symbolizing the four principle directions. The four parts of *Going for the Rain* mirror a Pueblo rain ritual in which the rain must be brought back from a long journey, what Ortiz calls the poet's "travelling prayer." This is one level of experience on which the book takes place, the one calling on ancient journey stories. Another level, demonstrated well in "Hunger in New York City," is the experience of what it is like to be an Acoma poet in an industrial, non-Acoma society.

Still another level to the book is found in Ortiz's construction of the journey; we are invited to travel outside the self and back inward again, which is triggered by a long train trip the poet has made to New York to visit a friend and give the friend a gift of Arizona sage. It is important to know these larger issues about *Going for the Rain* in order to appreciate what is underneath "Hunger in New York City." It fits in the perspective of the poet's train trip across the country from the ancient South-

> *Simon Ortiz has brought th[e] ideas of minimalism and social intelligence together in his work, through a voice that is both Acoma and American, both ancient and contemporary. ..."*

western desert, his inward journey, and his encounter with a megalopolis. Simon Ortiz calls his use of the ancient and the introspective in a present-time story a "sense of continuity essential to the poetry and stories in the books, essential to Native American life in fact." In "Hunger in New York City" we get an example of one moment of observation in the midst of that continuity, which tells us many things about the larger issues addressed in *Going for the Rain.*

Ortiz often uses the term "story" in reference to a poem. We are so used to being trained in the meter, rhyme, and other technicalities of poetry (which certainly affect how it works) that we may forget the role of *narrative* in any form of writing. The narrative line tells a story, and in Ortiz's work the story that happens right in front of us—in this case, in the poem—is often only a small part of a much larger story of history, spirituality, or self-understanding.

Consider, for instance, what you mean when you say "I'm hungry." You might be thinking of eating a meal, but you might hunger for something else as well. This is where the big questions surface again. If you are lonely, though you have a full stomach, you may hunger for companionship. If you are away from home, perhaps you hunger to return. Many books considered holy by those who believe in their teachings contain metaphors about hunger and thirst to represent the yearning for God or enlightenment. All these things are happening in "Hunger in New York City," beyond the visible hungers of the poor and starving created by the same conditions that built the new England. "Hunger in New York City" seems, on the surface, to be sparse and simple, but is rich and multi-layered.

The poem takes place when the poet is at the farthest point away from his home. He has just gotten off of a train in New York, and this is the poem he writes out of his initial impressions. He introduces us immediately to hunger and tells us first that it comes from outside of us, is a force coming from somewhere else, not only from the physical muscles and moving inward, but from concrete, land, or wind. So we are introduced to hunger, but we still do not know what kind of hunger the poet means. This will become our quest through the entire poem, with Ortiz feeding us little bits of which kind of hunger he might mean.

How we think of hunger is important to how we read the poem, because our imaginations and the material world may often be at odds. For example, if we say that Ortiz "personifies" hunger, we risk some oversimplification, obvious as the technique might seem. To personify means to give personhood, that is, identity (especially in human terms) to something inanimate. But in Acoma belief, life extends beyond what is animal and may be present in all things. So saying that hunger has life may not mean "personifying" it to an Acoma poet. Therefore, hunger is permitted to ask questions that not only the poet, but the reader, must try to answer.

In the second stanza, hunger is asking "for" many abstractions, ideas that do not stand for material things—"wisdom," for instance. In the third stanza, hunger asks yes-or-no questions, the most basic kind, and maybe the most important kind, because these basic questions are about what it means to survive. They are all about, literally, what gives us life.

The fourth stanza of the poem raises an issue found in much of Ortiz's work—how to answer these basic questions in the midst of a technological and industrial world full of noise and light and distraction. There is some irony here as well. If we are tempted to think of reservation life as impoverished, or to associate hunger with material goods alone, we may not notice the poverty found in the dominant culture's supposedly greatest achievement—its cities. The poet has come from the desert to New York and immediately thinks to write about hunger, which (we know by the title) lives in New York City just as in other places.

When the poet tells us, "I have hungered, truthfully and honestly," for the things of the city, he is confessing that this great machinery has lured him even as it has failed to feed him with what he needs. Ortiz has written other works about those hungers unfulfilled by technology, as in his short story "Man on the Moon" and in another poem from *Go-*

ing for the Rain, "Washyuma Moter Hotel." In the midst of the city, and at the halfway point of his long journey before returning home (which happens in the next section of the book), the poet remembers in the final stanza of "Hunger in New York City" what does feed him.

First, he prays by singing to himself, finally asking for blessing from mother earth. Then he tells us which kind of hunger we met at the beginning of the poem. In the middle of the stanza, quietly situated between the song and the request for blessing, the poet tells us that what feeds his hunger is "the humble presence / of all around me."

In those lines we learn much about Simon Ortiz's work. Since he uses poetry to demystify language, he has chosen methods of telling that are particular to the way we live today in order to teach in practical terms about yesterday as well. He does so by writing about fundamental objects and ideas and about those who are struggling along what the Acoma call the *heeyaanih,* the road of life.

When modernists such as Robert Lowell or William Carlos Williams wrote in this clear, simple language of things, they called it "minimalism" or "imagism." The Beat Poets of the 1950s, who inspired Ortiz as a poet, also used accessible language written in unconventional ways to talk about the common and struggling person in the city, about the land outside the city, and about the hungers that live in either place. Simon Ortiz has brought these ideas of minimalism and social intelligence together in his work, through a voice that is both Acoma and American, both ancient and contemporary, and toward his goal that "through poetry, prose, and other written works that evoke love, respect, and responsibility, Native Americans may be able to help the United States of America to go beyond survival."

Source: Sean Robisch, in an essay for *Poetry for Students,* Gale, 1998.

Sources

Berner, Robert L., "A Good Journey," in *World Literature Today,* Vol. 59, No. 3, Summer 1985, p. 474.

Bruchac, Joseph, *Survival This Way: Interviews with American Indian Poets,* Tucson: University of Arizona Press, 1987.

Gingerich, Willard, "'The Old Voices of Acoma': Simon Ortiz's Mythic Indigenism," in *Southwest Review,* Vol. 64, No. 1, Winter, 1979, pp. 18-30.

Hobson, Geary, in a review of "A Good Journey," in *Western American Literature,* Vol. XIV, No. 1, May, 1979, pp. 87-9.

Jaffe, Harold, "Speaking Memory," in *The Nation,* Vol. 234, No. 13, April 3, 1982, pp. 406-08.

Ortiz, Simon, "Man on the Moon" in *Virtually Now: Stories of Science, Technology, and the Future,* edited by Jeanne Schinto, Persea Books, 1996.

Ortiz, Simon, *Woven Stone,* Tucson: The University of Arizona Press, 1992.

Schein, Marie M., "Simon Ortiz" in *Dictionary of Literary Biography,* Volume 120: *American Poets Since World War II, Third Series,* edited by R. S. Gwynn, Detroit: Gale Research, 1992.

For Further Study

Niatum, Duane, *Harper's Anthology of 20th Century Native American Poetry,* Harper, San Francisco, 1988.
> Niatum places Ortiz within a larger framework of Native-American poets spanning almost a century, offering us over 350 pages of stunning work.

Wiget, Andrew, *Simon Ortiz,* Boise State University Press, 1986.
> In this book of criticism, Wiget explores Ortiz's role as both modern poet and traditional storyteller, emphasizing his connection with the land, and through it, with history.

Oysters

Anne Sexton

1972

"Oysters" appeared in 1972 as the first section of the six-part poem "The Death of the Fathers" in Anne Sexton's sixth published book of poetry, *The Book of Folly*. Sexton's earlier work had dealt with the subjects of mental illness, the suicidal impulse, romantic and sexual love, and the sexual connotations of fairy tales, as well as relationships between mothers and daughters. The theme of "The Deaths of the Fathers" was a departure for her. This was perhaps due to the fact that she was working with a woman therapist instead of a man. Or perhaps she felt the need to re-examine incestuous feelings for her father now that she had discovered he was not in fact her biological father.

The central images of the poems in this sequence seem almost like snapshots from a bizarre family photo album. The first is of a girl at fifteen eating a grown-up dinner alone with her father. The second, "How We Danced," presents the image of a young woman of nineteen dancing at a wedding with her father and discovering that he is sexually aroused by their contact. "The Boat" isolates a dangerous moment for the seven-year-old Anne riding in a sailboat with her mother and her father at the helm. "Santa" conflates the death of the father with the death of Santa. "Friends" examines a memory of a stranger who visited when her father was gone. In "Begat," the sixth and final poem of the sequence, the poet tries to focus on "father," to determine who he is. The exploration of the father-daughter relationship becomes increasingly disturbing, logically following the implication of

every little girl's belief that she can grow up to be her father's wife. "Oysters" marks the confusing rite of passage into the adult relationship between the daughter and the father.

Author Biography

Sexton, the daughter of Ralph and Mary Harvey, was born in 1928 and raised in suburban Boston. When she was nineteen she married Alfred Muller Sexton II. During her early twenties Sexton began experiencing severe bouts of depression. After the birth of her second daughter in 1955 she attempted suicide and was hospitalized under the care of Dr. Martin Orne, who encouraged her to write poems as a form of therapy. Sexton subsequently participated in several writing courses and attended the Antioch Writer's Conference on scholarship, studying under W. D. Snodgrass. Sexton produced extremely personal verse relating her experiences with mental illness. Her first collection, *To Bedlam and Part Way Back,* was published in 1960. As she gained a reputation as an important new poet, Sexton was invited to teach at high schools and universities, such as Harvard and Radcliffe. She also co-wrote several highly regarded children's books. And, in 1967, Sexton received the Pulitzer Prize in poetry for her third collection, *Live or Die.* Despite her literary success Sexton continually battled depression and psychosis. Twice her family was forced to have her committed to mental institutions. She ended her own life in 1974.

Poem Text

Oysters we ate,
sweet blue babies,
twelve eyes looked up at me,
running with lemon and Tabasco.
I was afraid to eat this father-food   5
and Father laughed
and drank down his martini,
clear as tears.
It was a soft medicine
that came from the sea into my mouth,   10
moist and plump.
I swallowed.
It went down like a large pudding.
Then I ate one o'clock and two o'clock.
Then I laughed and then we laughed   15
and let me take note—
there was a death,
the death of childhood
there at the Union Oyster House

Anne Sexton

for I was fifteen   20
and eating oysters
and the child was defeated.
The woman won.

Poem Summary

Line 1:

The poem inverts the standard syntax, or sentence structure, which would be "We ate oysters," to open with the word "[o]ysters," signalling their importance as an image within the context of the poem.

Line 2:

Rather than presenting the oysters as food, the poet describes them as helpless small creatures. The adjective "sweet" is clearly not in reference to their taste, but in conjunction with the word "babies" it must be used in its sense of "dear." The odd characterization of their color as blue creates a startling image of death with the word "babies."

Lines 3-4:

This refers to the fact that raw oysters are typically served by the dozen, with lemon wedges and hot pepper sauce. The persona of the poem per-

Media Adaptations

- Various audio recordings of Sexton's readings and interviews are available on cassette, including *Anne Sexton Reads her Work* (1973) and *Anne Sexton Reads Her Kind / Divorce, Thy Name is Woman / Little Girl, My String Bean, My Lovely Woman & Other Poems* (Caedmon Audio, 1973), both released near the time of her death.

- The National Endowment for Television spent several days at Sexton's house in 1965 filming a documentary about her life titled *Anne Sexton* (1966). The half-hour film, which was heavily edited in order to portray Sexton as an "ideal housewife and writer," is available at local libraries

- After her death, another film crew uncovered over an hour and a half of footage cut from the original 1966 documentary *Anne Sexton*. The version they released in 1973, *Sexton,* includes revealing out takes and readings that give a more complete portrayal of the talented and tormented poet.

ceives them as round eyes tearing with the sour juice and hot sauce.

Lines 5-6:

Eating raw oysters is an acquired taste, and usually not for children's super-sensitive taste buds. In this poem the persona associates this food with her adult father. (Other implications of the term "father-food" emerge in lines 10 to 13.) The father's laugh is, presumably, at his child's squeamishness.

Lines 7-8:

The sophisticated adult food being consumed is accompanied, for the father, by a sophisticated martini, obviously straight up rather than on the rocks so that the clarity of the liquid in the glass is noticeable to the child, who associates it with the teary running of the oyster-eyes, as well as with some apparent sadness.

Line 9:

This line does double duty, referring to the sedative effect of the martini on the father, as well as going on to describe the beginnings of the taste of the first oyster.

Lines 10-13:

It is obvious from the other poems in the sequence "The Death of the Fathers" (which "Oysters" opens) that a heavy aura of sexuality is meant to surround this poem. For example, it is believed that oysters are an aphrodisiac, a strange food for a father and daughter to be eating alone together. And, given the subject of incest explored in the other poems, it is difficult to read the poem as simply a very detailed description of a young girl eating oysters for the first time. In fact, it seems to be the interpretative consensus that the eating of oysters becomes an analogy for a sexual attraction between the girl and her father, and that the sea taste of the oyster's "soft medicine" is his semen.

The shock of this realization leads to a retrospective impact of the images of "babies" and "father-food" and "tears." Some critics read this poem as a mix of fantasy with memory, as a grown woman looks back and admits a sexual attraction to her father, then allows sexual fantasy to color the memory.

Lines 14-15:

Raw oysters are usually served circled on a plate with the lemon wedges and Tabasco in a dish in the middle. Evidently the girl had first eaten the very top oyster, midnight or noon, and then went in an organized fashion from there. It is typical "Anne Sexton" to place such a comic image after the shocking one of the preceding lines. As if to guide the reader further away from the horror, line 15 introduces laughter, although the lightening of the mood does not last for long.

Lines 16-23:

The poet in line 16 introduces herself retrospectively into the girl's experience to adamantly announce "the death of childhood." The "blue babies" of line 2 were, in one aspect of their multifaceted image function, a forewarning of something dark and secret and sexual. Now we see them as a premonition of the "death" of the "child" in this young woman. However, the poet next places us matter of factly in the restaurant, and the situation seems unexceptional. But while the poem never returns to the level of the shock of the incest analogy in lines 10 to 13, there is still an ambivalence in the final lines.

Certainly line 22 can be read as a rite of passage as the child learns to begin to adjust her palate to adult food. But line 23 has a strange double meaning. It reads first, perhaps, as though the woman in the persona has won out over the child, and the oysters were eaten to prove her adulthood. However, it can also mean that it is a woman now having dinner with a man, and not a child having dinner with a father. And the phrase can be read as "The woman [was] won," as in "winning a romantic conquest." There is enough evidence of misplaced romantic emotions in the other poems in the sequence that it does not seem a stretch to read this line both ways. In fact, given the emotional horror of the later poems, the ambivalence present in this poem seems "true," and in keeping with the emotional reality of such a father-daughter relationship.

Themes

Change and Transformation

In the poem "Oysters," Sexton details an adolescent girl's transformation from innocence to adulthood through an account of a single meal eating oysters with her father. At first a simple description of a father and daughter sharing a meal at a restaurant, the poem touches on important themes of sexual maturation and incest as the young speaker discovers the sexually charged implications of her actions. While change can be triggered by many catalysts, it seems here a single but profound realization that signals for the speaker the passing of childhood. This realization takes place as the speaker, sitting with her father, swallows the moist, salty oysters "that came from the sea into my mouth." This challenge to "eat the father-food" is so laden with sexuality it embarrasses the father and daughter. They both laugh uncomfortably to cover their discomfort.

To make sure both the speaker and reader agree exactly what change took place at that moment, Sexton pauses the scene (as the girl laughs with her father) to say: "and let me take note— / there was a death, / the death of childhood / there at the Union Oyster House." In every death there is rebirth, and in every defeat a side wins out. In this case "the woman won," Sexton concludes, though we know the opponents really inhabit the same body. Like

Topics for Further Study

- Write a poem about a food that you especially hated eating when you were young and describe a time when you could not avoid eating it.

- Explain how laughter is used in this poem. Is it a sign of amusement? Does it mean the same thing for each person in the poem?

the shells that litter her plate after she devours the raw oysters inside, the young girl finishes the meal transformed by experience.

Rites of Passage

Each culture has a unique rite or ceremony to mark a child's passage from innocence into adulthood. Most commonly, traditional rites take the form of a symbolic action; either the youth has to overcome a challenge, complete a journey, or endure physical pain. Although modern American culture may have abandoned most traditional ceremonies, the speaker of "Oysters" discovers a rite of passage in the everyday act of eating a plate of seafood with her father.

The restaurant scene Sexton describes holds several characteristics of ceremony: the young girl invited into the "adult" world; the father challenging her to overcome her fear and eat the slimy and spicy oysters; and finally, the act of eating, which places a part of the sea on her tongue like a sacrament. Through these actions, in turn, the fifteen-year-old girl leaves childhood behind and passes into the world of adults, suddenly a woman in her father's world. Underlying all of these actions is an uncomfortable sense of sexuality between the father and daughter as they eat the oysters (often rumored to be an aphrodisiac). The act of sex itself is a rite of passage from inexperience to experience.

Sex

Many critical interpretations of this poem are based on the action of the speaker eating oysters with her father. From this provocative action, critics conclude that an incestuous relationship between the pair exists. As the line-by-line explication of this poem illustrates, Sexton arranges the details and dramatic movement of "Oysters" in such a way as to craft an underlying theme of sexual attraction between father and daughter.

It is the realization of this attraction which perhaps changes the speaker that afternoon at the Union Oyster House. The details of the scene resemble a sexual encounter between the two: the girl afraid to "eat this father food"; the half-drunk man laughing (though what he drinks reminds her of tears); and the salty, moist and plump oysters which she swallows down "like a large pudding." Reinforcing this interpretation is the presence of terrible guilt or grief which would naturally accompany such a relationship.

Style

"Oysters" is written in free verse. It is constructed in one stanza of 23 lines, punctuated as five relatively middle-length sentences and one long final sentence extending from lines 15 to 23.

The lines vary in length from four syllables to ten, and lineation focuses an image per line, such as "and Father laughed" in line 6, "and drank down his martini," in line 7.

The poet utilizes alliteration as a means of focusing attention on the images of "blue babies" in line 2; of "father-food" and "Father" in lines 5 and 6; of "martini," "medicine," "mouth," and "moist and plump" in lines 7, 9, 10, and 11; and of "woman won" in line 23. She uses internal rhyme in "clear as tears" in line 8 to the same purpose. The repetition of the word "laughed" three times with "Father," then "I," and then "we" charts an emotional progression in lines 6 through 15, and the repetition of "death" in lines 17-18 emphasizes this emotional rite of passage.

The poem is written in the first person "I," although this is not evident until line 5. Furthermore, it is not revealed that the "I" is fifteen years old until line 20, after the rite of passage has been established.

Historical Context

"Oysters," published in 1972, is not informed as much by the historical events of the decade in which it was written as much as it was influenced by the movement of writers of which Sexton was a central figure. Known as the Confessionalists, this group of New England writers which gained popularity during the 1950s and early 1960s also included W. D. Snodgrass, Robert Lowell, and Sylvia Plath. Together they turned poetry in a direction so completely introspective and intimately revealing that many critics of the time admitted being too embarrassed by the details of sexual trauma and psychological illness to comment objectively on the books reviewed. As details from her biography account, Sexton suffered severe bouts of depression which led her to several suicide attempts. She finally succeeded in 1974, only two years after publishing "Oysters" and barely a decade after her close friend Sylvia Plath took her own life.

Plath and Sexton met in Robert Lowell's graduate writing seminar at Boston University, where they both learned how to use confessional poetry as a means of dealing with mental illness and emotional trauma. Plath attempted suicide so many times as to think of herself a artist at the craft of dying. In her poem "Lady Lazarus," written several years before Sexton wrote "Oysters," Plath confesses:

…The second time I meant To last it out and not
    come back at all. I rocked shut
As a seashell. They had to call and call And pick
    the worms off me like sticky pearls.
Dying Is an art, like everything else. I do it
    exceptionally well.

There is little doubt Sexton read Plath's poems before publication, and perhaps offered workshop suggestions to the fellow poet. Possible too is the chance Sexton had the image of her friend "rocked shut / As a seashell" in the back of her mind as she began the poem that would describe a young girl sitting at a table with her father, a plate of fresh oysters between them.

The popular psychoanalytical method of Sigmund Freud is a significant component to the critical interpretations of "Oysters." Ironically, Sexton may have been including Freudian imagery in her poems as a direct response to her years of psychotherapy. Sexton participated in various forms of therapy with a variety of doctors during the late 1950s and early 1960s, and even in 1972 it was not uncommon for psychiatrists to use Freudian psychoanalysis to help patients search out the roots of their illness.

This method often depends on a list of set symbolic images or relationships in order to interpret our actions. For example, Freud claimed that all water and fish images are "feminine" sexual sym-

Compare *&* *Contrast*

- **1972:** Britain imposes direct rule over Northern Ireland after thirty years of fighting between Catholics and Protestants. Over 467 Northern Irish are killed during the year, including thirteen Catholics shot dead by British troops at the Londonderry riots on January 30th, the day to be known infamously as "Bloody Sunday."

  1978: The Irish Republican Army (IRA) regularly attacks British Government officials in protest of British rule over Northern Ireland. IRA terrorists plant a bomb on Lord Mountbatten's yacht, killing the cousin of Elizabeth II, his young grandson and a friend. Later the same year IRA members ambush and kill eighteen British soldiers on a road south of Belfast.

  1998: After years of violence, both IRA and British leaders hope for peace by signing an agreement on April 9th which will turn direct rule of Northern Ireland back over to Irish officials.

- **1972:** President Nixon signs a bill January 5th authorizing a $5.5 billion, 6-year program to develop a space shuttle that will lift off as a rocket and return to earth as an airplane.

  1984: The space shuttle *Discovery*, the world's first spacecraft with the capability to be piloted back to earth, launches its maiden voyage. Television networks cancel a majority of the day's regular programming to offer viewers live coverage of the launch.

  1985: A horrified national audience watches live from home and schools as space shuttle *Challenger* explodes shortly after take-off, killing all crew aboard.

  1998: With very few mishaps since the *Challenger* disaster, NASA's space shuttle program schedules dozens of regular launches and re-entries of its small fleet of craft. Television coverage of the launches on national networks now rarely consists of more than brief blurbs about the event.

- **1972:** A new Surgeon General's report first warns of the dangers of "second-hand smoke" after studies warn that the carbon monoxide and other toxins are actually more harmful to non-smokers than to the smokers themselves. The news forces agencies to reconsider where smoking should be allowed, which at the time included grocery stores, airline flights and city offices.

  1998: Both state and federal government agencies seek compensation from big tobacco companies for billions of dollars spent treating smoking-related illnesses. Smoking is banned in all government buildings, most airline flights, and in many restaurants and bars.

---

bols and that many young girls, like mythical Elektra, are sexually attracted to the first males they love—their fathers. Whether this was true or not for Sexton is debatable, but it is highly likely her intensive therapy during the same years she published "Oysters" included discussions in which this Electra complex relationship with her father may have been discussed. She considered poetry a form of therapy and may have been using the prevalent analytical method of the time to handle her own confusion and obsession surrounding this complex relationship.

Critical Overview

Many critics have applauded confessional poetry for its move away from typically "academic" or intellectual contemporary poetry. In fact, a feature of confessional poetry is that it is very personal. Consequently, the question for many readers of confessional poetry is just how much of the work is autobiographical. While it is instructive to know Sexton's life story in order to grasp the technique and craft operating in her poems, J.D. McClatchy makes it clear in *Anne Sexton: The Artist and Her*

Critics that "Sexton is sharply aware ... of the difference between factual truth and poetic truth—of the need to 'edit' out, while trying not to distort." McClatchy is adamant that the value of Sexton's poetry is "as art, rather than as mere self-expression."

Lynette McGrath, like McClatchy, sees real value in the open forms of Sexton's later poetry. She notes in *Original Essays on the Poetry of Anne Sexton* that "as Sexton's poems become less structurally controlled, they begin to incorporate the loose syntax of conversation ...." McGrath maintains that Sexton's earlier formal structures closed out the reader, whereas later poems such as "Oysters" "encourage the reader to participate in or learn from the poet's own experience."

Helen Vendler, on the other hand, states in *The New Republic* that such a poem sequence as "The Deaths of the Fathers" "sounds entirely too much like an echo of [confessional poet Robert] Lowell, and a bad one...." Even such an appreciative critic as Katha Pollitt in *The Nation,* who admires the "daring rhymester" of Sexton's early work, suggests that, while it is commendable to want to grow as a writer, Sexton has "moved away from form as she matured, but without having worked out ways of achieving in free verse what form makes so easy: the use of structure and sound to delimit a drama, intensify emotion and clarify meaning." Pollitt is only one of many critics to see Sexton's later free verse as self-indulgent rambling. The fault is thought to be Sexton's approach to her work as more therapy than poetry.

J. D. McClatchy in *Anne Sexton: The Artist and Her Critics,* however, sees "The Deaths of the Fathers" as "one of Sexton's triumphs, daring in its explorations and revelations, its verse superbly controlled as the voice of each poem is modulated to its experience." According to McClatchy, "Oysters" is set in childhood and written in "the declaratives of a child."

While it presents Sexton's initiation, a rite of passage into the adult world, it simultaneously examines both her memory of her father's response to her and her own desire for him as a father, and a fantasy of adult desire for him as a man. "She is," as McClatchy sees it, "Daddy's Girl having lunch with her father at a restaurant." She "fearfully eats her oysters—'this father-food,' his semen."

Furthermore, McClatchy believes "that the patterns [the later poems] assume [in open forms] and by which they manage their meanings are those which more closely follow the actual experiences

they are recreating—forms that can include and reflect direct, personal experience...." It is his opinion that there is such a "blend of memory and fantasy" in the poems of this sequence that each interpenetrates and thus reinforces the other. For him, "Oysters" and the other poems of "The Deaths of the Fathers" are "the culmination of Sexton 's confessional style."

Criticism

Chris Semansky

Chris Semansky teaches writing and literature at Portland Community College in Portland, Oregon, and is a frequent contributor of poems and essays to literary journals. In the following essay, Semansky asserts that "Oysters" is a "confessional" poem that explores Sexton's childhood relationship with her father.

In the 1950s and 1960s poets such as Theodore Roethke, Allen Ginsberg, Robert Lowell, and John Berryman began writing and publishing poems that detailed intimate aspects of their personal lives. Unlike other poets who wrote about their own experiences, circumstances, and situations, these poets wrote about such taboo subjects as sex, mental illness, and drugs. Because these subjects often form the staples of psychoanalysis—a kind of talk therapy—the poets who wrote about these subjects were labeled confessional. Readers, then, were put in the position of therapist and the poet was the patient, or client. This relationship is especially appropriate for confessional poet Anne Sexton, who used her poetry to delve into her own troubled relationships and personal history.

The first poem of a six poem sequence called "The Death of The Fathers," from her 1972 collection, *The Book of Folly,* "Oysters" imagistically recalls a key event in the author's emotional development—the poet's memory of eating oysters with her father at the Union Oyster House when she was a young girl. For Sexton, this seemingly mundane event marked her own growth from adolescence to adulthood, from innocence to experience.

Poets often use imagery to make their writing concrete. Teachers of both poetry and fiction writing are fond of telling their students to show, not tell. This (theoretically) enables the readers to re-experience the event described rather than having it explained to them. Poetic imagery, however, is not only language used to describe what we see; it refers to all the objects and qualities of sense perception referred to in a poem or work of literature. These qualities can include touch, taste, smell, hearing, sensations of movement, etc. Sexton uses imagery associated with all of the senses, not just vision, to produce a poem meant to be read with the whole body, to be felt as well as understood. So, for instance, when she describes the oysters as "sweet blue babies, / twelve eyes look[ing] up at me" we understand the comparison between oysters and human babies while also being a little repulsed by the description. Sexton plays with this kind of tension throughout the poem as she recounts her sexual fantasies about her father.

The scene of the poem has all of the adult trappings so mysterious to children: not only oysters themselves (and the associations they have as an aphrodisiac) but the butter and lemon and tabasco, the father's martini, and the fact that they are eating alone. If, as some critics suggest, the oysters can be considered the father's semen, the scene takes on a more mysterious aura. If Sexton actually did eat her father's semen, we would be appalled. Incest, after all, remains taboo in almost all societies, but because Sexton's description merely uses her memory of oyster eating with her father to suggest desires that are often misunderstood, we are instead intrigued, drawn into a poem that can be read no other way than as confession.

Themes of passage and healing inform the poem. Swallowing oysters—"a soft medicine / that came from the sea into my mouth, / moist and plump"—not only suggest the act of incestuous fellatio, but it also suggests doing something that you might not like but that is good for you. For Sexton, this is expressing the desire she had as an adolescent to please her father, to be an adult like him and to do adult things. Sexton's use of tactile imagery—her description of the food and how the oyster went down "like a large pudding"—underscores the link between sex and food and keeps our attention focused on the body. Just as food passes through the body, so too has Sexton passed through adolescence into adulthood.

Similarly, the line "Then I ate one o'clock and two o'clock," not only describes the position of the oysters on her plate, but it also highlights the passing of time. By delving into her past, Sexton both waxes nostalgic and unearths memories that might have better been left alone. Psychoanalysis, sometimes called the "talking cure," works when psychologists prod their patients to remember trau-

What Do I Read Next?

- In 1958, Anne Sexton attended a poetry workshop that would forever change her writing style. There she worked with W. D. Snodgrass, who's "Heart's Needle" she would always credit as a major inspiration for her work.

- A revealing look at Anne Sexton's life is documented by her own letters to friends and family members. Her daughter Linda compiled and edited many in the book *Anne Sexton: A Self-Portrait in Letters,* published in 1992.

- Sexton considered poet Sylvia Plath a good friend. Her similar biography and confessional writing style makes her an ideal next read. Her poem "Mirror" is included in the first volume of *Poetry for Students,* and her book *Ariel* is widely available in bookstores.

- Yet another poet included in the "Confessionalists" with Sexton is Robert Lowell. He was her graduate school instructor at Boston University where she also met Sylvia Plath. Lowell's book *Life Studies* is perhaps his most famous work.

matic events in their pasts that supposedly can help to explain their current crises. Sexton was in psychoanalysis and various forms of psychotherapy a good portion of her adult life, and in her own writings she often claimed to make little distinction between poetry and therapy.

Arranged in chronological order, the other poems in the sequence similarly recount events with her father that marked passages in the author's emotional development. These events both literally and metaphorically detail Sexton's conflicted relationship with her father. Sexton biographer, Diane Wood Middlebrook, writes that during the holiday season of 1970 an old family friend, Azel Mack, convinced Sexton that he had had a lengthy affair with Sexton's mother and was in fact Sexton's biological father. This information touched off powerful emotions for Sexton, emotions that she incorporated into her poetry.

In her *Anne Sexton,* 1991, Middlebrook writes that "the emotional dynamic in 'The Death of Fathers' is complex and radically interesting. The series asserts the reality of various kinds of incestuous wishes in two kinds of fathers, one treacherously fixated by instinct, the other domineering, asserting rough sex play as his father-right." In "Begat," the last poem in the sequence, the speaker finally makes peace with the memory of her dead father.

Other writers were not as convinced by the poems. In a letter to Sexton, poet-critic (and friend) C. K. Williams wrote: "There isn't enough dumbness in the poems, enough of that language that floats just above incoherency, the incoherency of those mysteries of time and love that fatherhood and childhood embody."

Such blatant use of biographical material, especially material so sexually explicit, garnered some negative reaction from critics and readers. In *Oedipus Anne: The Poetry of Anne Sexton,* Diana George Hume writes that:

> If the response of [Sexton's] contemporaries to "confessional poetry" was sometimes sharply negative, it was specially inflected with contempt for "her kind." When [Robert] Lowell confessed, at first we slapped his patrician hand and told him to shape up and put back the stiff in his upper lip. When Sexton confessed, we sharpened the knife and heated the pot.

Indeed, male poets dominated the landscape of confessional poetry before Anne Sexton. One of her own chief influences was W. D. Snodgrass, to whom she wrote in a letter that "I want everyone to hold up large signs saying YOU'RE A GOOD GIRL." This desire to please men, and the emotional damage it can do to women, formed not only a recurrent theme in Sexton's poetry but in the poetry of Sylvia Plath as well, whose difficulties coming to terms with the memory of her own father are well-documented in her poems and prose. Commenting on the importance of the father figure in Sexton's poetry, Hume emphasizes:

> Sexton's search for the traditional Father-God in dozens of poems that may be failures in the feminist sense is an eloquent representation of an entire culture's quest for the same God. The loving and admonishing Father for whom she searches is the same Father for whom we have all searched.... Even those of us who have rejected him outright in favor of no gods at all—or of gods that offend our sensibilities less, match our politics or gender better, or seem to us truer, more imaginative—catch ourselves wishing, or fearing, that he might exist. Sexton's failing Father-God is, in short, our own; I cannot see how it could be otherwise in a patriarchy as old and enduring as ours.

Source: Chris Semansky, in an essay for *Poetry for Students,* Gale, 1998.

Suzanne Juhasz

In the following excerpt, Juhasz discusses the "end of Sexton's career and poetry" and "looks at the role that her poems played in her life and in ours."

If you are brought up to be a proper little girl in Boston, a little wild and boy crazy, a little less of a student and more of a flirt, and you run away from home to elope and become a proper Boston bride, a little given to extravagance and a little less to casseroles, but a proper bride nonetheless who turns into a proper housewife and mother, and if all along you know that there lives inside you a rat, a "gnawing pestilential rat," [as stated in the poem "Rowing,"] what will happen to you when you grow up? If you are Anne Sexton, you will keep on paying too much attention to the rat, will try to kill it, and yourself, become hospitalized, be called crazy. You will keep struggling to forget the rat and be the proper Boston housewife and mother you were raised to be. And into this struggle will come, as an act of grace, poetry, to save your life by giving you a role, a mission, a craft: an act, poetry, that is you but is not you, outside yourself. Words, that you can work and shape and that will stay there, black and true, while you do this, turn them into a poem, that you can send away to the world, a testimony of yourself. Words that will change the lives of those who read them and your own life, too. So that you can know that you are not only the wife and mother, not only the rat, but that you are the poet, a person who matters, who has money and fame and prizes and students and admirers and a name, Anne Sexton.

But what about the mother and wife, and what about the rat, when Anne Sexton becomes a poet? This essay is about the end of Sexton's career and poetry, and it looks at the role that her poems played in her life and in ours. It is a tale for our times, because it is also about what poetry can do for women and what it cannot do for women. Something we need to know....

[F]or Sexton the poem existed as a measure of control, of discipline, for one whom she defined as "given to excess." "I have found that I can control it best in a poem," she says. "If the poem is good then it will have the excess under control ... it is the core of the poem ... there like stunted fruit, unseen but actual" [*Anne Sexton: A Self-Portrait in Letters,* 1977].

Yet the poem had another function in her life, the one which gives rise to that label "confessional," which has always dogged her work and is not usually complimentary. Her poetry is highly personal. She is either the overt or the implicit subject of her poem, and the she as subject is the person who anguishes, who struggles, who seems mired in the primary soil of living: the love/hate conflict with mother and father, the trauma of sex, the guilt of motherhood. The person in the poem is not the proper lady and mother and wife who is always trying her best to tidy up messes and cover them with a coating of polish and wax. Rather, it is the rat, a creature of nature rather than culture, who is crude and rude, "with its bellyful of dirt / and its hair seven inches long"; with its "two eyes full of poison / and routine pointed teeth." The rat person, with her "evil mouth" and "worried eyes," knows that living is something about which to worry: she sees and tells. In form her poem often follows a psychoanalytic model, as I have pointed out in an earlier essay [titled " 'The Excitable Gift': The Poetry of Anne Sexton"], beginning in a present of immediate experience and probing into a past of personal relationships in order to understand the growth (and the damaging) of personality. As such, the poem for Sexton is an important agent in her quest for salvation: for a way out of the madness that the rat's vision engenders, a way that is not suicide.

Very early in her career, in "For John, Who Begs Me Not to Enquire Further," she presents an aesthetics of personal poetry which is conscious that the poem, because it is an object that communicates and mediates between person and person, can offer "something special" for others as well as oneself....

In such poetry, she warns, there is no "lesson," no universal truth. What there is is the poem of herself, which, as she has made it, has achieved an order; that very order a kind of hope (a belief in salvation) that might be shared. The poem of herself is, however, not herself but a poem. The imagery of this poem attests to that fact, as it turns self into object, a bowl, an orange, a sun, while it turns the poem about self into a coating or covering that surrounds the self. The bowl is like a planet in a heaven of "cracked stars shining / like a complicated lie"; if he should turn from this poem, she promises to "fasten a new skin around" or "dress" her orange, that strange sun.

Of course Sexton was right when she said that there ought to be something special in that gesture

> *She was often, although not always, a good poet, a skilled poet, whose words worked insight upon her subject matter and irradiated it with vision."*

her poems made toward others. People responded to her poetry because she had the courage to speak publicly of the most intimate of personal experiences, the ones so many share. She became a spokesperson for the secret domestic world and its pain. And her audience responded as strongly as it did, not only because of what she said but because of how she said it. She was often, although not always, a good poet, a skilled poet, whose words worked insight upon her subject matter and irradiated it with vision.

But what about herself, in the process? What did her poems do for her?

In a letter [reprinted in *Anne Sexton: A Self-Portrait in Letters*] she speaks of the necessity for the writer to engage in a vulnerable way with experience.

> I think that writers ... must try *not* to avoid knowing what is happening. Everyone has somewhere the ability to mask the events of pain and sorrow, call it shock ... when someone dies for instance you have this shock that carries you over it, makes it bearable. But the creative person must not use this mechanism anymore than they have to in order to keep breathing. Other people may. But not you, not us. Writing is "life" in capsule and the writer must feel every bump edge scratch ouch in order to know the real furniture of his capsule.... I, myself, alternate between hiding behind my own hands protecting myself anyway possible, and this other, this seeing ouching other. I guess I mean that creative people must not avoid the pain that they get dealt. I say to myself, sometimes repeatedly "I've got to get the hell out of this hurt"... But no. Hurt must be examined like a plague.

The result of this program, as she says in a letter to W. D. Snodgrass, is writing "real." "Because that is the one thing that will save (and I do mean save) other people."

And yet the program is not only altruistic in intent. Personal salvation remains for her an equally urgent goal. As she writes in "The Children," from one of her last books, *The Awful Rowing Toward God* (1975):

> The place I live in
> is a kind of maze
> and I keep seeking
> the exit or the home.

In describing this position of vulnerability necessary for poetry, she tells Snodgrass that a poet must remain "the alien." In her vocabulary for herself, that alien is of course the rat. But there is a serious problem here, because Anne Sexton the woman (who is nonetheless the poet, too) does not like the rat. The existence of the rat obstructs salvation. In "Rowing," the opening poem of *The Awful Rowing Toward God,* salvation is described as an island toward which she journeys. This island, her goal, is "not perfect," having "the flaws of life, / the absurdities of the dinner table, / but there will be a door":

> and I will open it and I will get rid of the rat inside
> me, the gnawing pestilential rat.

In the "Ninth Psalm" (ED. "Tenth Psalm" in *CP*) of her long poem "O Ye Tongues" (*The Death Notebooks*), an extended description of the state of salvation includes this vision: "For the rat was blessed on that mountain. He was given a white bath."

In other words, Sexton, recognizing at the age of twenty-eight her possession of a talent, turned her mad self to good work (and works): into a writer, an active rather than a passive agent. For she had defined madness as fundamentally passive and destructive in nature. "Madness is a waste of time. It creates nothing…. Nothing grows from it and you, meanwhile, only grow into it like a snail." Yet the rat who is the mad lady is also the poet. To have become a poet was surely an act toward salvation for Sexton. It gave her something to do with the knowledge that the rat possessed. Left to her silence, the rat kept seeing too much and therefore kept seeking "the exit." Words brought with them power, power to reach others. They gave her as well a social role, "the poet," that was liberating. Being the poet, who could make money with her poetry, who could be somebody of consequence in the public world, was an act that helped to alleviate some of the frustration, the impotence, the self-hatred that Sexton the woman experienced so powerfully in her life. The poet was good: how good she was Sexton, as teacher and reader and mentor, made a point of demonstrating.

But the rat was not good; in yet another image of self-identification, Sexton called that hated, evil, inner self a demon.…

The poems can never offer personal salvation for their poet, and she has come to understand why. First, because she defines salvation as a life freed at last from the rat and her pain ("I would sell my life to avoid / the pain that begins in the crib / with its bars or perhaps / with your first breath"), and yet she cannot kill the rat without killing the vision that is the source of her poetry. Second, because the poems themselves are a kind of suicide. She knows that poetry must be craft as well as vision; that the very act of crafting objectifies the poem's content. What has lived within her, externalized and formalized by art, becomes something other than herself; it is form but not flesh.

She expresses this new knowledge in the only way she knows, by making poetry of it.…

In an earlier essay on Sexton, I maintained that poetry had saved her from suicide. It did, for the years in which she wrote and was the poet. But it is equally true that poetry could not prevent her death, "the exit," because it could not bring her to salvation, "the home."

For Sexton salvation would have meant sanity: peace rather than perpetual conflict, integration rather than perpetual fragmentation. Sanity would have meant vanquishing at last her crazy bad evil gnawing self, the rat, the demon. Yet the rat was, at the same time, the source of her art. Its anxious visions needed to be nurtured so that she might be a poet. Sanity might bring peace to the woman, but it would destroy the poet. And it was not the woman, who made the peanut butter sandwiches and the marriage bed, whom Sexton liked. It was the poet. The discipline of her craft and the admiration, respect, and power that it brought allowed her to feel good about herself. That the woman and the poet were different "selves," and in conflict with each other, she was well aware. "I do not live a poet's life. I look and act like a housewife," she wrote. "I live the wrong life for the person I am." Although this fragmentation of roles wrought conflict and confusion, it nonetheless made possible the kind of poetry that Sexton wrote. But more and more in her final years she seemed to have come to despise the balancing act itself, demanding all or, finally, nothing.

Perhaps the kind of salvation that Sexton sought was unattainable, because its very terms had become so contradictory. Certainly, her poetry could not offer it. In poetry she could make verbal and public what she knew about her private self; she could shape this knowledge, control it, give it a form that made it accessible to others. But she could not write what she did not know, so that while her poems document all the rat has seen, they never offer an alternative vision. They are always too "close" to herself for that. And they are at the same time too far from her. By creating through externalization and formalization yet another self with which to deal, her poetry increased her sense of self-fragmentation in the midst of her struggle toward wholeness.

Yet Sexton's poetry has offered salvation to others. Personal poetry of this kind, a genre that many women, in their search for self-understanding and that same elusive wholeness, have recently adopted, must be understood to have a different function for its readers and for its writers. Art as therapy appears less profitable for the artist, who gives the gift of herself, than for its recipients. I think that I can learn from Sexton's poems as she never could. They project a life that is like my own in important ways; I associate my feelings with hers, and the sense of a shared privacy is illuminating. At the same time, they are not my life; their distance from me permits a degree of objectivity, the ability to analyze as well as empathize. Possibly I can use the insights produced by such a process to further change in my own life. For the artist, however, because the distance between herself and the poem is at once much closer and much greater, it is more difficult, perhaps impossible, to use the poem in this way. Salvation for the artist must come, ultimately, from developing a life that operates out of creative rather than destructive tensions. Sexton's life, art, and death exemplify some of the difficulties faced by women artists in achieving this goal and also dramatically underline the necessity of overcoming them.

Source: Suzanne Juhasz, "Seeking the Exit or the Home: Poetry and Salvation in the Career of Anne Sexton," in *Sexton: Selected Criticism,* edited by Diana Hume George, University of Illinois Press, 1988, pp. 303–11.

Sources

George, Diana Hume, *Oedipus Anne: The Poetry of Anne Sexton,* University of Illinois Press, 1987.

McClatchy, J. D., "Anne Sexton: Somehow to Endure," in *Anne Sexton: The Artist and Her Critics,* edited by J D. McClatchy, Indiana University Press, 1978, pp. 244-90.

McGrath, Lynette, "Anne Sexton's Poetic Connections: Death, God, and Form," in *Original Essays on the Poetry of Anne Sexton,* edited by Francis Bixler, University of Central Arkansas Press, 1988, pp. 138-63.

Middlebrook, Diane Wood, *Anne Sexton,* Random House, 1991.

Pollitt, Katha, "'The Awful Rowing,'" *The Nation,* Vol. 233, No. 17, November 21, 1981, pp. 533-37.

Sexton, Linda Grey, and Lois Ames, eds., *Anne Sexton: A Self-Portrait in Letters,* Houghton-Mifflin, 1979.

Stauffer, Donald Barlow, *A Short History of American Poetry,* E. P. Dutton, 1974.

Vendler, Helen, "Malevolent Flippancy," *The New Republic,* Vol. 185, No. 19, November 11, 1981, pp. 33-6.

For Further Study

Markey, Janice, *A New Tradition? The Poetry of Sylvia Plath, Anne Sexton and Adrienne Rich: A Study of Feminism and Poetry,* European University Studies Series 14, Volume 133.

> Places interpretation Sexton's work within the context of two other contemporary women poets in order to reveal a larger scope of feminist criticism often ignored by those studying the Confessionalists.

Sexton, Linda, *Searching for Mercy St: My Journey Back to My Mother, Anne Sexton,* Little Brown, 1996.

> Mixing heart-wrenching biography with objective criticism of her mother's work, Sexton's daughter Linda talks about life growing up with the mentally ill and sometimes abusive poet/parent.

Wagner, Linda, *Critical Essays on Anne Sexton,* G.K. Hall & Company, 1989.

> This anthology of essays about Sexton's work balances both critical interpretation and historical record.

Psalm 23

King James Bible

1611

A psalm is a sacred song, hymn, or poem; usually, the term is associated with the Book of Psalms, a book in the Bible containing 150 of these sacred works. Most of the psalms were originally believed to be written by David, the Hebrew king who lived around 970 B.C.E. Biblical scholars of recent centuries, however, have come to agree that the psalms are, at least in part, the work of many authors. The Old Testament of the King James Version of the Bible contains the most famous English translation of the psalms. Although the King James Version was finished in 1611, the original Hebrew psalm texts are thought to date between the thirteenth and the third centuries B.C.E. The predominant theme of the Book of Psalms is the expression of faith in God, but the individual poems have been classified into many forms, including hymns, laments, songs of confidence, and songs of thanksgiving. Psalm 23 is perhaps the most universally recognized of the psalms. Its popularity over the centuries stems from both the beauty of its poetry and the intensity with which the psalmist expresses trust in God. The psalm's chief poetic device is the metaphor: God is portrayed as two different archetypal figures in ancient Near Eastern culture, the shepherd and the host. As the shepherd, He guides and protects his flock, which is humankind. As host, God provides for humans, allowing them to celebrate His blessings. Through these metaphors, the psalmist presents a childlike trust in God. This trust is perhaps the purest manifestation of faith: although death and misfortune threaten the speaker, he or she be-

lieves in the protection of God. As a result, the speaker has no fear.

Poem Text

The Lord is my shepherd; I shall not want.

He maketh me to lie down in green pastures: he
    leadeth me beside the still waters.

He restoreth my soul: he leadeth me in the paths of
    righteousness for his name's sake.

Yea, though I walk through the valley of the
    shadow of death, I will fear no evil: for thou
    art with me; thy rod and thy staff they
    comfort me.

Thou preparest a table before me in the presence of   5
    mine enemies: thou anointest my head with
    oil; my cup runneth over.

Surely goodness and mercy shall follow me all the
    days of my life: and I will dwell in the
    house of the Lord for ever.

Poem Summary

Line 1:

The first line is perhaps the most famous in all the psalms. Its power derives from the crisp use of metaphor—the assumed, rather than directly stated, comparison between God and a shepherd. The nature of this comparison must have been evident to ancient Hebrews who meditated upon this poem. Like most Near Eastern peoples, the Hebrews relied on a herding economy, and the importance of the shepherd-figure derives not only from the necessity of sheep to that economy but also from the hostile nature of the environment. Because of the predators, poachers, and harsh desert conditions that threatened grazing lands, the shepherd needed to take great care to protect the sheep. The qualities of sheep complete the psalm's main metaphor. By calling God his shepherd and himself God's lamb, the psalmist expresses a specific relationship between the two. The psalmist is helpless, innocent, and utterly dependent on God. God, for his part, fulfills his role as shepherd by protecting the psalmist. Thus, the psalmist "shall not want."

Lines 2-3:

The second two verses describe God as a guide. The images in verse 2 are entirely pastoral: the shepherd leads his lamb to "green pastures" and "still waters." In verse 3, the implications are spir-

Media Adaptations

- A recording of the entire King James Bible, narrated by Alexander Scourby, can be heard on the Internet at http://www.audio-bible.com/.

- Psalm 23 in Middle English can be found on the Web at http://www1.cord.edu/faculty/sprunger/e315/psalm23.htm.

- Johann Sebastian Bach's Cantata 85, "Ich bin ein guter Hirt" (I am the good Shepherd) is based on the shepherd theme in the Bible. It includes a solo chorale based on Psalm 23. Psalms 18 through 29 in various musical settings, including Psalm 23 arranged by Charles Hylton Stewart, are available on *Psalms from St. Pauls,* Volume 2, performed by the St. Paul's Cathedral Choir on Hyperion Records.

itual: God still leads the psalmist, but the metaphor of the shepherd is no longer evident. This second type of "leading" involves the psalmist's soul, which God "restoreth" by guiding the psalmist "in the paths of righteousness." Righteousness here probably refers to the Hebrew law, which is extensively delineated throughout the first books of the Old Testament and was regarded by the Hebrew people as a direct expression of God. By following the Hebrew law, the psalmist is paying tribute to God and furthering God's influence. Thus, it is in his own "name's sake" that God leads the speaker to righteousness.

Line 4:

In the fourth verse the psalmist discusses faith in terms of trust—which is perhaps the purest expression of faith. The verse also contains implications of misfortunes in the speaker's life. These are conveyed through the second-most famous metaphor in the poem: "the valley of the shadow of death." Valleys in ancient Palestine represented many good and terrifying aspects of life. They were places for grazing sheep and for building cities but also for battles. In this verse, the valley is one of death and evil, but because the speaker has utter trust in God as shepherd, he or she is free from fear. God is close by, protecting the speaker with the shepherd's tools: a rod for use as a weapon, and a staff for support. The psalmist's sense of personal closeness with God is emphasized by the shift from third to second person: whereas before he referred to God as "He," now he uses "Thou."

Line 5:

In verse 5, the metaphor for God shifts from shepherd to host. The role of host in most ancient civilizations was an important one. A host was obligated to provide his guests with comfort and pleasure, but he was also responsible for the protection of anyone staying in his house. God as host provides a table for a feast, perhaps the sacrificial feast conducted in the Temple as part of Hebrew religious ceremony. This feast includes an abundance of wine ("my cup runneth over") as well as oil. Oil in ancient Hebrew culture had many uses. It was often a sign of opulence, and people who could afford oil applied it to their bodies as an expression of gladness and refreshment. Oil was also used to soften wounds, which in this verse might reflect the danger implied in verse 4. But most significant is the ritual of "anointing" in which the Hebrews applied oil to the foreheads of kings, priests, and the sick to symbolize blessing and purification. Though the psalmist is a helpless lamb, he or she is also like a king by virtue of closeness with God. At the same time, however, the speaker is like the sick, vulnerable to death and in need of God's blessing.

Line 6:

The last verse is a final declaration of hope and faith. The hope is eternal: the psalmist's faith transcends the barriers of time and thus makes the stay in "the house of the Lord" one that will last "for ever." Since all guests must eventually leave, the last line suggests the psalmist is in fact not a guest but rather a member of the household. As such, he or she is indefinitely entitled to the shelter of the house and the pleasures offered by God.

Themes

Protection and Security

A major theme in the psalm is the security that the Lord provides and will continue to provide; this security includes such things as food and drink, shelter from enemies, and protection in hostile circumstances. This theme is introduced in the psalm's famous first line, "The Lord is my shepherd." In this line and the following three verses, the speaker proclaims that the Lord will care for him the same way a shepherd cares for his flock. When the speaker announces "I shall not want," he is confident that his shepherd will provide everything he needs. Some scholars see an ambiguity in this line as well. They believe that the ancient Hebrew can also mean "I shall not go missing" or "I shall not become separated from the flock," which for a sheep in the wilderness would be fatal.

Later the Lord is portrayed as a host who provides shelter from one's enemies. Although the speaker sits "in the presence of mine enemies," he is in no danger from them. Indeed, he will be protected from *all* danger, even if he walks "through the valley of the shadow of death." The Lord's staff will provide guidance, his rod defense. Verse 4 is the only depiction of this very real and powerful danger. The Lord's abundant protection eliminates any fear the speaker would otherwise have.

Trust

Psalm 23 is a celebration of trust in the Lord, in his protection and goodness. The simple, direct language of the psalm conveys utter confidence. When the psalmist writes "I shall not want" in the first verse, it is obvious he feels no doubt whatsoever. In the fourth verse, halfway through, the speaker expresses his unwavering conviction in the protection the Lord provides. Regardless what happens, no matter how threatening the situation, "I will fear no evil." The speaker knows the Lord will protect him. The final verse of Psalm 23 sums up the speaker's faith. "Surely goodness and mercy shall follow me all the days of my life." Based on what the Lord does for him everyday, he concludes that he has nothing to fear in the future.

The psalmist expresses his trust in the Lord in two ways. In the first three and a half verses, he proclaims his trust in the Lord's goodness to the world. When he writes "he restoreth my soul," readers have the impression that they are being addressed personally, that the psalmist is telling them of his trust in the Lord. Midway through verse 4, however, the form of address abruptly changes. The speaker no longer refers to the Lord as "He" but as "Thou." Describing the moment of greatest danger, the psalmist speaks to the Lord directly and makes a personal confession of trust.

Rites of Passage

The psalm depicts a journey, similar to that in Exodus in which the Israelites were led out of Egypt across the desert to the Promised Land. At the beginning of the psalm, the speaker compares himself to a sheep guided by a shepherd. "He maketh me to lie down in green pastures: he leadeth me beside the still waters ... he leadeth me in the paths of righteousness."

In the Exodus story, Moses led his people out of Egypt. Midway through the psalm, the speaker passes through "the valley of the shadow of Death," similar to the forty years of wandering in the desert. The danger is only imagined by the speaker. Nevertheless the threat has been overcome, the passage complete, and the speaker is welcomed into the safety of Lord's household. At first the speaker is a guest. But ultimately, in the psalm's final "passage," the speaker is adopted as a member of the Lord's own family.

So the psalm depicts a rite of passage that begins with faith in the Lord, faith that leads through danger to salvation. That it is movement toward greater good is obvious in the steady improvement in the status of the speaker. He begins as a sheep in a flock, is welcomed as a guest by the Lord, and ultimately attains the status of family member.

The Covenant

The Covenant was the solemn agreement that established a special relationship between the Lord and the Jewish people. As a result of the relationship, the Jews were marked as the Lord's chosen people on earth. Psalm 23 depicts this holy covenant; as the first sign, the speaker addresses the Lord as "Thou" rather than referring to him as "He," which suggests a much more personal relationship. In verse 5, the Lord is portrayed as host who takes the speaker in and provides food and protection. Significantly, the Lord surpasses the normal expectations of a host; for example, "thou annointest my head with oil," a ritual usually reserved for honored guests, suggests a very special relationship.

In ancient Israel, covenants were sealed with a meal. That the meal has sealed a special relationship between the Lord and the psalmist is obvious when he writes "I will dwell in the house of the Lord for ever." The Lord has made the speaker a member of his immediate family. Family bonds imply the special relationship, for family members have duties toward the rest of the family, and they reap special benefits from their place in the family.

Topics for Further Study

- What contemporary profession could you use as a metaphor for God? Write a poem that extends the metaphor, showing specific parts of the job and explaining how these are similar to things God does.

- Which one stanza do you think fits most awkwardly into the poem? Which one stanza do you think best captures the thought and feeling of the entire poem? Explain the reasons you came to these conclusions.

Style

In ancient Hebrew poetry, the verse comprises the basic unit of thought. Generally the verse is broken into two parts in which the idea expressed in the first is balanced or expanded in the second. This characteristic is called parallelism, and there are several types common in the psalms. One type, synthetic parallelism, involves the explanation or elaboration in the second part of an idea presented in the first part. This is the chief device used in Psalm 23, and good examples of it can be seen in verses 4 and 5. In verse 4, the first part declares that the speaker walks "through the valley of the shadow of death," but is not afraid. The second part explains why: God is with the speaker, protecting him or her the way a shepherd protects a lamb. Verse 5 shows a slightly different type of synthetic parallelism. While the first part introduces the idea of a "table" that God has prepared for the psalmist, the second part elaborates the idea with specific images. The table becomes a feast, replete with "oil" and a cup that "runneth over."

Historical Context

The Composition of the Psalms

The precise date of their composition has never been firmly established by scholars. Traditions extending back to ancient times credit them to King

Compare & Contrast

- **1611:** Shakespeare completes his last play, *The Tempest,* and retires from the theater.

  Today: Andrew Lloyd Weber's plays, such as *Cats, Phantom of the Opera,* and *Evita,* have dominated theater the world over for more than two decades.

- **1611:** Blocked by ice the entire winter, seamen mutiny against Captain Henry Hudson during a voyage in search of a Northwest Passage to China. Hudson is put ashore on the bay that will later bear his name. He is never heard from again.

  Today: American astronauts and Russian cosmonauts work together on the MIR space station despite a series of mishaps, including malfunctioning oxygen systems, corroded hull sections, and occasional fires.

- **1611:** Johannes Kepler invents the astronomical telescope.

  Today: Built at a cost of more than $1 billion, the Hubble Space Telescope, from its orbit high over the earth, provides 100 times better resolution than the best earth-based telescopes.

- **1611:** John Rolfe learns tobacco cultivation from the Indians. The first crop is introduced at Jamestown, Virginia, and provides the financial stability the colony desperately needs.

  Today: The tobacco industry, accused of selling products harmful to public health, is forced to pay a government settlement totaling billions of dollars.

- **1611:** George Chapman completes the first great English translation of Homer's *Iliad.*

  Today: Computer scientists struggle without success to develop software that will enable a computer to make accurate translations from one natural language to another.

David who lived around 1000 B.C.E. It is known that David had a reputation as a skilled lyre player and composer, and was supposed to have organized the guilds of temple singers and musicians that would have performed the psalms. In addition to this evidence, Davidic authorship is often supported by lines in the psalms themselves. For example, the end of Psalm 72 states: "The prayers of David son of Jesse are ended." However, some scholars believe these lines were added sometime after the original composition.

Experts now believe that the psalms were written by several authors over a long period extending from the time of David, through the Babylonian exile (587-539 B.C.E.), to the period of Persian domination (539-450 B.C.E.) when Israel enjoyed a time of religious and cultural revival. It is known that a collection of psalms were sung in the Second Temple of Jerusalem built under the Persians.

A Greek translation that corresponds to the Book of Psalms and to older Hebrew documents found among the Dead Sea Scrolls was made in Alexandria circa 130 B.C.E. for Jews living in Egypt. It seems probable that the Greek translators had problems with the Hebrew, much of which was completely obsolete by their time. This indicates to historians that a considerable time, probably measuring in centuries, had passed since the original collection had been put together.

The King James Version

In January of 1604, King James I proposed that a new English translation of the Bible be made. At that time, there were two English versions in widespread use which reflected the split in the English church. The Church of England used the Bishops Bible; the Puritan sect preferred what was known as the Geneva Bible. King James called for a Bible "consonant as can be to the original Hebrew and Greek ... without any marginal notes." Marginal notes in earlier English versions had been used less for biblical exegesis than for political and theological attacks on opponents. The king wanted a uniform version that would cut across denominational lines.

Fifty-four translators, both Anglican and Puritan, organized into six groups and took nearly five years to compete the work. The translation was never intended to be a completely original translation. The King James translators were instructed use the Bishops Bible as the basis for their work and to compare it with the Hebrew and Greek originals. However, they were allowed—even encouraged—to consult other works; for example, they looked at the Latin Vulgate version, earlier English translations, Martin Luther's famous German translation, and translations into other European languages. They also consulted with other biblical scholars and translators.

In the course of their work, the King James translators read every verse of the bible aloud to better measure their rhythm and balance. The King James Bible was thus eminently suited to be preached aloud in church. It was published in 1611, and the king stipulated that it was to be read in every English church, a fact which contributed greatly to its quick popularity. One hundred and eighty–two editions were published by 1644; it eventually supplanted even the Puritan's Geneva Bible.

The language of the King James Bible is conservative. The translators consciously favored older, even obsolete forms (for example, "Thou preparest a table before me in the presence of mine enemies" in Psalm 23) over more modern forms that were already in common use in the 1600s. The archaic language gave the Bible an austerity, even at its time of publication. This was felt to be more appropriate than everyday speech for the Holy Scriptures.

However, the overall language of the Bible was kept relatively simple. It has a vocabulary of less than 8,000 words, which is less than half the total vocabulary in the works of William Shakespeare, considered the other great influence on modern English. Among the many expressions from the King James Bible that have passed into everyday use are "an eye for an eye," "the skin of my teeth," "the apple of his eye," "a man after his own heart," "out of the mouths of babes," and "at their wits' end."

Critical Overview

The eighteenth-century critic J. G. Herder writes about the sudden transition in metaphor from God as shepherd to God as host. He speculates that Psalm 23 was composed while its author was in exile from Palestine, which explains the psalm's emphasis on the idea of a secure resting place, the "house of the Lord." It also explains the significance of the feast spread out in "the presence of mine enemies" and the urgent shift from the valley to the table. "The sudden transition from one image to another," he writes, "is in the spirit of the Oriental ode. Yet but one feeling pervades the whole." Psychoanalyst Erich Fromm contrasts the mood of Psalm 23 with that of some other psalms. Rather than boasting "that he is good, that God will reward him, and that the wicked shall perish," writes Fromm, the psalmist conveys a quieter but perhaps more convincing resolve. "The elements of smugness, self-righteousness, and indignation are lacking," Fromm writes, "and instead we find a mood of quiet confidence and inner peace."

Criticism

Jhan Hochman

Jhan Hochman is a writer and instructor at Portland Community College in Portland, Oregon. In the following essay, Hochman examines the metaphorical language used in Psalm 23.

The word *psalm* is derived from a Greek word meaning a twitching, or to twitch or strum, especially the strings of a harp, lyre, or kithara. One of the Greek forms of the word also refers to a song sung to the accompaniment of the lyre, an early form of the guitar. In the context of the Old Testament psalms, of which Psalm 23 is a part, a psalm is not just any song sung to the accompaniment of a stringed instrument. It is a religious song—or better, a hymn. Psalms are most often spoken or chanted because their melodies have been lost to us.

The Old Testament Psalter, that is, the Book of Psalms, is comprised of 150 psalms divided into five parts in imitation of the Pentateuch, the first five books of the Old Testament (Genesis, Exodus, Leviticus, Numbers and Deuteronomy). The psalms have been classified into the following kinds: hymns (acts of praise); laments (solicitations by individuals for deliverance from sickness or

What Do I Read Next?

- The Book of Genesis in the King James Bible is one of the most celebrated renditions of the story of creation.

- William Tynsdale was the first great English Bible translator and much of his work found its way into the King James Version. David Danielle's *William Tyndale: A Biography* relates the story of Tyndale's work and his eventual martyrdom.

- The poet John Donne was alive at the time the King James Bible was published. Later in his life Donne gave up poetry and turned to religion. His *Sermons* combine beautiful language and deep religious insight.

- John Bunyan's allegory, *The Pilgrim's Progress,* was written nearly seventy years after the King James Bible. A best-seller in its day, it describes the Puritan's view of a Christian's pilgrimage toward salvation.

- *The Anatomy of Melancholy* by Robert Burton is a famous early work of human psychology published in 1621.

- In contrast to the Bible, John Locke's *Essay Concerning Human Understanding* (1690) attempts to explain human knowledge from a strict empiricist or scientific point of view.

---

false accusations, or solicitations by a nation for help in times of crisis); songs of trust (expressions of confidence in God's readiness to help); thanksgivings (gratitude for deliverance); sacred histories (recountings of God's dealings with the nation); royal psalms (accompaniments for coronations and royal weddings); wisdom psalms (meditations on life and God); and liturgies (compositions for specific occasions). Psalm 23 is considered a song of trust as are Psalms 11, 16, 27, 62, 131. Psalm 23 is one of the best known of all the psalms, chanted in churches and synagogues throughout America, and even occasionally making an appearance in popular culture. For example, it was prominently featured in Quentin Tarantino's film *Pulp Fiction.*

More than half of the psalms were thought to be composed by David, the second King of Israel who reigned from 1010 to his death in 970 B.C. The singer is none other than David, the boy who killed the giant Goliath with a slingshot. Before David became king he was a young shepherd, visited by Samuel and told that he had been chosen by God to be the next king of Israel. The interested student can find out more about David from Samuel 1 (16:1) and Samuel 2.

Psalm 23, composed by David, is meant to soothe the tortured soul and promote trust in God. The setting is peaceful pastureland, an area with which David, as a shepherd, was once familiar. David notices that like himself, God, too, is a "shepherd," and that David, the shepherd, is himself led by God like a sheep or lamb.

In other psalms, we find a variety of metaphors for God. Psalm 62 is perhaps the most fertile. First, God is a rock—rocks appear to last forever without changing, are often immovable, and have a homogeneous oneness about them that other natural entities lack. It is no surprise then that the next metaphor in Psalm 62 is God, the fortress; as a fortress protects from one's enemies, so, hopefully, will God. Notice that in Psalm 23, a fortress would have been more comparable to God's house (the temple) or the shepherd's pasture than to God Himself. In other words, the metaphorical leap is larger, and arguably more provocative in Psalm 62 than in Psalm 23.

The next metaphor in Psalm 62 is God as a refuge, a place of safety from one's enemies. In other psalms, God is light (27), a cup (16), and a mother (131). Perhaps it is not difficult then to understand how God is so conducive to a broad panorama of metaphors since a common comment about God—itself a metaphor—is "God is all."

In another metaphor, God's "lambs" are people. This is the predominant metaphor of the psalm, or more precisely, of the first two stanzas; people are lambs, God is the shepherd. Because a metaphor is a comparison between unlike things, or a yoking together of what is different, metaphors have both strengths and weaknesses. Psalm 23 is no exception.

Let us begin with the strengths of the metaphor. As a shepherd protects his flock from wolves or other predators, God is said to protect people—some or all depending upon your religious belief—from harm. In terms of sheep, "green pastures" and "still waters" (an alternative translation from the Hebrew is "waters of rest") are settings of peace and plenty, places where sheep can drink, eat, and lie down without fear, provided the shepherd is there to guard them. And even when the shepherd leads his flocks to or from the pastures through dangerous territories ("the valley of the shadow of death," alternatively translated as "the valley of deep darkness"), he watches over them, rod ready at hand to scare off or strike at predators.

But among these analogies, David—or far more likely, the translator—moves beyond the metaphor by personifying sheep instead of "sheep-ifying" people. For instance, it is said that God will restore the soul. Sheep seldom are thought to have souls. The Hebrew word, however, could have more accurately been translated as "lives" which would have still maintained the analogy in David's metaphor. In a second example, there are the "paths of righteousness." Sheep are seldom thought to be concerned about issues of morality, religious right and wrong. Again, however, the Hebrew is more accurately translated as "right paths," which is in keeping with David's noticing that both sheep and people walk on paths through pastures, valleys, or forests.

The psalm's central weakness, more attributable to David than the translator, is that the psalm can be read in a different way. Shepherds guard sheep only from *other* predators. When the sheep have been readied or the shepherd is ready, sheep are shorn for their wool and later killed for food. In this way shepherds are more like prison guards in charge of a prisoner readied for execution. The guards look out for the prisoner; they feed him, talk to him, make sure he does not get killed by other prisoners. If the metaphor is read in this way, a way David surely did not mean, the psalm turns sinister and contradictory.

The metaphor of the lamb as a victim of the Shepherd (God) is pertinent when Christ is called the "Lamb of God"; according to God's plan, he is slaughtered like a scapegoat for the sake of all people. And as lambs are eaten by people, so is Christ also "eaten" in Mass as the host, or wafer, for the purpose of sustaining those who partake.

David as a killer of lambs becomes a more feasible perception when we learn from Samuel 1 that David left his sheep shortly before killing Goliath, telling King Saul that he was able to fight the far more experienced and larger warrior because he previously killed lions and bears who had threatened his sheep. Not only did David fell Goliath with a stone, but David stabbed him with a sword and then cut his head off. Later, he killed 200 Philistines and, in a rather curious method of scalping, brought home the Philistinian foreskins to King Saul, which enabled David to marry King Saul's daughter. Perhaps in this light, the role of the shepherd as killer of sheep and their predators is not, after all, so distant from that of the warrior, especially since the shepherd often castrates his sheep like David mutilated the genitals of his slain foes.

In the third stanza of Psalm 23, the metaphor of sheep and shepherd is abandoned. David now imagines himself a "kind of guest in "the house of the Lord"—that is, the Jewish synagogue or temple, sitting at a table with God as the generous host. God consecrates, or makes sacred, his follower with a cleansing oil and fills David's cup until it overflows, the overflowing cup as a symbol of life's bounties. As long as people worship in the temple, David seems to say, they will have good lives.

The third stanza's central metaphor, temple as pasture, implies that for David the "house of the Lord" is protected and bountiful due to God's generous hospitality, much like pastures are protected and bountiful for sheep because of shepherds. Here, we might notice that as pasturing sheep are threatened by "evil" in "the valley of the shadow of death," the worshipper in the synagogue is threatened by "enemies" ready to slander or assault the righteous dining "in the house of the Lord." Some readers have confused the "house of the Lord" with heaven, primarily because of the last words in the line "I shall dwell in the house of the Lord *for ever.*" But the translation, "for ever" can be replaced by the alternative, "as long as I live." Such a translation lends clarity to the locale of the temple. The temple protects the person who worships there and follows the path created by God.

In summary, then, David's metaphorical language expresses these concepts: pasture as temple of Israel, sheep are like worshippers, shepherd equals God. Only by trusting in the Lord within the temple, David implies, are worshippers able to escape one's enemies.

Source: Jhan Hochman, in an essay for *Poetry for Students,* Gale, 1998.

Gene Rice

In the following essay, Rice elaborates on the metaphors and imagery used in Psalm 23.

In times of anxiety, danger, or sorrow, Psalm 23, as few other passages of Scripture, mothers the human heart. Although Psalm 23 is one of the most familiar texts of the Bible, there is a perennial freshness about it. Deep wells of meaning are opened by the metaphors of shepherd and sheep, of host and guest, and they speak to one at whatever one's level of sophistication.

The LORD is my shepherd, I shall not want (v. 1; RSV).

For a people with arable land, fenced fields, and an urban, industrial way of life, the metaphor of shepherd may not resonate with its full measure of meaning. Even if one knows something about sheep and the care of them, the grazing land of Palestine is quite unlike that of contemporary America. For the most part, the pastures of Palestine consist of trackless, arid hillocks and jagged ravines, rained upon only for a few months out of the year and beaten upon relentlessly by the sun during the summer. But the harshness of the landscape is occasionally relieved by "hollows as gentle and lovely as those ravines are terrible, where water bubbles up and runs gently between grassy banks through the open shade of trees" [according to George Adam Smith in his *Four Psalms,* 1896]. It is in such a setting as this that we are to visualize the shepherd at work in Psalm 23.

The demands on the shepherd are eloquently described by Jacob in his defense of himself to Laban. "It was like this with me: by day the heat consumed me, and the cold by night, and my sheep fled from my eyes" (Gen. 31:38–40). God's promise to the exiles in Babylon to be a shepherd to them calls attention to the many tasks of the shepherd. "I will make them lie down, says the Lord GOD. I will seek the lost, and I will bring back the strayed, and I will bind up the injured, and I will strengthen the weak" (Ezek, 34:15; cf. Luke 15:3–6). And the tenderness of the shepherd is touchingly pictured in the Isaianic picture of the return from exile, when God will "gather the lambs in his arms, … carry them in his bosom, and gently lead those that are with young" (Isa. 40:11).

The metaphor of shepherd thus reverberates with tones of selfless devotion, alertness, concern, tenderness, and security. Not surprisingly, it is a favorite image in the biblical world and is applied to judges, kings, prophets, and especially God.

The metaphor of sheep is likewise used to express Israel's relation to her leaders and to God. Without her king, Israel was like sheep without a shepherd. Israel was God's flock and the sheep of God's pasture. Normally, God as shepherd was thought of in relation to Israel as a flock. It is a rare and bold act when the psalmist claims the LORD as personal shepherd (elsewhere only by Jacob in Gen. 48:15). By doing so, the psalmist gives the metaphor its greatest intimacy and depth.

When the psalmist claims God as shepherd, the psalmist implicitly likens himself or herself to a sheep—not a very flattering comparison. One of the most vulnerable of animals, a sheep is helpless without leadership, guidance, care, and protection. And sheep are prone to get lost, injure themselves, and blindly follow the impulses of the flock. By this comparison, the psalmist acknowledges inadequacy, dependence, and need for a Shepherd; thus the psalmist becomes like a little child (Mark 10:15).

The psalmist completes the initial confession of faith with the affirmation, "I shall not want," *lo' 'eshsar,* a verbal phrase without an object. The lack of an object opens this affirmation to the widest possible meaning. Material well-being is certainly embraced within this statement but is by no means its sole content. The psalmist's religion embraces the totality of life, both spiritual and material.

Content is given to the psalmist's opening confession in the following description of the shepherd's feeding, guiding, and protecting the sheep. First the image of feeding.

He makes me lie down in green pastures; he leads me beside still waters; he restores my soul.

Skillfully wending his way through endless tracts of scrubby, tough, dried-up herbage, the shepherd guides the sheep to those special places, known only to himself, where the grass is fresh, tender, and succulent. There the shepherd lets the sheep graze leisurely so that they may relish their food. "After the sheep have eaten their fill, he does not immediately lead them to drink; otherwise, some of them might bloat to death" [according to Samuel Terrien in *The Psalms and Their Meaning for Today*]. Avoiding those places where the stream is rapid and dangerous, the shepherd seeks out a place where the water is calm and restful so that the sheep may safely slake their thirst, rest, and be renewed.

This is a strikingly "materialistic" picture. There is unconcealed delight in food, rest, and renewal, unmarred by consciousness of a distinction between sacred and secular. It should be noted, however, that what the sheep delights in are the basic and simple things of life. While the sheep are free of want and relish those things that satisfy their basic needs, their life is not one of luxury and indulgence, nor is their life a sated seeking after plea-sure for its own sake.

The meaning of this imagery is transparent. The psalmist is alluding to the task of earning a livelihood and to the simple, everyday activities of life. As the sheep travel far and endure the hard-ships of the journey, so the psalmist most likely works hard to supply the material needs of life. Yet the psalmist knows zest, joy, and serenity in earning a livelihood because even in this area of life God is shepherd. Living in trustful surrender to God, the psalmist is not anxious about life, about what to eat or drink or wear (Matt. 6:25). The psalmist is not one with tension headaches or high blood pressure, nor one feverishly caught up in the lust for things or in need of mood-altering drugs. The psalmist's faith has permeated every-day events and work and has made of them a sacrament.

The psalmist next pictures the guidance of the shepherd.

He leads me in paths of righteousness for his name's sake.

Because the choice nooks of pasture and of safe watering places are few and far between, the shepherd and his sheep need to be constantly on the move. The shepherd guides his sheep so that at the end of the day they arrive at a suitable lodging place for the night. In the open pasture land of Palestine is a bewildering maze of paths. But God, the shepherd, knows the right paths, the paths that lead to the desired goal and that fulfill the purpose of the journey. Such guidance is part of the re-sponsibility of a shepherd. The shepherd's name (i.e., character and reputation) are at stake. And as a Near Eastern shepherd, God leads rather than dri-ves the sheep.

As paths that lead to the desired goal are im-portant in the pasture land of Palestine, so are paths in life. Just as a sheep is inadequate to make its way in a trackless pastureland, so the psalmist affirms that we are not able to make our way in life on our own. The psalmist knows that some paths seem right, but their end is death (Prov: 14:12). The psalmist also knows that although life is like the pastureland of Palestine, there is One whose very nature it is to lead a person in paths of righteousness, paths that give meaning and pur-pose to life, paths that lead to the fulfillment of a person's God-appointed destiny. Even with the best guidance, however, life is not free of anxiety and danger.

The metaphors of shepherd and sheep perfectly capture the trustful submission and the care, provision, guidance, and protection that flow from this relationship."

Even though I walk through the valley of the shadow of death, I fear no evil; for thou art with me; thy rod and thy staff, they comfort me.

The words of the psalmist suggest a time in the late afternoon when the sun is about to set and the valleys are slowly filling up with shadows. This gloom provides a hiding place for beasts of prey and robbers. It is a place where death is a real pos-sibility. (*Tzalmaweth* means literally "darkest val-ley."…) If they are to reach the desired lodging place for the night, the shepherd and the sheep will have times when there is no choice but to go through such a valley. But even in that situation the sheep proceed with confidence because their shep-herd is with them, going ahead, picking out a se-cure path, and staying ready with a rod to ward off preying animals or robbers and with a staff to give the shepherd sure footing and to keep the sheep in good order.

Again, the landscape of Palestine serves as a counterpart of life. The deep, dark gorge is as much a part of the scene as the trackless pastureland, the glens of green grass, and the still waters. Life, too, has its anxieties and dangers, and sometimes one cannot escape them. The psalmist's life has not been all serenity and repose. That a real experience underlies the imagery of the valley of the shadow of death is suggested by the unconscious turning from the third to the second person: "For *thou* art with me." A life-threatening experience may have been the occasion that inspired this psalm. In any case, it is because of the experience of God's pres-ence in the midst of anxiety and danger that the psalmist can speak with such assurance. Trust in God does not exempt one from the valley of the shadow of death. But when God is with us—and this is "the salvation word par excellence of Scripture" [According to Patrick D. Miller Jr., in *Interpreting the Psalms*]—even this valley can be traversed victoriously.

With the scene of the sheep negotiating the dark, dangerous valley at the end of the day under the watchful and protective care of the shepherd, the psalmist concludes the use of the metaphors of shepherd and sheep. In the series of scenes illustrating the shepherd's care of the sheep, the psalmist encompasses experience in the world and shows how life has been illumined and blessed because of this special relationship to God. The metaphors of shepherd and sheep perfectly capture the trustful submission and the care, provision, guidance, and protection that flow from this relationship. Turning next to the experience of worship at the house of the LORD, the temple, the psalmist describes what happens there and uses the metaphors of host and guest.

> Thou preparest a table before me in the presence of my enemies; thou anointest my head with oil, my cup overflows.

This verse transports one into a completely different setting and atmosphere. The psalmist is now present at the temple and is made to feel like a welcomed and honored guest of the LORD.

Shepherd is a powerful metaphor and tends to dominate the interpretation of Psalm 23, but the metaphor of host is not without its own richness of meaning. The Near Eastern host is unrivaled for cordiality, graciousness, generosity, and attentiveness. These qualities are vividly illustrated by Abraham's treatment of the three (divine) travelers who visit him at Hebron in Genesis 18. The venerable patriarch is so pleased that the three strangers have turned aside to his tent that he runs to meet them, bows to the ground, and entreats them to honor him with their presence. Assuming that they are hot, tired, and thirsty, he urges them to stop and rest in the shade of the trees so that they may have their feet bathed and eat a "morsel." Pleased and excited by their acceptance, Abraham hastens into the tent and urges Sarah to quickly prepare generous portions of bread from the finest meal. Then he runs to the herd, chooses a calf "tender and good," and has his servant, who catches Abraham's excitement, hasten to prepare it. As his guests eat, Abraham hovers by them, attentive to their every need.

As the metaphor of shepherd is paired with that of sheep, so the metaphor of host is paired with that of guest. As anyone who has known genuine hospitality can testify, such an experience is a high mo-

ment in human relationships. The metaphors of host and guest have a dimension of depth and intimacy that is not true of the metaphors of shepherd and sheep. A sheep may delight in the security of being provided for, guided, and protected by its shepherd, but a guest may enjoy full rapport with his or her host. Thus the metaphors of host and guest complement and add a significant dimension to the metaphors of shepherd and sheep. As the guests of Abraham were made welcome, accepted, and honored, so is the psalmist in the experience of worship at the temple. Is it not the experience of being God's guest at the temple that is the basis of the psalmist's knowing God as shepherd in the world?

As a guest of the LORD, the psalmist participates in a communion sacrifice in which part of an animal is offered to God and the rest is eaten in a festive meal by the psalmist with family and friends. Such a meal was a joyful, sacramental occasion in which one renewed one's bond with God and one's fellow worshipers (cf. Ps. 22:26). Since the meal was eaten in the temple precincts and those participating were the LORD's guests, it was appropriate to refer to the LORD as preparing a table for the psalmist.

The quality of the LORD's reception of the psalmist is illustrated by the reference to the anointing of the head with oil and the filling of the cup of wine to overflowing. The anointing with oil tangibly expresses the acceptance, the cordiality, and the care with which the psalmist is received in God's house. The overflowing cup of wine symbolizes the blessing and exhilaration of communion with God and fellow worshipers. The psalmist has drunk from the rivers of God's delights (Ps. 36:8); the psalmist's soul is feasted as with marrow and fat (Ps. 63:5).

As a guest of the LORD, the psalmist also enjoys the protection of the host and, in the LORD's presence, feels secure from enemies. The enemies are not identified nor is there any indication of why the psalmist regards them as such. Are the enemies persons who have accused the psalmist of some offense that required trial by a religious tribunal, and is the psalmist giving thanks for having been vindicated? Or are the enemies hostile, foreign troops stationed in Palestine? Or are the enemies godless members of the psalmist's own society who scoff at and oppose the psalmist? Is there a connection between the enemies and the psalmist's experience of going through the valley of the shadow of death?

The reference to the psalmist's enemies is too general and brief for us to be able to identify them and to know the cause of their enmity. Still, the reference is a reminder that the life of the psalmist is not sheltered and idyllic, removed from hostility and threat. And it is significant that the psalmist does not curse the enemies or ask God to destroy them, as some psalmists do. Whoever the enemies are and whatever the reason for their enmity, they are no longer a threat to the psalmist who, because of God's presence, is secure and triumphant.

Still aglow with the companionship and hospitality of the host at the temple, the psalmist's thoughts turn to the time of leaving this blessed place.

> Surely goodness and mercy shall follow me all the days of my life; and I shall dwell in the house of the LORD forever.

As the psalmist anticipates leaving the temple, it is with the certainty that one is not abandoned upon leaving the holy place. While God's presence and companionship are known in a special way at the temple, they are by no means confined to it. The psalmist knows that God's presence, personified as goodness and mercy, follows (literally, "pursues" translated from *radap*) one in the world. And this pursuit is not momentary, but all the days of one's life. Goodness (*tob*) and mercy (*hesed,* elsewhere translated "steadfast love") are basic attributes of God that evoke thanksgiving and praise. Goodness is the gracious, compassionate benevolence of God demonstrated in creation and in deliverance from oppression and want. Mercy is the commitment that maintains the integrity of a relationship. The pairing of mercy with goodness expresses God's determination to see that goodness prevails.

The traditional translation, "and I shall dwell in the house of the LORD," follows Syriac, Targum, and Vulgate (*weyāšabtî*). The Septuagint and Symmachus translate, "And my dwelling shall be in the house of the LORD" (*wešibtî*). But the Hebrew (MT) reads, "and I shall return to the house of the LORD" (*wešabtî*). The word translated "forever," *le'ōrek yāmîm,* means literally, "for length of days" (i.e., a very long time, note the parallel with "all the days of my life" and cf. NRSV, "my whole life long"). Because of the reference to being pursued by goodness and mercy, it seems clear that the psalmist contemplates returning to the world. And from the psalmist's description of life in the world in verses 1–4, it does not appear that the psalmist wishes to retreat from the world. Prob-ably the intention of the psalmist is best represented by the Hebrew text (MT) and its sense is best expressed by the translation, [by Bernard W. Anderson in *Out of the Depths: The Psalms Speak for Us Today,*] "And I shall be a guest in Yahweh's house as long as I live." Yet the traditional translation is true to the inherent depths of the passage and should be retained, for it is clear that the psalmist is sure that the communion experienced as God's guest will not be broken (cf. Rom. 8:39).

Great literature has such depth and breadth that it may reveal its total meaning only over a period of time or that it may assimilate new meaning. The change from return of the Hebrew (Masoretic) text to dwell by the Greek, Syriac, Targum, and Vulgate shows that the deeper implications of the text were felt within Judaism. And because Jesus identified himself as the good shepherd and laid down his life for his sheep (John 10:1–18; cf. 1 Pet. 2:25; 5:4), the words of Psalm 23 have been filled with new meaning for the Christian. Jesus, for the Christian, is the shepherd who "restores our souls, leads us in paths of righteousness, accompanies us through danger, spreads the holy supper before us in the presence of sin and death, and pursues us in his gracious love all the days of our lives" [remarks James L. Mays in *Psalms* 1994]. And the comfort this psalm gives at funerals attests the fuller meaning given to dwelling in the house of the LORD by Jesus' victory over death and preparation of a place for his followers (John 14: 1–3). "The Lord has touched it with his finger, and enlarged its horizons" [according to J.R.P. Schlater in an article in *The Interpreter's Bible*].

The word *faith* is not found in Psalm 23, but here is one of the finest expressions of the reality of faith in the Bible. The metaphor of sheep eloquently captures the trustful dependence of the life of faith, and the metaphor of guest vividly pictures the joyous fellowship of the faith relationship. Both metaphors emphasize that faith is a living relationship to a person who is like a shepherd and a host. Together, the metaphors of sheep and guest define faith in its full range of meaning and consequences. The psalm has a hymn-like quality, celebrating the goodness of life lived in trustful companionship with God. By contrast, the psalm exposes the poverty of the Godless person. The psalm is a testimony that knowing God as shepherd and host brings freshness and zest to routine activities, direction and meaning to the competing pressures and demands on life, confidence and courage in the face of danger, triumph and fullness in spite of adversity, and assurance of victory over death and uninterruped communion with God.

Source: Gene Rice, "An Exposition of Psalm 23," in *The Journal of Religious Thought,* Vol. 52, No. 1, Summer/Fall 1995, pp. 71–78.

Sources

Fromm, Erich, "The Psalms," in *You Shall Be As Gods: A Radical Interpretation of the Old Testament and Its Traditions,* Holt, Rinehart and Winston, 1966, pp. 201-24.

Herder, J. G., *The Spirit of Hebrew Poetry,* translated by James Marsh and Edward Smith, 1833, pp. 222-46.

Lundblom, Jack R., "Psalm 23: Song of Passage," in *Interpretation,* Vol. XL, No. 1, January, 1986.

Tappy, Ron, "Psalm 23: Symbolism and Structure," in *The Catholic Bible Quarterly,* Vol. 57, No. 2, April, 1995.

For Further Study

The New Interpreter's Bible, Vol. IV, Abingdon Press, 1966.
    A massive reference work that provides a line-by-line analysis of the Bible.

Wenham, G. J., J. A. Motyer, D. A. Carson, and R. T. French, *New Bible Commentary,* 21st Century Edition, Intervarsity Press, 1994.
    A useful reference book, with interesting notes on variants between English translations and the original Hebrew text.

Richard Cory

E. A. Robinson
1897

First published in E. A. Robinson's second book of poems, *Children of the Night,* "Richard Cory" is one of the short, lyrical and dramatic character sketches that Robinson is now best known for, although during his life he was most famous for the long poems he wrote later in his career. Robinson created an imaginary place called "Tilbury Town," which he peopled with various failed and frustrated people. Richard Cory is one of those people. The poem may be read as an ironic commentary on the American dream of wealth, success, and power. The very embodiment of that materialistic dream, Cory kills himself for some unspecified reason, perhaps a spiritual emptiness or alienation from his fellow human beings. His death leaves the people who wanted to be like him wondering about the purpose of life. The speaker, a representative of the working-class people who admire and envy Cory, thought of the man in medieval terms as a king. Robinson seems to question the values of both Cory and the speaker, as well as that of the American dream.

Author Biography

A descendent of the colonial poet Anne Bradstreet, Robinson was born in Head Tide, Maine, in 1869 and grew up in the nearby town of Gardiner, his model for the fictitious Tilbury Town that figures prominently in his early verse. His father, Edward Robinson, and mother, Mary Elizabeth Palmer

Edwin Arlington Robinson

Robinson, were descended from old New England families. Robinson's father retired from his successful mercantile business at the age of 51, moving the family to Gardiner at that time so his sons could enjoy a better education.

Robinson's early years were marked by the advantages of an upper middle-class upbringing. He developed an interest in poetry while still in high school, and he was encouraged by a physician neighbor who shared his interest. He published his first poems in a local newspaper and, when he attended Harvard University for two years, in the school's publication *The Harvard Advocate*. But a decline in the family's circumstances forced him to return home. His father died in 1892; a recession in 1893 devastated the family's finances; and his brother Dean, a doctor, developed a drug addiction that eventually cost him his practice and led him to suicide. In 1896 Robinson's mother died of black diptheria, just weeks before *The Torrent and the Night Before,* the author's first, self-published book of poetry appeared.

Robinson lived in the family house with his two brothers and their families until 1897 when, following a dispute with his brother Herman over his wife, Emma, Robinson left for New York City. Some critics surmise that Robinson's recurring po-

etic theme of a triangular love relationship comes from this incident. In 1897 *The Children of the Night,* a gathering of Robinson's poems from his first collection and supplemented with others, was published. In New York Robinson shared an apartment with a friend and became acquainted with a more cosmopolitan society than he had previously known. Among the new people he met in New York was a charming derelict named Alfred H. Louis, who served as a model for the disreputable title character of Robinson's long poem *Captain Craig,* which was published in 1902.

Partly because of the lukewarm critical response to *Captain Craig,* Robinson did little writing for the next several years. He worked for brief periods at a number of jobs, including an office assistant, an advertising editor, and as a time-checker. It was during this period that Robinson also began drinking heavily. But in 1904 *The Children of the Night* attracted the attention of President Theodore Roosevelt after his son sent him a copy of the book from school. Roosevelt was impressed with Robinson's work and recommended it to Scribner's publishing house, which issued a new edition. In addition, Roosevelt gave Robinson a position with the New York Customs House so that he could write without financial worry. Robinson's finances, however, remained insolvent until the late 1920s.

Robinson made his sole trip overseas in 1923, visiting England for six weeks in reaction, so he claimed, to the passage of Prohibition. In 1927 he published his one commercial success, the long poem *Tristram,* based on an ancient legend. The book sold some 57,000 copies in its first year. In 1935 Robinson was diagnosed as having cancer and died just hours after completing corrections to the galleys of his final book. Although Robinson endured early neglect of his poetry, he eventually received three Pulitzer Prizes for his work. He was also awarded the Levinson Prize, a gold medal from the National Institute and the American Academy of Arts and Letters, and several honorary degrees.

Poem Text

Whenever Richard Cory went down town,
We people on the pavement looked at him:
He was a gentleman from sole to crown,
Clean favored, and imperially slim.

And he was always quietly arrayed,   5
And he was always human when he talked;
But still he fluttered pulses when he said,
"Good-morning," and he glittered when he walked.

And he was rich—yes, richer than a king—
And admirably schooled in every grace: 10
In fine, we thought that he was everything
To make us wish that we were in his place.

So on we worked, and waited for the light,
And went without the meat, and cursed the bread;
And Richard Cory, one calm summer night,   15
Went home and put a bullet through his head.

Poem Summary

Lines 1-4:

In the first stanza, the speaker of the poem, one of the "people on the pavement," implies by contrast that Richard Cory is not on the pavement with him and his lower-class peers. The speaker calls Cory a "gentleman," suggesting his upper-class status, and he makes puns on "sole," meaning both the bottoms of shoes and a person's spiritual essence, and "crown," meaning both the top of one's head and a symbol of royalty worn on the head. The word "imperially" also suggests royalty. And the expression "clean favored" may imply both that Cory is well groomed and that he is clearly a man of privilege.

Line 5:

The description of Cory as "quietly arrayed" is an oxymoron because it seems to contradict itself. The word "quietly" implies that Cory is dressed conservatively rather than in loud clothing, but the word "arrayed" means that he is dressed in fancy clothing. "Arrayed" also implies orderliness, and may mean dressed or ordered for battle, suggesting—like the word "crown" earlier—Cory's kingliness. The whole expression may literally refer to a fine, well-pressed, dark-colored suit, but the conflict between the definitions of the two words, when they are applied to clothing, also reflects the speaker's perception of Cory as both normal and superior.

Lines 6-8:

The speaker comments that Cory was "human," or normal, in conversation, yet that he created abnormal excitement ("fluttered pulses") with such regular expressions as "Good-morning." The line break and the comma after "he said" in line 3 allow for an abnormal pause before "Good-morning." This pause dramatizes the second of anticipation one of the people on the pavement might feel in awaiting the simplest of pronouncements from the kingly Cory. Literally, "glittered" may re-

fer to some watch chain or jewelry or tie-pin that Cory wears catching the sunlight, but figuratively it may refer to the armor of a king ready for battle or to the unusual spiritual aura that seems to surround the man.

Lines 9-10:

The speaker compares Cory to a king, at least in wealth, and he remarks that Cory has a good education "in every grace," suggesting both that Cory is well read and may speak several foreign languages, and that he has excellent manners, can make small talk easily, and knows which fork to use at a fancy dinner. The word "grace" also has religious significance; in Christian belief, people are saved from eternal damnation by the grace of God. The speaker's use of the word may imply that he looks upon Cory as blessed.

Lines 11-12:

These lines explain that the speaker and his class ("us") wish that they could be Richard Cory. But the phrasing may indicate rather that they want his kinglike "place" in society. The apparently throwaway phrase "In fine" in line 11 is loaded with possible significance. "Fine" can mean "finery," referring to Cory's clothes, wealth, manners, and education. Or it can mean "the end" (in music), foreshadowing Cory's tragic death. Or it can mean "a monetary penalty"; Cory loses everything when he commits suicide. When these three definitions are read in the poem, they suggest that Cory is everything in finery, in death, and in monetary punishment that could make the speaker wish to be dressed in fine clothes, dead, and with his money taken from him.

Lines 13-16:

At the time he addresses the reader, the speaker already knows that Richard Cory has shot himself in the head. For maximum irony, and to achieve as much shock effect as possible on his audience, the speaker saves this revelation until the end, but he may feel that his behavior and attitude previous to Cory's suicide were inappropriate. He and his working-class peers worked and expected "the light" to come. Meanwhile, they could not afford meat because it was too expensive, and they were unsatisfied with the bread they could afford. "The light" is a vague expression, traditionally suggesting a mental, spiritual, or religious revelation. "The meat" and "the bread" are more concrete physical images, but in sequence with "the light," they may take on more symbolic significance as synecdoches, or ex-

Media Adaptations

- An audio cassette, *Edwin Arlington Robinson,* from the Cross-Cultural Review Chapbook is available from Imperial International Learning.

- Part of the Sound Seminars series, *Robert Pack: On Edwin Arlington Robinson* was released by Jeffrey Norton Co. in 1962.

amples used to represent what they are examples of. "The meat" may represent and be an example of everything they could not afford to have but wanted badly and valued highly, and "the bread" may represent and be an example of everything they could have but did not enjoy or appreciate. Given that Richard Cory kills himself at night, "the light" may suggest a dawn of some sort, one which Richard Cory does not live to see. What seemed a "calm summer night" to the speaker was apparently not so calm for Richard Cory, even if it had the ultimate calming effect on him. And the dawn or revelation that the narrator seems to expect—how to be in Richard Cory's place—ironically come like a bullet in the speaker's head. Richard Cory's place during his life was to be a kingly, upper-class, wealthy gentleman in fine clothes, but after the suicide, Richard Cory's place is a grave. Since the speaker's aim in life seems to have been to be like Richard Cory, Cory's death brings his goals into question, if it does not outright kill them.

Themes

Wealth and Poverty

The poem's last line is pivotal and surprising because Richard Cory is powerful and in control, and a man such as that would seem to have no reason to kill himself. In the first stanza, he is shown to be different from the "people on the pavement," because he is wealthy and powerful. The glamour of Cory's appearance seems to be more impressive than the size of his bank account; his wealth is only

mentioned once, in line eight, and even then it is put in terms of his likeness to royalty and not in terms of what he could actually buy. The reason his wealth is important is that it is thought to have made him a better person—glamorous and cultured—than most people. For those not financially wealthy, it was difficult to just afford meat or fuel for their lamps. They were too busy keeping life and limb together to pay attention to the luxuries of life, like higher education and social status.

With Cory's suicide, it becomes clear that happiness has escaped him. Because he had material success, everyone just assumed he had attained a spiritual peace and emotional fulfillment. They misjudged him because of superficial appearances. Like the narrator, readers are left wondering what money really buys, other than material goods. It turns out that the rich are afflicted with the same despair and spiritual bankruptcy as the rest of the population.

Success and Failure

As this poem demonstrates, success is relative. Richard Cory evidently was not satisfied with what he had accomplished in his life. Many of the townspeople admired him and envied his privileged life. The "light" referred to in the poem's ninth line is just barely symbolic, a mixture of the actual means to pay for gas or electric lighting, of enlightenment, and of God's grace. The people want some sort of approval that would let them feel that they are not failures, that their lives had attained some level of success. Richard Cory evidently did not feel the light's salvation, even though the people of the town all felt that he, if anyone, would have.

Public vs. Private Life

So much attention is given to Richard Cory throughout the first twelve lines of the poem that it is difficult to believe that the poem's speaker did not know him well enough to anticipate the unhappiness that led to his suicide. Looking back, though, after the surprise ending, it is clear that the description of Cory's virtues were superficial and the speaker did not really know him.

Why would a wealthy man like Richard Cory even have a public persona? Assuming that he is not an entertainer, and his income is not dependent on his popularity, why should he hide his despair? Cory's motive for disguising his true self cannot be determined with any certainty from the facts given in this poem. The fact that he seems to be "admirably schooled" is given from the perspective of one of his admirers, making this a very unreliable witness. His outward self may have shown many signs of the coming tragedy that might have been noticed by someone who was less in awe of him. It is almost impossible to tell who created Richard Cory's public image.

Style

"Richard Cory" is a dramatic monologue, meaning that the speaker is assumed to be speaking to an audience. It is divided into four verses of four lines apiece. Each line is in iambic pentameter, meaning that it can be divided into five pairs of accented and unaccented syllables, with the unaccented syllable first. The first line may thus be read in a singsong fashion, as if someone were skipping while reciting:

When **e** / ver **Rich** / ard **Cor** / y **went** / down**town** …

The correct way to read poetry is to downplay these accents and to speak as naturally as possible, but the poet creates effects by varying this expected rhythm pattern to mimic the more complex patterns of human speech. Since it is impractical for a poet to write down every change in tone and voice he wants the reader to intone, the poet plays the reader's tendency to read in a singsong pattern against the reader's wish to read the poem as prose. The conflict between the two readings encourages the reader to find a compromise, and by varying the degree to which the reader is able to read singsong or prosy, the poet guides the reader to use the desired tone.

Other devices modify the accent pattern. For example, words with alliteration tend to be accented. In "Peter Piper picked a peck of pickled peppers," for example, the syllables that start with "p" are read with more emphasis than the other syllables. In line two of "Richard Cory," the singsong reading puts the emphasis on the word "on," but the alliteration with "people" and "pavement" gives more emphasis to the accents on the first syllables of those words and reduces the relative importance of the accent on "on."

The rhyme scheme for "Richard Cory" is *abab cdcd efef ghgh.* This scheme with the last two lines repeating the rhythmical and rhyme pattern of the first two lines creates balance between these pairs of lines, which Robinson uses effectively to give a sense of control to the poem's tone. Robinson ends sentences at the end of each pair of lines, and he slows the reading of the poem by ending clauses

Topics for Further Study

- Write a dialogue between Richard Cory and a Tilbury citizen. Let Cory explain his feelings at the time of his suicide and anticipate the response of the listener. Do they find common ground?

- Write Richard Cory's suicide letter. In it, explain what he was upset about. Did he feel that the world had treated him unjustly, or was he suffering some sort of guilt about the way he had behaved? Be sure to address specific details to the relatives and friends that you think he left behind.

- Why did the people curse the bread? What does that tell you about their feelings about and opinion of Richard Cory?

and phrases at the end of lines and putting commas, colons, and periods there. This technique is called end-stopping because it forces the reader to stop briefly at the end of each line.

Historical Context

The Robber Barons

The last decade of the nineteenth century is considered "The Gay Nineties," implying that it was a festive era during which Americans forgot their worries. This may have been true for the fortunate ones, the millionaires and children of millionaires who enjoyed great fortunes, but, as "Richard Cory" implies, many people at the time were not financially comfortable.

Between the end of the Civil War and the end of the century, America expanded westward, relocating indigenous peoples onto reservations and encouraging Americans to settle on their land. This expansion was driven by railroads, which needed steel, investment capital, and cheap labor. The key industries of the time—including railroads—were controlled by just a few individuals, who are re-

Compare & Contrast

- **1897:** Gold discovered in Alaska the previous year started reaching the United States. Prospectors looking to get rich quickly moved to Alaska, creating the Alaska Gold Rush. By the end of the year, the territory had produced gold worth $22 million dollars.

  1968: Oil was discovered in Alaska's Prudhoe Bay, on the Arctic Circle. During the 1970s environmentalists and indigenous peoples fought construction of the Alaskan Pipeline, which was constructed across thousands of miles of virgin wilderness to pump oil from Alaska's northern coast to Valdez, in the south.

  1989: A tanker loaded with oil from the Alaskan Pipeline crashed a few miles out of Valdez, spilling the million gallons of oil and creating an ecological disaster.

  Today: Alaska still provides approximately one fourth of the oil produced in the United States, but the Prudhoe Bay fields will reach depletion soon.

- **1897:** The population of the United States was estimated around 72,189,000.

  Today: The population of the United States is estimated to be around 250,000,000, with a growth rate of 10 percent per decade.

- **1897:** United States auto manufacturers produced 100 cars, up from 25 the year before.

  Today: The top three auto manufacturers in the United States produce over $375 billion annually.

---

ferred to as the Robber Barons because of the unscrupulous tactics they used to amass their wealth. Today, the names of Jay Gould, Cornelius Vanderbilt, Andrew Carnegie, John D. Rockefeller and J. P. Morgan are most often recognized for the schools, libraries, buildings, and foundations that their money helped to build. Yet citizens of the time knew that these men had built their fortunes by exploiting weak labor laws, bribing public officials, and, in general, transforming the government that the Founding Fathers dreamed of into a government run by wealthy interests.

The lives of these powerful men seemed to follow the same general pattern: they rose from humble, working-class families; accumulated great fortunes by recognizing growing industries; bribed government officials to ensure continuing success; and finally, driving their competitors out of business. For example, J. P. Morgan was a banker who controlled so much wealth that the federal government came to him for a loan during the financial crisis of 1895. He refused because the United States lacked the collateral for a loan, but he was willing to buy millions of dollars in United States bonds, which he quickly resold for an astronomical profit. Cornelius Vanderbilt and Jay Gould made their fortunes building railroads on government land, reasoning that westward expansion was in the public interest, and using steel rails provided by Carnegie's U.S. Steel Corporation. By the 1890s, Rockefeller's Standard Oil Corporation provided 90 percent of all petroleum products used in America.

The Robber Barons were able to control entire segments of the economy by buying up all competition—they were large enough to accept short-term losses if they lowered their prices until their competitors went bankrupt, and then bought the bankrupt business. To get around laws that prohibited owning manufacturing facilities in several states or holding stock in out-of-state companies, Rockefeller legally made Standard Oil into a "trust," which was not legally a company and therefore could do business in all states. Other companies followed; by the early 1890s, 5,000 separate companies were classified under 300 trusts. The Sherman Anti-Trust Act of 1890 was supposed to curb this practice of market control, but the pro-business government seldom enforced it, and numerous exceptions were allowed. In a 1895 case, for example, the Supreme Court refused to apply the antitrust laws to the company that owned 98 percent of the country's sugar-refining capacity, maintaining it was a manufacturing monopoly and not a commercial monopoly, and therefore exempt. By 1900, America was well on its way to becoming one of the world's great industrial giant, but it reached that point by granting favors to a few enterprising individuals.

Organized Labor

At the same time that some individuals were amassing unprecedented fortunes through their control of vital industries and their government connections, most Americans were laboring in unsafe working conditions for wages that barely kept them and their families alive. Trade unions have existed in the United States since the 1790s, and striking had been found legal in court in 1842; but the Civil War devastated the American economy and made it difficult for unions to interest workers in walking away from the jobs they had.

In the 1870s, unions began to gain popularity. The growth of unions can be traced to a few important reasons: the shamelessness of the richest Americans and their conspicuous wealth and indifference to their workers; and newspaper publicity—especially humorous cartoons—depicting the Robber Barons as pigs gorging themselves at the public trough. In addition, the indignation of the workers was compounded by unfair collusion between the wealthy and the government; for example, when several strikers were convicted without any evidence following a bomb explosion at the infamous Haymarket Riot in 1894, occurring during a strike against the McCormick reaper company, workers across the country were enraged.

Some union organizers were inspired by the works of Karl Marx, whose *Communist Manifesto* was published in 1848. This significant political tract inspired people all over the world to explore the relationship between workers and wealth. Two of the most powerful and influential union leaders in the country's history emerged during the 1880s and 1890s: Samuel Gompers, who was the president of the American Federation of Labor from its inception in 1886 until his death in 1924; and Eugene V. Debs, who led the powerful American Railway Union from 1893 to 1897 and then ran for president on the Socialist ticket in 1900, 1904, 1908, 1912 and once again in 1920, while he was serving a jail sentence for his vocal opposition to World War I.

Critical Overview

Robinson is most admired for his ability to write lyric and dramatic poetry. Allen Tate states that "Mr. Robinson's genius is primarily lyrical" and that "Richard Cory" is "a perfect specimen of Mr. Robinson's dramatic powers—when those powers are lyrically expressed."

W. R. Robinson points to "Richard Cory" as one of several poems set in the fictional Tilbury Town, a place of "spiritual crassness and blindness" that links Robinson "with small-town New England, the repressive, utilitarian social climate customarily designated as the Puritan ethic." (The Puritan ethic is the Christian emphasis on good works as evidence that one is saved from eternal damnation in Hell.) Robinson is often compared to Edgar Lee Masters, who wrote similar short-lyric poems on the citizens of a small town in the book *Spoon River Anthology*. Louis Untermeyer says that Robinson is "at his height" in such poems and that "none of the people in *Spoon River* (to which many of these characters bear a sort of avuncular relation) is pictured more surely and unforgettably than ['Richard Cory']."

Since the ending is so important to understanding the poem, critics often judge "Richard Cory" based on whether they like how it ends. Richard P. Adams reads the poem as an anti-materialistic poem and says that Cory's suicide "leaves the reader free to decide, if he has his own courage to do so, that working and waiting and going without, and even cursing on occasion, may be a pretty good life after all." William H. Pritchard seems to agree. He sees Robinson as "someone who relished ironic incongruities" such as the difference between the way the speaker of "Richard Cory" sees Cory and the way Cory's inner life really is. However, Yvor Winters does not value the poem as highly; he calls it a "superficially neat portrait of the elegant man of mystery," and he calls Cory's suicide "a very cheap surprise ending," saying that "all surprise endings are cheap in poetry, if not, indeed, elsewhere, for poetry is written to be read not once but many times."

Criticism

David Kelly

David Kelly is a writer and instructor at Oakton Community College in Des Plaines, Illinois. In the following essay, Kelly examines the role of

What Do I Read Next?

- The connection between Robinson's poems about Tilbury Town, including Richard Cory, and the poems of Edgar Lee Masters' *Spoon River Anthology,* published in 1915, has frequently been noted—both poem sequences provide a view of small-town America.

- Reviewers often compare Robinson to Henry James, a novelist who also explored the American attitude toward wealth. The Dial Press collection from 1944, *The Great Short Novels of Henry James,* includes the classics *Daisy Miller, The Turn of the Screw,* and more.

- All of Robinson's poems, including "Richard Cory," are gathered in *The Collected Poems Of Edwin Arlington Robinson,* published in 1937.

- Sherwood Anderson's classic *Winesburg, Ohio* (1919), tells the stories of citizens in a small town in Ohio.

- A great but often-neglected novel, Ford Madox Ford's *The Good Soldier: A Tale of Passion* also explores human the inner lives of privileged people. The character Richard Cory would fit comfortably into this novel.

---

wealth in the poem, focusing on how it influences the reader.

Americans can rest comfortably with the knowledge that Richard Cory, miserable wretch, pulled the trigger on himself, thereby assuring us that the wealth most of us will never know is not worth having anyway. If Cory actually was the person the poem tells the reader he was, not just rich but also human, graceful and kingly, it would have been proof that one can rise to the top without getting a swelled head or losing touch with the people, and, frankly, that sort of unbridled success has to be treated with suspicion.

Interestingly, if Cory's story happened today, someone would make a point to investigate this humanitarian millionaire, to find the business deal in his past that he concluded less than civilly, or the abandoned relative, or the pills or surgery that kept him so slim, or the child he bounced on his knee just a little too long.

The secret about Richard Cory's suicide is not why it happened—the reader has some idea of why—but the fact that it seems so natural that he would do it. In theory, accumulation of wealth is what America's economy is built on. Capitalism makes our society work, motivating citizens to get up out of their chairs, to build new things, to think and create and search for new solutions. Wealth is quite a motivator. Research scientists, for example, might drive themselves day and night in their search to cure diseases, simply out of love for mankind—but for the rest of us, it takes the promise of something more, in the way of recognition and financial rewards, to get us to do our jobs.

Without trying to belabor the obvious, in our society superior achievement is rewarded with wealth and prestige. We do not know how Richard Cory earned money, but we can see in the poem what an inspiration he was to the people on the pavement.

In its purest form, wealth can motivate people to do their best work, until they ascend to that category we call "the rich." The correlation between work and money is not pure; being who we are, humans tend to add moral implications to the equation, so that making money is more than a measure of work but also a measure of how good one is at heart.

To some degree, this explains why corporations also bestow benefits on chief executives—great benefits like cars, club memberships, vacations, and even homes. Companies consider these perks to be important because an executive who is living well will inspire junior executives to rise to his level by working hard. These fringe benefits convey approval and success in a way that cold hard cash does not. For example, after the first inauguration of Ronald Reagan in 1981, Nancy Reagan replaced the tableware in the White House with $209,000 worth of Lennox china. To some, this seemed like egotistical waste of money, but it was intended as an inspirational message, to show "the people on the pavement" the extreme luxury that one can earn from working hard and rising to the top of one's field.

Regardless of how economic theory justifies building one's fortune, America has never been completely comfortable with limitless acquisition of wealth. This philosophy can be traced to the Puritans, a sect of English Protestants whose religious beliefs opposed luxury and welcomed hardship. A number of religious and philosophical orders settled in America during colonial times, but the Puritans were able to leave their mark on the way the culture developed because they survived. They accepted the difficulties of living in the strange wilderness without requiring worldly gratification or reward. For Puritans, work was itself a way of following God's will, just as comfort was the devil's way of luring men away from God. We still use the phrase "Puritan work ethic" today to describe that specifically American drive to keep working regardless of the reward, for the sake of work alone.

And so Americans have two opposing views of wealth. Economically, greed is good; it inspires people to work harder to buy more and then find ways to work even harder. Yet spiritually the belief is prevalent that the pursuit of material goods is a futile, empty endeavor that isolates people from what is really important. Ours is supposed to be classless society, dedicated to the proposition that all people are created equal—but that basic principle is contradicted if wealthy people are considered better than ordinary people. To put it another way, we all want to be in Richard Cory's place, but that does not keep us from thinking the worst of him.

Richard Cory's suicide at the end of the poem seems natural, even if it does come as a shock, because the reader is prepared to believe that a wealthy man is hiding either shame or misery. One reason for this is that sometimes the rich *are* hiding something; it is naive to assume that the morals of the rich are better than anybody else's.

Another reason the reader may be suspicious is that the rich have more resources and therefore have more places to hide their secrets, from secret walled-up rooms to undeveloped plots of land to Swiss bank accounts. A rich man may have paid people to be silent about what he has done. A poor man almost surely has not.

Finally, we accept that Richard Cory had something hidden all along because he just seemed too good to be true throughout the poem. If anyone can create a false impression, an educated, wealthy person can. Modern readers are just too sophisticated to rely on outward appearances, as the poem's narrator apparently did, perhaps because he needed someone to look up to.

Wealth makes us suspicious and wealth makes us jealous, and when it comes to comparing our-

> *Americans can rest comfortably with the knowledge that Richard Cory, miserable wretch, pulled the trigger on himself, thereby assuring us that the wealth most of us will never know is not worth having anyway."*

selves to someone who has more, we remind ourselves about the camel who can pass through the eye of a needle easier than a rich man can get into heaven. We have more rich people to look at today than Robinson did in his time. They serve the same basic intellectual and moral needs for us that they served when this poem was written. In Robinson's day, the models of unrestrained wealth, such as Andrew Carnegie or Cornelius Vanderbilt or John D. Rockefeller or Andrew Mellon, were people who had built their astronomical fortunes from scratch, feeding both the hopes for personal growth and the fear of corruption that rich people are bound to stir up in common folk. There was a greater distance between wealthy people and average people.

Today we do not believe that the divide is that great. We believe that the person next door might win tonight's lottery and be a millionaire in the morning. We believe that any one of our acquaintances who can read a teleprompter, walk a runway, chat amicably, or catch a ball—that is, just about anyone—might just be considered as talented as Carnegie or Vanderbilt and be showered with just as much money. We believe that the rich are more like us than Edwin Arlington Robinson believed, but we also have a more steady barrage of scandals, exposed by the same media culture that is producing these instant millionaires. Every day the newspapers and television remind us that rich people have secrets, that they are vulnerable to scandal.

The other thing that we like to believe about the rich is that those who do not have secrets are lonely, too far removed from "the real world" to really enjoy life. Alienation is a common cause of suicides, and it would certainly apply to Richard Cory; for all of the talk about him, he is kept at a distance, treated like an object, forced to live a role, different than the common people with no rich friend or even a complacent chauffeur to talk to.

In modern American life the image of the isolated billionaire is a steady fixture: the character of Charles Foster Kane in the movie *Citizen Kane* dies wealthy but friendless; and in real life, Howard Hughes was unbelievably rich but so phobic about germs that he sealed himself off in a disinfected room and died, in 1976, like a hermit. Common sense implies that the very wealthy would have countless friends, but those "friends" are more likely to be attracted by money and therefore not true friends at all. Believing that it is lonely at the top makes life more bearable to those who do not think they will ever get there anyway.

It is an American tradition to want to be rich, but at the same time to wish the rich person unhappiness. The converse of this is, of course, the tradition of the rich person to not care who thinks ill of him or her. In Richard Cory's death, there is a kind of justification for the rest of us, the people on the pavement, the ones who are waiting for the light—we can rest assured that money does not buy happiness after all.

Source: David Kelly, in an essay for *Poetry for Students,* Gale, 1998.

Sources

Adams, Richard P., "The Failure of Edwin Arlington Robinson," in *Tulane Studies in English,* Vol. 11, 1961, pp. 97-151.

Chernow, Ron, "The Lady and the Titan," in *Vanity Fair,* May, 1998, pp. 224-38.

Currie, Harold, *Eugene V. Debs,* Twayne Publishers, 1976.

Lindsey, Almont, *The Pullman Strike,* The University of Chicago Press, 1942.

Pritchard, William H., "Edwin Arlington Robinson: The Prince of Heartbreakers," in *The American Scholar* Vol. 40, No. 1, Winter, 1978-79, pp. 89-100.

Robinson, W. R., "The Alienated Self," in *Edwin Arlington Robinson: A Poetry of the Act,* The Press of Western Reserve University, 1967, reprinted in *Edwin Arlington Robin-*

son: A Collection of Critical Essays, edited by Francis Murphy, Prentice-Hall, 1970, pp. 128-47.

Tate, Allen, "Edwin Arlington Robinson," in *Reactionary Essays on Poetry and Ideas,* Charles Scribner's Sons, 1936, pp. 123-201.

Trachtenberg, Alan, *The Incorporation of America: Culture and Society in the Gilded Age,* Hill and Wang, 1982.

Untermeyer, Louis, "Edwin Arlington Robinson," in *American Poetry since 1900,* Henry Holt and Company, 1923, pp. 40-66.

Winters, Yvor, *Edwin Arlington Robinson,* New Directions, 1946, 162 p.

For Further Study

Barnard, Ellsworth "'Of This or That Estate': Robinson's Literary Reputation," in *Edwin Arlington Robinson: Centenary Essays,* The University of Georgia Press, 1969, pp. 1-14.

The poet's reputation has changed in the past thirty years, since this essay was published; still, this account of Robinson's fluctuating reputation during his lifetime and in the decades soon after makes an interesting lesson in the history of American poetry.

Coxe, Louis O., *Edwin Arlington Robinson: The Life of Poetry,* Pegasus Press, 1969.
Biographical and critical study.

Franchere, Hoyt C., *Edwin Arlington Robinson,* Twayne Publishers, Inc., 1969.

This book-length survey of Robinson's life and work provides basic biographical and critical information, without breaking new ground. A useful all-around reference.

Fussell, Edwin S., "One Kind of Traditional Poet," in *Edwin Arlington Robinson: A Collection of Critical Essays,* edited by Francis Murphy, Prentice-Hall, Inc., 1970, pp. 95-109.

Contrasts Robinson's works with his reputation as an "old-fashioned" poet. Fussell also reports on how Robinson answered his younger critics.

Stovall, Floyd, "The Optimism Behind Robinson's Tragedies," in *Appreciation of Edwin Arlington Robinson,* edited by Richard Cary, Colby College Press, 1969, pp. 55-74.

This book was published "for the 100th anniversary of Maine's most illustrious poet," according to the title page. Stovall's essay examines Robinson's whole career, mentioning "Richard Cory" in passing.

Winters, Yvor, *Edwin Arlington Robinson,* New Directions Books, 1971.

Considered one of the definitive texts of literary criticism of Robinson. Important reading for anyone studying this poet.

The Rime of the Ancient Mariner

Samuel Taylor Coleridge
1798

"The Rime of the Ancient Mariner" is the first poem in *Lyrical Ballads*, the collaborative effort of Samuel Taylor Coleridge and William Wordsworth designed to explore new directions in poetic language and style, and move away from the formal and highly stylized literature of the eighteenth century. This collection is considered by many critics to be the first expression of what has come to be the Romantic movement in English poetry. Coleridge's contribution, "The Rime of the Ancient Mariner," was written in imitation of the form, language, and style of earlier ballads, but it embodied Romantic characteristics with its use of supernatural and Gothic imagery. The first publication of the poem in 1798 was received with little enthusiasm. Several critics objected to Coleridge's misuse of Old English, and (Wordsworth included) the over-extravagance of his supernatural imagery. Subsequently Coleridge, for the 1800 edition of the work, eliminated many Gothic elements and antiquated words. However, in an 1817 edition of his collected poems, *Sybilline Leaves*, Coleridge replaced some of the language he had previously deleted. Since the plot and theme had been considered confusing, he also included a marginal gloss, or set of notes, explaining the action of the poem. This is the version of "The Rime of the Ancient Mariner" that currently appears in most anthologies and textbooks.

On its simplest level, "The Rime of the Ancient Mariner" is a tale of crime, punishment, and redemption: a Mariner shoots an albatross (a bird

Samuel Taylor Coleridge

of good fortune) and is gravely punished by an extraneous force for this act. By learning to love, however, the Mariner partially redeems himself: for his penance he must wander the earth and retell his tale, explaining to people he encounters the lessons he has learned. Beyond this basic level of comprehension, critics seldom agree on a standard interpretation of the poem. With the richness and variety of the imagery, the complexity of the symbols, and the multiple levels of meaning, "The Rime of the Ancient Mariner" still retains its magic for the reader.

Author Biography

Coleridge was born in 1772 in the town of Ottery St. Mary, Devon, England, the tenth child of John Coleridge, a minister and schoolmaster, and his wife, Ann Bowdon Coleridge. Coleridge was a dreamy, isolative child and read constantly. At the age of ten his father died and he was sent to Christ's Hospital, a boarding school in London where he was befriended by fellow student Charles Lamb. In 1791 he entered Cambridge University, showing promise as a gifted writer and brilliant conversationalist. He studied to become a minister, but in 1794, before completing his degree, Coleridge left Cambridge. He went on a walking tour to Oxford

where he became friends with poet Robert Southey. Inspired by the initial events of the French Revolution, Coleridge and Southey collaborated on *The Fall of Robespierre. An Historic Drama* (1794). As an outgrowth of their shared belief in liberty and equality for everyone, they developed a plan for "pantisocracy," an egalitarian and self-sufficient agricultural system to be built in Pennsylvania. The pantisocratic philosophy required every member to be married, and at Southey's urging, Coleridge wed Sarah Fricker, the sister of Southey's fiancee. However, the match proved disastrous and Coleridge's unhappy marriage was a source of grief to him throughout his life. To compound these difficulties, Southey later lost interest in the scheme, abandoning it in 1795.

Coleridge then moved to Nether Stowey in England's West Country. Lamb, William Hazlitt, and other writers visited him there, making up an informal literary community. In 1796 William Wordsworth, with whom Coleridge had exchanged letters for some years, moved into the area. The two poets became instant friends, and they began a literary collaboration. Around this time Coleridge composed "Kubla Khan" and the first version of "Rime of the Ancient Mariner"; the latter work was included as the opening poem in Coleridge and Wordsworth's joint effort, *Lyrical Ballads, with a few Other Poems,* which was published in 1798. That same year, Coleridge traveled to Germany where he developed an interest in the German philosophers Immanuel Kant, Friedrich von Schelling, and the brothers Friedrich and August Wilhelm von Schlegel; he later introduced German aesthetic theory in England through his critical writing. Soon after his return in 1799, Coleridge settled in Keswick near the Lake District, which now gained for him—together with Wordsworth and Southey who had also moved to the area—the title "Lake Poet." During this period, Coleridge suffered poor health and personal strife; his marriage was failing and he had fallen in love with Wordsworth's sister-in-law, Sarah Hutchinson—a love that was unrequited and a source of great pain. He began taking opium as a remedy for his poor health.

Seeking a more temperate climate and to improve his morale, Coleridge began a two-year trip to Italy, Sicily, and Malta in 1804. Upon his return to England Coleridge began a series of lectures on poetry and Shakespeare, which are now considered the basis of his reputation as a literary critic. Because of Coleridge's abuse of opium and alcohol,

The Rime of the Ancient Mariner

Samuel Taylor Coleridge
1798

"The Rime of the Ancient Mariner" is the first poem in *Lyrical Ballads*, the collaborative effort of Samuel Taylor Coleridge and William Wordsworth designed to explore new directions in poetic language and style, and move away from the formal and highly stylized literature of the eighteenth century. This collection is considered by many critics to be the first expression of what has come to be the Romantic movement in English poetry. Coleridge's contribution, "The Rime of the Ancient Mariner," was written in imitation of the form, language, and style of earlier ballads, but it embodied Romantic characteristics with its use of supernatural and Gothic imagery. The first publication of the poem in 1798 was received with little enthusiasm. Several critics objected to Coleridge's misuse of Old English, and (Wordsworth included) the over-extravagance of his supernatural imagery. Subsequently Coleridge, for the 1800 edition of the work, eliminated many Gothic elements and antiquated words. However, in an 1817 edition of his collected poems, *Sybilline Leaves*, Coleridge replaced some of the language he had previously deleted. Since the plot and theme had been considered confusing, he also included a marginal gloss, or set of notes, explaining the action of the poem. This is the version of "The Rime of the Ancient Mariner" that currently appears in most anthologies and textbooks.

On its simplest level, "The Rime of the Ancient Mariner" is a tale of crime, punishment, and redemption: a Mariner shoots an albatross (a bird

Samuel Taylor Coleridge

of good fortune) and is gravely punished by an extraneous force for this act. By learning to love, however, the Mariner partially redeems himself: for his penance he must wander the earth and retell his tale, explaining to people he encounters the lessons he has learned. Beyond this basic level of comprehension, critics seldom agree on a standard interpretation of the poem. With the richness and variety of the imagery, the complexity of the symbols, and the multiple levels of meaning, "The Rime of the Ancient Mariner" still retains its magic for the reader.

Author Biography

Coleridge was born in 1772 in the town of Ottery St. Mary, Devon, England, the tenth child of John Coleridge, a minister and schoolmaster, and his wife, Ann Bowdon Coleridge. Coleridge was a dreamy, isolative child and read constantly. At the age of ten his father died and he was sent to Christ's Hospital, a boarding school in London where he was befriended by fellow student Charles Lamb. In 1791 he entered Cambridge University, showing promise as a gifted writer and brilliant conversationalist. He studied to become a minister, but in 1794, before completing his degree, Coleridge left Cambridge. He went on a walking tour to Oxford

where he became friends with poet Robert Southey. Inspired by the initial events of the French Revolution, Coleridge and Southey collaborated on *The Fall of Robespierre. An Historic Drama* (1794). As an outgrowth of their shared belief in liberty and equality for everyone, they developed a plan for "pantisocracy," an egalitarian and self-sufficient agricultural system to be built in Pennsylvania. The pantisocratic philosophy required every member to be married, and at Southey's urging, Coleridge wed Sarah Fricker, the sister of Southey's fiancee. However, the match proved disastrous and Coleridge's unhappy marriage was a source of grief to him throughout his life. To compound these difficulties, Southey later lost interest in the scheme, abandoning it in 1795.

Coleridge then moved to Nether Stowey in England's West Country. Lamb, William Hazlitt, and other writers visited him there, making up an informal literary community. In 1796 William Wordsworth, with whom Coleridge had exchanged letters for some years, moved into the area. The two poets became instant friends, and they began a literary collaboration. Around this time Coleridge composed "Kubla Khan" and the first version of "Rime of the Ancient Mariner"; the latter work was included as the opening poem in Coleridge and Wordsworth's joint effort, *Lyrical Ballads, with a few Other Poems,* which was published in 1798. That same year, Coleridge traveled to Germany where he developed an interest in the German philosophers Immanuel Kant, Friedrich von Schelling, and the brothers Friedrich and August Wilhelm von Schlegel; he later introduced German aesthetic theory in England through his critical writing. Soon after his return in 1799, Coleridge settled in Keswick near the Lake District, which now gained for him—together with Wordsworth and Southey who had also moved to the area—the title "Lake Poet." During this period, Coleridge suffered poor health and personal strife; his marriage was failing and he had fallen in love with Wordsworth's sister-in-law, Sarah Hutchinson—a love that was unrequited and a source of great pain. He began taking opium as a remedy for his poor health.

Seeking a more temperate climate and to improve his morale, Coleridge began a two-year trip to Italy, Sicily, and Malta in 1804. Upon his return to England Coleridge began a series of lectures on poetry and Shakespeare, which are now considered the basis of his reputation as a literary critic. Because of Coleridge's abuse of opium and alcohol, his erratic behavior caused him to quarrel with Wordsworth, and he left Keswick to return to London. In the last years of his life Coleridge wrote political and philosophical works, and his *Biographia Literaria*, considered his greatest critical writing, in which he developed artistic theories that were intended to be the introduction to a great philosophical work. Coleridge died in 1834 of complications stemming from his dependence on opium.

Poem Text

Part the First

It is an ancient Mariner,
And he stoppeth one of three.
"By thy long grey beard and glittering eye,
Now wherefore stopp'st thou me?

The Bridegroom's doors are opened wide,   5
And I am next of kin;
The guests are met, the feast is set:
May'st hear the merry din."

He holds him with his skinny hand,
"There was a ship," quoth he.   10
"Hold off! unhand me, graybeard loon!"
Eftsoons his hand dropped he.

He holds him with his glittering eye—
The Wedding-Guest stood still,
And listens like a three years' child: 15
The Mariner hath his will.

The Wedding-Guest sat on a stone:
He cannot choose but hear;
And thus spake on that ancient man,
The bright-eyed Mariner.   20

"The ship was cheered, the harbour cleared,
Merrily did we drop
Below the kirk, below the hill,
Below the lighthouse top.

The Sun came up upon the left,   25
Out of the sea came he
And he shone bright, and on the right
Went down into the sea.

Higher and higher every day,
Till over the mast at noon—"   30
The Wedding-Guest here beat his breast,
For he heard the loud bassoon.

The Bride hath paced into the hall,
Red as a rose is she;
Nodding their heads before her goes   35
The merry minstrelsy.

The Wedding-Guest he beat his breast,
Yet he cannot choose but hear;
And thus spake on that ancient man,
The bright-eyed Mariner.   40

"And now the storm-blast came, and he
Was tyrannous and strong:
He struck with his o'ertaking wings,
And chased us south along.

With sloping masts and dipping prow,   45
As who pursued with yell and blow
Still treads the shadow of his foe
And forward bends his head,
The ship drove fast, loud roared the blast,
And southward aye we fled.   50

And now there came both mist and snow
And it grew wondrous cold:
And ice, mast-high, came floating by,
As green as emerald.

And through the drifts the snowy clifts   55
Did send a dismal sheen:
Nor shapes of men nor beasts we ken—
The ice was all between.

The ice was here, the ice was there,
The ice was all around: 60
It cracked and growled, and roared and howled,
Like noises in a swound!

At length did cross an Albatross:
Thorough the fog it came;
As if it had been a Christian soul,   65
We hailed it in God's name.

It ate the food it ne'er had eat,
And round and round it flew.
The ice did split with a thunder-fit;
The helmsman steered us through!   70

And a good south wind sprung up behind;
The Albatross did follow,
And every day, for food or play,
Came to the mariners' hollo!

In mist or cloud, on mast or shroud,   75
It perched for vespers nine;
Whiles all the night, through fog-smoke white,
Glimmered the white moonshine."

"God save thee, ancient Mariner!
From the fiends that plague thee thus!—   80
Why look'st thou so?"—"With my crossbow
I shot the Albatross.

Part the Second

"The Sun now rose upon the right:
Out of the sea came he,
Still hid in mist, and on the left   85
Went down into the sea.

And the good south wind still blew behind,
But no sweet bird did follow,
Nor any day for food or play
Came to the mariners' hollo!   90

And I had done a hellish thing,
And it would work 'em woe:
For all averred, I had killed the bird
That made the breeze to blow.
Ah wretch! said they, the bird to slay,   95
That made the breeze to blow!

Nor dim nor red, like God's own head,
The glorious Sun uprist:
Then all averred, I had killed the bird
That brought the fog and mist.   100
'Twas right, said they, such birds to slay,
That bring the fog and mist.

The fair breeze blew, the white foam flew,
The furrow followed free;
We were the first that ever burst   105
Into that silent sea.

Down dropt the breeze, the sails dropt down,
'Twas sad as sad could be;
And we did speak only to break
The silence of the sea!   110

All in a hot and copper sky,
The bloody Sun, at noon,
Right up above the mast did stand,
No bigger than the Moon.

Day after day, day after day,   115
We stuck, nor breath nor motion;
As idle as a painted ship
Upon a painted ocean.

Water, water, everywhere,
And all the boards did shrink;   120
Water, water, everywhere,
Nor any drop to drink.

The very deep did rot: O Christ!
That ever this should be!
Yea, slimy things did crawl with legs   125
Upon the slimy sea.

About, about, in reel and rout
The death-fires danced at night;
The water, like a witch's oils,
Burnt green, and blue, and white.   130

And some in dreams assurèd were
Of the Spirit that plagued us so;
Nine fathom deep he had followed us
From the land of mist and snow.

And every tongue, through utter drought,   135
Was withered at the root;
We could not speak, no more than if
We had been choked with soot.

Ah! well-a-day! what evil looks
Had I from old and young!   140
Instead of the cross, the Albatross
About my neck was hung.

Part the Third

"There passed a weary time. Each throat
Was parched and glazed each eye.
A weary time! a weary time!   145
How glazed each weary eye!
When looking westward, I beheld
A something in the sky.

At first it seemed a little speck,
And then it seemed a mist;   150
It moved and moved, and took at last
A certain shape, I wist.

A speck, a mist, a shape, I wist!
And still it neared and neared:
As if it dodged a watersprite,   155
It plunged and tacked and veered.

With throats unslaked, with black lips baked,
We could not laugh nor wail;
Through utter drought all dumb we stood!
I bit my arm, I sucked the blood,   160
And cried, A sail! a sail!

With throats unslaked, with black lips baked,
Agape they heard me call:
Gramercy! they for joy did grin,
And all at once their breath drew in,   165
As they were drinking all.

See! See! (I cried) she tacks no more!
Hither to work us weal;
Without a breeze, without a tide,
She steadies with upright keel!   170

The western wave was all a-flame.
The day was well-nigh done!
Almost upon the western wave
Rested the broad bright Sun;
When that strange shape drove suddenly   175
Betwixt us and the Sun.

And straight the Sun was flecked with bars,
(Heaven's Mother send us grace!)
As if through a dungeon-grate he peered
With broad and burning face.   180

Alas! (thought I, and my heart beat loud)
How fast she nears and nears!
Are those her sails that glance in the Sun,
Like restless gossameres!

Are those her ribs through which the Sun   185
Did peer, as through a grate?
And is that Woman all her crew?
Is that a Death? and are there two?
Is Death that woman's mate?

Her lips were red, her looks were free,   190
Her locks were yellow as gold:
Her skin was as white as leprosy,
The Nightmare Life-in-Death was she,
Who thicks man's blood with cold.

The naked hulk alongside came   195
And the twain were casting dice;
'The game is done! I've won, I've won!'
Quoth she, and whistles thrice.

The Sun's rim dips; the stars rush out:
At one stride comes the dark;   200
With far-heard whisper, o'er the sea,
Off shot the spectre-bark.

We listened and looked sideways up!
Fear at my heart, as at a cup,
My life-blood seemed to sip!   205
The stars were dim, and thick the night,
The steersman's face by his lamp gleamed white;
From the sails the dew did drip—
Till clomb above the eastern bar
The hornèd Moon, with one bright star   210
Within the nether tip.

One after one, by the star-dogged Moon,
Too quick for groan or sigh,
Each turned his face with a ghastly pang,
And cursed me with his eye.   215

Four times fifty living men,
(And I heard nor sigh nor groan)
With heavy thump, a lifeless lump,
They dropped down one by one.

The souls did from their bodies fly,—   220
They fled to bliss or woe!
And every soul, it passed me by,
Like the whizz of my cross-bow!"

Part the Fourth

"I fear thee, ancient Mariner!
I fear thy skinny hand!   225
And thou art long, and lank, and brown,
As is the ribbed sea-sand.

I fear thee and thy glittering eye,
And thy skinny hand, so brown."—
"Fear not, fear not, thou Wedding-Guest!   230
This body dropt not down.

Alone, alone, all, all alone,
Alone on a wide wide sea!
And never a saint took pity on
My soul in agony.   235

The many men, so beautiful!
And they all dead did lie:
And a thousand thousand slimy things
Lived on; and so did I.

I looked upon the rotting sea,   240
And drew my eyes away;
I looked upon the rotting deck,
And there the dead men lay.

I looked to Heaven, and tried to pray;
But or ever a prayer had gusht,   245
A wicked whisper came, and made
My heart as dry as dust.

I closed my lids, and kept them close,
And the balls like pulses beat;
For the sky and the sea and the sea and the sky,   250
Lay like a load on my weary eye,
And the dead were at my feet.

The cold sweat melted from their limbs,
Nor rot nor reek did they;
The look with which they looked on me   255
Had never passed away.

An orphan's curse would drag to hell
A spirit from on high;
But oh! more horrible than that
Is a curse in a dead man's eye!   260
Seven days, seven nights, I saw that curse,
And yet I could not die.

The moving Moon went up the sky,
And nowhere did abide:
Softly she was going up,   265
And a star or two beside—

Her beams bemocked the sultry main,
Like April hoar-frost spread;
But where the ship's huge shadow lay,
The charmèd water burnt away   270
A still and awful red.

Beyond the shadow of the ship,
I watched the water-snakes:
They moved in tracks of shining white,
And when they reared, the elfish light   275
Fell off in hoary flakes.

Within the shadow of the ship
I watched their rich attire:
Blue, glossy green, and velvet black,
They coiled and swam; and every track   280
Was a flash of golden fire.

O happy living things! no tongue
Their beauty might declare:
A spring of love gushed from my heart,
And I blessed them unaware: 285
Sure my kind saint took pity on me,
And I blessed them unaware.

The selfsame moment I could pray;
And from my neck so free
The Albatross fell off, and sank   290
Like lead into the sea.

Part the Fifth

"O sleep! it is a gentle thing,
Beloved from pole to pole!
To Mary Queen the praise be given!
She sent the gentle sleep from Heaven,   295
That slid into my soul.

The silly buckets on the deck,
That had so long remained,
I dreamt that they were filled with dew;
And when I awoke, it rained.   300

My lips were wet, my throat was cold,
My garments all were dank;
Sure I had drunken in my dreams,
And still my body drank.

I moved, and could not feel my limbs: 305
I was so light—almost
I thought that I had died in sleep,
And was a blessèd ghost.

And soon I saw a roaring wind:
It did not come anear;   310
But with its sound it shook the sails,
That were so thin and sere.

The upper air burst into life!
And a hundred fire-flags sheen,
To and fro they were hurried about!   315
And to and fro, and in and out,
The wan stars danced between.

And the coming wind did roar more loud,
And the sails did sigh like sedge;
And the rain poured down from one black cloud;   320
The Moon was at its edge.

The thick black cloud was cleft, and still
The Moon was at its side:
Like waters shot from some high crag,
The lightning fell with never a jag,   325
A river steep and wide.

The loud wind never reached the ship,
Yet now the ship moved on!
Beneath the lightning and the Moon
The dead men gave a groan.   330

They groaned, they stirred, they all uprose,
Nor spake, nor moved their eyes;
It had been strange, even in a dream,
To have seen those dead men rise.

The helmsman steered, the ship moved on;   335
Yet never a breeze up blew;
The mariners all 'gan work the ropes,
Where they were wont to do;
They raised their limbs like lifeless tools—
We were a ghastly crew.   340

The body of my brother's son
Stood by me, knee to knee:
The body and I pulled at one rope,
But he said nought to me."

"I fear thee, ancient Mariner!"   345
"Be calm, thou Wedding-Guest!
'Twas not those souls that fled in pain,
Which to their corses came again,
But a troop of spirits blest:

For when it dawned—they dropt their arms,   350
And clustered round the mast;
Sweet sounds rose slowly through their mouths,
And from their bodies passed.

Around, around, flew each sweet sound,
Then darted to the Sun;   355
Slowly the sounds came back again,
Now mixed, now one by one.

Sometimes a-dropping from the sky
I heard the skylark sing;
Sometimes all little birds that are,   360
How they seemed to fill the sea and air
With their sweet jargoning!

And now 'twas like all instruments,
Now like a lonely flute;
And now it is an angel's song,   365
That makes the Heavens be mute.

It ceased; yet still the sails made on
A pleasant noise till noon,
A noise like of a hidden brook
In the leafy month of June   370
That to the sleeping woods all night
Singeth a quiet tune.

Till noon we quietly sailed on,
Yet never a breeze did breathe:
Slowly and smoothly went the ship,   375
Moved onward from beneath.

Under the keel nine fathom deep,
From the land of mist and snow,
The Spirit slid: and it was he

That made the ship to go.   380
The sails at noon left off their tune,
And the ship stood still also.

The Sun, right up above the mast,
Had fixed her to the ocean:
But in a minute she 'gan stir,   385
With a short uneasy motion—
Backwards and forwards half her length
With a short uneasy motion.

Then, like a pawing horse let go,
She made a sudden bound: 390
It flung the blood into my head,
And I fell down in a swound.

How long in that same fit I lay,
I have not to declare;
But ere my living life returned,   395
I heard and in my soul discerned
Two voices in the air.

'Is it he?' quoth one, 'Is this the man?
By Him who died on cross,
With his cruel bow he laid full low   400
The harmless Albatross.

The Spirit who bideth by himself
In the land of mist and snow,
He loved the bird that loved the man
Who shot him with his bow.'   405

The other was a softer voice,
As soft as honeydew:
Quoth he, 'The man hath penance done,
And penance more will do.'

Part the Sixth
First Voice

"'But tell me, tell me! speak again,   410
Thy soft response renewing—
What makes that ship drive on so fast?
What is the ocean doing?'

Second Voice

'Still as a slave before his lord,
The Ocean hath no blast;   415
His great bright eye most silently
Up to the Moon is cast—

If he may know which way to go;
For she guides him smooth or grim.
See, brother, see! how graciously   420
She looketh down on him.'

First Voice

'But why drives on that ship so fast,
Without or wave or wind?'

Second Voice

'The air is cut away before,
And closes from behind.   425

Fly, brother, fly! more high, more high!
Or we shall be belated:
For slow and slow that ship will go,
When the Mariner's trance is abated.'

I woke, and we were sailing on   430
As in a gentle weather:
'Twas night, calm night, the Moon was high;
The dead men stood together.

All stood together on the deck,
For a charnel-dungeon fitter: 435
All fixed on me their stony eyes,
That in the Moon did glitter.

The pang, the curse, with which they died,
Had never passed away:
I could not draw my eyes from theirs,   440
Nor turn them up to pray.

And now this spell was snapt: once more
I viewed the ocean green,
And looked far forth, yet little saw
Of what had else been seen—   445

Like one that on a lonesome road
Doth walk in fear and dread,
And having once turned round walks on,
And turns no more his head;
Because he knows a frightful fiend   450
Doth close behind him tread.

But soon there breathed a wind on me,
Nor sound nor motion made:
Its path was not upon the sea,
In ripple or in shade.   455

It raised my hair, it fanned my cheek
Like a meadow-gale of spring—
It mingled strangely with my fears,
Yet it felt like a welcoming.

Swiftly, swiftly flew the ship,   460
Yet she sailed softly too:
Sweetly, sweetly blew the breeze—
On me alone it blew.

Oh! dream of joy! is this indeed
the lighthouse top I see?   465
Is this the hill? is this the kirk?
Is this mine own countree?

We drifted o'er the harbour-bar,
And I with sobs did pray—
O let me be awake, my God!   470
Or let me sleep alway.

The harbour-bar was clear as glass,
So smoothly was it strewn!
And on the bay the moonlight lay,
And the shadow of the Moon.   475

The rock shone bright, the kirk no less,
That stands above the rock:
The moonlight steeped in silentness
The steady weathercock.

And the bay was white with silent light,   480
Till rising from the same,
Full many shapes, that shadows were,
In crimson colours came.

A little distance from the prow
Those crimson shadows were: 485
I turned my eyes upon the deck—
O, Christ! what saw I there!

Each corse lay flat, lifeless and flat,
And, by the holy rood!
A man all light, a seraph-man,   490
On every corse there stood.

This seraph-band, each waved his hand:
It was a heavenly sight!
They stood as signals to the land,
Each one a lovely light;   495

This seraph-band, each waved his hand,
No voice did they impart—
No voice; but oh! the silence sank
Like music on my heart.

But soon I heard the dash of oars,   500
I heard the Pilot's cheer;
My head was turned perforce away,
And I saw a boat appear.

The Pilot and the Pilot's boy,
I heard them coming fast: 505
Dear Lord in Heaven! it was a joy
The dead men could not blast.

I saw a third—I heard his voice:
It is the Hermit good!
He singeth loud his godly hymns   510
That he makes in the wood.
He'll shrieve my soul, he'll wash away
The Albatross's blood.

Part the Seventh

"This Hermit good lives in that wood
Which slopes down to the sea.   515
How loudly his sweet voice he rears!
He loves to talk with the marineres
That come from a far countree.

He kneels at morn, and noon, and eve—
He hath a cushion plump: 520
It is the moss that wholly hides
The rotted old oak-stump.

The skiff-boat neared: I heard them talk,
'Why this is strange, I trow!
Where are those lights so many and fair,   525
That signal made but now?'

'Strange, by my faith!' the Hermit said—
'And they answered not our cheer!
The planks look warped! and see those sails,
How thin they are and sere!   530
I never saw aught like to them,
Unless perchance it were
Brown skeletons of leaves that lag
My forest-brook along;
When the ivy-tod is heavy with snow,   535
And the owlet whoops to the wolf below,
That eats the she-wolf's young.'

'Dear Lord! it hath a fiendish look—'
(The Pilot made reply)

'I am a-feared'—'Push on, push on!' 540
Said the Hermit cheerily.

The boat came closer to the ship,
But I nor spake nor stirred
The boat came close beneath the ship,
And straight a sound was heard. 545

Under the water it rumbled on,
Still louder and more dread:
It reached the ship, it split the bay;
The ship went down like lead.

Stunned by, that loud and dreadful sound, 550
Which sky and ocean smote,
Like one that hath been seven days drowned
My body lay afloat;
But swift as dreams, myself I found
Within the Pilot's boat. 555

Upon the whirl, where sank the ship,
The boat spun round and round;
And all was still, save that the hill
Was telling of the sound.

I moved my lips—the Pilot shrieked 560
And fell down in a fit;
The holy Hermit raised his eyes,
And prayed where he did sit.

I took the oars: the Pilot's boy,
Who now doth crazy go, 565
Laughed loud and long, and all the while
His eyes went to and fro.
'Ha! ha!' quoth he, 'full plain I see,
The Devil knows how to row.'

And now, all in my own countree, 570
I stood on the firm land!
The Hermit stepped forth from the boat,
And scarcely he could stand.

'O shrieve me, shrieve me, holy man!'
The Hermit crossed his brow. 575
'Say quick,' quoth he, 'I bid thee say—
What manner of man art thou?'

Forthwith this frame of mine was wrenched
With a woeful agony,
Which forced me to begin my tale; 580
And then it left me free.

Since then, at an uncertain hour,
That agony returns:
And till my ghastly tale is told,
This heart within me burns. 585

I pass, like night, from land to land;
I have strange power of speech;
That moment that his face I see,
I know the man that must hear me:
To him my tale I teach. 590

What loud uproar bursts from that door!
The wedding-guests are there:
But in the garden-bower the Bride
And Bride-maids singing are:
And hark the little vesper bell, 595
Which biddeth me to prayer!

O Wedding-Guest! this soul hath been
Alone on a wide wide sea:
So lonely 'twas, that God Himself
Scarce seemèd there to be. 600

O sweeter than the marriage-feast,
'Tis sweeter far to me,
To walk together to the kirk
With a goodly company!—

To walk together to the kirk, 605
And all together pray,
While each to his great Father bends,
Old men, and babes, and loving friends,
And youths and maidens gay!

Farewell, farewell! but this I tell 610
To thee, thou Wedding-Guest!
He prayeth well, who loveth well
Both man and bird and beast.

He prayeth best, who loveth best
All things both great and small; 615
For the dear God who loveth us,
He made and loveth all.

The Mariner, whose eye is bright,
Whose beard with age is hoar,
Is gone: and now the Wedding-Guest 620
Turned from the Bridegroom's door.

He went like one that hath been stunned,
And is of sense forlorn:
A sadder and a wiser man,
He rose the morrow morn. 625

Poem Summary

Lines 1-4:

The poem opens with a simple factual statement: An old sailor stops one of three men walking by who are on their way to a wedding. The fact that he chooses only one individual out of the three will be mentioned again at the end of the poem. The dialogue begins at line three with the guest asking the old man why he has stopped him. He also comments on the Mariner's glittering eye, a detail that will be repeated twice more in the first six stanzas. Lines 2 and 4 are exemplary of Coleridge's use of archaic words: "stoppeth" and "stopp'st."

Note

An Ancient Mariner meeteth three Gallants bidden to a wedding-feast and detaineth one.

Lines 5-8:

The focus of these lines is on the guest's desires and responsibilities. He is the groom's closest relative, so it is his duty to attend the wedding and the feast that follows.

Lines 9-16:

Coleridge uses the following two stanzas to illustrate the power of the Mariner's gaze. Although the Mariner physically restrains the guest in line 9, he drops his hand quickly when challenged. Line 13 explains that his true power thus lies in the hypnotic quality of his gaze and not in his physical strength. The guest is transfixed like prey held fast by the unblinking stare of a predator; his will is surrendered to the Ancient Mariner.

Note

The Wedding-Guest is spell-bound by the eye of the old sea-faring man, and constrained to hear his tale.

Lines 17-24:

Like many Gothic tales, the story opens with an ordinary setting—the wedding guest is on his way to a joyous, but ordinary, function—when suddenly he is trapped by the Mariner and his tale. The Mariner's own story begins in a very ordinary, and somewhat similar, manner—the ship sets off, and the entire town celebrates the joyous occasion. Soon, however, the Mariner's tale changes from the realm of everyday activity into the world of spirits and the supernatural. In this retelling, he will bring the guest along on his journey.

Lines 25-30:

The sun, which will later be shown to be an important symbol, is used to convey geographic details accurately. Coleridge's note reinforces this point. Because the sun rises on the left side of the boat, the reader knows the vessel is heading south. Coleridge's details about geography and nature are frequently quite specific and for the most part accurate. Thus, the farther south the ship goes, the more directly overhead the sun will be. For Coleridge, the "line" always refers to the equator.

Note

The maniner tells how the ship sailed southward with a good wind and fair weather, till it reached the line.

Lines 31-36:

The focus of the poem returns to the world of the ordinary, to the wedding, with its music and celebration. The wedding guest beats his breast, symbolizing his frustration and longing to attend the wedding as he hears the music playing.

Note

The Wedding-Guest heareth the bridal music; but the Mariner continueth his tale.

Lines 37-40:

Repetition is often an important poetic element in ballads. Here, Coleridge uses it to reinforce the power of the Mariner's gaze. The wedding guest is trapped by a power he cannot resist. Line 37 repeats line 31; although he beats his breast, he cannot break the Mariner's spell. Lines 38 to 40 are also a repetition, of lines 18 to 20.

Lines 41-44:

Up to this point, the voyage has been normal, but then a storm sets in. Coleridge uses personification, attributing human characteristics to that which is not human, when he describes the storm as a tyrant chasing the ship. The feeling conveyed is such that it seems that a malevolent force has deliberately targeted this ship.

Note

The ship drawn by a storm toward the South Pole.

Lines 45-50:

Varying the stanza length and rhyme scheme, Coleridge makes the lines of poetry flee just like the ship.

Lines 51-57:

In these stanzas, the ship enters a totally new and frightening world of mystery and cold. The strangeness of the environment is developed with a series of vivid images: emerald icebergs, ice that moans and cries, lifeless vistas. While these may sound fantastic, even to a modern reader, John Livingston Lowes, in his *The Road to Xanadu: A Study in the Ways of the Imagination,* reinforces the accuracy of Coleridge's details by providing several sources on which he based these descriptions. In addition, the development of an atmosphere of uncertainty and imminent danger in an unnatural setting is a common element in Gothic literature.

Note

The land of ice, and of fearful sounds, where no living thing was to be seen.

Lines 58-62:

Line 58 indicates that the ship is surrounded by ice. The next line reinforces it. Coleridge repeats the word ice four times in lines 58 to 60, so that the lines themselves are filled with ice.

Lines 63-66:

Coleridge stages a dramatic introduction by making the albatross materialize out of the fog. It soon becomes apparent that the albatross plays a key role in the poem, though many critics differ on its importance. He is seen by some as merely a bird, while others view him as a Jesus-like figure. In lines 65 and 66 the albatross is greeted as a Christian soul, hailed in God's name.

Note

Till a great sea-bird, called the Albatross, came through the snow-fog, and was received with great joy and hospitality.

Lines 67-74:

These lines further discuss the special relationship between the bird—the only living creature seen in the land of ice—and the crew. They offer the bird hospitality and encourage it to remain with them. Shortly thereafter there is a split in the ice. Coleridge's marginal gloss explains that the bird is a good omen.

Note

And lo! The Albatross proveth a bird of good omen, and followeth the ship as it returned northward through fog and floating ice.

Lines 75-77:

Coleridge emphasizes the loyalty of the albatross that comes each evening to sit on the ship. Vespers are evening prayers said by Catholics, but they also may refer to the evening.

Line 78:

Coleridge introduces the moonlight in this line. The moon will later assume an important symbolic role in the poem.

Lines 79-82:

Without any apparent motive or reason, the Mariner shoots and kills the albatross. Part 1 of the poem ends very abruptly, as it began, with this event. It is possible to interpret the Mariner's act in many ways: a simple violation of hospitality, a symbolic act of murder, a recreation of Adam's fall in the Garden of Eden, or a reenactment of the crucifixion of Christ.

Note

The Ancient Mariner inhospitably killeth the pious bird of good omen.

Lines 83-86:

In these lines, Coleridge reverses lines 25 to 28 as to indicate a change in the ship's direction as it heads north. The reader is now as aware as the Mariner of the details of the voyage. The ship has passed Cape Horn, the southernmost part of South America. The word "Sun" is now capitalized, indicating that it is symbolically important.

Lines 87-90:

The second stanza in this section reiterates the details of lines 71 through 74. The contrast, however, now has a far more important emotional meaning, for the sense of joy in the earlier lines has been destroyed. The crew is once again alone on the empty seas, and the bird's absence constantly reminds them of their isolation; there are no other living creatures around.

Lines 91-102:

These two longer stanzas that describe the crew's changing attitude are very important because they implicate the crew for the Mariner's sin. Although the crew at first denounces the Mariner, describing his deed as hellish, they applaud the killing of the albatross after the sun shines through the polar mists. The marginal note explains that with the crew's betrayal, they participate in the Mariner's sin.

It is ironic that the appearance of the sun causes the change of attitude of the crew. Although Coleridge describes the sun as glorious in line 98, it will soon change.

Note

His shipmates cry out against the Ancient Mariner for killing the bird of good luck.

But when the fog cleared off, they justify the same, and thus make themselves accomplices in the crime.

Lines 103-106:

In these lines, Coleridge describes the ship's passage into the Pacific Ocean using sound to reinforce his meaning. The alliteration in this stanza begins a light "f" sound: "fair," "free," "flew." It is then accompanied by the more forceful "b" sound: "burst," "blew." The words themselves convey the airy, floating sense of the breeze. Lines 103 to 105 describe the ship as returning to normal conditions, but the description of the silent sea in line 106 hints at the impending disaster. Though it is unclear in the poem, the marginal note informs the reader that the ship continues north until it reaches the equator.

Note

The fiar breeze continues; the ship enters the Pacific Ocean and sails northward, even till it reaches the line.

Lines 107-110:

The wind stops and leaves the crew motionless, indicating that their punishment is close at hand. Coleridge also alliterates the "s" sound.

Note

The ship hath been suddenly becalmed.

Lines 111-114:

Coleridge provides many powerful images to convey the ship's plight. He describes the sky, for example, as hot and copper. Copper is an excellent conductor of heat, and thus magnifies the waves of heat that are beating down upon the crew. The sun has now turned bloody instead of glorious.

Lines 115-118:

Coleridge repeats the phrase "day after day" to emphasize the passage of time. A simile in lines 117 and 118 reinforces the stillness; the ship has no more movement than a ship in a picture.

Lines 119-122:

This powerful image emphasizes the lack of fresh water. The boards are shrinking because the heat and absence of fresh water to moisten them. It is ironic that the crew virtually dies of thirst while they are surrounded by an endless expanse of undrinkable saltwater.

Note

And the Albatross begins to be avenged.

Lines 123-126:

Coleridge evokes a nightmarish description of rot and decay. Water is typically a life–giving force, but in line 123 it decays. Later, in lines 129 and 130, it burns. The repetition of "slimy" adds to the unpleasant imagery. Coleridge chooses the word "things" to describe the crawling creatures. The very vagueness of the term indicates that these are so unpleasant that they have no name. Lowes, seeking the source for such creatures, found travel books that mention seas rotting with sea weed, slime fish, and burning water. This description, however, is used for its nightmarish quality rather than its accuracy.

Lines 127-130:

Coleridge emphasizes the supernatural quality of the burning water by using the simile "like witch's oils."

Lines 131-134:

The punishment is given by a spirit from the land of the albatross. The marginal note discusses at length the nature of these invisible spirits.

Note

A Spirit had followed them; one of the invisible inhabitants of this planet, neither departed souls nor angels; concerning whom the learned Jew, Josephus, and the Platonic Constantinopolitan, Michael Psellus, may be consulted. They are very numerous, and there is no climate or element without one or more.

Lines 135-138:

Coleridge vividly describes the suffering of the entire crew.

Lines 139-142:

The cross is apparently a symbol of Christ. The cross around the Mariner's neck is replaced by the albatross, a highly symbolic action. Again, there are many different interpretations of this act. First, the Mariner may no longer deserve to wear the cross of Christianity and must replace it with the symbol of his sin. Second, he figuratively carries the albatross around his neck as Christ carried the cross. The marginal note explains that the crew wishes to throw the guilt totally on the mariner. Thus, like Christ, he bears the guilt for all.

Note

The shipmates, in their sore distress, would fain throw the whole guilt on the Ancient Mariner: in sign whereof they hang the dead sea-bird round his neck.

Lines 143-148:

Part 3 is the most Gothic section of the entire poem, full of nightmarish images and supernatural beings. The stanzas themselves are the most varied here, as the unsettling images distort everything, including the structure of the poem itself. The six lines in the first stanza emphasize the words weary and glazed. Everything is dull and devoid of hope unlike the glittering gaze of the Mariner in the opening stanzas. Coleridge's marginal notes in this section are particularly helpful in comprehending the poem.

Note

The Ancient Mariner beholdeth a sign in the element afar off.

Lines 149-156:

Repetition is used to signal the Mariner's growing hope as the dot in the distance draws closer.

Lines 157-161:

Because there is no water, the crew cannot speak. The Mariner sacrifices himself by biting his arm and drinking his own blood and notifying the crew of the approaching ship.

Note

At its nearer approach it seemeth him to be a ship; and at a dear ransom he freeth his speech from the bonds of thirst.

Lines 162-170:

Coleridge contrasts the initial joy of the crew at the thought of rescue with the fear that follows when they realize that the ship is moving by some supernatural power.

Note

A flash of joy;

And horror follows. For can it be a ship that comes onward without wind or tide?

Lines 171-176:

Coleridge's vivid description of nature reinforces the mood as the sun lights up the western sky with flames. This red backdrop highlights the ghostly ship that approaches. In the next four stanzas and accompanying note, Coleridge will repeat "Sun" six times as he describes the ship that has appeared between the Mariner and the sun.

Lines 177-184:

The note stresses the skeletal nature of the ship. Although the Mariner begs Mary for grace here, he will soon discover himself unable to pray.

Note

It seemeth him but the skeleton of a ship.

Lines 185-194:

Coleridge continues to develop Gothic visions as he further describes the skeleton ship. As the vessel approaches, the Mariner wonders about its inhabitants. In the marginal note, Coleridge answers the Mariner's questions.

Coleridge's description of the woman is puzzling. Red lips, golden hair, and fair skin are considered signs of beauty, and the phrase "Her looks were free" implies sexual awareness. The woman on the vessel, however, is hideous. Contrast the use of color in this description with that of the bride in line 24. While the bride's redness is compared to that of a rose, the white of Spectre-Woman's skin bears the decay of leprosy.

Note

And its ribs are seen as bars on the face of the setting Sun. The Spectre-Woman and her Death-mate and no other on board the skeleton ship.

Like vessel, like crew!

Lines 195-198:

It is necessary to read the note here in order to understand the nature of the stakes in this dice game between death and death-in-life. The victory of death-in-life explains the Mariner's unique fate. He is condemned to suffer endlessly, without ever having death to end the suffering.

Note

Death and life-Death have diced for the ship's crew, and she (the latter) winneth the Ancient Mariner.

Lines 199-202:

Night falls suddenly, as Coleridge's note explains, since there is no period of twilight at the equator.

Note

No twilight within the courts of the Sun.

Lines 203-211:

Coleridge's vivid images render this night as particularly mysterious and dark. His use of the metaphor "thick" to describe the night magnifies the fearfulness and darkness of the waiting. When the crescent moon rises, it appears with one star: the planet Venus.

Lines 212-223:

Coleridge stresses the death of each crewman, "one after one," in order to intensify the devastating effect this has on the Mariner. Although each dies without a word, they turn to curse the Mariner with a look. When the spirits leave the dead bodies "one by one," each spirit reminds the Mariner of his sin as they pass "like the whizz of my cross-bow."

Note

At the rising of the Moon,
One after another,
His ship-mates drop down dead;
But Life-in Death begins her work on the Ancient
    Mariner.

Lines 224-231:

Coleridge begins Part 4 with the Mariner pausing his tale of horror and returning the focus on the confounded guest. This has the effect of lessening the tension after the extremely dramatic, supernatural life and death quality of Part 3.

Note

The Wedding-Guest feareth that a spirit is talking to him;

But the Ancient Mariner assureth him of his of his bodily life, and proceedeth to relate his horrible penance.

Lines 232-235:

Repetition of the word "alone" reinforces the Mariner's sense of isolation.

Lines 236-243:

In this stanza, Coleridge contrasts the beauty of the men while they were alive with the multitude of slimy creatures in the sea. Because he lives, the Mariner feels that he is a part of the world of slime and decay that surrounds him. Several critics stress the importance of Coleridge's note that the Mariner's despising the sea creatures and himself indicates that he despises nature itself, and thus has learned nothing.

Note

He despiseth the creatures of the calm.

And envieth that they should live, and so many lie dead.

Lines 244-247:

With this stanza, Coleridge emphasizes a key Christian symbol: souls that are damned are unable to pray. The Mariner's soul, too, is rotting like everything else around him.

Lines 248-262:

Coleridge describes the Mariner's torment, again using the image of the weary eye. He cannot avoid the eyes of the dead men, and accepts their curse as he feels that he is the one who brought about this destruction.

Media Adaptations

- *English Romantic Poetry*, read by Sir Ralph Richardson, Claire Bloom, Sir Anthony Quayle, and Frederick Worlock includes "The Rime of the Ancient Mariner" and "Kubla Khan" by Coleridge, Harper Caedmon.

Many of Coleridge's poems are accessible on the World Wide Web. The S.T. Coleridge Home Page URL is http://www.lib.virginia.edu/etext/stc/Coleridge/stc.htm A very comprehensive listing of other Samuel Taylor Coleridge resources on the Internet is available at http://www.lib.virginia.edu/etext/stc/Coleridge/ internet.html

Note

But the curse liveth for him in the eye of the dead men.

Lines 263-271:

Coleridge fills this section with contrasting images: the moon travels gently in its path, welcomed everywhere, while the ship is trapped in the burning water; the moon is described as cool and restful, while the ship is described as red and filled with heat. Again the color red is used, but this time it connotes hell-fire and terror.

Note

In his loneliness and fixedness he yearneth towards the journeying moon, and the Stars that still sojourn yet still more onward; and everywhere the blue sky belongs to them, and is their appointed rest, and their native country and their own natural homes, which they enter unannounced, as lords that are certainly expected and yet there is a silent joy at their arrival.

Lines 272-276:

Coleridge continues contrasting images with vivid descriptions in the next two stanzas. Beyond the shadow of the ship, the water snakes seem to shimmer in the moonlight that reflects off of them as they move.

Note

By the light of the Moon he beholdeth God's creatures of the great calm.

Lines 277-281:

In the ship's shadow, however, the water snakes take on an even more beautiful aspect as they glow with color and light. This is a large contrast from the ship's presentation as a place of desolation and despair after the death of the albatross. The color red had previously conveyed images of fire and death, but in line 281, the tracks of the snakes flash with "golden fire," a phrase that is warm and comforting. This shift foreshadows the change which will occur in the Mariner himself in the next stanza.

Lines 282-287:

Part 4 ends with the freeing of the Mariner's soul. He blesses the snakes, "unaware" of the forgiveness bestowed on him.

Note

Their beauty and their happiness. He blesseth them in his heart.

Lines 288-291:

Once he is forgiven, the Mariner can pray again. As he prays, the enormous weight of the albatross and his crime is released. Coleridge uses the simile "like lead" to convey the enormous burden which is now lifted.

Note

The spell begins to break.

Lines 292-296:

As Part 5 begins, Coleridge uses a series of images to convey the peace and comfort that comes to the Mariner; he is finally able to sleep.

Lines 297-308:

When the Mariner dreams of rain, it rains. He feels light in his body and soul. This atmosphere is in contrast to the previous section where there was a predominance of weariness, loneliness, and decay.

Note

By grace of the holy Mother, the Ancient Mariner is refreshed with rain.

Lines 309-317:

The calm and quiet of the last verses disappear as the Mariner is surrounded by strange sights and sounds. The fires in the sky, which make the stars seem pale in comparison, sound like the Aurora Borealis. It would make geographical sense if this were the case, since the ship must leave the Pacific and round Cape Horn at the tip of South America again in order for the Mariner to return home. Coleridge does not stress the geography, but his awareness of it in other parts of the poem makes this a possibility. The fires may also be seen as a manifestation of the spirit world.

Note

He heareth sounds and seeth strange sights and commotions in the sky and the element.

Lines 318-326:

Coleridge uses vivid imagery to describe the supernatural phenomena in this storm.

Note

The bodies of the ship's crew are inspired, and the ship moves on;

Lines 327-340:

These lines demonstrate more examples of Gothic influences on the story. When the dead return to life and the Mariner assumes his place beside them, there is a deep sense of terror and oppression.

Lines 341-344:

Coleridge adds a very poignant quality to the tale with these lines. Perhaps more than any other in the poem, they serve to remind the reader of the normal world to which the Mariner once belonged. It is ironic that he is seen as having a family only after he is forced to work next to his nephew, with whom there is no longer any possibility of love or communication.

Lines 345-349:

The ghastly quality of the story frightens the guest. When the Mariner reassures him that the spirits who possessed the dead are "blest," it contrasts the picture of them in line 340 as "a ghastly crew."

Note

but not by the souls of the men, nor by daemons of earth or middle air, but by a blessed troop of angelic spirits sent down by the invocation of the guardian saint.

Lines 350-357:

The contrast continues in these lines. When the dead first rose, they groaned (a typical Gothic detail). As the day dawns, the spirits become music, creating a marvelous mixture of sounds and notes. In these lines, sound and music are used to create a sense of peace. Another interesting contrast is with the spirits that gather around the mast at dawn: before its death the albatross perched there every evening.

Lines 358-366:

Coleridge uses natural and musical imagery to convey the beauty of the music the Mariner hears.

Lines 367-372:

After the music of the spirits ceases, Coleridge continues using sound imagery, creating a simile: the sails sound like a hidden brook providing a lullaby to the wood. Interestingly, Coleridge uses sound to convey a sense of quiet.

Lines 373-382:

Coleridge supplies details about the voyage itself in these two stanzas and in the accompanying note that explain how the ship moves without a breeze. The Spirit of snow and ice is carrying the ship from below. The note makes it clear that this spirit resents helping the Mariner and wants him to receive further punishment for the murder of the albatross.

Note

The lonesome Spirit from the South Pole carries on the ship as far as the Line, in obedience to the angelic troop, but still requireth vengeance.

Lines 383-392:

Coleridge once again reestablishes clear geographic details with a metaphor. The sun, straight above the mast, pins the ship to the water at the equator. When the ship moves again, the motion causes the Mariner to faint.

Lines 393-405:

When the Mariner regains partial consciousness, he hears the voices of spirits. Coleridge uses these voices to review the details of the poem. The note identifies the speakers as fellow daemons of the Polar Spirit. The word daemon is not the same as the modern word, demon. Rather, daemons are invisible spirits, living in the world. They may be patterned after similar spirits in Greek mythology who lived in nature, serving as messengers between the gods and man. The first voice restates the Mariner's sin. The gentle albatross loved and trusted the Mariner, who shot him. The reference to Jesus in line 399 serves to reinforce the Christian symbolism of the albatross.

Note

The Polar Spirit's fellow daemons, the invisible inhabitants of the element, take part in his wrong; and two of them relate, one to the other, that penance long and heavy for the Ancient Mariner hath been accorded to the Polar Spirit, who returneth southward.

Lines 406-409:

This final stanza in Part 5 foreshadows the rest of the poem. The peace of this section is only transitory; the Mariner will suffer more.

Lines 410-413:

Coleridge continues to use the spirit voices to clarify the poem for the reader. In lines 411 through 439, they explain how the ship is moving.

Lines 414-417:

The second voice points out the still ocean that is waiting for directions from the Moon. Line 414 contains a simile in which there is a slave before a master, that is used to illustrate the calm.

Lines 418-421:

Since the moon controls the tides, it gives the ocean its direction.

Note

The Mariner hath been cast into a trance; for the angelic power causeth the vessel to drive northward faster than human life could endure.

Lines 422-429:

In answer to the repeated query, the second voice explains that the ship is being driven by a power that parts the air so that it may pass through. The marginal note adds that this is an angelic power, and that the ship is moving so swiftly that the Mariner could not survive if he were fully conscious.

Lines 430-441:

Coleridge returns to the Gothic imagery of Part 3, providing a distinct contrast to the peaceful descriptions of Part 5. As the Mariner wakes, he finds the dead men staring at him. He describes them as fit for a "charnel-dungeon"—a place where dead bodies are kept. The moonlight, usually peaceful, is reflected in their eyes. As the guest is trapped by the Mariner's stare, so too is the Mariner transfixed by the dead men. These lines also recall Part 4 when the Mariner finds himself momentarily unable to pray.

Note

The supernatural motion is retarded; the Mariner awakes, and his penance begins anew.

Lines 432-445:

The spell is broken and the Mariner can look to the ocean.

Note

The curse is finally expiated.

Lines 446-451:

Coleridge uses a powerful extended simile that continues throughout the six-line stanza to describe the Mariner's fear about what may lie ahead of him.

Lines 452-459:

The wind returns, but now it is a supernatural force that touches only the Mariner and not the objects around him.

Lines 460-463:

There is an alliteration of "swiftly" and "sweetly" in lines 460 and 462. In fact, the entire stanza contains many instances of alliteration.

Lines 464-467:

The Mariner sees his home. For consistency, Coleridge is careful to mention the landmarks in the reverse order from which he first described them during the ship's farewell in lines 23 and 24.

Note

And the Ancient Mariner beholdeth his native country.

Lines 468-471:

In these lines, the Mariner's questions emphasize his disbelief that he is truly home. He prays that if this is only a dream, it will be one from which he will never waken.

Lines 472-479:

The moon provides a benevolent guiding light revealing to the Mariner his home in a series of vivid images.

Lines 480-487:

The crimson shapes filling the bay in the moonlight seem to be living, supernatural creatures. They may be the daemons or spirits of the Mariner's own land. Nevertheless, these beings have played a prominent role in the Mariner's voyage all along.

Note

The angelic spirits leave the dead bodies, and appear in their own forms of light.

Lines 488-499:

The spirits within the crew leave and the Mariner sees that they are angels. They bid the Mariner farewell and, in their silence, bless the Mariner. The phrase "By the holy rood" refers to the crucifix.

Lines 500-507:

With the sound of oars, Coleridge reintroduces the ordinary world. The Mariner recognizes the voices of people he knew, and the supernatural realm vanishes. His happiness is so great that even the realization that he, alone, is returning from the voyage cannot diminish it.

Lines 508-513:

Coleridge includes the hermit as the third passenger in the boat. Part 6 ends with the Mariner's hope that this good man will forgive his sins.

Lines 514-522:

Coleridge opens Part 7 with a description of the hermit: a good man who lives in harmony with God, man, and nature. These characteristics are important since the Mariner has been out of harmony with all three.

Note

The Hermit of the wood

approacheth the ship with wonder.

Lines 523-526:

The lights from the seraph band had drawn the men toward the ship. Now that the angels have departed, the ship lies in darkness.

Lines 527-537:

As the three men approach the ship, they are shocked by its ragged condition. Coleridge uses a simile comparing the ship's sails to leaves in the winter.

Lines 538-541:

In these lines, Coleridge contrasts the fear of the pilot with the open-hearted optimism of the hermit.

Lines 542-549:

For the last time, the world of the supernatural intrudes. There is a sound under the water and the the bay splits open. The ship then disappears exactly as the albatross disappeared: "like lead." Gothic literature is filled with similar visions where the earth splits so that people and objects can be dragged down beneath the earth.

Note

The ship suddenly sinketh.

Lines 550-559:

The Mariner, thrown clear, is rescued by the boat as the hills reverberate with sound. The little boat is caught up in the whirlpool created by the sunken ship.

Note

The Ancient Mariner is saved in the Pilot's boat.

Lines 560-569:

The three rescuers thought the Mariner was dead, and are horrified when he begins to speak and move.

Lines 570-577:

On land, the Mariner begs the hermit to forgive him.

Note

The Ancient Mariner earnestly entreateth the Hermit to shrive him; and the penance of life falls on him.

Lines 578-581:

The Mariner is handed his punishment: he is forced by an uncontrollable urge to tell his story.

Lines 582-590:

The Mariner is forced to travel from land to land searching for certain individuals to whom he must relate his story. This is why he stopped the guest. It was his destiny was to hear the tale and to learn from the Mariner's suffering.

Critics have found parallels between the ancient Mariner and Cain, who was forced to wander the earth after the murder of his brother, Abel. He has also been compared to the legendary figure of the Wandering Jew, who was supposedly so cruel to Christ during the crucifixion that he is forced to wander the earth forever.

Note

And ever and anon throughout his future life an agony constraineth him to travel from land to land,

Lines 591-596:

The poem returns to the present, where the wedding ceremony is over. It is the Mariner who mentions this, now that his tale has been told. The guest offers no protests and seems unaware of the wedding feast.

Lines 597-600:

The Mariner repeats line 234 to remind the guest of the terrible isolation that he went through, where he was separated from all other living things. Even God seemed absent from him.

Lines 601-609:

The Mariner reminds the guest of the simple pleasure that comes in prayerful company.

Lines 610-617:

In these lines, Coleridge states the moral of the poem: that one must necessarily love all living things. Many critics object to this simple message, Coleridge, himself, being among them.

Note

and to teach, by his own example, love and reverence to all things that God made and loveth.

Lines 618-625:

The Mariner, his eye still bright, disappears, leaving the last stanzas of the poem to the wedding guest. No longer interested in the wedding feast, he holds still within the trance of the Mariner's gaze. The poem ends with the guest having learned the Mariner's lesson.

Themes

Sin

The poem "The Rime of the Ancient Mariner" revolves around a single action, the killing of a bird, known as the albatross, and its horrible consequences. The repercussions of the Mariner's crime are puzzling at first. However cruel the killing might have been, why should two hundred men die and the Mariner himself be driven nearly insane as a result?

But the Mariner's action cannot be judged in these simple terms, for it is far more than a secular crime, like robbing a bank or even killing a man. That the murder is deeply religious in nature is shown when the dead albatross is equated with Christ: "Instead of the cross, the Albatross / About my neck was hung," the Mariner says. Killing the bird was more than an ordinary crime because it violated the sacred natural order, an order encompassing the visible and the invisible, the spiritual, the natural, and the human. It included the Polar Spirit and other spirits, the albatross, the ice and sea and sun and moon, as well as the men on the ship. All are bound by an intricate series of connections, of which the Ancient Mariner is completely unaware. He is able to kill the albatross without a thought. But like Adam's sin, the simple act of eating an apple, the Mariner's violence calls for a harsh punishment.

Like the biblical Adam, who ate the apple because he wanted to be like God himself, the Mariner places himself on a par with God above nature. As far as he is concerned, humans are the measure of all things. In such an order, he can kill the bird without a second thought; to him, there is no deeper moral order. It is clear after the other sailors have died that the Mariner feels mankind is better than the rest of nature. Looking at the sea, he regrets the deaths of "the many men so beautiful" while "a thousand thousand slimy things," the ocean creatures, still live. The Ancient Mariner will not begin atoning for his sin until realizes that he is not master of the world, but part of it.

Atonement

Like the story of Adam and Eve, the Mariner's sin is eventually followed by redemption. Gazing at the ocean, he sees schools of sea snakes glistening in the moonlight. They are no longer "slimy things," they are bathed in beautiful "golden fire." "A spring of love gushed from my heart, / And I blessed them unaware." This moment is the poem's turning point and it mirrors the casual, ignorant murder of the bird.

It might seem odd that such a moment could save him. What is important is that his essential nature has changed, the nature that led him to kill the albatross in the first place. The Mariner realizes that he had nothing to do with that change—it was a gift from a higher power. "Sure my kind saint took

pity on me / And I blessed them unaware," he says. No one can *choose* to love. Love is a gift that springs from the heart; we either love or we do not.

The instant he blesses the water snakes, he is saved and can return home. His punishment has been severe: the death of his crew, thirst, and fearful visions. But he continues to carry his guilt with him, even after his redemption. When the Mariner returns to his country, he turns to the hermit. "He'll shrieve my soul, he'll wash away / The Albatross's blood." He confesses his guilt to the hermit. But after he has been forgiven, the Mariner's atonement continues. By the end of the poem, he "hath penance done and penance more will do." So the Mariner wanders the earth telling his story, to "teach" others.

Imagination

Imagination plays a special role in "The Rime of the Ancient Mariner." In the poem imagination has transformative powers. It is a special form of knowledge more true and insightful than other forms. The sailors employ a scientific approach to life and therefore misconstrue many of the spiritual events and their consequences.

When the Mariner kills the albatross, for example, and the ship begins to drift through the fog, he says, "all averred, I had killed the bird / That made the breeze to blow." But the next day the "glorious sun" rises and the sailors change their tune. "Then all averred, I had killed the bird that brought the fog and mist." Their reasoning is superficial and fails to go beyond their own limited momentary self-interest. It lacks any broader moral basis.

The Mariner and his men have unwittingly sailed into a universe full of spirits and ghostly ships and roaring ice that cannot be known by the common modes of perception. No one on the ship is aware of the deeper realities that surround the ship. The Mariner does not realize the albatross's place in the mysterious unseen order and he kills it. He does not understand his *own* place in the world. The world he finds himself in cannot be grasped by mere reason. It has the shape and feel of a dream where the rules of logic no longer apply. It can only be grasped by the imagination.

In the poem imagination is represented by wind blowing and moonlight shining down on the sea. The first sign is the appearance of the albatross, "the bird that made the breeze to blow." The Mariner kills the bird, and his punishment is to be eventually left alone on a rotting ship, the rest of the crew dead.

An artist's rendition of the Mariner and albatross.

The world without imagination is a dead world, and it is a world the Mariner chooses because of his murder of the bird. The spirit of imagination is there, in the form of the Polar Spirit deep below the water. The Polar Spirit is like the creative spirit; it comes unseen and may be benign or destructive. The Mariner is like a dead man himself, doomed to "death-in-life." The Mariner finally turns in disgust from the empty world around him. "I closed my eyes, and kept them closed … for the sky and the sea and the sea and the sky / Lay like a load on my weary eye / And the dead men at my feet."

The doors to imagination open for the Mariner when he turns his back on the superficial world of sensory perception. The moon rises, new light shines, and a different world is revealed. The creatures of the sea look so different that normal, logical speech does not describe them. They can only be experienced directly. "Oh happy living things! No tongue / Their beauty might declare."

After his experience in the moonlight, the Mariner realizes that there is a moral order in the universe. He knows that that order encompasses him and every other creature.

When the spirit of the air says "the Spirit who bideth by himself / In the land of mist and snow, / He loved the bird that loved the man / Who shot him with his bow," it is describing an unending

Topics for Further Study

• The Mariner of this poem is sent out to travel the world and teach about love and reverence. Imagine this happening now. What occupation, other than mariner, might be given a person responsible for this chore? Since albatrosses are rare today, what other crime against nature might a contemporary person commit to bring this punishment upon him or herself? Write a scenario that would retain the emotions of guilt and redemption from this poem, but transfer them to the world in which you live.

• The third section of the poem concerns the approach of the skeleton ship, with Death and Death-in-Life coming to meet the Ancient Mariner. To what extent is he glad to see them? Has his loneliness increased his interest in the macabre? How can you tell? What do the details of their appearance tell the Mariner he can expect out of life in the future?

chain of love that binds all beings. The Mariner's senseless murder broke that chain. Afterward, wandering the earth, he remains intensely sensitive to this awareness and tries to communicate it to the Wedding Guest. The most important thing, he asserts, is to worship God.

Alienation and Loneliness

The Ancient Mariner is an outsider. He leaves his countrymen to sail off into the unknown. He is confronted with real isolation for the first time when ice traps the ship in the south polar seas. "Nor shapes of men nor beasts we ken / The ice was all between." The spell of isolation is broken by the arrival of the bird. The seamen greet it "as if it had been a Christian soul" and share their food with it. It remains with them and breaks up the ice, eventually enabling the ship to sail free. Once free, the Mariner murders the bird. He is the ultimate outsider, an anti-social outlaw who has violated the most basic rules about hospitality toward guests.

The Mariner's isolation deepens. His shipmates hang the dead bird around his neck as a mark of his exclusion. All communication on the ship ceases and the Mariner is alone in his own thoughts. "Through utter drought all parched we stood." After he hails the ship that bears Death and Death-in-Life, his alienation is total, "alone, alone, all all alone / Alone on the wide wide sea."

The Mariner remains alone on the sea, in a condition one critic has described as schizophrenic. He is on the edge of madness, in such a deep existential crisis that he is alienated from himself as well.

After his mystical experience with the water snakes, he begins to recover from his psychotic trance. Suddenly he is no longer alone, life is everywhere around him and the revelation saves him. "The upper air burst into life!" Suddenly the air is full of music "like all instruments / Now like a lonely flute; / And now it is an angel's song." Even the dead men move again as if they were alive.

The Ancient Mariner is a changed man after his experience but remains alone. He tells the Wedding Guest he values nothing more than the company of other people, yet he wanders the earth alone. He does not join the wedding feast. The effect of the story is to make the Wedding Guest a more lonely, solitary person. He does not join the wedding celebration although he was he was anxious to do so. He simply leaves, "stunned." And it is surely significant that his new-found knowledge not only makes him "a wiser man," but "a sadder" one as well.

Style

"The Rime of the Ancient Mariner" is mostly written in the traditional ballad stanza: a series of four-line verses, the first and third of which are written in iambic tetrameter, and the second and fourth written in iambic trimeter.

In order to analyze the rhythm or meter of a line of poetry, the line must first be divided into syllables. An iamb is a metrical unit consisting of one unstressed syllable followed by one stressed syllable. In Coleridge's poem, for example:

> In **mist** / or **cloud** / on **mast** / or **shroud**
> It **perched** / for ves / pers **nine**

When the iambs above are read aloud, the emphasis falls on every second syllable. The meter of the first line is in iambic tetrameter because it contains four iambic units in each line (totalling eight syllables), whereas the meter of the second line is in iambic trimeter because it contains only three iambic units (totalling six syllables).

Ballad stanzas also employ a set rhyme scheme. In the traditional schematic form, the second and the fourth lines rhyme, whereas the first and third lines do not. Coleridge followed this pattern, frequently adding additional rhyming elements. In the lines above, "cloud" and "shroud" are examples of internal rhyme, because they rhyme within a single line. Furthermore, the line contains alliteration, a rhyming element that repeats the beginning sounds of words (e.g. "mist" and "mast"). Coleridge also uses the rhyming element assonance, in which there are repeated verb sounds within words (e.g. in the second line: "per," "ves," "pers").

Although most of the verses follow the four-line stanza, Coleridge deliberately varies the poem's pattern to illustrate certain points or to help develop an idea, because it calls the reader's attention to a particular section. For example, the first eleven stanzas of the poem follow the basic pattern very closely. In the twelfth stanza, however, both the number of lines and the rhyme scheme change. Of the six lines that form this stanza, the first two employ eye rhyme—"prow" and "blow"—where the words' endings are spelled similarly but differ in their pronunciation. Moreover, Coleridge uses internal rhyme—"fast" and "blast—in the fifth line of this stanza. In this passage, Coleridge also describes the ship as fleeing before the storm. These variations serve to move the poem along more quickly, i.e. the lines of poetry themselves speed up or "flee." Coleridge also utilizes stanzaic changes throughout the poem to emphasize his meaning.

The poem is divided into seven parts that are written in dialogue form, with occasional descriptive comments added by the poet. Another important detail in the poem's organization is the inclusion of a series of marginal notes which were added in the 1817 version of the poem. These notes provide a great deal of information—some of which appearing exclusively in the notes—that may help a reader to better understand the poem's sense or meaning.

Historical Context

The French Revolution

In 1798, England was still reacting to the ideas and events of the French Revolution. The French ideology and army both continued to threaten England at that time. The slogan *Liberte, Egalite, Fra-* *ternite*—Liberty, Equality, Brotherhood—that inspired the French masses to overthrow, and eventually kill, the French king and queen led the ruling houses of Europe to oppose the French Republic. Bitter opposition to royalty and church, an integral part of France's liberal political philosophy, concerned the conservative rulers of Britain. These radical ideas, it was feared, could lead to unrest in the British lower classes.

France was also a real military threat to Britain. The fear of a French invasion was constant through much of the 1790s. Revolutionary France had threatened to invade neighboring Holland earlier in the decade. In 1796, a French force set out to assist Irish rebels planning an uprising against the English government and only a bad storm kept French troops from landing in Ireland. In 1798, Napoleon massed troops just across the English Channel in preparation for an invasion that never took place.

French intentions seemed clear. England's suspicions spurred many to support the old traditional English values and oppose the new France.

The Irish Rebellion

Britain faced the prospect of revolution in its nearest colony in the second half of the 1790s. Irish Roman Catholics had been demanding religious freedom and reform of the Irish parliament for a few years; and when they went ignored, Irish radicals and members of the working class joined forces to form United Irishmen in 1795. The group was secret, organized along on military lines, and dedicated to radical action in order to reform Ireland. It was also militantly Catholic and targeted its attacks exclusively against Protestants.

Between 1796 and 1798 the situation grew very serious. In 1796, the French attempted an unsuccessful expedition to Ireland with the Irish radical leader Wolfe Tone. As a result of the growing trouble, the English government instituted a series of draconian measures. In 1796 the Insurrection Act was passed, followed by the suspension of the right of *habeas corpus.* The following year the English attempted to seize all private arms in Ireland and suppressed publication of a radical newspaper in Belfast.

In 1798, as the United Irishmen prepared an armed rebellion, the English authorities arrested the main rebel leaders. Local uprisings erupted and a number of battles were fought. In the end, the Irish were defeated at the Battle of Vinegar Hill. Following their victory, the English government abol-

Compare & Contrast

- **1798:** Napoleon Bonaparte conquers Egypt on July 22, but on August 1 the British navy under Admiral Horatio Nelson destroys the French fleet and strands Bonaparte and his army in Africa.

  Today: The United States together with the United Nations threaten Saddam Hussein and Iraq with sanctions and military action if weapons inspectors are not allowed to inspect key weapon sites.

- **1798:** Irish resistance to British rule is brutally broken at the Battle of Vinegar Hill.

  Today: Ireland and Great Britain continue to try to work out a plan to bring peace to embattled Northern Ireland.

- **1798:** Eli Whitney, the inventor of the cotton gin, develops a system for producing firearms from interchangeable parts. The invention sets the stage for the industrial revolution in America.

  Today: Personal computers, based on the mass-production of silicon chips, are a multibillion dollar industry.

---

ished the Irish parliament completely. They allowed the Irish to be represented only in the English parliament.

Lyrical Ballads

The publication of *Lyrical Ballads,* a book written by Samuel Taylor Coleridge and William Wordsworth, is considered the beginning of the Romantic movement in English literature. The idea to collaborate on a book of poetry was conceived by Wordsworth and Coleridge at the same time they formulated the idea for the *Ancient Mariner,* a work which was initially planned as a collaboration.

The project was forgotten for three or four months, only to be raised again by Coleridge in 1798. He proposed that they, along with Wordsworth's sister, travel together to Germany in order to learn German, study natural science, and explore German philosophy. The book was intended first and foremost as a way to raise money for the long trip. When *Lyrical Ballads* was published, it opened with "The Rime of the Ancient Mariner"; all but four of its poems were written by Wordsworth.

Lyrical Ballads was revolutionary because it used the language of the working classes. In his preface to the second edition, Wordsworth argued explicitly that this was necessary. He maintained that the language of the lower classes was superior

to the elevated, self-consciously poetic language of English poetry. In plain, straightforward language, Wordsworth wrote, "the passions of the heart find a better soil in which they can attain their maturity … and speak in plainer and more emphatic language."

That essay became a manifesto for other Romantic poets. In the aftermath of the French Revolution, the essay and the poetry in *Lyrical Ballads* was viewed as incendiary and dangerous by some critics. It was dangerous because by leveling the language of different social classes, the book implied a similar leveling of *all* class distinctions. It was perceived to oppose to the age-old English system of noble and subject. Wordsworth wrote that through the ability to feel the "great and simple affections" of human nature—an ability this common language conferred—"one being is elevated above another."

Critical Overview

Nineteenth-century critics had somewhat mixed reviews regarding "The Rime of the Ancient Mariner." They lauded the poem's brilliant imagery, but found the story unconvincing, the language distracting, and the theme incomprehensible.

Twentieth-century critics cannot agree on a standard interpretation of the poem. In *The Road to Xanadu*, John Livingston Lowes argues that the moral of the poem only has validity within the special world that Coleridge created. He notes, however, that the death of an entire crew is a rather harsh punishment for the death of a bird. Lowes contends that the poem operates on three "interlocking" levels: the voyage, the spirit world, and the tale of crime and punishment. He fails, however, to regard the poem's effectiveness as a tale of salvation and redemption. Nevertheless, Lowes's greatest contribution to the study of "The Ancient Mariner" is his intensive investigation into Coleridge's sources that sparked a renewed interest in his poetry.

In "A Poem of Pure Imagination," Robert Penn Warren disagrees with Lowes's views on the triviality of the Mariner's act, contending that the poem's primary theme is one of sacramental vision; of "One Life" for all creatures. The Mariner's crime represents humankind's fall from grace, like original sin. Warren also points out that "the bird is hailed 'in God's name,' both literally and symbolically, and in the end we have, therefore, in the crime against Nature a crime against God." For Coleridge, then, God is nature, and in doing this act, the Mariner separates himself from nature and ultimately from God. In *Coleridge: The Clark Lectures,* Humphry House discusses the importance of Coleridge's use of natural imagery in developing the poem's main theme. He points out that the elements of nature not only provide key insights into the Mariner's spiritual state, but they also provide "the link between the Mariner as an ordinary man, and the Mariner as one acquainted with the invisible world, which has its own sets of values." House cautions the reader against wholeheartedly adopting any single interpretation of the poem, as he contends that any such action may limit, and ultimately prevent, the reader from gaining valuable insight from issues that he may have overlooked.

Criticism

Jhan Hochman

Jhan Hochman is a writer and instructor at Portland Community College in Portland, Oregon. In the following stylistic and thematic analysis of "The Rime of the Ancient Mariner," Hochman focuses on the role of the albatross in the poem.

Samuel Taylor Coleridge's "The Rime of the Ancient Mariner" is one of the most scrutinized works in English poetry. A multi-volume set could be devoted to commentaries and criticism alone. Why such an abundance of commentary when the poem, at least as a story, seems in so little need of explanation?

There are many reasons this poem is worth our attention. First, there is the fact that the poem has been changed and appended since its first appearance in Wordsworth's and Coleridge's *Lyrical Ballads* (1798). The original poem's archaic language and derivative poeticisms, such as "Or my staff shall make thee skip" and "Like chaff we drove along," were updated for publication in 1800 due to the urgings of Coleridge's closest peer, Wordsworth, who felt "the old words and the strangeness of it have deterred readers from going on."

Another major change to the poem appeared in 1817 when marginal glosses (summations of the action) were added. Regarding these, William Empson has written extensively; he casts a suspicious eye on their reliability since Coleridge's mental condition was supposed to be of dubious clarity.

The point is that change to a major literary work produces interest and work for scholars. Comparisons made between earlier and later versions, and an addition of notes or glosses become a major preoccupation and reason for publication.

A second reason for the amount of criticism on "The Rime of the Ancient Mariner" is to determine the various works that contributed to the poem's composition. Inspirations for the poem are though to include travel narratives such as Shelvocke's *A Voyage Around the World by the Way of the Great South Sea* and Bligh's *A Voyage to the South Sea,* both of which recount killings of albatrosses.

Poems that influenced Coleridge include those in Percy's collection *Reliques of Ancient English Poetry.* In addition, one scholar believes an influence on Coleridge was an ancient Indian work translated from Sanskrit, *The Laws of Manu,* a work describing punishments for killing birds.

Finally, another reason for the large body of commentary is that "The Rime of the Ancient Mariner" provides fertile ground for the study of literature, philosophy, and psychology: from arguments for less poetic language and syntax in poems; to a defense for animal rights and of Christian devotion to God's great accomplishment, na-

What Do I Read Next?

- In later years, when he was no longer writing poetry, Coleridge commented on his work as an author in his *Biographia Literaria.*

- Some biographers have blamed Coleridge's decline as a poet on his long addiction to opium. Thomas de Quincey, a friend of Coleridge's, described his own opium addiction in the fascinating *Confessions of an English Opium Eater.*

- Coleridge was inspired by his readings on voyages of exploration made at the time. Captain James Cook describes his voyages around Antarctica and the South Seas in *Voyages of Discovery.*

- The Ancient Mariner was partially intended to capitalize on the interest in Gothic literature at the time. The craze for the Gothic was set off by Horace Walpole's *The Castle of Otranto,* a novel that retains many of its eerie qualities today.

- Nearly one hundred years after Coleridge wrote this poem, Friedrich Nietzsche wrote a long prose-poem, *Thus Spoke Zarathustra,* about another lonely man searching for meaning in life.

---

ture; to more recent theories, for example, Julia Kristeva's eruption of the semiotic (primitive response) into the realm of the symbolic (language and the social order).

One could say that ever since its appearance in 1798, the "The Rime of the Ancient Mariner" itself has been on a long voyage through English literature.

The poem is a ballad, a narrative song form written primarily in four-line stanzas (quatrains) of alternating lines of tetrameter (four accented beats per line) and trimeter (three accented beats). In the quatrains, second and fourth lines end-rhyme. "The Rime of the Ancient Mariner" depicts a ship captain's odyssey, as does its much earlier predecessor, the anonymous ballad "Sir Patrick Spens," also a ballad of sea and death.

Two stories dominate the action in "The Rime of the Ancient Mariner," the frame story describing an ancient mariner telling a story to a guest at a wedding, and the internal story about the mariner's bizarre tale of murdering a sea bird and suffering the consequences.

Perhaps it would be best to start with the frame story. The most obvious question that the reader might ask is, Why does the mariner's telling take place at a wedding? A likely answer is that weddings are declarations of love often made in a church. As the internal story is about Christian love for "all things both great and small," a church wedding is perhaps the closest ceremony expressing the sentiment of love between beings. The mariner's story expands the mutual declaration of love for two people into a declaration of love for all animals. At the wedding, the mariner is seized with the urge to tell his story. The mariner's glittering eye spots the correct listener, because at the end of the poem the wedding guest awakes the morning after the mariner's tale "a sadder and a wiser man."

What makes the wedding guest sadder and wiser? Of course, the tale of the mariner's unexplained murder of an albatross and his explained punishment for killing the sea bird. The reader might be prone to reflexively see this albatross as white. However, in Shelvocke's travel narrative mentioned above, the albatross is black. Further, Coleridge does not specify the bird's color, which in fact does vary. The absence of described color—especially whiteness—is telling: less is the sea bird an analogue of the Christ-dove (recall the lines, "as if it had been a Christian soul"), or a white bird symbolizing purity, than it is, plain and simple, a bird.

If the albatross is anything, it is a synecdoche, a concept or figure of speech by which a part is used to stand for the whole. In this case the albatross stands for all animals. By coupling the absence of described color with the unexplained murder, the killing can be viewed as a synecdoche for all killing of animals apart from that of killing to eat. That is, killing an animal apart from the purpose of survival, Coleridge seems to say, is a crime, i.e., murder, not only against the animal but against all of nature, especially one policed by spirits.

The crew cannot quite make up its mind whether the bird brings favorable or unfavorable sailing weather. First it blames the mariner for killing the bird that brought good weather, then praises him for killing the bird that brought bad weather, then finally blames him again, hanging the albatross around his neck like a punishing millstone or crucifix. What is the reader to think about the connection of the albatross to the weather?

Since the weather itself is both favorable and unfavorable for sailing immediately after the mariner kills the albatross, readers are left to form their own interpretation. It is most likely that the bird is neither symbol nor portent, but meant as a representative of nature, and for killing a representative of nature, the weather eventually turns bad. Coleridge might have thought that while people should not kill animals except for food (he was not a vegetarian), animals should be used for human gain, despite occasional cruelty since animals are of a lower order. Coleridge was, after all, a Christian, a religion that was not exactly consistent in its views of animals.

Whatever the finer points of Coleridge's view of animals, the mariner is indeed punished for his murder—though it might be said that it is the crew who suffers most since they all die. Are they killed simply for having thought for a brief moment that the mariner had done the right thing killing the albatross? Is not the death of all these men a rather heavy penalty to pay for thinking a wrong thought?

But asking this question seems to lead us astray. Instead, the death of the crew is better understood as a punishment directed at the mariner more than the crew: "The souls did from their bodies fly,—They fled to bliss or woe! And every soul, it passed me by, Like the whizz of my crossbow!" The whizz of souls punishes the mariner for his doubly fatal act. Still the expendability of the crew does seem severe, perhaps even a flaw despite the explanation that the punishment comes about due to a game of chance between death and death-in-life in Part III.

The last bit of penance the mariner must do before finishing his odyssey is confess to the hermit in Part VII. The threesome of the pilot, pilot's boy, and the hermit suggest an earthly holy trinity. If so, the hermit might be the analogue of the Holy Spirit, a kind of breath or voice from God, especially that voice manifested in sages and prophets. While the hermit of the poem makes no contact with serpents, one tradition of the hermit dictates that if he finds serpents, a symbol of the instincts, in his path, he is not to harm them but instead charm them into swirling around his walking staff like one hermit, Aesculapius, did (the image of staff and coiling snakes has become a Western symbol for medical science). Aesculapius not only marshalled the instincts/serpents to heal the sick—serpents were thought sacred to Aesculapius—but could bring the dead to life.

The hermit is therefore a fitting choice to rescue—with the help of the pilot and his son—the mariner after his death cruise, and finally to "heal" the mariner by hearing, as a priest would, the mariner's confession. The hermit, it seems, is the first of those the mariner must tell his story to in order to expiate his sinful killing of the albatross.

After the crew dies, the mariner himself becomes a wise hermit of the sea, for whom eventually serpents, or in this case, water snakes, become sacred (recall Aesculapius's ability to revive the dead). While the mariner did not revive the revenant crew himself, the crew revives following a lightning storm in which the moon is strangely visible. The constant references to moon, sun, the mariner's own glittering eye, and the evil one-eyed gaze of the crew in Part IV might remind readers of the one-eyed cyclops. The cyclops fashioned thunder and lightning for Zeus, the chief sky god who used them to kill Aesculapius. The mariner is not killed but somewhat punished by the terror of the crew being reanimated.

In the most important ways, however, the evil eyes of sun and moon become good ones after the mariner understands his mistake and the albatross falls from his neck. Even the reanimation of the crew is favorable in that the dead crew sails the ship that gets the mariner home. The mariner's change of heart regarding animals makes evil eyes turn good, the sun less hot, and the moon less cold.

With the mariner's new understanding—or perhaps better, his new vision—he is also able to pray. Ancient Egyptians defined the eye as the sun within the mouth. They were on target, for the mariner's new improved vision not only turns sun and moon hospitable, but transforms his fearful glittering eye into a wise one—a kind of third eye—that allows him to pray and, more importantly for this poem, to tell his story to those needing to hear it. Perhaps Coleridge was a little more astute than even the ancient mariner since Coleridge decided that not just certain people, but most everyone would wake up a little sadder and wiser after reading the "The Rime of the Ancient Mariner."

Source: Jhan Hochman, in an essay for *Poetry for Students,* Gale, 1998.

Raimonda Modiano

In the following essay, Modiano investigates "some aspects of the discrepancy between the ex-

perience the Mariner is likely to have undergone and his subsequent account of it."

With its first appearance in *Lyrical Ballads* (1798), *The Rime of the Ancient Mariner* emerged as a perplexing and highly controversial poem. To Coleridge's contemporaries it seemed a "rhapsody of unintelligible wildness and incoherence," occasionally redeemed by passages of unusual craftsmanship. To modern readers the poem is neither absurd nor spoiled by "great defects" of diction, character, and morality, and certainly no one today would want to call it a "Dutch attempt at German sublimity," as Southey mockingly described Coleridge's venture [in] *Coleridge: The Critical Heritage.* Yet although readers no longer dispute the coherence and quality of the poem, they hardly agree on what it means. *The Ancient Mariner* has been variously interpreted as a sacramental vision of crime, punishment, and salvation; as a nightmarish tale of senseless suffering; as a discourse on prayer; as a parody of the Christian doctrine of atonement; as an elaborate structure of occult symbolism; as a poetic workshop for Coleridge's later metaphysics; and as a prophetic allegory of Coleridge's personal life.

The myriad of critical interpretations points to a fundamental center of ambiguity in the poem. In his narrative the Mariner conspicuously relies on Christian rituals and beliefs, and yet the Christian doctrine fails to explain his world of excessive suffering and irrational events. Much of the Mariner's fate seems bleakly absurd, and yet he moves in an ordered universe where crime leads to suffering, however disproportionate, and blessing brings about redemption, however temporary. Natural forces such as the sun and the moon appear to form unified symbolical patterns, but contrary to what [American novelist and poet] Robert Penn Warren once tried to demonstrate, not everything good happens under the moon and everything bad under the sun. The poem teasingly gravitates toward coherent systems of thought, and yet no mythic or philosophical tradition, be it Christian, Egyptian, Neoplatonic, or the like, is large enough to contain it.

The Ancient Mariner raises special problems of interpretation because while it involves us in a series of captivating incidents and continuously tempts us to decipher some meaningful order which holds them together, it draws its dramatic action not from events as such which correspond to any one particular world view, but from the manner in which a deeply troubled character, laboring under various delusions, fears, and anxieties, is able to re-

construct a painful episode of his past. The poem does not offer an objective account of an adventurous voyage at the time when it originally occurred, but merely a later *version* of that voyage told by an old and lonely man who can neither explain nor fully describe what happened to him on a "wide wide sea."

From Coleridge's own statements about the composition of *The Ancient Mariner* and from the testimony of his contemporaries, it appears that Coleridge intended to explore precisely the discrepancy between actual experience and the recounting of experience by a character with a "most believing mind." Until late in his life Coleridge maintained his view that the true subject of a supernatural poem is the mentality of its narrator and the circumstances that cause him to confuse reality with his distorted apprehension of it. In a notebook entry written in 1830, Coleridge points out that, to insure the credibility and success of a supernatural tale, the poet "of his free will and judgement" must do "what the Believing Narrator of a Supernatural Incident, Apparition or Charm does from ignorance and weakness of mind,—i.e. mistake a *Subjective* product (A saw the Ghost of Z) for an objective fact—the Ghost of Z was there to be seen." The poet must also take into account the psychological forces that play upon the witness of an unfamiliar object, namely, [as noted in *Inquiring Spirit,* edited by Kathleen Coburn] "the magnifying and modifying power of Fear and *dreamy* Sensations," the "additive and supplementary interpolations of the *creative* Memory and the inferences ... of the prejudiced Judgement," which tend to slip into and are "confounded with the *Text* of the actual experience."

My interest here is to investigate some aspects of the discrepancy between the experience the Mariner is likely to have undergone and his subsequent account of it. I shall pay particular attention to the Wedding Guest's controlling influence on "the additive and supplementary interpolations" of the Mariner's "*creative* Memory" and the inferences of his "prejudiced Judgement." I would also like to show that language itself, although it is the only means by which the Mariner can relive his past, finally binds him to an inaccurate view of it. In many ways *The Ancient Mariner* draws our attention to the distance between private history and its narratives, between attempted "texts" and [as noted in *The Notebooks of Samuel Taylor Coleridge,* Volume III, edited by Kathleen Coburn] "the thousand indescribable things that form the whole reality of the living fuel." The poem tests the limits of man's power to convey through language the inner life of self which is intrinsically mysterious, prerational, and mute; it points to "the inadequacy of Words to Feeling, of the symbol to the Being" (*Notebooks,* II).

For the moment I would like to mention two hints by which the poem alerts us to this question. When the Mariner kills the Albatross, he not only alienates himself from nature, his shipmates, and God, but also loses his speech:

> And every tongue, through utter drought,
> Was withered at the root;
> We could not speak, no more than
> if We had been choked with soot.

Consequently, the Mariner remains silent during most of the action recorded in his tale. In Part III, upon apprehending the oncoming bark, he performs a sacrificial gesture to regain speech, biting his arm to draw blood. But the words he is able to utter ("A sail! a sail!"), words of hope and salvation, so blatantly conflict with the events that follow that the Mariner immediately reverts to his mute mode of perceiving, dreaming, enduring.... [T]he Mariner is cursed with the extinction of language. Indeed, how is one to name and encode that most bizarre apparition of a spectral bark with a deathly crew on it? The Mariner's world is full of sights "to dream of, not to tell." But although the Mariner, ... suffers the pain of inexpressible solitude after the contact with an unfamiliar world, he carries an even greater burden: all his life he *must* tell a story about an experience that has deprived him of a corresponding language, a story that will inevitably disclose its limitations.

This is one of the central paradoxes of the Mariner's situation. He can relieve himself of his inner agony and retain his sanity after his return from the vast solitudes of the ocean only by shaping an otherwise formless, incomprehensible, and unbearable past into a structured narrative with a beginning, climax, ending—and a moral lesson as well. Despite its inadequacies, language provides the Mariner with the means of expression and conceptual categories by which he can make sense of his experience and share it with an auditor. But through the very process of turning his recollections into a tale that must account for his endless wandering, and must also be credible to an auditor, the Mariner endows his past with a coherence and meaning which it did not originally possess. At an uncertain hour, the narrative that has temporarily given form and value to the Mariner's life is doomed to disintegrate, and his labor to "bring back fragments of former Feeling" begins anew (*Notebooks,* III).

Coleridge gives us yet another clue to the poem's concern with the disparity between discourse and experience. In 1817, when he revised *The Ancient Mariner* for *Sibylline Leaves,* he added an explanatory gloss which, allegedly, was meant to clarify the poem's geographical and moral directions. Wordsworth regarded the gloss as a superfluous afterthought, and later critics have likewise had difficulties in defining its function. Recently, William Empson [in *Coleridge's Verse: A Selection*] has made a strong case against the inclusion of the gloss in modern editions of *The Ancient Mariner,* for he believes that it is nothing but a "parasitic growth" which makes nonsense of the poem. It is true that, as Empson demonstrates, the gloss tends to misrepresent the poem by translating its ambiguities into simplistic equations. For example, the speaker of the gloss attributes the persecution following the killing of the Albatross to the Mariner's breach of the laws of hospitality, which hardly explains the cause of the Mariner's torment. To justify the presence of spirits in the Mariner's narrative, the speaker pedantically refers the reader to a scholarly source, and later he conveniently identifies the spirits animating the dead crew as a "troop of angelic spirits, sent down by the invocation of the guardian saint." Are we to agree with Empson that the gloss should be discarded as an entirely mistaken frame of reference for the poem, composed by a poet who had fallen out of sympathy with his earlier ideals and grown more conventional in his old age? I think not, for one good reason: the incongruities between the gloss and the Mariner's tale are much too obvious not to become suspect. It is hard to imagine that Coleridge could have misunderstood his own work to such a degree or that he would have compromised this artistic standards in order to suit the orthodox norms of the public of his time. Clearly, Coleridge did not want us to take the moralistic judgments proposed in the gloss at their face value. Rather, he uses the gloss to show what can happen to a work if clarity and secure moral explanations replaced its vastly nebulous universe....

It would, however, be a simplification to regard the gloss merely as Coleridge's answer to contemporary critics and reviewers who found *The Ancient Mariner* offensively obscure and lacking in moral sentiments. For one thing, the speaker of the gloss is not hopelessly unperceptive; in some instances he understands quite well the psychic factors that influence the Mariner's acts. Perhaps we can gain a fuller sense of the persona of the gloss through a comparison with [Scottish essayist and historian Thomas] Carlyle's *Sartor Resartus.* Like Teufelsdröckh's editor, the narrator of the gloss approaches a strange piece of imaginative literature from a rational position which is bound to be inadequate and is exposed for its inefficiencies. And like Carlyle's editor, the speaker of the gloss shows a capacity for imaginative growth and is drawn into the center of the hero's world to the point of stylistic imitation. And yet, very much like Carlyle's editor, the speaker can grow only so much in the direction of the hero's values, so that his distinctive sensibility is always in view.

The gloss, in effect, duplicates and is meant to highlight a particular situation dramatized in the poem. Within the narrative the Mariner tries to communicate to a conventionally-minded auditor a deeply personal experience of his past; in the gloss an editor tries to make that same experience accessible to readers who may share the biases of the Wedding Guest. Although the editor is often entranced by the strange fortunes that befall the Mariner, his responsibility toward the public makes him adopt a more sensible and ethical approach to the Mariner's story, an approach that results in gross misrepresentations. But the Mariner's need to maintain a dialogue with the Wedding Guest forces him to adopt the same approach with similar disadvantages. It is the Mariner who winds up his tale with a perfectly orthodox moral which contrasts with the pain and inexplicable suffering he had described all along. Thus, the editor's overt practice of translating the Mariner's narrative into a public language of familiar beliefs reflects a less perceptible process by which the Mariner gradually produces a socially acceptable account of his voyage. This process has as its source the Wedding Guest's resistance to the Mariner's tale.

The confrontation between the Mariner and the Wedding Guest is one of the most obvious features of surface plot in the poem, so obvious, in fact, that few critics have cared to discuss its significance at any length. The Mariner's unusual character has so absorbed critics that the minor appearance of the Wedding Guest has slipped by unattended. A few have tried to rescue him from neglect, showing that he, like the Mariner, is capable of conversion and changes from a stubbornly conventional man to a "sadder and wiser" member of his community. But no matter how generous we want to be with the Wedding Guest, it is the Mariner who engages our interest, and although one might want to know to what extent he influences the Wedding Guest's life, it is more important to investigate whether the Wedding Guest affects the Mariner in any way or, rather, whether the Mariner is affected by his own compulsion to speak to the Wedding Guest.

Critics have not sufficiently recognized the Mariner's vulnerable susceptibility to the Wedding Guest, in part because they have mistakenly seen their relationship as one of the master-pupil kind. The Mariner is often taken to be the impersonated figure of the artist-missionary who wants to inform the Wedding Guest about a different, more problematic reality beyond the kirk, hill, and lighthouse top of the shore. From this perspective the Wedding Guest is reduced to a frivolous and naïve man who must be taught that there are more things on earth than marriage feasts. But the Mariner does not simply have a mission; he has a fate as well. When he meets the Wedding Guest, he has one possession; a story. His monomania, his sole mode of being, is an oral recapitulation of a devastating experience of his past. Unless his ghastly tale is told, he can never escape, not even momentarily, the most "woful agony." The Mariner desperately needs the Wedding Guest, because through his confession he hopes to wrench himself free of his painful loneliness and find some continuity between the chaos of his past life and the Wedding Guest's world of communal rituals. His need for the Wedding Guest is so urgent that at the beginning he resorts to physical force to make him listen to his tale. His dependence upon the Wedding Guest's continuous attention will significantly influence the very way in which he shapes his narrative, as I shall show in the following discussion.

To my knowledge, no critic has noticed that an abrupt shift takes place in the Mariner's story when the Wedding Guest interrupts him in Parts IV and V of the poem. In each case, and more prominently in the latter, the Mariner interpolates calm scenes of beauty in a context that does not assimilate them. Preceding the Wedding Guest's intervention in Part IV, for instance, is the scene of the Mariner's shipmates dropping dead one by one, each turning his face with a "ghastly pang" and cursing the Mariner "with his eye." This gruesome moment is followed, after the Wedding Guest's outburst of fear and the Mariner's haunting cry of loneliness, by a return to the scene of death which, surprisingly, becomes quite attractive to view:

> The many men, so beautiful!
> And they all dead did lie:
> And a thousand thousand slimy things
> Lived on; and so did I.

Having previously witnessed the pang of death in the sailors' eyes, one would expect to see ugly faces distorted by pain rather than serene bodies merging quietly with the general calm of life. The incongruity of this scene is intensified by the fact that in the stanzas immediately following, the beauty of death vanishes completely and in its stead terror creeps in. There is nothing aesthetically pleasing about the sight of a "rotting deck" on a "rotting sea," or of "cold sweat" melting from dead limbs. What is it, then, that causes the Mariner's brief and rather unnatural perception of beauty? It is possible to speculate that, given the proximity of this scene of restful calm to the Wedding Guest's intervention, it might be in some way related to it. This suggestion gains support from the fact that, with the next intervention of the Wedding Guest in Part V, a parallel though much more emphatic change occurs in the Mariner's narrative from supernatural horror to humanized beauty.

Before the Wedding Guest interrupts him in Part V, the Mariner relives one of the most frightening episodes of his past. The dead sailors suddenly rise like ghosts, without speaking or moving their eyes. They begin to work the ship as "they were wont to do," but their motions are lifeless and their silence eerie. The sailors are indeed "ghastly," as the Mariner describes them, and their miraculous reanimation is even more horrifying than their previous dying. At this point the Wedding Guest breaks in, voicing his anxiety; to placate his fears, the Mariner provides him with the following explanation:

'Twas not those souls that fled in pain,
Which to their corses came again,
But a troop of spirits blest.

Although the Wedding Guest might buy this explanation, the reader will not and should not. The metamorphosis of the "ghastly crew" into a disembodied troop of angelic spirits is much too obvious a tour de force to be credible. It looks like a "supplementary interpolation" prompted by the Mariner's need to respond to and pacify the Wedding Guest. It is important to note that the lines just quoted were not part of the original composition of *The Ancient Mariner;* Coleridge inserted them in 1800 when he revised the poem for the second edition of *Lyrical Ballads.* Empson, [in *Coleridge's Verse,*] uses this example to demonstrate how Coleridge manages to ruin his work by trying to cover up its unchaste strangeness. But to read the passage this way is to lift it out of its dramatic context and forget that it is the Mariner who speaks it, not Coleridge. When Coleridge added these lines in 1800, he made another important change in the original text: in the second version, the Wedding Guest ad-

dresses himself to the Mariner just before the blest spirits enter into the Mariner's tale. Viewed from this perspective, the lines do not emphasize Coleridge's orthodox leanings; rather, they identify the Wedding Guest as a source for the Mariner's orthodox vocabulary. They indicate that the presence of the Wedding Guest forces the Mariner to mold his unfamiliar past into a more conventional and communicable story. The lines also establish a link between the intervention of the Wedding Guest and the following episode of enchanting sights and sounds, a link that is vaguely suggested in the 1798 text.

Since this episode is central to my thesis, I shall quote it in full and examine it in detail:

For when it dawned—they dropped their arms,
And clustered round the mast;
Sweet sounds rose slowly through their mouths,
And from their bodies passed.

Around, around, flew each sweet sound,
Then darted to the Sun;
Slowly the sounds came back again,
Now mixed, now one by one.

Sometimes a-dropping from the sky
I heard the sky-lark sing;
Sometimes all little birds that are,
How they seemed to fill the sea and air
With their sweet jargoning!

And now 'twas like all instruments,
Now like a lonely flute;
And now it is an angel's song,
That makes the heavens be mute.

It ceased; yet still the sails made on
A pleasant noise till noon,
A noise like of a hidden brook
In the leafy month of June,
That to the sleeping woods all night
Singeth a quiet tune.

This is a beautiful reverie, but it remains a reverie nonetheless, a distorted apprehension of the Mariner's existence on the ocean. It is difficult to believe with J. B. Beer [in his *Coleridge the Visionary*] that the episode marks the culmination of the Mariner's process of regeneration, the completion of his vision of the ideal universe "which was only prefigured to him in the sight of the moon and the water-snakes." Nothing happens to the Mariner himself at this time. He is able to apprehend harmonious sounds, but that does not transform him in the way the blessing of the water snakes did. The act of blessing had immediate and major psychic effects on the Mariner: "the self-same moment" he could pray, the Albatross fell off his neck, he was able to sleep, and he was released from thirst. No such positive consequences follow from the

Mariner's entranced vision of sweet sounds. The ship moves on quietly for a while, "Yet never a breeze did breathe"—a statement with an ominous ring in view of previous scenes of terror when motion took place "Without a breeze, without a tide." Indeed, no sooner does the sun fix itself upon the bark than the Mariner is knocked down senseless by the ship's sudden bound.

There is a fundamental difference, both in the manner of the Mariner's composition and in its content, between the scene of blessing and that of divine music. In the former instance the Mariner's experience takes in beings which inhabited his world all along: the slimy water snakes. He can therefore focus on them sharply and perceive them vividly. Although, as he declares, no human tongue could describe their beauty, he is able to represent in detail their shapes, colors, and movements. In the latter example, on the other hand, the Mariner has difficulties in identifying the things he perceives. Unable to determine the source of the sounds he hears or their exact quality, he proceeds to name them through a series of analogies, constantly shifting the terms of comparison. The sounds come to him now mixed, now one by one; they seem to originate from the song of a skylark or other little birds and resemble in turn the collective tune of "all instruments" or the individual voice of a lonely flute, an angel's song, or a hidden brook. The whole scene is cast in an unreal light. Nothing is what it is but seems to be like something else. Moreover, all the terms of this rich metaphoric exchange come from a realm that is essentially foreign to the ocean. (There are no skylarks on the ocean.) It is quite apparent that the Mariner borrows the metaphors composing his aural reverie from a landscape that belongs entirely to the Wedding Guest's shore world. Only in this world would one normally hear sounds of skylarks, lonely flutes, or hidden brooks, and would such time references as "the leafy month of June" have any significance. For the Mariner whose ship is stalled on a silent sea, time extends indefinitely, and conventional month-counts have ceased to matter.

It appears, then, that the Wedding Guest's intervention in Parts IV and V of the poem occasions a sudden shift of narrative perspective in the Mariner's tale which meliorates the horror of previous scenes. This shows that the Mariner's story is a composite of his past and present, of the time of his voyage and the time of dialogue about it. At crucial moments the present invades the Mariner's past, clouding his memory of what that past really

was, giving him fantasies of little birds exchanging "sweet jargoning" in the midst of a grotesque spectacle of bodies that mimic the actions of live men. The episode of angelic sounds makes two important suggestions: one, that the Wedding Guest has a direct impact on the course of the Mariner's story, and two, that the Mariner's tale and the life behind it do not always coincide. The episode also reveals the Mariner's particular habit of metaphoric expression which will eventually distance him from his own past, leaving him in the end with a dry moral that falls flat even on the Wedding Guest's ears. As I shall show in the rest of the paper, the Mariner is subject to linguistic forces which finally defeat him, mocking the pride he takes in his "strange power of speech."

A close look at the vocabulary of the poem indicates that the Mariner resorts to two modes of language which, though mixing with each other, remain relatively distinct. When he is deeply immersed in his past and oblivious to his auditor, he speaks in a language that is primarily sensorial and concrete. Objects and actions are named as they are perceived without taking on conceptual meanings external to their immediate experiential value. On the other hand, when the Mariner is influenced by a social situation—a debate with his shipmates, a dialogue with the Wedding Guest, or a discussion between two spirits apprehended from a trance—he tends to use a language that does not merely record objects but assigns them meanings dependent upon a system of shared mythology.

For convenience I would like to label the former type as the language of self and the latter as the language of social discourse. A complex process of transfer from one type of language to the other governs the development of the Mariner's narrative. As the Mariner departs from the shore and advances toward the climactic event of his journey, the encounter with the specter-bark, his tale gradually empties itself of metaphors which link him to the safe public world he has left behind. After the intervention of the Wedding Guest in Part IV, this process reverses itself. The Mariner is increasingly tempted to find Christian equivalents in his mysteriously demonic universe and begins to draw upon orthodox analogies to characterize unique experiences. The language of metaphor, however, has dangerous pitfalls. By using metaphor, one may easily end up being used by it; that is, one may cease to distinguish between models of comparison and the reality they were meant to illustrate. This is, I believe, what happens to the

Mariner. Having borrowed his terms of description from the Wedding Guest's world in order to make himself understood to his listener, the Mariner soon begins to confuse it with his own world, and in the end he identifies himself completely with the public values represented by his auditor.

In Part I, the Mariner uses a mixed language which contains both vivid pictorial and auditory imagery and conventional perceptions of Christian heritage. To say that the ice is "As green as emerald" and sounds "Like noises in a swound" is to establish an analogy in which both terms belong to the same level of physical reality and which functions to intensify the sensory qualities of the objects perceived. On the other hand, to say that the ship drove fast "As who pursued with yell and blow / Still treads the shadow of his foe," or that the arrival of the Albatross was "hailed … in God's name," as "if it had been a Christian soul," is to build up a quite different kind of analogy which refers particular objects to concepts of a well-established tradition ("foe," "God's name," "Christian soul"). When at the end of Part I the Wedding Guest invokes "God" to "save" the Mariner from the "fiends" that plague him, he expresses himself precisely in the language of that tradition.

These two types of analogy illustrate the linguistic trends I wish to trace here, one based on concrete perceptions of individual objects, the other on more abstract and conceptual interpretations of events. Both trends recur throughout the poem, but their frequency and distribution vary from part to part. In Part II, for instance, the action of sensory language is more intense than in Part I, where it frequently mixes with the language of social discourse. This mixture is due in part to the Wedding Guest's interruption and in part to the circumstance that the Mariner still speaks collectively for himself and his shipmates. As the Mariner becomes an isolated voice after killing the Albatross, and his ship enters an unknown world ("We were the first that ever burst / Into that silent sea"), unusual events begin to happen, all demanding an acute sensory awareness. The ship is stopped in the midst of a "copper sky," "As idle as a painted ship / Upon a painted ocean"; an infinitude of water surrounds the crew only to remind them of their thirst; slimy things crawl upon the sea, and the water burns at night "like a witch's oils," "green, and blue and white."

Despite the increase of sensory data, the language of social discourse is not extinct in this section of the poem. It occurs before the Mariner's ad-

> *[T]he Mariner desires to make sense of chance and irrationality in terms of accepted myths in order to maintain control over an experience that borders on madness."*

vent into the silent sea, toward the beginning of Part II. Here the shipmates gather to discuss the Mariner's act of shooting the Albatross. They refer to it in turn as "hellish" and "right," appealing to conventional though opposite moral absolutes. In the midst of this debate the Mariner notices the rising of the sun: "Nor dim nor red, *like God's own head,* / The glorious Sun uprist" (my italics). There are many different suns and moons in the poem, some more symbolic than others. The sun that rose upon the right at the beginning of Part II is a merely physical sun engaged in its daily activities. But the sun of this passage is primarily a symbolic object; it is a Christian sun and glorious. The point I want to stress is that in the context of a social dialogue, the Mariner's perception of the surrounding universe is conceptualized. As soon as the dialogue is over, the narrative turns to sensory objects and immediate experiences of physical suffering (unbearable thirst, the withering of speech organs).

The language of social discourse reasserts itself at the end of Part II, where the Mariner directs his attention to his shipmates. He detects "evil looks" in their faces and finds the Albatross hung around his neck instead of the cross. The exchange of the cross for the slain Albatross summons again the Christian doctrine as a mythological frame of reference. But this replacement does not simply establish a symbolic association between the Albatross and Christ; it also marks the Mariner's separation from a world represented by the cross, a world of redemptive suffering and just order. In Part III, this separation grows wider. As the specterbark approaches the ship from a distance, the Mariner's universe becomes increasingly mysterious and its morality increasingly dubious. The fact that his fate is decided by an irrational fortune game played by frightening and alien figures undermines the logic of a Christian world view, as Edward Bostetter [in his "The Nightmare World of *The Ancient Mariner*"] convincingly demonstrates. The Mariner still attempts ritualistic invocations to protective powers ("Heaven's Mother send us grace!") and gestures of sacrifice to regain speech (the biting of his flesh), but these prove to be meaningless. Familiar assumptions about reality, such as "a sail is a ship which means people which means aid," are no longer functional in a universe policed by Death and Life-in-Death. The very nature of knowing has become problematic.

By the time the Mariner encounters the specter-bark, he is completely divorced from communal ties: he has been separated from nature, from his shipmates, from God, and from language itself. Significantly, his narrative loses many of its conceptual referents to an established order and marks his immergence into a private world which has no correlation to reality as commonly understood. The episode of the encounter with the specter-bark is composed of a series of concentrated and fast-moving actions, and the Mariner uses strikingly unusual analogies to describe them:

> A speck, a mist, a shape, I wist!
> And still it neared and neared:
> As if it dodged a water-sprite,
> It plunged and tacked and veered.
>
> And straight the Sun was flecked with bars,
> (Heaven's Mother send us grace!)
> As if through a dungeon-grate he peered
> With broad and burning face.
>
> Are those *her* sails that glance in the Sun,
> Like restless gossameres?
>
> And every soul, it passed me by,
> Like the whizz of my cross-bow!

Although they contain words that connote social or metaphysical concepts (dungeon, soul), these analogies are essentially concrete. The reference to a dungeon grate emphasizes the physical appearance of the sun. Likewise, the last analogy focuses not on the metaphysical status of the sailors' departing souls, but on their movement and quality of sound.

After the intervention of the Wedding Guest in Part IV, a change in the Mariner's use of language becomes noticeable. Although the narrative maintains stretches of sensory descriptions (the sight of the water snakes in the moonlight, for instance), a different mode of discourse begins to emerge. The narrative moves from a world commanded by Death and Life-in-Death to one where a "saint" is

supposed to "take pity" on the Mariner, and finally does, as the Mariner interprets it, when he blesses the water snakes. The Mariner turns to traditional concepts, such as heaven, hell, and religious rituals of blessing and praying. He had previously described his experiences through the action of physical objects; now he resort to familiar metaphors ("My heart as dry as dust") or to analogies that appeal to an orthodox mentality:

> An orphan's curse would drag to hell
> A spirit from on high;
> But oh! more horrible than that
> Is the curse in a dead man's eye!

This is not the way the Mariner projects horror in Part III. In this passage he insists that his experience is horrible through a conspicuous social rhetoric. He refers to "An orphan's curse," to "hell," to spirits "from on high," and uses conventional phrases such as "the curse in a dead man's eye." These lines do not advance the action of the narrative or add new descriptive details; instead, they offer an explanation that demands the exercise of a traditional imagination. The Wedding Guest, for example, might understand the Mariner's situation if he were to think of an orphan's curse and accept the fact that a curse in a dead man's eye is even more horrible. As this example shows, there are parts of the Mariner's narrative in which he does not describe anything new but reflects on his experience, and these parts tend to attract a social mode of discourse. The same thing happens at the end of Part IV, where the Mariner explains the blessing of the water snakes as the merciful act of a saint, and at the beginning of Part V, where he attributes the long-awaited sleep to "Mary Queen" of Heaven.

In Part V we are plunged again into the center of acute sensory perceptions and dynamic action. Refreshed by rain during sleep, the Mariner awakes to an animated landscape of explosive fire-flags, dancing stars, roaring wind, and torrential rain. He continues to observe the activity of nature and the ghostly reanimation of the crew until the Wedding Guest interrupts him. As the Mariner's dream soliloquy is shattered ("It had been strange, even in a dream, / To have seen those dead men rise"), his narrative takes an orthodox turn which conceptualizes and tames his previous account of events. What follows is the episode of sweet sounds already discussed, where we find metaphors drawn from a common stock of religious vocabulary ("And now it is an angel's song, / That makes the heavens be mute"), as well as from a hospitable shore landscape.

From this point on, the rich sensorial language and swift-moving narrative of earlier episodes give way to a more pronounced trend of social discourse. The end of Part V and the beginning of Part VI consist of a rather long dialogue between two spirits which recasts the entire sequence of calamities suffered by the Mariner in the light of Christian morality. The killing of the Albatross is related to the Crucifixion, and the Mariner's subsequent punishments are interpreted as a trial of "penance." The dialogue prefigures both the concepts and the conventional rhythms of the Mariner's concluding moral; lines like " 'He loved the bird that loved the man / Who shot him with his bow' " sound close to

> He prayeth best, who loveth best
> All things both great and small;
> For the dear God who loveth us
> He made and loveth all.

The Mariner soon adopts the Christian explanation provided by the two spirits and believes that he is in a world where crime leads to punishment and penance to salvation. When he sees the hermit on the shore, he hopes to be released from his sin through the ritual of confession: "He'll shrieve my soul, he'll wash away / The Albatross's blood."

As the Mariner approaches the shore, elements of a familiar landscape and concepts of a familiar world begin to invade his narrative. The wind feels "Like a meadow-gale of spring," and the sailors' bodies, which were "flat, lifeless and flat," are miraculously transformed into a "heavenly sight" of seraphs. Even when the Mariner concentrates on physical objects and actions, he uses a language that is more commonplace than before. Analogies such as "The harbour-bay was clear as glass," "Like one that hath been seven days drowned / My body lay afloat," or "But swift as dreams, myself I found / Within the Pilot's boat" are pale and lack the unusual imaginative quality of previous images such as sails "Like restless gossameres" or souls rushing by like the whizz of the crossbow.

I do not mean to claim that the distinction between sensory and conceptual language has mathematical precision. My purpose has been to point out some linguistic strategies employed in *The Ancient Mariner* to show the modifications undergone by individual experiences during the process of their transfer into verbal structures which make possible the communication between speaker and listener. I have also tried to establish a critical perspective from which the Mariner's concluding moral no longer appears as a feeble tag unconnected with the content of his story, as critics have often argued. The moral represents the culmination of a tendency that is apparent throughout the Mariner's tale and is only given a more emphatic form toward the end. As I have shown, the Mariner erects orthodox structures out of unorthodox experiences when he interprets events or when the Wedding Guest claims his attention. The Mariner is in many ways a Wedding Guest himself, and his exchange with his auditor reflects an inner conflict. Like the Wedding Guest, the Mariner desires to make sense of chance and irrationality in terms of accepted myths in order to maintain control over an experience that borders on madness. In light of the changes that occur in the Mariner's narrative when his auditor interrupts him in Parts IV and V, it is not at all surprising that the Mariner, when he reaches out for the Wedding Guest for the last time, utters a moral extracted from the codes by which the Wedding Guest leads his life. The irony of the Mariner's fate is that, while trying to overcome the resistance of the Wedding Guest by exposing his auditor to a more imaginative way of thinking and at the same time by drawing closer to his values, the Mariner succeeds in alienating both himself and the Wedding Guest from their own respective worlds. When the Mariner delivers his closing moral, the Wedding Guest is "stunned" and "of sense forlorn," a state hardly suitable for the wise lesson of love and prayer the Mariner tries to teach him. He has been initiated indeed into a universe where God "Scarce seemed … to be," and naturally he goes neither to the marriage feast nor to the church. On the other hand, the tale which ends with the moral is a tale gone wrong for the Mariner too, and he is the first to feel it. The memory of green ice, slimy water snakes, and the revengeful specter-bark continues to haunt the mind and demands a new story. But every time the Mariner begins his tale again, trying to seize upon his past as firmly and urgently as he commands a Wedding Guest to listen, he is bound to fall into the same trap of dialogued experience and to construct a narrative that will provide a Christian abstract of a far more mysterious and in part untranslatable episode of his past.

The search for an adequate medium of expression that could accommodate the deepest demands of the self without sacrificing either the authenticity or the intelligibility of the artistic product has a long and tortuous history in Coleridge even prior to the composition of *The Ancient Mariner,* and it forms the subject of many reflections in his later work. Coleridge's views on the suitability of language to self-expression and to the representation of fundamental intuitions gained through the imagination are not consistent, varying according to his moods and the specific purpose of his arguments. At times Coleridge regards language as a potent and elevated means of articulating the poet's visionary perceptions of reality. As "the medium of all Thoughts to *ourselves* of all Feelings to others, & partly to ourselves," language partakes of "the two things mediated," participating in the unified entity which it represents [from *The Notebooks of Samuel Taylor Coleridge*]. Coleridge agrees with his contemporary, [as noted in the preface to *Aids to Reflection,*] the philologist Horne Tooke, that words are the wheels of intellect, "but such as Ezekiel beheld in 'the visions of God.' ... Whithersoever the Spirit was to go, the Wheels went, and thither was their Spirit to go; *for the Spirit of the living creature was in the wheels also.*" But this great credit granted to language is often undermined by Coleridge's gloomy awareness of the abstractness of words and their power to chain, distort, and impoverish the experiences of the self. In one notebook entry he says:

> It is the instinct of the Letter to bring into subjection to itself the Spirit.—The latter cannot dispute—nor can it be disputed for, but with a certainty of defeat. For words express generalities that can be made *so* clear—they have neither the play of colors, nor the untranslatable meaning of the eye, nor any of the thousand indescribable things that form the whole reality of the living fuel. (*Notebooks,* III)

Like other Romantic writers, including Wordsworth and Shelley, Coleridge believed in the existence of a prelinguistic level of consciousness which cannot be fitted into any one objectified verbal structure. The poet's innermost feelings and impressions are, as he puts it in a notebook entry, "languageless." Words convey "generalities, tho' some less than others," and they "not only awake but really involve associations of other words as well as other Thoughts—but that, which I see, must be felt, be possessed, in and by its sole self!" (*Notebooks,* III). The stronger the desire to possess an emotion or image in its unadulterated form, the more frustrating it is to try to break through the abstract network of language. Who, Coleridge asks,

> has deeply felt, deeply, deeply! & not fretted & grown impatient at the inadequacy of Words to Feeling, of the symbol to the Being?—Words—what are they but a subtle *matter?* and the meanness of Matter must they have, & the Soul must pine in them ... O what then are Words, but articulated Sighs of a Prisoner heard from his Dungeon! powerful only as they express their utter impotence! (*Notebooks,* II)

To escape the prison of language, Coleridge tries out various means of nonverbal representation only to discover that while they supplement language, none of them is a fit measurement for the noblest parts of one's nature:

> Without Drawing I feel myself but half invested with Language—Music too is wanting in me.—But yet tho' one should unite Poetry, Draftsman's-ship & Music—the greater & perhaps nobler certainly all the subtler parts of one's nature, must be solitary—Man exists herein to himself & to God alone /—Yea, in how much only to God—how much lies *below* his own Consciousness. (*Notebooks,* I)

If poetry, drawing, and music together fail to communicate the voice of self, what can one expect from language alone? Moreover, how does one share with readers or listeners impressions which they have never experienced in their own lives, "material Objects, Landscapes, Trees, ... they have never seen"? "Assuredly, the impressions received by the words are very faint compared with the actual impression—it is but a dim abstract at best—and most often a Sort of *tentative process* now by this analogy, now by that, to recall the reader to some experiences, he must have, tho' he had not attended to them" (*Notebooks,* III). The Mariner too draws upon the resources of analogies to make himself intelligible to the Wedding Guest, but what he offers his auditor is an imperfect copy of an inimitable original. The actual impressions and memories of his past cry out for words. The inner anguish generates the tale, and the tale once told perpetuates the anguish. The Mariner is trapped in a Sisyphean labor to articulate his solitary voyage on a "wide wide sea."

Source: Raimonda Modiano, "Words and 'Languageless' Meanings: Limits of Expression in 'The Rime of the Ancient Mariner,'" in *Modern Language Quarterly,* Vol. 38, No. 1, March 1977, pp. 40–61.

Sources

Boulger, James D., *Twentieth Century Interpretations of The Rime of the Ancient Mariner,* Prentice Hall, Inc., 1969.

Empson, William, "The Ancient Mariner: An Answer to Warren," in *Kenyon Review,* Winter, 1993, pp. 155-77.

House, Humphry, in *Coleridge: The Clark Lectures, 1951-52,* Rupert Hart-Davis, 1953, 167 p.

Knox-Shaw, P. H., "The Eastern Ancient Mariner," in *Essays in Criticism,* April, 1996, pp. 115-35.

Lowes, John Livingston, in *The Road to Xanadu: A Study in the Ways of the Imagination,* Houghton-Mifflin Company, 1927, 639 p.

Stevenson, Warren, "The Case of the Missing Captain," in *The Wordsworth Circle,* Winter, 1995, pp. 12-18.

Warren, Robert Penn, "A Poem of Pure Imagination: An Experiment in Reading," in *The Rime of the Ancient Mariner* by Samuel Taylor Coleridge, Reynal and Hitchcock, 1946, pp. 59-117.

Watkins, Daniel P., "History as Demon in Coleridge's *The Rime of the Ancient Mariner,*" in *Papers on Language and Literature,* Vol. 24, No. 1, Winter 1988.

Williams, Anne, "An I for an Eye," in *PMLA,* October, 1993, pp. 1114-127.

Wordsworth, William, and Samuel Taylor Coleridge, *Lyrical Ballads,* Methuen, 1968.

For Further Study

Buchan, A. M., "The Sad Wisdom of the Mariner," in *Twentieth Century Interpretations of The Rime of the Ancient Mariner,* Englewood Cliffs, NJ: Prentice Hall, Inc., 1969.

An accessible essay that considers deeper implications of the killing of the Albatross, and the guilt and loneliness it causes.

Holmes, Richard, *Coleridge,* New York: Oxford University Press, 1982.

Discusses the world of chaos and chance in *The Ancient Mariner.*

Purser, J. W. R., "Interpretation of *The Ancient Mariner,*" in *The Review of English Studies,* Vol. VII, No. 31, August 1957.

Purser glosses the most important symbols in the poem in this readable article.

Radley, Virginia L., *Samuel Taylor Coleridge,* Twayne English Authors Series, New York: Twayne Publishers, 1966.

A general introduction to Coleridge's major work, including *The Ancient Mariner.*

Twitchell, James, "The World above the Ancient Mariner," *Texas Studies of Literature and Language,* Vol. 17, No. 1, Spring 1975.

A study of the invisible world of spirits through which the Ancient Mariner sailed.

Whalley, George, "The Mariner and the Albatross," in *Twentieth Century Interpretations of "The Rime of the Ancient Mariner,"* Englewood Cliffs, NJ: Prentice Hall, Inc., 1969.

Whalley discusses the symbolism of the Albatross and how the Mariner's experience mirrored Coleridge's own life.

Shine, Perishing Republic

Robinson Jeffers

1925

"Shine, Perishing Republic," published in 1925 in the collection *Roan Stallion, Tamar and Other Poems,* is one of Robinson Jeffers's most anthologized pieces. This book's publication marked the beginning of his fame as a poet and the start of a career that would garner as much acclaim as it would harsh criticism. Written in a prosperous American period typically remembered as the Roaring Twenties, "Shine, Perishing Republic" reveals an extreme distaste for the underlying national trend toward corruption and dictatorship. Using long lines and an anthem-like tone reminiscent of Walt Whitman, Jeffers uses the poem to express a philosophy he would continue to explore throughout his career: Inhumanism. Jeffers sees the core of America hardening into the "mould of its vulgarity," corrupt and self-centered, man's relationship with fellow man like that of "clever servant" and "insufferable master."

Author Biography

Born in Pittsburgh, Pennsylvania in 1887, Robinson Jeffers was the son of a professor of theology and, thus, no stranger to the academic world. He began tutorials at the age of three and a half with his parents, studying biblical history and Greek mythology. By the age of twelve young Jeffers was well read in French, German, Latin, Greek, and English. The University of Western Pennsylvania accepted him for admission when he was fifteen, but his father's failing health prompted the family

to move to California. He remained there for the majority of his life, where he came to be known as a "Californian landscape painter," due to his abundance of vivid nature poems. At his new university, Occidental, Jeffers edited the school's literary magazine while taking classes in astronomy, ethics, geology, history, economics, biblical literature, and rhetoric. While later pursuing a graduate degree in literature at the University of Southern California (USC), by then only eighteen years old, Jeffers fell in love with fellow student Una Call Kuster. At the time of their affair she was two years older and already married. Jeffers soon left the country to study philosophy in Switzerland, where he picked up what he would later term "inhumanism," before returning to USC to study medicine for three years. Although he attempted to avoid Una and their affair by moving to Seattle, when he inherited almost $10,000 in 1912 and moved back to southern California, they were soon reunited.

After marrying Una in 1913, upon her divorce from her first husband, and tragically losing their baby daughter, Jeffers and his wife moved to Carmel, California, where he built by hand a granite house complete with stone tower. With a clear view of the ocean and the mountains, Jeffers rarely left his isolated fortress, writing more than nineteen volumes of poetry from within "Hawk Tower's" stone walls. He used part of his inheritance to self publish his first volume, *Flagons and Apples,* that same year, which critics ignored; he later wished that he had instead destroyed the collection of "embarrassingly stilted love poems." The southern California landscape, which he compared to the "magnificent unspoiled scenery" of Homer's Ithaca, became his new passion and would dominate the majority of his work after 1914. Highly disturbed by two horrific world wars, Jeffers experienced what he later called "the accidental new birth" of his mind, which revealed to him the beginnings of his isolationist philosophy of "inhumanism." His wife considered the act of building the stone tower the source of his new vision. "As he helped the masons shift and place the wind and water-worn granite," she later noted, "I think he realized some kinship with it and became aware of strengths in himself unknown before." Jeffers found a strange escape in stone imagery from the suffering in the world. He considered it inhuman but beautiful, permanent, and universal compared to our fleeting time in this world.

Jeffers and Una had twin sons while living in the stone house. Over the course of his career Jeffers drew the attention of many critics. Some re-

Robinson Jeffers

jected his work outright as pseudo-prophetic and bloated, while others praised him as the most original of visionary poets of this century. He was the recipient of numerous awards, including *Poetry* magazine's Levinson, Eunice Tiethens Memorial and Union League Civic and Arts Foundation Prizes, The Borestone Mountain Poetry Award, and an Academy of American Poets Fellowship. A prolific poet and playwright, self-declared philosopher and prophet, Robinson Jeffers died in his sleep in 1962 after four years of quickly degenerating health.

Poem Text

While this America settles in the mould of its
    vulgarity, heavily thickening to empire,
And protest, only a bubble in the molten mass,
    pops and sighs out, and the mass hardens,

I sadly smiling remember that the flower fades to
    make fruit, the fruit rots to make earth.
Out of the mother; and though the spring
    exultances, ripeness and decadence; and
    home to the mother.

You making haste haste on decay: not   5
    blameworthy; life is good, be it stubbornly
    long or suddenly

A mortal splendor: meteors are not needed less
    than mountains: shine, perishing republic,

But for my children, I would have them keep their
    distance from the thickening center;
    corruption

Never has been compulsory, when the cities lie at
    the monster's feet there are left the
    mountains.

And boys, be in nothing so moderate as in love of
    man, a clever servant, insufferable master.

There is the trap that catches noblest spiritts, that   10
    caught—they say—God, when he walked on
    earth.

Poem Summary

Lines: 1-2

Jeffers wastes no time in revealing the target of his anthem: the "perishing republic" from the title is America. While a republic is a nation that is supposed to be ruled equally by all of its people, Jeffers sees the United States instead settling "in the mould of its vulgarity, heavily thickening to empire." In steel factories like those of his boyhood Pittsburgh, workers pour thick, glowing, molten ore into molds to be cast into parts for warships and automobiles. Jeffers uses this direct comparison, or metaphor, to hold the shape of his extreme distaste for America's corruption. Unlike a republic of equal voters, an empire is ruled by a small group of powerful people determined to expand their national territory. Social "protest," which is a republic's most powerful tool, means little according to Jeffers, who sees it as "only a bubble in the molten mass [that] pops and sighs out, and the mass hardens." Such a dire image sets the mood for the rest of the poem, which itself is a form of protest against this America "heavily thickening to empire."

Early on it is important to note that although these two lines are broken by the editor into four in order to fit the page, Jeffers intends for the reader to read them as just two metrical line units. In cases where the poetic line unit cannot physically fit completely across the page, editors will break the line, but indent it to indicate it is a continuation rather than the start of a new poetic thought.

Lines: 3-4

After lamenting the direction America seems to be heading, in these next lines the speaker tries to find some consolation. Typical of Jeffers, he looks to nature for perspective. There he "sadly

smiling remembers" that perhaps in everything there is a cycle. Although America is settling into vulgarity and any protest to that fact "pops and sighs out," he remembers that "the flower fades to make fruit, the fruit rots to make earth." Out of death comes life; from decay, fertilizer for new growth. Note in line 4 his use of the word "decadence," which literally means a period of decay, but was also a popular phrase at the time for describing a sinful or corrupt lifestyle.

This is a fairly optimistic shift in tone from the first two lines. Perhaps in alluding to "mother earth," Jeffers reiterates the idea of a cycle in line 3, in which "Out of the mother" comes a circle of spring flowers, ripened fruit and decay, then "home" again "to the mother." By looking to nature to find the "larger scope of things," the speaker is hoping that out of America's "decadence," will come an era of rebirth.

Line: 5

Here the speaker turns his voice from an introspective pose to direct address, telling the reader, "You making haste haste on decay: not blameworthy; life is good…." Again playing with the double meaning of "decadence" as introduced in the previous lines, Jeffers seems to say that no matter how fast we allow our own decay, it is not something he is going to blame us for. Diffusing his earlier harshness, here the poet shows he recognizes that "life is good, be it stubbornly long or suddenly / a mortal splendor." No matter how wild and fast or stubbornly long our lives are, generally things are good. The phrase "suddenly / a mortal splendor" may foreshadow the ending of the poem, which alludes to a time when God took mortal form to walk the earth.

Line: 6

In line 6, Jeffers introduces two polar images: the bright splendor of a meteor streaking across the sky versus the immovable and stoic mountain below. This dual image is typical of Jeffers, who often placed dynamic or spiritual images next to those of permanence. The most famous of these image pairs are the Rock and the Hawk, which appear again and again in his work. In this poem, the meteor and the mountain are "needed" equally, like the two forces of yin and yang that work against each other in order to create the circle of life. Having reached this point in the poem, the speaker pauses to refrain, or repeat, the title "Shine, perishing republic." After accompanying the speaker through a landscape of molten vulgarity, fruit ripening and decaying, and meteors streaking over mountains, the phrase holds a new meaning, a significance earned from the journey.

Lines: 7-8

While he does not blame those of us who lead decadent lives, in these lines the speaker has a different attitude about how his children should live. Pivoting on the word "but," Jeffers informs us, "But for my children, I would have them keep their distance from the thickening center" (first introduced in lines 1 and 2). Like any protective parent, he does not want his children exposed to vulgarity and an empire of greed. "Corruption," he continues, "Never has been compulsory," or required. The "monster" in line 8 might be the same grotesque mass that began the poem. As the speaker predicted, the center of the monster has hardened, turning to mountains.

Note where Jeffers decided to break line 7, though a single sentence flows through both lines and into line 8. By breaking the line after the word "corruption," Jeffers causes us to read the end of line 7 as " … the thickening center; corruption." Although grammatically the word "corruption" is the beginning of a new thought (corruption / Never has been compulsory), for an instant the reader is reminded that corruption is also the center of the hardening mass from the first lines of the poem.

Line: 9

In this line Jeffers shifts his voice again, this time speaking directly to his young boys. He seems to advise them to be wary of becoming too attached to fellow man, or humankind. This is the basic tenant of his self-proclaimed philosophy of "Inhumanism," which asserts that the root of most evil can be found in mankind's relationship to itself; man is cruelest to fellow man. He continues his warning with an analogy, comparing this relationship to that of "clever servant" to "insufferable master," where, like in an empire, there is a severe imbalance of power.

Line: 10

This final line widens the scope of the poem even further, targeting the very basis of Christianity. "There is the trap," Jeffers concludes, "that catches the noblest spirits, that caught—they say—God, when he walked the earth." Like the "mortal splendor" from line 6, many Christians believed that God took human form in the body of Christ to walk among men. According to the New Testa-

ment, ("they say") God sent his son to spread the new gospel to a world that had become afflicted with corruption and vulgarity, just as Jeffers saw America in the 1920s. But Jesus walked the earth for only 33 years before his fellow man "trapped him" and sent him to his death on the cross. Ending the poem on such a dark note, Jeffers seems to point out that man's cruelty to fellow man is "a trap" that does not discriminate what it captures, be it human, animal, or even the "noblest spirit" we worship.

Themes

Patriotism

Although the portrayal of America in "Shine, Perishing Republic" is not flattering, the poem is written from the point of view of a speaker who still feels patriotic enough to cry out against the forces of corruption and vulgarity that threaten his country. The poem is written in the same anthem-like tone and long lines as Whitman's patriotic "O Captain, My Captain," written upon the occasion of President Lincoln's assassination. As harsh as the speaker's views may be, describing America as a monster settling into "the mould of its vulgarity, heavily thickening to empire," he does so with a sad nostalgia for the country he perceives as burning out like the last streak of a comet across the night sky. He realizes that even this type of protest is perhaps useless, "only a bubble in the molten mass [that] pops and sighs out."

Many critics place Jeffers at the center of the long American tradition of individualist anarchism. He believed in the importance of individual freedom and an ideal government comprised of a loose confederation of small communities. Contrary to this, at the time of the poem's publication in 1925, America was emerging from two decades as a rising world power and entering an era that would show sharp social and economic divide among its people. The prosperity of the twenties benefited a specific segment of society, but at the expense of a great mass of factory workers and common laborers who were underpaid and nonunionized. Rural areas of the country declined economically while the corporate business world grew in the heart of cities. These trends culminated in the late 1920s and the 1930s as the Great Depression, and against this inevitable calamity the speaker summons up perhaps a last ounce of patriotism to call out, "shine, perishing republic."

Topics for Further Study

- Do you feel America today is better or worse than the nation Jeffers describes? Have we as a people settled into "a mould of vulgarity?" Use recent news items as examples to discuss your answers.

- For some, the thought of a poet living alone in a stone tower seems to perfectly fit the cliche of an artist as solitary figure. Do you believe artists—poets, painters, dancers, etc.—are more isolated from society than others? Give examples to explore and develop your viewpoint.

- Write a poem protesting a trend you see in terms of the environment, the military, economy, religious attitudes, etc. Use the first half of your poem to directly address those causing the problem. In the second half, shift your point of view and speak to your future children. Compare poems and discuss.

Cycle of Life

It is common for the poems of Robinson Jeffers to turn to nature when faced with the evils of man. In "Shine, Perishing Republic," the speaker "sadly smiling" recalls the natural cycle of life and death to find comfort. After beginning the poem with images of death and decay, he reminds the reader and himself that "the flower fades to make fruit, the fruit rots to make earth." Playing with the word "decadence," which was a popular way to describe the bohemian lifestyle, Jeffers hopes that, like in nature, every period of "decay" is followed by rebirth and "spring exultances." Similarly, perhaps after America's period of decay will come a better time, though this type of optimism in his poems is rare and often short-lived. Jeffers generally believed that man should reject all relationships with fellow man, choosing instead a deeper relationship with nature in order to understand the larger cycles of life and death, as "Out of the mother" we are born, live and die, returning again "home to the mother."

God and Religion

The poem, which begins as a patriotic outcry and then turns to nature's cycle of life for comfort, eventually concludes on a religious note. While carefully distancing himself (with the interjection "—*they* say—") from the Christians he alludes to, Jeffers ends the poem with an example of what he considers man's biggest "trap." Reminiscent of his inhumanist philosophies that rejected organized religion and found man's relationship to man the main source of corruption, Jeffers uses Christ's crucifixion as the prime example of how cruel we can be to each other. Our cruelty is like a "trap" that can snare even the noblest spirits; man is so cruel to fellow man that even God, whom Christians believed walked the earth in the body of Jesus Christ, could not escape.

Style

"Shine, Perishing Republic" is written in free verse, which means Jeffers did not use a set rhyme pattern or traditional form of line length to construct this poem. "Free" does not necessarily mean without form; rather, the poem's shape grows organically from its content, similar to how a river carves its own banks. Jeffers believed poems should balance both "substance and sense, a physical and psychological reality." Perhaps driven by this logical instinct, the poem is divided into unrhymed couplets, or two-line stanzas. "Stanza" literally means "room" in Italian, and in this poem Jeffers carefully organizes his shifts of voice and tone inside these five rooms.

Jeffers uses long, Whitman-like lines throughout the poem, some extending further than this book's margins allow (such lines broken by the editor rather than the poet are continued as indented lines). These long lines seem to build a momentum of their own, the poet's voice building force as it stretches out across the page. Jeffers uses these extended lines to perhaps mirror the speaker's anger at witnessing America's republic decline into a bubbling mass of vulgarity. The lines of the poem do not follow a set rhythmic pattern of accented stresses; as in the sonnet form, each line's heavy beat matches the forceful and angered voice of a father worried about his children's future, pounding like a fist:

"I would **have** them **keep** their **dis**tance from the **thick**ening **cen**ter, cor**rup**tion."

Compare & Contrast

- **1925:** Transatlantic telephone service begins between London and New York, costing $25 per minute and restricted to 3 minutes total.

  Today: The internet, or World Wide Web, provides nearly instant communication and distribution of information over an international network of telephone lines and satellites.

- **1925:** Television gets its first demonstration in the auditorium of New York's Bell Telephone Labs. Closer to the first video conference than television as we know it today, audience members watch Herbert Hoover address them from Washington, D.C., while listening to his voice over telephone wires.

  Today: International businesses, universities, and classrooms widely use integrated video con-

ferencing systems for Distance Learning, employee training, and political debates.

- **1925:** Police arrest over 75,000 people for drinking alcohol, which is strictly prohibited. Some 1,565 Americans die from drinking bad homemade liquor, hundreds are blinded, and many are killed in bootlegger wars.

  Today: Alcohol companies advertise widely on television and in the print media, convincing the nation any cause for celebration is "Miller Time." Over 100,000 Americans die each year of alcohol poisoning alone; countless others are injured or killed in alcohol-related auto accidents and alcoholism-based domestic violence.

Jeffers uses similar tensions between content and form throughout the poem to give an otherwise "free verse" poem a solid and sustaining structure.

Historical Context

At the time of the poem's publication in 1925, America was emerging from two decades as a rising world power and entering an era that would feature sharp social divide and poverty. The prosperity of the 1920s benefited a specific segment of society at the expense of a great mass of factory workers and common laborers who were underpaid and nonunionized. Rural areas of the country declined economically, while the corporate business world grew in power and wealth. A leisure class emerged in the suburbs as well as in the bohemian quarters of larger cities, and with it came a lack of morality and values that disturbed many. Among these angered outsiders was Jeffers, who some critics describe as an prophet scolding his tribe for their greed.

The 1920s were also a time of literary exploration and vision. Many noted "lost generation" writers like Hemingway traveled the world in search of purpose and inspiration. This was also the decade in which Charles Lindbergh completed the first solo, nonstop transatlantic flight, Albert Hegenberger made the first successful flight from San Francisco to Hawaii, and Amelia Earhart scouted her first transatlantic flight with two other pilots.

Contrary to this national fever for travel and exploration, Jeffers instead chose to move his family to southern California and build a granite house by hand complete with an observation tower (known as "Hawk Tower"). Virtually isolated in his stone house perched on a remote rocky shore, Jeffers spent the rest of his life composing books and philosophical essays.

Critical Overview

It is difficult to find much specific criticism of "Shine, Perishing Republic" and Jeffers's other early, shorter poems. But critical commentary discussing Jeffers as a philosophical poet and writer of long, narrative pieces is easier to find.

Many critics begin their discussion of his nature poetry with a synopsis of his fairly obscure personal philosophy. "Inhumanism," as Jeffers called it, "is a shifting of emphasis from man to not man. It offers a reasonable detachment as rule of conduct, instead of love, hate and envy." This was a repugnant idea to many, including several critics who find contradictions in Jeffers's work.

Some critics dismissed his body of work outright. Kenneth Rexroth, in his book *Assays,* commented, "[In Jeffers's] philosophy I find a mass of high-flown statements indulged in for their melodrama alone, and often essentially meaningless." Robert Boyers, writing for the *Sewanee Review,* similarly writes, "Structurally, [his poems] are sound enough, but the texture of these poems is swollen by effusions of philosophizing and by attempts to impose representative signification on characters and actions."

Other critics view Jeffers and his "philosophic-dramatic" poetry as revolutionary and prophetic work worthy of high accolades. James Dickey praises Jeffers in *Babel to Byzantium* by observing that he "fills a position in this country that would simply have been an empty gap without him: that of the poet as prophet, as large-scale philosopher, as doctrine-giver." Perhaps the greatest praise comes from Nobel-winning poet Czeslaw Milosz, who was quoted in the *Los Angeles Times* as calling Jeffers "undoubtedly … one of the great poets of this century."

Criticism

Sean Robisch

Sean Robisch teaches composition and literature at Purdue University and holds a Ph.D. in American Literature. His fiction has appeared in Hopewell Review *and* Puerto del Sol. *In the following essay, Robisch explains why Jeffers seems so critical of humanity and notes our personal responsibility as citizens of any "republic."*

We are taught to love our nation, just as, when he was a young poet, Robinson Jeffers was taught to love his nation. But for each of us, the dilemma always exists as to how we are to love an entity so difficult to define as a nation, which changes over time and is something both greater than and less than the geographical area inside its boundaries.

Just because you draw a line on a map, have you made, for instance, a Republic? And how are we to know whether or not this territory will endure, as much as we champion its existence? In "Shine, Perishing Republic," written in 1925, Jeffers addresses these questions.

I say "addresses," and and not answers, because Jeffers was not prone to deliver easy, closed-ended conclusions (even in such poems as "The Answer"). Instead, his poems are filled with paradoxes, dilemmas, and uncomfortable situations. If the first time you read "Shine, Perishing Republic" you think of it as an unpatriotic poem, then the second time through, knowing what Jeffers was apt to do in his work, you might have a much different response. It is true that Jeffers is hard on nationhood; in fact, much of his work is critical of humanity in general. Humanity can be "slavish in the mass," he writes, "but at stricken moments it can shine terribly against the dark magnificence of things." In many of his poems, Jeffers expresses this position by pitting human indulgences against the purities of the natural world (which preceded humanity), and he often concludes that people fall short of an acceptable standard for behaving properly in their environment. Awareness of this underlying philosophy is necessary when considering Jeffers's writing in general and "Shine, Perishing Republic" in particular.

In this poem, Jeffers employs the concept of nationhood to analyze the value of human endeavor in terms of the earth's lifetime and its systems. When he writes that he is "sadly smiling," the poet might be sarcastic, cynical, or even prophetic. Although the statement that the Republic is perishing may seem ominous and pessimistic, it is really a simple declaration of the predictable. If we judge this viewpoint as too harsh, however, it may just speak to our tendency of avoiding criticism while simultaneously seeking praise. It is important to be demanding of humans and the nations they form, Jeffers implies, because if we are too quick with our allegiances we may not ask the difficult questions necessary for improvement and future survival. Corruption, the poet tells us, is "never compulsory," meaning that we have choices to do what is pure or vulgar. If we do not avoid corruption, we may march forward in blind loyalty until we finally commit the horrible act of sacrificing someone— even God. So while Jeffers explains that blame does us no good, he also, in the second-to-last line, warns "his boys" not to put so much faith and love in humanity that they absolve them of any wrongdoing. However, if we are all part of the Republic, and part of humanity, then we also must be part of what is poured into the "mould" and therefore be a little "vulgar" ourselves. How are we to handle this position? The poem's last stanza tells us: we are to be wary, cautious, and to remember that the Republic itself, the hardening "mass" (he surely intends the pun) will meet its end, to begin something new.

Poets are experts at metaphor, and in this poem Jeffers demonstrates his ability to help us see what he means, since what he is trying to express is both paradoxical and complex. First, he gives us a familiar metaphor, the image of the mould. Because of its once-generous immigration policy that welcomed people from all nations, the United States has, for many years, been called a "melting pot," in which races, genders, classes, and creeds all blend together into a kind of alloy. If this is so, then what shape does the molten material form when it cools and hardens? Jeffers decides here that the shape, the mould into which the liquid is poured, is "vulgarity." He then extends this metaphor. What if someone decided to openly criticize the Republic? According to Jeffers, in America a protest is only a bubble in the mixture. He uses the phrase "sighs out" to imply the tiny puff of air when a bubble bursts, likening it to a small voice briefly noted that soon disappears. The mass takes its place and hardens over the vacated spot. This is a seemingly pessimistic way to talk about one's own country, but Jeffers immediately follows that image of the hardening mass with organic images of rebirth in the next stanza. Now, the death of that bubble in the mix may take on some importance; it reminds us that out of mortality may come fertility.

This is also a crucial point in Jeffers's work, as Robert Brophy has explained. Jeffers works with mythic-ritual cycles, which do not consider death an end, but as a marker for the next phase of the cycle. One of the images prominent in myths about the cycle of death and life is the blood sacrifice, in which a scapegoat would take on the sins of the community and be ritually killed, ushering in a new era or "season." After insisting for two stanzas that the Republic will not outlast the mountains—that whether "stubbornly long or suddenly a mortal splendor," all nations will inevitably end—Jeffers closes the poem by making reference to the crucifixion of Christ. In this way, Jeffers delivers a complex message about what benefits (freedom and loyalty) and what evils (entrapment and murder) might grow out of the same Republic.

What Do I Read Next?

- Many critics trace Jeffers's theories of inhumanism back to his years of philosophical studies in Zurich. While at the university he read Schopenhauer and Nietzsche, two philosophers whose works shed interesting light on his later poems.

- Robinson Jeffers's complete body of poetry, titled *The Collected Poems of Robinson Jeffers,* is collected in two 300-page volumes, edited by Tim Hurt.

- David Brower recently re-released a book of poems and photographs originally published in 1965 by the Sierra Club. *Not Man Apart: Photographs of the Big Sur Coast* combines Jeffers's poems with photos by several famous artists, including Edward Weston and Ansel Adams.

- You can read Jeffers's censored poetry in the book *In This Wild Water: The Suppressed Poems of Robinson Jeffers.*

If we were to believe that death sends us to a better place, then wouldn't it be a compliment to wish death on the Republic? We are tempted to say no, of course; wishing death on anyone, let alone an entire nation, is usually thought to be morally unacceptable. However, the nation, as all human-made things, will eventually end, so wishing its death and predicting its death may be easily confused, depending on the language used. Nations are finite, and according to the worldview we get in the poem, this is not bad, but merely inevitable. One image that has been used for many centuries to articulate this idea of death's inevitability as a way of keeping nations humble is the image of the toppling ruin. In the United States it is sometimes demonstrated in the paintings of the Hudson River School, notably in Thomas Cole's series *The Course of Empire.* The image of a building's broken stone overgrown with foliage reminds us that even the greatest of human works is subject to the force of time. Therefore, the first two words in Jeffers's title, "Shine, Perishing" both command the

> *During times when many poets were testing the intellectual possibilities of poetry, Jeffers was testing how it might contribute to what he saw as the most fundamental force, that of a planet spinning in the cosmos.*"

nation to be a good one and predict its imminent decline. When, in the middle of the poem, Jeffers writes that we make the process of decay speed up in our haste (he doubles the haste), he also tells us that blame has no place in the cycle. "Life is good," he writes, but it will end. Therefore, we are called to look beyond our Republic and beyond blame for what is most valuable and necessary.

In his *Shine, Perishing Republic: Robinson Jeffers and the Tragic Sense in Modern Poetry*, Rudolph Gilbert points out that Jeffers "draws his meanings from age-old symbols, never from arguments." This may one reason he earned such high praise at the beginning of his career and such criticism (even lessening attention from critics) toward its end. While "Shine, Perishing Republic" does not involve the intense experiments with language that "high modernists" such as Ezra Pound, Gertrude Stein, and T. S. Eliot were trying during the 1920s, it does provide complex moral dilemmas about what we mean by the concepts of "civilization" and "progress." This poem was not Jeffers's only comment about such things: in 1935 he wrote "Shine, Republic," a poem investigating how freedom might become itself a trap, and in 1944 he wrote "Shine, Empire." In both of these works, Jeffers criticized the human obsession with freedom, which was to him both a great result of democracy and, in the larger sense, an illusion. In "Shine, Empire" he took an unpopular stance by criticizing the participation in war of both Axis and Allied forces. As he continued to address such issues, some critics accused his work of having lost its polish and having turned into a series of outbursts. Other com-

mentators, including Brother Antoninus and Rudolphe Louis Megroz, defended him for both his vision and craft in responding to the conditions not only of his present, but of humanity's possible future.

In "Shine, Perishing Republic" Jeffers's use of the word "Republic" is an allusion to the Roman Empire, the great power of the ancient world that toppled. An indication of this allusion is in the Christian reference in the poem's closing lines. As in his poem "Meditation on Saviors," Jeffers frequently presents the reader with a struggle between the force of materialistic civilization and its constructs versus spirituality and the organic earth. The industrial and material is Caesar's world, while the organic and spiritual is Christ's—the same struggle Plato gives us in *Phaedrus* with the Temple of Reason. In this metaphor, Caesar becomes the savior of the Republic, and Christ the scapegoat who is sacrificed at the end of a season in the mythic cycle. This may be why the "mould" in the poem, that image of what is humanly made with machinery and liquid alloys, is called "vulgarity." Jeffers invites us to become upset with a criticism of nationhood and civilization, because when we do so we might respond, line-by-line through the poem, with the same logic used both to forge empires and to sacrifice individuals.

Robinson Jeffers was regularly "ahead of his time." In the 1960s, his reputation was revitalized by the various environmental movements that found him willing to take a hard look at what human beings were doing to the nonhuman. The work environmentalist thinkers often considered had been written before there was an "environmental movement" as such, and in between the most prolific periods of national policy-making about how the "Republic" would consider "the mother" (a popular metaphor for Earth, as in the Greek goddess Gaia). These periods were the 1850s-1860s and the 1960s-1970s. Jeffers's most noteworthy poems were written during the business and mechanization booms of the 1920s-1940s. During times when many poets were testing the intellectual possibilities of poetry, Jeffers was testing how it might contribute to what he saw as the most fundamental force, that of a planet spinning in the cosmos. In this light, his views of nationhood as finite, of blame as useless, and of blind loyalty as destructive, are worth considering in order to make us better readers of poetry, which in turn might make us more responsible children of empires.

Source: Sean Robisch, in an essay for *Poetry for Students*, Gale, 1998.

David J. Rothman

David J. Rothman is the executive director of the Robinson Jeffers Association, the author of several books of poetry, and a contributor of articles, essays, and poetry to numerous journals and books. In the following essay, Rothman describes how Jeffers's clear language and complex syntax enchance the poet's commentary on the rise and decline of societies, and he also provides a sympathetic examination of Jeffers's often-maligned philosophy of "Inhumanism."

Robinson Jeffers (1887-1962) was one of the most famous American poets of the twentieth century, and he led a career that ranks as one of the most fascinating, productive, and controversial of all American artists. In 1925, already in his late 30s, Jeffers was the author of two virtually unknown volumes of verse that were very different from his mature work. Then, with the publication of *Roan Stallion, Tamar, and Other Poems* in 1925, he rocketed to a fame shared by only a handful of contemporary writers. In the following twelve years, his output was tremendous: seven lengthy volumes of new poetry, each of which contained one or more long, tragic, narrative poems along with visionary lyrics about nature and the fate of civilization. Several of the books also included verse plays, often based on free adaptations of Greek tragedies. Many of these volumes were highly praised best-sellers, and some are still in print. In 1932, with the publication of *Thurso's Landing and Other Poems,* his photograph, a portrait by Edward Weston, appeared on the cover of *Time* magazine. The anonymous reviewer referred to Jeffers as a writer "whom a considerable public now considers the most impressive poet the U.S. has yet produced."

After this high point, Jeffers's star sank rapidly beginning in the mid-1930s. The causes included his continuing emphasis on what was viewed as social detachment, in a time when more and more writers were calling for politically engaged art; his occasionally bitter philosophy of "Inhumanism," in which Jeffers argued that human beings should turn away from human problems to contemplate the more lasting beauty and significance of the inhuman, natural world; his advocacy of isolationism during World War II, including poems highly critical of both Hitler and the Allies; and the harsh judgment by many critics that his poems lacked erudition, complexity, and craft, and were hysterical, by which the critics meant excessively violent and shrill. Although Jeffers published more work

of high quality, and his free adaptation of Euripides's *Medea* enjoyed a highly successful run on Broadway in the late 1940s, by the time of his death in 1962 he had been all but forgotten by scholars and critics, although he has always retained a popular following, especially as a poet of the natural world.

Today Jeffers is primarily known through a few anthologized lyrics, including "Shine, Perishing Republic," and some of the shorter narratives (such as "Roan Stallion"). This is unfortunate, because he wrote a tremendous body of work, much of it at the same level of intensity. Despite general critical indifference and lingering scholarly hostility, he has directly influenced not only poets such as William Everson (who credited his exposure to Jeffers's work as one of the most important events of his life) and, more recently, Mark Jarman, but also figures as different as O'Neill and Faulkner, along with artists in other fields, such as photographers Edward Weston and Ansel Adams. The list of recent and contemporary writers who claim to admire him includes Charles Bukowski, Robert Bly, Diane Wakoski, Edward Abbey, Dana Gioia, John Haines, Czeslaw Milosz, Gary Snyder, and many others. As Gioia has pointed out, Jeffers remains the greatest poet to date of the American West; one of the greatest American poets of the natural world, indeed one of the greatest visionary poets of the natural sublime ever to have written, and a crucial influence on the entire modern environmental movement; and one of the greatest narrative poets America has produced. I would add that he is one of the greatest verse dramatists this country has ever seen, perhaps surpassed only by T. S. Eliot. Most important, he conveys his vision of the poet's place in the world so powerfully that even many who do not agree with him feel compelled to address his art and its claims.

"Shine, Perishing Republic" remains the most widely anthologized Jeffers poem. First published in *Roan Stallion, Tamar, and Other Poems,* the 1925 volume that made Jeffers's reputation, the title may have the most lasting resonance of any phrase Jeffers ever coined. Among many others, Edward Abbey quotes it in *Desert Solitaire,* and Robert Frost uses it as the epigraph to his late poem "Our Doom to Bloom" (from *In the Clearing,* 1961). It is one of Jeffers's earliest lyrics in his mature style, and it announces a resigned political pessimism that would characterize his political and social poetry for the following four decades. On the basis of this poem and others, Jeffers was often accused of being a misanthrope. While there is a good

> *Looking out at a society that he considers corrupt, Jeffers does not choose to engage in protest, but rather to remember the cycle of nature in which even rotting fruit has a constructive role to play in the life of the world ...."*

deal of skepticism in the poem about humanity's ability to create a society worth joining, it is a serious mistake to treat this skepticism as the only tone in the poem, because that approach obscures Jeffers's complex view of love.

The poem appears to begin with a metaphorical description of political decay that will lead to a call to action. In clear, forthright language radically at odds with the complexity and obscurity of many contemporary modernist lyrics (Eliot, Pound, Stevens, H.D. and others), Jeffers compares America to a tremendously hot, but slowly cooling and hardening, molten mass:

> While this America settles in the mould of its
>   vulgarity, heavily thickening to empire,
> And protest, only a bubble in the molten mass,
>   pops and sighs out, and the mass hardens ...

While the language is clear, the syntax is complex, containing no fewer than four dependent clauses all predicated on the initial word "While," one of which contains a complex adverbial modifier ("And protest, only a bubble in the molten mass, pops and sighs out"). Also, while the imagery seems clear at first, Jeffers leaves things a bit vague. Is America being compared to a river of volcanic lava that has run its course and is now cooling? That would make some sense, as the country began in a fiery political revolution. But lava runs where it wishes, not settling "in a mould." So is Jeffers comparing it to some artificially heated substance, perhaps metal, that is being forged?

Jeffers does not resolve the question, but it seems clear that he sees his country as having once been fiery and dynamic, whether through natural or artificial heat, but now as a cooling substance being cast into a "mould of vulgarity," in which protest is merely an ineffectual bubble. The imagery of scorching heat and the mention of protest suggest that some kind of response is forthcoming. Jeffers holds us in suspense for quite some time, forcing us to wait through an entire stanza for the main clause of the sentence. Yet when this clause comes, at the beginning of the next stanza, it involves not action, but only wistful, personal observation and an instruction to himself to remember something:

> I sadly smiling remember that the flower fades to
>   make fruit, the fruit rots to make earth.
> Out of the mother; and through the spring
>   exultances, ripeness and decadence; and
>   home to the mother.

This second stanza is nothing less than a philosophical theory or myth of history as an organic cycle that Jeffers probably picked up from his readings in writers such as Vico and Spengler. Looking out at a society that he considers corrupt, Jeffers does not choose to engage in protest, but rather to remember the cycle of nature in which even rotting fruit has a constructive role to play in the life of the world; decay is as natural as growth. As many had done before him, Jeffers compares the rise and decline of civilizations to the natural life of plants. Whereas in the first stanza society was compared to something fiery where no life could possibly live, "the molten mass," in the second stanza it is compared to "the mother," the earth and all the life it creates, sustains, and gathers back into itself in death.

While Jeffers's language seems simple, the richness of his intertwined metaphors is part of what makes the poem far more than a sermon about how societies rise and fall. Consider the simple phrase "spring exultances." What are those? Are they the flowers of spring mentioned earlier in the same line? If so, in what sense are flowers "exultances?" To exult means to rejoice jubilantly, and derives from a Latin root that means roughly "to leap up." The word, therefore, does make sense to connect the literal thing, the flower, with the quality of exultation in spring. It is through this careful and extremely clear joining of real things with seasons and metaphorical structures of history—both at the level of words and in the social myth Jeffers sketches—that the poem gains its force. Just as flowers have the quality of "spring exultances," fruit gains the quality of "ripeness" and rotting gains the quality of "decadence," all of which are also terms with moral and historical connotations.

Astonishingly, most critics have downplayed Jeffers's interest in poetic language, as he did not dwell upon it in his writing about poetry and his meanings appear at first to be fairly straightforward. Yet, if read with care, "Shine, Perishing Republic" reveals a rich and deeply satisfying set of metaphorical associations that harken back at least as far as the prophetic language of the Old Testament. At the same time Jeffers's poem is quite different from any simple fire-and-brimstone sermon about corruption, even though Jeffers obviously saw America as in decline, and in the poem warns his sons to keep their distance from it.

We can see more clearly what Jeffers is doing in this regard if we compare his descriptions of a corrupt America to a passage from Jeremiah, perhaps the fieriest book in the Old Testament. Jeremiah, like other books of the Hebrew bible, is even written in rhythms that Jeffers echoes in his poetry:

> 1.21 A voice was heard upon the high places, weeping and supplication of the children of Israel: for they have perverted their way, and they have forgotten the Lord their God.
>
> 1.22 Return, ye backsliding children, and I will heal your backslidings. Behold, we come unto thee; for thou art the Lord our God.
>
> 1.23 Truly in vain is salvation hoped for from the hills, and from the multitude of mountains; truly in the Lord our God is the salvation of Israel.

Jeffers was often called a prophet, and there is no doubt that his voice contains a prophetic tone. Yet instead of counseling others or himself to pursue protest, or even virtuous action, as Jeremiah does, Jeffers suggests that all one can do is recall and meditate on the cycles of history, which proceed as inevitably as the life of a pear.

At the same time, Jeffers also does not want to be misunderstood as attacking those who are "making haste," whatever their project. As if anticipating a critical response to his self-imposed isolation, the poem's third stanza turns directly to someone with whom Jeffers appears to be having a conversation or argument. The poem suddenly becomes suddenly more intimate as Jeffers addresses this hypothetical "You."

> You making hast haste on decay: not blameworthy;
>   life is good, be it stubbornly long or
>   suddenly
> A mortal splendor: meteors are not needed less
>   than mountains: shine, perishing republic.

The passage gives the sense that the poem began in response to something that someone else may have said about the need for action. Jeffers's response is first that things are pretty much hopeless; second, that this is not really a problem, as all societies develop and decline in predictable ways that are similar to natural cycles; but third, that, despite such facts, action (by which he presumably means some kind of political or social activism) is "not blameworthy," because it is all part of a larger, cosmic vitality that transcends mere human concerns.

At this point, we need to have a somewhat better sense of what Jeffers meant by "Inhumanism," the name he later gave to what he called his "philosophical attitude." Inhumanism undergirds all of Jeffers's work, including his poems, with political and social themes. As Jeffers recognized, it is not a philosophy in the analytical sense, but rather a way of trying to relate to reality in a particular way and answer perennial questions. In a lyric from just a few years after "Shine, Perishing Republic," called "Credo," Jeffers wrote that "The beauty of things was born before the eyes and sufficient to itself; the heart-breaking beauty / Will remain when there is no heart to break for it." In other words, as he repeated throughout his life, the beauty of nature, in ocean, rock, hawk, sky, and star, has absolutely no need of human beings. In one of his longer poems, the narrative poem "Roan Stallion," he actually called humanity "the last, least taint of a trace in the dregs of the solution" of the universe.

In Jeffers's view, many of civilization's problems—that led during his lifetime to two devastating world wars—grew out of a childish insistence on still seeing ourselves as the center of the universe and always looking inward when we should be looking outward, away from human concerns and toward the wild beauty of all creation. So Jeffers defined Inhumanism as "a shifting of emphasis and significance from man to not-man; the rejection of human solipsism and recognition of the transhuman magnificence." Hostile critics often called this attitude hateful and misanthropic, when it is probably more appropriate to say that Jeffers felt we should not exaggerate our own importance in the cosmic scheme of things. In Jeffers's view, as he wrote in a poem called "The Answer":

> ... the greatest beauty is Organic wholeness, the
>   wholeness of life and things, the divine
>   beauty of the universe. Love that, not man
>   Apart from that, or else you will share
>   man's pitiful confusions, or drown in
>   despair when his days darken.

This is the approach to life, deeply influenced by modern science as well as traditional Christianity, that has led many to see Jeffers as one of the spiritual founders of the modern environmental movement. The emphasis on loving the universe, not merely man apart from it, is Jeffers's solution to the problem of how to confront the horrible truths of human history in many poems, including "Shine, Perishing Republic." Jeffers's response to the horrors of World War I and the developments that ultimately led to World War II is literally to try to put them in perspective by placing them in a much larger framework of contemplation—the realm of meteors and mountains. If we, like so many of Jeffers's weaker critics, see only Jeffers's denunciations of human behavior, we miss this crucial element in his poetry, which transforms it into something quite different.

At the same time as he denounces "America … thickening to empire," Jeffers also makes it clear that the intimate circle of his own family is still very much at stake. His work is that of a poet's and therefore intimately involved with people, not merely that of a philosopher contemplating ideas. In the poem's final two stanzas, he first talks about how he would convey his ideas to his sons, and then shifts the address of the poem directly to them:

> But for my children, I would have them keep their
>   distance from the thickening center;
>   corruption
> Never has been compulsory, when the cities lie at
>   the monster's feet there are left the
>   mountains.
> And boys, be in nothing so moderate as in love of
>   man, a clever servant, insufferable master.
> There is the trap that catches noblest spirits, that
>   caught—they—say God, when he walked on
>   earth.

Notice that where Jeremiah says "Truly in vain is salvation hoped for from the hills, and from the multitude of mountains; truly in the Lord our God is the salvation of Israel," Jeffers seems almost to reverse this. If not salvation, then at least freedom from corruption will be found in the mountains, in the "inhuman" world.

Garth Jeffers, one of Jeffers's two sons addressed in the poem (Jeffers and his wife Una had no daughters who lived past infancy), died in the spring of 1998. When Jeffers wrote this poem Garth and his brother Donnan were quite young—less than 10 years old—and certainly not mature enough to understand it. Despite Jeffers's dim view of human beings' ability to live together, and his acknowledgment of our fate and the fate of the societies in which we live, I have to think that "Shine, Perishing Republic" is a love poem to these boys, albeit one filled with sadness. Motivated by both both apprehension and joy, its ultimate counsel is

to be "moderate … in love of man," exactly because Jeffers knows the attraction of such love. After all, there is no need to counsel against immoderate love for man if it is not a temptation. And the reason it is a temptation is because love holds out the hope of improving the world, which Jeffers sees as illusory even though it appeals to "noblest spirits," such as Jesus.

The most important thing to realize is that, despite Jeffers's apparent conclusion on the matter, it is his very poem that keeps alive the conversation among the various positions Jeffers elaborates. How can we love each other in the face of social corruption? How can we do anything in society if all action only participates in the general decay? What is the significance of our relation to "the mountains" as opposed to our relation to "the cities?"

It is Jeffers himself who is torn by love for suffering humanity and a recognition of how little he can do about its fate. In the end, his Inhumanism and his critique of Christianity are only consolations for the agony of being a witness to history, a fate no thinking person can avoid in this century. It is himself Jeffers is warning, as much as his children.

The reason the poem has survived for 75 years and is likely to continue to do so is not because it offers some simple truth, though its attitudes are powerful. It is because Jeffers captures his own ambivalence of heart and mind in such a careful way that the poem itself becomes a manifestation of a deeply lived and contemplated vitality. On the one hand Jeffers knows that social life is deeply flawed, that republics become corrupt and crumble, because of the generally foolish behavior of human beings. Yet his poem is fired with love for his own sons, as emblems of a larger humanity for whom he wishes a good life, for "life is good." Even the "perishing republic" is blessed as a natural phenomenon, like a "meteor" that should in fact shine forth even as it dies. These are not the words of a simple, uncomplicated misanthrope. In the end, it is Jeffers's agonizing effort to find a way to live in the world that gives this poem, like much of his best work, its force. The poem's power grows out of adoration for the world and the vitality of creation, mixed with anguish at its suffering, all dissolved into a philosophical attitude that emphasizes but never achieves detachment. The unnamed "they" in the last line, the "they" who suppposedly say that Jesus was caught in a trap of love, is purposefully unnamed, because it is Jeffers himself.

The emotional and intellectual richness of Jeffers's lyric focuses a complex moment of consciousness, relating family, society, history, nature, love, and death in a highly compressed and memorable way.

Source: David J. Rothman, in an essay for *Poetry for Students,* Gale, 1998.

Gilbert Highet

In the following excerpt, written in 1953, Highet discusses the themes of Jeffers's poems and how they reflect Jeffers's attitudes toward humanity and nature.

It is sad that the word *romantic* has been so misused and vulgarized. If it had not been, we could call this American poet a romantic figure. Most of the many meanings implied in the word would fit him: unorthodox, strongly individual, imaginative and emotional, daring, careless of routine success, a lover only of the material things which can be loved without desire (not money and machines, but mountains, waters, birds, animals); lonely, too, lonely. Yes, he is a romantic figure.

His name is Robinson Jeffers. He lives in Carmel, California, in a house which he and his sons built, stone by stone. He is getting on toward seventy now. When he first settled in Carmel, it was a small windswept village smelling of trees and the sea, inconveniently simple, unfrequented, unfashionable, a good place for a man to be himself and nobody else. Now—at least in the summer— it is a bright and busy seaside town, with a beach, cocktail bars, branches of very chi-chi metropolitan stores, and a rich flow of traffic from the rest of California. Why, in those quaint narrow streets there is hardly room for all the Cadillacs. This is the same kind of change which, in our own lifetime, has infected many other places: Montauk, Acapulco, Oxford, Provincetown, you can fill out the list yourselves. Mr. Jeffers does not enjoy the change. He did not expect it when he built his home there on the lonely peninsula near Point Lobos. But he is a pessimist, and he has long been convinced that mankind spoils nearly everything it touches. He does not, therefore, see much of the beauties of prosperous California. He prefers to watch the ocean which is full of life but which is too cold and powerful for us to swim in, the rocky hills which will not grow grapefruit, but have a superhuman dignity of their own.

Mr. Jeffers is not a popular poet. He never wished to be a popular poet, he has shunned every device which leads toward popularity, he avoids publicity, he will not lecture and give readings and play the guitar, he has no immediate disciples, and has formed no school. It is not that he is deliberately obscure. You can understand all his poetry, if you read it with care: far more easily than the work of his contemporaries Eliot and Pound and Valéry. It is not that he was once ambitious, and is now soured by lack of recognition: far from it. His poetry is not meant to be liked. It is meant, I think, to do people good.

But it is very remarkable poetry, and he is a very distinguished man. America has produced great statesmen, soldiers, engineers, explorers, civilizers, inventors, and actors. It has produced—in nearly two centuries—very few great poets. Robinson Jeffers may prove to be one of those great poets. I say *may,* because I honestly do not know whether he will or not. But if he does, he will be like some other solitary artists who were recognized during their lives as odd, provocative, masterful, self-sufficient, and eccentric; and whose work turned out to be as durable as stone. Such was Euripides, whom Mr. Jeffers admires and something resembles; such was Lucretius; such was Dante; such were Breughel, and Monteverdi, and Poe. It takes time … it takes at least a century for a good work of poetry to prove what it is.

If you have not read Mr. Jeffers' poems, there is a handsome one-volume edition of his *Selected Poetry.* When you look over it, what you will see is this: a single, comparatively small book about 600 pages in all. Not much for a life's work, you may think; but many of these poems are the result of thirty or forty years of thought, and they are intended to live ten times, or a hundred times, as long.

You will see that Mr. Jeffers writes three different types of poem. Some are meditative lyrics, anywhere between ten and forty lines long—a thought, a brief description of something seen, a memory or a vision. Some are long narrative poems—that is a good form which we are foolish to neglect nowadays: a story told in verse is harder to do, but often far more effective, than a story told in prose. There are about a dozen exciting, lurid, visionary narrative poems set in the wild hill-country of central California near Monterey. They are about bitter loves, and hatreds more satisfying than love. Crime, sensuality, madness haunt them. Brothers kill each other. Fearful illicit passions rage through them like forest fires.

In the same form Mr. Jeffers has also written several dramas, and poems partly narrative and partly dramatic, most of them on plots from Greek tragedy. The best known is his adaptation of the

> *[Jeffers's] poetry is not meant to be liked. It is meant, I think, to do people good."*

Medea which was (he says himself) inspired by Judith Anderson's art and personality, and which showed us her magnificent acting in New York during the winter of 1947–8. These pieces also move among the grim ideas which have long filled his mind and which are the basis of his poetry.

Both the lyrics and the stories are written in large, muscular, unrhymed lines, with an irregular pulse which is basically a new sort of blank verse, with a long rhythm (about ten beats to the line) which reminds me irresistibly of the Pacific hammering at the rocks. It is intended to echo the ebb and flow of excitement, the interchange of narrative and speech. For my taste it is usually too irregular, because I can remember poetry only when it has a fairly steady pattern; still, it is free and powerful and eloquent, anything but monotonous and conventional.

Now, if I try to explain what Mr. Jeffers' themes are, I shall risk distorting them, oversimplifying them, making them too naive or brutal, breaking up their subtle interrelations, vulgarizing a poetic statement by changing it into a Message. And yet his work is very cohesive, so that one can bring out its leading motives, as one could not do with a wayward poet like Yeats; and his ideas are so strange that unless we are boldly introduced to them, we may not comprehend them at all. He is a tragic poet; and tragedy is a truth which is hard, hard to understand.…

Mr. Jeffers, you see, believes a number of terrible things. They are not all true for Christians, who believe in redemption; but they are true for many other inhabitants of this world.

First, he believes that men and women are animals. For him, there is *no difference* between a delicatessen, or a fur store, and a pack of coyotes hunting down a deer … except that the coyotes hunt and devour in hot blood, whereas we breed the meat-cattle and slaughter them and trap the furry animals and skin them with a cold greedy purposefulness

which is more disgusting. Many animals are cruel and noble. Their cruelty contains style and courage, the cougar and the hawk. Men and women are usually cruel. When they are cruel and mean, they are loathsome … animals. When they are cruel and noble, they may be noble animals.

Then, Mr. Jeffers utterly abominates war, modern war. He sees it as a symptom and a cause of what he considers the decadence of our civilization. He believes that growing populations and multiplying machines all over the world have distorted the balance of nature, and that war is now the greatest of all such distortions. His last book was full of violent isolationism. One might expect him to regard the whole of warfare as an understandable activity like the ferocity of animals: to think of the shark when he sees a submarine, to admire the flight of bombers as much as the flight of the hawks; but he cannot.

Third, he is unlike most of us in his view of happiness. Most people, I think he would say, want easy pleasure and drowsy happiness. But real fulfillment is not pleasure: it is something more powerful. Effort and suffering are more natural than rest and enjoyment. Pain lasts longer and is more real than pleasure.

Fourth—the fourth of Mr. Jeffers' themes is the grandest of all, and the most wretched, and the most difficult. It is this. *The human race is not needed.* It is an infestation from which the planet is suffering. Look at a wooded mountainside, with the bear and the deer in the forests, the badger and the fox in the brush, birds and their cousins the reptiles crawling and flying above and below. Can you truthfully say that it would improve that scene to drive a six-lane motor-highway across it? Or to put a town in the middle of it? And when people say that it would be a terrific disaster if another war blotted out the human race, do they mean it? Do they mean that the mountains would weep, the rivers run backward with grief, and the animals and the birds go into mourning? Or would the earth begin its peaceful work of purification, covering up—with falling leaves and drifting dust and sifting earth and growing plants and moving hillsides and encroaching forests—our cities, our factories, and our prisons? And then would the whole planet, with its other children, heave a single, long, unanimous sigh of relief?

These are some of the ideas which—unless I have gravely misunderstood him—Robinson Jeffers holds. He also has an extremely complex and difficult conception of sex, and the family, as a source of tragedy. He has made these themes into fine poetry. He does not think they are pleasant ideas. But he thinks they are true. He thinks that they have the truth of nature; that they are somehow part of nature. And he loves nature, wild nature. In this he is more like a primitive American than a modern man—like the Indian who climbed Chief Mountain to be alone and see visions, or the early white hunters who went west because they loved land and animals without humanity. But he is also like several distinguished American artists: Thoreau; Melville; Martha Graham; and Ernest Hemingway. Most of nature, he knows, is not pleasant; but it is—well, what is a thunderstorm? What is a forest fire? What is a north wind bringing bitter snow over the mountains? Or the ocean surging against a rocky cliff? The sound, the power, the terror, and the nobility of these things make the truth of Robinson Jeffers' poetry.

Source: Gilbert Highet, "An American Poet," in *Critical Essays on Robinson Jeffers,* edited by James Karman, G. K. Hall and Co., 1990, pp. 201–04

Sources

Abbey, Edward, *Desert Solitaire: A Season in the Wilderness,* New York: Simon and Schuster, [1968] 1990.

Antoninus, Brother, *Robinson Jeffers: Fragments of an Older Fury,* Oyez, 1968.

Beach, Joseph Warren, *The Concept of Nature in Nineteenth Century English Poetry,* The Macmillan Company, 1936.

Boyers, Robert, "A Sovereign Voice: The Poetry of Robinson Jeffers," in *The Sewanee Review,* Vol. VII, No. 3, Summer, 1969.

Brophy, Robert J., *Robinson Jeffers: Myth, Ritual, and Symbol in His Narrative Poems,* The Press of Case Western Reserve University, 1973.

Brophy, Robert J., ed., *The Robinson Jeffers Newsletter: A Jubilee Gathering 1962-1988,* Occidental College, Los Angeles, 1988.

Dickey, James, *Babel to Byzantium,* Farrar, Straus, 1968.

Frost, Robert, *The Poetry of Robert Frost,* edited by Edward Connery Lathem, New York: Holt, Rinehart and Winston, 1975.

————, *Robinson Jeffers: Fragments of an Older Fury,* Berkeley: Oyez Press, 1968.

Gilbert, Rudolph, *Shine, Perishing Republic: Robinson Jeffers and the Tragic Sense in Modern Poetry,* Boston: Bruce Humphries, Inc., 1936.

Gioia, Dana, "Strong Counsel" in *Can Poetry Matter?,* Saint Paul: Graywolf Press, 1992, pp. 47-60.

"Harrowed Marrow," *Time* April 4, 1932, pp. 63-64.

Hass, Robert, introduction to *Rock and Hawk: A Selection of the Shorter Poems by Robinson Jeffers,* edited by Robert Hass, New York: Random House, 1987, pp. xv-xliii.

Hunt, Tim, ed., *The Collected Poetry of Robinson Jeffers,* three vols., Stanford University Press, 1988.

Jarman, Mark, *Iris,* Brownsville, OR: Storyline Press, 1992.

Rexroth, Kenneth, *Assays,* New Directions, 1961.

Whitman, Walt, *Leaves of Grass: Comprehensive Reader's Edition,* edited by Harold W. Blodgett and Sculley Bradley, New York: New York University Press, 1965.

Zaller, Robert, *Centennial Essays for Robinson Jeffers,* University of Delaware Press, 1991.

————, *The Cliffs of Solitude: A Reading of Robinson Jeffers,* Cambridge University Press, 1983.

For Further Study

Brophy, Robert, *Robinson Jeffers: Myth, Ritual, and Symbol in His Narrative Poems,* Shoe String Press, 1976.
  In this book of criticism, Brophy traces connections between Jeffers's deep understanding of Greek and Christian mythology and the symbols which recur in his narrative poems.

Coffin, Arthur, *Robinson Jeffers: Poet of Inhumanism,* University of Wisconsin Press, 1971.
  Coffin searches out examples from Jeffers's large body of work to illustrate the role of "Inhumanism" in the poet's life and writing.

Everson, William, *Excesses of God: Robinson Jeffers as a Religious Figure,* Stanford University Press, 1988.
  Provides a biographical and critical overview.

Zaller, Robert, *The Cliffs of Solitude: A Reading of Robinson Jeffers,* Cambridge University Press, 1983.
  Views Jeffers's work through the lens of the poet's solitary personal life on the coast of Big Sur.

Sir Patrick Spens

Anonymous

1765

"Sir Patrick Spens" is a traditional ballad, which means 1) that it was originally written to be sung, 2) that it is anonymous because the names of the original author or authors have been lost to us over time, and 3) that the ballad often exists in several versions. Ballads tell mostly tragic stories, and "Sir Patrick Spens" explores two primary themes. One is mortality: people are born and must die. This is related to the second theme, the role of fate or accident in peoples' lives.

Ballads may or may not have some basis in fact. According to Francis James Child's *English and Scottish Popular Ballads,* other versions of "Sir Patrick Spens" suggest it may be combining three historical events. In 1281, Scottish King Alexander III's daughter Margaret was married to Norway's King Eric, but on her voyage home, the ship sank and all perished. Eric and Margaret were survived by a daughter, also named Margaret. She was to be married to a son of England's King Edward I, but died while sailing from Norway. There is no historical link between Sir Patrick Spens and these events, though chronicles indicate that there was a Spens and that he may have been a Captain, not a Lord. Finally, there was a famous shipwreck off the coast of Aberdour near Papa Stronsay Island, which claims to be the burial place of Sir Patrick Spens. Though it is unlikely the events in this poem are true in the historical sense, we can see that they may refer to these actual events. More importantly for us, these events help explain a bit about why

the king ordered Spens to sail at such a dangerous time of year.

Although ballads such as "Sir Patrick Spens" are traditional and anonymous, many poets copy the traditional ballad form. You might want to compare "Sir Patrick Spens" with such ballads as William Blake's "The Tyger," Samuel Taylor Coleridge's "Rime of the Ancient Mariner," John Keats's "La Belle Dame Sans Merci," and Walter Raleigh's "The Nymph's Reply to the Shepherd."

Poem Text

The king sits in Dumferling toune,
    Drinking the blude-reid wine:
O quhar will I get guid sailor,
    To sail this schip of mine?
Up and spak an eldern knicht,   5
    Sat at the king's richt knee:
Sir Patrick Spens is the best sailor
    That sails upon the sea.
The king has written a braid letter,
    And signed it wi' his hand;   10
And sent it to Sir Patrick Spens,
    Was walking on the sand.
The first line that Sir Patrick red,
    A loud lauch lauchèd he:
The next line that Sir Patrick red,   15
    The teir blinded his ee.
O quhar is this has don this deid,
    This ill deid don to me;
To send me out this time o' the yeir,
    To sail upon the sea?   20
Mak haste, mak haste, my mirry men all,
    Our good schip sails the morn.
O say na sae, my master deir,
    For I feir a deadlie storme.
Late late yestreen I saw the new moone   25
    Wi' the auld moone in hir arme;
And I feir, I feir, my deir master,
    That we will come to harme.
O our Scots nobles wer richt laith
    To weet their cork-heild schoone;   30
But lang owre a' the play were played,
    Their hats they swam aboone.
O lang, lang may the ladies stand
    Wi' their fans into their hand,
Or e'er they see Sir Patrick Spens   35
    Come sailing to the land.
O lang, lang, may the ladies stand
    Wi' their gold kems in their hair,
Waiting for their ain deir lords,
    For they'll see them na mair.   40
Have owre, have owre to Aberdour,
    It's fifty fadom deip:
And thair lies guid Sir Patrick Spens,
    Wi' the Scots lords at his feit.

Poem Summary

Line 1:

The ballad begins by introducing the main characters. Here, we meet the king, who is in Dumferling, Scotland. The king "sits," in that he "reigns" and his throne is a "seat" of his power. He also "sits" in the sense of being stationary. He does not move, though his actions will make others move.

Line 2:

The wine that the king drinks is "blood red," suggesting his power over life and death, as well as the ease with which he controls other people's lives. He sends men to their deaths as casually as one might drink a glass of wine.

Lines 3-4:

"Oh where will I get a good sailor, to sail this ship of mine?" the king asks. Soon, the king will choose Sir Patrick Spens. Although being selected by the king is an honor, it also means that Spens must undertake an impossible journey. As a sailor, Spens is a "good," skillful sailor and because he is brave, he is a good man as well; but this cannot save him from his fate. No matter how skillful a sailor he is, no human can withstand the fury of nature. And no matter how loyal and true he is, like all people, Spens must die.

Lines 5-6:

An "elder" knight speaks up. The fact that the knight is an elder suggests that he is respected, a senior advisor to the king. The knight also has power in court because he sits at the king's side—i.e., at his right knee. As we will see, because the knight speaks "up," Spens and his ship are sent down "fifty fadom deip."

Lines 7-8:

The elder knight praises Sir Patrick Spens as the world's best sailor. Notice the sibilance in lines 7 and 8; the repetition of "s" sounds imitates the sound of waves crashing on the shore.

Lines 9-10:

The king writes a broad letter of command, ordering Spens to sail the royal ship. It is signed with the king's hand, the royal signature, and must be obeyed.

Lines 11-12:

The letter is sent to Spens as he walks along the beach. Notice that the word "who" seems to be

Media Adaptations

- Fairport Convention performed a version of "Sir Patrick Spens" on their 1970 album *Full House,* available from Rykodisc.

- Geoff Kaufman produced *Fair Stood the Wind,* available in cassette from Folk-Legacy Records.

omitted from line 12; it is not stated, but implied (The line might read "who was walking on the sand"). This kind of omission is called an ellipsis. Just as the "who" is absent from the line, so Spens will be absent from the earth when the letter sends him to his death.

Lines 13-14:

Spens reads the first line of the letter and laughs. Perhaps it praises his skill as a sailor, or perhaps it identifies his assignment, the impossible journey, and Spens laughs because he thinks it is a joke. In a sense, it is a joke, played on him not by the king or the knight, but by fate.

Lines 15-16:

Spens reads further and realizes that the king is serious about sending him on a dangerous voyage. His fate is sealed, but his tear-blinded eye is ironic. Irony is wit or mockery that usually means the opposite of what is said. Destiny or fate are traditionally represented as "blind"—think of Oedipus, Homer, and Milton, whose blindness is seen as a sign that they "see" a higher truth. Like them, Spens can "see" his fate, his inevitable death after the impossible voyage, though tears "blind" him.

Lines 17-18:

Spens asks who has done this ill deed to him and the reader begins to suspect the motives of the elder knight. Does he have some secret motive for sending Spens to certain death? We are not told, but wonder about the court, where things are not always what they seem, where illusion can be confused with reality. But the courtly world's deception does not allow it to escape from life's only cer-

tainty: death. Consider the inversion from "done ... deed" to "deed done" in lines 17 and 18. Just as Spens's reaction while reading the letter went from laughter to tears, so the poem's word order changes to show how his world has been turned upside down.

Lines 19-20:

Spens knows that the weather at this time of year is treacherous.

Lines 21-22:

Although the assignment is dangerous, the men must hurry. They follow Spens's orders as he follows the king's. Notice how the repetition of "m" and "s" in lines 21 and 22 emphasize the irony. While the men make "haste," they are anything but "merry." The sailors know they are sailing off to die, and while the ship may be "good," no ship can withstand the violence of natural elements.

Lines 23-28:

In lines 23 through 28, a sailor speaks up, hoping his master will say it is not so, that they are not really going to sail. The sailor is apprehensive because he has seen the new moon in the old moon's arms, that is, the dark shape of the new moon and only the hint of a crescent of the old moon. This is an evil omen that predicts bad weather, and the sailor fears, correctly, the ship and crew will come to harm. This is the poem's most famous image and is used by Samuel Taylor Coleridge in his "Rime of the Ancient Mariner." In lines 27 and 28, note the repetition of "ei," "e," and "r" sounds, which call to mind the ocean's waves moving up and down, tossing a ship at sea.

Lines 29-30:

The ship has now sailed, but the nobles are "loath" to "wet" their shoes. This is ironic, because soon not only their shoes, but their entire bodies will be wet, and they will be drowned. The reader compares the nobles, who fear wetting their shoes, with Spens, who knows they are all doomed to drown in the storm. The nobles' concerns are petty in comparison with Spens, who is a brave soldier fatalistically following orders. Though they are noble because of their family titles, Spens is noble because of his actions.

Lines 31-32:

The shipwreck is a "play," like a trick of fate or an event in the sense of a sports figure who makes a play. Play also suggests a child's game, for the sailors are like toys in the hands of nature. The fact that we see the nobles' hats and not the nobles themselves is synecdoche, the substitution of the part for the whole. The hats themselves can be seen as a sign of worldly vanity, and it is ironic that the hats swim, but the nobles themselves cannot; they drown.

Lines 33-36:

The ladies stand waiting for Spens and their men to return. They stand, while the king sits, and by the poem's end, the men lay. Their fans are a sign of vanity, but fans are also used to control the weather by making one more comfortable when it is too hot. At sea, however, the weather cannot be controlled, and the storm kills their men. Recall that the king signs the letter with his hand, which leads to the deaths of Spens and the nobles, that the ladies wait with fans in their hands for men who will never return. This repetition of "hand" links cause and effect, the king, who caused the men to go to sea, and the effect, the men's demise and their women's sorrowful waiting.

Lines 37-38:

Again, gold is a gold traditional symbol of worldliness, and while the gold combs will remain shiny, the women's hair will turn grey with time. Their attention to gold is misplaced, for like their men, they too will pass away.

Line 39:

The women wait for their "own dear lords," but their men belong no longer to them but to death.

Line 40:

The women will never see their men again, though ironically, the reader sees them lying on the ocean floor. The women hope to see their men alive, but the reader sees the men's dead bodies.

Lines 41-44:

Half the way over to Aberdour, the ship is wrecked in the storm. Now the "good" Spens, like the good ship, is fifty fathoms beneath the sea. The poem's ending is ironic when we consider the ways the positions of the body have indicated social status (for example, remember the knight who sat at the king's right knee). At the end, while the lords may outrank Spens socially (note that some versions of the poem have Spens not a "Sir," but merely a Captain), their cowardice and concern for worldly things—their failure to comprehend their situation and act accordingly—sets Spens above the lords in the end. Significantly, they lie at his feet, not he at theirs.

Themes

Power and Authority

In the eighteenth century, when "Sir Patrick Spens" was written, European society was still rigidly hierarchical. Power was concentrated at the top. This structure is reflected in "Sir Patrick Spens." Most obvious is the power of the king, who holds the power of life and death, first symbolized in the "blude-reid wine" he drinks on his throne. It is more than symbolic, because he does send Sir Patrick and his men to their deaths "fifty fathom deep."

The king exercises his power with startling ease. To issue the command that will have terrible import for Sir Patrick and his crew, he has only to write "braid letter" and "sign it with his hand." And he does this without a single consideration of the consequences for the men and their ship. Although the command saddens Sir Patrick, he never questions the right of the king to send him on such a deadly mission.

Others beside the king also exercise power. The "eldern knicht" occupies a position of power. He "sat at the king's right knee" which makes him the second most powerful man at court. More significantly though, he has the king's ear. When he recommends Sir Patrick as a good sailor, the king listens. This senior knight may even be the real power in the poem, for when Sir Patrick receives the letter sending him out to sea in winter he suspects almost immediately that someone has "an ill deed don" to him. He believes some force is plotting against him on purpose, probably to kill him.

Sir Patrick's authority over his men is impressive. His power seems to issue more from his moral force and personality rather than from his place in the social hierarchy. The king must sign a formal order to send the men to sea; Spens merely calls his "mirry men" to prepare to sail and they follow their "dear master" despite unfavorable omens and deep misgivings. Sir Patrick's authority is emphasized in the final lines, where in death at the bottom of the sea, the Scottish nobles occupy a position of subservience at the feet of Sir Patrick.

Topics for Further Study

- Write a letter from Sir Patrick Spens to the king, explaining that he will not sail as requested and giving valid reasons for this decision.

- Do you believe that Sir Patrick Spens was brave or foolish? Explain what you would do in his situation, using lines from the poem to support your position.

Death

As in many ballads, death is a dominant force in "Sir Patrick Spens." It is a force that no human can escape. Death is personified in the figure of the king drinking blood on his throne. He is far away from Sir Patrick and his men, "in Dumferling toune," and until his letter comes they can live as if he does not exist. But when death calls in the form of the king's order, it is a command that they cannot defy.

First, Sir Patrick refuses to believe the fateful notice he is given. Then "the teir blinded his ee," and he is overcome by sorrow. He becomes angry, crying out, with a touch of paranoia, that someone must be out to get him, "to send me out this time o' year, / to sail upon the sea." But no one can choose the time death calls. And despite the omens of doom that his men point out and their desire to avoid death, Sir Patrick and his crew must accept their fate.

Some of the crew and bystanders are in denial, or are so wrapped up in other things that they are completely unaware of it. The Scottish nobles sailing with Sir Patrick seem to think more about getting their fine shoes wet than they do about their own imminent deaths. Waiting for their men to return, ladies stand on the shore waiting with fans and gold combs in their hair. These glittering signs of the world's transient pleasures highlight their ignorance of the fate of their men, indeed the fate that awaits them sometime in the future. The images recall the famous words from the Book of Ecclesiastes: "Then I looked on all the works that my hands had wrought, and on the labour that I had laboured to do: and, behold, all was vanity and vexation." And so "lang, lang, may the ladies stand," waiting with their baubles and fashion as if everything were fine and in the end there would be a happy ending.

Style

A ballad tends to be a purely narrative poem—that is, it tells a story—as a rule concentrating on a single incident or situation. In "Sir Patrick Spens," that event is a shipwreck. Written in a traditional ballad form, the poem is composed of four-line stanzas. Typically, the first and third lines of each stanza have four accents, while the second and fourth lines have three accents. Although ballads are usually unrhymed, they were originally composed to be sung. Their accents form a rhythm, and ballads have a musical quality and regular beat when read. Notice the accents in the first four lines of "Sir Patrick Spens".

> The **king** sit in Dumfer*ling* **toune**,
> **Drink**ing the **blude**–reid **wine**:
> O **quhar** will I **get guid sail**or
> To **sail** this **schip** of **mine**?

The ballad's rhythm is reinforced by the repetition of sounds. In "Sir Patrick Spens," we find consonance, (repetition of consonants), assonance (repetition of vowels), and sibilance (repetition of the sounds of "s" and "c"). Notice the ways that repetitions of "i" sounds in "king, "in," "drinking," and "wine" and of "d" sounds in "Dumferling," "drinking," and "blude-reid" reinforce the rhythm.

Historical Context

Scotland in the United Kingdom

Scotland was in a transition period when "Sir Patrick Spens" first appeared in print. It had been an independent kingdom until 1707, when the Treaty of Union was signed with Great Britain, making Scotland part of the United Kingdom. The Union was long in coming, considering the two kingdoms had been ruled by the same monarch for more than one hundred years. Both countries had their own reasons for wanting union. For Britain it meant security from attacks by her old enemy from the south, France. For Scotland it meant economic assistance from her more prosperous neighbor.

Compare & Contrast

- **1765:** The English Parliament passes the Stamp Act. Later in the year, the law gives rise to the slogan "No taxation without representation" and contributes to the mood of discontent that eventually leads to the American Revolution.

  Today: Growing numbers of Americans are dissatisfied with the federal tax system. The Republican Party makes tax reform a major part of its party platform.

- **1765:** James Watt invents an efficient steam engine that will help usher in the industrial revolution.

  Today: Micromachines, often too small to be visible to the naked eye, are prevalent in the automobile industry. It is predicted that they will

  soon be able to be implanted in human bodies where they will monitor and correct health problems.

- **1765:** The world's first savings bank opens.

  Today: Banks are becoming more and more "virtual" with transactions handled electronically by telephone or computer.

- **1765:** The Portuguese Inquisition abolishes the auto-da-fe (burning at the stake) as a punishment for Jews and heretics.

  Today: The execution of Karla Faye Tucker, a brutal murderer and self-proclaimed reborn Christian, rekindles the debate over the legitimacy of capital punishment in the United States.

Most overt Scottish resistance to the union was put down within a few decades. However, the spirit of rebellion lived on in Scotland in the eighteenth century. In fact, Scotland provided support to the Jacobites in their attempt to overthrow the British Hanoverian monarch in the Glorious Revolution of 1688. Scottish Jacobite uprisings were squelched in 1715 and 1745.

In an attempt to root out the last traces of Scottish disloyalty, parliament enacted the Abolition of Heritable Jurisdictions (Scotland) Act in 1747. Since prehistoric times the Scottish highlands had been ruled by the clan system. Clan members and warriors swore their allegiance to the clan chieftain. The Act abolished the clan system with a single blow. The wearing of kilts and tartans was forbidden; clan members were made to swear oaths to the British monarch. Clan chiefs lost their feudal rights and became mere landowners.

Prosperity integrated Scotland into the British realm better than any legislation. English farming methods were introduced, and by the end of the century Scottish farmers were teaching the English. With access to English markets, linen production doubled between 1750 and 1775. The Scottish min-

ing industry grew rapidly as well. Missionary activity and a road-building program into the Highlands also increased Scotland's contacts with the outside world.

Aftermath of War with France

War broke out between England and France in 1756. Known as the Seven Years War, the conflict is considered an early "World War," in which Britain and Prussia were allied against France, Austria, Spain and Russia. English and French armies fought in Europe, India, the Caribbean, and North America.

When the Treaty of Paris ended the war in 1763, it was viewed as a great triumph in England. Canada was ceded to Britain by the treaty; this greatly strengthened the English position in North America. The merchant class savored the victory. Trade, they thought, would flourish with new supplies of raw materials and new markets for English goods the colonies could provide.

The war, however, proved costly for England. Rather than boosting the English economy, the high cost of the war served to depress it. Because of the enormous strain it placed on the English treasury, parliament and the Crown had to create new sources of revenue. This situation resulted in various tax measures, like the Stamp Act in 1765.

The Stamp Act caused growing dissatisfaction with English rule in the American colonies. And with Canada under English control, the American colonists had less use for English armies for protection from the threat of a French invasion. An important tie to England was suddenly cut. The high cost of the war also led to the deterioration of the British military, in particular the Royal Navy. That decline played an important role in England's defeat in the American Revolution.

Critical Overview

"Sir Patrick Spens" is a Scottish folk ballad, which was probably composed sometime during the 15th century. It was first published in 1765 in Thomas Percy's famous collection, *Reliques of Ancient English Poetry* (most often referred to as Percy's *Reliques*). While ballads tell stories, they do so in special ways, generally by presenting events without much descriptive detail and sometimes leaving out key events entirely.

In "Sir Patrick Spens," for example, we never see the storm or the shipwreck. Instead, as Lloyd Frankenberg writes in his book *Invitation to Poetry,* all the action "is about to take place or has already gone by. The shipwreck is hats bobbing on the water." M. J. C. Hodgart's book *The Ballads* suggests that there are similarities among the ways ballads, cartoon strips, and films tell stories. In all of these forms, the narrative is presented not "as a continuous sequence of events but as a series of rapid flashes." The ballad's effect on us depends on which scenes are presented and how individual scenes are situated in the story as a whole. Also, ballads' stories focus on the specific, rather than the general. As Arthur K. Moore writes in an essay in *Comparative Literature,* a ballad's representation of a "particular disaster … tends to merge with the multiple of other fatal misadventures dogging the footsteps of mankind." Ballads generally include little description and few observations about the action by the poem's speaker (its persona), according to Gordon Hall Gerould's book, *The Ballad for Tradition.* The significance of the events is left to the reader to decide. This means that although ballads may appear simple, they are deceptively so.

Criticism

Jhan Hochman

Jhan Hochman is a writer and instructor at Portland Community College in Portland, Oregon. In the following essay, Hochman discusses the role of loyalty in the poem "Sir Patrick Spens."

The king's drinking of the blood-red wine in the first stanza of the anonymous ballad, "Sir Patrick Spens," provides a foreshadowing of the tragic deaths of Sir Patrick and his crew. While it is uncertain whether the Scottish king is aware of the risks of such a dangerous mission on the high seas, it hardly matters—Sir Patrick must do his duty, even if he and his crew of Scottish lords will end up forever on the ocean floor.

"Sir Patrick Spens" is considered a ballad, an old-English, rhymed-song form that tells a story. The poem is one of the oldest examples of the ballad in English; it was found by Thomas Percy (1729–1811) in what is now known as the Percy Folio, a handwritten manuscript of the mid-seventeenth century once owned by Humphrey Pitt of Shifnal. Percy included the ballad of "Sir Patrick Spens" in his *Reliques of Ancient English Poetry* (1765), still the most important source of old English ballads.

As a narrative poem, "Sir Patrick Spens" is in the tradition of Homer's great epics *The Iliad* and *The Odyssey.* In fact, "Sir Patrick Spens" bears comparison to *The Odyssey.* In Sir Patrick's odyssey, however, it is uncertain whether Sir Patrick, unlike Odysseus, is a hero or a fool for having followed the king's orders.

The ballad is composed of eleven quatrains (four-line stanzas), in which the second and fourth lines rhyme. The first and third lines contain four beats (tetrameter) and the second and third contain three beats (trimeter). Composed of five dramatic scenes, the poem utilizes a rather contemporary, sudden cinema-like cutting or montage between each scene.

The scenes are as follows: the first is of the elder knight recommending Sir Patrick for the mission. In the second, Sir Patrick reads the letter from the king as he walks the beach along the ocean where he eventually will drown. The third scene depicts Sir Patrick talking to his fearful crew. The fourth scene is of the wives of the ship's crew waiting—somewhat like Odysseus' wife Penelope—for the ship to return. The fifth and final scene shows Sir Patrick and his men drowned at the bottom of the ocean.

While these scenes now seem abrupt in transition, musical interludes played between scenes might once have prepared the listener for the radical changes. Stanza eight is the only exception to this list of scenes because it does not show a concrete scene but instead comments on the fear, or perhaps cowardice, of the crew.

Not only is "Sir Patrick Spens" a poem of scenes, but of images. The ballad is held together by bookend stanzas harboring similar tableau: the elder knight sitting at the right knee of the king in the first stanza, and the final stanza with the lords around the feet of Sir Patrick at the bottom of the ocean. The difference in position between king and knight and of Sir Patrick and his lords suggests a relationship of command and of loyalty. In his essay "Seven Types of Accuracy," which appeared in *The Iowa Review,* Richard Moore has remarked that the men gathered around Sir Patrick at the end of the ballad poses a riddle: Why are the men gathered there?

Moore's answer is that they had gathered at the feet of Sir Patrick in the final moments of the shipwreck in hopes he would save them. This contention could also indicate a newfound solidarity or resolution in the face of their collective end—especially if we recall that prior to the mission the men were worried about going on the voyage.

The men's hesitation reminds the reader of the omen the men had seen the evening before, the new moon with the old moon in her arm described in stanza seven. This is the phase of the moon known as the waning crescent that "holds" the darkened portion in the hollow of its arc, the next phase of the moon being the darkened new moon. In some cosmologies, the moon corresponds to the changing phases of human life, and the completely invisible new moon on the cusp of two successive months would indicate death. It is possible the men believe the voyage will be dangerous because it will take place just prior to this deathly new moon. While this might be mere superstition, it is grounded in a bit of science since the moon does have a profound effect on the earth's oceans and tides.

Still, Sir Patrick does not respond to this fear even though he must be aware of it; in stanza five, when he is seen walking the beach and reading the king's letter, Sir Patrick remarks on the evil deed done to him by the king (or is it the elder knight?) for sending him and his men out on the sea during this time. One may also conjecture that the king knows this will be a dangerous mission because he is not interested in just any sailor but the best one available.

Another question must be asked at this point. What is this mission, anyway, and why is it so important that the king must risk all these lives and perhaps a precious cargo? Even with extensive historical research, this riddle is likely to remain unanswered.

A compelling image in the poem is that of lord's ladies waiting for their men to return from the mission. The ladies' fans and combs suggest a life of leisure and wealth that are powerless in buying off the weather in hopes of keeping their husbands alive. Folding fans—traditional symbols of the moon—also suggest the successive phases of the moon and the passage of time. The waiting of the women might also imply their helplessness. The women cannot search and rescue their husbands, nor can they easily move on and marry again. They are doomed to wait, perhaps long after they feel certain their husbands have perished. Was it for the precious goods like fans and gold combs that the men lost their lives?

If, as Sir Patrick says, this command that he sail at a bad time of the year, was an evil deed, why was it evil? Was it because he suffered the unluckiness of the draw? Or was it, as some critics suggest, because the elder knight was an enemy of Sir Patrick and he set Sir Patrick up for such a dangerous mission?

Another critic, Richard Moore, rejects this conjecture as absurd, and posits that the elder knight's suggestion is merely to help the king and advance himself. Perhaps Moore is correct, for if the knight were an enemy, the theme would have been reinforced at the end of the poem and would show how one's vaunted reputation (like that of Sir Patrick) can eventually destroy one.

This theme is touched on briefly when Sir Patrick reads the letter and laughs in stanza four. Moore asserts the laugh is provoked by the king's remark that Sir Patrick has been recommended as the best sailor on the seas. If so, this is not just a laugh of humility, but a laugh acknowledging that Sir Patrick has been done in by his own renown.

So what, then, is the point of this poem? Is it a morality tale about how one should not obey the king when it means a suicide mission? Or a lesson on how honorable it is to do one's duty, no matter what the consequences? In choosing the second answer, the poem seems to celebrate the fearless hero-

What Do I Read Next?

- Like the sailors in "Sir Patrick Spens," Dylan Thomas struggles against the inevitability of death in his poem, "Do Not Go Gentle into That Good Night."

- In the *Book of Job,* the righteous man, Job, is beset by the loss of everything he holds dear and confronts God about his unjust fate.

- A modern American ballad about a sea tragedy is "The Titanic" by Leadbelly. The lyrics can be found in *Folk Songs of North America* by Alan Lomax.

---

ism of Sir Patrick. The poem should then be considered a heroic epic, not a tragedy.

Why does the balladeer conclude the poem with the overwhelming image of death, of corpses submerged at the bottom of the ocean? To answer this, the last two lines must get special attention. In one interpretation, the final image could reinforce the concept of loyalty, whether to king or captain. Another interpretation might be that the final image is not dramatic, but absurd, like a surreal and morbid group portrait. To see the image as absurd leads the reader to conclude that suicidal loyalty is ridiculous. Sir Patrick becomes a negative example, a fool who obeyed his king. By the same token, Sir Patrick's men would also be fools who, against their better judgment, did their duty so as not to be branded traitors or cowards.

Whatever the truth of either interpretation, the reader's conclusion will likely depend on his or her view of loyalty—a twentieth-century perspective, influenced by the largest number of men and women in any century that maimed and killed out of loyalty to leader, country, and honor.

Source: Jhan Hochman, in an essay for *Poetry for Students,* Gale, 1998.

Carolyn Meyer

Carolyn Meyer has a Ph.D. in Irish and British literature and has written numerous articles on contemporary Irish poetry. In the following essay,

Meyer analyzes how "Sir Patrick Spens" fits into the category of ballad and comments on the poem's ultimately tragic storyline.

Simple, spirited and singable, a folk ballad is a poem of rhythmically distinctive style that tells a story in an engaging and accessible way. It owes its origins to Europe of the late Middle Ages, where it began as "a song sung while dancing," a meaning that still holds true for the modern folk songs that are its musical descendants. As part of the oral tradition, ballads survived in the collective consciousness of cultures across Europe and North America, having been transmitted from generation to generation as a kind of verbal legacy until they eventually found their way into print, in important compilations such as Francis J. Child's *The English and Scottish Popular Ballads* (1882-98) and Thomas Percy's *Reliques of Ancient English Poetry* (1765). Anonymous compositions whose origins are a source of endless debate, ballads may be the works of individuals or the creations of entire communities. Each new singer of a ballad, in the course of its successive re-telling, becomes as much an original composer as a preserver or guardian of tradition. Given the margin for error and individual embellishment, variations are bound to occur, and this explains why some ballads exist in several different versions.

Renaissance poet Sir Philip Sidney called medieval ballads "the darling songs of the common people." Their authorship resides with the people, as do their themes, which are more inclined to appeal to the heart than the head. Their main function is, of course, to entertain, yet as living artifacts of pre-literate and illiterate folk cultures, they also tend to mirror common fears, fantasies, and aspirations; comment on life; and offer strategies for living. The events they describe have closest affinity with what ballad scholar Alfred B. Friedman has called in his introduction to *The Viking Book of Folk Ballads of the English-Speaking World* "the stuff of tabloid journalism—sensational tales of lust, revenge and domestic crime," whose substance never strays far from the twinned themes of love and death. Acts of betrayal, infidelity, incest, murder, even parricide and infanticide, abound, as do jealous husbands, heartless stepmothers, parted lovers, and women cruelly wronged or spurned. There are also ballads of the supernatural and those that recount the deeds of gallant knights and heroic adventurers. Of this final ballad grouping, one of the best known is "Sir Patrick Spens," a traditional folk ballad in Scottish dialect that tells the tragic tale of a dauntless sea captain who, at his king's commanding, must undertake an ill-timed sea voyage that he knows will spell his doom. Sir Patrick is a hero who knows his fate, who bitterly declaims his misfortune, but who has the fortitude and resilience to overcome his grief and bewilderment and persevere in spite of that knowledge. Achieving a realism and immediacy through devices which prolong the intensity of its highly charged moments, "Sir Patrick Spens" is remarkable among ballads for its fine use of dramatic irony, contrast, and terse understatement.

While its ironic vision is rare in traditional balladry, "Sir Patrick Spens" is united with ballads the world over through a number of standard conventions, rhetorical devices, and formulaic features. A ballad is essentially a compact story-poem in which the narrative is related impersonally and with rigid economy—stripped down to the bare bones and often leaving gaps that the reader is relied upon to bridge, much like the technique of cinematic montage. A ballad usually focuses on a single crucial episode, plunging almost immediately into the climactic event and then proceeding swiftly toward an outcome that is, almost without exception, an unhappy one. (Appropriately most ballad tunes are written in a minor key.) In the rush to reach the all-important catastrophe, there is little time to supply circumstantial details, delineate character, probe psychological motivation, or draw a moral. The poet, functioning as an anonymous communal voice, keeps himself out of the poem, rarely intruding to offer his own subjective comments. Instead, events are shown or dramatized and protagonists are given the opportunity to speak for themselves in plentiful, though mostly untagged, exchanges of dialogue. The language is simple, unequivocal, and concrete, punctuated by the occasional stock phrase or epithet, such as "lily white hands" or, in the case of "Sir Patrick Spens," "my mirry men." Repetition, in the form of the rhyme, assonance, and refrain which bulk large in ballads, not only assists memorization but helps to thicken the emotional atmosphere, or as poet Samuel Taylor Coleridge explained, "to discharge emotion that could not be exhausted in one saying." Incremental repetition, a type frequently found in ballads like "Sir Patrick Spens" (see stanzas nine and ten), advances the story through minor successive changes to repeated lines and phrases. A ballad is also instantly recognizable by its short, four-line stanzas (called quatrains) of alternating iambic tetrameter and iambic trimeter (lines of four and three stressed syllables respectively) that rhyme abcb and give what critic Paul Fussell has described in *Poetic Me-*

> *..'Sir Patrick Spens' is remarkable among ballads for its fine use of dramatic irony, contrast, and terse understatement.*"

ter and Poetic Form as "the illusion of primitive sincerity and openness."

Robust yet full of foreboding, "Sir Patrick Spens" exposes the harsh machinations of fate that govern human life and make for both its glory and impermanence. Sir Patrick's narrative begins with a ballad's characteristic abruptness, and, at once, it introduces the dichotomy of king and subject that continues as the action moves rapidly from the pleasures of the Scottish court, to the dangers of life on the high seas, back to the splendors of aristocratic society, and finally to the obscure ocean depths. The first three stanzas concern the inciting action—the king's need for a "guid sailor / To sail this schip of mine"—followed by his decision, made on his elderly knight's recommendation, to secure the services of Sir Patrick Spens. Where the ship is bound for is not indicated in the most widely anthologized version of the poem. Other, later versions of the ballad, however, name Norway as the voyage's destination. These versions apparently have historical foundation in two conflated events from the late-thirteenth-century reign of Alexander III of Scotland: one being the wreck of a vessel ferrying Scots nobles on their homeward journey from the nuptials of Margaret, Alexander's daughter, and Eric, King of Norway; the other, the disappearance of Alexander's granddaughter, the Maid of Norway, on her way to wed Edward I of England. But in this particular version of the poem, the lack of any reason for the voyage, coupled with the questionable circumstances in which the plan is hatched and the shadowy motives of the king and his company, only add to the injustice of Sir Patrick's inescapable situation. While everything about Sir Patrick is uniformly "guid" or good—his seamanship, the ship, and his character—the king is subtly implicated in the captain's undoing. The king, along with his knights, not only appears sedentary—for he "sits in Dumferling toune," the royal capital—but seems devoted to the good life, "[d]rinking the blude-reid wine" as he conducts important affairs of state. The life of ease and repose he leads contrasts sharply with the physical hardships endured by the men of action, such as the vigorous Sir Patrick "walking on the strand," who carry out his orders. In one of the ballad's few details, the wine the king drinks is said to be not merely red, but a vivid "blude-reid," an ominous symbol of the monarch's complicity in shedding the blood of his countrymen. Letters seldom bring good news in the realm of balladry, and the king's "braid letter" is no exception, since by it Sir Patrick's fate is quite literally "signed," sealed and delivered. "Broad" may simply mean bold or unequivocal, but it may also imply a drunken coarseness or crudity of expression; both meanings seem applicable since the letter's contents are enough to move Sir Patrick to both laughter and tears.

Sir Patrick's life lies not only in the king's hands, but in those of his elderly advisor, quite literally his "right-hand man" (sitting "at the king's richt kne"), who responds to the king's question in a familiar ballad formula: "Patrick Spens is the best sailor / That sails upon the se." Sir Patrick is paradoxically condemned by praise, his reputed excellence as a mariner the indirect cause of his undoing. But if the circumstances in which he receives the letter are any indication—he is first seen taking his daily constitutional on a beach—he fully lives up to his reputation as a man of the sea.

Stanzas four and five trace Sir Patrick's gradual realization of the letter's grave implications, portraying a welter of emotions, from initial shock and stunned disbelief to doleful melancholy and reproachful suspicion. Suspense is generated by a device common to ballads, a sequence ("first … then") which is then combined with incremental repetition to capture Sir Patrick's rapid alteration from laughter (perhaps at the thought that the king is joking) to tears:

> The first line that Sir Patrick red,
>   A loud lauch lauchèd he:
> The next line that Sir Patrick red,
>   The teir blinded his ee.

Sir Patrick racks his brain for a possible reason for his seeming persecution, feverishly stumbling over the same thoughts again and again. Intuitively, he already seems to understand that this will be his final voyage. Experience has taught him that "this time o' the yeir" is inopportune, even hazardous, for sea travel:

> O wha is this has don this deid,
>   This ill deid don to me,

To send me out this time o' the yeir,
>   To sail upon the se?

A rapid jump in the narrative, further contributing to the ballad's montage effect, finds Sir Patrick on board his ship, putting on a brave face for the sake of his crew as they ready to make sail the next morning. Undaunted, perhaps even accepting or defiant of his fate, Sir Patrick assumes command with an air of business as usual; he even sounds a good deal like Robin Hood as he addresses his crew as "my mirry men all" and exhorts them to "[m]ak haste, mak haste" with their preparations. But these good-natured gestures, aimed at boosting morale, are fraught with irony. There is no cause for merriment: the sailors make haste toward certain danger and their "guid schip," as at least one of the crew suspects, will be the means to their demise. In answer to Sir Patrick's forced optimism, one anxious crew member, so overwrought he says "I feir" not once but twice, predicts disaster on the basis of an omen he had read in the previous night's sky—"the new moone, / Wi' the auld moone in hir arme." This singularly beautiful poetic image is one that otherwise spells disaster for the superstitious mariners.

With another abrupt transition, stanza eight marks a shift from the narrative of Sir Patrick to a vignette of the vain and haughty Scots nobles who travel on his ship. By virtue of their titles and all that hereditary privilege bestows, they deem themselves much too good to wet even the cork heels of their shoes. But what fate has in store for them will prove this petty concern laughable. In due course, much more than their shoes will get wet—in fact their shoes are more likely to float than they will be. Nor will their wealth and power save them. The finality of their situation is rendered with the stanza's shift from present to past tense:

> O our Scots nobles wer richt laith
>   To weet their cork-heild schoone;
> Bot lang owre a' the play wer playd,
>   Thair hats they swam aboone.

As in Shakespeare's famous lines "All the world's a stage, / And all the men and women merely players" (*As You Like It,* 2.7.139-40), real life here is compared with play-acting, only in this case misadventure stops the proceedings and the play goes unfinished. In an indictment of materialism sharpened through a mordantly satirical comment on the pretensions of the upper classes, the rich are deprived of their belongings as well as their dignity as the ship goes down. With a bold stroke of physical humor that seems not only ludicrous but pathetic, their fine hats float above them, the only markers of their watery grave. It is thus through understatement that the ballad's central event, the tragic shipwreck, is suggested rather than painstakingly described. In the few details that show how the mighty are fallen, a powerful statement is made on the vanity and ephemeral precariousness of human life. Paths of glory lead but to the grave.

Two parallel stanzas, nine and ten, enlarge upon this theme by contrasting the resplendent Scottish noblewomen, ever expectant of their husbands' return, with the stark reality that no such return will be possible. The ladies are lavishly outfitted with fans and adorned with gold combs, but the implication is clearly that their riches will do them no good in bringing back their lost lords or in serving as a replacement for their loved ones. Their long and patient vigil, made to seem more tragic, protracted, and suspenseful by the doubled adverbs "O lang, lang" and by incremental repetition—"lang, lang may their ladies sit" and "lang, lang may the ladies stand"—will ultimately prove futile. They may well wait forever, as the austere comment closing the section states with a resonant finality: "For they'll se thame na mair."

What remains unanswered until the end of the poem is the exact fate of Sir Patrick Spens. The concluding stanza specifies the whereabouts of his vessel at the time of its sinking, "haf owre to Aberdour," a potent reminder of a destination within reach but forever unattainable. In a parting irony, Sir Patrick's body is revealed to lie "fiftie fadom deip … Wi' the Scots lords at his feit," as if symbolically paid homage in a justly fitting—if macabre—tribute to his true nobility. "Sir Patrick Spens" tells the tragic tale of a shipwreck where the spectacle of the event itself is overshadowed by its emotionally charged prelude and aftermath. Sir Patrick does what no one should be forced to do-to enter into dangerous circumstances knowing he will not come out alive. Nevertheless, Sir Patrick's example shows how this should be done—with a resolve outfacing death. He is both a hero for the glory of his perseverance and a victim for his subordination to the whims of politics and to the insidious workings of fate, which neither worldly wealth and power nor love can alter or deter.

Source: Carolyn Meyer, in an essay for *Poetry for Students,* Gale, 1998.

William M. Ryan

In the following excerpt, Ryan examines the ways in which version A of "Sir Patrick Spens" deviates from the formula of most traditional ballads and, in particular, deems it "distinctive in lacing ... tragedy with dramatic irony."

Two overlapping fallacies which go their perennial way in oppressing the popular taste in literature are the seldom examined beliefs that old is good *per se* and that all of the old pieces within a certain period and genre are equal parts of the whole. The drab and the mediocre have been indiscriminately dissected along with masterpieces, and students have been fed a diet mixed with both the poor fare and the good. Medieval drama is a case in point; the "English and Scottish popular ballads" are another. By lifting one ballad out of its crowded depository and demonstrating its superiority over other ballads which have formulaic similarities, the present article pays tribute to a great poem that is deserving of more attention than critics have been wont to give it. The relative merit of "Sir Patrick Spens" [version A, in *The English and Scottish Popular Ballads,* 1956] is my only concern. Authorship and date of composition of almost all medieval and Renaissance ballads being presently and perhaps everlastingly beyond reach, those containing parallels to "Sir Patrick Spens" have been selected irrespective of chronology, and possible direction of influence has been ignored.

The stage on which "a' the play wer playd" is a large one—many actors, a wide frame of action—and "Sir Patrick Spens" consequently does not cast an incantatory spell as darkly and deeply as does, for example, "Bonny Barbara Allen" with its warping combination of intimacy and alienation. "Sir Patrick Spens," however, treating as it does of a king and a powerful nobleman who suffers violent death, contains the kernel of true dramatic tragedy and is, moreover, distinctive in lacing this tragedy with dramatic irony of such bitterness and weighted implication that it compensates for slight substance and the relative lack of narrative development. The stanzas are carefully laid, and because so much is implied, so little given, the ending comes almost as suddenly as the losing of the boat and the drowning of its crew. Yet, despite this brevity, the poem sets up suspense for a few lines; e.g. through Sir Patrick's horrified "O wha is this has don this deid" and the "I feir a deadlie storme" of one of his men.

Special use is made of meter. We have not entered as far as the third foot of the opening line, have read only the first word of the second foot, when a mild metrical shock occurs. Unlike the nursery rhyme king and queen who were *in* the counting house and parlor, respectively, with the stress falling on the preposition (not the verb *was*), the ballad's king *sits,* and as it happens, he sits in Dumfermline, where he is expected to be found sitting, since it is the royal burgh. For a verb like *sits* to receive stress is quite normal, just as it is for the verb-to-be not to receive it. What is *not* normal, however, is for a monosyllabic verb to constitute an internal foot. Attention is shortly drawn to another sitter, the elder knight at the king's right knee, because the verb is again stressed following a noun phonologically similar to "king," the noun "knicht." This repetition contrasts with the single appearance of the related verbs "walking," "lies," and "stand," which add something, however little, to the impression that there is peculiarity in the king's sitting and his minister's too. As the story progresses it is clearly seen to be concerned with men of physical action and other men who, in the manner of the brass in any war, precipitate the action by issuing commands from behind desks which are behind the lines. The simple repetition would seem to contribute to the linkage of the two characters.

No sooner is the first line finished than meter again makes itself felt, this time in a telling participle at the beginning of line two—"drinking." The stem *drink* is the first foot, and in this position of emphatic prominence, coming as it does after the even more conspicuous "sits," it directs attention to the king's second condition, as it were. He sits; he drinks. Others go out onto the cold, rough sea. Discovery that the wine is red and not only red but blood-red (note the natural stress pattern /x) adds to the subtle impression that this drinking is of particular importance to the story, an impression soon confirmed by the king's metaphorical shedding of the blood of his subjects.

The reader generally acquainted with the popular ballads will appreciate the strokes of elaboration in our poem, clear sign of a special talent, as a formula is adopted, then built upon. Someone sits and drinks wine in other ballads—"Lamkin," "Brown Robin," "The White Fisher"—but only in "Sir Patrick Spens" is the combination found of *sits* as monosyllabic foot and wine that is "blude-reid" (the stress is on *blude*), adding a splash of color and an ominous symbol, both of which were welcomed by the medieval audience. Blood and wine were, moreover, commonly associated in popular literature and therefore in people's minds, quite apart from the sacrament of the Eucharist....

When the king, perhaps on drunken impulse, sings out "O whar," he sounds like many another ballad character; the two words are heard in at least twelve ballads, by my count, and continue in modern usage in popular songs like "Billy Boy" and "Where and O Where Is My Little Wee Dog?"... In eight of the old ballads the query regards a "lit-

tle" or "wee" or "bonny" boy, who is said to be used in almost all instances a messenger. As we have seen and shall see repeatedly, familiar matter is handled differently in "Sir Patrick Spens" A: it is a "guid sailor" who is called for, a man to serve as ship's master, not a boy to go aloft as a lookout.... The king specifies not only a sailor but a "gúid sailór" (à la Française), and the stress pattern is repeated to strong effect in the following stanza when Sir Patrick is called "the bést sailór."...

With abruptness typical of medieval narrative, going all the way back to Anglo-Saxon heroic poetry, the king writes Sir Patrick a letter—a broad letter perhaps so called for one of two reasons: its wasteful calligraphy, the result of a drinker's loss of motor control; its unusual length, product of drunken garrulousness as he first, presumably, greets his noble reader with some flattering salutation or other and a few pleasantries before coming to the point. No reason is implied for the letter's misleading first part. Not only did someone's writing a letter usually presage disaster in ballads; a long or broad letter, signed with the writer's own hand or sealed by him, was even worse. Again a poor choice is avoided in "Sir Patrick Spens" A: instead of specifying the familiar bonny boy as deliverer of the letter, the letter is simply "sent."...

When the letter was delivered, Sir Patrick was walking. Now, walking, of itself does not seem to have much traditional significance in this poetry. Characters walk here or there in a few of the ballads, just as characters sit by windows or on castle walls in others, but these have none of the ironic association conveyed by the king's sitting in "Sir Patrick Spens."... At most, walking is being set as a counterweight against thematic dying—motion against repose. From a more general point of view, however, "walking" is probably best taken as mere formulaic filler, as in "The Twa Corbies," "Captain Car," and many other ballads.

Again, as we have come to expect, "Sir Patrick Spens" A works the old into something fresh. The good sailor is "walking on the sand"—beach or strand presumably being his habitual choice for constitutionals and dramatically the most appropriate place for a sea dog who is already in a state of nervous apprehension.

With "first line" and "next line" the poem conforms to a catalogue of enumeration that is ubiquitous in the world of balladry. Even here, however, a point can be made in defense of "Sir Patrick Spens A, for at least fifteen of the ballads with a "first ... next" or "first ... second" sequence and an equal number with tear-blinded eyes are happy affairs, belying the seemingly implicit threat in the stages of the action.…"Sir Patrick Spens" is not … the first or the only ballad but is a rare one in making tighter suspense through this sequence.

Unconsciously mimicking the king's "O whar," "O wha," says Sir Patrick, "… has don this ill deid," and like the king he is of course perfectly aware of the answer to his own question. That is, if the king was determined to do an ill deed it was no doubt poor Patrick who must fall victim to it. The stricken man's woeful cry repeats "deid," adding "ill" to the second. He is in effect saying, "How could you do this to me?," "How can this happen to me?," "Who ever heard of such a thing?" He may also be indicting the prompter who named him to the king, but the idea loses cogency when the facts of dreadful hardship and all but certain death are considered; in this extremity, the king's orders to sail in the morning being already signed and sealed, court politics will not matter much and there is too little time to seek a remedy.…

"Mak hast, mak haste" is, like various duplicate imperatives in the ballads, spoken with tension at a critical moment. So far as I know it is unique except for its appearance in the inferior "Bonny Birdy" where the voice that utters the taut injunction is no less and no more than that of the bird itself, a far cry, if a pun may be allowed, from the anxious skipper's order to his crew, whom he addresses as "my mirry men all." Considering the universal popularity of "merry men," it was almost inevitable that the phrase, rather than a plain "my men," would appear in "Sir Patrick Spens." The fact that it is a tragic ballad would be no deterrent; in the majority of instances the poems with "merry men" end unhappily, and in a few there is cruel irony like that of "Sir Patrick Spens" A, where the master is speaking to men who must die with him.…

If "Sir Patrick Spens" A must be said to have admitted an overworked formula in its single use of "my mirry men" it may also be said to have done so with restraint.

There is a touch of mild irony in "our guid ship" in the sixth stanza: with no cause for optimism the captain and the crew will not be thinking positively about the craft which, so it seems, is to take them to their death. Sir Patrick's forced cheeriness is calculated, of course, to keep the "merry" men's spirits as high as possible. Irony is more pointed in the following stanza as one of the crew expresses the dismay he felt at sight of the old-new moon, an omen to be perhaps taken seriously in one of the other seasons but a mere redundancy in the present perilous situation.

Stanza 8 possesses the most obvious specimens of ironical humor—the litotes of the sailors' being loath to wet their corkheeled shoes and the floating-hat property familiar in slapstick comedy. (A clumsy put-down that was popular in the nineteen forties enjoined the object of displeasure to "walk west till your hat floats." The comedian Buster Keaton—but not his funny hat—disappears underwater as his boat goes down.) In this case the headgear of the noblemen constitute the only marker their grave will ever have, and appropriately the vestigial hats are set afloat in a context and atmosphere, briefly created in line 31, of play-acting, a calculated use of man's ancient practice of referring to real-life events—any accident of misadventure—in terms of plays and stories, as in "news story," "play a heroic part," "dénouement."

An adverb heard once in stanza 8 is used with duplication in the following two stanzas. With a metrical break similar to that in the first line of the poem, "lang, lang" receives two stresses.…

In these closing stanzas of "Sir Patrick Spens" the ladies' fans are a reminder that the lost crew were not ordinary seamen but the cream of Scottish knighthood, a further irony insofar as wasting of human life may be calibrated relatively. The ladies' gold combs share this significance and have also perhaps a deeper one, for at least it may be noted in passing that combs have been objects of superstition since their earliest use and in all parts of the world. In the time of St. Cuthbert in Anglo-Saxon England combs were buried with the illustrious dead because of a belief that "by combing his hair a man tidied his brains which lay beneath it" [according to Peter Hunter Blair in his *Northumbria in the Days of Bede*]. James G. Frazer cites comb superstitions among natives of Sarawak, ancient Romans, Choctaw, Omaha, and Natchez American Indians [in his book *The Golden Bough*].

The comb, then, as token of both life and death, would have definite associations in the medieval mind, and the gold combs in "Sir Patrick Spens" A, though they figure as ornaments, not as utensils, may have been intended as portents or symbols of ill fortune.…

Even the ladies' waiting brings ironic hint of the comic, in the same manner as Chaucer's very numerous *occupationes* suddenly abandon someone or other, to the reader's amusement. The closing stanza conveys the information that the distance the storm-racked boat was able to make was "half owre to Aberdour." To indicate similar limitation of distance, lesser balladeers, including revisers of "Sir Patrick Spens," usually fell back on "had not … a league (but one, three, etc.)." As poet and reader take leave forever of the sunken boat and its lifeless crew, Sir Patrick is shown somewhat elevated even in death "Wi the Scots lords at his feit," probably by virtue of his having been lashed to the rudder during the storm. The king still "sits in Dumferling toune," while the good sailor holds his rightful place over his men, all unbeknownst to them and to anyone who has eyes to see, to all, alas, but the fishes of the deep.

Source: William M. Ryan, "Formula and Tragic Irony in 'Sir Patrick Spens,'" in *Southern Folklore Quarterly,* Vol. 44, 1980, pp. 73–83.

Sources

Brooks, Cleanth, and Robert Penn Warren, *Understanding Poetry,* Holt, Rinehart and Winston, 1960.

Child, Francis James, "Sir Patrick Spens," in *English and Scottish Popular Ballads,* Dover Publications, Inc., 1965, Vol. 2, pp. 17-33.

Drabble, Margaret, *The Oxford Companion to English Literature,* Oxford University Press, 1991.

Frankenberg, Lloyd, "Sir Patrick Spens," in *Invitation to Poetry: A Round of Poems from John Skelton to Dylan Thomas Arranged with Comments,* Garden City: Dolphin Books, 1956, pp. 113-15.

Friedman, Alfred B., introduction to *The Viking Book of Folk Ballads of the English-Speaking World,* New York: Viking, 1956.

Fussell, Paul, *Poetic Meter and Poetic Form,* New York: Random House, 1965.

Gerould, Gordon Hall, "The Nature of Ballads," in *The Ballad of Tradition,* Gordian Press, 1974, pp. 1-14.

Hodgart, M. J. C., "The Poetry of Ballads," in *The Ballads,* Hutchinson University Library, 1950, pp. 27-35.

Moore, Arthur K., "The Literary Status of the English Popular Ballad," *Comparative Literature* Vol. 10, No. 1, 1958, pp. 1-20.

Moore, Richard, "Seven Types of Accuracy," in *The Iowa Review,* Spring 1982, pp. 152-63.

For Further Study

Frankenberg, Lloyd, *Invitation to Poetry,* Doubleday & Company, 1956.
Explores how the fragmentary technique of "Sir Patrick Spens" contributes to the poems allusive richness.

Hodgart, M. J. C., *The Ballads,* Hutchinson's University Library, 1950.
Compares the technique in "Sir Patrick Spens" with jump-cutting techniques of modern movies.

Van Doren, Mark, "On *Sir Patrick Spens,*" in *Introduction to Literature,* edited by Louis G. Locke, William M. Gibson, and George Arms, Holt Rinehart and Winston, 1963.
Van Doren examines the emotional force of "Sir Patrick Spens."

Sonnet 30

William Shakespeare
1609

In *Palladis Tamia: Wit's Treasury* (1598), Francis Mere writes that a man named William Shakespeare was known for "his sugared sonnets among his private friends." Though the melancholy tone of most of "Sonnet 30" (first published in 1609) can hardly be characterized as sweet, the final couplet does have a saccharine quality that many of Shakespeare's critics have found distasteful. After the speaker has been overwhelmed with sadness for twelve lines, can he really solve all of his problems and find happiness in a couplet's time? Perhaps his friend is indeed his savior, possessed with the wealth, power, or influence to replace the speaker's mysterious "losses" (line 14). But the speaker's quick and easy change of heart in the last two lines may be a sign that his grief is not as deep as it seems. Indeed, the sonnet's difficult phrasings, heavy alliteration, and deliberate drag of repeated words lend a theatrical tone to his moans and sighs; the reader is left wondering if the speaker's eye is, in fact, "unused to flow" (line 5).

Author Biography

Shakespeare was born in Statford-upon-Avon on or about April 23, 1564. His father was a merchant who devoted himself to public service, attaining the highest of Stratford's municipal positions—that of bailiff and justice of the peace—by 1568. Biographers have surmised that the elder Shakespeare's social standing and relative prosperity at

William Shakespeare

this time would have enabled his son to attend the finest local grammar school, the King's New School, where he would have received an outstanding classical education under the direction of highly regarded masters. There is no evidence that Shakespeare attended university. In 1582, at the age of eighteen, he married Ann Hathaway of Stratford, a woman eight years his senior. Their first child, Susanna, was born six months later, followed by twins, Hamnet and Judith, in 1585. These early years of Shakespeare's adult life are not well documented; some time after the birth of his twins, he joined a professional acting company and made his way to London, where his first plays, the three parts of the Henry VI history cycle, were presented from 1589 to 1591. The first reference to Shakespeare in the London literary world dates from 1592, when dramatist Robert Greene alluded to him as "an upstart crow." Shakespeare further established himself as a professional actor and playwright when he joined the Lord Chamberlain's Men, an acting company formed in 1594 under the patronage of Henry Carey, Lord Hunsdon. The members of this company included the renowned tragedian Richard Burbage and the famous "clown" Will Kempe, who was one of the most popular actors of his time. This group began performing at the playhouse known simply as the The-

atre and at the Cross Keys Inn, moving to the Swan Theatre on Bankside in 1596 when municipal authorities banned the public presentation of plays within the limits of the city of London. Three years later Shakespeare and other members of the company financed the building of the Globe Theatre, the most famous of all Elizabethan playhouses. By then the foremost London Company, the Lord Chamberlain's Men also performed at Court on numerous occasions, their success largely due to the fact that Shakespeare wrote for no other company.

In 1603 King James I granted the group a royal patent, and the company's name was altered to reflect the King's direct patronage. Records indicate that the King's Men remained the most favored acting company in the Jacobean era, averaging a dozen performances at Court each year during the period. In addition to public performances at the Globe Theatre, the King's Men played at the private Blackfriars Theatre; many of Shakespeare's late plays were first staged at Blackfriars, where the intimate setting facilitated Shakespeare's use of increasingly sophisticated stage techniques. The playwright profited handsomely from his long career in the theater and invested in real estate, purchasing properties in both Stratford and London. As early as 1596 he had attained sufficient status to be granted a coat of arms and the accompanying right to call himself a gentleman. By 1610, with his fortune made and his reputation as the leading English dramatist unchallenged, Shakespeare appears to have retired to Stratford, though business interests brought him to London on occasion. He died on April 23, 1616. and was buried in the chancel of Trinity Church in Stratford.

Poem Text

When to the sessions of sweet silent thought
I summon up remembrance of things past,
I sigh the lack of many a thing I sought,
And with old woes new wail my dear time's waste:

Then can I drown an eye, unused to flow,   5
For precious friends hid in death's dateless night,
And weep afresh love's long-since-cancelled woe,
And moan th' expense of many a vanished sight:

Then can I grieve at grievances foregone,
And heavily from woe to woe tell o'er   10
The sad account of fore-bemoanèd moan,
Which I new pay as if not paid before.
    But if the while I think on thee, dear friend,
    All losses are restored and sorrows end.

Poem Summary

Lines 1-2:

As in Shakespeare's "Sonnet 29," the speaker sets up an "if-then" statement by using the word "when." This allows him to describe his feelings and actions in the present tense, even though he is not experiencing them at the time of composition. The description thus possesses a sort of false immediacy.

The speaker begins to implement a financial or legal metaphor from the word "sessions"; though it generally designates a period of activity, the word also describes the periodic sittings of judges in a court of law. In the next line, "summon up" possesses a similar double entendre: its broader definition is "to call forth," but it also means "to order an appearance before a court." The metaphor is continued throughout the sonnet, with words such as "cancelled" (line 7), "expense" (line 8), "account" line 11), and "paid" (line 12). Thus, though "Sonnet 30" tells a rather unspecific tale of a friend in need and a friend indeed, the related metaphors tell their own story: the speaker has incurred debts or the wrath of the law, and only his "dear friend" can get him out of trouble.

Lines 3-4:

In these lines, the speaker is in essence "crying over spilled milk," as the old saying goes. Past losses and problems plague the speaker once again, and the reader can almost hear him stutter and sob, thanks to the tripping rhythm of line 3, and the dragging alliteration and the series of gasp-like stresses in line 4.

"Dear time's waste," an emphasized phrase because of its three consecutive accented syllables, may mean a single missed opportunity, a misspent lifetime, or a squandering of valuable time; the reader is left to decide whether time was wasted inside or out of the courtroom.

Lines 5-8:

Though he claims that he rarely sheds a tear, the speaker continues to cry throughout the second and third quatrains. The memory of dead friends, lost loves, and faded visions keeps his eyes moist. He seems to hiccup his way over consecutive accented syllables in lines 6 and 7; the profusion of "and"s and "then"s beginning the lines make him sound as if he were blubbering with grief.

Despite the sonnet's gushing emotion, a Renaissance reader may have found cause to chuckle in line 7. "Woe" and "woo" were homonyms dur-

Media Adaptations

- There are several audio recordings of readings of Shakespeare's sonnets, including *Sonnets of Shakespeare,* by Spoken Arts, Inc.; *Living Literature: The Sonnets of Shakespeare,* by Crown Publishers, Inc.; and *Shakespeare: The Sonnets,* by Argo Records.

- *Shakespeare's Sonnets* is a "Films for the Humanities & Sciences" video featuring an indepth look at the poems and recitals of selected sonnets by such actors as Ben Kingsley and Claire Bloom.

ing Shakespeare's time; their interchangeability makes the speaker sound as if he has given up on the possibility of love—preferring, perhaps, to wallow in self-pity.

Lines 9-12:

The phrase that runs through the third quatrain means little more than, "I continue to dwell on the bad aspects of the past." The speaker not only stretches this idea, but the language and rhythm of the quatrain as well. Each of the first three lines contains a twice-repeated word that is nearly synonymous with the repeated word in the next line: "grieve" and "grievances" of line 9 are echoed by "woe" and "woe" of line 10, and "moaned" and "moan" of line 11. These words, as well as those of line 12, "pay" and "paid," are all comprised of long vowelled sounds associated with wailing and weeping. Going back to the figure of speech in line 5, the speaker is indeed "drowning"—in his own language as well as in tears.

The speaker's actual causes of sorrow remain unknown throughout the sonnet, though the legal or financial metaphor which persists through this quatrain affords one interpretation. For example, a "sad account" may be a sorrowful tale, but it also may be a very sorry-looking record of finances; perhaps the records are so sloppy that the speaker is repaying bills already paid, or perhaps he is being charged an unfortunately high interest rate.

Lines 13-14:

The language in line 14 once again suggests that the speaker's grief may have been related to his financial situation. Perhaps the friend is a wealthy patron; "dear," used also in line 4, has the meaning "of a high value" as well as "much loved." The reader of "Sonnet 30" may indeed be this friend: one who has patiently listened to the speaker's problems, and perhaps rescued him from debt by buying his book of sonnets!

Themes

Memory and Reminiscence

The opening lines of "Sonnet 30" establish the central theme of the poem as the speaker, writing to a friend, shares "remembrances of things past" with much heartache. Ironically, it is the vague way Shakespeare handles this theme which many critics cite as the poem's fatal flaw. The speaker never focuses his details enough for the reader to connect on an emotional level and share these feelings of "woe" and "grief." Instead Shakespeare provides abstractions, never telling us exactly what were the "many a things" he sought during his life. Who are the friends now "hid in death's dateless night?" Whose "love long since canceled woe" is making him well up with tears? What are the "many a vanished sight" and the "grievances forgone" which are making him moan from line to line?

This type of writing makes communication on an emotional level difficult between poet and reader. Some literary critics seem to enjoy having the chance to "solve" a vague poem's "mystery," as if poets intended that only professors are intellectually abstract enough to decipher even their worst writing. In turn Shakespeare's critics claim this poem's "hidden" theme is more about money than memory, citing the repetition of "financial" metaphors throughout.

The theme of memory and reminiscence also deflates the sonnet form's traditional "if:then" construction. The poet develops the first two stanzas like a legal premise and nails down a conclusion with the final couplet's two-beat anvil strike. If we examine the clauses in the poem, the argument proves itself circular: "When to the sessions of sweet silent thought / I summon up remembrance of things past / … Then can I drown and eye … / … Then can I grieve at grievances forgone." This has confused many a reader expecting the sonnet's traditional specific and forward development to-

Topics for Further Study

- Say you are Shakespeare's friend, and the last couplet of the sonnet is addressed to you. Write a letter in response to Shakespeare asking him to clarify any lines which seemed vague to you. If a good friend says to you "I sigh the lack of many a thing I sought," would you let him or her end there, or would you demand details?

- Thinking of the sonnet form in terms of an engine, take some time to disassemble its parts and explore what makes it work. How do the end-rhymes help each line fit together like teeth on a gear? How does the rhythmic structure from word to word in each line help move the reader's eye across the page? Do think there are any parts of the poem you could exclude and still get the sonnet to "work" properly? Why or why not?

ward a one-two punch ending. But this poem's theme seems to make the speaker's wheels spin in self-pity, the argument instead seeming to say "when I think back on things past I can cry and can grieve at things gone." And the final couplet which we might hope to leave us with surprise turn instead gives the speaker a chance to "duck out" of this poem, seeming to say "but when I think of you, old friend, everything's OK. Bye."

Shakespeare wrote "Sonnet 30" less than a decade before his death, and the theme of memory for memory's sake may have come from a man realizing his life is more behind him than ahead. In this case, the act of reminiscence itself becomes more heart-wrenching for the speaker than any one specific memory, a lifetime of woes behind him, though younger readers (even readers in their forties) may find it difficult to connect with the power of emotion he was trying to express so abstractly.

Friendship

The extended sequence of which "Sonnet 30" was a part conveys a strong theme of friendship. Many of the sonnets were written to a young male friend whom Shakespeare loved dearly (and platonically), often commenting on his beauty, urging him to marry a nice woman and have children. "Sonnet 30," though too abstract to find any specific mention of this common character in the sequence, is most likely written as a direct address to a friend.

It is difficult to tell exactly, but Shakespeare could have been speaking to a friend about all the things past which make him sad and how he finds comfort when his thoughts turn toward their friendship, as the closing lines suggest: "But if the while I think on thee, dear friend, / All losses are restored and sorrows end." Or the speaker, who mentions "precious friends hid in death's dateless night," is really just sitting in a room writing to himself and to his friends who have passed away, the memories of the good times shared the real source of the old man's comfort.

Style

The sonnet (from the Italian "sonnetto," meaning "little song") owes much of its long-standing popularity to the Italian poet, Petrarch. By the mid-sixteenth century, this fixed poetic form was adopted by the English, who borrowed the fourteen-line pattern and many of Petrarch's literary conventions. English writers did, however, work out an alternate rhyme scheme that allows for more variety in rhyming words: while an Italian sonnet might rhyme *abbaabba, cdccdc,* an English or Shakespearean sonnet rhymes *abab, cdcd, efef, gg.*

In all but three of Shakespeare's 154 sonnets ("Sonnet 99," "Sonnet 126," and "Sonnet 145"), the first three groups of four lines each are known as quatrains, and the last two lines are recognized as a couplet. The three breaks between the quatrains and the couplet serve as convenient places where the writer's train of thought can take a different direction. In "Sonnet 30," a dramatic—and controversial—change in the writer's emotional state takes place in the final couplet, and is signalled by the word "but."

"Sonnet 30" is written in iambic pentameter. Iambic meter, the most familiar rhythm in the English language, is simply the succession of alternately stressed syllables; an iamb, a type of poetic foot, is a group of two syllables in which the first is unstressed and the second is stressed. The use of "penta" (meaning "five") before "meter" means that there are five iambs per line.

Stresses embody meanings; both variety and emphasis are added to lines in which the regular

rhythm is broken. "Sonnet 30" is for the most part regular in meter, but this only draws more attention to the few breaks in the lines. The phrases "sweet silent thought" (line 1) and "death's dateless night" (line 6) are noticeable stumbling blocks to a reciter of this poem, thanks to their use of two consecutive accented syllables (known as spondees) and alliteration. Additionally, Shakespeare could have written "many things" and "many vanished sights" in lines 3 and 8, but chose instead to include the tripping rhythms of "many a thing" and "many a vanished sight"; in each case, the extra syllable embellishes upon the notion of plentifulness.

Historical Context

Although it is one of the more abstract poems in the sequence, our understanding of "Sonnet 30" grows as we discover the context in which Shakespeare wrote the poem and the rest of the lengthy sequence. He wrote the poem less than a decade before his death, an older poet reminiscing back on his long life, reflecting on his regrets and woes. Some critics point to the repeated use of "legal" and "financial" terms peppered throughout the poem to conclude Shakespeare is specifically griping about his many debts. On the other hand, since the speaker of the poem is remembering himself as a younger man, the repeated use of those terms may reflect the position Shakespeare's father held as the poet began his career in the theater.

Having grown up with a father in one of Stratford's highest municipal positions, bailiff and justice of the peace, he surely developed a strong legal vocabulary. Also contradicting the popular interpretation of the poem is the evidence that Shakespeare enjoyed prosperity from childhood to retirement, sending his children to the finest grammar schools, profiting handsomely from his long career in the theater and his real estate investments.

In order to gain a wider context surrounding the publication of these poems, it is important to note the drastic changes that occurred across Europe. Shakespeare lived and wrote his famous sonnet sequence during the Renaissance, a period of sweeping cultural, social, and political change. The influence of the Catholic Church, an institution that had dominated all aspects of life throughout Europe during the medieval times, was giving way to more secular, less spiritual forces. The religious Reformation challenged the absolute authority of the pope in spiritual matters and em-

Compare
&
Contrast

- **1558:** Elizabeth I becomes Queen of England and will rule until her death in 1603. She survives several assassination attempts made by English Catholics, reflecting a sharp ideological divide between the Protestant-ruled government and Catholics both native to England and abroad. Suspicions of spying, treachery, and outright attack were well-justified throughout Elizabeth's reign.

  Today: Elizabeth II has ruled Britain since 1952. She began her reign at the height of the Cold War, in which Western democratic countries such as Britain and the United States were in a continual state of hostility with the communist countries, such as the Soviet Union and China. An era of spying, treason, and general mistrust pervaded the national psyche. Since the collapse of communism in the late 1980s, however, Britain has entered a period of relative peace, a condition never enjoyed by the first Queen.

- **1600:** A French commercial partnership secures a monopoly on fur trade in the New World, while the English East India Company is established with hopes of challenging Dutch control of the spice trade.

  Today: England, France and other continental countries are moving to form the European Economic Community, a union designed to help Eu-

  ropean countries compete more effectively in the truly global marketplace, which is dominated by such economic giants as the United States and Japan.

- **1604:** King James I publishes his *Counterblaste to Tobacco,* describing smoking as "a custome loathsome to the eye, hatefull to the nose, harmfull to the braine, dangerous to the lungs, and in the blacke stinking fume thereof, nearest resembling the horrible Stigian smoke of the pit that is bottomlesse."

  Today: Over fifty million Americans still smoke, despite its being identified as a cause of heart disease, emphysema, and lung cancer. More than 390,000 Americans die each year from the effects of smoking.

- **1609:** Part of convoy sailing to the aid of starving English settlers in the Virginia colony, the ship *Sea Venture* blows off course and becomes shipwrecked on an unexplored island. The Isle of Devils, as it was called, was rumored to be inhabited by demons.

  Today: The Isle of Devils is now called Bermuda. It remains a colony of Great Britain and is one of the oldest members of the British Commonwealth. Because of its pleasant subtropical climate, it is a popular vacation destination.

---

phasized the faith and devotional practices of the individual.

Along with this dispersion of spiritual authority came a redistribution of political power to individual states, which were throwing off the control of the pope in Rome. Art and culture, too, experienced a reawakening ("renaissance" means "rebirth"), as sacred themes in painting, drama, and poetry were replaced by human concerns, such as love, honor, and physical beauty. Writers and painters sought to create new standards, new definitions of what was true, good, or beautiful, based

on direct experience rather than on received knowledge or traditions.

The sonnet itself has a strong historical foundation; it is a form Shakespeare both followed and innovated for future generations of writers. He followed a tradition of sonnet (from the Italian *Sonnetto,* or *little song*) writing that dates back to the fourteenth-century *Rime* of the Italian poet Petrarch.

The first English sonneteer of note was Sir Thomas Wyatt, who, by the mid-sixteenth century, translated a number of Petrarch's sonnets into English and wrote original compositions closely modeled on Italian patterns. Along with his friend Henry Howard, Earl of Surrey, Wyatt is credited with introducing a vogue for sonnet writing in England that lasted until the end of the sixteenth century. Although the English writers borrowed many poetic conventions already established by Petrarch, including adopting the fourteen-line format of the sonnet, they altered the rhyme scheme in order to increase the scope of the rhyming words. After each quatrain (*abab cdcd, efef*) the writer can either continue developing a single idea, or pursue another.

Surrey's contribution to sonnet writing is significant in one important respect, and that is he always ended his sonnets with a rhymed couplet (*gg*). This practice, which was followed by most Elizabethan sonneteers, also became Shakespeare's own. Although Shakespeare's sonnets were first published in 1609, at least some were written a decade or more earlier, and circulated in manuscript among the author's friends.

Critical Overview

The praise of "Sonnet 30" has been tempered by the strong negative opinions of its final couplet. In *Shakespeare's Sonnets,* Kenneth Muir declares the poem "one of the most highly wrought of all the sonnets," noting the poem's richly varied meter and extensive word play; however, he also acknowledges that the last two lines destroy the languid, dramatic movement of the first twelve. Quoting from Mark Van Doren's *Shakespeare,* Muir agrees that the final couplet of "Sonnet 30" runs with "perfunctory and absurd rapidity to fabricate a concluding statement."

Other discussions of "Sonnet 30" have centered upon its legal or financial metaphor. In their books on Shakespeare's sonnets, both Stephen Booth and Gerald Hammond trace the metaphor's path through the entirety of the poem; Hammond claims in *The Reader and Shakespeare's Young Man* that "Sonnet 30" possesses "one of the most exhaustive metaphors in [Shakespeare's sequence of] sonnets."

Criticism

Jhan Hochman

In the following essay, Hochman surveys stylistic aspects of "Sonnet 30," and determines why the poem is perceived as a failure.

"Sonnet 30" is part of Shakespeare's sequence of 154 sonnets, all of which were published in 1609. The first 126 sonnets are thought to be addressed to a handsome, young aristocrat who was likely Shakespeare's sponsor. It is not surprising then that the tone of these sonnets is exceedingly praiseworthy or obsequious toward the sponsor, and sometimes even self-effacing of the poet.

The first 126 sonnets contain what is now assumed to be occasional homosexual content (especially "Sonnet 20"), formerly a source of contentious argument in Shakespearean criticism. Homosexuality would have been perceived as more of a slight to the great Shakespeare's reputation than it is now.

The sonnets were written in the heyday of sonnet writing, from 1591-1597, a period beginning with Sir Philip Sydney's *Astrophel and Stella.* Shakespeare's contribution to the development of the English sonnet is his emphasis on friendship more than on love. Like the first 126 sonnets, "Sonnet 30" is a panegyric, that is, a form of verbal praise. The panegyrical aspect of the poem, however, is not introduced until the last couplet which serves as a punch line, that while surprising in relation to the rest of the poem, tends less to knock readers out than let them down. This probably has more to do with satisfying the sponsor than Shakespeare's failure in this poem.

Shakespeare follows the form of the English sonnet introduced by Wyatt and developed by Sidney. The English form bundles the fourteen sonnet lines into four groups: three groups of four lines (quatrains) and one group of two lines (couplet). The predecessor of the English or Shakespearean sonnet is the Italian or Petrarchan sonnet, also fourteen lines but internally divided into two groups, one of eight lines (octave) and the other six lines (sestet). Lines are generally of ten syllables, five accents per line, and have an end-rhyme scheme of *abab cdcd efef gg.* Not only is there end-rhyme, but a kind of internal rhyme or "consonance," the repeating of consonant sounds in every line. In fact, every line is dominated by at least one consonant sound, sometimes two.

For example, in line four there are five "w" or semivowel sounds: with, woes, new, wail, waste. In line nine, there are three "g" or affricate sounds: grieve, grievances, foregone. There is also an overall pattern of voiced and voiceless consonants. The poem begins and ends in voiceless consonants, especially "s" sounds or sibilants in the first three lines and the final line.

What Do I Read Next?

- The sonnet is perhaps the most popular form in English verse. Two of Shakespeare's contemporaries also writing thematically related sonnet sequences were Sir Philip Sidney and Edmund Spenser. Sidney's *Astrophil and Stella* was published in 1591, and Spenser's *Amoretti* was published in 1595.

- The fourteenth century Italian poet Petrarch was a significant innovator of the sonnet form, and his works influenced Shakespeare and other poets. His sonnets are available in a number of English translations, including *Rime Disperse* (1991), translated by Joseph A Barber.

- Many contemporary American poets still use the sonnet form to craft their poems, and many still collect their work into thematic sequences. Most recently, Ron Wallace, a poet living and teaching in Madison, Wisconsin, published his latest sonnets in a collection titled *The Uses of Adversity and Blessings* on University of Pittsburgh Press, 1998.

On the other hand, the vast majority of sounds in the body of the poem are voiced sounds of various kinds—semivowels (woe, wail), stops (death's, dateless) nasals (moan, many), and fricatives (thee, the). With voiceless sibilants at the beginning and end of the sonnet, it can be said that the poem begins and ends in a kind of whispering silence, those "sessions of sweet silent thought." The body of the poem, meanwhile, is louder, appropriate to the "testimony," and the accompanying moaning, wailing, and crying the writer exhibits.

The focus of "Sonnet 30" is the memory of past events. It is subdivided into three quatrains as follows: the first quatrain has memory trained on old goals; in the second, on old, dead friends; in the third, on old grievances. Let us then proceed quatrain by quatrain. In the first two lines remembrances of things past are established within a metaphor of a court ("sessions").

As a judge or lawyer would, the "I" of the poem "summons" up his memories as if they were witnesses in a court of law coming to testify on the stand. As the court room demands silence in order to hear and give proper respect to the proceedings, so are memories summoned up to remembrance during times of quiet, of "sweet silent thought." The first group of memories to take the stand (the plaintiff) tells its tale of time wasted on goals sought but never reached. The testimony is accompanied by sighs and wails. The fourth line is specifically interesting in that it can be read in at least three ways, especially in regard to the way the line is punctuated:

> 1) And with old woes, new(ly) wail, my dear time's waste.
>
> 2) And with old woes new, wail my dear time's waste.
>
> 3) And with old woes, new(ly) wail, my dear, time's waste.

In versions (1) and (3) "new" is read as an adverb and in version (2) as a postmodifying adjective. In (1) and (2) "dear" means valued or scarce, but in (3) "dear" means beloved.

In the second quatrain, the memories that testify in the "court" are those of dearly loved friends who have died. The account of these is accompanied by moaning and a rare bout of crying ("drown an eye, unus'd to flow"), a crying that takes up the wailing of the fourth line. These memories speak of friends lost in eternity and timelessness ("death's dateless night"). In this quatrain, the focus is on the eye drowned with tears and darkness that cannot see "many a vanish'd sight." The blind eye of the plaintiff might bear some relation to the symbol of justice blindfolded in order not to be swayed by age, race, gender, or wealth in her decisions, all of these categories also cancelled by death, or what some call the ultimate justice.

The last quatrain is taken up with memory's testimony about old grievances. To "grieve at grievances foregone" has several possible interpretations. First, grievances can mean former bouts of grieving, memories of which can make one grieve again. Second, the line might mean regret for not having voiced grievances, that is, complaints, when the "I" of the poem had the opportunity. This relates to the first quatrain's regret over having not got all the things the speaker sought. Third, grievance can mean a wrong done to a person; thus the speaker grieves over past wrongs done to him.

The last two interpretations relate to not only the telling of memory but the testimony in a law court—a plaintiff has a grievance toward a defendant because the plaintiff feels she has been wronged, or had a grievance committed against her. In closing statements, then, the metaphor of the court and memory can be fleshed out as follows: the mind is the court wherein the memory testifies. As a witness or plaintiff testifies about the past, so too does the faculty of memory retell its story in the court, or mind, of the present.

But there is another correlation with "sessions" of court made in "Sonnet 30," this one having to do with what are now called "damages," or rewards to plaintiffs for wrongs done them, most often in the form of money. Memory takes the stand in this court of the mind and testifies as to how it has had to "pay" and make "account" of past grieving. These words have double meaning relating not only to money but to having suffered the real event ("paid"), and additionally suffered for being made to tell about it (made "account"). Memory, the plaintiff in this case, would like some damages for the wrongs and pain it has suffered.

The verdict, as in a court of law, is delivered in the last moments of the session, or, in this case, the sonnet. Justice is done; the memory is compensated for not getting the things it sought, for losing the friends it loved, and for suffering grievances. Justice is delivered in the couplet. The memory or image of the living friend in the mind's eye restores the losses the memory grievingly tells about. The poet's eye is thereby unblinded; the tears and darkness evaporate and the mental image of the poet's friend appears clearly in the mind's eye. A kind of blind justice has been done and the plaintiff/poet can see.

Still, one element appears missing from the poem and this discussion. I have already mentioned the court, or the mind, the place where memory is summoned to the stand like a plaintiff or witness; and there is the judge, implicit as that part of the mind which summons up memory; and finally, there is the compensation for damages, the friend. But nowhere is there mentioned a defendant, the personification of the source of the wrongs suffered by the plaintiff. Who might qualify?

It seems there is but one best choice: Time, or more specifically, the Past. It is the Past that has caused the loss of goals sought, the death of friends had, and the grieving over grievances foregone. Why did Shakespeare not figure the Past or Time as the defendant in this sonnet? Perhaps because the metaphor becomes quite weak here. In this court, because there is the reward of the friend for

the damages suffered, the defendant (the Past) can be said to have lost. But of course, the Past suffers no loss at the court's reward, for the Past, even if it can be called guilty, cannot be punished nor avenged.

The presence of the Past, unavoidably arising from the deep of memory, can only be, Shakespeare writes, tolerated by the substitution of a living friend. But is this not the weakness of the poem I spoke of at the beginning, that the whole of Past regret is saved by one friend? Perhaps if Shakespeare felt that he did not have to heap cloying praise on his sponsor, the poem might have been better and might have said something more general regarding friendship and the present—something to the effect that if the Past can become an enemy, the Present must be made a friend.

Source: Jhan Hochman, in an essay for *Poetry for Students,* Gale, 1998.

Bruce Meyer

Bruce Meyer is the director of the creative writing program at the University of Toronto. He has taught at several Canadian universitites and is the author of three collections of poetry. In the following essay, Meyer provides an in-depth analysis of "Sonnet 30," including a discussion of its place in Shakespeare's sonnet sequence, its distinct language, and its message about the meaning of friendship.

Of all of the 154 sonnets written by or attributed to William Shakespeare in the collection known simply as *The Sonnets* (1609), "Sonnet 30" is possibly the one poem that speaks more than the others about the nature of the sonnet form. "Sonnet 30" takes as its chief theme the concept of memory in much the same way that the sonnet form itself is a poetic vehicle for stasis, memory and eternal life. When reading "Sonnet 30," one is reminded of the closing lines of another famous Shakespeare poem, "Sonnet 18" ("Shall I compare thee to a summer's day?"), which closes with a profound statement on the role that poetry and literature play in making time stand still: "So long as men can breathe or eyes can see / So long lives this and this gives life to thee." "Sonnet 18," which declares that poetry and its "eternal still" (as Keats called it) can capture a single moment's apprehensions, tensions, and desires, is a parallel statement to the message of "Sonnet 30"—that the power of memory contained in a single poem can restore life to the lifeless and beauty and youth to that which has long since turned to grief and dust.

The exact date of composition for "Sonnet 30" is unknown. According to most scholars, it was composed sometime before 1598, which sets it in the same period during which Shakespeare wrote some of his best early plays—*Romeo and Juliet, Richard II* and *The Merchant of Venice.* Because they are the works of a younger poet who had not yet achieved the full stride of greatness that would produce such later works as *Othello, Hamlet,* and *King Lear,* the sonnets are an impressive, if uneven collection of poems that feature such pinnacles of the sonnet form as "Sonnet 30." For Shakespeare, the sonnet was an intimate form of writing, if not a non-public piece of work. What is likely is that Shakespeare's sonnets were well circulated among a select group of writers and friends prior to their publication in 1609. When the sonnets were collected and printed by Thomas Thorpe in 1609, probably without Shakespeare's consent, they may have been arranged with only a casual eye to matters such as chronology, thematic development, and completeness. The Sonnets as we have them today read as if they are fragments of a much larger poetic work. The gaps of connection between individual poems, the shifts in focus that form several narrative threads within the larger collection, and the strange, almost hurried sense of resolution presented by the final two sonnets ("Sonnet 153" and "Sonnet 154"), have left critics and readers with many unanswered questions. Did Shakespeare write the sonnets with a particular order in mind and is this order reflected in the current system of arrangement? Are the sonnets a complete collection or are we missing important pieces of a much larger puzzle? Are Shakespeare's sonnets only half of a dialogue, a debate with another poet about the fate and the life of a young man who figures as a key character in the narrative of the overall sequence?

Shakespeare's sonnets are part of a collection known as a sonnet sequence, much like the works devoted to Astrophel and Stella by Sir Philip Sidney. A sonnet sequence is a gathering of a number of sonnets that, when grouped together, present an examination of a large theme or narrative. In the case of Shakespeare's sonnets, the sequence of 154 sonnets tells the story of a complex triangular relationship between an older, established poet; a young man who cannot decide whether or not he should marry; and a mysterious dark woman who has tempted and emotionally wronged the older poet. Elusive and inconclusive, the Sonnets still puzzle scholars with the question of the identities of the young man and the dark woman. The dedi-

cation at the opening of the sequence, to a "Mr. W. H." only serves to confound the matter.

What we do know is that the Sonnets, as we have them, appear to tell us a story. Sonnets "1" to "17" are the older poet's advice to the young man, in which the poet appeals to his junior to marry. Sonnets "18" to "126"—of which "Sonnet 30" is a significant statement—celebrate the life of the young man and the importance of his relationship to the older poet. A major shift in the narrative implications of the Sonnets occurs at "127," where the emphasis suddenly is placed on the thorny relationship that the older poet has had with a mysterious dark woman. While the earlier sonnets in the sequence deal with persuasion, friendship, memory, time and the fragile fleeting beauty of youth, the latter sonnets mingle passion with loathing, as the older poet, who was the dark woman's lover, warns his young charge about the "forsworn wife" who wishes to get her claws into the unwary youth. The relationship between the older poet and the young man is further complicated from "79" to "86" when the older poet is temporarily displaced in the younger poet's favour by a rival. The entire sequence concludes with the final two sonnets, "153" and "154," the "Cupid" sonnets, which some critics suggest are of doubtful authorship, but which act as a fitting envoi or "sign-off" to the entire sequence. Although it can be argued that these final two sonnets do not fit the narrative that the Sonnets imply, they are the natural conclusion to a typical sonnet sequence. Sidney's *Astrophel and Stella,* for example, ends with the exhaustion of love, and its narrator simply washes his hands of the whole matter of love. Shakespeare's conclusion is that everyone is, in one way or another, a slave to love, whether that love be lust, friendship, or the still-warm embers of a lost love. What matters most, Shakespeare reminds us throughout the sequence, is the value of love that defines friendships, memories, and poems.

"Sonnet 30" encapsulates the very nature of the Sonnets, in which the great battle of the universe is that perpetual struggle not only between life and death but also between mutability and perpetuity. In the mortal combat against time, man's great weapons are memory and poetry, where poetry is perceived as a vehicle for memory. "Sonnet 30" opens with the memorable lines, "When to the sessions of sweet silent thought / I summon up remembrance of things past," suggesting that the power of memory is akin to a court, where experiences are tried and weighed and verdicts are pronounced on their value. Shakespeare maintains this legal language throughout the poem and gradually transforms the language of jurisprudence into the language of accounting. In the end, "All loses are restored," and a balance, not only of experience but of absence against presence, is tipped in favour of friendship and solace. Shakespeare uses words such as "lack," "precious," "cancelled," "expense," and "grievances," and phrases such as "sad account," "new pay," and "if not paid before" to suggest that beneath the surface of a world that is legalistic—an account in arrears—there is something that cannot be taken away; the solace of black ink in nature's ledger of debits and credits. But the experience of retaining something of value in the face of time's ravages is not without its price. With an almost elegiac note of lament, ("Then can I drown an eye, unused to flow, / For precious friends hid in death's dateless night, / And weep afresh love's long since cancelled woe,") the weight of grief caused by the loss of friends and the passage of time causes the persona almost to lose heart. Yet in the end, the recompense of friendship with the object of the persona's admiration not only balances out the account, but puts it in profit so that "sorrows end." The account of the world is settled by friendship—the achievement of the Platonic ideal in which friendship, loyalty and asexual love are the only true and lasting foundations for human values. And ideally, the sonnet is the form that best conveys these ideals. As a poetic form the sonnet is associated most often with love and with considerations and reasoning in pursuit of high-minded and often abstract concepts.

The "English" or "Shakespearean" sonnet was an English language hybrid of a form that had developed in Italy and southern France during the late Middle Ages. Rooted in the hymns of praise that were associated with the cult of the Virgin Mary during the eleventh century, the sonnet evolved via the secular songs of the Provencal troubadours into a vehicle for praising the attributes of a woman. The Italian sonnet, more lyrical than its English successor, possessed a rhyme scheme of *abbaabba cdccdc* which, in Italian, is highly musical with the repeated resonances and vowel end rhymes. In English, however, the repetition of end rhymes is a test of the language even in couplet rhymes. Due to the limitations of language and the diminished possibilities of rhyme in the English language, the Shakespearean sonnet took on a less lyrical pattern of rhyme repetition and resonance. Instead, English sonneteers based their sonic systems on alternating rhymes (which Shakespeare employs in "Sonnet 30"): *abab cdcd efef gg*. The final

> " In the mortal combat against time, man's great weapons are memory and poetry . . . . "

"rhyming couplet" is usually applied in the Shakespearean sonnet to the reinforcement of a conclusion as in the solacial lines, "But if the while I think on thee, dear friend, / All loses are restored and sorrows end." Both the iambic pentameter line and the rhyme scheme combined to make the English sonnet a form in which the emphasis is on a brief but considered topic that is expressed in verse meant to be spoken rather than sung. In this vein, the English sonnet, such as it is in "Sonnet 30," carries with it a personal quality of intimate communication—an expression of sincere and reasoned thought that is fleeting, short, and bound by a very measured period of time. In short, it is a reflection of a mind at work as it thinks out loud. And what is more, the sonnet as a literate or spoken form rather than a lyrical or sung form implies the concept of confession where the listener is either being addressed directly or is eavesdropping on a soliloquy.

"Sonnet 30" articulate the beauty and justice of friendship as it argues its way to a rational conclusion. What should be remembered about the sonnet form is that it is more rhetorical than lyrical in its structure. The word "sonnet" is derived from a number of sources, chiefly the Italian word *sonetto* meaning "a little sound or song" or *suono* meaning "sound." As a poetic form, the sonnet lives up to its name in that it is a bridge between the lyric and the spoken utterance. Fourteen lines in length and adapted in English into an iambic pentameter line (the line of the spoken rather than the sung phrase), the sonnet does not sing as much as it persuades. In short, it is a "thinking" form of poetry that argues, tests and weighs ideas first and sings about them (either to celebrate or lament) second.

The antecedant to the Shakespearean sonnet, the Italian sonnet, is much less complex rhetorically than its English counterpart. The typical Italian sonnet, such as that written by Petrarch or Dante (see Dante's wonderful study of the sonnet form, "La Vita Nuovo") is comprised of two rhetorical sections, the opening eight lines known as the octave and the final six lines called the sestet. The usual format, as Dante explains in "La Vita Nuovo" was for the octave to present a dilemma, a condition, or a problematic experience to which the answer or resolution is to be found in the concluding sestet. The English sonnet, however, is broken down into smaller, more subtle developments of three groups of four lines followed by a concluding and very clear-cut statement in the couplet.

"Sonnet 30," as an argument opens (lines 1–4) with a discussion of how memory leads the persona to the lamentable discovery that his life has been wasted. Lines 5 to 8 are pure lamentation bordering on elegy in which the persona sheds tears ("drown an eye") and feels woe for all those people and things that he has lost. In the grief that he feels calls him into account and during the third portion of the poem, lines 9 to 12, he uses a series of "accounting" words to show that his experience is truly in a state of debit. The situation, which is terribly sad up to this point, is suddenly and miraculously reversed by the realization that he has the friendship of the young man to whom the sonnet is addressed. The recollection and friendship of this young man makes the losses disappear and the persona is restored to happiness by the mere power of thought, memory, and presence.

"Sonnet 30" addresses not only to the matter of friendship but the issue of time and what time does to the world. In its statement, it is a reflection of the ironic nature of the sonnet form, for the sonnet (in its short format) is both an acknowledgment of brevity and a vehicle for the stasis of considered reflection and memorialized ideals. The persona of "Sonnet 30" laments the passage of time and the discovery of mutability triggered by the power of memory and the realization of loss. It is the power of memory and the perspective of reasoned thought, however, that allows him to appreciate the beauty of friendship and its value as a peg on which he can hang his hopes that all is not lost in the course of living. The true hero in the world of this poem is the power of the human mind, and "Sonnet 30" celebrates not just mere cerebral acts but the wonder of recall, the power of the imagination, and the consolation of meditation. What is miraculous about "Sonnet 30" is that it thematically treads a fine ironic line between loss and recompense. Time and entropy destroy that which is of this world; yet what is left through the power of consolation, in an almost Boethian sense, is of true and lasting value. The poem shows us the dark side of life, but it also permits us to travel and articu-

late that fine and often difficult pathway to solace. As a poetic vehicle it acknowledges the ravages of time, yet, by its very nature as a poem, it protects and shields from the grips of loss and endless grief that is most important to us as human beings. It is this fine balance between extremes that makes "Sonnet 30" a remarkable testament to the power of the mind—so much so that the English translator of Marcel Proust's voluminous and heroic attempt to recapture the "lost time" of an entire lifetime and its epoch in *A la recherche du la temps perdu* found its English title, *Remembrance of Things Past,* in the second line of "Sonnet 30." In this simple, all-too-brief poem, Shakespeare gives us both an examination of time and a consolation for loss.

Source: Bruce Meyer, in an essay for *Poetry for Students,* Gale, 1998.

Murray Krieger

In the following excerpt, Krieger discusses the interplay of both financial and sentimental metaphors in "Sonnet 30" and explains how its incongruous conclusion is "rationalized."

[T]he mythology proclaimed by love's mystic can take its meaning only in its relations to the cold-blooded world. At his best, as we have repeatedly seen, Shakespeare is most aware of the stubborn persistence of niggardly marketplace facts that demand recognition even by him who would transcend them. His most satisfying attempts to produce the poetry that is love's self-justifying discourse are those—like Sonnet 74 or 87 among many I might mention—that arise out of, and remain responsive to, the common world's apparent truths. It is this extraordinary juxtaposing of the most factual and most supernal—or rather the rendering of the second by means of the first—that makes the unit comprised of Sonnets 30 and 31 among the most rewarding in [Shakespeare's Sonnet] sequence....

In Sonnet 30 the poet indulges in just the sort of mourning that we saw him asking his friend—if somewhat ironically—to reject coldly in Sonnet 71 ("No longer mourn for me"). There are other relations between Sonnets 30 and 71, especially in the tone of the two sonnets with their opposition between sentiment and marketplace. Indeed, perhaps it is the futility of marketplace methods in Sonnet 30 to appreciate the powers and needs of affections that leads in Sonnet 71 to the somewhat self-pitying indictment of the "vile world" in its emotional unresponsiveness.

Shakespeare's strategy in Sonnet 30 of using the language of law and bookkeeping should by now be familiar to us. His joining in metaphor the world of sentiment and of the marketplace has been effective in many of the sonnets (I need mention only Sonnets 4, 74, and 87). Such bits of soft sentiment as "sweet silent thought," sighs, wails, drowning eyes, grievings and moans, are held in the businesslike framework of "sessions" to which one is harshly summoned up, of woes that are "cancell'd," of "expense," accounts, and payments. We must be puzzled by a phrase like "precious friends," which can be read into either world, or both; or by the telling over the "sad account," which can refer to the narrating of his sentimental tale or to the "telling" activity of the auditor. But it is just this language which has a foot in both worlds that seems to prove how thoroughly the poet has proved their union. And yet this union should be a shocking one, a yoking of elements that are indeed most heterogeneous. What business can these disparate areas of human experience have with each other, especially in these sonnets which have emphasized the polar conflict between matter, in all its niggardliness, and the open generosity of spirit?

It is precisely the poet's error that he tries to submit his woes to the auditor's assumptions and operations. He is so subdued by common-sense worldliness that he feels forced to render the intangible as tangible, the immeasurable sorrows as measurable items. At the same time, he undercuts his sentimental insistences, presented too howlingly in the most obvious and unimaginative terms of lamentation (four uses of "woe," three of "moan," alliterative emphasis on "woes," "wail," and "waste," among the many obvious devices), by enclosing them within the matter-of-factness of marketplace reduction. The dominant frustration in the poem is the poet's inability to make this reduction work, as the world of lamentation resists being converted into items in a ledger. Distressed by the endlessly resistant ineffability of lamentation, the poet still seeks to be an auditor of the affections and discovers in the sonnet how unsuccessful this procedure is fated to be. He treats his various mournings as items to be entered in the account book (especially lines 7–12), but the things persist in refusing to act accordingly: the woes, grievances, and moans will not permit themselves to be balanced. They never cease their demands for further payment. Endlessly costly, they cannot be isolated, made into finite entities that have an end. The auditor-poet thinks he has paid them off, only to have them still unremoved on the debit side. That

he must ever "new wail" "old woes," ever spending his sorrow anew, leaves him at the end of his arithmetical tether. The "woe" is "long since cancell'd" and thus ought to be done with; but there it is, still agonizingly there, demanding to be wept "afresh." It is this persistence of sorrow that makes the repetitions in each line of the third quatrain so effective ("grieve at grievances," "woe to woe," "fore-bemoaned moan," "pay as if not paid"). The sorrow will continue to be repeated again and again—grievances to be regrieved, the account of woes to be told over and over as the moans are to be always bemoaned. For lamentation is turned into a most unsuccessful business enterprise that must pay and pay for what has been many times paid for. The repetition shifts from the commonplace emotional terms in lines 9–11 (grieve, woe, moan) to that most central marketplace term, "pay," in line 12. The latter reveals the framework in which the others have been considered all along—and suggests why this consideration has been inadequate to the needs of the poet in his lament. Affection cannot be reduced to ledger entries; what can take care of items in an account is inapplicable to the immeasurable world that is beyond cancelling. Perhaps we should think of that star in Sonnet 116, "Whose worth's unknown, although his highth be taken." For once again we are faced with truth's inaccessibility to troth.

The couplet reveals how thoroughly—and futilely—the poet has exhausted his marketplace methods, which have at once lent specificity to his lament and revealed their own bankruptcy. After all the payments and repayments which leave the pain still there and unalleviated, suddenly there is the cavalier gesture of the couplet and an unearned leap to total release:

> But if the while I think on thee, dear friend,
> All losses are restor'd and sorrows end.

All reasonable ways out having failed, the poet turns to the present friend, and the endlessly troublesome troubles are at an end. The "sessions of sweet silent thought" are adjourned for him to "think on" his dear friend. The attempt to make legal and financial sense of his thought is abandoned for the sheer, unreasoning immediacy of love. Affection's past laments can be resolved not by submitting them to the consolations of normal reason but by transforming them into affection's present joys. With the mere thought of the friend, then, the bottomless pit of payment no longer yawns. The finality of the reversal in the poem's last word is total: sorrows are at once at an absolute "end." Fur-

> *[Shakespeare] treats his various mournings as items to be entered in the account book ..., but the things persist in refusing to act accordingly: the woes, grievances, and moans will not permit themselves to be balanced."*

ther, not only is there no need to pay further, but all that has been paid is "restor'd." Of course, the double action of "losses" is like that of other words in the poem that reach at once toward the financial and the sentimental poles: the "losses" are also the human losses, those "precious friends hid in death's dateless night" for whom he has so endlessly mourned. For, as Sonnet 31 insists, the poet has lost no one.

The shift from the futility of the auditor's care in the first twelve lines to the success of the lover's reckless leap in the couplet—the sudden replacement of affection by affection instead of the sensible replacement of affection by measurement—these leave us at the end of Sonnet 30 perhaps unconvinced, but persuaded of what the ardor of love can lead the lover to insist upon, and to deny, in his transcendence of the world. But the poetic entity is not yet complete, since its second half in Sonnet 31 is undertaken in order to earn metaphorically the rash extravagance of the couplet of Sonnet 30, its total restoration of "*all* losses" and its "end" to endless sorrows. The dead he has mourned are literally resurrected—indeed reincarnated—in the collective and yet uniquely singular entity of the beloved friend, who becomes their magical mirror-window. They were only "supposed dead." The poet suggests that he was misled by his missing their appearance into making this supposition: that he was deluded by his trust in flesh into seeing it as the sole form of living and was unprepared for the flowing together of "distincts." Thus they were wrongly "thought buried" (line 4). But later in the sonnet, as his metaphor develops, we find them "buried" after all (line 9)—buried in the

friend, of course, and there living still—though as "things remov'd," "hidden" in him (line 8) rather than in "death's dateless night" (Sonnet 30, line 6). If "hidden," then "buried"; but as "buried *love*" in him it can *live*. How different this burial is from that supposed burial which led to the mourning of Sonnet 30, and how different this "grave," this tomb which is the womb of further and more complete life ("Thou art the grave where buried love doth live").

In this sonnet the poet can afford to look back upon the "supposed" burial and the mistaken mourning it caused. After acknowledging in the first quatrain his supposition as a worldling, he speaks of the tears that love has stolen from his eye. He is in effect referring to his endless lamentation in the first twelve lines of Sonnet 30, except that he now sees these tears as being unjustly stolen rather than as being justly collected, since his trothful vision is leading him to see the burial of his friends as a form of rebirth, an occasion that merits joy rather than sorrow. The tears were taken before "as interest of the dead"—that is, on behalf of the (seeming) dead and their just claim upon his affections. But there has been too much financial terminology in Sonnet 30 for us to ignore the other sense of "interest"—especially when it has been used in just the bank-clerk's sense of increment with respect to the dead in Sonnet 74 ("My life hath in this line some interest," line 3). Thus "interest" must also refer to what is left over as surplus and memorial. As we have seen in Sonnet 30, tears are the sole possible survivors, the sole proper "interest" of the materialistic version of death. With the end of matter in death and his worms, the auditor's mentality must demand something tangible, material, as *its* surviving "interest" (and we know how the very poem itself, the "this," functioned to elevate and even spiritualize this demand in Sonnet 74). The only material "interest of the dead," so long as they are seen as merely dead, is "many a holy and obsequious tear," referred to in Sonnet 31 after having been dwelled upon in Sonnet 30. But if love suspends the material sense of "property," it gives rise to the magical "interest" of the new entity, the beloved friend, who is the corporate resurrection of all the old entities. That other financial term, "due" ("That due of many now is thine alone"), indicates what happens to "interest" in the new irrational consideration: the friend, as the miraculous "grave" that allows "buried love" to "live," now has as his "due" or "interest" not the sad matter of tears (which were both inadequate and, it turned out, uncalled for) but the just inheritance of all the affection that love has stored through his predecessors who have become himself. The final line insists that the identity, the incarnation, be seen as complete, with no one and nothing held back: "And thou— *all* they— hast *all* the *all* of me." The unqualified "all" has been prepared for from the final line of Sonnet 30 ("*All* losses are restor'd and sorrows end"), through Sonnet 31, lines 1 ("*all* hearts"), 3 ("*all* love's loving parts"), and 4 ("*all* those friends"), to the climactic line 11 ("Who *all* their parts of me to thee did give"). No wonder the friend now is nothing less than *all* of them and has nothing less than *all* of the poet. The poet sees that selfhood has merged with thou-ness and them-ness. In this marriage of *all* true minds, the distinctness of subject and object, and the distinctness of persons past and the person present have been obliterated into a present union that is total and transcendent in its sovereign invulnerability to the "impediments" of "state." The union is consummate in the identities that are lost in it even as they achieve their fulfillment—their reborn and still living incarnation—in it.

Nowhere does Shakespeare more ambitiously and explicitly lay claim to the miracle that approaches eschatology through incarnation, coming at them out of the "common things" of the marketplace in all their precious distinctness. The couplet of Sonnet 30, with its seemingly sentimental leap out of the common-sense hopelessness that precedes it, comes to be justified by the poet's creating his beloved friend, in Sonnet 31, as the total and crowning summation of individuated histories, which have now retreated into mere "images" (Sonnet 31, line 13). But these images do not "die single," as does that of the Narcissus of Sonnet 3, since they die to a new life through love, becoming a constitutive part of the friend as the total reality that lives now as the corporate past. Of course, compared to the rhapsodic historic sweep of sonnets like 106 and 53, Sonnets 30–31 would appear to urge a more modest and personal eschatology: the end and transcendence of the poet's private emotional history. Still for his subjectivity and its troth, this history is enough, for it is total. This history has been the cosmos of the entire sonnet sequence; and only the magical discourse of poetry— and of these poems—could create the cosmology that both permits and resolves the mysteries of a substance that flows among its shifting entities. The discreteness of their images that "die single" (Sonnet 3, line 14) is dissolved into unions that defy the more common reason of our world.

We may freely admit that Sonnet 31, as microcosm of the workings of the entire sequence, finally only "rationalizes" the hasty miracle of Sonnet 30 into the special terms of the unreasonable reason of the system—which is to say that it converts the mere claim to miracle into substantive metaphor. It turns the claim into a mirror-window by making a mirror-window of the friend. In this sense, we may say that Sonnet 31 earns the claim of the couplet of Sonnet 30 rather than proves it. For the mode of discourse of a poem as a mirror-window must, like the metaphor at its root, only earn and never try to prove lest it convert itself into another mode of discourse. So Sonnet 31 gives us the miracle still, though now in an embodiment analogous to the Christian Trinity, and keeps it unreduced and unreducible—as unreducible as metaphor. This is the discourse of love's mystic, using the reason of love's unreason. As such, these sonnets are discursive testimony of how love's unreason must work: they represent the way love's unreason speaks. They become both act and repository of faith.

Source: Murray Krieger, *A Window to Criticism: Shakespeare's Sonnets and Modern Poetics,* Princeton University Press, 1964, pp. 178–87.

Sources

Booth, Stephen, "Sonnet 30," in *Shakespeare's Sonnets,* Yale University Press, 1977, pp. 181-83.

Fineman, Joel, *Shakespeare's Perjured Eye,* University of California Press, 1986.

Hammond, Gerald, *The Reader and Shakespeare's Young Man Sonnets,* Barnes and Noble Publishing, 1981, pp. 40-2 and 166-68.

Landry, Hilton, ed., *New Essays on Shakespeare's Sonnets,* AMS Press, 1976.

Muir, Kenneth, *Shakespeare's Sonnets,* George Allen and Unwin, 1979, pp. 57-8.

Pequigney, Joseph, *Such Is My Love,* University of Chicago Press, 1985.

Shakespeare, William, *The Complete Works of Shakespeare: Revised Edition,* edited by Hardin Craig and David Bevington, Scott, Foresman and Company, 1973.

For Further Study

Auden, W. H., introduction to *The Sonnets* by William Shakespeare, edited by William Burto, New American Library, 1964, pp. xvii-xxxvii.

A wide-ranging discussion touching on several issues related to the sonnets, including style, themes and form.

Muir, Kenneth, *Shakespeare's Sonnets,* George Allen & Unwin, 1979.
    A concise overview of major issues in criticism of Shakespeare's sonnets, including style, dates of composition, and publication, sequence and relation to other of Shakespeare's works.

Smith, Barbara Hernstein, ed., *Sonnets,* by William Shakespeare, New York University Press, 1969.
    This edition offers students a glossed collection of the sonnets, supported by an introduction, commentary and thematic index.

Wilson, John Dover, ed., *The Sonnets* by William Shakespeare, Cambridge University Press, 1966.
    Wilson's writing is academic but accessible to younger readers, offering extensive introductory material and notes to the collected sonnets.

Strong Men, Riding Horses

Gwendolyn Brooks
1960

While Gwendolyn Brooks has more than established her place in the world of poetry, she did not do so without receiving criticism. During her early years, other African–American writers argued not against the presence of her talent, but that she did not use her poetic gifts to speak directly to the experience of blacks in America. The key to this seems to be the word "directly"; one could argue that she did indeed write of her experiences of oppression and hardship, but did so indirectly. Much of her early work not only was written in traditional forms, but was also written about mythological figures in the European language of the time. "Strong Men, Riding Horses" provides an excellent example of how Brooks might have gone about writing of personal, timely issues by using a mythological veil. It is a poem predominantly about the mythic figure of the Westerner: the strong, male, frontiersman who headed west to explore or confront whatever challenge presented itself. She uses this to set up the contrast of the weakness and fear the speaker of the poem feels, as the second and third stanzas state, with a first person "I," the feelings of inadequacy. The turn is made with this short, two-line stanza that follows the first. If one were to read just these two lines, and even the final stanza that follows, they would be hard pressed to locate this in the myth of the West. They might instead think it to be the words of someone trapped and unhappy in a contemporary urban area or a poor rural town. It is this combination of mythological subject matter and subtle contemporary reference—of which this poem is an excellent example—that brought Brooks into the poetry world. And even though she would alter her style years later and become much more directly political, these poems have a certain solidity and power, in addition to their control of language, that should be studied as well.

Author Biography

Combining a commitment to racial identity and equality with a mastery of poetic techniques, Brooks has bridged the gap between the academic poets of her generation in the 1940s and the young militant writers of the 1960s. Born in Topeka, Kansas, in 1917, but raised in Chicago, Brooks started writing poetry as a child. She was inspired by her parents, Keziah Wims Brooks, a schoolteacher, and David Anderson Brooks, a janitor who had failed to achieve his dream of becoming a doctor because of insufficient funds for tuition. By the late 1930s Brooks had published some seventy-five poems and had been encouraged in her efforts by Langston Hughes. Following graduation from Wilson Junior College in 1936, she worked briefly as a maid and then as a secretary to Dr. E. N. French, a "spiritual advisor" who sold potions and charms out of a Chicago tenement building known as the Mecca. In 1938 Brooks joined the NAACP Youth Council, where she met Henry Lowington Blakely II. The two were married the following year and in 1940 saw the birth of their son, Henry Lowington Blakely III.

In 1941 Brooks attended poetry workshops at Chicago's South Side Community Art Center, producing poems which would appear in her first published volume, *A Street in Bronzeville* (1945). This work was a poetic description of the everyday lives of the black people who occupied a large section of Chicago called "Bronzeville." Its themes would feature prominently in Brooks's works during the next two decades: family life, war, the quest for contentment and honor, and the hardships caused by racism and poverty. *Annie Allen* (1949), her next book of poems, continued the movement of Brooks's poetry toward social issues. The book won the Pulitzer Prize in 1950, the first time that the award had been presented to a black honoree. Brooks's daughter Nora was born the next year and in 1953 the author published *Maud Martha*, a novel.

Over the next several years, Brooks produced a book of poetry for children and worked on a novel

Gwendolyn Brooks

which she later abandoned (although the first chapter was published as both a story and a poem). Her next major collection, *The Bean Eaters* (1960), details the attempts of ghetto inhabitants to escape feelings of hopelessness. The importance of the volume derives from Brooks's continued mastery of poetic forms and her movement away from autobiographical tensions and toward social concerns. Brooks's popularity and national visibility increased in the 1960s—in 1962 President John F. Kennedy invited her to read at a Library of Congress poetry festival. New pieces in *Selected Poems* (1963) reveal the author's growing interest in the civil rights movement; among the new poems was a salute to the Freedom Riders of 1961.

Brooks experienced a change in political consciousness and artistic direction after observing the combative spirit of several young black authors at the Second Black Writers' Conference at Fisk University in 1967. This inspiration helped inform the volume *In the Mecca* (1968), in which Brooks abandoned traditional poetic forms in favor of free verse and increased her use of vernacular to make her works more accessible. In *Riot* (1969) and *Family Pictures* (1970) Brooks evoked the revolutionary legacy of such slain black activists as Medgar Evers, Malcolm X, and Martin Luther King, Jr., and examined the social upheavals of the late 1960s. And in the nonfiction book *A Capsule Course in Black Poetry Writing* (1975) Brooks advised beginning poets.

The 1980s continued to bring Brooks honors and awards—in 1980, she read her works at the White House with Robert Hayden, Stanley Kunitz, and eighteen other distinguished poets. Now holding over forty honorary doctorates and having served as Consultant in Poetry to the Library of Congress from 1985 to 1986, Brooks continues to read her works throughout the United States.

Poem Text

Lester after the Western

Strong Men, riding horses. In the West
On a range five hundred miles. A Thousand.
    Reaching
From dawn to sunset. Rested blue to orange.
From hope to crying. Except that Strong Men are   5
Desert-eyed. Except that Strong Men are
Pasted to stars already. Have their cars
Beneath them. Rentless, too. Too broad of chest
To shrink when the Rough Man hails. Too flailing
To redirect the Challenger, when the challenge   10
Nicks; slams; buttonholes. Too saddled.

I am not like that. I pay rent, am addled
By illegible landlords, run, if robbers call.

What mannerisms I present, employ,
Are camouflage, and what my mouths remark   15
To word-wall off that broadness of the dark
Is pitiful.
I am not brave at all.

Poem Summary

Line 1:

This is an interesting subtitle in which we can see Brooks combining the modern with the traditional, as the rest of the poem will do. "After the Western" evokes the Old West but suggests that the subject of the poem comes later, "after" the West of American legend is gone. The phrase also evokes the "Western" as a movie genre, and suggests that Lester "takes after," or resembles, images from film. Immediately, therefore, Brooks is suggesting the source of the patterns after which men model their "strength."

Lines 2-3:

Echoing the actual title, the most substantial stanza of the poem begins. It continues to empha-size the western mythology in use and leads us into huge open spaces. The open range, miles and miles, and in such space, a "reaching." Notice how Brooks chose to place the word "reaching" at the end of the line, as if it is doing what it says, into the white space of the page.

Lines 3-4:

The description of the West continues as two more measurements of the journey are offered. In addition to the geographical miles in line 3, there is now a measurement of time, and then a more imagistic version of color, as "rested blue to orange" can be seen as another way to describe the move from dawn to sunset.

Line 5:

Here there is one final way of measuring the journey, though it is quite different. The similarity is established with the parallel structure, which implies that the subjects are related or meant to be compared. The parallel structure here is the use of the sentence with the "From ... to ... " rhetoric. This last version of it though, "From hope to crying," is more abstract. In fact, one could argue that the three different descriptions move from the fairly concrete world of specific events ("From dawn to sunset") to the abstract world of colors ("blue to orange"), to the even more abstract world of emotions ("From hope to crying"). This line also begins a series of reasons why these western men, these strong men, are able to survive such a journey.

Line 6:

The first thing that makes the men exceptional in the face of the hardship they encounter is that they are "desert-eyed." This could mean several things. It could mean the eyes are open and expansive. Given the lack of water and life in a desert it could offer the connotation of a lack of emotion, or humanness. Most likely though it refers back to the journey "from hope to crying" to say that the strong man's eyes are dry, without tears.

Line 7:

Here the admirable exceptions continue as the strong man is "pasted to the stars." The most logical meaning here might be that the man is already drawn to and connected to another world, the world of stars, and not to an earthly one that takes us through a cycle of hope and grief. There are of course other possibilities; for instance it might mean the man is seen a particular way by others,

Media Adaptations

- An audio cassette titled *Gwendolyn Brooks and Lucille Clifton* was released in 1993 by the American Academy of Poets Tape Program.

- A recording of "Gwendolyn Brooks Reading Her Poetry" is available from Caedmon press.

admired and raised above other people, as the speaker of the poem is doing. There is also then an unexpected detail in this line, that of the car. Thus far the poem has stayed within a traditional western landscape, an old western scene. Suddenly there is an automobile. This is Brooks's subtle way of approaching the contemporary world through the mythic.

Lines 8-9:

This line continues the description of characteristics that seem, with another unexpected element, to make the Strong Man admirable to the speaker of the poem. He is "rentless." This again could be said to evoke a more modern scene as it is far more common to rent a place to live, or a car, in the mid-twentieth century in which Brooks writes than in the traditional, or even contemporary West. Regardless, it reaffirms the idea that the man is free from obligation to others.

The poem then turns to a different rhetorical structure to continue the description of such a man. The use of "too" at the beginning of several phrases serve to show how he is adequately prepared for what he confronts. In this case, and leading into line 9, he is "too broad of chest," too big and strong to falter when the "Rough Man"—another mythic figure it seems—challenges him.

Lines 10-11:

Here the description continues from line 9 as the man is now "too flailing" to "redirect the challenger." This seems to imply that the strong man is so involved, so caught up in the action of defending himself that he doesn't even think to evade his challenger. He confronts him head-on. This

could be seen as less of a strength, as it implies that he to a certain extent has lost his head, his ability to make wise choices. In fact one could argue that many of the qualities attributed to the Strong Man aren't necessarily positive or admirable qualities. But it seems here that the speaker of the poem intends them to be. In this case the man takes on his challenges directly, and struggles with what will become an issue toward the end of the poem, bravery.

There are then, in line 11, different ways with which the challenge confronts the man. They range from subtle ("nicks") to forceful ("slams"), to odd ("buttonholes"). This last one refers to a way of detaining someone, often with conversation, as if you are barely holding them there, perhaps by the edge of their shirt or garment. This adds an interesting, intellectual element to the challenges that might face the man—they might include verbal skills and discourse. This might also be seen as a reference to the poem itself, a challenge of words that Brooks is trying to confront. "Too saddled" is a final, interesting descriptive reference which could be intended to offer the image of the man firm and stable upon the saddle of his horse. It could also mean too burdened to worry about anything or anyone else, as to saddle a horse is to burden it.

Lines 12-13:

This short stanza is the major turn in the poem. Up until this point, except for the reference to the car, the poem has taken place exclusively in the landscape of the rural West. It has also been written in third-person narrative referring to the Strong Man. Suddenly here, with a stanza break the poem shifts to a first person "I" and, one could argue, a more urban landscape. The speaker is admitting that he or she is not like the Strong Man described previously, and talks of having to pay rent to "illegible landlords" and having to avoid robbers. This person is held down by having to pay rent and cannot confront danger when it presents itself. Notice too in all of this that the word "illegible" to describe the landlord provides more evidence that this poem has some connection to the written word. As "buttonholes" introduced the idea of conversation in the context of the Strong Man defending himself, the landlord is criticized for not being clear, or readable. This might be a reference to the landlord's dishonesty. Regardless of this, it seems more and more likely that Brooks intends use of language, or writing in particular, to be another place in which this struggle continues.

Lines 14-17:

In this final stanza the speaker of the poem continues with the confession of shortcomings. He or she admits that whatever effort might be made to defend, it is only in the name of disguise, of hiding one's self from the threat. Offered too are two more references to the role of words or speech in all of this, as line 15 mentions the mouth and line 16 uses the inventive and hybrid verb, "word-wall." The speaker does not just wall off the coming threat, but uses words to do so. This additional mention of the role of words in the speaker's defense seems enough to conclude that the writing of the poem has been metaphorically represented by the tale of the Westerner.

This brings up the compelling idea that Brooks might be talking of her own attempts to write poetry. It is well known that she was criticized by some for not writing more directly of the experience of blacks in America. And though in the poem she refers to the enemy as "that broadness of the dark" and no doubt means that powerful and mysterious experience of the unknown and of night, she might also be alluding to the darkness within, the personal sufferings kept hidden. It could even be interpreted to be the darkness of her skin, or the mass of blacks who have suffered great oppression in America. The challenge of representing them, and speaking for them might well be what Brooks realizes she has been avoiding. This is a touchy issue, given that the narrative speaker of any poem doesn't necessarily have any connection to the writer of the poem. And the poem could certainly exist just as a description of having to confront great odds, "dark" of any sort. But it seems too that one could read this poem as representative of the difficult position Brooks was in as an individual artist on the one hand, and a member of an oppressed race of people on the other.

Line 18:

This final line is stark and powerful after such long lines. It re-invokes the landscape of the West and the Strong Man by talking of bravery, the quality he was being praised for earlier in the poem, but does so without shifting the focus from the speaker of the poem, the first person "I." This is a good example of when it is important to keep in mind that the writer of a poem and the speaker in the poem are often separate. Here, the speaker is admitting his or her lack of bravery in the face of a world that is threatening, economically and physically. Gwendolyn Brooks, however, as the author of the poem, displays great bravery in confronting

such a subject, such an idea, and writing about it with strength and grace.

Themes

Strength and Weakness

"Strong Men, Riding Horses" begins right after the final credits roll, the Western movie and its images of strength still fresh on Lester's mind as he heads back out into the bright, downtown street. Brooks does not specify which movie, or what characters, but it does not matter because Lester has named them for himself as he plays scene after scene back in his mind: Strong Man, Rough Man, Challenger. The names are capitalized as if proper, and to Lester, each character becomes more real for what they represent than for who they are.

We do not learn what kind of person Lester is until later in the poem, but in the first stanza we gain insight into his psyche by what he remembers most from the movie. He remembers their broad chests that stretched larger than life across the screen, implying tremendous physical strength in the face of danger. He remembers their eyes, the camera zoomed in close enough to see the whole sunset reflected there, "blue to orange," though they are too emotionally strong for any tears to well up: "From hope to crying. Except that Strong Men are / Desert-eyed." And beyond this physical and emotional strength there is a sense of determination, to make it alone with the land; no matter what, they are staying outdoors, in the open, part of them permanently "pasted to the stars."

Courage and Cowardice

After comparing himself to the characters in the Western, Lester admits "I am not like that." While cowboys live in the land of endless horizons and burning sunsets, dodging danger left and right, Lester realizes he lives in the city of rent and "illegible landlords," a downtown where muggers lurk in the shadows of alleys. He is no cowboy. His actions, he admits, are "camouflage," a poor disguise for someone he is not. He does not have the courage or vocabulary to build a wall with his words against the "broadness of the dark" which surrounds him. Instead, he concludes, compared to the cowboys, he is "pitiful" and "not brave at all."

American Dream

Underlying this poem is the theme of the American Dream. Strangely, in the middle of a

Topics for Further Study

- Think of a movie you have seen recently that featured a character you admired for her/his physical or emotional strength. Write a poem describing this character in the face of a conflict, but end the poem by admitting how you would have reacted in the same situation. Remember to use specific images to paint the scenes with sensory details. Compare poems and discuss.

- What do you think the speaker means when he says "What mannerisms I present, employ, / Are camouflage …" in the final stanza? How would you paraphrase that line?

- Brooks describes a speaker who cannot live up to the ideal hero in the western movie he just saw. Do you think there is more pressure today on youth from the media to be somebody you are not? Discuss your answers.

scene describing the wide landscape, endless sunsets, and cowboys dodging bullets, an automobile appears in the line "they have their cars beneath them." We can guess that the cowboys really have their horses beneath them, but for Lester the message is the same; they are free, they go where they please, they are independent. What still lingered from the Old West in the late 1950s and early 1960s was a sense of "rugged individualism," or the belief that anyone could succeed with enough determination and raw strength. This was an essential personal characteristic on the western frontier, where everyone stood equal against forces—wild animals, natural disasters, murderous invaders—that could literally kill you if you were not strong enough.

Although the idea of rugged individualism is the foundation of the American Dream, the dream did not hold up against changing times. It was soon clear for many people that anyone had an equal chance to have a house in the suburbs, a nice job, 2.3 kids and a car to drive them to Sunday school—that is, unless you were Hispanic, Black, a woman, a Jew, or homosexual.

When the house lights in the theater are still down, the American Dream can survive in the hopes of cowboys and strong men. But for Lester, a black man with rent and muggers on his mind, that dream fades as soon as the credits roll, the curtain closes, and he steps back out onto the bright street.

Style

Though "Strong Men, Riding Horses" isn't written in a traditional form, it does, like most of Brooks's work, have internal structure and deliberateness. The poem is written primarily in free-verse, though many of the lines are exactly, or one syllable more or less than, ten syllables long. One gets the feel that this poem, the first stanza especially, could very well have been a sonnet. But it does break up and establish its own form as it proceeds, using amidst the free-verse some internal rhyme to hold it together. One could argue that Brooks, by having the form close to that of a sonnet but then breaking from it and opening it up, creates the effect of letting the language and the form mimic the mythological subject of the poem, which has to do with the idea of breaking free from the east, going west into the open range.

Historical Context

In 1960, the year "Strong Men, Riding Horses" appeared in *The Bean Eaters,* the Civil Rights Act was still four years to fruition. It was legal in some states for employers to discriminate against applicants based on their race. Southern Senators fought vehemently from February 29 to March 5 in an attempt to block a civil rights act that would allow federal referees to monitor polling locations where discrimination had been reported. With a national mood still resistant to civil change in some areas and outright hostile in others, many urban blacks found themselves struggling just to get by in the ghetto, trapped by economic and racial barriers. These are the people who inhabit Brooks's collection *The Bean Eaters,* in which she begins many poems with a brief epigraph introducing the characters in her poems. Everyone we meet—whether it is Roger of Rhodes, Leslie Eileen, Lester just walking out of a movie theater after seeing a Western, or the famous seven hanging out in front of the pool hall in "We Real Cool"—share a common

Compare & Contrast

- **1960:** America's relationship with Cuba quickly deteriorates after Fidel Castro signs an agreement at Havana on February 13th with Soviet first deputy premier Anastas Mikoyan. The paper strongly ties the neighboring island to Communist Russia both politically and militarily. Tensions caused by both American and Russian threats of nuclear action over the tiny country later come to a head in a naval standoff to be known as The Cuban Missile Crisis.

  1998: Although Cuba is one of only a very small handful of Communist countries remaining, the relationship between Castro, still in power, and the American government, improves. Castro shows a sign of goodwill by allowing the visit of Pope John Paul II, and American business investors pressure Washington to ease sanctions on Cuba so they may invest in the fertile market there.

- **1960:** Hughes Laboratory in Malibu, California introduces the first commercial lasers. They will be used for industrial metalwork cutting and welding.

  1998: Lasers are widely used in a variety of diverse applications, from corrective eye and dental surgery to military targeting and "smart bombs." Scientists and science-fiction writers alike perceive lasers as being the eventual first line of defense against any stray asteroids heading toward Earth.

---

goal: to escape their hopelessness and get out of the ghetto.

Movies are a form of escape, and for a young urban kid there must have been nothing more inviting than the wide expanse of a western sunset across the theater screen. By 1960 the Western as movie genre had settled into some common thematic and cinematographic devices you can expect to see in any movie released today. These devices include: panoramic landscape shots so wide the characters are mere dots against the horizon; the loner who is strong and unfaltering against any challenge; the ambiguous "Indians" who attack without warning; and, of course, the cowboy in his white hat riding off into the sunset. This romantic portrayal of the frontier days was attractive to a nation which believed that anyone with enough courage and common sense could make something of himself.

Movies during this time did not offer African Americans many positive role models. Most black actors and actresses still played stereotypical roles of chauffeur or housemaid in the Hollywood lives of the rich. There is little surprise in the conclusions Lester makes for himself, holding his life up against the template of the strong white men riding around in the absolute freedom and limitless opportunity of the open frontier. "I am not like that," he sadly concludes. "I am not brave at all."

Critical Overview

"Strong Men, Riding Horses" provides an excellent example of Gwendolyn Brooks's early work, for which she both won a Pulitzer Prize (1949 for her second volume of poems, *Annie Allen*) and received fair amounts of criticism. Criticism, when it came from the mainstream, predominantly white critics, while acknowledging Brooks's skill, cautioned her against what some saw as a quaint portrait of American life—motherhood, family, the poor. But a large amount of criticism came from other black writers and activist who felt that Brooks was avoiding a direct confrontation and examination of the black experience in 1950s America. In this poem for instance, one of these critics may have found fault with the fact that the poem only addressed the speaker's real situation vaguely and near the end, while spending much of the poem talking of a mythic western figure. In doing this, writing mythological and close to traditional European forms, writer and black activist Don L. Lee claimed that by using "their language … [Brooks] suffers by not communicating with the masses of black people." Brooks would finally come to agree in 1967 when she attended the Black Writers' Conference at Fisk University, and from then on she wrote largely in free-verse, and went more directly at the emotional and political issues of racial injustice in America.

Throughout all of the criticism and change though, few could argue Brooks's inherent skill and brilliance with language. American writer Stanley Kunitz commented that "Miss Brooks is particularly at home in the sonnet, where the tightness of the form forces her to consolidate her energies and to make a disciplined organization of her attitudes and feelings." And always in her work were the moving portraits of families, cities, and other characters of the American landscape. As poet Langston Hughes noticed very early on in Brooks's career, "the people and the poems [of] Gwendolyn Brooks … are alive, reaching, and very much of today."

Criticism

Marisa Anne Pagnattaro

Marisa Anne Pagnattaro is writer and teaching assistant at the University of Georgia. In the following essay, Pagnattaro notes how, in altering the sonnet form, Brooks further emphasizes the contrast between the life of her subject with that of the movie's hero.

The advent of "Strong Men, Riding Horses" in *The Bean Eaters* (1960), Gwendolyn Brooks's third volume of poetry, marks the beginning of a shift in her literary career. Brooks was initially praised for her technical ability and for the clear images in her first two books, *A Street in Bronzeville* (1945) and *Annie Allen* (1949). For example, in his review of *Annie Allen* for *Poetry* magazine, critic Stanley Kuntz noted that "Brooks is particularly at home in the sonnet, where the tightness of the form forces her to consolidate her energies and to make a disciplined organization of her attitudes and feelings." Brooks applied this technical expertise to very commonplace subject matter, drawing on what Langston Hughes called "the ordinary aspects of black life." In 1949, Brooks won a Pulitzer Prize for *Annie Allen*, becoming the first African American to be honored with the award for poetry.

The Bean Eaters, however, reflects what Brooks has called "a turning point, 'politically' "— a slightly more critical look at black life in America. Accused by some of not confronting the plight of the black community and criticized by others of "forsaking lyricism for polemics," this collection was met with a mixed reception by both black and white critics. "Strong Men, Riding Horses" is representative of Brooks's more reflective posture. In this poem, Brooks breaks free of traditional form in her grim psychological portrait of one urban man's experience. The title invokes an image of great physical power, of men confidently traveling on the backs of horses. Subtitled "Lester after the Western," the poem opens with Lester's unbridled enthusiasm for the mythic West. It is as if Lester has escaped into the movie theater for the afternoon, steeped himself in the hope of the frontier, and filled his mind with remnants of great gusto for a lost time. Lester's own life, however, pales in comparison. He is embattled with trepidation and concerns over the practical and mundane.

Brooks seems to be playing with the sonnet in "Strong Men, Riding Horses," manipulating this traditional form to make a social point about the contrast between the fictionalized promise of the frontier and urban reality. Instead of a single, four-teen-line stanza in iambic pentameter, Brooks has seventeen neatly divided lines. The first ten-line stanza re-creates the expansiveness of the West. This vista is then abruptly followed by a couplet that catapults the poem into the present. In these two lines, the poem becomes personal, contrasting Lester's life with those of his heros'. The concluding stanza is half as long as the first, a mere five lines underscoring Lester's failure to measure up to what he has seen on the big screen. This calculated breaking up of the sonnet form in favor of free verse challenges conventional expectations about the structure of Brooks's poetry.

The first line of the poem echos the title, reiterating the power of the men in the movies. This stanza takes readers out of the pre-civil rights present of the poem and summons forth the mythic West. These American legends are on a "range five hundred miles" or, perhaps, it is a "Thousand." Their world is expansive, "Reaching / From dawn to sunset." Ostensibly, the cowboys' life is full of freedom and possibility. The parallel structure in the next two lines further emphasizes the extremes between which the men operate: "Rested blue to orange. / From hope to crying." They live life to the fullest extent. Lester is quick to point out that the Strong Men are "desert-eyed." Coupled with the previous line, this observation seems to say that they could cry if they wanted to, but do not need to shed any tears. These men epitomize the American ideal of independence, unencumbered by earthly constraints. Moreover, the men are "Pasted to stars already," as if to say that they are memorialized in the grandest celestial fashion. At this point, Lester cannot see through their unemotional facade.

In the second half of the first stanza, however, the tone becomes darker. The sudden intrusion of automobiles reels the poem into the twentieth century. The speaker says: "Have their cars / Beneath them." This fragmentary thought—equating the horses with a contemporary mode of transportation—places the strong men in the present. It also signals the speaker's edginess, which continues in the next phrase: "Rentless, too." Not only are the strong men in command of their lives and their locomotion, they are not tied to a monthly demand for money. This first use of "too," meaning also, is then contrasted with the repetition "too" meaning in excess of an amount that is desirable. This latter reference hints at what seems to be Lester's irritation about the mythical men. They are "Too broad of chest / To shrink when the Rough Man hails. Too flailing / To redirect the Challenger, when the challenge / Nicks; slams; buttonholes. Too saddled." These lines express Lester's mounting ambivalence toward men who first appeared to be the subject of his respect and awe. This may also be Lester's way of expressing his own resentment toward the stereotyped masculine ideal.

The couplet that separates the first and last stanzas is a first-person interjection of Lester into the poem. His abrupt confession is in sharp contrast to the strong men: "I am not like that. I pay rent, am addled / By illegible landlords, run, if robbers call." Instead of being stoic and confident, Lester, by his own admission, is fearful. Brooks's interesting choice of language—"addled" and "illegible"—suggests that the world is a muddled and confusing place for Lester. Additionally, the deliberate rhyming juxtaposition of "addled" with "saddled" separates Lester's world of uncertainty from the security of the ensconced cowboys who sit tight when confronted with adversity. Lester is flighty; when faced with the deprivation of his property, he flees. Unlike the quintessential masculine American male from the Old West, he retreats from any possible battle.

What Do I Read Next?

- An extensive selection of Brooks's poems is collected in *Blacks,* available from Third World Press, Chicago, 1994.

- Brooks is included in a 1989 anthology called *An Ear To the Ground* which celebrates a diverse selection of multicultural writers.

- Margaret Abigail Walker is a lesser-known African-American poet contemporary to Brooks. Her book *For My People,* though more formally structured, overlaps some of the same thematic territories as the Pulitzer Prize-winning poet.

- Brooks, Keorapete Kgositsile, Haki R. Madhubuti, and Dudley Randall each offer ideas relevant to younger black writers in their textbook *A Capsule Course in Black Poetry Writing* (Broadside Press, 1977). Brooks initiated the project to cover issues normally excluded from the typically white-dominated classrooms at that time.

The third and final stanza provides a glimpse into Lester's cowardly life. He offers insight into the persona he tries to project: "What mannerisms I present, employ, / Are camouflage." Lester's outward appearance is mere subterfuge for the insecurity that lurks below the veneer of his body language. Likewise, he says "what my mouths remark / To word-wall off that broadness of the dark / Is pitiful." Lester is a big talker, but there is no internal fortitude to back up his rhetoric. He deems himself deserving of contempt, because he is "not brave at all." This concluding line strikes to the core of Lester's self-doubt and weakness.

At the end of "Strong Men, Riding Horses," Brooks leaves readers to ponder Lester's sense of hopelessness; she offers no indication that Lester will ever be able to rise above his present limited circumstances. This statement is particularly grim in light of the literary resonances in the poem. In 1931, Sterling A. Brown (1901-1989) published the poem "Strong Men." In an epigram at the beginning of the poem Brown quoted Carl Sandburg

In this poem, Brooks breaks free of traditional form in her grim psychological portrait of one urban man's experience."

(1878–1967): *"The strong men keep coming on."* As a folk poet of the Harlem Renaissance, Brown continues in Sandburg's populist tradition, celebrating the working urban masses in this poem. Brown, however, invokes a different nineteenth-century landscape than Brooks. Instead of the manifest destiny of the West, Brown begins with the institution of slavery in the South. Unlike Brooks's "Strong Men, Riding Horses," this poem is a tribute to the ability to overcome great adversity. It opens with the horror of enslavement, *"They dragged you from homeland, / They chained you in coffles,"* yet concludes with a growing sense of power. Blacks may have been relegated to living in *"slums"* and segregated, *"'Reserved for whites only,'"* but they are not defeated. The last stanza proclaims: *"One thing they cannot prohibit— / The strong men ... coming on / The strong men gittin' stronger. / Strong men .... / Stronger...."* This sense of building strength and hope is nowhere to be found at the end of Brooks's poem.

The difference between Brown's and Brooks's "strong men" is indicative of Brooks's overall lack of activism in her early career. Even though some critics thought *The Bean Eaters* was "getting too social," many black critics felt that Brooks was not doing enough to directly address the concerns of the black community. As Don L. Lee observes in his essay "The Achievement of Gwendolyn Brooks," even though Brooks was "deeply involved with black life" in her early work, she was "not communicating with masses of black people." "Strong Men, Riding Horses" is particularly vulnerable to criticism that Brooks was continuing to write for a primarily white audience. In this poem, Brooks merely gives a glimpse into what appears to be the speaker's unfocused rage about his circumstances. Lester's "confessional" does little to confront the social roots of his limited existence.

There is no real momentum for resistance or change.

The rudiments of a more political stance in Brooks's poetry in *The Bean Eaters* were greatly enlarged after Brooks attended the 1967 Second Black Writers' Conference at Fisk University in Nashville. Brooks describes how she was "'loved' at South Dakota State College," but at Fisk she was "coldly Respected." In her essay "The Field of the Fever, the Time of the Tall Walkers," Brooks continues expounding on the evolution of her sensibility: "I—who have 'gone the gamut' from an almost angry rejection of my dark skin by some of my brainwashed brothers and sisters to a surprised queenhood in the new Black sun—am qualified to enter at least the kindergarten of new consciousness now. New consciousness and trudge-toward-progress." "Strong Men, Riding Horses" bears the beginnings of what would later develop into Brooks's poetic and social activism. Excited by the energy of the black movement and its celebration of African heritage, Brooks entered a new consciousness in her work that far exceeded her pre-1967 poetry.

Source: Marisa Anne Pagnattaro, in an essay for *Poetry for Students,* Gale, 1998.

Chris Semansky

Chris Semansky teaches writing and literature at Portland Community College in Portland, Oregon, and is a frequent contributor of poems and essays to literary journals. In the following essay, Semansky explores the symbolism of the American cowboy in "Strong Men, Riding Horses."

Most of us are familar with myths, the stories cultures tell themselves to explain phenomena and reasons for why things happen. America also has its myths; for instance, the myth of the how the West was settled. In one version of this myth, cowboys represent the self-reliant, self-motivated pioneers who made their own way across the country, conquering hostile Indian tribes, dispensing justice as they saw fit, drinking black coffee, and sleeping under the desert stars. Macho, confident, and masters of their own world, cowboys embodied the spirit of adventure and freedom that came to characterize the American West. Gwendolyn Brooks uses both the figure and the myth of the cowboy in her poem "Strong Men, Riding Horses" as foils to underscore the powerlessness and despair of African Americans.

Lester, an inner-city black man and the speaker of "Strong Men," muses on the life of the cowboy after watching a Western film. All of the images he details mark a stark contrast to his own life. Cowboys are strong men who live lives of possibility. Their home, the range, reaches from "Dawn to sunset. Rested blue to orange." Lester is plainly awed by this. Cowboys have a natural entitlement to space. Embodying the stereotype of the macho man, they are "Too broad of chest / To shrink when the Rough Man hails." Think of John Wayne or Clint Eastwood, two icons of Western films. Invariably these actors play "desert-eyed" heroes who challenge or are challenged by an authority (the "Rough Man") who is attempting to take away their freedom or space. Through cunning, wit, strength, and their own superior moral position they defeat the "Rough Man." Lester, however, is "addled" by the "Rough Man"—for him "illegible landlords"—whereas cowboys are "saddled" and fearless in their cars. Cowboys represent the vastly superior white world for Lester, distant and unattainable.

Lester survives in a blighted urban environment, fearful of being robbed. Brooks views this syndrome as a kind of spiritual death because it induces a feeling of homelessness, of powerlessness. Compare this to where and how cowboys live. Writing of the meaning of the West (the cowboys's "home") in popular culture and film, Jane Tompkins in her *West of Everything* asserts:

> The West functions as a symbol of freedom, and of the opportunity for conquest. It seems to offer escape from the conditions of life in modern industrial society; from a mechanized existence, economic dead ends, social entanglements, unhappy personal relations, personal injustice. The desire to change places [for the audience] also signals a powerful need for self-transformation. The desert light and the desert space, the creak of saddle leather and the sun beating down, the horses' energy and force—these things promise a translation of the self into something purer and more authentic, more intense, more real.

The significance of these images is that although they are the stuff of Hollywood, one of the largest purveyors of myth and illusion in the modern world, Lester takes them seriously. However, instead of identifying with the cowboys in the movie, Lester *compares* himself to them, coming up short. "The effect of the contrast between Lester and the cowboys," critic Harry Shaw notes in his study *Gwendolyn Brooks*, "is sharpened by the poem's being presented from Lester's point of view. This allows the poet to restate or distort reality in order to focus attention on ironies in the overall situation." Irony, a popular literary device, is a way of meaning the opposite of what you say.

Here, Lester is unintentionally ironic in describing his own verbal impotence:

> What mannerisms I present, employ,
> Are camouflage, and what my mouths remark
> To word-wall off that broadness of the dark
> Is pitiful.
> I am not brave at all.

Although Lester feels inferior because he considers himself a rent-paying coward who is unable to articulate his own miserable situation we, as readers, can see through his self-deception and feel empathy for Lester, who is more real than the white cowboys he valorizes. It is his own efforts to appear courageous that we admire, not the phony behavior of the cowboys who, after all, are "pasted to stars."

Another irony in Lester's monologue is that although he sees himself as inarticulate the language he employs belies this. He speaks like a poet, not like the stereotype we have of the disadvantaged urban poor. He does not use slang or speak in a dialect, both of which are conventional features of monologues. Rather his speech has a clipped, formal quality which itself contrasts with the silent, monosyllabic utterances of the cowboy, and contrary to what he claims, what Lester says is not pitiful but straightforward and honest. We admire his vulnerability and do not believe him when he says, "I am not brave at all."

Like other poems in *The Bean Eaters*, (1960), "Strong Men, Riding Horses" depicts characters despairing of their lives, who feel themselves trapped with little left to live for except their memories. The title poem of the collection describes a couple, "an old yellow pair," who have resigned themselves to going forward, though they have nothing for which to hope. Like Lester, theirs is a rented existence. Shaw writes: "While *The Bean Eaters* contains more on survival than [Brooks's] two previous books, it contains something on every major social theme …. the poetry is enriched by more complex themes than before, a development made possible and necessary by the mixture of efficient characterization and the presentation of a meaningful situation."

In his *A Life of Gwendolyn Brooks*, George Kent writes that "The universe of *The Bean Eaters* is a very complicated one. It has, when closely observed, numerous balances in the consideration of its issues: the racial and the intraracial; the social and the metaphysical; the individual and the group. The tumultuous outer universe is comprised of the tearing flesh and blood in Chicago and in the nation as a whole."

"Strong Men, Riding Horses" succeeds because like much conventionally successful poetry, it shows—not tells—us who the speaker is. When writers do this, they are practicing characterization. When such a technique works it is because readers are left to discover the meaning of the character's actions rather having the meaning spelled out for them by the author. This shows respect for the readers, because it asks them to infer things about characters by how they act.

"Strong Men" has been much anthologized because it, like much of Brooks's later poetry, demonstrates how blacks have come to internalize white oppression by letting it configure the very ways they think about themselves. It is apropos that Lester responds to cowboys, for although they have been romanticized as freedom-loving individualists, in reality many of them actively participated in the genocide and oppression of Native Americans.

Brooks frequently uses subjects of popular culture in her poetry as vehicles for addressing social themes. Sometimes, however, readers do not understand her point. Shaw notes that sometimes these subjects "are so innocent or asocial in appearance that they may beguile the unperceptive reader into a superficial reading and, therefore, perhaps a superficial appreciation, missing the heart of the poetry's black message." This might be especially true of non-black readers who, because they themselves have not experienced the world as Lester has, might have difficulty seeing the irony of her poem. Such readers might instead focus on Lester's lack of self-esteem and see the poem more as a lament of a life not lived rather than an indictment of the social relations which have oppressed and continue to oppress a large segment of the American population. This, of course, would be most ironic of all.

Source: Chris Semansky, in an essay for *Poetry for Students,* Gale, 1998.

Sources

Brooks, Gwendolyn, interview with Claudia Tate in *Black Women Writers at Work,* New York: Continuum, 1983, pp. 39-48.

————, interview by George Stavros, *Contemporary Literature* 1970, pp. 1-20.

————, "The Field of the Fever, the Time of the Tall-Walkers," in *Black Women Writers (1950-1980): A Critical Evaluation,* edited Mari Evans, Garden City, NY: Anchor Press, 1984, reprinted from *Report from Part One: An Autobiography by Gwendolyn Brooks* Detroit: Broadside Press, 1972.

Hughes, Langston, "Name, Race, and Gift in Common," in *Voices,* No. 140, Winter, 1950, pp. 54-6.

Kent, George E., *A Life of Gwendolyn Brooks,* Lexington, KY: University Press of Kentucky, 1990.

Kunitz, Stanley, "Bronze by Gold," in *Poetry,* Vol. 76, No. 1, April 1950, pp. 52-6.

Lee, Don L., "The Achievement of Gwendolyn Brooks," *The Black Scholar,* Vol. 3, No. 10, Summer 1972, pp. 32-41.

Shaw, Harry, *Gwendolyn Brooks,* Boston: G.K. Hall & Co., 1980.

Tompkins, Jane, *West of Everything,* London: Oxford University Press, 1990.

For Further Study

Clark, Norris, *A Life Distilled: Gwendolyn Brooks, Her Poetry and Fiction,* University of Illinois Press, 1987.
    Clark combines author biography with a close and comprehensive reading of Brooks's work to give us a picture of the poet within a broader social context.

Kent, George, *A Life of Gwendolyn Brooks,* University of Kentucky Press, 1990.
    Offers unique insight into the poet's life.

Melham, D. H., *Gwendolyn Brooks: Poetry and the Heroic Voice,* University of Kentucky Press, 1987.
    Mostly biographical, this text combines literary analysis with historical background in order to place each poem in its proper context.

Tears, Idle Tears

Alfred, Lord Tennyson
1847

"Tears, Idle Tears" was published in 1847, in a volume of poetry titled *The Princess*. After years of struggling with poverty, Alfred, Lord Tennyson was awarded a government pension in 1845, which allowed him to apply himself to longer works. *The Princess* was intended to be a long examination of a contemporary controversy, the education of women and the establishment of female colleges. The focus of *The Princess* shifted, though, while Tennyson was writing it, and it ended up giving more consideration to the roles of men and women in society, which the poet considered to be moving unnaturally toward each other. *The Princess* achieved popularity—when the first edition sold out, new editions appeared, year after year, for decades following—but critics considered it a failure of Tennyson's imagination, a sign of his inability to maintain a subject throughout an extended work. The same critics, though, did praise specific poems that had appeared as part of the larger work, in particular "Tears, Idle Tears."

This melancholy poem examines life from a perspective of life's end, with memories affecting the speaker in some indefinable way. Contrary to the common notion that equates death with sadness, Tennyson balances the sad part of the poem with sweetness, freshness, and love. Distant memories seem so real to the speaker that the past has a life of its own, and the poem suggests that this is the source of sadness that we get from "days that are no more."

Author Biography

Tennyson was born in 1809 in Somersby, Lincolnshire, England. The fourth of twelve children, he was the son of a clergyman who maintained his office grudgingly after his younger brother had been named heir to their father's wealthy estate. According to biographers, Tennyson's father, a man of violent temper, responded to his virtual disinheritance by indulging in drugs and alcohol. Each of the Tennyson children later suffered through some period of drug addiction or mental and physical illness, prompting the family's grim speculation on the "black blood" of the Tennysons. Biographers surmise that the general melancholy expressed in much of Tennyson's verse is rooted in the unhappy environment at Somersby.

Tennyson enrolled at Trinity College, Cambridge, in 1827. There he met Arthur Hallam, a brilliant undergraduate who became Tennyson's closest friend and ardent admirer of his poetry. Hallam's enthusiasm was welcomed by Tennyson, whose personal circumstances had led to a growing despondency: his father died in 1831, leaving Tennyson's family in debt and forcing his early departure from school; one of Tennyson's brothers suffered a mental breakdown and required institutionalization; and Tennyson himself was morbidly fearful of falling victim to epilepsy or madness. Hallam's untimely death in 1833, which prompted the series of elegies later comprising *In Memoriam,* contributed greatly to Tennyson's despair. In describing this period, he wrote: "I suffered what seemed to me to shatter all my life so that I desired to die rather than to live." For nearly a decade after Hallam's death Tennyson published no poetry. During this time he became engaged to Emily Sellwood, but financial difficulties and Tennyson's persistent anxiety over the condition of his health resulted in their separation. In 1842 an unsuccessful financial venture cost Tennyson nearly everything he owned, causing him to succumb to a deep depression that required medical treatment. Tennyson later resumed his courtship of Sellwood, and they were married in 1850. The timely success of *In Memoriam,* published that same year, ensured Tennyson's appointment as Poet Laureate, succeeding William Wordsworth. In 1883 Tennyson accepted a peerage, the first poet to be so honored strictly on the basis of literary achievement. Tennyson died in 1892 and was interred in Poet's Corner of Westminister Abbey.

Alfred, Lord Tennyson

Poem Text

> Tears, idle tears, I know not what they mean,
> Tears from the depth of some divine despair
> Rise in the heart, and gather to the eyes,
> In looking on the happy autumn-fields,
> And thinking of the days that are no more.   5
>
> Fresh as the first beam glittering on a sail,
> That brings our friends up from the underworld,
> Sad as the last which reddens over one
> That sinks with all we love below the verge;
> So sad, so fresh, the days that are no more.   10
>
> Ah, sad and strange as in dark summer dawns
> The earliest pipe of half-awakened birds
> To dying ears, when unto dying eyes
> The casement slowly grows a glimmering square;
> So sad, so strange, the days that are no more.   15
>
> Dear as remembered kisses after death,
> And sweet as those by hopeless fancy feigned
> On lips that are for others; deep as love,
> Deep as first love, and wild with all regret;
> O Death in Life, the days that are no more!   20

Poem Summary

Lines 1-5:

The poem begins by referring to tears that are "idle," not in the physical sense of "motionlessness" that we usually use the word for (they do have motion, moving from the heart to the eyes), but in the broader sense. Idle here means useless, creating nothing, causing nothing to happen. This could be what gives the poem its especially tragic mood: the speaker feels tears, and is very observant and clear in describing them, but there is nothing to be done about them. The speaker says that, though their meaning is unknown, the tears originate from a divine despair ("divine" here implies a connection to godliness, to forces beyond our physical world) and travel through the heart into the eyes. The last two lines of this stanza describe the circumstances under which these tears rise. There is a contradiction in line 4 that helps support the idea of idleness in the tears: the reference to "autumn fields" is clear enough, as autumn is a time when plants die and animals begin to migrate or hibernate, and this by itself would be appropriate for a discussion of despair and tears, but Tennyson adds the word "happy," which cancels out that gloomy effect. Throughout this poem he balances images of hope against images of depression. And so line 5's reference to "the days that are no more" is not so obviously a negative reference as it may seem upon first reading. If the author had meant to portray these memories as being awful to the poem's speaker, he could have strengthened the sense of hopelessness by using the description "days past" or "days gone by," which would emphasize the fact that they are lost, instead of their simple lack of existence.

Lines 6-10:

The "beam" referred to in line 6 is a sunbeam, the first one of the sunrise, an image of newness and beginning that has the opposite implication as the autumn field mentioned in line 4. That this dawn sunbeam is hitting a ship's sail offers a sense of newness, especially when we find out in the next line that the ship is bringing friends. But then, in line 7, the poem shows its contradictory nature again by saying that these friends are arriving from "the underworld." Literally, this reference would have referred to the Southern Hemisphere, notated on Victorian era maps with upside down type, as the bottom of the globe: however, there is no way to deny that, going back to Greek mythology and beyond, "the underworld" has referred to the realm of the dead. The only way these friends could return from the underworld would be through memory, but the poet infuses these memories with life by connecting them to freshness and daybreak.

Media Adaptations

- An audio cassette read by Tony Church titled *Alfred, Lord Tennyson* was released by Argo (London, England) in 1963.

- An audio cassette titled *Alfred, Lord Tennyson: Portrait of a Poet* is available from CMS Records.

- Caedmon released *Poetry of Tennyson,* an audio cassette, in 1972.

- A set of 5 LP albums titled *Great Poets of English Literature* was released by Encyclopedia Britannica Films in 1969.

Line 8 follows the mention of the underworld with sadness, reversing the sunrise imagery with the last beam of sunset, that reddens the sky and then sinks, like the same ship departing, below the horizon. While the "underworld" reference in line 7 brought up the idea of memories of loved ones, line 9 implies that the speaker is actually facing death (what else could take away, not just specific loved ones, but "*all* we love"?). With no future, this speaker talks of exploring the present and the past equally as the same sort of sensations, using "fresh" and "sad" to describe both everyday occurrences of the sun's motion and also the days that are no more.

Lines 11-15:

This stanza expands upon the imagery of the stanza which came before it, but the relationship is brought out more clearly. Since the dawn has already been mentioned in line 6, and the speaker's approaching death is implied in line 9, this stanza takes the time to consider in detail what sadness the coming dawn would create in a dying person, and in the end relates that sadness to memory. Line 11 repeats the contradiction of line 4's "happy autumn-fields" with "dark summer dawns," since both summer and dawn are associated with brightness, not dark. The song (or "pipe") of birds before sunrise, so early that the birds themselves are only half awake, is a sound that is seldom heard, but we can infer that dying ears are aware of this sound precisely because they are dying, and are absorbing worldly experiences while they can. This is clearly the case with the dying eyes that focus on the window frame (casement) in the dark and stay on it until the sunrise slowly makes it "glimmer," or glow. There is a sense of desperation, of hunger, implied in the way the dying person seeks out even the slightest physical experience, and in the last line of this stanza the memories of the dying person are given equal importance with the current experiences.

Lines 16-20:

In line 16, the three ideas that Tears, Idle Tears is concerned with—memory, death, and, as implied by "kisses," life—are brought together. The next three lines use the imagery of romantic love, which has not played a part earlier in the poem. Even hopeless love, symbolized by the imaginary kisses given to someone who belongs to another and is thus unobtainable, is introduced in the poem as sweet. The poem goes on to demonstrate just how deeply the "days that are no more" extend into a dying person's existence by comparing those days to first love, which is presented as the deepest experience life has to offer. Tennyson attempts, too, to convey how the loss of the past can evoke wild regret, even as love remembered can. Line 20 compares the days irretrievably lost to "Death in Life," rendering the poem's images of idle tears and dying hours relevant to those who have not experienced either.

Themes

Death

The speaker of this poem is mystified by the tears that he (assuming that the speaker, like the poem's author, is a man) is shedding. In contemplating this mystery, the speaker explores the idea of death. In the first stanzas, death is only implied, as the poem mentions the things that are gone forever; it is the finality of death that is implied here, its ability to shut a final door, since death is the ultimate irreversible experience. The speaker knows that his strange anguish stems from the one-way nature of life, and he uses imagery that refers to death in the first two stanzas: autumn (when summer blooms go into dormancy) and the underworld (which in classical mythology is the land of all dead, not just the hell of sinners).

The references to death reach a new level in stanza 3, when the speaker mentions "dying ears"

Topics for Further Study

- Write a poem in four stanzas about the futility of a particular emotion: joy, sorrow, anger, etc. Use physical objects to symbolize ideas as much as possible.

- Compare this poem to William Cullen Bryant's "Thanatopsis." Are the two authors talking about the same thing? What clues do you have that they are? What clues tell you that they are not?

- Explain how you think this speaker feels about death.

that hear the morning song of birds and "dying eyes" that watch the casement, or window, when it starts glowing with sunrise. The implication that someone is sick and bedridden might lead readers to believe that the poem is about a specific dying person, but it might also be a comment on the situation all humans face—inevitable death. The speaker's awareness of this gruesome truth would account for the inexplicable "divine despair" that pervades the whole poem. By the final stanza, death is present. Rather than the vague notion it was before, it is presented as a concrete reason for the speaker's tears. In the end, death is used for its emotional impact in common conversation; "death in life" is an oxymoron, a self-contradiction, unless the word "death" is understood as the worst type of misery.

Love

This poem views the two most significant motivating factors in life as death and love, and it turns to these two factors when trying to make sense of the speaker's sorrow, which has no specific cause. Death is made more vivid by showing it beside its opposite, the beauty and liveliness of nature. Like death, love is considered almost casually at first, and grows to major significance only in the end. The first time the word is used, it is not a reference to romantic love, but an affirmation of life; "all we love" is brought up in line 9 to emphasize the thoroughness of death, as represented by the setting sun. The last stanza of the poem gives great attention to the role romantic love plays.

In order to examine love in its extreme, Tennyson specifies that his subject is "first love," the most pure and spontaneous kind. There are two types of love that he presents as possible causes of his sorrow. The first he represents as "remembered kisses after death," which indicate a love affair that lives on in a person's mind but can never be continued because the other lover is gone. The second image of love introduces a human into this poem that is mostly about human nature; for example, the untrue lover who kisses one person while actually loving another. This deceit earns special attention in the poem as the only thing one human can do to another that would cause this kind of deep sorrow, to inspire these idle tears. Romantic treachery is treated here as the equal of death in its ability to wring the joy out of the human soul.

Permanence

The impression Tennyson gives in this poem is that all sorrow stems from the fact that beautiful days and wild first love eventually end. He uses imagery, in particular sunrise and sunset, to indicate that life follows a progression from beginning to end. He also utilizes the idea of death to show that, unlike days or seasons, life is not a cycle.

Each stanza ends with a reflection on "the days that are no more," a phrase that is constructed to bring out the sadness and strangeness of what is lost. The poem does not reflect on the benefits of time's passage—how one outlives diseases and grows wiser—because it is an emotional examination of the mysterious, unexplained tears, in no way pretending to give a balanced view. Tennyson's explanation of this mystery leads him to a central problem of human existence, the fact people cannot hold onto the things they would like to freeze in time. It was an idea that remained a central theme of his; almost forty years after this poem, in 1886, he wrote in "Locksley Hall Sixty Years After" (which was itself a sequel of an earlier work), "Let us hush this cry of 'Forward' til ten thousand years have gone."

Style

"Tears, Idle Tears" is written in blank verse, which means that there is no definite rhyme scheme. It consists of four cinquains (stanzas of five lines each). Each stanza develops its own idea for the first four lines, and then, at the end of the fifth line, returns to the refrain of "the days that are no more."

Although there is no strict meter (pattern of rhythm) or rhyme scheme in "Tears, Idle Tears," the poem does rely upon some devices that are related to rhyme to bind it together musically. While rhyme relies upon the repetition of the final vowel and consonant sounds, as in "where / fair" or "spill / thrill," Tennyson connects his ideas together with alliteration, the repetition of the first sound in a word. This can be seen in the "d"s of the second line ("depth of some divine despair"); the "s"s of the fifteenth line ("So sad, so strange"); and in the numerous places where two or more words with the same initial sound appear near each other, if not on the same line, then in close proximity. Tennyson also weaves this poem together with approximate rhymes, which do not necessarily have their final consonant in common but share a similar vowel sound. This can be heard in the "i" sound of "divine" and "rise"; "friends" and "reddens"; and in "Dying eyes." Both alliteration and approximate rhymes give the reader a feeling of wholeness and completeness about the poem.

Historical Context

Alfred, Lord Tennyson is considered by many readers to be the epitome of Victorian Era poets. After all, he was a favorite of Queen Victoria herself, and was appointed by her to be England's Poet Laureate, a position he held from 1850 until his death in 1896. On the other hand, he was almost thirty years old when Victoria ascended to the throne in 1837, and most of his ideas and sensibilities had been formed during the era now referred to as the Age of Romanticism. Both schools of thought show themselves to some degree in "Tears, Idle Tears."

Romanticism is thought to have been inspired by the great social revolutions of the late eighteenth century: the American Revolution of 1776 and, even more influential to life in Europe, the French Revolution of 1789. Politically, these events signified a new mood, a swing toward individual rights and away from repressive governments.

Romanticism in the arts was brought to life in the introduction to William Wordsworth and Samuel Taylor Coleridge's poetry collection *Lyrical Ballads,* published in 1798. Among the themes often covered in Romantic poetry were a glorification of nature, as opposed to the world of mankind,

Compare & Contrast

- **1847:** The potato famine that had ravaged Ireland for the previous two years showed signs of letting up, but new potato crops could not be planted quickly enough for the growing season. As a result, 200,000 Irish citizens emigrated.

  Today: Many analysts theorize that the unrest in Northern Ireland today results from the way the potato famine weakened the country almost 150 years ago.

- **1847:** Karl Marx and Fredrich Engels published *The Communist Manifesto,* urging the workers of the world to unite and assuring them, "The proletariat have nothing to lose but their chains."

  1917: A revolution in Russia overthrew the ruling czar; after a brief period of rule by a moderate government, a Communist government, following Marx's ideas, was installed. Four years later the Union of Soviet Socialist Republics, the Soviet Union, was officially chartered.

  1991: Because of economic and political problems, the Soviet Union was dismantled. With few exceptions, including China and Cuba, most of the countries of the world have turned away from Communism.

- **1847:** Former slave Frederick Douglass, who had escaped slavery and then bought his own freedom with money made on lecture tours in Europe, started *The North Star,* an abolitionist newspaper which he co-edited until 1860.

  1865: As a result of the Union's victory of the American Civil War, the 13th Amendment abolished slavery.

  1964: One hundred years after slavery ended, President Lyndon Johnson signed the Civil Rights Act of 1964, prohibiting segregation of public accommodations and discrimination in employment and education.

  Today: Civil rights issues are complicated by the addition of charges of "reverse discrimination" by members of the majority classes.

---

as well as a nostalgia for the past that cannot be recaptured. Both of these are apparent to some degree in this poem. Romanticism also gave us the popular image of the doomed, hedonistic poet who defies all moral conventions and dies young, as Romantic poets Lord Byron and John Keats did.

Romanticism's rejection of society and science eventually wore thin, especially as the turmoil at the turn of the century gave way to relative peace, prosperity, and scientific progress. One of the most significant changes was the locomotive. The first steam engine was invented in 1804, and tracks were installed soon after that. Considered noisy and ugly, the train was also barely quicker than a horse, with top speeds reaching twelve or so miles per hour. In 1829 engineer George Stephenson introduced his design for the *Rocket,* a steam engine that could carry freight and passengers at an incredible forty to fifty miles per hour. No mode of transportation

had ever moved like it before, and it changed the way that people thought about their world, redefining distances as if the land itself had somehow been altered. Romantics were able to look back to simpler times, when the world moved at a slower pace—just as modern romantics are apt to recall the pre-computer world of written information—but their discomfort did not stop the world from changing.

The England of 1837 was experiencing vibrant economical and scientific changes that were too powerful to ignore, and that resulted in a new artistic sensibility. Groundbreaking discoveries in every aspect of life made progress unavoidable. For example, in 1840 James Prescott Joule formulated the theory that would become the First Rule of Thermodynamics (regarding conservation of energy). In the mid-1840s, Louis Pasteur discovered bacteria and determined how they caused disease. Around the same time commercial sewing machines made mass production of clothing possible.

England celebrated these advances in 1851 with an exhibition at the Crystal Palace, a tall shining building that was built especially for the occasion and was in itself a milestone of architectural achievement. The theme of the exhibition, "universal prosperity," pointed out the problems that plagued the Victorian Age. As the economy stabilized and machines accelerated the pace of life, poverty grew rampant and cities became overcrowded and polluted.

Novels of the late 1800s, especially those written by Trollope and Dickens, described the devastation of modern urban life, such as Dickens's description of London keeping its streetlights on during the day when pollution blocked out the sun. Children in Victorian England worked in factories from sunup to sundown; poor people who did not or could not work were sent to rot in debtor's prisons. The vague unhappiness expressed in "Tears, Idle Tears" is linked to "the days that are no more"—a perspective that was even more heartbreaking during Victorian times.

Critical Overview

"Tears, Idle Tears" was published as a part of a longer poem, *The Princess,* which was Tennyson's first long work and his first attempt to apply his lyrical talent to a social issue. The idea for such a project came from outside of Tennyson's normal sphere of inspiration, from the urging of friends, who convinced him that a poet's duty to society required him to go beyond the comforts of what is familiar and address problems directly. "Tennyson himself was never satisfied with [*The Princess*]," wrote critic George O. Marshall Jr., in *A Tennyson Handbook,* "although he considered some of the blank verse among the best that he ever wrote." Modern critics agree. Although *The Princess* was received with mixed reviews when it was published, the long work has declined in critical esteem to the point where the book is seldom read in its entirety anymore, although particular poems, including "Tears, Idle Tears," are still highly regarded. Tennyson's lack of success with the long, sustained form and success with short subjects may be the result of what W. H. Auden, himself one of the most successful poets of the twentieth century, noted in a 1944 essay: "[Tennyson] had the finest ear, perhaps, of any English poet; he was also un-

doubtedly the stupidest; there was little about melancholia that he didn't know; there was little else that he did."

Marshall lists critics throughout the years who have expressed admiration for "Tears, Idle Tears," including Douglas Bush and Herbert J. C. Grierson, who called the poem "the most moving and finely wrought lyric Tennyson ever wrote." Writing about "Tears, Idle Tears," as well as other notable examples, Herbert Foltinek stated the opinion that "these are among Tennyson's most delicate and evocative creations; here, if anywhere, art aspires toward the creation of music." Critic Cleanth Brooks, whose long essay "The Motivation of Tennyson's Weeper" focuses on "Tears, Idle Tears," concludes that "when the poet is able, as in 'Tears, Idle Tears,' to analyze his experience … he secures not only richness and depth but dramatic power as well."

Criticism

Chris Semansky

Chris Semansky teaches writing and literature at Portland Community College in Portland, Oregon, and is a frequent contributor of poems and essays to literary journals. In the following essay, Semansky derides "Tears, Idle Tears" as cliche and banal.

Many critics have praised Alfred, Lord Tennyson's poem, "Tears, Idle Tears," a song from his long narrative poem, *The Princess.* Cleanth Brooks, for example, one of the most well-known and well-respected critics of the twentieth century, claims in his *The Well Wrought Urn* that the poem's success lies in its capacity to use paradox and ambiguity to represent the conflicting and complex inner life of its speaker. Claiming that critics who oppose emotion to intellect in poetry have done not only a disservice to poetry, but to Tennyson's poem as well, Brooks wrote, "The opposition is not only merely superficial; it falsifies the real relationships. For the lyric quality, if it be genuine, is not the result of some transparent and 'simple' reduction of a theme or a situation that is somehow poetic in itself; it is, rather, the result of an imaginative grasp of diverse materials—but an imaginative grasp so sure that it may show itself to the reader as unstudied and unpredictable without for a moment relaxing its hold on the intricate and complex stuff which it carries." To understand Brooks's comment about Tennyson's poem we must first understand what the critic means by "lyric quality."

A lyric is usually a short poem consisting of the words of a single speaker. Employing the first person "I," the lyric most often revolves around or expresses the feeling or state of mind of the speaker. Matthew Arnold's popular poem, "Dover Beach," for example, expresses the speaker's attempt, through observation and meditation, to resolve an emotional problem. Though the genre of the lyric includes many kinds of utterances (the love lyric, dramatic lyric, and ode among them), most critical attention has been aimed at understanding the emotional content of the lyric, to interpreting the speaker's feeling. So, when Brooks argues that "lyric quality" not be simplified, he means that in reading lyric poems we should take into consideration the head as well as the heart of the speaker and recognize that feeling consists of perception, thought, observation, and other variables.

I have no problem with this statement in general. However, "Tears, Idle, Tears" is not a sophisticated rendering of complex experience, as Brooks would have us believe; or rather, it is not a poetically sophisticated rendering of experience. It is an exercise in banalities and cliches. A cliche is a phrase or word that has been used so much it becomes hackneyed or trite. Cliched language is language that has lost its capacity to convey a vivid idea or image to the reader. For example, some popular poets—in terms of sales and readership—accused of writing in cliches are branded as trite and amateurish by critics. Tennyson's poetry, on the other hand, though regularly studied in classrooms, is rarely bought or read for pleasure. The critical apparatus that has been responsible for valorizing Tennyson's poetry is the same apparatus responsible for ignoring or condemning seemingly similar work by others.

Let us take a look at what Brooks has written about "Tears, Idle Tears" and see if it holds up. In his essay, "The Motivation of Tennyson's Weeper," Brooks spends close to a page inquiring into the nature of the tears introduced by the speaker in the first stanza.

> Tears, idle tears, I know not what they mean,
> Tears from the depth of some divine despair
> Rise in the heart, and gather to the eyes,
> In looking on the happy Autumn-fields,
> And thinking of the days that are no more.

"Are they idle tears?" Brooks asks. "Or are they not rather the most meaningful of tears?" He comes to the conclusion that the speaker is unaware of the exact origin of his tears. Do we as readers, though, really care where they came from? Tennyson's speaker is distraught; he is crying. He says the tears "rise in the heart." Historically the heart (even in Tennyson's time) has been the seat of emotion, so there is no surprise or freshness in using the image of the heart as the (metaphorical) place where the tears begin. Similarly, saying that the tears "gather to the eyes" introduces nothing new to our understanding of how crying happens. Tennyson is belaboring the obvious. Then we are told that the speaker is "looking on the happy Autumn-fields." "The happy Autumn-fields"? Can there be a more a more vague, more banal, indeed a more vapid image to use than "happy Autumn-fields" to describe what the speaker looks at while thinking about the past?

Brooks concludes that "the first stanza seems, not a meditated observation, but a speech begun impulsively—a statement which the speaker has begun before he knows how he will end it." Fair enough, but what kind of a speaker thinks or talks in iambic pentameter? And what kind of a poet would use such generic images to illustrate a (supposedly) complex emotional state?

After spending a good deal of ink and words attempting to make a case for the poem's use of paradox, ambiguity, and ironic contrast, and hence justify Tennyson's poem as worthy of being read, Brooks writes that "The last stanza evokes an intense emotional response from the reader." Not this reader. Tennyson ends the poem with the same kind of banal images and cliches as he started it.

> Dear as remember'd kisses after death,
> And sweet as those by hopeless fancy feign'd
> On lips that are for others; deep as love,
> Deep as first love, and wild with all regret;
> O Death in Life, the days that are no more!

Regardless of Brooks's elaborate attempts to ferret "deep meaning" from these lines by insisting that the poem's tight organization "represents an organic structure," he is wrong when he writes that the reader "will probably find himself [sic] in accord with this [his] general estimate of the poem's value." It is not the theme of Tennyson's poem that is unappealing. After all, almost all poets worth their salt (or metaphors) have written in one way or another about loss: loss of love, loss of life, loss of the past. Arguably, the bulk of poetry from the Romantics to the present deals in some way or another with loss. It is the imagery and figurative language that Tennyson chooses to convey his sense of loss that are unappealing.

For example, calling "the days that are no more.... Deep as first love, and wild with all regret" trivializes a very real human response to the passing of time and to the sense that one has missed opportunities in life. The comparison is weak between the items being compared—the past and deep love—because the words he chooses are abstract and vague. We cannot see days or love, and using the adjective "deep" to describe both of them adds nothing new to our understanding of the ideas of time or love.

"Tears, Idle Tears" embodies cliches even as it seeks to transcend them. Its inability to accomplish the latter makes the poem more like a sappy lyric than a complex rendering of human emotion, as Cleanth Brooks would have his readers believe. Tennyson can get away with it because of his place in literary history as a canonical figure. Brooks can "read into" the poem poetic strategies because of Tennyson's reputation and the reception of his other poetry. It is comforting to know that academically sanctioned poets such as Tennyson can write poems as bad as some by popular poets. The real irony is that while he crafted a poem that failed to express his emotions, that work was embraced by an audience unable to express its own feelings as well.

Source: Chris Semansky, in an essay for *Poetry for Students,* Gale, 1998.

J. Hillis Miller

In the following excerpt, Miller explains that "Tears, Idle Tears" "expresses a profound apprehension of temporality" and discusses the effects of several poetic devices used in the poem.

We ordinarily distinguish sharply between criticism and poetry. Some poets, we say—Coleridge, Arnold, and T. S. Eliot, for example—were also great critics, but other poets—Shakespeare, Byron, Browning, or Thomas Hardy—were not critics at all or not critics of distinction. We would usually put Tennyson in the latter category. For one thing, he is supposed to have had no aptitude for reflection or for theoretical generalization. W. H. Auden said of Tennyson: "He had the finest ear of any English poet. He was also the stupidest." Tennyson left no body of criticism. Such observations by Tennyson about poetry as exist, for example in the *Memoir* by Hallam Tennyson, are, as Gerhard Joseph shows in an admirable recent book on Tennyson [titled *Tennyson and the Text: The Weaver's Shuttle*], a version of Victorian commonplaces about the general superiority of symbol over alle-

What Do I Read Next?

- Peter Levi's 1993 biography, simply named *Tennyson,* contains all of the information currently known about Tennyson's life, rendered beautifully. Levi, one of England's best poets and scholars, gives a poet's perspective to his understanding of his subject.

- Another excellent biography was written by famed Tennyson scholar Christopher B. Ricks. Also titled *Tennyson,* it was first published in 1972 and revised for the second edition in 1989.

- "Tears, Idle Tears" is included with all of Tennyson's others in the definitive edition *The Poems of Tennyson,* edited by Christopher Ricks, most recently published in 1987.

- The poet Robert Browning lived at the same time as Tennyson and is considered to embody the socially elevated side of Victorianism that complements Tennyson's earthiness. *The Poetical Works of Robert Browning* was published in 1974 by Houghton Mifflin, with an introduction by G. Robert Stange,

- Many students are familiar with the works of Charles Dickens, whose novels are considered to have captured the embodiment of the Victorian Age. In particular, *Bleak House* gives a good sense of the futility felt by the common people (who were Tennyson's greatest supporters). It was published in 1853, just six years after this poem.

gory, though he sometimes speaks of using a "sort of allegory" in the weak and conventional sense of a rationally concocted "*this* for *that.*" Tennyson favors latitude of subjective interpretation. He refuses to pin down definitely the meanings of his poems. He speaks of an "allegory in the distance" or of a "parabolic drift" in the *Idylls of the King* [as noted in Hallam Tennyson's *Alfred Lord Tennyson: A Memoir*], but he always refused to fix that "drift" with exact interpretations. Tennyson is committed to the idea that poetry should be socially useful.

Perhaps letting his readers make what they like of it is part of that program.

In any case, no one in his right mind would claim that Tennyson is an important critic in the sense that Arnold, Pater, Eliot, and even Gerard Manley Hopkins are important critics. Nevertheless, I shall show that one significant dimension of Tennyson's poems is the way they represent what might be called "poetic thinking" about the nature and powers of poetry. And I shall show that what Tennyson's poems obliquely say about poetry is far more interesting than the relatively conventional views about poetry expressed outside the poetry, or even inside the poetry when he makes overt assertions. If Tennyson was stupid, his poems are far from stupid about the nature of what they themselves are and what they do. As theoretical reflection about poetry they are deep, profound, as I shall show through the example of "Tears, Idle Tears."…

Much has been written about this powerful and moving poem. I shall not try to recapitulate that commentary here, but shall try to read the poem afresh. Though "Tears, Idle Tears" has its own integrity, is usually read outside its context, and was probably written without *The Princess* in mind, nevertheless the poem is inserted at a dramatic moment in *The Princess.* The singing of it by one of Princess Ida's "maids" helps precipitate the catastrophe of the poem: the revelation that Princess Ida's female college has been invaded by three men disguised as women. "Tears, Idle Tears" is therefore placed against a background of questions about gender roles and women's liberation.…

["Tears, Idle Tears"] speaks poetically for a view of time as generated by difference, non-presence, distance, unattainability, and loss that can never be made up by a recovered presence in the bosom of God. God, in fact, suffers from a "divine despair" at not being able to recuperate and encompass all the times and places of his creation. By "speaking poetically," I mean speaking through image and rhetorical structure rather than through conceptual formulation.…

As Heidegger observes in *Sein und Zeit,* the terminology available in Western languages for expressing time is remarkably impoverished. Since we lack adequate specifically temporal language, we Westerners always express time (and falsify it) in some spatial image or other, for example in the movement of the hands of a clock.…

The project of "Tears, Idle Tears" is to find a way with spatial images to express Tennyson's peculiar apprehension of human time, especially his sense of the past. Tennyson must, that is, try to turn time into language or make time of words. This is both a poetic and a theoretical project. For Tennyson one of the major uses of poetry is to express the human sense of time. This is an example of what I mean when I say Tennyson's critical and theoretical thinking about poetry takes place in his poems, not in prose about poetry.

Temporal distance is associated with spatial distance in the first stanza of "Tears," when the theme of the poem is announced. "[L]ooking on the happy Autumn-fields / And thinking of the days that are no more" makes the speaker of the poem cry, but the tears are idle and without ascertainable meaning. Though the poem is sung by one of the Princess's maidens, no doubt it expresses Tennyson's own obsession with what he called the "passion of the past." Twice in comments about the poem he asserted that it was written at a particular "mouldered lodge" of the past, Tintern Abbey: "This song came to me on the yellowing autumn-tide at Tintern Abbey, full for me of its bygone memories. It is the sense of the abiding in the transient." Tennyson does not mention Wordsworth, but "Tears, Idle Tears" has the same theme as Wordsworth's poem and might almost be called Tennyson's "Tintern Abbey." Among the "bygone memories" was surely this one of Wordsworth's many poems about memory, as well as the memory of the history that is inscribed materially in the ruined abbey. Tennyson insisted, however, that the tears of the poem were not generated by "real woe, as some people might suppose; 'it was rather the yearning that young people occasionally experience for that which seems to have passed away from them for ever'."

This is an important clue. The poem, Tennyson is saying, with however much or little of denegation, does not express sorrow about separation from any real person, for example his separation by death from Hallam, who is buried not far from the ruins of Tintern Abbey. All the images in the poem about separation from friends and the woe of unfulfilled desire are just that, merely images, prosopopoeias for something that is imageless and has nothing to do with persons. They are images, that is, for human temporality.

The pattern of repeated adjectives woven and interwoven as the grammatical armature of the poem names no specific sorrow or loss. The adjectives name rather the quality that "the days that are no more" have just because they are no more: "Fresh"; "Sad"; "So sad, so fresh"; "sad and strange"; "so sad, so strange"; "Dear"; "sweet"; "deep"; "Deep"; "wild." Even a child who has had no actual loss to weep, says Tennyson, experiences this sense of loss as an intrinsic and apparently causeless feature of consciousness itself. To mourn this loss is the human condition. The problem for poetry is to find words to express what is outside specific experiences, even prior to them, something that has nothing to do with intersubjective relations. It is something, moreover, that seems even prior to language, at least the language of direct reference.

One mode of figurative expression exploited in this poem is to personify that primordial sense of loss by embodying it in something that can be put in words, that is, in a series of situations embodying loss or separation: friends returning by boat but not yet here; friends leaving by boat and disappearing over the horizon; a dying man or woman waking at dawn; the memory of kisses given a dead loved one when he or she was alive; the unassuagable desire to kiss "lips that are for others"; the desire of first love, a desire so deep that somehow it cannot be distinguished from regret for something lost. These personifications are explicitly labeled similes by the "as" that follows each adjective: "Fresh as," "Sad as," and so on. These images are systematically genderless....

[T]he primary figure in the poem is of course the tears. What can be said of them? Tears are an extraordinary phenomenon. They are not articulate speech. They are mute; but no one can doubt that they are signs. They say even more than words do. Oozing involuntarily from the intimacy of the body as it is moved by thoughts and feelings, they betray that intimacy, speak for it, whether the one who cries wishes to or not. They break down the chaste division between inside and outside. They turn the body inside out. As bodily fluids that are at the same time unmistakably signs they break down the division between spirit and body. Tears are profoundly embarrassing or shocking because they are the involuntary making material of what, we think, ought to be secret and immaterial. Much has been written recently about "the materiality of the sign." Tears are a paradigmatic example of such a sign. The tears in "Tears, Idle Tears" are particularly indiscrete and troubling just because they have no sufficient cause. Looking on the happy Autumn-fields and thinking of the days that are no more hardly seems something to cry about. But the tears rise to the singer's eyes."

If the tears have no sufficient cause, their meaning is also unknown. "I know not what they

> *["Tears, Idle Tears"] speaks poetically for a view of time as generated by difference, non-presence, distance, unattainability, and loss that can never be made up by a recovered presence in the bosom of God."*

mean," says the singer. If the tears are signs, they are signs in an unknown language....

The world of Tennyson's "Tears, Idle Tears" is like the world of those baroque mourning plays that Walter Benjamin, in *Ursprung des deutschen Trauerspiels,* defines as a realm of nature (*physis*) bereft of any divine presence. Tennyson's poem, like those mourning plays, is a work of mourning not for any particular death, but for the loss of redeeming relation to transcendence. Tennyson's tears of mourning are brought back up like Eurydice from the underworld, but their function as communicating messengers is lost along the way. They connect this world with the other one, but in the mode of non-connection. The message the tears bring is lost in the transition from the depths of some divine despair to the singer's heart to her or his eyes. They are now signs in an unknown language, unreadable....

The tears are "idle" presumably because they are generated in a moment of idleness, whether "silken-folded" or not. In this moment the speaker or singer has turned away from the future-oriented work that normally occupies human beings just to look at the happy Autumn-fields and think of the days that are no more. This is an activity that is idle in the sense of accomplishing nothing, as the tears, so it seems, accomplish nothing. Nothing can be done to alter the non-being of the past. Or can it? The tears appear to be "idle" because they do not work. They do not do anything. The days that are no more are no more. No words can bring them back. If the tears are cognitively empty ("I know not what they mean"), they also appear to be performatively void....

On the other hand, by a paradox that is at the center of what this poem says about poetry, the poem about the tears, the naming of the tears in poetry, is performatively efficacious.... These tears are generated by the song or they are the very ones the song names, though it is not autumn and the maid has presumably not suffered the various losses or unassuaged desires that are named in the poem. Nevertheless, "the tears come to her eyes," as we say. Sing this poem and you will cry. But you will cry tears not for your own loss but for a generalized loss, loss in general, a loss that is, for Tennyson, the essential feature of the human sense of time past. To sing about these tears is to bring them up from the depths and to confront them again as signs whose meaning is unknown. If the tears rise up, they then fall....

Another odd fact about these tears, or about tears in general, is that they obscure clear vision of what generated them. We speak of how someone's eyes are "misted with tears." The weeper in this poem can no longer clearly see the happy autumn fields that brought on the tears through their association with the past. Tennyson himself was extremely near-sighted. He had to hold a book close to his eyes in order to read it. The happy autumn fields always presumably looked misty to him, as if he were crying, even when there were no tears in his eyes. When what is seen is seen obscured by tears, its deeper meaning is at the same time revealed, in the case of this poem by the crescendo of sideways displacements into one simile or another. Tears are apocalyptic. They unveil and veil at the same time.

Tears are ruined symbols, symbols that do not communicate that for which they stand. If this is so, a more proper name for the tears would be "allegorical sign," defining "allegorical sign" as a symbol turned inside out....

Tennyson's idle tears are a paradigmatic example of an allegorical sign as opposed to a symbol. Such a sign is defined in terms of temporal distance, not spatial contiguity, by its unlikeness to what it stands for, not its similarity to the symbolized, by its opacity and lack of discernible meaning, not by its transparency. An allegorical sign is characterized by its failure to put the one who contemplates it in present possession of what it stands for, not by its cognitive efficacy. It has performative force, not a constative function. The tears work as signs through a strange efficacy of putting weeper, singer, and listener or witness in touch at a distance with what they cannot name as perspic-

uous meaning. This failure of the tears to express what they mean makes them function admirably as allegorical signs for temporality, the strange non-being of the days that are no more as Tennyson experienced them....

The singer of "Tears, Idle Tears" mocks and contradicts the concept of time so confidently expressed by the Princess a little earlier in the poem and replaces it with an allegorical time of perpetual loss and absence.

Tennyson's final name for this perpetual loss and absence is "Death in Life." The phrase is a prosopopoeia, the culmination of the chain of images personifying the days that are no more as like one or another person or interpersonal situation. But like all prosopopoeias, this one is as much an invocation as a name. It can be read either as an exclamatory definition, a constative assertion: "'O Death in Life,' that is what the days that are no more are," or as a performative vocative or apostrophe, a prosopopoeia or trope of address to the absent, the inanimate, or the dead, that is, the days that are no more. Like Christ's "Lazarus, come forth" Tennyson's speaker implores the days that are no more to come forth and manifest themselves in the form of an allegorical personification: "O Death in Life." Like Wordsworth's "Ye knew him well, ye cliffs and islands of Winander," Tennyson's address to "Death in Life" presupposes that this being or personage might appear or answer back. But the poem ends abruptly with this line. No evidence is given that the days that are no more appear in answer to the speaker's call. "O Death in Life" is a failed prosopopoeia, the ruin of the trope of personification that has been a chief rhetorical tool in the poem for naming by one catachresis or another something that has no proper name, or for performatively invoking it. Insofar as the days that are no more are accurately described as death in life they could not manifest themselves except as an absence, as a ghost....

"Death in Life" names the undermining of all presence and possession in this life by a principle of loss.

Tennyson here names that principle of loss, appropriately enough, "Death." This death is not a future end but a dimension of separation, loss, or difference that permeates life from childhood to old age, from birth to "death" in the usual sense. As Dylan Thomas said, "After the first death there is no other." The "first death" occurs the moment we are born. Human life thereafter is undermined by this constant presence of death.

I claim to have fulfilled the promise made at the beginning of this paper. I have shown that if Tennyson's abstract thinking was conventional and traditional, his poetic thinking went against that conventional thinking. "Tears, Idle Tears," as one example of that, expresses a profound apprehension of temporality as well as a profound sense of the way the poetic devices of allegorical sign, prosopopoeia, and catachresis can be used performatively to call forth that apprehension of temporality.

Source: J. Hillis Miller, "Temporal Topographies: Tennyson's Tears," in *Victorian Poetry,* Vol. 30, Nos. 3-4, Autumn-Winter 1992, pp. 277–88.

Sources

Altick, Richard D., *Victorian People and Ideas,* W. W. Norton & Co., 1973.

Auden, W. H., "Tennyson," in *Forwards and Afterwards,* edited by Edward Mendelson, Random House, 1973, p. 223.

Barnard, Robert, *A Short History of English Literature,* Blackwell Press, Inc., 1994.

Bloom, Harold, ed., *Alfred Lord Tennyson,* Chelsea House, 1985.

Brooks, Cleanth, "The Motivation of Tennyson's Weeper," in *The Well Wrought Urn: Studies in the Structure of Poetry,* Harcourt Brace Jovanovich, 1956, pp. 166-77.

Burton, Elizabeth, *The Pageant of Early Victorian England, 1837-1861,* Charles Schribner's Sons, 1972.

Jump, John D., *Alfred Tennyson: In Memoriam, Maud, and Other Poems,* J.M. Dent and Sons, Ltd., 1974, pp. vii-xx.

Morse, David, *High Victorian Culture,* New York University Press, 1993.

For Further Study

Altholz, Josef L., ed., *The Mind and Art of Victorian England,* The University of Minnesota Press, 1976.
> This collection of scholarly essays captures the broad panorama of cultural influences that were at work while Tennyson was working.

Gordon, William Clark, *The Social ideals of Alfred Tennyson as Related To His Time,* Haskell House, 1966.
> This scholarly monograph concisely links history and literature in terms of Tennyson's career.

Marshall, George O., Jr., *A Tennyson Handbook,* Twayne Publishers, 1963.
> Provides a brief summary and history for each of Tennyson's poems.

Pattison, Robert, *Tennyson and Tradition,* Harvard University Press, 1979.
> The poetic forms that Tennyson would have been familiar with and the ways that he incorporated them are examined in this dense, scholarly work.

Shannon, Edgar Finley, Jr., *Tennyson and the Reviewers,* Archon Books, 1952.
> Surveys reader responses to Tennyson, from 1827 to 1851, tracing how his reputation grew and how his work was affected by critical response.

Shaw, W. David, *Tennyson's Style,* Cornell University Press, 1976.
> In this overview of Tennyson's works, Shaw provides abundant annotations and cross-references.

This Is My Letter to the World

Emily Dickinson
c. 1862

"This Is My Letter to the World" is believed to have been written in 1862, the year during which Dickinson first began to share her poetry with Thomas Wentworth Higginson, a minister, writer, and editor who had a special interest in struggling young writers. Although Higginson was not successful in helping Dickinson present her work to the world during her own lifetime, he did offer her advice and personal support throughout her prolific writing career. This poem was finally published four years after Dickinson's death, in a collection edited by Higginson called *Poems by Emily Dickinson.*

It is usually unwise to assume that the poet is the same as the speaker in a poem; however, "This Is My Letter to the World" is strikingly descriptive of Dickinson's literary career. Although Dickinson wrote some 1,800 poems, only seven of them were published in her lifetime, and those were all greatly altered by editors who did not always comprehend Dickinson's unconventional poetic style. Dickinson may have been frustrated by the poor reception that her work received from her contemporaries, but she also seemed to recognize that true genius is often misunderstood in its own time. As the poem indicates, Dickinson kept writing her poetry with the confidence that some day its proper audience would discover it.

Author Biography

Dickinson was born in Amherst, Massachusetts, in 1830 and lived there all her life. Her grandfather

Emily Dickinson

was the founder of Amherst College, and her father, Edward Dickinson, was a lawyer who served as the treasurer of the college. He also held various political offices. Her mother, Emily Norcross Dickinson, was a quiet and frail woman. Dickinson went to primary school for four years and then attended Amherst Academy from 1840 to 1847 before spending a year at Mount Holyoke Female Seminary. Her education was strongly influenced by Puritan religious beliefs, but Dickinson did not accept the teachings of the Unitarian church attended by her family and remained agnostic throughout her life. Following the completion of her education, Dickinson lived in the family home with her parents and younger sister, Lavinia, while her elder brother, Austin, and his wife lived next door. She began writing verse at an early age, practicing her craft by rewriting poems she found in books, magazines, and newspapers. During a trip to Philadelphia in the early 1850s, Dickinson fell in love with a married minister, the Reverend Charles Wadsworth; her disappointment in love may have brought about her subsequent withdrawal from society. Dickinson experienced an emotional crisis of an undetermined nature in the early 1860s. Her traumatized state of mind is believed to have inspired her to write prolifically: in 1862 alone she is thought to have composed more than three hun-

dred poems. In that same year, Dickinson initiated a correspondence with Thomas Wentworth Higginson, the literary editor of the *Atlantic Monthly* magazine. Over the years Dickinson sent nearly one hundred of her poems for his criticism, and he became a sympathetic adviser and confidant, but he never published any of her poems. Dickinson's isolation further increased when her father died unexpectedly in 1874 and her mother suffered a stroke that left her an invalid. Dickinson and her sister provided her constant care until her death in 1882. Dickinson was diagnosed in 1886 as having Bright's disease, a kidney dysfunction that resulted in her death in May of that year.

Poem Text

This is my letter to the World
That never wrote to Me—
The simple News that Nature told—
With tender Majesty

Her Message is committed   5
To Hands I cannot see—
For love of Her—Sweet—countrymen—
Judge tenderly—of Me

Poem Summary

Lines 1-2:

In these lines, the "letter" is a written message, quite possibly meaning this poem or a whole body of poetic work. The letter is addressed to the world, which could be the planet Earth or the whole natural universe; the reading public or the whole human race. It is not clear which specific meaning is intended here, and it is possible that all these meanings are implied. The letter is unrequited, for the speaker never received any letters from the world. Perhaps this is a metaphor for the experience of the artist who is lonely and misunderstood. If the speaker is writing poetry, perhaps the world, or the public, has never appreciated the poet's unique talents and creative vision. However, the speaker is not discouraged. Even if the communication is in only one direction, it still continues.

Lines 3-4:

Here, the speaker humbly stresses the simplicity of the "news," or new information, contained in the writing. The speaker goes on to claim that the letter's contents were inspired by the "ten-

Media Adaptations

- There are a variety of recordings available of fellow poets reading Dickinson's work. Audio cassettes include "Fifty Poems of Emily Dickinson," "Dickinson and Whitman; Ebb and Flow," "Heaven Below, Heaven Above," "The Enlightened Heart" and "Poems and Letters of Emily Dickinson," all of which are available from the Audiobooks.com website.

der Majesty," or delicate power, of nature itself and not by the author's will alone. If the speaker is an artist, then this statement is in keeping with the philosophy that art is an imitation or celebration of the natural world, and that the artist's will has less to do with the creative process than the powers of creation itself. In other words, nature and the whole of creation speak through the artist's work. This surrender of power can be seen both positively and negatively, for it can mean that the speaker accepts the role of the godhead in all human creativity, or it can mean that the speaker is afraid to take responsibility and risk misunderstanding and ridicule.

Lines 5-6:

In the first line of the second quatrain, the pronoun "Her" refers to nature, in this case perhaps Mother Nature. The poem's speaker has captured nature's message in poetry, and that message is "committed," or delivered for safe keeping, to "Hands" that the speaker will never meet. Here, "Hands" is an example of a figure of speech called synecdoche, for the whole future generation of possible readers is represented by their hands alone. This "letter" is the speaker's legacy to posterity, and it is a great act of faith to leave one's art to the care of strangers.

Lines 7-8:

The poem ends with the speaker pleading to "Sweet—countrymen," or future readers, for a compassionate understanding of the "letter to the world." The speaker makes this appeal in the name of nature itself, as it is nature who is the inspiration behind the work. This request is almost pitiful, for it seems to predict a potentially negative reaction from readers. It asks the reader to think of the speaker's predicament and to show mercy accordingly.

Themes

Alienation and Loneliness

One of the central themes of "This Is My Letter to the World," is alienation; many readers agree that the poem seems to be written by a speaker who has waited so long for outside contact she finally decides to complete the message for herself. The poem, like many found after her death, balances a love for solitude with a loneliness for outside contact, or as Dickinson says of herself in another piece, it is a "Joy to be Hidden but a Disaster not to be Found."

During Dickinson's time and still today, the act of writing can be a lonely process. She did not care about being published, a process that involves sending poems out to a magazine editor you have never met and waiting months for a response. A majority of her communication with other human beings was done through letters, so it seems a natural metaphor for Dickinson to use in representing her alienation—writing a letter to the world after waiting a whole life for the world to write her first.

Unlike Whitman, who populated his poems with the many individuals he knew and observed during his lifetime, Dickinson's poem is devoid of individuals. Instead she writes from a point of view so isolated from her readers we appear small on her world's horizon, a mass of "Sweet—countrymen." Dickinson, typically awkward with human contact, even seems to diminish her own poetic role as a creator in the poem, referring to herself instead as a kind of journalist reporting "the simple news that nature told."

Art and Experience

Many critics consider this speaker's "letter to the world" a metaphor, or analogy, for the role of art itself as a message from poet to reader, dancer to audience, painter to those who stand and gaze with arms crossed. How many times have you heard the question "what is art?" Unlike the cliche answer—that there is no answer, only something to be pondered over espresso in museum coffee shops—a simple but accurate response may be that

Topics for Further Study

- Dickinson packs whole volumes of interpretation into a poem the size of a matchbook. Although she wasn't known to read Japanese haiku, her ability to "spread out" in such a small space is reminiscent of the three-line form. Read Basho's "Falling upon Earth," included in Volume 2 of this textbook series. Which poem do you feel is more effective at expressing the poet's emotions? Why? Discuss your answers.

- Write your own letter to the world, in paragraph form, speaking to a reader who will find your note 50 years after your death. Fill more than half a notebook page. Then go back and circle the phrases and lines which surprised you the most while you were writing, and "cut and paste" these into a poem on a separate sheet. The poem must fit in two quatrains (four-line stanzas) and each line may not exceed seven words. Proper punctuation is strictly prohibited except for the use of a long dash (—). Compare your results and discuss.

it is a form of communication between two human beings. Or more specifically, an *inside* person speaking to another *inside* person. The most powerful art is that which carries an emotion from deep within one person and places it quickly and honestly into another at an equal emotional depth. In "This is My Letter to the World," Dickinson imagines that other person, her reader, as "Hands I cannot see," distant and hidden, but open and waiting nonetheless for the letter. This image of hands may remind us of another of her poems, in which she describes writing poetry as "spreading wide my narrow hands / To gather Paradise." These same narrow hands, in turn, carry paradise to us, her anonymous readers.

The common poetic device of "metaphor," literally takes its meaning from the Greek *meta,* "over, across, behind," and *phoreo,* "to bring, carry, bear." If you travel to Athens, you can watch the huge moving company vans with the word *metaphora* lettered across their sides grow smaller down the street. So art carries its heavy cargo of emotions from one human to another, a package delivered from narrow hand to narrow hand. There is risk involved in art as well, the artist's emotions gathered from such a personal center, so easily bruised. Perhaps any artist's biggest fear is to have one's work rejected or ignored. Dickinson ends this poem with perhaps this same fear, evident in the form of a plea for us to please receive the news she reports from Nature, but "For love of Her—countrymen— / Judge tenderly—of Me."

Style

"This Is My Letter to the World" is a lyric written in two quatrains, or four-line verses, arranged in alternating lines of eight and six iambic syllables, the so-called common meter of the English hymns Dickinson knew from childhood. The uncomplicated syllabic and rhyme systems of common meter allowed Dickinson to showcase the power of language without distraction, and more than half of her published poems employ this traditional hymn form.

The poem rhymes in the second and fourth lines of each stanza with words that share a common long "e" sound, including a repeated "Me," and there are other echoing "e" sounds throughout. Dickinson's abundant use of consonants, another device that enhances her rhyme, is demonstrated in the poem's many "s," "t," "n," and "d" sounds.

Historical Context

Emily Dickinson may be one of the few poets we read today who seems to resist her historical context, yet for that same reason she is one of the most personally accessible. With some poets, our full understanding of their work depends heavily upon our understanding of the historical and cultural context surrounding it before each line can expand like thin sponges dipped in water. Our understanding of Allen Ginsberg's poem "Howl," for example, grows as we learn about the conservative political environment of America in the 1950s; similarly, our reading of Gwendolyn Brooks is informed greatly by our understanding of the Civil Rights movement of the 1960s.

Compare & Contrast

- **1862:** Congress passes the Homestead Act, which gives 160 free acres of Western land to any individual who could productively farm the soil for five years. The arid climate and nutrient-poor soil proved stubborn to yield produce, and many farmers failed.

  Today: Many Western farmers successfully raise cattle on the difficult land, though some feel government regulations today hinder their ability to conduct their farming.

- **1862:** President Lincoln issued the Emancipation Proclamation, declaring that on January 1, 1863, that all persons held as slaves in the United States would be free.

1865: Freedom of slaves did not actually take effect until the Confederacy was defeated in the Civil War. Almost immediately, laws were enacted that required blacks to be treated differently than whites in almost all social circumstances.

1964: After increasing gains made in the cause of equality, the Civil Rights Act of 1964 put an end to legal discrimination in public accommodations, unions, and federally funded programs.

Today: We have laws to punish racial discrimination, although American attitudes still show extreme racial consciousness.

But Dickinson, who rarely left her small village of Amherst and, later in her life, never left her small room in her father's house, wrote poems with far more inward vision than out. The extent of her seclusion was to the point that when her father died in 1874, she did not attend his funeral; rather, she listened to the service at the nearby cemetery through a window in her upstairs bedroom. She would write many poems about death in that room, having listened to numerous funerals sitting at her desk by the window, though she would never reveal the source of that procession or the Civil War that raged in the South during her lifetime. The context surrounding Dickinson was simple: wooden chair, white dress, a fly buzzing against a glass pane. Her gaze was deeply inward, and in the closely held mirror of her poetry, we perhaps find it easiest to see ourselves.

Many critics categorize Dickinson with Walt Whitman, another poet living and writing at the same time, though the two never met or even acknowledged each other's existence. Some critics call them the parents of American poetry as we know it today. In the late 1850s, during the same years Emily Dickinson scratched out "This Is My Letter to the World" (the poem itself on the page no larger than a matchbook), bundled it tightly with the other hundreds of poems and tucked it into a corner chest in her room, Whitman was writing, self-publishing, revising, and publishing again his manifesto-length "Song of Myself." Both poems come from the same autobiographical center and aim themselves directly at the reader; Emily's a quick arrow, Whitman's a sawed-off shotgun blast: he would publish seven different editions of the poem during his lifetime. When Dickinson's friend and future editor Thomas Westworth Higginson wrote to ask her if she had read Whitman's work, she replied "You speak of Mr. Whitman—I never read his Book—but was told that he was disgraceful."

We do know from the same exchange of letters that she did read Keats, Browning, Ruskin, the Book of Revelation, and Ralph Waldo Emerson. From Emerson we can guess she gained her eagerness to treat Nature as an emblem. Most of our understanding of Dickinson's life is through the collected correspondences with Higginson. Through these letters we have a glimpse inside her quiet life and the few delicate relationships she tended. That one act of courage on her part in writing Higginson and including a few of her poems—her first "Letter to the World"—initiated a correspondence which would grow to reveal a patchwork of the life of whom William Carlos

Williams would later call his "Patron Saint" of poetry.

Chris Semansky

Chris Semansky teaches writing and literature at Portland Community College in Portland, Oregon, and is a frequent contributor of poems and essays to literary journals. In the following essay, Semansky discusses how "This Is My Letter to the World" provides insights into Dickinson's poetic identity and philosophy.

Critical Overview

"This Is My Letter to the World" has received special attention from critics because of the verse's apparent relevance to Dickinson's career as a writer. The great Dickinson scholar Thomas H. Johnson, editor of the first complete edition of Dickinson's poetry and author of the influential book *Emily Dickinson: An Interpretive Biography,* views the poem as one of Dickinson's "verses on the function and status of the poet." According to Johnson, the poet is "blessed, but isolated," performing the role of an interpreter of nature for the benefit of the world from which she is alienated.

A second critic, William Robert Sherwood, examines the poem more closely in his book *Circumference and Circumstance.* According to Sherwood, the poem illustrates Dickinson's decision "to avoid the complications of notoriety, to trust to fame." Sherwood believes that Dickinson's religious background influenced her decision to avoid seeking popularity in her own lifetime. He explains that "the distinction Emily Dickinson made between fame and notoriety" relates to "the Puritan discrimination between the elect and the unregenerate." In the Puritan tradition, the elect are those chosen by God, and the unregenerate are those who have not been spiritually reborn and who seek their approval from other people instead of from God. In addition, Sherwood argues that Dickinson was far too dedicated to her art to sacrifice her integrity in order to achieve public success. Because Dickinson felt that great art is divinely inspired, "the very source of poetry made its exploitation a sacrilege."

Inder Nath Kher, in his book *The Landscape of Absence: Emily Dickinson's Poetry*, believes that the poem illustrates a paradox, or seemingly contradictory statement. Kher explains that "the artist withdraws from his fellow men into the world of art, only to enter more deeply into dialogue with humanity." For Kher, the poem represents the difficult decision that the artist makes when choosing "the tragic position of being neglected by the world she aims to transform." Later in his book, Kher goes on to explain that the poem illustrates "the importance of creative self-reliance" and teaches the reader that one must first acquire self-knowledge before attempting to know the world.

Written in 1862, the year she tackled the subject of poethood in many of her verses, "This Is My Letter to the World" provides us with a glimpse into how Dickinson thought about the art of poetry and about her own identity as a poet.

In his *Portrait of Emily Dickinson: The Poet and Her Prose,* David Higgins notes that for Dickinson the act of letter writing and of composing poetry were virtually interchangeable: "When she wrote letters she chose appropriate fragments and worked them into her prose. Sometimes the letter as a whole would pass through two or more drafts before it satisfied her. Meantime she would have chosen poems from the scrap basket or from her 'packets' and fitted them also into her letter. The final writing—the letter her correspondent actually received—might look spontaneous, but it was the last of several creative stages." Letter writing is frequently an intimate act, even more so in the mid-nineteenth century. That Dickinson used the genre of the letter as a kind of model for some of her poems (and vice versa) gives us an idea of the intimate relation she had to writing both letters and poetry.

Rather than a complaint that she was ignored by others, Dickinson's opening lines must be read as a statement of faith. The "world" for Dickinson is not society or friends or her family, but rather an imagined space in which her relationships to these entities are negotiated, but never defined. A virtual recluse in her father's house, Dickinson derived much of her emotional sustenance from her correspondence. In his *Emily Dickinson,* critic Paul Ferlazzo writes:

> What she may have lost in the spontaneity and warmth we associate with lively human exchange, she made up for with a deepened verbal precision and psychological investment. In some cases she was able to carry on a more enriching emotional communication through the mail than many of us are able to do in our more immediate face-to-face contacts. She seemed to thrive on the power of the disembodied idea, on the essence of the mind captured on paper and unencumbered by matter.

What Do I Read Next?

- Walt Whitman, who lived and wrote during the same period as Dickinson, handled similar themes in an entirely different style. His *Leaves of Grass,* a book-length poem, is widely available and anthologized.

- It was common practice for publishers to freely edit and change a writer's poems before going to print; in some cases, as with Dickinson, what readers viewed barely resembled the poems as she intended. When Harvard University acquired the rights to the Dickinson estate in 1950, they published the poems true to the original manuscripts. All 1775 poems are available in *The Complete Poems of Emily Dickinson,* published by Little, Brown and Co.

- A good deal of biographical insight into Dickinson's life can be discovered by reading *The Letters of Emily Dickinson,* edited by Thomas Johnson and published in 1958 by Harvard University Press.

Indeed, brevity and intensity mark Dickinson's letters and poems. She put so much of her life into her writing that the argument could be made that language is the real house in which Dickinson lived, not the white-shuttered house in Amherst where biographers and historians locate her. Dickinson corresponded with more than one hundred people during her life and developed elaborate rituals, not only for writing letters but for reading them as well. She describes her own finely tuned ritual of letter reading in "The Way I read a Letter's—this—":

The Way I read a Letter's—this—
'Tis first—I lock the Door—
And push it with my fingers—next—
For transport it be sure—
And then I go the furthest off
To counteract a knock—
Then draw my little Letter forth
And slowly pick the lock—

The elaborately precise detail of Dickinson's description, a staple of her verse, demonstrates an almost obsessive relation the poet had towards language. As much an act of seduction as it is an act of decoding, Dickinson's approach to reading letters as well as writing them was to delve into the mystery of language. Rather than using accessible language, however, she frequently employed metaphors and images whose references were not always clear. What are we to make, for instance, of "That simple news that Nature told— / With tender Majesty"? Does it refer to what the "World" never told her? And is Nature for Dickinson synonomous with the world?

There are no easy answers, for Dickinson's own relation to poetry, to Nature, to others, to life itself, was complicated. Indeed, it would be incorrect to claim that she distinguished among them. Biographer Thomas Johnson claimed in *Emily Dickinson: An Interpretive Biography* that "among artists, she best understood poets, and had intimate knowledge of the poetic process. It is coeval with love, she knows but it cannot be explained…. Her letter to the world from which she is shut away will transmit such news about nature as she has received through her senses."

But what is this news that she is sending to the world, and what is the "Message" that nature commits to invisible hands? Dickinson's message is that she is a poet and that she has submitted herself in faith to others, history, god, nature with faith that she will be judged favorably.

Her Message is committed
To Hands I cannot see—
For love of Her—Sweet—countrymen—
Judge tenderly—of Me

Such an attitude exemplifies the difficulty of living a life in uncertainty, yet trusting that wisdom can be gained from such a commitment. Nature, for Dickinson, was the source of wisdom and was at root inscrutable. Ferlazzo reminds us that "Dickinson believes that a separation exists between the world of nature and that of man. We live outside of nature and are permitted to observe it, experience it, and enjoy it if we can; but we are not privileged to enter into its secret." At times conventionally religious, but most times not, Dickinson was heavily influenced by Ralph Waldo Emerson, who encouraged others to reject European values and modes of belief and to think for themselves. Emerson's writing championed transcendentalism, a philosophy that saw in nature a realm of possibilities rather than prescriptions, an idea Dickinson heartily embraced.

Dickinson was not only comfortable writing about Nature's inscrutability, about its "secret" but she did it with a style which itself was often difficult to comprehend. Eschewing periods for dashes, ignoring or reinventing rules of punctuation and word order, Dickinson wrote in a spare, elliptical manner, inviting readers to make their own connections among her words. An iconoclast more intent on opening up the possibilities of language rather than providing definitive interpretations of experience, Dickinson explored connections between the seen and the unseen worlds and, as Peggy McIntosh and Ellen Louise Hart write, she "indicate[d] finally that human beings in our arrangements of life seldom attain what we need, desire, and are capable of understanding."

When Thomas Wentworth Higginson and Mabel Loomis Todd edited the first edition of Dickinson's poems in 1890 they placed "This Is My Letter to the World" just after the table of contents and before the first page of selections, though no evidence has ever been produced that Dickinson intended it as an introduction to any of her poems. It has since been anthologized and reprinted countless times, and pointed to as the representative poem for how Dickinson conceived of her poetic identity. It is important to remember, though, that rather than representing an experience or an idea, Dickinson's poems were experiences themselves. In writing about the uncertainties of "poethood," the mystery of nature, and the (tentative) faith she had in the world, Dickinson enacted these same fears and desires. The secret of the code she wrote in, then, became the mysteries of writing and living themselves. Rather than pointing outward towards some definitive answer or truth, her poems pointed inward towards more questions.

Source: Chris Semansky, in an essay for *Poetry for Students,* Gale, 1998.

Donald E. Thackrey

In the following excerpt, Thackrey considers that, for Emily Dickinson, the writing of poetry was a mystical experience.

From what origin or impulse in the poet does poetry come? An answer to this question necessitates a brief glance at the poet herself. To any reader of her poems or letters, the emotional resources of Emily Dickinson seem boundless. She exhibits the capacity to experience the fullness and variety of an emotional life which the great mystics testify exists beyond the horizons of ordinary experience....

In conjunction with a rich emotional nature can usually be found a highly imaginative life. The letters as well as the poems of Emily Dickinson testify to her imaginative powers....

Two salient characteristics of Emily Dickinson's mind as exhibited in her poems and letters seem to be a result of her abundant emotional and imaginative resources. As we might expect, these characteristics display a typical counterbalance in point of view. There is first of all the supremely intense joy of life. The evidence of this ecstatic joy could be accumulated from innumerable poems and letters....

The second and probably more significant direction taken by her intense emotional and imaginative nature is a thorough awareness of the suffering in life. Suffering seemed to be a basic, unavoidable element of human life, and this fact weighed heavily on a person as capable of profound feeling as Emily Dickinson....

Whatever the cause of suffering, the poems of Emily Dickinson give ample evidence that she had a capacity for experiencing suffering far beyond that of the ordinary person....

One can conclude from the evidence in her poems that Emily Dickinson's emotional and imaginative life was developed to an amazing extent. Joyous ecstasy and the antithetic bleak despair— not to mention the other shades of emotional feeling for which she is noted—possessed her life and gave to it a direction which resulted in a dedication to poetry.

The question which was probably unexpressed but was nevertheless an essential one to Emily Dickinson can now be asked. What course of action was necessary for such a person to achieve some sort of realization of her nature? First of all we must note that history has shown that artists act as if they were under a tremendous compulsion to express whatever vision they have seen....

Thus, for Emily Dickinson, poetry was undoubtedly an unavoidable necessity. Still there were certain rational justifications for turning to poetry....

[In his book *Emily Dickinson,*] Richard Chase maintains that Emily Dickinson regarded poetry as "one of the stratagems by which she was empowered to endure life," and this view is supported by ... excerpts from her letters. She strove to raise bloom on the bleakness of her lot, as one of her poems expresses it....

If, however, poetry for Emily Dickinson began as an anodyne for life, it soon developed into some-

> *One can conclude from the evidence in her poems that Emily Dickinson's emotional and imaginative life was developed to an amazing extent."*

thing infinitely more important to her—so important in fact, that after Emily Dickinson's maturity, it would scarcely be possible to separate any aspect of her life and personality from her poetry. Poetry became the meaning, the very essence, of life.

Several of her poems speak specifically of poetry. The opening poem in Madame Bianchi's volume is a significant comment.

This is my letter to the world,
That never wrote to me,—
The simple news that Nature told,
With tender majesty.

Her message is committed
To hands I cannot see;
For love of her, sweet countrymen,
Judge tenderly of me!

Nature's simple news, of course, inspired more than just her so-called nature poems. All her poetry was dependent upon the secrets she thought of as coming from nature. But what, exactly, is poetry?...

Emily Dickinson is consistent in regarding the poet as a divine magician, dealing with familiar things, but transforming them into piercing, ravishing "pictures" that so overpower the human imagination that they can only be described in terms of "thunder," "immense attars," and "divine insanity." Words, the mighty, electric elements of poetry, fuse into the incandescent instruments of the divine which one experiences as poetry. It is the use of *words* which effects the magical transformation of existence from "ordinary meanings" into "divine intoxication." But notice also the implication that no one may completely experience poetry, for poetry, like love, has for Emily Dickinson the mystical significance of God. We can prove either love or poetry by the effects they have upon us; yet there remains the awareness that the essence of love

or of poetry, their ultimate potentiality, is forever denied us. Thus poetry, for Emily Dickinson, in spite of the almost illimitable power of words, offers a challenge and a medium by which one can attempt to transcend the normal limits of perception (even highly-developed artistic perception) and enter into the transcendent, mystical awareness that is "intimate with madness." The supreme worth of poetry, consequently, is self-evident....

The position of a poet in relation to the reading public is always interesting and especially so in Emily Dickinson's case because of the unusual manner in which her poems were written, stored away, and finally edited and published. It has often been assumed that Emily Dickinson secluded herself from the world and turned to writing poetry because of an unhappy love affair. To assume that frustrated love was the sole genesis of Emily Dickinson's unusual life and work is, I think, to underestimate her. Emily Dickinson herself suggests that her retirement may have been prompted, in part, by a desire to escape the shallow loquaciousness of ordinary social intercourse....

It may be added, from the general tenor of her work, that the seclusion was not only to avoid certain things but also to gain a positive advantage. Her withdrawal from the world brings to mind again her ever-present tendency toward a mystical view of life. It is well known that mystics are eager to sacrifice their whole lives to a certain object, a certain vision of truth. Such sacrifices are not self-denial in the mystical philosophy, but rather self-fulfillment. Whatever rationale Emily Dickinson conceived for her seclusion, it is certain that this privacy allowed her the time and opportunity to nourish and maintain her poetic genius....

The position of Emily Dickinson as a poet, then, was this: to utilize the tremendous resources of her emotional and imaginative energy to create poetry which in turn provided her with an outlet or an anodyne for this energy which might otherwise have destroyed her sanity. Words, the powerful agents of thought, became the instruments by which she projected herself into first one relationship and then another with the natural world and with that other more elusive world of her mystical intuitions....

Her goal was sometimes obscured, but she nevertheless was determined to approach a complete comprehension of the mysteries of life and death by means of mystical experience recorded and examined through the discipline of the communication of words in the framework of poetic creation. A mystical vision first experienced and then assimilated into her understanding by the expression of it in poetry established the foundation for further exploration of her consciousness which in turn led to new levels of mystical experience. Perhaps her mystical experiences may be thought of as the climb of a giant mountain slope reaching ever upward but interrupted by frequent ledges upon which she paused for orientation, a view of the ground covered, and the gathering of forces for the next ascent. Her ultimate goal will be achieved at death when she becomes the bride of the Father and of the Son and of the Holy Ghost. Until then her position as a poet must reflect the "compound vision" which depends upon the awareness of death.

Source: Donald E. Thackrey, "The Position of the Poet," in *Emily Dickinson's Approach to Poetry,* University of Nebraska Press, 1954, pp. 52–75.

Sources

Ferlazzo, Paul, *Emily Dickinson,* Boston: Twayne, 1976.

Garbowsky, Maryanne M., *The House without the Door: A Study of Emily Dickinson and the Illness of Agoraphobia,* Teaneck, NJ: Farleigh Dickinson University Press, 1989.

Higgins, David, *Portrait of Emily Dickinson: The Poet and Her Prose,* New Brunswick, NJ:, Rutgers University Press, 1967.

Johnson, Thomas H., "The Business of Circumference: Meaning in Poetry," in his *Emily Dickinson: An Interpretive Biography,* Belknap Press of Harvard University Press, 1967, pp. 134-54.

Juhasz, Suzanne, ed., *Feminist Critics Read Emily Dickinson,* Bloomington: Indiana University Press, 1983.

Kher, Inder Nath, "Landscapes of Absence: Mansions of Mirage," and "Self: The Quest for Identity," in his *The Landscape of Absence: Emily Dickinson's Poetry,* Yale University Press, 1974, pp. 47-84.

Kirkby, Joan, *Emily Dickinson,* Women Writers Series, New York: St. Martins, 1991.

Lauter, Paul, ed., *The Heath Anthology of American Literature,* NY: Houghton Mifflin, 1998.

Rich, Adrienne, "Vesuvius at Home: The Power of Emily Dickinson" in *On Lies, Secrets and Silence,* New York: W.W. Norton and Co., Inc., 1979, pp. 157-184.

Sewall, Richard B., ed., *Emily Dickinson, A Collection of Critical Essays,* New York: Prentice-Hall, 1963.

Sherwood, William Robert, *Circumference and Circumstance,* Columbia University Press, 1968, 302 p.

Smith, Robert McClure, *The Seductions of Emily Dickinson,* Tuscaloosa: University of Alabama Press, 1996.

For Further Study

Aiken, Conrad, "Emily Dickinson," in *Emily Dickinson: A Collection of Critical Essays,* edited by Richard Sewall, Prentice Hall, Inc., 1963.
    Provides a critical and biographical overview.

Boruch, Marianne, "Dickinson Descending" in *Poetry's Old Air,* University of Michigan Press, 1995.
    Explores biographical elements and the "cottage industry" of critics still writing about Dickinson's life.

Dobson, Joanne, *Dickinson and the Strategy of Reticence,* Indiana University Press, 1989.
    Views Dickinson's verse from a perspective of contemporary feminist literary theory. Her interpretations of the poems are refreshingly different than any other published, including those in this textbook series.

Toads

Philip Larkin
1955

First published in Philip Larkin's second collection of poetry, *The Less Deceived,* in 1955, "Toads" is one of his more popular poems. It was this second collection which introduced Larkin to poetic recognition at the age of 33. Over the years, this humorous and sardonic look at nine-to-five office life has provided both a window into the author's biography and an anthem for those who share the poem's central question: "Why should I let the toad *work* / Squat on my life?" Like so many in England during the 1950s who found themselves spending a majority of their time sitting in an office at a desk in order just to pay off "a few bills," the speaker of the poem dreams of telling his boss "Stuff your pension!" Featuring Larkin's distinctive mix of "everyday" language crafted into metered verse, many critics and readers perceived the poem as Larkin's stand against office life. Less than ten years later, he returned to the same subject in a follow-up "sister" poem, "Toads Revisited."

Author Biography

Although Philip Larkin only published five slim volumes of poetry during his lifetime, by the time *High Windows* was published in 1974, he was regarded as one of the greatest British postwar poets, commonly known as "England's *other* Poet Laureate." In fact, he was officially offered the position when it became available in 1984, but he politely declined, insisting instead on keeping a more pri-

vate life away from the public eye. Even when his work was most popular, he refused to choose a career exclusively in poetry, working instead as a librarian while also writing novels, criticism, and essays on jazz.

Born August 9, 1922, in Coventry, Warwickshire, England, Philip Arthur Larkin was the second child of Sydney and Eva Larkin. His father being the city treasurer, he grew up in a "quite respectable house" in a middle class neighborhood. His poems reflect a negative view of these early years, which he described as an "opaque childhood" punctuated by "forgotten boredom." An undiagnosed near-sightedness, combined with a speech stammer, caused Larkin to withdraw from other children, learning instead to dislike them outright. After years of considering himself an "unsuccessful schoolboy," he began feeling more comfortable during his final terms at the King Henry VIII high school, where he learned to balance his love for cricket, football, jazz music, and reading in his father's extensive library. It was during these late teen years when Larkin began writing prose and poetry, inspired by the lush novels of Henry James, whom many critics consider his biggest writing influence. He continued to write at Oxford in 1940, where he enrolled in St. John's College and, later that year, published his first poem, "Ultimatum," in the school literary magazine *The Listener.*

World War II required many college students to join the British military, but due to his poor eyesight, Larkin was free to finish up his schooling in English language and literature. Acquiring a deep love for W. H. Auden's and W. B. Yeat's poetry, he remained at the university until 1943, when he received a First Class bachelor's degree. Larkin received his master's degree from Oxford in 1947. Larkin decided not to pursue a teaching career due to his stammer, which persisted late into his life. Instead, he chose to work as a librarian at the Wellington urban district council in Shropshire while completing a professional accreditation in a librarianship correspondence course. In 1946 he was appointed assistant librarian at the University College in Leicester, and shortly after that appointed sublibrarian at Queen's University in Belfast, Northern Ireland. Perhaps faster than expected, Larkin was settling into his lifetime career; in 1955 he became librarian of Brynmor Jones Library of the University of Hull in Yorkshire, where he worked until his death in 1985.

The drudgery of work became a common theme throughout Larkin's work, most notably in the two half-serious poems "Toads" and "Toads

A drawing of Philip Larkin

Revisited." "Why should I let the toad *work* / Squat on my life? / Can't I use my wit as a pitchfork / And drive the brute off?" the speaker of "Toads" asks. As a younger poet Larkin told an interviewer for the *Guardian,* "Work encroaches like a weed over the whole of my life … It's all the time absorbing creative energy that might have gone into poetry." But an older Larkin learned to balance work with his creative vocation. As the speaker of "Toads Revisited" writes, "No, give me my in-tray, / My loaf-haired secretary / … Give me your arm, old toad; / Help me down Cemetery Road." It was while working at the public library in Shropshire that Larkin wrote his first two novels, *Jill* (1945) and *A Girl in Winter* (1947). Stories of "displaced working-class heroines," they reflect a cheerless and gloomy postwar England. Both novels were critically praised for their carefully textured landscapes, and *A Girl in Winter* was so well received that Larkin's publisher pressured him for a third book of prose, though by this point his energies were shifting back toward poetry.

Although Larkin's first collection of poetry, *The North Ship,* was published before his two novels, it was not until Marvell Press published *The Less Deceived* in 1955 that he began to gain a reputation as a poet. His inclusion in the influential anthology *New Lines,* in which editor Robert Conquest first dubbed Larkin a member of "The Movement," further reinforced his place in modern British literature. Larkin's work appeared regularly in such notable journals as *Atlantic Monthly* and *The Partisan Review*. These poems were later collected in the book *The Whitsun Weddings* in 1964. It was another ten years, in 1974, before *High Windows* appeared as his final collection of poetry.

Publishers Faber and Faber celebrated Larkin's 1982 birthday with the publication of *Larkin at Sixty,* which was a collection of tributes from friends and colleagues. By this point in his life Larkin had earned an international reputation as, in the words of Alan Brownjohn, "the most technically brilliant and resonately beautiful, profoundly disturbing yet appealing" poet to be writing in the second half of this century. He received many honors, including several doctorates, appointments to the National Manuscript Collection of the Contemporary Writers Committee and the literature panel of the Arts Council for Great Britain, as well as such literature awards as the Queen's gold medal for Poetry in 1965 and the Lioness Award for Poetry in 1974. In addition, Larkin was made a Companion of Honour in the Queen's Birthday Honours List. A man who saw life "more as an affair diversified by company than as an affair of company diversified by solitude," Larkin died shortly after an operation for throat cancer in 1985.

Poem Text

Why should I let the toad *work*
   Squat on my life?
Can't I use my wit as a pitchfork
   And drive the brute off?

Six days of the week it soils   5
   With its sickening poison—
Just for paying a few bills!
   That's out of proportion.

Lots of folk live on their wits:
   Lecturers, lispers,   10
Losels, loblolly-men, louts—
   They don't end as paupers;

Lots of folk live up lanes
   With fires in a bucket,
Eat windfalls and tinned sardines—   15
   They seem to like it.

Their nippers have got bare feet,
   Their unspeakable wives
Are skinny as whippets—and yet
   No one actually starves.   20

Ah, were I courageous enough
   To shout *Stuff your pension!*

But I know, all too well, that's the stuff
   That dreams are made on:

For something sufficiently toad-like   25
   Squats in me, too;
Its hunkers are heavy as hard luck,
   And cold as snow,

And will never allow me to blarney
   My way of getting   30
The fame and the girl and the money
   All at one sitting.

I don't say, one bodies the other
   One's spiritual truth;
But I do say it's hard to lose either,   35
   When you have both.

Poem Summary

Lines: 1-4

In this first stanza the speaker introduces the poem's central question: "Why should I let the toad *work* / Squat on my life?" By comparing day-to-day office life to a toad, Larkin depicts the tedium of years sitting behind a desk. Squat, slimy, and fat, the toad seems to sit on the speaker of the poem and leave no room for fun. But Larkin can think of a possible escape—his intelligence. Like a sharp tool, perhaps he can "use [his] wit as a pitchfork / and drive the brute off." Can he utilize his good education and sharp sense of humor in order to find a better way to survive?

By directly comparing work to a toad, Larkin sets up a central *metaphor* which the remainder of the poem will extend and explore. Metaphors enable us to describe otherwise vague or difficult subjects—emotions, attitudes, etc.—in terms readers can "grasp" and understand with their senses.

Lines: 5-8

Continuing the metaphor, the speaker uses the second stanza to elaborate on the questions asked in the first stanza. We learn that work dominates his life six days out of seven each week, month after month, year to year. The proportion seems unreasonable, even dangerous. The toad *work* "soils" the speaker "with its sickening poison," painting a grotesque picture of a man covered in poisonous slime while being crushed by the squatting weight. And what for? the speaker wonders. "Just for paying a few bills!"

Lines: 9-12

In the third stanza, the speaker defends his question by pointing out that many people "live on their wits," as he had initially proposed in the first stanza. But the list Larkin offers us does not catalog the "witty" types we would first expect. Other than lecturers, who support themselves by teaching, the rest of the "folks" living on their wits—"lispers, / Losels, loblolly-men" and "louts"—may have had difficulties finding work. Lispers are those having or affecting the air of sophisticated culture, not persons with a speech impediment. A losel is a literally a "worthless person"; a lout is considered a "clumsy, stupid fellow."

Perhaps a British expression from the 1950s, it is difficult to tell what exactly a "loblolly-man" is, though the term "loblolly" itself refers to a thick, sloppy liquid. From this and the context of the word, readers can assume that is probably not a complimentary title. But no matter what the reason, these folks manage to "live on their wits" without ending up as paupers, or common beggars, as perhaps society expects of those who reject conventional careers.

Perhaps reflecting the whimsical intention of this list, Larkin uses alliteration, or a repeated sound, to craft the third stanza. When we read this list aloud, the repeating "L" sound is almost humorous in its echo, reminding us of the "la la" babble of a losel, loblolly-man or lout.

Lines: 13-16

The speaker provides additional examples of people able to survive on very little in these lines. They do not need much—a fire in a bucket, a tin of sardines, a windfall of luck or money now and then—and they even "seem to like it." Rather than spending six days of the week in an office in order to pay a few bills, these people manage to get by on what little is given to them.

Lines: 17-20

In the fifth stanza the speaker continues to focus his descriptive eye on the people who seem to get by without working. He notices that their nippers (a British slang for young boys) "have got bare feet," perhaps because they are too poor to buy shoes. Similarly, their "unspeakable wives / are skinny as whippets," those terribly-thin racing dogs. Although these families show distinct signs of severe poverty—barefoot children, emaciated parents—the speaker points out that no one actually starves.

Note that in this stanza Larkin has provided gender information for his characters without explicitly referring to their sex. In line eighteen Larkin refers to "their unspeakable wives," imply-

Media Adaptations

- Readings (by The Poets): Philip Larkin; Thom Gunn; Ted Hughes; Seamus Heaney; Douglas Dunn; Tom Paulin; Paul Muldoon. Audio cassette and paperback, 1995.

- Douglass Dunn and Philip Larkin/Book and Cassette (Faber Poetry Cassettes). Faber & Faber, 1984.

ing that the male made the decision on work. Reflecting the "male as breadwinner" attitudes of the 1950s, Larkin crafts his lines perhaps confident his readers would not have to be told which gender he is referring to in his verse.

Lines: 21-24

In these lines, the speaker wishes he could summon up the courage to tell his boss "stuff your pension!" Common to many careers, many companies reward their long-time employees by offering them a pension, or paid compensation, at the time of their retirement. So even if you have to "slave away" your life for twenty years or more, at least when you reach a certain age you can stop working and continue to collect monthly paychecks. Perhaps tired of working with the reward so far in the future, the speaker just wants to say "take this job and shove it." But quickly the speaker's rational side kicks in, reminding him that he knows, "all too well, that's the stuff / That dreams are made on."

Lines: 25-26

Here the speaker turns his attention back on himself and questions if a life without work would really suit him. In these lines we learn the toad work might not be alone sitting on him, "for something sufficiently toad-like / Squats in me, too." Perhaps it is in his nature to work six days a week.

Lines: 27-33

In these lines the speaker wonders if any other way of life is possible for him. Unlike the folks he described in the fourth stanza who are able to survive on windfalls and sardines, Larkin fears this cold weight inside him "will never allow [him] to blarney," or sweet talk, his "way to getting / The fame and the girl and the money / All at one sitting."

It is in these lines the speaker perhaps defines what he thinks are the two possible ways of succeeding in life: either by being a lucky sweet-talker or by working six days a week at the office. Although the latter is like having a toad squatting on you, he knows that he may have to settle for living that way since he has never had the luck or flattering nature to succeed any other way.

Lines: 34-36

This final stanza seems to summarize the debate. The tone of this stanza becomes fairly abstract, never fully answering the question raised in the first stanza. Void of any concrete images we can understand through using our senses, these lines read almost like a philosophical statement. "I don't say, one bodies the other / One's spiritual truth" may mean that the speaker does not intend to make a moral judgment, or that one way of living—by luck or hard work—holds more spiritual significance than the other.

Or maybe the speaker is making a distinction between the "inner" and "outer" toads in his life. It is no surprise that Larkin's critics do not agree on an interpretation for these closing lines. And perhaps Larkin does not intend for us to choose one or the other, but a combination of the two, as the speaker concludes "but I do say it's hard to lose either, / When you have both."

Themes

Search for Self

The two questions that open the poem—"Why should I let the toad *work* / Squat on my life? / Can't I use my wit as a pitchfork / And drive the brute off?"—are both questions of identity. In an attempt to define who he is, the speaker examines his life. He finds that he spends six days a week at the office in order to pay a few bills. Perhaps in 25 years or more he will earn his pension and be able to retire with financial security, a check arriving on schedule as it always has, even though he will not be sitting behind a desk any longer. But the ratio of work versus financial reward does not seem fair. Surely he can find another way, one that provides spiritual fulfillment and a little fun.

Topics for Further Study

- Write a similarly structured poem which begins with the question "Why should I let the toad *school* / Squat on my life?" Using the hymnal measure form Larkin employs, rhyme your quatrains *abab*, keeping your lines under seven words each. Compare results and discuss.

- Imagine you are Philip Larkin having received this poem rejected from a publisher, a terse note attached: "This poem ends in a fog of abstraction. Rewrite the last stanza!" Cover the last four lines with a blank sheet of paper, reread the poem from the top (at least three times), then write your new and improved ending. Compare results and discuss.

- Share this poem with a parent or other adult. Then ask if they too think of work as a toad squatting on their life. Have they ever wanted to shout "stuff your pension?" What is keeping them at their current job? Demand an honest, specific answer, then ask yourself what do you expect out of the career you will eventually choose? Demand the same.

How can he make his life different? Is he "courageous enough / To shout *Stuff your pension!*" to his boss? As the poem nears closure, he begins to wonder if "something sufficiently toad-like" squats in him too, that perhaps what he begins the poem fighting against is really part of his own identity. Although the poem ends without the speaker or reader really finding the answer to these questions, the speaker has learned something about himself.

Duty and Responsibility

Underlying the questions about work in "Toads" is the implicit assumption that the speaker feels a duty and responsibility *to* work. He is expected to be at his desk six out of seven days a week in order to be a productive and valued employee. At the time of the poem's publication, Larkin worked as a librarian at Brynmor Jones Library of the University of Hull in Yorkshire, and stayed at that same job until his death in 1985. He managed a staff of more than a hundred employees. Both students and staff depended on him to organize a wealth of University resources.

This sense of responsibility is so strong for the speaker of "Toads" that even when he considers quitting, another part of himself speaks up, reminding like a parent "But I know, all too well, that's the stuff / That dreams are made on." His dreams, we learn later, also include fame, women, and money, at least two of which we know from Larkin's biography he achieved. If the toad which squats on the speaker is daily grind at the office, then the toad which squats in him might be an inner duty, a self-discipline that keeps him at his desk.

Style

Considered a "traditionalist" poet and a master in his craft, Larkin combines formal poetic structure with colloquial language to create an interesting speaker's voice in "Toads." Using traditional poetic devices borrowed heavily from William Butler Yeats and Thomas Hardy, Larkin contains his humorous and pessimistic voice inside nine quatrains, or four-line stanzas. The stanzas themselves are built on an *abab* rhyme scheme, which means that the first and third lines rhyme *a*, as do the second and fourth lines *b*. This is traditionally known as *hymnal measure*.

Larkin bends his own rules with the use of "slant rhymes," or words which may have matching consonant or vowel sounds, but not both. An example of this is in the first stanza, which rhymes "life" with "off," or the third stanza which matches "lispers" with "paupers." This use of "half" or "slant" rhymes, made famous by Emily Dickinson, help to soften and hide a traditional form so the content of the poem is not overshadowed by its "container."

Historical Context

Although "Toads" reads like a manifesto of a person jailed for years, the poem is actually written by a man taking his first few steps into a lifelong career. In 1954, Larkin had just begun his new position as a librarian at the Brynmor Jones Library of the University of Hull in Yorkshire.

Perhaps aware of the magnitude of this decision when he wrote the poem, Larkin remained at that same job until his death in 1985. He managed a steadily growing staff of librarians until eventually more than a hundred employees worked under him. "Toads" not only reflects Larkin's feelings at that time, but perhaps spoke for a generation finding themselves at the beginning of a long, narrow road.

Unlike the "blue collar" industrial jobs which dominated the workplace toward the beginning of the twentieth century, the 1950s signaled a shift to more "white collar" desk jobs. Society was headed into the "information age." Jobs changed. Instead of manufacturing steel to build railroads or weaving fabric to clothe children, more and more people found themselves formulating reports or routing office memos.

The 1950s was a period of homogenization, a time of conformity over individuality. Symbolizing the time was the charcoal grey suit and narrow dark tie for businessmen who drove into the city by day and returned home to white picket fences and suburbs by night.

Newspapers reported the escalating tensions between Russia and England, France, and America. Cold war paranoia spread worldwide. Citizens were expected to be productive and conformist. The pressure to fit in meant that those who found themselves in the margins—those who did not put on a grey suit and head to the office each day—were often considered to be "losels" and "louts" and were met with suspicion by most citizens.

Robert Lowell, an American poet contemporary to Larkin, described the decade as the "tranquilized fifties," capturing the distilled boredom and routine of the time. As Larkin grumbled about work, across the Atlantic a generation of writers raised their voices against the conservative standards and expectations. In the same year Larkin asks his readers "Why should I let the toad work / Squat on my life? / Can't I use my wit as a pitchfork / And drive the brute off?," Beat poet Allen Ginsberg writes in his poem *America,* "America I've given you all and now I'm nothing / ... When can I go into the supermarket and buy what I need with my good looks?"

Both poets searched for an alternative to the pervasive attitude of the 1950s, and ironically, both come to similar poetic conclusions. Just as Larkin eventually discovers something toad-like squatting inside which keeps him from the lucky life of fame and women, Ginsberg too resigns himself: "Amer-

Compare & Contrast

- **1955:** Beat poet Allen Ginsberg reads his poem "Howl" for the first time to a captivated audience at the Six Gallery in Berkeley. Jack Kerouac passes a jug of wine around. The whole room yells "Go! GO!" after each long line Ginsberg reads. The poem, later published by City Lights Books, becomes the "beatnik bible" for a generation of teens dissatisfied with the establishment.

  1997: Allen Ginsberg dies of natural causes in New York. Having influenced a generation of writers worldwide during his lifetime, obituaries run in literary and counter-culture magazines alike, from the *Paris Review* to *Rolling Stone Magazine.*

- **1955:** IBM introduces its first business computer. The compact mainframe is large enough to fill an entire room.

1998: More than one in four families own personal computers, or PCs. These desk or laptop machines run on microprocessors far more powerful than the first IBMs, yet the chips are smaller than a fingernail.

- **1955:** Both Ann Landers and "Dear Abby" first appear as columnists in syndicated newspapers, answering readers's confidential questions and offering advice.

  1998: There are virtually thousands of columnists, call-in radio shows, and television programs dedicated to answering a public's endless need for advice on day-to-day matters, from choosing clothes to soul mates.

---

ica this is quite serious. / … I'd better get right down to the job."

Critical Overview

While much commentary of "Toads" focuses on the speaker's ambivalent and sardonic tone as he debates the necessity of work, critics do not seem to agree on an interpretation of the speaker's conclusions. Martin Scofield, writing for *The Massachusetts Review* in his essay "The Poetry of Philip Larkin," writes "The last stanza is perhaps equivocal; despite [Larkin's] disclaimer, work does seem to be propping up 'spiritual truth'."

In his *Out of Reach: The Poetry of Philip Larkin,* critic Andrew Swarbrick views the speaker's conclusion as more of attempt to dodge blame for being in the situation he so vehemently gripes about. He writes: "In the poem's conclusion, the speaker tries to argue that his having to settle

for the world of work is not his fault: but almost buried within the poem is a more personally discrediting admission." Perhaps Swarbrick speaks for first-time readers and seasoned critics alike when he complains that "Toads" "ends in a fog of abstraction."

Criticism

Jhan Hochman

Jhan Hochman is a writer and instructor at Portland Community College in Portland, Oregon. In the following essay, Hochman discusses how various aspects of the poem—structure, symbolism, and tone—depict Larkin's inner struggle between responsibility and freedom.

In "Toads" (1955), Philip Larkin depicts what is perhaps one of the more prevalent conflicts between need and desire—the need to work for money and the desire to live by one's wits.

In "Toads," work is embodied as a crouching, noxious toad (whose handling perhaps leads to calluses rather than warts). At least since the Book of Genesis, work has been called toil, and was the punishment for Adam and Eve. "Toads" maintains the Eden myth could do with some revision; Adam and Eve would now be less tempted to eat from the tree of knowledge than from the tree of financial success.

With this updated myth, work as a punishment is more directly reflective of contemporary economic necessity since it is less the desire for knowledge than it is the *need* for money which drives people to work. Larkin, however, is ashamed of the way he lets the toad squat upon his freedom. He uses the poem to work through his self-disgust. Eventually he arrives at an understanding, one that might be called anti-heroic; the toad, while no dragon, is damnably hard to chase away with the pitchfork of wit, and so must be accepted. Philip Larkin is no dragon-slayer.

Neither is he a romantic poet. Larkin, at least in his poems, is less interested in promoting romanticized sentiment than in accepting life as it must be lived. As with other contemporary poets of "The Movement," a group of poets that also included Thom Gunn and Donald Davie, Larkin avoided rhetorical excess and cosmic heaviness, instead mining more mundane existences and conversational language for his poetry.

Larkin's primary model was Thomas Hardy (1840-1928), a poet who goaded readers to realize that love is fleeting and death just around the corner. Larkin, however, appears skeptical that people like Hardy can so easily accept the worst, and so uses his poetry to come to terms with what most think it best or easy to avoid. His attempt to deal with the worst is one reason Larkin said he wrote his poems, the others being that he felt they needed to be written. He criticized W. H. Auden for continuing to write poems; Larkin felt that Auden's need to write had vanished.

Just as Larkin composed "Toads" out of a need to accept or reframe his cowardice before the toad of work, his poem, "At Grass" (1950), is working towards an acceptance of, perhaps even contentment with, the absence of notoriety. And there is also the poem, "Aubade" (1977), an attempt to come to terms with the fear of impending death.

It might be said that "Toads," more than "At Grass" or "Aubade," is more complex since the poet is torn between two alternatives, work and wit. Work is called a toad, a specific metaphor called *theriomorphism,* a figurative transformation whereby concepts or creatures are made into animals. Theriomorphism's more well-known sister-metaphor is *personification,* wherein concepts or creatures become not animals, but persons or person-like, for example, when liberty is called "Lady Liberty," and even becomes a statue greeting ships sailing into New York harbor.

Toads are considered by some the negative flip side of frogs who, with the notable exception of the abnormally large population of frogs sent as a plague by God in Exodus, usually herald desired rain and fertility. The toad is a negative symbol because some varieties of toad secrete a skin-irritating fluid as a defense against being eaten, and also because toads have bumps on their skin wrongly thought to cause warts on the people who handle them.

Larkin's toad is a little different because its major negative trait seems to be squatting, a squatting that weighs the speaker down with hunkers (hips or thighs) heavy as the hard luck and cold snow he fears he will have to withstand if he gives up his job. The fear of the unknown and the security of predictability prevent him from *hopping* with the force of a toad into adventure and risk. Lest we forget, toads hop as well as squat. Larkin's ignoring the fact that toads hop with incredible strength only goes to show that in order for most metaphors to function (good metaphors, by the way, leap from one concept to another like toads), they must focus on similarities and ignore a great deal of difference.

Toads, weighed down with the Larkin-imposed trait of being unwilling to jump, are counterposed to wit, blarney, and courage, i.e., the courage to wing it. In spite of Larkin, it might be helpful to think of the wit/soul/mind/spirit complex as a bird. At least since ancient Egypt, the bird has been a symbol of spirit/soul/mind, of activation and aspiration toward higher planes.

But perhaps the opposition between toad and bird can be distilled even further: squatting versus flying and "singing." For example, Larkin wants to flee work, to escape toil by using the gift of wit, of enchanting speech, by using "winged words" as do "lecturers and lispers." Lispers are those having or affecting the air of sophisticated culture, not persons with a speech impediment. Larkin thinks he might also avoid work by employing the wheedling talk of "losels" (scoundrels, con men) and "loblolly men" (boors or clowns), summed up as those with the gift of "blarney." The Blarney Stone is a stone high in the wall of Blarney Castle and said to confer the gift of flattery upon those who can kiss it.

What Do I Read Next?

- Larkin saved over 700 of his personal letters, revealing fascinating biographical information. Anthony Thwaite edited *Selected Letters of Philip Larkin 1940-1985.*

- To get a sense of how Larkin's work relates to a larger poetic context, read Calvin Bedient's *Eight Contemporary Poets: Charles Tomlinson, Donald Davie, R. S. Thomas, Philip Larkin, W. S. Graham.*

- Salem Hassan explores Philip Larkin's role in the British poetic "movement" in his book *Philip Larkin and His Contemporaries: An Air of Authenticity.*

- Another British poet who wrote during the same period as Larkin, and who shared his distaste for public life, is Stevie Smith. Her *Collected Poems* is available from University of Oxford Press.

And if Larkin is not able to wing his way through life by the bird-like lilt of lingual flourish, perhaps he might scavenge like an abandoned dog, or like the desperately poor who Larkin naively thinks—-probably because he has not seen it happen—never starve. But alas, Larkin knows too well he will never be able to take the leap and try to survive either by his mouth, or by a hand-to-mouth existence. His toad is not one who leaps, but lolls. It is not, as he says, that the toad weighs down his bird and keeps it from singing and flying, that the body weighs down the mind ("It is not that the one bodies the other / One's spiritual truth"), but that when you have both a body that needs security and a mind that needs freedom, it is difficult to disregard ("lose") either. Larkin's conclusion is neither a reconciliation between body and mind, nor a decision to give up his fantasy of wit for mere toadish reality. Larkin is instead ambivalent; he must live with—must accept—the opposition between his ineradicable need to squat and his desire to fly, sing, or live by his wits.

Larkin's uncomfortable dilemma of work versus "freedom" is thus maintained, not conveniently ignored. As if to mimic the ongoing battle between the need to work and the need to live with no obligations, the form of "Toads" exhibits repeated oppositions: the rhyme scheme, *abab,* is grounded in what is called "half-rhyme," where, for example the final consonant "k" sound of "work" is forced to rhyme with "pitchfork" and the final consonant "f" sound of "life" with "off" in the first quatrain. Full rhyme might lessen the impact of the poem, would blend different sounds into a reconciliation at odds with a content focused on conflict. Even the number of lines and stanzas are divisible by two with opposing indentations in each stanza. No final stanza of say, three lines can reconcile Larkin's opposition between the need to work and the desire to flee it. Furthermore, each stanza follows a beat pattern of *3232,* that is, a first and third line of trimeter and second and fourth line of dimeter. Opposition is built into the very warp and weft of "Toads."

Contrast "Toads" with Larkin's "Toads Revisited" (1962). The latter poem is not only a revisitation, but a revision of Larkin's perception of work. In "Toads Revisited," work is accepted as the better alternative to the hard lives of the aged, the mentally unstable, and the homeless poor Larkin sees in the park. He no longer feels the temptation to stop working and has realized that work is better than destitution.

And the poem's form largely reflects his revised sentiment: no pattern of opposing line indentations; nine stanzas instead of eight, the ninth as a resolution; lines almost exclusively of trimeter, the number three being a number not of opposition but resolution; a rhyme scheme of *aabb* instead of *abab* (though still employing slant rhyme, perhaps a minor weakness); and finally the last two lines of full rhyme, virtually a blended couplet that speaks to Larkin's perhaps grudging acceptance of the toad, work.

By the end of reading both "Toads" and "Toads Revisited," there is no blinding insight; instead there is an unsolvable conflict ("Toads") and then resignation to the way things are ("Toads Revisited"). Larkin slays no dragons, cannot even chase away a toad. But then it takes a certain kind of un-toadlike creature to convert toadlike conflictedness and resignation into the decisive and winged words of poetry.

Source: Jhan Hochman, in an essay for *Poetry for Students,* Gale, 1998.

Bruce Meyer

Bruce Meyer is the director of the creative writing program at the University of Toronto. He has taught at several Canadian universitites and is the author of three collections of poetry. In the following essay, Meyer explores Larkin's ruminations concerning life and work in his poem "Toads."

When asked by Robert Phillips of *The Paris Review* how he arrived at the idea of "toads" as an image for working and the relationship between the individual and his daily job, Philip Larkin responded "Sheer genius." As critics such as Andrew Motion, in his essay "Philip Larkin and Symbolism," have suggested "Toads" is one of the poet's most curious pieces, "tak[ing] the form of a debate between two sides of his [Larkin's] personality— with the rebellious, freebooting, anti-authoritarian aspect having the first say." On one hand, the persona of "Toads" feels secure in his working life, yet on the other hand he sees the possibilities of freedom in those who have shed the cloak of responsibility and respectability. As Larkin's close friend, the poet and critic John Wain pointed out in *Professing Poetry,* "Ordinary life, Toad-land, is a touching dream. And also a dazzling vision. And intensely sad. And an empyrean where stones shine like gold above each sodden grave. This is the Larkinian imperative, the point at which his poetry assumes its authority and speaks out. Into this dailiest of daily lives comes the priest and the doctor, running, in their long coats; into this most prosaic of prose chronicles come the limbs crying for stillness ..." Philip Larkin's poetry is that of the common man in search of the balance that will make life livable and acceptable. Larkin concerns himself with the dichotomies that face the individual, in this case the choice between freedom and responsibility. The tough answer that he finds in "Toads" is the painful realization that he has chosen one way of life at the cost of the other and that existence is sadder because he can acknowledge and even understand what it would be like to be different. Larkin commented in *The Listener* in 1972 that "What I should like to do is write different kinds of poems that might be by different people. Someone said once that the great thing is not to be different from other people, but to be different from yourself." For Larkin, the great observer of common life, the sadness lies imbedded in this realization. He is not a poet of dreams, but of realities and the way one confronts and lives up to those impositions of life that represent not the possible but the actual.

Philip Larkin's poem, "Toads" (composed in 1953 and published in *The Less Deceived,* 1955) is about the relationship between the working man and his job. From Larkin's perspective, a job is something one must do "six days a week" to the point that "it soils / with sickening poison." What, he asks, is the price of work? He considers the alternatives to work—unemployment and even vagrancy—and weighs the benefits of "folk" who "live up lanes / With fires in a bucket, / Eat windfalls and tinned sardines." Those who turn their backs upon the daily drudgery of a regular job and the way that a job wears one down are compared to "toads." They bear an unseemliness, like their namesakes, and although they may fascinate the observer and even entice him to imagine himself as a work-free individual, they are, after all, slightly repulsive. This is something that the poet finds hard to understand because that very repulsiveness is part of his own personal make-up—the desire to find an alternative way to spend one's life. After all, Larkin remarks, life as a jobless and homeless vagrant might not be so bad: "Lots of people live on their wits," he notes, comparing the "toad" people to "Lecturers, lispers, / Losels, lobolly-men, louts," and suggesting that "No one actually starves." That toad-like quality, the desire to shuffle off the demands of respectability and professional dedication is something that "Squats in me, too." For Larkin, the spirit of uselessness is something he must accommodate in his being, a dilemma that he faced as he began his career as a noted librarian at the University of Hull. It is the realization of "the toad work," the concept of an alternative existence in a virtual "Land of Cockaigne," being part of his nature that he struggles to resolve in the poem "Toads."

Peter Breughel the Elder produced a fascinating painting titled *The Land of Cockaigne* in which a group of Renaissance period peasants laze about in a field, their stomachs full, on a warm summer day. This notion of dispensing with the pressures and obligations of daily responsibility in favor of an existence in which sustenance is provided almost by default rather than pursuit is an age-old concept. In nineteenth-century poetry, the concept of "vagabondia" as developed by American poet Richard Hovey and Canadian poet Bliss Carman in a series of poetry volumes, is viewed as an almost Utopian offshoot of the Wordsworthian Romantic ideal of man living in harmony with Nature. In the code of "vagabondia," Nature provides miraculously for those who choose to pursue freedom rather than position, and the carefree vagabond is

> *A subtheme that runs throughout Larkin's entire oeuvre is the bitter realization that the gap between poetry and reality dictates that the poet redefine his position in the contemporary world ...."*

happy just to walk the world, unbridled from obligation and responsibility. This concept of "vagabondia" had a number of key offshoots that, in terms of literary development, have led in different directions. In one manifestation, the vagabonds of Carman and Hovey's nineteenth-century happy wanderings have manifested themselves as Samuel Beckett's clown-like tramps of the Theatre of the Absurd in *Waiting for Godot.* But the thread from which Larkin takes his cue in "Toads" comes down to him via the poetry of W. H. Davies, Robert Frost, and Edward Thomas.

W. H. Davies, a popular Georgian poet of the early twentieth century, wrote a number of well-received books which evolved the vagabond figure into the British idea of "the tramp" (a major influence on the comedy of Charlie Chaplin). Davies's most significant work, *Autobiography of a Supertramp* (1908), came from his experiences a vagabond in North America following his introduction to the poetry of Carman and Hovey. Aside from the influence of Davies, Larkin was also a great admirer of the poetry of Edward Thomas who (when teamed in writing relationship with American poet Robert Frost who had met Hovey at Dartmouth College) further evolved the concept of the "free life" as a literary motif in twentieth-century English poetry.

Unlike his "vagabondia" predecessors, however, Larkin's ideal is not rooted in freedom but in necessity. Larkin realizes that freedom is a literary illusion, and a rather weak one at that. He acknowledges actuality with a constancy that sets him apart among twentieth-century poets; yet there is a playfulness in Larkin's choice of structure for "Toads." He applies his observations and consid-

erations in an *abab* rhymed stanza which, for all the prosaic tone and cadence of the lines, is actually a song stanza in much the same way that previous "vagabondia" lyrics used the element of song to celebrate freedom. Larkin turns the stanza structure on its head, almost in a gesture of black comedy, to effect an additional layer of irony (which in this case lies at the core of the poem's essential dichotomy) to his conclusion that he has "both" worlds within his own. Andrew Motion suggests that this "conclusion in the final stanza is disarmingly compacted." Motion continues that the poem's statement, by the final stanza should "be obvious: that working and not working complement each other. The compression itself forms a crucial part of the poem's meaning. It conveys a sense of being trapped in an argument, and of a deliberate, difficult effort at self-persuasion."

What is intriguing, biographically, about "Toads" is that it was written so early in Larkin's own professional life, at the outset of his long and distinguished career as librarian at the University of Hull's Brynmor Jones Library. In a letter to Robert Conquest written on April 14, 1955, about the time Larkin's *The Less Deceived* went to press, Larkin commented that "Hull has me shagged out at the moment, partly through work," and quoted "Toads" almost as an emblem or motto for his existence at that time: "('six days of the week it soils' etc.) and partly through living in an awful hostel where I can get no peace. But that will soon be altered, whether for better or not I can't say yet. In the meantime, poetry is impossible." This last statement suggests that Larkin may have felt a connection between the "work" in "Toads" and the process of poetic composition, or the painful experience of not being able to write. For poets, this is the worst kind of experience. The debate, it can be argued, at least on a compositional level, is not between daily work and freedom, but between life and the desire to write. The playful pursuit of song through the ironic misuse of the song stanza for humorous purposes contains a rather bleak message of the relationship between the poet and his world. A subtheme that runs throughout Larkin's entire oeuvre is the bitter realization that the gap between poetry and reality dictates that the poet redefine his position in the contemporary world—a belief that was held not only by Larkin but by his compatriots of the period. In the introduction to the anthology *New Lines* (1956), the poets who became known as The Movement—Larkin, Kingsley Amis, Robert Conquest, and John Wain—suggested that the role of poetry was not to pursue typically "poetic" ideals but to articulate a vision that was "anti-phony, anti-wet." In other words, Larkin and others held the belief that poetry should turn away from "petered out sentimentalism" and "combat" the trend toward poetry as a vehicle for the poetic ideal and opt for a "reverence for the real person or event." Larkin continued to assert this belief throughout his poetic career and commented to *The Times* in February of 1974 that he wanted his readers to come away from the poem not with "the poem, but the experience; I want them to live something through the poem, without necessarily being conscious of the poem as a poem."

In a voice typical of The Movement poets, Larkin draws a clear line in "Toads" between daily reality and the way literature makes us think the world should be. The sixth-stanza lament, "Ah, were I courageous enough / To shout *Stuff your pension!* / But I know, all too well, that's the stuff / That dreams are made on" echoes Prospero's lines that close the comic masque betrothal revels of Ferdinand and Miranda in Act IV, Scene i of Shakespeare's *The Tempest*. Like Prospero in that famous speech on the nature of illusion, Larkin seems to be implying that the illusion of freedom that the persona sees in the world of the jobless is actually a "baseless fabric of this vision" where all "shall dissolve, / And like this insubstantial pageant faded, / Leave not a rack behind." Such is the message of many of Larkin's finest poems: "Aubade," "The Whitsun Weddings," and the sequel poem to "Toads" from his next volume, *The Whitsun Weddings,* "Toads Revisited." For Larkin, however, the fleetingness of life is nothing to sentimentalize; yet the sadness of the "insubstantial pageant" remains to haunt his work.

In "Toads Revisited" Larkin considers those who have dodged "the toad work" as "being stupid or weak" while at the same time imagining himself in their place. He opts for his "in-tray," his "loaf-haired secretary," and his menial power to keep a caller waiting on the phone. In the end, however, Larkin surmises that both lives, the life of the free vagabonds and those who pursue "toad work," lead to the same conclusion: "Help me down Cemetery Road." In an almost elegiac note reminiscent of Thomas Gray in "An Elegy in a Country Church-yard," the paths of glory, drudgery, or simple indifference to the responsibilities of life "lead but to the grave." What is key in all this, perhaps the saving grace of a rather bleak vision, is that Larkin teaches us to be able to imagine something different for ourselves; for a moment we learn how we can transport ourselves into another reality if only to realize the certainty and fixity of our own conditions. The end result of "such stuff as dreams are made on" is the power not to see ourselves differently, but as ourselves. After all, the hardest thing to imagine is oneself and the purpose of "Toads" and its successor poem is to lead the reader through the harsh and ironic dilemma of otherness to the clarity of self-realization.

Source: Bruce Meyer, in an essay for *Poetry for Students,* Gale, 1998.

Sources

Brownjohn, Alan, *Philip Larkin,* Longman Group, 1975.

Larkin, Philip, *Collected Poems,* Farrar, Straus, and Giroux, 1989.

Motion, Andrew, *Philip Larkin,* Methuen, 1982.

Rossen, Janice, *Philip Larkin: His Life's Work,* University of Iowa Press, 1989.

Scofield, Martin, "The Poetry of Philip Larkin" in *The Massachusetts Review,* Summer, 1976.

Swarbrick, Andrew, *Out of Reach: The Poetry of Philip Larkin,* Macmillan, 1995.

Timms, David, *Philip Larkin,* Oliver and Boyd, 1973.

For Further Study

Latre, Guido, *Locking Earth to the Sky: A Structuralist Approach to Philip Larkin's Poetry,* Peter Lang Publishing, 1995.

    Exploring Larkin's use of traditional form, Latre discovers many fascinating relationships between his tight poetic structure and everyday language.

Motion, Andrew, *Philip Larkin: A Writer's Life,* Farrar Straus & Giroux, 1993.

    Motion draws from Larkin's entire archive of work to make both literary and psychological conclusions regarding the "cranky" and "overwhelmingly humorous" poet.

The Tropics in New York

Claude McKay

1922

Claude McKay was a major figure in the Harlem Renaissance, a time of unprecedented artistic achievement from African Americans during the 1920s and early 1930s. McKay grew up in Jamaica, which influenced much of his work. Both in his poetry and fiction writing, McKay frequently profiled the life of the common people, whose vitality and spontaneity he contrasted with a restrictive and inhuman social order. In "The Tropics in New York," published in *Harlem Shadows: The Poems of Claude McKay* (1922), McKay portrays the speaker as a prisoner in a foreign country, expressing a lyrical nostalgia for his homeland.

Author Biography

Born in 1899 in the hills of Jamaica, McKay was the son of peasant farmers. His parents' sense of racial pride greatly affected the young McKay. When he was growing up, his father would share folktales about Africa as well as stories about McKay's African grandfather's enslavement. Educated by his brother, a schoolteacher and avowed agnostic, McKay was imbued with freethinking ideas and philosophies. Walter Jekyll, an English linguist and specialist in Jamaican folklore, played an equally important role in the education of McKay, introducing him to works by such British masters as John Milton, Alexander Pope, and Percy Bysshe Shelley and encouraging him to experiment with verse in his native Jamaican dialect. Moving to Jamaica's capital when he was nineteen, McKay

was exposed to extensive and brutal racism, the likes of which he had not experienced before in his predominantly black native town of Sunny Ville. The caste society of principally white Kingston, which placed blacks below whites and mulattoes, revealed to McKay the alienating and degrading aspects of racism. The overt racism in Kingston soon led McKay to sympathize strongly with the plight of blacks, who, he saw to his alarm, there lived under the near-total control of whites.

In 1912, with Jekyll's assistance, McKay published his first volumes of poetry, *Songs of Jamaica* and *Constab Ballads.* Later in the same year, McKay became the first black awarded the medal of the Institute of Arts and Sciences in Jamaica for his poetry, and he used the money from this award to travel to the United States to study agriculture. He attended Tuskegee Institute in Alabama and Kansas State College before he decided to quit his studies in 1914 and move to New York City. By 1917 McKay established literary and political ties with left-wing thinkers in Greenwich Village, and during this time he published his most famous poem, "If We Must Die." In 1923 McKay left America for twelve years, traveling first to Moscow, where he was extolled as a great American poet. He grew disillusioned with the Communist Party when it became apparent that he would have to subjugate his art to political propaganda, and by 1923 he left for Paris. Later, he journeyed to the south of France, Germany, North Africa, and Spain, concentrating on writing fiction. Once back in New York he wrote his autobiography, an attempt to bolster his financial and literary status. He developed his interest in Roman Catholicism and became active in Harlem's Friendship House, a Catholic community center. By the mid-1940s his health began to deteriorate. On May 22, 1948, McKay died of heart failure in Chicago.

Claude McKay

Poem Text

Bananas ripe and green, and ginger-root,
   Cocoa in pods and alligator pears,
And tangerines and mangoes and grape fruit,
   Fit for the highest prize at parish fairs,

Set in the window, bringing memories   5
   Of fruit-trees laden by low-singing rills,
And dewy dawns, and mystical blue skies
   In benediction over nun-like hills.

My eyes grew dim, and I could no more gaze;
   A wave of longing through my body swept,   10
And, hungry for the old, familiar ways,
   I turned aside and bowed my head and wept.

Poem Summary

Lines 1-4:

The first stanza is filled with the names of luscious, exotic fruit from a land other than America. It ends with a festive outdoor activity, a parish fair, which would have been a social event that gathered together a dispersed agricultural community. It is the sort of event that a stranger in a strange land would remember longingly.

Lines 5-8:

The speaker mentions a window, which serves a dual purpose: fruits bought at a market in the city would be put on a window sill to ripen, but the window is also a vehicle for the speaker's memory to be cast outside, leading into this stanza's memories of the tropical landscape.

Lines 9-12:

The warm nostalgia the speaker related toward his homeland in the first two stanzas now makes him sad in his longing for it. Not being able to live there, he feels helpless and alienated in his new surroundings. The hunger in line 11 ties the end of the poem to the luscious fruits at the beginning.

Topics for Further Study

- Write a poem about something you see in your ordinary life that reminds you of "the old familiar ways," which could include the time before you were born. Make the details vivid, appealing to the five senses.

- Do you think that this speaker is usually nostalgic for the old ways, or is this a mood that comes up once in a while? Explain your answer.

Themes

Culture Clash

The title of this poem is a contradiction, a clash of landscapes. New York City in the 1920s thrived with diverse immigrant cultures all living within a few city blocks of each other. Just as diverse were the fruits, vegetables, and other foods sold on the street or from merchant's carts. The narrator of the poem arranges an exotic grocery list on his windowsill for us to view: "Coco pods and alligator pears, / tangerines and mangoes and grape fruit." Almost all of these foods are not native to our American culture, and in the second stanza the speaker reveals neither is he.

Although McKay does not describe the urban New York landscape in detail, we can imagine the harsh contrast of what the speaker sees looking through his downtown apartment window and what the exotic fruit reminds him of: "trees laden by low-singing rills, / And dewy dawns, and mystical blue skies." The Jamaican-born speaker finds himself in a new landscape but recalls old memories triggered by the discovery of this exotic fruit on his windowsill.

Reminiscence and Memory

The odd contrast between the exotic fruit set against the New York urban landscape inspires the speaker to reminisce and long for his homeland. After he surveys the tropical arrangement of fruits set in his windowsill, the speaker looks out the window into what should be downtown New York, but instead sees scenes from his childhood in Jamaica. Through this window into the past he sees "fruit trees laden by low-singing rills, / And dewy dawns."

Memory can be triggered by many things: an aunt's perfume, the sound of popcorn on the stove, a faded picture from your sixth birthday party. The speaker of McKay's poem fills his apartment with fragrant ginger and bright green bananas, sweet mangos, and tart pink grapefruit inside thick rinds. He fills his senses with the tropics, "bringing memories / of ... mystical blue skies / In benediction over nun-like hills." By the end of the second stanza the speaker is overcome with the weight of his emotions, and his memories flood him with longing.

Alienation and Loneliness

A stranger in a strange landscape, the speaker first finds comfort in the familiar fruits he has placed on his windowsill to ripen, but soon he is overcome by the memories they evoke, as well as feelings of alienation and loneliness. Like the alligator pear strangely out of place against a backdrop of brownstone apartments, taxis, and fire escapes, the speaker is alien to his environment. "A wave of longing through [his] body swept, / And hungry for the old, familiar ways, / [He] turned aside and bowed my head and wept." McKay describes his longing as a hunger, connecting the theme of loneliness to the exotic foods that first triggered the powerful childhood memories.

Style

"The Tropics in New York" is structured in three stanzas; each stanza is a quatrain—that is, it consists of four lines. The rhyme scheme of each quatrain is *abab*. The rhythm of each line is iambic pentameter. Iambic refers to the fact that each line is made up of pairs of syllables, the first unstressed and the second stressed. Pentameter means that there are five of these pairs per line ("penta" is the Greek word for five), meaning that there are ten syllables per line. Iambic pentameter is one of the most common rhythms used in poetry, because it follows the natural rising-and-falling pattern of English speech. Taken along with the simple, almost song-like swaying of the *abab* rhyme pattern, we can assume that this is a poem with simple, direct intentions, with no deep mystery for the reader to unravel. In the first stanza, the use of words like "ginger-root," "cocoa in pods," "alligator pears,"

Compare & Contrast

- **1922:** The new Ku Klux Klan gains political power in the United States.

  1979: Still a strong force in the South, Klansmen in Greensboro, N.C., fire on members of the Workers Viewpoint Organization, killing three and wounding twelve.

- **1922:** Following the Russian Revolution, the Soviet Union is created.

  1990: Russian President Gorbachev convinces the congress to surrender power September 5th, ending the Union of Soviet Republics and communist rule.

  1998: Although capitalist democracy has replaced communist rule for more than eight years, polls indicate that almost half of Russian citizens asked feel their quality of living has actually decreased with the advent of democracy and capitalism.

- **1922:** The IRA, or Irish Republican Army, declares its formal constitution. The aim of the organization is to "safeguard the honor and independence of the Irish Republic."

1978: A bomb planted by IRA terrorists on a royal yacht kills Lord Mountbatten, cousin of Elizabeth II. The blast also kills his young grandson and a young friend. Many other British soldiers and politicians are killed within weeks of the bombing in similar ambushes and sniper attacks.

1998: After years of violence, both IRA and British leaders take a significant step toward peace by signing an agreement on April 9th. This agreement will turn direct rule of Northern Ireland back over to Irish officials.

- **1922:** The Federal Reserve Board establishes the first bank-wire system to eliminate physical transfer of funds in order to avoid theft, loss, or destruction of treasury certificates.

  1998: New encryption methods allow secure transfer of funds over the Internet. Families who rarely make cash purchases due to the ease of credit cards now have the option of booking flights, ordering groceries, buying rare books, and even gambling via their home personal computer on the Internet.

---

and "mangoes" conjures up an exotic land, unfamiliar to Americans. The second stanza continues the faraway remembrances that began in the first. The descriptions are of the countryside. The tone of the third stanza changes abruptly from the first and second. Whereas the first two talk about an open, fertile countryside, the third stanza draws back to the internal struggle of the speaker, an isolated individual far away from home.

Historical Context

During the Summer of 1919, only a few years before the publication of "Tropics in New York," there were violent race riots in Chicago. These riots inspired McKay's poetic anthem *If We Must*

Die, a piece that spoke powerfully to the atmosphere of oppression and race-fueled murder. Many critics cite his poems of social protest and racial injustice as what best characterize his writing as a whole. McKay mostly rejected any ties between his race and possible interpretations of his work.

As a Jamaican native living in New York, McKay was among more than one million new immigrants to enter the United States in the early 1920s. America during that time was fiercely segregated. "White only" sports teams, restaurants, theaters, and water fountains were a part of the American landscape. Eighty-five percent of all blacks lived in the South, and 23 percent of those families were illiterate. In New York, the artistic and social scene flourished, where the Harlem Renaissance was also at its height.

But even McKay, the man some consider the father of this artistic and intellectual black movement of the postwar 1920s, could not avoid the prejudice that pervaded every aspect of day-to-day living. Invited to write a theater review of Leonid Andreyev's *He Who Gets Slapped,* McKay was questioned by management when he tried to take his assigned seat in the front row—the row reserved for whites only.

This type of hypocritical treatment forced many to question the democratic system, intrigued instead by the promise of a truly equal society as described by the Marxists. Claude McKay grew more and more interested in socialism, hanging out with "left-wing" society types like Frank Harris, editor of *Pearson's Magazine.*

In the 1922, the same year he published his first acclaimed work *Harlem Shadows,* the Union of Soviet Socialist Republics (USSR) was established. McKay was so impressed with the social and political change in Russia he traveled there. Over the course of the rest of his life he lived in and out of the country for more than twelve years.

The 1920s was a time of literary revolution worldwide. During the same year Claude McKay published *Harlem Shadows* while living in urban New York, England's T. S. Eliot and Ireland's James Joyce published their own hallmark pieces. Each work, Eliot's *The Wasteland* and Joyce's *Ulysses,* drew immediate attention for their innovative forms and voices, just as *Harlem Shadows* had crafted immigrant voices into verses.

Critical Overview

In *The Nation,* Walter F. White wrote of *Harlem Shadows,* which includes "The Tropics in New York," that "[McKay's] work proves him to be a craftsman with keen perception of emotions ... and an adept in the handling of his phrases to give the subtle variations of thought he seeks." Jean Wagner also commented positively about *Harlem Shadows* in *Black Poets of the United States: From Paul Laurence Dunbar to Langston Hughes,* saying "The languorous sweetness of [the nature poems] is like a cool breeze from the Isles, introducing a note of most welcome tranquillity into the militant fierceness of the poems of rebellion." "The Tropics in New York" is about a man who feels imprisoned in America because he cannot return to his native country. Geta J. LeSeur, in *CLA Journal,* writes that McKay in "The Tropics in New

York" "speaks for the hundreds of West Indians who became exiles away from their homeland primarily because of economic and diplomatic reasons.... The alienation felt is one of time and distance, and the consequence and helplessness is clearly felt in the last three lines. The progression is from glorious song to despair. It is one of his most moving poems on this theme ... "

Criticism

David Kelly

David Kelly is a writer and instructor at Oakton Community College in Des Plaines, Illinois. In the following essay, Kelly discusses how, within this poem of the immigrant experience, McKay uses cinematic techniques that were advanced for his time and raises several racial issues concerning black Americans.

Claude McKay's poem "The Tropics In New York" is probably the most anthologized of all of the author's works, which means that it is the work that the greatest number of readers will think of when McKay's name comes to mind. To some degree, there is a great irony to this, because the poem depicts McKay—who so often played the role of the angry radical—as a vulnerable, lonesome foreigner, not challenged by the racial politics of his new land but reduced to tears by his sense of nostalgia. Some critics would say that this nostalgia is a reason why black Americans have a difficult time formulating a complete cultural identity, and they would encourage poems such as this one that are willing to examine that sense of loss. Other commentators would suggest that this poem plays to old stereotypes developed during slavery—that the author is playing the minstrel show character of the freed slave in the North, longing for the simple days back on the plantation when he wasn't troubled to think independently. The subject matter of the poem, comparing a natural, primitive world to the civilized "urban jungle," is bound to invite speculation about which one McKay thinks is more powerful, which one he deems righteous, as well as the implications of these settings on the role of blacks in America.

Most readers of the poem would not be inclined, on first reading, to see it in terms of racial identity at all. It is about loneliness and memory, experiences that cross all social boundaries. America is a land of immigrants, and immigrants naturally look back longingly to the circumstances of their youth. McKay does, as a matter of fact, capture the feeling that anyone who has moved to a new land is bound to have. He accomplishes this by having the objects that trigger his nostalgia be innocuous objects, more tantalizing to the senses than they are provocative to the intellect. While a Jamaican such as McKay might be transported back in memory by the fruits that grow in Jamaica, a Lithuanian immigrant may relate to the experience because it is the same one he or she gets from barley husks, a Mexican might pine for yucca, a Malian for millet or dates. And seen with the fuzzy lens of nostalgia, every country has dewy dawns and mystical blue skies and nun-like hills (whatever those are). McKay lures out the sentiment buried within immigrants, as well as in people whose families have been here for generations but who have kept their ties to their motherland, by downplaying what America has to offer. How is New York represented in this poem? As a window sill. The window doesn't look out over a new land with gold-paved streets or over a dirty and dangerous ghetto, it looks magically out on Jamaica. Many transplanted persons live this way: in denial of their circumstances, with little sense of "now," but only of "then."

It is interesting that this poem, the nostalgic wail of a speaker "hungry for the old ways," cries out for nature, but it views the world in terms of technology, with an eye that was apparently trained by the cinema. In 1922, the year this poem was first published, movies were (of course) not as sophisticated as they are today. They were filmed in black-and-white, and the only sound they had was that of a live organ playing while the picture ran. Still, they had worked out the visual language of motion pictures to a great degree. One needs only look at such classic silent films as *Nosferatu, Blood and Sand,* and *The Cabinet of Dr. Caligari* to know that McKay would have been familiar with such techniques as the close-up, the fade, and the dissolve. In "The Tropics in New York," he directs the viewer's eye the way that a camera does. The opening "scene," in the first stanza, could be the work of a still camera, but it nonetheless bears the mark of a camera of some sort: what else in human experience could focus one's attention on one set of objects, ignoring the context they are in? What marks this poem as a visual equivalent of motion pictures, though, is the widening angle from the tight shot in the first stanza to the second stanza, which includes the window behind the fruit. The objects do not move, it is the reader's view of them that moves. Between lines 5 and 6 comes an even more specific movie trick, a dissolve as bleary and

wavy as the transition from Kansas to Oz, taking us out of a New York apartment to a lush utopia, springboarding off of the word "memories." The human eye does not fade out and then fade in on a different scene like that: movie footage does.

So the poem conveys a longing for the old, natural home of fruit trees and blue skies, but it shows its mixed intentions by framing its longing for nature in (what was then) a high-tech way. Unfortunately, this division between forward-looking technology and the simplicity that excludes technology happens to correspond to a long-standing philosophical problem for African Americans, with the love of technology indicating a love of the European culture that created slavery and love of nature indicating a resistance to progress that some feel has held blacks back. Framed as a racial issue, it would appear that there was no way for Claude McKay to crawl away from the culture/primitivism question without looking like a traitor to somebody. Unfortunately, because of who he was and when and where he worked, any poem by Claude McKay is bound to be examined from a racial perspective.

Any basic search for information on McKay is likely to turn up the words "Harlem Renaissance" within the first sentence or two. He was a black man who worked in Harlem during the early 1920s, and so he is grouped into this category by definition. What made McKay stand out from his African-American peers is that he grew up in Jamaica and came to experience America's particular form of racism only later in life, during his two years at Kansas State College, after he had already tasted success as a published poet in his home land. In Harlem he was involved with the Socialist Party as an associate editor of *The Liberator,* a Marxist publication. This sort of radicalism was not at all unusual for that time and place. Edward Margolies's critical study of black authors, *Native Sons,* published in the politically charged climate of 1968, tells us that "McKay's best writings are found in his early Harlem poems, which alternate between a celebration of the Harlem proletariat and a clarion call for racial militancy."

As a native of Jamaica, McKay formed a tight relationship with the countryside; the land and sky that are described in this poem are contrasted with the concrete corridors that define New York City. It is understandable that, when he thought of his own people living their lives freely and productively without the degrading roles society had cast blacks of the 1920s in, he saw them surrounded by nature—at one with the trees and free under the

What Do I Read Next?

- Claude McKay was perhaps better known for his prose than his poetry. For a healthy sampling of both verse and prose spanning his writing career, check out *The Passion of Claude McKay: Selected Poetry and Prose, 1912-1948* (1973).

- Although many critics may say McKay's autobiography is included in his poetry, *Harlem Glory: A Fragment of Aframerican Life* (1988), is one of his self-portraits. A critical look at his fellow African Americans, this book continues to stir emotions and raise questions of the role of ethnicity in writing.

- Two recent books that look at the Harlem Renaissance not only in terms of literature, but art, music, and sculpture as well, are George Hutchinson's *The Harlem Renaissance in Black and White* and Cory Winz's *Black Culture and the Harlem Renaissance*. Both books are also exceptional sources for gaining a better understanding of the cultural context surrounding the black intellectual movement.

open sky. As the world has become more crowded and industrial, with society and its by-products pressing in from every direction, it is quite high praise to consider any one group as being in touch with nature, or connected to the world as it was before civilization arrived to corrupt it. "And yet," Margolies points out, and many critics agree, "at the root of McKay's radicalism is the ancient stereotype of the primitive Negro." Writers of all races have excused the way that blacks locked out social progress by assuming that an extra degree of spirituality in the "primitive" people makes everything equal. Treating blacks as a group with different abilities and different historical needs than whites may be a way of facing reality, but when this idea is misapplied it leads to such weird cultural phenomena as the nightclubs of the celebrated Harlem Renaissance being staffed by black entertainers while the owners and patrons were white, or the professional sports that have mostly minor-

ity players but few nonwhite coaches. A poem such as "The Tropics in New York" can, unfortunately, be read to mean that Negroes were a people of the land, with no competence as leaders of society.

McKay didn't stay in Jamaica, though: he left the tropics for America, showing a personal appreciation for civilization and technology that is not shown in this poem. In his life he was an ambitious man, leaving tiny Jamaica for the big time, New York, confident that he had the talent to make a name for himself. After struggling with American racism for a few years, he left Harlem to spend some of his most productive years traveling to England, France, Germany, Russia, and several African nations, experiencing particular types of racial stereotypes in each one. While it is any person's right to live the way they choose, and to once in a while look back with some sorrow on "the old, familiar ways," black writers have considered it no favor that he indulged in the Western culture that oppressed blacks, and that he struggled so hard to be accepted by it. He disliked and feared many of the blacks he met in Africa and felt more comfortable among whites, even while, as the poem implies, feeling alienated in white American society. As African critic Femi Ojo-Ade put it, for McKay, "America, the civilized, is hard to reach. Africa, the savage, though easily accessible, is repulsive."

As fine as it is that McKay would move to the largest country in the Western Hemisphere and aspire to conquer the social order, there is an undeniable hint of self-loathing detectable when an author leaves his past behind and at the same time writes about the "hunger" he feels for the old ways. If this is a common immigrant experience, then McKay's dilemma was and is repeated thousands of times each day by everyone who is separated from their past. If, as his harshest critics put it, McKay's stance represents an abandonment of blacks, either by playing to the "noble savage" stereotype or by accepting the values of the oppressors, then his perpetually being defined as a Harlem Renaissance author takes on a tone of sad irony.

Source: David Kelly, in an essay for *Poetry for Students,* Gale, 1998.

Chris Semansky

Chris Semansky teaches writing and literature at Portland Community College in Portland, Oregon, and is a frequent contributor of poems and essays to literary journals. In the following essay, Semansky explores how McKay's vivid and evocative imagery functions in "The Tropics in New York."

In the first stanza of his poem, "The Tropics in New York," Claude McKay describes a veritable cornucopia of fruits and plants. After we finish reading this stanza we can almost taste these exotic delicacies, the ripe bananas, the ginger-root, the alligator pears. The words seem to have a power of their own to make our mouths water. This is the power of imagery.

Imagery, when effective, has the ability to make the reader experience the thing or things being described, in this case the tropical fruits of McKay's birthplace, Jamaica. It is not only the naming of the fruit that makes McKay's imagery effective, but the manner in which he does it—by listing the different kinds. A list by its very definition is an accumulation of details and remains a popular poetic device writers use to achieve an almost photographic effect of the things described. In this case, the sense stimulated is not only vision but taste as well, for these are perfect specimens, "fit for the highest prize at parish fairs."

We learn in the second stanza that the delicacies described are not in fact in Jamaica but in New York City, a steamy place in the summer but definitely not the tropics. McKay might be using irony by titling his poem, "The Tropics in New York," then, or he simply might be using "tropics" as a rough synecdoche. A synecdoche is a figure of speech in which a part of something is used to signify the whole.

In this case "tropics" might be (metaphorically) read as tropical fruit, but simultaneously stand in for all of the tropics. However, these tropical treats *do* remind the speaker of his homeland. The sight of them brings memories "of fruit-trees laden by low-singing rills / And dewy dawns, and mystical blue skies / in benediction over nun-like hills." Rills are small brooks or streams that lace Jamaica's countryside, and the hills are nun-like because blue skies are offering a blessing.

This stanza also signals a move from the specific to the general, as the sight of individual pieces of fruit (possibly in a bowl) moves the speakers so that he remembers the conditions that physically enabled their existence (dawn, skies, hills). The reader can also consider the present, in which the speaker initially sees the fruit in the window as the fruit of the past. That is, the speaker's initial experience of his homeland made possible the nostalgia and longing he feels when seeing a bowl of fruit years later.

Nostalgia is a fitting theme for a poet who left his native country as a young man to come to the United States. It is also a subject made popular by English Romantic poets such as William Wordsworth, who wrote many poems mourning the loss of traditions, people, and humanity's relationship to nature. McKay, in "The Tropics in New York," is not merely expressing his yearning for Jamaican fruit. He is showing the reader through his choice of details *what* he misses about his country: its spectacular landscape; its spirituality; its sheer fecundity. McKay could have written a poem about how after stumbling across seashells at a corner store he was suddenly reminded of the Jamaican coast, but writing about such a commonplace item as fruit allowed him to pack more resonance in his images.

We associate ripe fruit, especially tropical fruit, with abundance, with the sheer headiness of being alive and growing. It is exotic and sweet and pleasurable, much like many of our own (good) memories of childhood. Though as readers we are not consciously aware of these associations, they are there nonetheless and affect our reception of the poem.

After two stanzas of description, the narrator discusses its significance. We now understand that we were seeing what the speaker was seeing, that the narrator's "I" was the photographic eye. This stanza, however, contains no description because the speaker's "eyes grew dim." Instead we have a comment on the previous description, which allows us to understand the description's purpose. This stanza *tells* us the meaning of what the first two stanzas *showed* us. The speaker is hungry, not for bananas, cocoa, mangoes, and grapefruit, but "for the old, familiar ways." McKay's use of the word "hungry" to describe his desire is appropriate, given the poem's imagery.

In "Claude McKay's Romanticism," in *CLA Journal*, Geta LeSeur writes that "the progression [from the first two stanzas to the third] is from glorious song to despair. It is one of his most moving poems on this theme." The reader must keep in mind, however, that the despair is also informed by the speaker's implicit recognition of the discrepancy between New York City, one of the largest urban centers in the world, and the pastoral, idyllic setting McKay portrays as his home.

"The Tropics in New York" first appeared in 1920 in *The Liberator,* a radical socialist newspaper. There is nothing, however, explicitly or implicitly radical about the poem. In fact, an argument could be made that the piece is conservative because of the (implicit) desire the speaker expresses to go home again.

Though a communist sympathizer for a good part of his adult life, many of McKay's early poems deal with traditional themes and subject matter. In many ways he was a modern romantic. Like the Romantics, McKay frequently wrote out of personal experience; the "I" in the poem was more often than not McKay. LeSeur observes that "McKay obviously is the speaker in this poem, although he speaks for the hundreds of West Indians who became exiles away from their homeland primarily because of economic and diplomatic reasons. The poem, therefore, does have a oneness of feeling about it. The alienation felt is one of time and distance, and the consequence and helplessness is clearly felt in the last three lines."

Though McKay wrote about his hunger for the old ways of his native land, we can also read this poem as an example, though not the best, of McKay's own theory of poetry. In his theory, he frequently promoted traditional poetic forms. In his introduction to *Harlem Shadows,* his only book of verse, McKay writes that the eighteenth-century Scottish poet, Robert Burns—a traditionalist—was a primary influence on his work. McKay believed that the traditional should "work best on lawless and revolutionary passion and words, so as to give the feeling of the highest degree of spontaneity and freedom."

However, it is hard to see exactly how lawless and revolutionary McKay's own words and passions are in "The Tropics." Written in iambic pentameter and employing an *abab cdcd efef* rhyme scheme, this lyric poem focuses on the lament of one individual, not, as LeSeur suggests, the numerous exiles from the West Indies. A lyric is usually a short poem consisting of the words of a single speaker. Employing the first person "I," the lyric most often revolves around or expresses the feeling or state of mind of the speaker.

Burns's poem, "O my love's like a red, red rose," for example, expresses the speaker's passion for his sweetheart. Lyrics may or may not be written in iambic pentameter. Iambic pentameter means that each of the poem's lines consist of five (penta) feet. Meter is measured in feet, and a foot usually contains a stressed syllable and one or more unstressed syllables. An "iambic" foot, the most common in English poetry, consists of an unstressed syllable followed by a stressed syllable. The first line of "The Tropics,"—"Bananas ripe and green, and ginger-root"—contains ten syllables, alternately unstressed and stressed.

McKay uses a traditional form to write about traditional subjects, loss and nostalgia. It is pre-cisely his use of tradition that critics have applauded, viewing him as a poet whose work embodies universal rather than African American ideals. Perhaps better examples of his theory of how traditional forms can give shape to radical content are his Shakespearean sonnets, "America" and "The White City." Both of these poems criticize America and the cultural oppression of African Americans but they do so in a way that conventional critics appreciate. Said another way, critics have praised McKay because he played by the rules.

Source: Chris Semansky, in an essay for *Poetry for Students,* Gale, 1998.

P. S. Chauhan

In the following excerpt, Chauhan disagrees with those who think McKay's works reflect the consciousness of the Harlem Renaissance, instead pointing out a "colonial sensibility" that stems, he believes, from the poet's Jamaican heritage.

If McKay's conflicting views were an enigma to his friends, the ambiguities of his work are a bafflement to his critics. Naturally, the variant readings of the man and his fiction today constitute the central problem of McKay scholarship. Wayne Cooper, McKay's biographer [who wrote *Claude McKay: Rebel Sojourner in the Harlem Renaissance*], trying to find an acceptable solution, locates the source of all ideological paradoxes in the personal pathology of a personality "characterized always by a deep-seated ambivalence" that was caused mainly by "dependence upon a succession of father figures."

There is another way, however, to explain the presence of incongruous elements in McKay's work. It is more than likely that his work seems paradoxical because it has been read in an inappropriate context. Beginning with James Weldon Johnson's *Black Manhattan* (1930), critics have concluded, certainly to their satisfaction, that McKay was "of the Harlem group," indeed that he was "one of the movement's ornaments" [according to George E. Kent in his article "Patterns of the Harlem Renaissance"]. In the latest study of the Harlem School, *The Harlem Renaissance: Revaluations* (1989), Geta LeSeur affirms that "Claude McKay remains today part of the acknowledged literary triumvirate of the Harlem Renaissance. He shares this prestigious position with Langston Hughes and Jean Toomer." Her view is typical of the current scholarship's understanding of McKay's affiliations.

One fruitful close reading of McKay's work—
a reading heretofore denied him—however, forces
us to the conclusion that to anchor his consciousness in Harlem is to dislocate his true emotional
geography; it is, indeed, to misread the map of his
political awareness. If we would account for all the
elements of his thought, we might have to take
McKay for what he really was in life: a colonial
writer who happened to stop over in Harlem on his
lifelong quest for a spiritual home, on a quest, incidentally, that no colonial writer has ever effectively escaped. His association with Harlem, it can
be affirmed, was no more than what Harlem itself
has been to Afro-American letters: "a moment in
renaissancism" [according to Houston A. Baker, Jr.
in his *Modernism and the Harlem Renaissance*].
Such being the case, by continuing to identify his
work exclusively with Harlem's ethos, we have not
only robbed it of its uniqueness but also denied it
the central place it deserves in the global discourse
of black writers that McKay so ably initiated. Ar-
bitrary points of reference have led us only to
skewed inferences.

Unable, or unwilling, to read McKay as a
writer from Jamaica, then a British colony, and
hence as one with a mind-set entirely different from
that of the Harlemite, many critics have landed
themselves in a puzzle. James Weldon Johnson, a
person whom McKay in the dedicatory note to
Harlem: Negro Metropolis (1940) calls a "friend
and wise counselor," finds McKay's lifelong nostalgia for Jamaica intriguing. "Reading McKay's
poetry of rebellion," says Johnson, "it is difficult
to conceive of him dreaming of his native Jamaica
and singing," Such perplexity results, obviously,
from an ignorance of, or from ignoring, a basic fact
about the colonial sensibility: that it straddles two
worlds—the one of its origin, the other of its adop-
tion. Politically, its values and attitudes derive
from, and swing between, the two sets. It sides, at
once, with each of the two antagonists: the victim
and the victimizer.

That McKay should have been assimilated into
the Harlem Renaissance looks rather natural in retrospect. For one thing, noticed when literary history understood artistic works in terms of schools
or movements, Claude McKay was bound to be
read as part of the Harlem Renaissance, especially
since to be black and to have a powerful literary
voice was considered nothing less than miraculous.... [According to Alain Locke in *The New Negro: An Interpretation,*] his poems truly served as
a clarion call to the New Negro, "the younger gen-

> *Unable, or unwilling,
to read McKay as a writer
from Jamaica, then a
British colony, and hence as
one with a mind-set
entirely different from that
of the Harlemite, many
critics have landed
themselves in a puzzle.*"

eration [that was] vibrant with a new psychology."
But to credit McKay with the boom and bloom of
black art and literature, or with the general growth
of interest in Harlem, is to be guilty of the *post hoc,
ergo propter hoc* fallacy. That the birth of the Renaissance followed McKay's departure from
Harlem need not argue for his paternity of the
movement.

McKay's own comments about the Harlem Renaissance, distant and mocking, would argue
against his incorporation into the movement. Invited by James Weldon Johnson "to return to America to participate in the Negro renaissance movement," McKay found himself loathe to return to
Harlem, for, he explained years later [in his *A Long
Way from Home*], "if I did return I would have to
find a new orientation among the Negro intelli-
gentsia." This is hardly the sentiment of an author
who is said to have been the progenitor of the Renaissance. Even when he did devote a book to the
Negro Metropolis [titled *Harlem: Negro Metropolis*], McKay could not bring himself to say anything
more sympathetic about the Renaissance than the
following:

> New Yorkers had discovered the existence of a fash-
> ionable clique, and an artistic and literary set in
> Harlem. The big racket which crepitated from this
> discovery resulted in an enormously abnormal ad-
> vertisement of bohemian Harlem. And even solid real
> estate values were affected by the fluid idealistic art
> values of Harlem.

The truth is that McKay was even less responsible for the Harlem Renaissance than Pound
had been for the Chicago School of Poetry. He was
for the Harlem Renaissance, but certainly not *of* it.

Yet to stress McKay's colonial heritage is by no means to minimize his value to the movement or the overall worth of his work. To the contrary, his work did, indeed, carve out a path which black writers all over the world, not only the Harlemite, could, if they would, follow. Some of them … dared not follow McKay's lead. But a few others did. Aimé Césaire, according to the interview published in *Discourse on Colonialism* (1955), was inspired by McKay's novel *Banjo* (1930), which for him was "really one of the first works in which an author spoke of the Negro and gave him a certain literary dignity." That McKay's self-assurance, like his passionate devotion to the cause of the black race, did a yeoman's service to the advancement of African American literature is a fact widely, and correctly, accepted.

What is little suspected, however, is the pervasive presence of the colonial sensibility in his work. This essay seeks to identify only a few of the traits distinguishing the colonial strain.…

Linguistically, his work bears the mark all too common to the writing done in colonies. It is pulled by two gravitational forces: the one of his native tongue, the other of the language of the colonizer. In his first book of poems published in the United States, *Harlem Shadows* (1922), McKay confesses to the linguistic tension that had been part of his upbringing. "The speech of my childhood and early youth," he writes, "was the Jamaica dialect … which still preserves a few words of African origin, and which is more diffcult of understanding than the American Negro dialect. But the language we wrote and read in school was England's English." The dual versions of the language, like those of the island culture, internalized during the period of his cognitive development, haunt McKay's work to the very end and affect its tone and texture in various ways.…

The argument of McKay's later poetry, like the diction of his earlier poems, is disposed around two poles: the vernacular and the metropolitan. The progression of his well-known poems readily reveals the bipolar tensions that underlie the conceptual design of his verses. Whether it be "To One Coming North," "North and South," or "The Tropics in New York," the absent landscape of Jamaica is so powerfully present in the poems as to displace the New York scene, the immediate locale and the subject of the poem.…

[F]or a poet grounded in British education and well versed in Milton, Wordsworth, Keats, and Hopkins, it was as natural that he should use the disciplined form of a sonnet as it was that he should possess "the classical feeling" which Frank Harris discovered in his poetry. Just as McKay's cynicism and invective came from his experience as a subaltern in an imperial colony, the sonnet form came from his formal education in the classics of the colonizer.

Even when McKay had managed to slough off the Jamaica dialect, he continued to be possessed by the memories of the Jamaican flora and fauna. It is only by reconginizing McKay's unconscious proclivity towards Jamaican animals that one may explain why his imagery militates against the texture of the traditional narrative. His yarn, spun with the staple of the English idiom, sets up expectations associated with the tenor of the average English novel. But before the reader has a chance to settle down, he is suddenly jolted as tropical imagery leaps at him.…

It seems that McKay's mind, harking back to the tropical landscape of his native island, quietly ushers its beasts into the parlors of Manhattan and the restaurants of Marseilles. Even as the author negotiates the surge and rhythm of the English sentence, his memory drags in the native creatures, populating, in consequence, the metropolitan English narrative with strange birds, beasts, and flowers.

His punctuating the English prose with the bestiary of Jamaica creates resonances that travel beyond the fictional narrative.…

McKay seems … to have picked up bits and pieces of the white colonizer's disdain for the native black community, for it is the Master's stance that comes through in the colonial author's unguarded moments.

One reason why McKay's attitude towards black characters is less than respectful is that, unlike Harlem writers—Jean Toomer, Zora Neale Hurston, and Rudolph Fisher—who went to their folk roots—McKay went for literary inspiration to Anglo-Saxon masters, to Dickens, Shaw, Whitman, and Lawrence. As a person raised in a colony, it was impossible for him totally to divest his mind of the literature and the attitudes of the colonizer and to adopt the literary genealogy of the African-American peers of his generation.

Nothing in McKay's writing so powerfuly registers his ambivalence towards the interest of the Harlem community as his shifting attitude towards the Harlem prostitute. If the narrator of the poem "Harlem Shadows" is the rueful patriarch bemoaning the corruption of the "little dark girls who in slippered feet / Go prowling through the night from street to street," that of the novel *Home to Harlem* gloats in the depredations of Jake and his associates who, like predators, go stalking through the night, always "hungry foh a li'l brown honey." The poem and the novel, read together, suggest an author running with the hare and hunting with the hound....

The only character of McKay's who ever finds a home is Bita (*Banana Bottom,* 1933), but such arrival for a fictional character becomes possible only when the writer's fancy returns to settle in his native land, as, for once, it did. The home for McKay was never Harlem, but Jamaica, where alone his characters could regain their integrity.

It can well be argued that McKay's vacillation between alternating preferences for the native culture and the metropolitan, like his pull between the pastoral and the urban, between an allegiance to Marxism and a desire for free peasantry, can be satisfactorily explained only in terms of the colonial's attachment to the simple rhythms of his native world and to a fascination for the metropolitan systems of the West, whose cruelty and inequity would constantly drive his thoughts back to the security of a remembered community. A creature of colonial experience, McKay was condemned to dwell in the limbo of the imagination of the colonized, unable forever to state a clear-cut preference. That is the primary reason why his work seems so paradoxical, why it bears the print of the journeys between the polarities of a divided mind.

To comprehend him satisfactorily, therefore, one must approach McKay not from one direction alone, but from two. One must read McKay, indeed one must re-read McKay, in a context different from that of the Harlem Renaissance, the context he has long been relegated to. In order to appreciate the nature of his ambiguities, one must recognize the intellectual baggage he brought with him to Harlem—the English attitudes, a European sen-

sibility, and the general impedimenta of a colonial mind, congnitive elements altogether unknown to most Harlemites.

Source: P. S. Chauhan, "Rereading Claude McKay," in *CLA Journal,* Vol. 34, No. 1, September, 1990, pp. 68–80.

Sources

LeSeur, Geta J., "Claude McKay's Romanticism," in *CLA Journal,* Vol. 32, No. 3, March, 1989, pp. 296-308.

Margolies, Edward, *Native Sons: A Critical Study of Twentieth-Century Black American Authors,* Philadelphia: J.P. Lippencott Company, 1968.

Ojo-Ade, Femi, "Claude McKay: The Tragic Solitude of an Exiled Son of Africa," in *Of Dreams Deferred, Dead or Alive: African Perspectives on African-American Writers,* Westport, CT: Greenwood Press, 1996.

Wagner, Jean, "Claude McKay," in *Black Poets of the United States: From Paul Laurence Dunbar to Langston Hughes,* translated by Kenneth Douglas, University of Illinois Press, 1973, pp. 197-257.

White, Walter F., "Negro Poets," in *The Nation,* New York, Vol. 114, No. 2970, June 7, 1922, pp. 694-95.

For Further Study

Cooper, Wayne, *Claude McKay, Rebel Sojourner in the Harlem Renaissance: A Biography,* Louisiana State University Press, 1996.

In this comprehensive biography, Cooper traces McKay's search for identity, from his Jamaican family background to his years in Harlem, Paris, England, and beyond.

Tillery, Tyrone, *Claude McKay: A Black Poet's Struggle for Identity,* University of Massachusetts Press, 1992.

Addresses McKay's "tough and angry" personality in a well-rounded look at the writer and his work. The study is as much of a look inside the thriving intellectual Harlem scene as it is a biography of the "black, radical, socialist" poet.

When I Was One-and-Twenty

A. E. Housman

1896

This poem, like nearly all of A. E. Housman's most famous poems, was written when the poet was a young man, and was originally published in 1896 as part of Housman's first book of poems, *A Shropshire Lad.* Its subject matter, contrasting the vivacity of youth with expressions of loss and sorrow, is a frequent theme of Housman's. In the speaker's narrative, or dramatic monologue, he tells of failing to heed the advice of an older man to guard his heart and consequently experiencing the pain of young lost love. "When I Was One-and-Twenty" may be seen as an example of the way in which Housman's poetry frequently creates or describes a world that provokes no response beyond a painful endurance. However, it many also be seen as an example of how Housman's poetry contains a lightness of verse and musicality that almost contradicts the expressed anguish.

Author Biography

Housman was born in 1859 in Fockbury, Worcestershire, England. The eldest of seven children in a family that would produce a famous dramatist (Housman's younger brother, Laurence) and a novelist and short story writer (his sister Clemence), Housman attended Bromsgrove School, a notable institution that emphasized Greek and Latin studies. Though successful academically, Housman was a small and frail boy who did not easily form friendships. When he was twelve, Housman's

mother died, the first of a number of events which would affect him profoundly and erode his religious faith. (Years later he would write that he "became a deist at thirteen and an atheist at twenty-one.") He also developed a pronounced facial tic that he never entirely overcame.

Housman earned a scholarship to St. John's College, Oxford, which he began attending in 1877. He immersed himself in the study of classical languages, particularly Latin and Greek, and he also helped to found *Ye Round Table,* an undergraduate magazine featuring humorous verse and satire (a skill in which he excelled, though critics would later condemn his poetry for being stark and humorless). While at college Housman established a friendship with a classmate, Moses Jackson, that would have an enormous impact upon his life. Jackson was a good-looking, athletic young man with whom Housman fell hopelessly and permanently in love. Jackson rebuffed his friend's affections, and Housman was heartbroken; many of his subsequent poems speak of unrequited love and refer to the rejection he suffered when he was "one-and-twenty." Initially, Housman excelled at his studies at Oxford. However, in 1879 he failed his final examinations; not only did he fail, he turned in answer books that were nearly blank but for seemingly random scribblings. The reason for this is generally attributed to some sort of nervous breakdown, though its origins are cause for speculation: some feel it may have been the result of overconfidence, others speculate that it was caused by his pining over Jackson, while still others conjecture that Housman failed deliberately, if subconsciously. Regardless of the cause, Housman returned home ungraduated and disgraced; though he returned to Oxford a year later and obtained a "pass" degree, it seemed the door to a career in academia was closed.

In 1882 Housman passed the civil service examination and took a position in a London patent office—a career decision that was influenced, no doubt, by the fact that Jackson was employed at the same office. For the first four years of his ten-year stay at the patent office he shared a West End apartment with Moses Jackson and his younger brother Adalbert Jackson. Housman spent his evenings at the British Museum library studying Greek and Latin. When, in 1888, Moses Jackson left England for a teaching position in Karachi, India, Housman withdrew into a monkish seclusion, occupied only with his studies and scholarly writing. A number of his articles were published in journals such as the *Classical Review* and the *Journal of Philology,* and they began to earn for Housman a reputation

A. E. Housman

as a brilliant and meticulous scholar. When the Chair of Greek and Latin at University College, London, became available in 1892, the institution overlooked Housman's academic falterings and appointed him to the vacant position. In November of 1892 Adalbert Jackson—who, since the departure of Moses, had been Housman's closest friend—died of typhoid. This trauma created an emotional explosion that resulted in Housman's composing *A Shropshire Lad,* a collection of sixty-three poems addressing the themes of unrequited love, the oblivion of death, and idealized military life. Because of the 1895 persecution and imprisonment of poet Oscar Wilde, Housman was careful to distance himself from the homosexuality depicted in *A Shropshire Lad,* often adopting the persona "Terence Hearsay." The first printing of Housman's collection, published in 1896, was done so at the poet's own expense; neither it nor a second edition, published two years later by a different publisher, sold particularly well. However, when the Boer War broke out in 1899, readers rediscovered the numerous patriotic military poems in the volume, and sales were quickly booming. After the publication of *A Shropshire Lad,* Housman's writing efforts were restricted to scholarly publications—and those limited chiefly to the study of a single classic Roman author of questionable skill and influence, Manilius. The reason for this somewhat odd choice of subject matter was simple: the decidedly shallow nature of Manilius's text allowed Housman to showcase his own editorial and critical talents, thus earning him greater professional distinction. He completed a total of five volumes on Manilius.

Housman's poetic output, which had previously gushed from him in a torrent, was reduced to a trickle. Thus it was not until 1922 that he produced his second collection of verse, the aptly titled *Last Poems*. Though more than a quarter century had elapsed since the publication of *A Shropshire Lad*, the poems contained in *Last Poems* were nearly identical in theme, form, and diction to those in the earlier volume. In 1923 Moses Jackson died, and with him went much of Housman's inspiration; he wrote only a few more lines of prose before his death in 1936. Housman continues to be a popular and frequently read poet despite the fact that since the initial publication of his verse, his work has been intermittently praised and rebuffed for what has been called its "obvious limitations." While his overriding morbidity of theme is often described as tedious and adolescent, Housman's open investigations of the mysteries of death and the dual nature of humankind have earned him acknowledgment as a precursor to the development of modern poetry.

Poem Text

When I was one-and-twenty
    I heard a wise man say,
"Give crowns and pounds and guineas
    But not your heart away;
Give pearls away and rubies   5
    But keep your fancy free."
But I was one-and-twenty,
    No use to talk to me.

When I was one-and-twenty
    I heard him say again,   10
"The heart out of the bosom
    Was never given in vain;
'Tis paid with sighs a plenty
    And sold for endless rue."
And I am two-and-twenty,   15
    And oh, 'tis true, 'tis true.

Poem Summary

Lines 1-4:

In the opening lines, the speaker begins his monologue by clearly expressing that at the age of

twenty-one he was warned, by a man the speaker considered "wise," not to give his heart away. Notice that the remembered warning is in the form of a quote, rather than a paraphrase, which makes the poem's imagery and emotions more immediate. A wise person can be thought to be one who has already experienced the pain of a lost or unrequited love. Here, the wise person, who, we assume in his wisdom, also knows the value of financial stability, and the attraction of money, has warned the young speaker of the poem that being poor is better than suffering the pain and despair of lost love—of living after having given your very heart away. The images of the currency become a concrete manifestation of the contrast between things of the heart and things of the world. The inherent message in the warning is that though you need money to buy food and shelter, it would be better to go without these necessities that keep us alive than to suffer in love.

Lines 5-6:

Here the speaker continues to quote the wise man exactly, remembering that he had warned the speaker to go even beyond giving away the standard monetary currency of "crowns," "pounds," and "guineas"; to give precious gems away, such as "pearls" and "rubies," rather than allow his "fancy," or love, to be restricted. This suggests that the heart is more precious than gems, and ought to be guarded even more carefully. Use of the images of "pearls" and "rubies" intensifies the emotional impact of the remembered warning expressed through the images of the "crowns," "pounds," and "guineas" of the previous lines.

Lines 7-8:

In these lines, the speaker admits that when he was twenty-one he wasn't in the habit of listening to or heeding lessons attempting to be taught by someone of experience. There is an implication here that youth not listening to those older or wiser is a universally understood concept.

Lines 9-14:

In this section of the poem, the speaker tells us that he was warned more than once. Here, Housman uses the word "paid" in line 13 to continue the imagery of monetary currency and gems in the previous stanza. The impact that this has, perhaps, is to make us feel even more intensely that there is always an exchange in life, that one can never get something for nothing. In this instance, the price for giving up "fancy" and the heart will be "endless rue," or sorrow. The new quotation marks at the beginning of line 11 and the end of line 14 serve to magnify how exactly the speaker remembers the second warning as well. By the end of the poem, we realize, this quotation has probably had the effect of taking us more directly into the speaker's agony by hearing the words even as he has gone over them in his "rue."

Lines 15-16:

In the final lines of the poem Housman completes the speaker's monologue in a simply and clearly expressed agreement with the wise man's warnings. Just one year older, and apparently now experienced in the pain of lost or unrequited love, he simply states "'tis true." However, he begins his expression with the word "oh," and repeats the phrase "'tis true," which suggests the intensity of the woe and sorrow felt, while continuing the poem's musicality. Here, the conciseness and simplicity of expression allow us, perhaps, to feel even more severely the impact of the warnings contained above.

Media Adaptations

- A phonographic record titled *On Wenlock Edge: Songs from A Shropshire Lad* was released by Arabesque Recordings in 1980.

- *Poems and Songs from A Shropshire Lad*, a two-album phonographic recording, was released by Hyperion, London, in 1995.

- In 1965 Caedmon released an audio cassette read by James Mason titled *A Shropshire Lad and Other Poetry*

Themes

Knowledge and Ignorance

The speaker of this poem admits that he did not, or could not, follow the advice given to him when he was twenty-one, even though it came from a wise man. There are two possible reasons for his failure to act. The first is that he did not recognize the wisdom of the wise man until he turned twenty-two and through experience came to see the wisdom of his advice. The other possibility is that the poem's speaker *did* realize that it was good advice at the time but was helpless to do anything about it because he was too young; when he had matured, it was as if a spell had been broken, and he realized the wisdom of the man's words.

Both of these ways of looking at the phrase "a wise man" illustrate the same thing about knowledge—that it can only be absorbed when one is ready for it—but each one implies a slightly different lesson about this particular character. The poem subtly draws the line between knowledge that is told by someone else and knowledge that is gained from experience, showing readers that experiential knowledge is the only kind that matters. Another issue that is left to interpretation is whether ignoring wise advice and only drawing from experience is meant to represent the human condition, as the poem's lofty tone implies, or if it is only a condition of youth.

Freedom

This poem conveys the message that a person in love is not free, that one must avoid giving their heart to another in order to keep their "fancy free." Money, it tells us, makes no such claim on personal freedom. The advice to "Give crowns and pounds and guineas" away contradicts common knowledge, which dictates that acquiring wealth gives a person the means with which to pursue happiness. Housman tells us, through the persona of the wise man, that acquired wealth has nothing to do with freedom and therefore does not affect happiness. Falling in love, on the other hand, does take one's freedom, and therefore leaves a person in misery, or "endless rue."

There is some historical precedent to his view of love, since the idea of "giving away" one's heart is a common way of speaking of love. Popular songs, for instance, tell us of being enslaved by love, of behaving how one otherwise would not behave, losing one's will and being made weak. In popular culture, though, this loss of freedom is presented as a positive thing, a feeling that the person in love welcomes; what "When I Was One-and-Twenty" adds is a sense of just how miserable an experience it is to lose one's freedom in this way. The poem never says whether its speaker is successful in love—that is, whether the person he has given his heart to loves him back—which leaves readers to assume that any sort of love will be "paid

Topics for Further Study

- This poem tells of a truth that the speaker cannot understand when he is twenty-one but does when he is twenty-two. Think of a piece of advice that you were not impressed with when it was given, but seems obvious now. Write a poem that shows concrete objects, the way that Housman does, to express your belief in a positive light.

- Write a short story about the old man who gives advice in this poem, showing your readers why he gives the advice that he does. Has he had good luck with love or bad luck? Do you think he is married? Did he give away large sums of money at one time, or did he just give away his love?

- This poem was published in 1896, at a time when the Industrial Revolution was at its height in England. At the time, young men would have been more familiar with commerce than earlier generations. How do you think the growth of cities might have affected Housman's decision to compare love to buying and selling?

with sighs a plenty," presumably because any person who is in love is not free.

Rites of Passage

Readers are told that something has happened to the speaker of this poem between the ages of twenty-one and twenty-two to make him realize that the wise man's advice about love was true. The new attitude is not presented as being a misstep, or as a temporary response to a situation; in fact, it is presented as the truth. The person in the poem is meant to have matured from ignorance to understanding in one year. Why, at the end of the poem, does he reflect on the wise man's words with, "'Tis true, 'tis true"? Age alone might be the cause: the poem might be saying that within the year between twenty-one and twenty-two just happens, for reasons sociological or biological, to be the time of life when this truth makes itself known.

More likely, though, this poem wants us to believe that something happened in the intervening year to change this speaker's perspective. The poem does not describe such an event, but it is unlikely that the sort of bitter disappointment described here could occur by itself, spontaneously. This seems like more of an absolute truth than a response to just one bad relationship. If the new understanding is true, and if most people come to this understanding as they age, then going through the experience can fairly be called a "rite of passage." The message of this poem seems to be that the effect of surviving one's First Big Love (or possibly one's First Big Disastrous Love) is to be elevated into the ranks of wise people who have already seen the light.

Style

"When I Was One-and-Twenty" is a dramatic monologue written in the form of a Scottish lyric ballad or song that exemplifies Housman's acknowledged influence by German lyric balladist Heinrich Heine, Shakespeare's songs, as well as the border ballads of Scotland. The poem consists of two stanzas of eight lines each. All of the even-numbered lines contain end rhymes, such as "say" and "away," while none of the odd-numbered lines rhyme, for a rhyme scheme of *abcb*. The end rhymes in the poem are considered perfect or full rhymes, because after their differing consonants they contain identical, accented vowel sounds, such as in "say" and "away." The poem also contains some near rhymes within individual lines of the poem; for example, "crowns" and "pounds" in line 3, and "not" and "heart" in line 4. A rhyme occurring within a line is called internal rhyme.

If the poem is read aloud, a certain rhythm or meter can be heard. Each of the odd-numbered lines contains seven syllables, and each of the even-numbered lines contains six syllables. This gives the poem a musicality, precision, and conciseness that can be seen as classical elements. There is also a definite beat recurring in each line, called iambic: segments of two syllables where the first is unstressed and the second is stressed. For example, look at the second line of this poem:

I **heard** / a **wise** / man **say** ...

All of the even-numbered lines of this poem contain three segments, or feet of iambs, which is called iambic trimeter. All of the odd-numbered lines of this poem contain one extra syllable in the

Compare & Contrast

• **1896:** L. Starr Jameson, a revolutionary who unsuccessfully lead a raid against the Boer government in South Africa, was sent to England for trial. He was found guilty but received an unusually light sentence, raising the suspicions of the Boers, who were the white descendants of Dutch settlers from the 1830s; they believed that the British wanted to rule South Africa because gold had been discovered there in 1884.

1899-1902: The Boer War between Great Britain and residents of Transvaal and Orange Free State in what is now South Africa ended with an uneasy peace settlement recognizing British sovereignty.

1948: The Republic of South Africa, populated mostly by Afrikaners (a modern name for Boers), voted for a system of racial segregation known as apartheid, which denied black Africans full social recognition and privileges.

1990: Finally succumbing to international pressure, the apartheid system was abolished in South Africa.

Today: Nelson Mandela, a black African who spent nearly thirty years in prison for his opposition to apartheid, has been president of South Africa since 1990.

• **1896:** In *Plessy v. Ferguson,* one of the most influential legal cases in U.S. history, the Supreme Court ruled that states could provide separate facilities for black citizens to use, creating a legal basis for "Whites Only" drinking fountains, public transportation, hospitals, rest rooms, etc.

1954: Ruling in the case of *Brown v. the Board of Education of Topeka, Kansas,* the Supreme Court ruled by a margin of 9 to 0 that "separate could never be equal," and therefore that separate schools for blacks and whites violated the U.S. Constitution.

1955: Rosa Parks refused to leave the section of a Montgomery, Alabama bus that was designated for white use only, and was arrested; the year-long boycott of the bus system following her arrest showed the power of blacks as consumers and helped bring an end to segregation.

Today: States and municipalities around the country are questioning whether "Affirmative Action" programs that are supposed to bring employment situations into racial balance are doing more harm than good.

• **1896:** The first public showing of a motion picture in the United States took place in New York.

Today: The American film industry makes almost six billion dollars in ticket sales annually.

• **1896:** The first motor car available to the U.S. public, the Haynes-Duryea, went on sale. Twenty-five cars were produced that year.

Today: The United States produces twelve million cars per year; worldwide production is approximately 50 million cars per year.

---

final segment, creating what is called a feminine ending, which means there is an extra unaccented syllable at the end of the line. Although it is possible to ascribe this detailed beat and meter to the poem, it is generally regarded simply as a ballad, or is sometimes referred to as a lyric ballad that contains classical overtones because of Housman's use of short words and precise and clear construction.

Historical Context

The literary world of Britain in the late 1800s was dominated by quiet traditionalism, continuing the mood of prosperity and complacency set by the reigning queen, Victoria, who had ascended to the throne in 1837. Today, the Victorian Age is remembered as a period of hypocrisy, when citizens adhered to strong codes of moral decency in public even if they behaved quite differently in private.

After the death of Victoria's husband, Albert, in 1861, the queen never remarried, spending the next forty years in mourning. Her stiff-lipped prudery set the pace for the rest of the country's mood. The economy of Great Britain prospered throughout the last half of the nineteenth century, mainly due to the expansion of the British Empire, as lands across the world became British colonies. While the country's upper class prospered, though, the poor suffered new and unimagined lows, especially in the cities. The Industrial Revolution affected most developed countries across the globe and brought millions of people from farms to take jobs in manufacturing. In the city, they crowded into slums and, among filth and unchecked pollution that blocked the sun so thoroughly that the street lamps in London often had to be left on during the day. Novelists such as Charles Dickens and George Meredith drew attention to the suffering and injustices in the Victorian system, but there was little incentive for those in power to change.

By the time Housman wrote this poem in the 1890s, the Victorian tradition of masking inner oppression with outward cheerfulness and respectability was starting to wear thin. In England, an artistic movement called "aestheticism" gained popularity. Its motto, "Art for art's sake," advocated beauty above all else, including morality. Rebelling against the prevailing ideas of goodness and evil, aesthetes drew attention to the distance between real experience and the necessary artificiality of art. As the 1890s progressed, the aesthetes took the name "decadents," which challenged polite society's conventions even further. Decadent poets include Dante Gabriel Rossetti and Charles Swinburne.

In 1895 one of the most famous decadents, Oscar Wilde, was brought to trial for homosexuality. Wilde, a flamboyant, attention-loving public figure, did much to bring the charges against himself; accused of homosexuality by a lover's father, he sued the father for slander, bringing attention to his private life and forcing the government to invoke an obscure law banning homosexuality. The fact that the case dominated the headlines undoubtedly affected Housman as he tried to find a publisher for *A Shropshire Lad.* He ended up publishing it with his own money in 1896. Wilde served two years in jail, then moved to Paris and changed his name, though, ironically, his case did help dissolve the piety of Victorianism by raising questions about whether the government should legislate morality.

A Shropshire Lad was not recognized as an important work when it was first published; in a few years, when Britain entered the Boer War in 1899, the book's war poems caught the public's imagination, raising it to a best-seller and establishing it as one of the great poetry collections of all time. There was much support in Britain for the war, but there were also great misgivings. It took place in what is now South Africa, between British settlers and the Afrikaners, known also as Boers, who were the descendents of the Dutch who had colonized the area earlier. The war lasted for three years and the British were victorious.

In 1914 World War I started, introducing the world to fighting and destruction on scales previously unheard-of; literature, in the early years of the century and then even increasingly after the war's end in 1919, turned toward modernism, focusing on the individual's feelings and encouraging artists to experiment with new, exotic forms that quickly left Victorian works looking old-fashioned and stuffy.

Critical Overview

In a 1923 *The Bookman* article, poet, novelist, and critic William Rose Benét noted that "there is, perhaps, nothing [in Housman's work] quite so perfect in its poignancy as was that first cry of youth, 'When I Was One-and-Twenty.'" William R. Brashear, however, in a 1969 essay in *Victorian Poetry,* wrote that the "narrowness" of Housman's subject matter may have "prevented him from coming into his own." Brashear refers here to the themes Housman frequently employs: unrequited love, grief, despair, bad luck, and "trouble" in general. Brashear states that the troubles and despair in the poems cannot be dismissed, and when fully apprehended, many of Housman's poems do contain "a unique starkness and power." But he argues that some of these poems of despair and bleakness "are not among Housman's greatest, though [they are] well-turned and eminently successful in the achievement of their limited effects." He writes that the effects, however, are "over-indulged," and that "there is relatively too much to do about a too little or common complaint." He calls them, without pointing to this particular poem, "the work of a diminutive Housman," and says "the author's preoccupations strike one as unwholesome and immature."

Nevertheless, this poem is seen by other critics as representative of Housman's practice of writing poems with painful themes which are, at the same time, highly musical, and replete with important ironies and paradoxes. Gordon B. Lea points to this duality in a 1973 essay published in the *The Colby Library Quarterly*. He asserts that Brashear has underestimated the dualities in Housman's poetry, and has failed to see that the poet creates in his work an "illuminating paradox" through which to explore the relationship between life and death. He calls these paradoxes "engaging discrepancies" and states that although they "occasionally accentuate the bleakness of Housman's vision, ... more frequently they relieve it, and, as a result, a poetry whose sentiments ought to depress us actually delights us." Lea points to "When I Was One-and-Twenty" as an example of the fascinating way in which Housman uses musicality to create this kind of discrepancy between subject and sound. He first says of Housman's poetry in general: "The poetry dramatizes that life is an agony and God an oppressor, but it does so to a music that is distractingly light and melodious, a music that often functions as an ironic descant to the bleak sentiments and painful experiences it accompanies." He writes that this incongruity is pronounced in "When I Was One-and-Twenty," explaining how "sound acts as a counterpoint" to the theme of the painful price of young love. He attributes this to the poem's "agile" iambic trimeter, and its short vowel sounds and words, which "combine merrily to undermine the sadness of the speaker, a rejected or abandoned lover."

Criticism

Jhan Hochman

Jhan Hochman is a writer and instructor at Portland Community College in Portland, Oregon. In the following essay, Hochman provides biographical information on Housman and discusses whether the reader should consider "When I Was One-and-Twenty" as a "portrait of adolescence" or an "adolescent poem."

By the time readers reach the end of A. E. Housman's "When I Was One-and-Twenty" (1895) they will likely be divided into at least two camps: the first comprised of those echoing Housman's twenty-two year old in an earnest chorus of "'tis true, 'tis true"; and the second, comprised of those that just smile at the earnest repetition of the antique phrase.

The former camp will, more likely than not, be young people well under the age of twenty-one since young people generally give their heart away at a much earlier age than twenty-one. The latter camp will likely be older, and these people have fallen in love. They will find the effusiveness of the poem overwrought and quaintly adolescent. In fact, there has been much critical agreement that Housman was a poet for adolescents, not for adults.

Before joining this critical multitude, however, readers should stop and ask: Is this poem adolescent, or is it better viewed as a portrait of adolescence? To answer, it would behoove readers to realize that Housman, no mere lad, was 36 when he wrote the poem, which was untitled and numbered thirteen in his first collection *The Shropshire Lad* (1896). Presumably he was experienced in the ways of love and of the disappointment love can bring.

This is confirmed with a little biographical information. Housman met Moses Jackson, a fellow Oxford student, and fell in love with him. Jackson, however, was heterosexual and did not return his feelings. The two, however, would remain friends for most of their lives. In verse published after he died, Housman wrote: "Because I liked you better / Than suits a man to say, / It irked you, and I promised / To throw the thought away." Housman worked and lived together with Jackson until 1886; at that time, Housman moved to another part of London, likely because it was too difficult to live so close to the man he loved. Later, Jackson married and moved away, and it was shortly thereafter that Housman wrote the bulk of his poetry: "I did not begin to write poetry in earnest until the really emotional part of my life was over."

If Housman had composed his love poems while experiencing emotional turmoil, the work might have suffered and indeed been merely self-centered—what some people think of as adolescent. But because he waited until he gained perspective on his feelings, it might be more prudent to think his poems transcended the merely personal, and became poems that might be called songs of adolescence—not adolescent songs.

The word *lyric* comes from *lyre,* a kind of harp Greek lyrics (singer-poets) they played as they sang. The lyric is a short poem often expressing the sentiments of the poet within stanzas or strophes (pronounced stro-feez). "When I Was One-and-Twenty" is composed of two stanzas or strophes, the second strophe called the antistrophe. The poem is in iambic trimeter (generally, three sets of unaccented and accented syllables per line), and with

What Do I Read Next?

- Housman rose to fame as one of England's pre-eminent poets on the basis of just one book, *A Shropshire Lad,* first published in 1896 and in print continuously throughout the past century. Included along with this poem are such standards of literature anthologies as "To An Athlete Dying Young," "Loveliest of Trees," and "Terrence, This IS Stupid Stuff."

- *The Letters of A. E. Housman* were edited and compiled by Henry Maas and published by Rupert Hart-Davis of London in 1971. To those even somewhat familiar with the poet's biography, cutting past things written about him and going straight to his words can be amusing, although those completely unfamiliar with his life will find these friendly but reserved letters irrelevant.

- In 1929, D. C. Somervell published the now-classic *English Thought in the Nineteenth Century;* it was published ten times in Great Britain before the first American edition in 1965. The book is not large or unduly complex, but very clear in following one social trend after another, right up to the end of the century, to the world Housman inhabited.

- A very good literary analysis of Housman's work in general is B.J. Leggett's 1978 study, *The Poetic Art of A. E. Housman: Theory and Practice,* published by the University of Nebraska Press. The author is a very perceptive Housman scholar; in particular, his line-by-line study of "When I Was One-and-Twenty" in a chapter titled "Songs of Innocence and Experience" is well-researched and clear, if slightly dry intellectually.

- One can get a good sense of the social pressures that affected the poet and (only slightly) cramped his subject matter from reading F. M. L. Thompson's *The Rise of Respectable Society: A Social History of Victorian Britain, 1830-1900.* Housman came at the very end of the Victorian era, too late to enjoy any of its splendor but in tome to suffer from its narrow-minded stuffiness. Thompson's book divides Victorian life by general categories, such as "Work," "Childhood," "Marriage," "Homes and Houses," making it easy to compare similar elements from our own world.

- Tom Burns Haber edited the centennial edition of Housman's poetry and wrote a 1967 biography entitled *A. E. Housman.* Of all of the Housman biographies available, this one is of particular interest to the student because it focuses most of its attention in the relationships between his life and particular poems. Casual readers might be bored with his explanations of how specific lines changed from their first written manuscript form to their publication, but writers and those familiar with the writing process will understand the significance of each minor correction.

---

slight variation, has an *abab* rhyme scheme. The song-like aspect of the poem fits a poem about adolescence, particularly since the song form has become the most popular form of music for young people—especially those songs with *lyrics* worshipping or denouncing love.

With this in consideration, it is not surprising that Housman was heavily influenced by the tradition of English ballads first collected in Percy's *Reliques of Ancient English Poetry* (1765), still the most important source of old English ballads. Nor should readers be surprised that more than most poems, Housman's have been turned into songs by modern songwriters.

Most contemporary criticism is wrong in that it relegates Housman to the status of "minor" and "adolescent" poet. This is not to assert that Housman is a major poet, but only that a dismissal of "When I Was One-and-Twenty" on the grounds it is simple and adolescent seems less interesting than investigating whether the poem maturely expresses, perhaps even pokes fun at, the voice(s) of adolescence. The persona of this poem looks back and understands his ignorance of what it means to give your heart away. The young man now recognizes the truth of the wise man's advice.

The wise man might be seen as a type, that of the isolated hermit. But it is unlikely the youth is himself an ascetic, and more likely is a young man subject to the temptations of society. After all, how can a vibrant, curious, young person avoid romantic entanglement? With this in mind, is the wise man's advice unwise or futile? Should the wise man not have said: "You *will* give your heart away and you *will* regret it. There is little you can do about it." But perhaps the wise man was wiser than that and said something else altogether: "Go out and have a wild time (spend lots of money on, and buy lots of jewelry for, your lovers), but stay unattached until you are more experienced in the ways of the world."

Would this version of the wise man's advice be useful for Housman himself, a man who devoted himself to unattainable love in a time hostile to homosexuals? This hostility hit home when Housman read about a young cadet who committed suicide over what Housman thought was homosexual desire. And when in 1895 Oscar Wilde was arrested for homosexuality and imprisoned for two years, Housman sent him a present, a copy of *The Shropshire Lad*.

Because the object of devotion in "When I Was One-and-Twenty" is presumably female—"Give pearls away and rubies"—readers might surmise that this poem is not about a young gay man. But it is more likely that Housman could not, without dire consequences, express homosexual love in a public, and, for safety's sake had to alter the poetic persona to that of a heterosexual.

If this is a poem about, or greatly influenced by, sexuality, it is no wonder the poem is fatalistic, whether humorously or seriously so. Notice that love is comparable to economic exchange. Love is like money paid for something in return, something beneficial like love, not unpleasant like sorrow.

In the first strophe, money facilitates fun of the sexual kind, and is a positive in that it helps the giver to avoid giving his heart away. In the antistrophe, money is cast as superior to love as a system of exchange, since what one gets in return is pleasure, not heartbreak. Is this true, or is it mock bitterness? Is this an adolescent poem or a poem about adolescence?

> *Most contemporary criticism is wrong in that it relegates Housman to the status of 'minor' and 'adolescent' poet. This is not to assert that Housman is a major poet, but only that a dismissal of 'When I Was One-and-Twenty' on the grounds it is simple and adolescent seems less interesting than investigating whether the poem maturely expresses, perhaps even pokes fun at, the voice(s) of adolescence."*

While most readers can agree that Housman, through his persona as a young man, is telling the reader that love is hard, is he trying to do more? Is the poem itself a poem of advice, where just as the wise man advises the youth, the youth advises his readers in a poem? And if this is a poem of advice, of what are we being advised? Is the youth sincerely telling us to never fall in love (a truly adolescent poem)? Is the youth mocking the futility of the knowledge that love hurts since one can hardly avoid falling in love (a more mature poem)? Or is it possible that the young reader is advised by both the wise man and the youth to go out and enjoy sexual involvement and leave emotional involvement and commitment for later (a poem about adolescence, and for both adolescents and adults)?

While this reading might seem a typical one to come out of the end of the twentieth century—an era of omnipresent sex and uncloseted homosexuality—there is, perhaps, one thing missing from the wise man's advice that could update Housman's "When I Was One-and-Twenty" for the end of the second millennium. It is this: while youth should have a good time and keep their fancies free they must also remember to protect themselves.

Source: Jhan Hochman, in an essay for *Poetry for Students,* Gale, 1998.

Sources

Abrams, M. H., ed., *The Norton Anthology of English Literature,* Vol. II, Norton, 1986.

Bayley, John, *Housman's Poems,* Oxford University Press, 1992.

Benét, William Rose, in a review of *Last Poems,* in *The Bookman,* Vol. 571, No. 1, March, 1923, pp. 83-5.

Brashear, William R., "The Trouble with Housman," in *Victorian Poetry,* Vol. 7, No. 2, Summer, 1969, pp. 81-90.

Caldwell, Theodore, ed., *The Anglo-Boer War: Why Was It Fought? Who Was Responsible?* D.C. Heath and Co., 1965.

Ellman, Richard, ed., *The Norton Anthology of Modern Poetry,* Norton, 1973.

Graves, Richard Perceval, *A. E. Housman: The Scholar Poet,* Scribner, 1980.

Halevy, Elie, *Imperialism and the Rise of Labour: A History of the English People in the Nineteenth Century,* volume five, Ernest Benn Limited, 1965.

Housman, A. E., *The Collected Poems of A. E. Housman,* Henry Holt, 1950.

Lea, Gordon B., "Ironies and Dualities in 'A Shropshire Lad,'" in *Colby Library Quarterly,* Series X, No. 2, June, 1973, pp. 71-9.

Leggett, B. J., *The Poetic Art of A. E. Housman,* University of Nebraska Press, 1978.

Ricks, Christopher, ed., *A. E. Housman: A Collection of Critical Essays,* Prentice Hall, 1968.

For Further Study

Graves, Richard Perceval, *A. E. Housman: The Scholar-Poet,* Charles Shribner's Sons, 1979.
   This very thorough and readable biography is not inspired, but it is solid and respectable, giving it a certain appeal to Housman's biggest fans. Graves has all the facts of Housman's life, but never turns the trick of making the man come alive on the page.

Hoagwood, Terrance Allan, *A. E. Housman Revisited,* Twayne Publishers, 1995.
   This book gives a quick, general biography of the poet, and then provides a brief interpretation of the poems in *A Shropshire Lad, Last Poems, More Poems,* and *Additional Poems.* This is a very useful source for any student doing a comparison of two or more of Housman's works.

Parkenham, Thomas, *The Boer War,* Random House, 1979.
   A history of the Boer war that provides a good sense of the British mindset at the turn of the century, when Housman's verse first caught the public's attention. War historians will love this book, and anyone doing research on the times ought to take a look at it.

Wilbur, Richard, "Round About a Poem of Housman's," in *A. E. Housman: A Collection of Critical Essays,* edited by Christopher Ricks, Prentice-Hall, Inc., 1968, pp. 85-105.
   Wilbur, a great poet himself, relates his own experience in World War II to Housman's poem "Epitaph on an Army of Mercenaries," and quickly dissolves into a twenty-page analysis of the poem.

Glossary of Literary Terms

A

Abstract: Used as a noun, the term refers to a short summary or outline of a longer work. As an adjective applied to writing or literary works, abstract refers to words or phrases that name things not knowable through the five senses.

Accent: The emphasis or stress placed on a syllable in poetry. Traditional poetry commonly uses patterns of accented and unaccented syllables (known as feet) that create distinct rhythms. Much modern poetry uses less formal arrangements that create a sense of freedom and spontaneity.

Aestheticism: A literary and artistic movement of the nineteenth century. Followers of the movement believed that art should not be mixed with social, political, or moral teaching. The statement "art for art's sake" is a good summary of aestheticism. The movement had its roots in France, but it gained widespread importance in England in the last half of the nineteenth century, where it helped change the Victorian practice of including moral lessons in literature.

Affective Fallacy: An error in judging the merits or faults of a work of literature. The "error" results from stressing the importance of the work's effect upon the reader—that is, how it makes a reader "feel" emotionally, what it does as a literary work—instead of stressing its inner qualities as a created object, or what it "is."

Age of Johnson: The period in English literature between 1750 and 1798, named after the most prominent literary figure of the age, Samuel Johnson. Works written during this time are noted for their emphasis on "sensibility," or emotional quality. These works formed a transition between the rational works of the Age of Reason, or Neoclassical period, and the emphasis on individual feelings and responses of the Romantic period.

Age of Reason: See *Neoclassicism*

Age of Sensibility: See *Age of Johnson*

Agrarians: A group of Southern American writers of the 1930s and 1940s who fostered an economic and cultural program for the South based on agriculture, in opposition to the industrial society of the North. The term can refer to any group that promotes the value of farm life and agricultural society.

Alexandrine Meter: See *Meter*

Allegory: A narrative technique in which characters representing things or abstract ideas are used to convey a message or teach a lesson. Allegory is typically used to teach moral, ethical, or religious lessons but is sometimes used for satiric or political purposes.

Alliteration: A poetic device where the first consonant sounds or any vowel sounds in words or syllables are repeated.

Allusion: A reference to a familiar literary or historical person or event, used to make an idea more easily understood.

Amerind Literature: The writing and oral traditions of Native Americans. Native American literature was originally passed on by word of mouth, so it consisted largely of stories and events that were easily memorized. Amerind prose is often rhythmic like poetry because it was recited to the beat of a ceremonial drum.

Analogy: A comparison of two things made to explain something unfamiliar through its similarities to something familiar, or to prove one point based on the acceptedness of another. Similes and metaphors are types of analogies.

Anapest: See *Foot*

Angry Young Men: A group of British writers of the 1950s whose work expressed bitterness and disillusionment with society. Common to their work is an anti-hero who rebels against a corrupt social order and strives for personal integrity.

Anthropomorphism: The presentation of animals or objects in human shape or with human characteristics. The term is derived from the Greek word for "human form."

Antimasque: See *Masque*

Antithesis: The antithesis of something is its direct opposite. In literature, the use of antithesis as a figure of speech results in two statements that show a contrast through the balancing of two opposite ideas. Technically, it is the second portion of the statement that is defined as the "antithesis"; the first portion is the "thesis."

Apocrypha: Writings tentatively attributed to an author but not proven or universally accepted to be their works. The term was originally applied to certain books of the Bible that were not considered inspired and so were not included in the "sacred canon."

Apollonian and Dionysian: The two impulses believed to guide authors of dramatic tragedy. The Apollonian impulse is named after Apollo, the Greek god of light and beauty and the symbol of intellectual order. The Dionysian impulse is named after Dionysus, the Greek god of wine and the symbol of the unrestrained forces of nature. The Apollonian impulse is to create a rational, harmonious world, while the Dionysian is to express the irrational forces of personality.

Apostrophe: A statement, question, or request addressed to an inanimate object or concept or to a nonexistent or absent person.

Archetype: The word archetype is commonly used to describe an original pattern or model from which all other things of the same kind are made. This term was introduced to literary criticism from the psychology of Carl Jung. It expresses Jung's theory that behind every person's "unconscious," or repressed memories of the past, lies the "collective unconscious" of the human race: memories of the countless typical experiences of our ancestors. These memories are said to prompt illogical associations that trigger powerful emotions in the reader. Often, the emotional process is primitive, even primordial. Archetypes are the literary images that grow out of the "collective unconscious." They appear in literature as incidents and plots that repeat basic patterns of life. They may also appear as stereotyped characters.

Argument: The argument of a work is the author's subject matter or principal idea.

Art for Art's Sake: See *Aestheticism*

Assonance: The repetition of similar vowel sounds in poetry.

Audience: The people for whom a piece of literature is written. Authors usually write with a certain audience in mind, for example, children, members of a religious or ethnic group, or colleagues in a professional field. The term "audience" also applies to the people who gather to see or hear any performance, including plays, poetry readings, speeches, and concerts.

Automatic Writing: Writing carried out without a preconceived plan in an effort to capture every random thought. Authors who engage in automatic writing typically do not revise their work, preferring instead to preserve the revealed truth and beauty of spontaneous expression.

***Avant-garde*:** A French term meaning "vanguard." It is used in literary criticism to describe new writing that rejects traditional approaches to literature in favor of innovations in style or content.

B

Ballad: A short poem that tells a simple story and has a repeated refrain. Ballads were originally intended to be sung. Early ballads, known as folk ballads, were passed down through generations, so their authors are often unknown. Later ballads composed by known authors are called literary ballads.

Baroque: A term used in literary criticism to describe literature that is complex or ornate in style or diction. Baroque works typically express tension, anxiety, and violent emotion. The term "Baroque Age" designates a period in Western European literature beginning in the late sixteenth century and ending about one hundred years later. Works of this period often mirror the qualities of works more generally associated with the label "baroque" and sometimes feature elaborate conceits.

Baroque Age: See *Baroque*

Baroque Period: See *Baroque*

Beat Generation: See *Beat Movement*

Beat Movement: A period featuring a group of American poets and novelists of the 1950s and 1960s—including Jack Kerouac, Allen Ginsberg, Gregory Corso, William S. Burroughs, and Lawrence Ferlinghetti—who rejected established social and literary values. Using such techniques as stream of consciousness writing and jazz-influenced free verse and focusing on unusual or abnormal states of mind—generated by religious ecstasy or the use of drugs—the Beat writers aimed to create works that were unconventional in both form and subject matter.

Beat Poets: See *Beat Movement*

Beats, The: See *Beat Movement*

Belles- lettres: A French term meaning "fine letters" or "beautiful writing." It is often used as a synonym for literature, typically referring to imaginative and artistic rather than scientific or expository writing. Current usage sometimes restricts the meaning to light or humorous writing and appreciative essays about literature.

Black Aesthetic Movement: A period of artistic and literary development among African Americans in the 1960s and early 1970s. This was the first major African-American artistic movement since the Harlem Renaissance and was closely paralleled by the civil rights and black power movements. The black aesthetic writers attempted to produce works of art that would be meaningful to the black masses. Key figures in black aesthetics included one of its founders, poet and playwright Amiri Baraka, formerly known as LeRoi Jones; poet and essayist Haki R. Madhubuti, formerly Don L. Lee; poet and playwright Sonia Sanchez; and dramatist Ed Bullins.

Black Arts Movement: See *Black Aesthetic Movement*

Black Comedy: See *Black Humor*

Black Humor: Writing that places grotesque elements side by side with humorous ones in an attempt to shock the reader, forcing him or her to laugh at the horrifying reality of a disordered world.

Black Mountain School: Black Mountain College and three of its instructors—Robert Creeley, Robert Duncan, and Charles Olson— were all influential in projective verse, so poets working in projective verse are now referred as members of the Black Mountain school.

Blank Verse: Loosely, any unrhymed poetry, but more generally, unrhymed iambic pentameter verse (composed of lines of five two-syllable feet with the first syllable accented, the second unaccented). Blank verse has been used by poets since the Renaissance for its flexibility and its graceful, dignified tone.

Bloomsbury Group: A group of English writers, artists, and intellectuals who held informal artistic and philosophical discussions in Bloomsbury, a district of London, from around 1907 to the early 1930s. The Bloomsbury Group held no uniform philosophical beliefs but did commonly express an aversion to moral prudery and a desire for greater social tolerance.

Bon Mot: A French term meaning "good word." A *bon mot* is a witty remark or clever observation.

Breath Verse: See *Projective Verse*

Burlesque: Any literary work that uses exaggeration to make its subject appear ridiculous, either by treating a trivial subject with profound seriousness or by treating a dignified subject frivolously. The word "burlesque" may also be used as an adjective, as in "burlesque show," to mean "striptease act."

C

Cadence: The natural rhythm of language caused by the alternation of accented and unaccented syllables. Much modern poetry—notably free verse—deliberately manipulates cadence to create complex rhythmic effects.

Caesura: A pause in a line of poetry, usually occurring near the middle. It typically corresponds to a break in the natural rhythm or sense of the line but is sometimes shifted to create special meanings or rhythmic effects.

Canzone: A short Italian or Provencal lyric poem, commonly about love and often set to music. The *canzone* has no set form but typically contains five or six stanzas made up of seven to twenty lines of eleven syllables each. A shorter, five- to ten-line "envoy," or concluding stanza, completes the poem.

Carpe Diem: A Latin term meaning "seize the day." This is a traditional theme of poetry, especially lyrics. A *carpe diem* poem advises the reader or the person it addresses to live for today and enjoy the pleasures of the moment.

Catharsis: The release or purging of unwanted emotions— specifically fear and pity—brought about by exposure to art. The term was first used by the Greek philosopher Aristotle in his *Poetics* to refer to the desired effect of tragedy on spectators.

Celtic Renaissance: A period of Irish literary and cultural history at the end of the nineteenth century. Followers of the movement aimed to create a romantic vision of Celtic myth and legend. The most significant works of the Celtic Renaissance typically present a dreamy, unreal world, usually in reaction against the reality of contemporary problems.

Celtic Twilight: See *Celtic Renaissance*

Character: Broadly speaking, a person in a literary work. The actions of characters are what constitute the plot of a story, novel, or poem. There are numerous types of characters, ranging from simple, stereotypical figures to intricate, multifaceted ones. In the techniques of anthropomorphism and personification, animals—and even places or things—can assume aspects of character. "Characterization" is the process by which an author creates vivid, believable characters in a work of art. This may be done in a variety of ways, including (1) direct description of the character by the narrator; (2) the direct presentation of the speech, thoughts, or actions of the character; and (3) the responses of other characters to the character. The term "character" also refers to a form originated by the ancient Greek writer Theophrastus that later became popular in the seventeenth and eighteenth centuries. It is a short essay or sketch of a person who prominently displays a specific attribute or quality, such as miserliness or ambition.

Characterization: See *Character*

Classical: In its strictest definition in literary criticism, classicism refers to works of ancient Greek or Roman literature. The term may also be used to describe a literary work of recognized importance (a "classic") from any time period or literature that exhibits the traits of classicism.

Classicism: A term used in literary criticism to describe critical doctrines that have their roots in ancient Greek and Roman literature, philosophy, and art. Works associated with classicism typically exhibit restraint on the part of the author, unity of design and purpose, clarity, simplicity, logical organization, and respect for tradition.

Colloquialism: A word, phrase, or form of pronunciation that is acceptable in casual conversation but not in formal, written communication. It is considered more acceptable than slang.

Complaint: A lyric poem, popular in the Renaissance, in which the speaker expresses sorrow about his or her condition. Typically, the speaker's sadness is caused by an unresponsive lover, but some complaints cite other sources of unhappiness, such as poverty or fate.

Conceit: A clever and fanciful metaphor, usually expressed through elaborate and extended comparison, that presents a striking parallel between two seemingly dissimilar things—for example, elaborately comparing a beautiful woman to an object like a garden or the sun. The conceit was a popular device throughout the Elizabethan Age and Baroque Age and was the principal technique of the seventeenth-century English metaphysical poets. This usage of the word conceit is unrelated to the best-known definition of conceit as an arrogant attitude or behavior.

Concrete: Concrete is the opposite of abstract, and refers to a thing that actually exists or a description that allows the reader to experience an object or concept with the senses.

Concrete Poetry: Poetry in which visual elements play a large part in the poetic effect. Punctuation marks, letters, or words are arranged on a page to form a visual design: a cross, for example, or a bumblebee.

Confessional Poetry: A form of poetry in which the poet reveals very personal, intimate, sometimes shocking information about himself or herself.

Connotation: The impression that a word gives beyond its defined meaning. Connotations may be universally understood or may be significant only to a certain group.

Consonance: Consonance occurs in poetry when words appearing at the ends of two or more verses have similar final consonant sounds but have final vowel sounds that differ, as with "stuff" and "off."

Convention: Any widely accepted literary device, style, or form.

Corrido: A Mexican ballad.

Couplet: Two lines of poetry with the same rhyme and meter, often expressing a complete and self-contained thought.

Criticism: The systematic study and evaluation of literary works, usually based on a specific method or set of principles. An important part of literary studies since ancient times, the practice of criticism has given rise to numerous theories, methods, and "schools," sometimes producing conflicting, even contradictory, interpretations of literature in general as well as of individual works. Even such basic issues as what constitutes a poem or a novel have been the subject of much criticism over the centuries.

D

Dactyl: See *Foot*

Dadaism: A protest movement in art and literature founded by Tristan Tzara in 1916. Followers of the movement expressed their outrage at the destruction brought about by World War I by revolting against numerous forms of social convention. The Dadaists presented works marked by calculated madness and flamboyant nonsense. They stressed total freedom of expression, commonly through primitive displays of emotion and illogical, often senseless, poetry. The movement ended shortly after the war, when it was replaced by surrealism.

Decadent: See *Decadents*

Decadents: The followers of a nineteenth-century literary movement that had its beginnings in French aestheticism. Decadent literature displays a fascination with perverse and morbid states; a search for novelty and sensation—the "new thrill"; a preoccupation with mysticism; and a belief in the senselessness of human existence. The movement is closely associated with the doctrine Art for Art's Sake. The term "decadence" is sometimes used to denote a decline in the quality of art or literature following a period of greatness.

Deconstruction: A method of literary criticism developed by Jacques Derrida and characterized by multiple conflicting interpretations of a given work. Deconstructionists consider the impact of the language of a work and suggest that the true meaning of the work is not necessarily the meaning that the author intended.

Deduction: The process of reaching a conclusion through reasoning from general premises to a specific premise.

Denotation: The definition of a word, apart from the impressions or feelings it creates in the reader.

Diction: The selection and arrangement of words in a literary work. Either or both may vary de-

pending on the desired effect. There are four general types of diction: "formal," used in scholarly or lofty writing; "informal," used in relaxed but educated conversation; "colloquial," used in everyday speech; and "slang," containing newly coined words and other terms not accepted in formal usage.

Didactic: A term used to describe works of literature that aim to teach some moral, religious, political, or practical lesson. Although didactic elements are often found in artistically pleasing works, the term "didactic" usually refers to literature in which the message is more important than the form. The term may also be used to criticize a work that the critic finds "overly didactic," that is, heavy-handed in its delivery of a lesson.

Dimeter: See *Meter*

Dionysian: See *Apollonian and Dionysian*

Discordia concours: A Latin phrase meaning "discord in harmony." The term was coined by the eighteenth-century English writer Samuel Johnson to describe "a combination of dissimilar images or discovery of occult resemblances in things apparently unlike." Johnson created the expression by reversing a phrase by the Latin poet Horace.

Dissonance: A combination of harsh or jarring sounds, especially in poetry. Although such combinations may be accidental, poets sometimes intentionally make them to achieve particular effects. Dissonance is also sometimes used to refer to close but not identical rhymes. When this is the case, the word functions as a synonym for consonance.

Double Entendre: A corruption of a French phrase meaning "double meaning." The term is used to indicate a word or phrase that is deliberately ambiguous, especially when one of the meanings is risque or improper.

Draft: Any preliminary version of a written work. An author may write dozens of drafts which are revised to form the final work, or he or she may write only one, with few or no revisions.

Dramatic Monologue: See *Monologue*

Dramatic Poetry: Any lyric work that employs elements of drama such as dialogue, conflict, or characterization, but excluding works that are intended for stage presentation.

Dream Allegory: See *Dream Vision*

Dream Vision: A literary convention, chiefly of the Middle Ages. In a dream vision a story is presented as a literal dream of the narrator. This device was commonly used to teach moral and religious lessons.

E

Eclogue: In classical literature, a poem featuring rural themes and structured as a dialogue among shepherds. Eclogues often took specific poetic forms, such as elegies or love poems. Some were written as the soliloquy of a shepherd. In later centuries, "eclogue" came to refer to any poem that was in the pastoral tradition or that had a dialogue or monologue structure.

Edwardian: Describes cultural conventions identified with the period of the reign of Edward VII of England (1901-1910). Writers of the Edwardian Age typically displayed a strong reaction against the propriety and conservatism of the Victorian Age. Their work often exhibits distrust of authority in religion, politics, and art and expresses strong doubts about the soundness of conventional values.

Edwardian Age: See *Edwardian*

Electra Complex: A daughter's amorous obsession with her father.

Elegy: A lyric poem that laments the death of a person or the eventual death of all people. In a conventional elegy, set in a classical world, the poet and subject are spoken of as shepherds. In modern criticism, the word elegy is often used to refer to a poem that is melancholy or mournfully contemplative.

Elizabethan Age: A period of great economic growth, religious controversy, and nationalism closely associated with the reign of Elizabeth I of England (1558-1603). The Elizabethan Age is considered a part of the general renaissance—that is, the flowering of arts and literature—that took place in Europe during the fourteenth through sixteenth centuries. The era is considered the golden age of English literature. The most important dramas in English and a great deal of lyric poetry were produced during this period, and modern English criticism began around this time.

Empathy: A sense of shared experience, including emotional and physical feelings, with someone or something other than oneself. Empathy is often used to describe the response of a reader to a literary character.

English Sonnet: See *Sonnet*

Enjambment: The running over of the sense and structure of a line of verse or a couplet into the following verse or couplet.

Enlightenment, The: An eighteenth-century philosophical movement. It began in France but had a wide impact throughout Europe and America. Thinkers of the Enlightenment valued reason and believed that both the individual and society could achieve a state of perfection. Corresponding to this essentially humanist vision was a resistance to religious authority.

Epic: A long narrative poem about the adventures of a hero of great historic or legendary importance. The setting is vast and the action is often given cosmic significance through the intervention of supernatural forces such as gods, angels, or demons. Epics are typically written in a classical style of grand simplicity with elaborate metaphors and allusions that enhance the symbolic importance of a hero's adventures.

Epic Simile: See *Homeric Simile*

Epigram: A saying that makes the speaker's point quickly and concisely.

Epilogue: A concluding statement or section of a literary work. In dramas, particularly those of the seventeenth and eighteenth centuries, the epilogue is a closing speech, often in verse, delivered by an actor at the end of a play and spoken directly to the audience.

Epiphany: A sudden revelation of truth inspired by a seemingly trivial incident.

Epitaph: An inscription on a tomb or tombstone, or a verse written on the occasion of a person's death. Epitaphs may be serious or humorous.

Epithalamion: A song or poem written to honor and commemorate a marriage ceremony.

Epithalamium: See *Epithalamion*

Epithet: A word or phrase, often disparaging or abusive, that expresses a character trait of someone or something.

Erziehungsroman: See *Bildungsroman*

Essay: A prose composition with a focused subject of discussion. The term was coined by Michel de Montaigne to describe his 1580 collection of brief, informal reflections on himself and on various topics relating to human nature. An essay can also be a long, systematic discourse.

Existentialism: A predominantly twentieth-century philosophy concerned with the nature and perception of human existence. There are two major strains of existentialist thought: atheistic and Christian. Followers of atheistic existentialism believe that the individual is alone in a godless universe and that the basic human condition is one of suffering and loneliness. Nevertheless, because there are no fixed values, individuals can create their own characters—indeed, they can shape themselves— through the exercise of free will. The atheistic strain culminates in and is popularly associated with the works of Jean-Paul Sartre. The Christian existentialists, on the other hand, believe that only in God may people find freedom from life's anguish. The two strains hold certain beliefs in common: that existence cannot be fully understood or described through empirical effort; that anguish is a universal element of life; that individuals must bear responsibility for their actions; and that there is no common standard of behavior or perception for religious and ethical matters.

Expatriates: See *Expatriatism*

Expatriatism: The practice of leaving one's country to live for an extended period in another country.

Exposition: Writing intended to explain the nature of an idea, thing, or theme. Expository writing is often combined with description, narration, or argument. In dramatic writing, the exposition is the introductory material which presents the characters, setting, and tone of the play.

Expressionism: An indistinct literary term, originally used to describe an early twentieth-century school of German painting. The term applies to almost any mode of unconventional, highly subjective writing that distorts reality in some way.

Extended Monologue: See *Monologue*

F

Feet: See *Foot*

Feminine Rhyme: See *Rhyme*

Fiction: Any story that is the product of imagination rather than a documentation of fact. characters and events in such narratives may be based in real life but their ultimate form and configuration is a creation of the author.

Figurative Language: A technique in writing in which the author temporarily interrupts the order, construction, or meaning of the writing for a particular effect. This interruption takes the form of one or more figures of speech such as hyperbole, irony, or simile. Figurative language is the opposite of literal language, in which every word is truthful, accurate, and free of exaggeration or embellishment.

Figures of Speech: Writing that differs from customary conventions for construction, meaning, or-der, or significance for the purpose of a special meaning or effect. There are two major types of figures of speech: rhetorical figures, which do not make changes in the meaning of the words, and tropes, which do.

Fin de siecle: A French term meaning "end of the century." The term is used to denote the last decade of the nineteenth century, a transition period when writers and other artists abandoned old conventions and looked for new techniques and objectives.

First Person: See *Point of View*

Folk Ballad: See *Ballad*

Folklore: Traditions and myths preserved in a culture or group of people. Typically, these are passed on by word of mouth in various forms—such as legends, songs, and proverbs— or preserved in customs and ceremonies. This term was first used by W. J. Thoms in 1846.

Folktale: A story originating in oral tradition. Folktales fall into a variety of categories, including legends, ghost stories, fairy tales, fables, and anecdotes based on historical figures and events.

Foot: The smallest unit of rhythm in a line of poetry. In English-language poetry, a foot is typically one accented syllable combined with one or two unaccented syllables.

Form: The pattern or construction of a work which identifies its genre and distinguishes it from other genres.

Formalism: In literary criticism, the belief that literature should follow prescribed rules of construction, such as those that govern the sonnet form.

Fourteener Meter: See *Meter*

Free Verse: Poetry that lacks regular metrical and rhyme patterns but that tries to capture the cadences of everyday speech. The form allows a poet to exploit a variety of rhythmical effects within a single poem.

Futurism: A flamboyant literary and artistic movement that developed in France, Italy, and Russia from 1908 through the 1920s. Futurist theater and poetry abandoned traditional literary forms. In their place, followers of the movement attempted to achieve total freedom of expression through bizarre imagery and deformed or newly invented words. The Futurists were self-consciously modern artists who attempted to incorporate the appearances and sounds of modern life into their work.

G

Genre: A category of literary work. In critical theory, genre may refer to both the content of a given work—tragedy, comedy, pastoral—and to its form, such as poetry, novel, or drama.

Genteel Tradition: A term coined by critic George Santayana to describe the literary practice of certain late nineteenth- century American writers, especially New Englanders. Followers of the Genteel Tradition emphasized conventionality in social, religious, moral, and literary standards.

Georgian Age: See *Georgian Poets*

Georgian Period: See *Georgian Poets*

Georgian Poets: A loose grouping of English poets during the years 1912-1922. The Georgians reacted against certain literary schools and practices, especially Victorian wordiness, turn-of-the-century aestheticism, and contemporary urban realism. In their place, the Georgians embraced the nineteenth-century poetic practices of William Wordsworth and the other Lake Poets.

Georgic: A poem about farming and the farmer's way of life, named from Virgil's *Georgics.*

Gilded Age: A period in American history during the 1870s characterized by political corruption and materialism. A number of important novels of social and political criticism were written during this time.

Gothic: See *Gothicism*

Gothicism: In literary criticism, works characterized by a taste for the medieval or morbidly attractive. A gothic novel prominently features elements of horror, the supernatural, gloom, and violence: clanking chains, terror, charnel houses, ghosts, medieval castles, and mysteriously slamming doors. The term "gothic novel" is also applied to novels that lack elements of the traditional Gothic setting but that create a similar atmosphere of terror or dread.

Graveyard School: A group of eighteenth-century English poets who wrote long, picturesque meditations on death. Their works were designed to cause the reader to ponder immortality.

Great Chain of Being: The belief that all things and creatures in nature are organized in a hierarchy from inanimate objects at the bottom to God at the top. This system of belief was popular in the seventeenth and eighteenth centuries.

Grotesque: In literary criticism, the subject matter of a work or a style of expression characterized by exaggeration, deformity, freakishness, and disorder. The grotesque often includes an element of comic absurdity.

H

Haiku: The shortest form of Japanese poetry, constructed in three lines of five, seven, and five syllables respectively. The message of a *haiku* poem usually centers on some aspect of spirituality and provokes an emotional response in the reader.

Half Rhyme: See *Consonance*

Harlem Renaissance: The Harlem Renaissance of the 1920s is generally considered the first significant movement of black writers and artists in the United States. During this period, new and established black writers published more fiction and poetry than ever before, the first influential black literary journals were established, and black authors and artists received their first widespread recognition and serious critical appraisal. Among the major writers associated with this period are Claude McKay, Jean Toomer, Countee Cullen, Langston Hughes, Arna Bontemps, Nella Larsen, and Zora Neale Hurston.

Hellenism: Imitation of ancient Greek thought or styles. Also, an approach to life that focuses on the growth and development of the intellect. "Hellenism" is sometimes used to refer to the belief that reason can be applied to examine all human experience.

Heptameter: See *Meter*

Hero/Heroine: The principal sympathetic character (male or female) in a literary work. Heroes and heroines typically exhibit admirable traits: idealism, courage, and integrity, for example.

Heroic Couplet: A rhyming couplet written in iambic pentameter (a verse with five iambic feet).

Heroic Line: The meter and length of a line of verse in epic or heroic poetry. This varies by language and time period.

Heroine: See *Hero/Heroine*

Hexameter: See *Meter*

Historical Criticism: The study of a work based on its impact on the world of the time period in which it was written.

Hokku: See *Haiku*

Holocaust: See *Holocaust Literature*

Holocaust Literature: Literature influenced by or written about the Holocaust of World War II. Such literature includes true stories of survival in concentration camps, escape, and life after the war, as well as fictional works and poetry.

Homeric Simile: An elaborate, detailed comparison written as a simile many lines in length.

Horatian Satire: See *Satire*

Humanism: A philosophy that places faith in the dignity of humankind and rejects the medieval perception of the individual as a weak, fallen creature. "Humanists" typically believe in the perfectibility of human nature and view reason and education as the means to that end.

Humors: Mentions of the humors refer to the ancient Greek theory that a person's health and personality were determined by the balance of four basic fluids in the body: blood, phlegm, yellow bile, and black bile. A dominance of any fluid would cause extremes in behavior. An excess of blood created a sanguine person who was joyful, aggressive, and passionate; a phlegmatic person was shy, fearful, and sluggish; too much yellow bile led to a choleric temperament characterized by impatience, anger, bitterness, and stubbornness; and excessive black bile created melancholy, a state of laziness, gluttony, and lack of motivation.

Humours: See *Humors*

Hyperbole: In literary criticism, deliberate exaggeration used to achieve an effect.

I

Iamb: See *Foot*

Idiom: A word construction or verbal expression closely associated with a given language.

Image: A concrete representation of an object or sensory experience. Typically, such a representation helps evoke the feelings associated with the object or experience itself. Images are either "literal" or "figurative." Literal images are especially concrete and involve little or no extension of the obvious meaning of the words used to express them. Figurative images do not follow the literal meaning of the words exactly. Images in literature are usually visual, but the term "image" can also refer to the representation of any sensory experience.

Imagery: The array of images in a literary work. Also, figurative language.

Imagism: An English and American poetry movement that flourished between 1908 and 1917. The Imagists used precise, clearly presented images in their works. They also used common, everyday speech and aimed for conciseness, concrete imagery, and the creation of new rhythms.

In medias res: A Latin term meaning "in the middle of things." It refers to the technique of beginning a story at its midpoint and then using various flashback devices to reveal previous action.

Induction: The process of reaching a conclusion by reasoning from specific premises to form a general premise. Also, an introductory portion of a work of literature, especially a play.

Intentional Fallacy: The belief that judgments of a literary work based solely on an author's stated or implied intentions are false and misleading. Critics who believe in the concept of the intentional fallacy typically argue that the work itself is sufficient matter for interpretation, even though they may concede that an author's statement of purpose can be useful.

Interior Monologue: A narrative technique in which characters' thoughts are revealed in a way that appears to be uncontrolled by the author. The interior monologue typically aims to reveal the inner self of a character. It portrays emotional experiences as they occur at both a conscious and unconscious level. images are often used to represent sensations or emotions.

Internal Rhyme: Rhyme that occurs within a single line of verse.

Irish Literary Renaissance: A late nineteenth- and early twentieth-century movement in Irish literature. Members of the movement aimed to reduce the influence of British culture in Ireland and create an Irish national literature.

Irony: In literary criticism, the effect of language in which the intended meaning is the opposite of what is stated.

Italian Sonnet: See *Sonnet*

J

Jacobean Age: The period of the reign of James I of England (1603-1625). The early literature of this period reflected the worldview of the Elizabethan Age, but a darker, more cynical attitude steadily grew in the art and literature of the Jacobean Age. This was an important time for English drama and poetry.

Jargon: Language that is used or understood only by a select group of people. Jargon may refer to terminology used in a certain profession, such as computer jargon, or it may refer to any nonsensical language that is not understood by most people.

Journalism: Writing intended for publication in a newspaper or magazine, or for broadcast on a radio or television program featuring news, sports, entertainment, or other timely material.

K

Knickerbocker Group: A somewhat indistinct group of New York writers of the first half of the nineteenth century. Members of the group were linked only by location and a common theme: New York life.

Kunstlerroman: See *Bildungsroman*

L

Lais: See *Lay*

Lake Poets: See *Lake School*

Lake School: These poets all lived in the Lake District of England at the turn of the nineteenth century. As a group, they followed no single "school" of thought or literary practice, although their works were uniformly disparaged by the *Edinburgh Review.*

Lay: A song or simple narrative poem. The form originated in medieval France. Early French *lais* were often based on the Celtic legends and other tales sung by Breton minstrels—thus the name of the "Breton lay." In fourteenth-century England, the term "lay" was used to describe short narratives written in imitation of the Breton lays.

Leitmotiv: See *Motif*

Literal Language: An author uses literal language when he or she writes without exaggerating or embellishing the subject matter and without any tools of figurative language.

Literary Ballad: See *Ballad*

Literature: Literature is broadly defined as any written or spoken material, but the term most often refers to creative works.

Lost Generation: A term first used by Gertrude Stein to describe the post-World War I generation of American writers: men and women haunted by a sense of betrayal and emptiness brought about by the destructiveness of the war.

Lyric Poetry: A poem expressing the subjective feelings and personal emotions of the poet. Such poetry is melodic, since it was originally accompanied by a lyre in recitals. Most Western poetry in the twentieth century may be classified as lyrical.

M

Mannerism: Exaggerated, artificial adherence to a literary manner or style. Also, a popular style of the visual arts of late sixteenth-century Europe that was marked by elongation of the human form and by intentional spatial distortion. Literary works that are self-consciously high-toned and artistic are often said to be "mannered."

Masculine Rhyme: See *Rhyme*

Measure: The foot, verse, or time sequence used in a literary work, especially a poem. Measure is often used somewhat incorrectly as a synonym for meter.

Metaphor: A figure of speech that expresses an idea through the image of another object. Metaphors suggest the essence of the first object by identifying it with certain qualities of the second object.

Metaphysical Conceit: See *Conceit*

Metaphysical Poetry: The body of poetry produced by a group of seventeenth-century English writers called the "Metaphysical Poets." The group includes John Donne and Andrew Marvell. The Metaphysical Poets made use of everyday speech, intellectual analysis, and unique imagery. They aimed to portray the ordinary conflicts and contradictions of life. Their poems often took the form of an argument, and many of them emphasize physical and religious love as well as the fleeting nature of life. Elaborate conceits are typical in metaphysical poetry.

Metaphysical Poets: See *Metaphysical Poetry*

Meter: In literary criticism, the repetition of sound patterns that creates a rhythm in poetry. The patterns are based on the number of syllables and the presence and absence of accents. The unit of rhythm in a line is called a foot. Types of meter are classified according to the number of feet in a line. These are the standard English lines: Monometer, one foot; Dimeter, two feet; Trimeter, three feet; Tetrameter, four feet; Pentameter, five feet; Hexameter, six feet (also called the Alexandrine); Heptameter, seven feet (also called the "Fourteener" when the feet are iambic).

Modernism: Modern literary practices. Also, the principles of a literary school that lasted from roughly the beginning of the twentieth century until the end of World War II. Modernism is defined by its rejection of the literary conventions of the nineteenth century and by its opposition to conventional morality, taste, traditions, and economic values.

Monologue: A composition, written or oral, by a single individual. More specifically, a speech given by a single individual in a drama or other public entertainment. It has no set length, although it is usually several or more lines long.

Monometer: See *Meter*

Mood: The prevailing emotions of a work or of the author in his or her creation of the work. The mood of a work is not always what might be expected based on its subject matter.

Motif: A theme, character type, image, metaphor, or other verbal element that recurs throughout a single work of literature or occurs in a number of different works over a period of time.

Motiv: See *Motif*

Muckrakers: An early twentieth-century group of American writers. Typically, their works exposed the wrongdoings of big business and government in the United States.

Muses: Nine Greek mythological goddesses, the daughters of Zeus and Mnemosyne (Memory). Each muse patronized a specific area of the liberal arts and sciences. Calliope presided over epic poetry, Clio over history, Erato over love poetry, Euterpe over music or lyric poetry, Melpomene over tragedy, Polyhymnia over hymns to the gods, Terpsichore over dance, Thalia over comedy, and Urania over astronomy. Poets and writers traditionally made appeals to the Muses for inspiration in their work.

Myth: An anonymous tale emerging from the traditional beliefs of a culture or social unit. Myths use supernatural explanations for natural phenomena. They may also explain cosmic issues like creation and death. Collections of myths, known as mythologies, are common to all cultures and nations, but the best-known myths belong to the Norse, Roman, and Greek mythologies.

N

Narration: The telling of a series of events, real or invented. A narration may be either a simple narrative, in which the events are recounted chronologically, or a narrative with a plot, in which the account is given in a style reflecting the author's artistic concept of the story. Narration is sometimes used as a synonym for "storyline."

Narrative: A verse or prose accounting of an event or sequence of events, real or invented. The term is also used as an adjective in the sense "method of narration." For example, in literary criticism, the expression "narrative technique" usually refers to the way the author structures and presents his or her story.

Narrative Poetry: A nondramatic poem in which the author tells a story. Such poems may be of any length or level of complexity.

Narrator: The teller of a story. The narrator may be the author or a character in the story through whom the author speaks.

Naturalism: A literary movement of the late nineteenth and early twentieth centuries. The movement's major theorist, French novelist Emile Zola, envisioned a type of fiction that would examine human life with the objectivity of scientific inquiry. The Naturalists typically viewed human beings as either the products of "biological determinism," ruled by hereditary instincts and engaged in an endless struggle for survival, or as the products of "socioeconomic determinism," ruled by social and economic forces beyond their control. In their works, the Naturalists generally ignored the highest levels of society and focused on degradation: poverty, alcoholism, prostitution, insanity, and disease.

Negritude: A literary movement based on the concept of a shared cultural bond on the part of black Africans, wherever they may be in the world. It traces its origins to the former French colonies of Africa and the Caribbean. Negritude poets, novelists, and essayists generally stress four points in their writings: One, black alienation from traditional African culture can lead to feelings of inferiority. Two, European colonialism and Western education should be resisted. Three, black Africans should seek to affirm and define their own identity. Four, African culture can and should be reclaimed. Many Negritude writers also claim that blacks can make unique contributions to the world, based on a heightened appreciation of nature, rhythm, and human emotions—aspects of life they say are not so highly valued in the materialistic and rationalistic West.

Negro Renaissance: See *Harlem Renaissance*

Neoclassical Period: See *Neoclassicism*

Neoclassicism: In literary criticism, this term refers to the revival of the attitudes and styles of expression of classical literature. It is generally used to describe a period in European history beginning in the late seventeenth century and lasting until about 1800. In its purest form, Neoclassicism marked a return to order, proportion, restraint, logic, accuracy, and decorum. In England, where Neoclassicism perhaps was most popular, it reflected the influence of seventeenth- century French writers, especially dramatists. Neoclassical writers typically reacted against the intensity and enthusiasm of the Renaissance period. They wrote works that appealed to the intellect, using elevated language and classical literary forms such as satire and the ode. Neoclassical works were often governed by the classical goal of instruction.

Neoclassicists: See *Neoclassicism*

New Criticism: A movement in literary criticism, dating from the late 1920s, that stressed close textual analysis in the interpretation of works of literature. The New Critics saw little merit in historical and biographical analysis. Rather, they aimed to examine the text alone, free from the question of how external events—biographical or otherwise—may have helped shape it.

New Journalism: A type of writing in which the journalist presents factual information in a form usually used in fiction. New journalism emphasizes description, narration, and character development to bring readers closer to the human element of the story, and is often used in personality profiles and in-depth feature articles. It is not compatible with "straight" or "hard" newswriting, which is generally composed in a brief, fact-based style.

New Journalists: See *New Journalism*

New Negro Movement: See *Harlem Renaissance*

Noble Savage: The idea that primitive man is noble and good but becomes evil and corrupted as he becomes civilized. The concept of the noble savage originated in the Renaissance period but is more closely identified with such later writers as Jean-Jacques Rousseau and Aphra Behn.

O

Objective Correlative: An outward set of objects, a situation, or a chain of events corresponding to an inward experience and evoking this experience in the reader. The term frequently appears in modern criticism in discussions of authors' intended effects on the emotional responses of readers.

Objectivity: A quality in writing characterized by the absence of the author's opinion or feeling about the subject matter. Objectivity is an important factor in criticism.

Occasional Verse: poetry written on the occasion of a significant historical or personal event. *Vers de societe* is sometimes called occasional verse although it is of a less serious nature.

Octave: A poem or stanza composed of eight lines. The term octave most often represents the first eight lines of a Petrarchan sonnet.

Ode: Name given to an extended lyric poem characterized by exalted emotion and dignified style. An ode usually concerns a single, serious theme. Most odes, but not all, are addressed to an object or individual. Odes are distinguished from other lyric poetic forms by their complex rhythmic and stanzaic patterns.

Oedipus Complex: A son's amorous obsession with his mother. The phrase is derived from the story of the ancient Theban hero Oedipus, who unknowingly killed his father and married his mother.

Omniscience: See *Point of View*

Onomatopoeia: The use of words whose sounds express or suggest their meaning. In its simplest sense, onomatopoeia may be represented by words that mimic the sounds they denote such as "hiss" or "meow." At a more subtle level, the pattern and rhythm of sounds and rhymes of a line or poem may be onomatopoeic.

Oral Tradition: See *Oral Transmission*

Oral Transmission: A process by which songs, ballads, folklore, and other material are transmitted by word of mouth. The tradition of oral transmission predates the written record systems of literate society. Oral transmission preserves material sometimes over generations, although often with variations. Memory plays a large part in the recitation and preservation of orally transmitted material.

Ottava Rima: An eight-line stanza of poetry composed in iambic pentameter (a five-foot line in which each foot consists of an unaccented syllable followed by an accented syllable), following the abababcc rhyme scheme.

Oxymoron: A phrase combining two contradictory terms. Oxymorons may be intentional or unintentional.

P

Pantheism: The idea that all things are both a manifestation or revelation of God and a part of God at the same time. Pantheism was a common attitude in the early societies of Egypt, India, and Greece—the term derives from the Greek *pan* meaning "all" and *theos* meaning "deity." It later became a significant part of the Christian faith.

Parable: A story intended to teach a moral lesson or answer an ethical question.

Paradox: A statement that appears illogical or contradictory at first, but may actually point to an underlying truth.

Parallelism: A method of comparison of two ideas in which each is developed in the same grammatical structure.

Parnassianism: A mid nineteenth-century movement in French literature. Followers of the movement stressed adherence to well-defined artistic forms as a reaction against the often chaotic expression of the artist's ego that dominated the work of the Romantics. The Parnassians also rejected the moral, ethical, and social themes exhibited in the works of French Romantics such as Victor Hugo. The aesthetic doctrines of the Parnassians strongly influenced the later symbolist and decadent movements.

Parody: In literary criticism, this term refers to an imitation of a serious literary work or the signature style of a particular author in a ridiculous manner. A typical parody adopts the style of the original and applies it to an inappropriate subject for humorous effect. Parody is a form of satire and could be considered the literary equivalent of a caricature or cartoon.

Pastoral: A term derived from the Latin word "pastor," meaning shepherd. A pastoral is a literary composition on a rural theme. The conventions of the pastoral were originated by the third-century Greek poet Theocritus, who wrote about the experiences, love affairs, and pastimes of Sicilian shepherds. In a pastoral, characters and language of a courtly nature are often placed in a simple setting. The term pastoral is also used to classify dramas, elegies, and lyrics that exhibit the use of country settings and shepherd characters.

Pathetic Fallacy: A term coined by English critic John Ruskin to identify writing that falsely endows nonhuman things with human intentions and feelings, such as "angry clouds" and "sad trees."

Pen Name: See *Pseudonym*

Pentameter: See *Meter*

Persona: A Latin term meaning "mask." *Personae* are the characters in a fictional work of literature. The *persona* generally functions as a mask through which the author tells a story in a voice other than his or her own. A *persona* is usually either a character in a story who acts as a narrator or an "implied author," a voice created by the author to act as the narrator for himself or herself.

Personae: See *Persona*

Personal Point of View: See *Point of View*

Personification: A figure of speech that gives human qualities to abstract ideas, animals, and inanimate objects.

Petrarchan Sonnet: See *Sonnet*

Phenomenology: A method of literary criticism based on the belief that things have no existence outside of human consciousness or awareness. Proponents of this theory believe that art is a process that takes place in the mind of the observer as he or she contemplates an object rather than a quality of the object itself.

Plagiarism: Claiming another person's written material as one's own. Plagiarism can take the form of direct, word-for-word copying or the theft of the substance or idea of the work.

Platonic Criticism: A form of criticism that stresses an artistic work's usefulness as an agent of social engineering rather than any quality or value of the work itself.

Platonism: The embracing of the doctrines of the philosopher Plato, popular among the poets of the Renaissance and the Romantic period. Platonism is more flexible than Aristotelian Criticism and places more emphasis on the supernatural and unknown aspects of life.

Plot: In literary criticism, this term refers to the pattern of events in a narrative or drama. In its simplest sense, the plot guides the author in composing the work and helps the reader follow the work. Typically, plots exhibit causality and unity and have a beginning, a middle, and an end. Sometimes, however, a plot may consist of a series of disconnected events, in which case it is known as an "episodic plot."

Poem: In its broadest sense, a composition utilizing rhyme, meter, concrete detail, and expressive language to create a literary experience with emotional and aesthetic appeal.

Poet: An author who writes poetry or verse. The term is also used to refer to an artist or writer who has an exceptional gift for expression, imagination, and energy in the making of art in any form.

Poete maudit: A term derived from Paul Verlaine's *Les poetes maudits* (*The Accursed Poets*), a collection of essays on the French symbolist writers Stephane Mallarme, Arthur Rimbaud, and Tristan Corbiere. In the sense intended by Verlaine, the poet is "accursed" for choosing to explore extremes of human experience outside of middle-class society.

Poetic Fallacy: See *Pathetic Fallacy*

Poetic Justice: An outcome in a literary work, not necessarily a poem, in which the good are rewarded and the evil are punished, especially in ways that particularly fit their virtues or crimes.

Poetic License: Distortions of fact and literary convention made by a writer—not always a poet—for the sake of the effect gained. Poetic license is closely related to the concept of "artistic freedom."

Poetics: This term has two closely related meanings. It denotes (1) an aesthetic theory in literary criticism about the essence of poetry or (2) rules prescribing the proper methods, content, style, or diction of poetry. The term poetics may also refer to theories about literature in general, not just poetry.

Poetry: In its broadest sense, writing that aims to present ideas and evoke an emotional experience in the reader through the use of meter, imagery, connotative and concrete words, and a carefully constructed structure based on rhythmic patterns. Poetry typically relies on words and expressions that have several layers of meaning. It also makes use of the effects of regular rhythm on the ear and may make a strong appeal to the senses through the use of imagery.

Point of View: The narrative perspective from which a literary work is presented to the reader. There are four traditional points of view. The "third person omniscient" gives the reader a "godlike" perspective, unrestricted by time or place, from which to see actions and look into the minds of characters. This allows the author to comment openly on characters and events in the work. The "third person" point of view presents the events of the story from outside of any single character's perception, much like the omniscient point of view, but the reader must understand the action as it takes place and without any special insight into characters' minds or motivations. The "first person" or "personal" point of view relates events as they are perceived by a single character. The main character "tells" the story and may offer opinions about the action and characters which differ from those of the author. Much less common than omniscient, third person, and first person is the "second person" point of view, wherein the author tells the story as if it is happening to the reader.

Polemic: A work in which the author takes a stand on a controversial subject, such as abortion or religion. Such works are often extremely argumentative or provocative.

Pornography: Writing intended to provoke feelings of lust in the reader. Such works are often condemned by critics and teachers, but those which can be shown to have literary value are viewed less harshly.

Post-Aesthetic Movement: An artistic response made by African Americans to the black aesthetic movement of the 1960s and early '70s. Writers since that time have adopted a somewhat different tone in their work, with less emphasis placed on the disparity between black and white in the United States. In the words of post-aesthetic authors such as Toni Morrison, John Edgar Wideman, and Kristin Hunter, African Americans are portrayed as looking inward for answers to their own questions, rather than always looking to the outside world.

Postmodernism: Writing from the 1960s forward characterized by experimentation and continuing to apply some of the fundamentals of modernism, which included existentialism and alienation. Postmodernists have gone a step further in the rejection of tradition begun with the modernists by also rejecting traditional forms, preferring the anti-novel over the novel and the anti-hero over the hero.

Pre-Raphaelites: A circle of writers and artists in mid nineteenth-century England. Valuing the pre-Renaissance artistic qualities of religious symbolism, lavish pictorialism, and natural sensuousness, the Pre-Raphaelites cultivated a sense of mystery and melancholy that influenced later writers associated with the Symbolist and Decadent movements.

Primitivism: The belief that primitive peoples were nobler and less flawed than civilized peoples because they had not been subjected to the tainting influence of society.

Projective Verse: A form of free verse in which the poet's breathing pattern determines the lines of the poem. Poets who advocate projective verse are against all formal structures in writing, including meter and form.

Prologue: An introductory section of a literary work. It often contains information establishing the situation of the characters or presents information about the setting, time period, or action. In drama, the prologue is spoken by a chorus or by one of the principal characters.

Prose: A literary medium that attempts to mirror the language of everyday speech. It is distinguished from poetry by its use of unmetered, unrhymed language consisting of logically related sentences. Prose is usually grouped into paragraphs that form a cohesive whole such as an essay or a novel.

Prosopopoeia: See *Personification*

Protagonist: The central character of a story who serves as a focus for its themes and incidents and as the principal rationale for its development. The protagonist is sometimes referred to in discussions of modern literature as the hero or anti-hero.

Proverb: A brief, sage saying that expresses a truth about life in a striking manner.

Pseudonym: A name assumed by a writer, most often intended to prevent his or her identification as the author of a work. Two or more authors may work together under one pseudonym, or an author may use a different name for each genre he or she publishes in. Some publishing companies maintain "house pseudonyms," under which any number of authors may write installations in a series. Some authors also choose a pseudonym over their real names the way an actor may use a stage name.

Pun: A play on words that have similar sounds but different meanings.

Pure Poetry: poetry written without instructional intent or moral purpose that aims only to please a reader by its imagery or musical flow. The term pure poetry is used as the antonym of the term "didacticism."

Q

Quatrain: A four-line stanza of a poem or an entire poem consisting of four lines.

R

Realism: A nineteenth-century European literary movement that sought to portray familiar characters, situations, and settings in a realistic manner. This was done primarily by using an objective narrative point of view and through the buildup of accurate detail. The standard for success of any realistic work depends on how faithfully it transfers common experience into fictional forms. The realistic method may be altered or extended, as in stream of consciousness writing, to record highly subjective experience.

Refrain: A phrase repeated at intervals throughout a poem. A refrain may appear at the end of each stanza or at less regular intervals. It may be altered slightly at each appearance.

Renaissance: The period in European history that marked the end of the Middle Ages. It began in Italy in the late fourteenth century. In broad terms, it is usually seen as spanning the fourteenth, fifteenth, and sixteenth centuries, although it did not reach Great Britain, for example, until the 1480s or so. The Renaissance saw an awakening in almost every sphere of human activity, especially science, philosophy, and the arts. The period is best defined by the emergence of a general philosophy that emphasized the importance of the intellect, the individual, and world affairs. It contrasts strongly with the medieval worldview, characterized by the dominant concerns of faith, the social collective, and spiritual salvation.

Repartee: Conversation featuring snappy retorts and witticisms.

Restoration: See *Restoration Age*

Restoration Age: A period in English literature beginning with the crowning of Charles II in 1660 and running to about 1700. The era, which was characterized by a reaction against Puritanism, was the first great age of the comedy of manners. The finest literature of the era is typically witty and urbane, and often lewd.

Rhetoric: In literary criticism, this term denotes the art of ethical persuasion. In its strictest sense, rhetoric adheres to various principles developed since classical times for arranging facts and ideas in a clear, persuasive, appealing manner. The term is also used to refer to effective prose in general and theories of or methods for composing effective prose.

Rhetorical Question: A question intended to provoke thought, but not an expressed answer, in the reader. It is most commonly used in oratory and other persuasive genres.

Rhyme: When used as a noun in literary criticism, this term generally refers to a poem in which words sound identical or very similar and appear in parallel positions in two or more lines. Rhymes are classified into different types according to where they fall in a line or stanza or according to the degree of similarity they exhibit in their spellings and sounds. Some major types of rhyme are "masculine" rhyme, "feminine" rhyme, and "triple" rhyme. In a masculine rhyme, the rhyming sound falls in a single accented syllable, as with "heat" and "eat." Feminine rhyme is a rhyme of two syllables, one stressed and one unstressed, as with "merry" and "tarry." Triple rhyme matches the sound of the accented syllable and the two unaccented syllables that follow: "narrative" and "declarative."

Rhyme Royal: A stanza of seven lines composed in iambic pentameter and rhymed *ababbcc*. The name is said to be a tribute to King James I of Scotland, who made much use of the form in his poetry.

Rhyme Scheme: See *Rhyme*

Rhythm: A regular pattern of sound, time intervals, or events occurring in writing, most often and most discernably in poetry. Regular, reliable rhythm is known to be soothing to humans, while interrupted, unpredictable, or rapidly changing rhythm is disturbing. These effects are known to authors, who use them to produce a desired reaction in the reader.

Rococo: A style of European architecture that flourished in the eighteenth century, especially in France. The most notable features of *rococo* are its extensive use of ornamentation and its themes of lightness, gaiety, and intimacy. In literary criticism, the term is often used disparagingly to refer to a decadent or over-ornamental style.

Romance:

Romantic Age: See *Romanticism*

Romanticism: This term has two widely accepted meanings. In historical criticism, it refers to a European intellectual and artistic movement of the late eighteenth and early nineteenth centuries that sought greater freedom of personal expression than that allowed by the strict rules of literary form and logic of the eighteenth-century neoclassicists. The Romantics preferred emotional and imaginative expression to rational analysis. They considered the individual to be at the center of all experience and so placed him or her at the center of their art. The Romantics believed that the creative imagination reveals nobler truths—unique feelings and attitudes—than those that could be discovered by logic or by scientific examination. Both the natural world and the state of childhood were important sources for revelations of "eternal truths." "Romanticism" is also used as a general term to refer to a type of sensibility found in all periods of literary history and usually considered to be in opposition to the principles of classicism. In this sense, Romanticism signifies any work or philosophy in which the exotic or dreamlike figure strongly, or that is devoted to individualistic expression, self-analysis, or a pursuit of a higher realm of knowledge than can be discovered by human reason.

Romantics: See *Romanticism*

Russian Symbolism: A Russian poetic movement, derived from French symbolism, that flour-

ished between 1894 and 1910. While some Russian Symbolists continued in the French tradition, stressing aestheticism and the importance of suggestion above didactic intent, others saw their craft as a form of mystical worship, and themselves as mediators between the supernatural and the mundane.

S

Satire: A work that uses ridicule, humor, and wit to criticize and provoke change in human nature and institutions. There are two major types of satire: "formal" or "direct" satire speaks directly to the reader or to a character in the work; "indirect" satire relies upon the ridiculous behavior of its characters to make its point. Formal satire is further divided into two manners: the "Horatian," which ridicules gently, and the "Juvenalian," which derides its subjects harshly and bitterly.

Scansion: The analysis or "scanning" of a poem to determine its meter and often its rhyme scheme. The most common system of scansion uses accents (slanted lines drawn above syllables) to show stressed syllables, breves (curved lines drawn above syllables) to show unstressed syllables, and vertical lines to separate each foot.

Second Person: See *Point of View*

Semiotics: The study of how literary forms and conventions affect the meaning of language.

Sestet: Any six-line poem or stanza.

Setting: The time, place, and culture in which the action of a narrative takes place. The elements of setting may include geographic location, characters' physical and mental environments, prevailing cultural attitudes, or the historical time in which the action takes place.

Shakespearean Sonnet: See *Sonnet*

Signifying Monkey: A popular trickster figure in black folklore, with hundreds of tales about this character documented since the 19th century.

Simile: A comparison, usually using "like" or "as", of two essentially dissimilar things, as in "coffee as cold as ice" or "He sounded like a broken record."

Slang: A type of informal verbal communication that is generally unacceptable for formal writing. Slang words and phrases are often colorful exaggerations used to emphasize the speaker's point; they may also be shortened versions of an often-used word or phrase.

Slant Rhyme: See *Consonance*

Slave Narrative: Autobiographical accounts of American slave life as told by escaped slaves. These works first appeared during the abolition movement of the 1830s through the 1850s.

Social Realism: See *Socialist Realism*

Socialist Realism: The Socialist Realism school of literary theory was proposed by Maxim Gorky and established as a dogma by the first Soviet Congress of Writers. It demanded adherence to a communist worldview in works of literature. Its doctrines required an objective viewpoint comprehensible to the working classes and themes of social struggle featuring strong proletarian heroes.

Soliloquy: A monologue in a drama used to give the audience information and to develop the speaker's character. It is typically a projection of the speaker's innermost thoughts. Usually delivered while the speaker is alone on stage, a soliloquy is intended to present an illusion of unspoken reflection.

Sonnet: A fourteen-line poem, usually composed in iambic pentameter, employing one of several rhyme schemes. There are three major types of sonnets, upon which all other variations of the form are based: the "Petrarchan" or "Italian" sonnet, the "Shakespearean" or "English" sonnet, and the "Spenserian" sonnet. A Petrarchan sonnet consists of an octave rhymed *abbaabba* and a "sestet" rhymed either *cdecde, cdccdc,* or *cdedce.* The octave poses a question or problem, relates a narrative, or puts forth a proposition; the sestet presents a solution to the problem, comments upon the narrative, or applies the proposition put forth in the octave. The Shakespearean sonnet is divided into three quatrains and a couplet rhymed *abab cdcd efef gg.* The couplet provides an epigrammatic comment on the narrative or problem put forth in the quatrains. The Spenserian sonnet uses three quatrains and a couplet like the Shakespearean, but links their three rhyme schemes in this way: *abab bcbc cdcd ee.* The Spenserian sonnet develops its theme in two parts like the Petrarchan, its final six lines resolving a problem, analyzing a narrative, or applying a proposition put forth in its first eight lines.

Spenserian Sonnet: See *Sonnet*

Spenserian Stanza: A nine-line stanza having eight verses in iambic pentameter, its ninth verse in iambic hexameter, and the rhyme scheme ababbcbcc.

Spondee: In poetry meter, a foot consisting of two long or stressed syllables occurring together. This form is quite rare in English verse, and is usually composed of two monosyllabic words.

Sprung Rhythm: Versification using a specific number of accented syllables per line but disregarding the number of unaccented syllables that fall in each line, producing an irregular rhythm in the poem.

Stanza: A subdivision of a poem consisting of lines grouped together, often in recurring patterns of rhyme, line length, and meter. Stanzas may also serve as units of thought in a poem much like paragraphs in prose.

Stereotype: A stereotype was originally the name for a duplication made during the printing process; this led to its modern definition as a person or thing that is (or is assumed to be) the same as all others of its type.

Stream of Consciousness: A narrative technique for rendering the inward experience of a character. This technique is designed to give the impression of an ever-changing series of thoughts, emotions, images, and memories in the spontaneous and seemingly illogical order that they occur in life.

Structuralism: A twentieth-century movement in literary criticism that examines how literary texts arrive at their meanings, rather than the meanings themselves. There are two major types of structuralist analysis: one examines the way patterns of linguistic structures unify a specific text and emphasize certain elements of that text, and the other interprets the way literary forms and conventions affect the meaning of language itself.

Structure: The form taken by a piece of literature. The structure may be made obvious for ease of understanding, as in nonfiction works, or may be obscured for artistic purposes, as in some poetry or seemingly "unstructured" prose.

***Sturm und Drang*:** A German term meaning "storm and stress." It refers to a German literary movement of the 1770s and 1780s that reacted against the order and rationalism of the enlightenment, focusing instead on the intense experience of extraordinary individuals.

Style: A writer's distinctive manner of arranging words to suit his or her ideas and purpose in writing. The unique imprint of the author's personality upon his or her writing, style is the product of an author's way of arranging ideas and his or her use of diction, different sentence structures, rhythm, figures of speech, rhetorical principles, and other elements of composition.

Subject: The person, event, or theme at the center of a work of literature. A work may have one or more subjects of each type, with shorter works tending to have fewer and longer works tending to have more.

Subjectivity: Writing that expresses the author's personal feelings about his subject, and which may or may not include factual information about the subject.

Surrealism: A term introduced to criticism by Guillaume Apollinaire and later adopted by Andre Breton. It refers to a French literary and artistic movement founded in the 1920s. The Surrealists sought to express unconscious thoughts and feelings in their works. The best-known technique used for achieving this aim was automatic writing—transcriptions of spontaneous outpourings from the unconscious. The Surrealists proposed to unify the contrary levels of conscious and unconscious, dream and reality, objectivity and subjectivity into a new level of "super-realism."

Suspense: A literary device in which the author maintains the audience's attention through the buildup of events, the outcome of which will soon be revealed.

Syllogism: A method of presenting a logical argument. In its most basic form, the syllogism consists of a major premise, a minor premise, and a conclusion.

Symbol: Something that suggests or stands for something else without losing its original identity. In literature, symbols combine their literal meaning with the suggestion of an abstract concept. Literary symbols are of two types: those that carry complex associations of meaning no matter what their contexts, and those that derive their suggestive meaning from their functions in specific literary works.

Symbolism: This term has two widely accepted meanings. In historical criticism, it denotes an early modernist literary movement initiated in France during the nineteenth century that reacted against the prevailing standards of realism. Writers in this movement aimed to evoke, indirectly and symbolically, an order of being beyond the material world of the five senses. Poetic expression of personal emotion figured strongly in the movement, typically by means of a private set of symbols uniquely identifiable with the individual poet. The principal aim of the Symbolists was to express in words the highly complex feelings that grew out of everyday contact with the world. In a broader sense, the term "symbolism" refers to the use of one object to represent another.

Symbolist: See *Symbolism*

Symbolist Movement: See *Symbolism*

Sympathetic Fallacy: See *Affective Fallacy*

T

Tanka: A form of Japanese poetry similar to *haiku*. A *tanka* is five lines long, with the lines containing five, seven, five, seven, and seven syllables respectively.

Terza Rima: A three-line stanza form in poetry in which the rhymes are made on the last word of each line in the following manner: the first and third lines of the first stanza, then the second line of the first stanza and the first and third lines of the second stanza, and so on with the middle line of any stanza rhyming with the first and third lines of the following stanza.

Tetrameter: See *Meter*

Textual Criticism: A branch of literary criticism that seeks to establish the authoritative text of a literary work. Textual critics typically compare all known manuscripts or printings of a single work in order to assess the meanings of differences and revisions. This procedure allows them to arrive at a definitive version that (supposedly) corresponds to the author's original intention.

Theme: The main point of a work of literature. The term is used interchangeably with thesis.

Thesis: A thesis is both an essay and the point argued in the essay. Thesis novels and thesis plays share the quality of containing a thesis which is supported through the action of the story.

Third Person: See *Point of View*

Tone: The author's attitude toward his or her audience may be deduced from the tone of the work. A formal tone may create distance or convey politeness, while an informal tone may encourage a friendly, intimate, or intrusive feeling in the reader. The author's attitude toward his or her subject matter may also be deduced from the tone of the words he or she uses in discussing it.

Tragedy: A drama in prose or poetry about a noble, courageous hero of excellent character who, because of some tragic character flaw or *hamartia*, brings ruin upon him- or herself. Tragedy treats its subjects in a dignified and serious manner, using poetic language to help evoke pity and fear and bring about catharsis, a purging of these emotions. The tragic form was practiced extensively by the ancient Greeks. In the Middle Ages, when classical works were virtually unknown, tragedy came to denote any works about the fall of persons from exalted to low conditions due to any reason: fate, vice, weakness, etc. According to the classical definition of tragedy, such works present the "pathetic"—that which evokes pity—rather than the tragic. The classical form of tragedy was revived in the sixteenth century; it flourished especially on the Elizabethan stage. In modern times, dramatists have attempted to adapt the form to the needs of modern society by drawing their heroes from the ranks of ordinary men and women and defining the nobility of these heroes in terms of spirit rather than exalted social standing.

Tragic Flaw: In a tragedy, the quality within the hero or heroine which leads to his or her downfall.

Transcendentalism: An American philosophical and religious movement, based in New England from around 1835 until the Civil War. Transcendentalism was a form of American romanticism that had its roots abroad in the works of Thomas Carlyle, Samuel Coleridge, and Johann Wolfgang von Goethe. The Transcendentalists stressed the importance of intuition and subjective experience in communication with God. They rejected religious dogma and texts in favor of mysticism and scientific naturalism. They pursued truths that lie beyond the "colorless" realms perceived by reason and the senses and were active social reformers in public education, women's rights, and the abolition of slavery.

Trickster: A character or figure common in Native American and African literature who uses his ingenuity to defeat enemies and escape difficult situations. Tricksters are most often animals, such as the spider, hare, or coyote, although they may take the form of humans as well.

Trimeter: See *Meter*

Triple Rhyme: See *Rhyme*

Trochee: See *Foot*

U

Understatement: See *Irony*

Unities: Strict rules of dramatic structure, formulated by Italian and French critics of the Renaissance and based loosely on the principles of drama discussed by Aristotle in his *Poetics.* Foremost among these rules were the three unities of action, time, and place that compelled a dramatist to: (1) construct a single plot with a beginning, middle, and end that details the causal relationships of action and character; (2) restrict the action to the events of a single day; and (3) limit the scene to a single place or city. The unities were observed faithfully by continental European writers until the Romantic Age, but they were never regularly observed in English drama. Modern dramatists are typically more concerned with a unity of impression or emotional effect than with any of the classical unities.

Urban Realism: A branch of realist writing that attempts to accurately reflect the often harsh facts of modern urban existence.

Utopia: A fictional perfect place, such as "paradise" or "heaven."

Utopian: See *Utopia*

Utopianism: See *Utopia*

V

Verisimilitude: Literally, the appearance of truth. In literary criticism, the term refers to aspects of a work of literature that seem true to the reader.

Vers de societe: See *Occasional Verse*

Vers libre: See *Free Verse*

Verse: A line of metered language, a line of a poem, or any work written in verse.

Versification: The writing of verse. Versification may also refer to the meter, rhyme, and other mechanical components of a poem.

Victorian: Refers broadly to the reign of Queen Victoria of England (1837-1901) and to anything with qualities typical of that era. For example, the qualities of smug narrowmindedness, bourgeois materialism, faith in social progress, and priggish morality are often considered Victorian. This stereotype is contradicted by such dramatic intellectual developments as the theories of Charles Darwin, Karl Marx, and Sigmund Freud (which stirred strong debates in England) and the critical attitudes of serious Victorian writers like Charles Dickens and George Eliot. In literature, the Victorian Period was the great age of the English novel, and the latter part of the era saw the rise of movements such as decadence and symbolism.

Victorian Age: See *Victorian*

Victorian Period: See *Victorian*

W

Weltanschauung: A German term referring to a person's worldview or philosophy.

Weltschmerz: A German term meaning "world pain." It describes a sense of anguish about the nature of existence, usually associated with a melancholy, pessimistic attitude.

Z

Zarzuela: A type of Spanish operetta.

Zeitgeist: A German term meaning "spirit of the time." It refers to the moral and intellectual trends of a given era.

Cumulative Author/Title Index

A

Ah, Are You Digging on My Grave?
  (Hardy): V4
Angelou, Maya
  Harlem Hopscotch: V2
  On the Pulse of Morning: V3
Angle of Geese (Momaday): V2
Anonymous
  Sir Patrick Spens: V4
  Swing Low Sweet Chariot: V1
Any Human to Another (Cullen): V3
A Pièd (McElroy): V3
Arnold, Matthew
  Dover Beach: V2
As I Walked Out One Evening
  (Auden): V4
Auden, W. H.
  As I Walked Out One Evening: V4
  Musée des Beaux Arts: V1
  The Unknown Citizen: V3
Auto Wreck (Shapiro): V3

B

Barrett, Elizabeth
  Sonnet 43: V2
Bashō, Matsuo
  Falling Upon Earth: V2
The Bean Eaters (Brooks): V2
Because I Could Not Stop for Death
  (Dickinson): V2
The Bells (Poe): V3
Blake, William
  The Tyger: V2
Brooks, Gwendolyn
  The Bean Eaters: V2
  The Sonnet-Ballad: V1

Strong Men, Riding Horses: V4
Browning, Elizabeth Barrett
  Sonnet 43: V2
Browning, Robert
  My Last Duchess: V1
Byron, Lord
  *The Destruction of
    Sennacherib*: V1

C

The Charge of the Light Brigade
  (Tennyson): V1
Chicago (Sandburg): V3
Clifton, Lucille
  Miss Rosie: V1
Coleridge, Samuel Taylor
  The Rime of the Ancient Mariner:
    V4
Concord Hymn (Emerson): V4
The Courage that My Mother Had
  (Millay): V3
The Creation (Johnson): V1
Cullen, Countee
  Any Human to Another: V3
cummings, e. e.
  l(a: V1
  old age sticks: V3

D

The Death of the Ball Turret Gunner
  (Jarrell): V2
The Death of the Hired Man (Frost):
  V4
The Destruction of Sennacherib
  (Byron): V1

Dickinson, Emily
  *Because I Could Not Stop for
    Death*: V2
  *"Hope" Is the Thing with
    Feathers*: V3
  *The Soul Selects Her Own
    Society*: V1
  This Is My Letter to the World:
    V4
*Do Not Go Gentle into that Good
  Night* (Thomas): V1
Donne, John
  Holy Sonnet 10: V2
Dove, Rita
  This Life: V1
Dover Beach (Arnold): V2

E

Eliot, T. S.
  *The Love Song of J. Alfred
    Prufrock*: V1
Emerson, Ralph Waldo
  Concord Hymn: V4

F

Falling Upon Earth (Bashō): V2
Fern Hill (Thomas): V3
Fifteen (Stafford): V2
Frost, Robert
  The Death of the Hired Man: V4
  Nothing Gold Can Stay: V3
  The Road Not Taken: V2
  *Stopping by Woods on a Snowy
    Evening*: V1

H

Hardy, Thomas
  Ah, Are You Digging on My Grave?: V4
  The Man He Killed: V3
Harlem (Hughes): V1
Harlem Hopscotch (Angelou): V2
Hawk Roosting (Hughes): V4
Hayden, Robert
  Those Winter Sundays: V1
Heaney, Seamus
  Midnight: V2
High Windows (Larkin): V3
The Highwayman (Noyes): V4
Holy Sonnet 10 (Donne): V2
"Hope" Is the Thing with Feathers (Dickinson): V3
Housman, A. E.
  When I Was One-and-Twenty: V4
Hughes, Langston
  Harlem: V1
  Mother to Son: V3
Hughes, Ted
  Hawk Roosting: V4
Hurt Hawks (Jeffers): V3
Hunger in New York City (Ortiz): V4

I

I Hear America Singing (Whitman): V3
In a Station of the Metro (Pound): V2
An Irish Airman Foresees His Death (Yeats): V1

J

Jarrell, Randall
  The Death of the Ball Turret Gunner: V2
Jeffers, Robinson
  Hurt Hawks: V3
  Shine Perishing Republic: V4
Johnson, James Weldon
  The Creation: V1

K

Keats, John
  Ode on a Grecian Urn: V1
  Ode to a Nightingale: V3
  When I Have Fears that I May Cease to Be: V2
King James Bible
  Psalm 23: V4

L

l(a (cummings): V1
Larkin, Philip
  High Windows: V3
  Toads: V4

Longfellow, Henry Wadsworth
  Paul Revere's Ride: V2
The Love Song of J. Alfred Prufrock (Eliot): V1

M

The Man He Killed (Hardy): V3
McElroy, Colleen
  A Pièd: V3
McKay, Claude
  The Tropics in New York: V4
Midnight (Heaney): V2
Millay, Edna St. Vincent
  The Courage that My Mother Had: V3
Milton, John
  [On His Blindness] Sonnet 16: V3
Mirror (Plath): V1
Miss Rosie (Clifton): V1
Momaday, N. Scott
  Angle of Geese: V2
Mother to Son (Hughes): V3
Musée des Beaux Arts (Auden): V1
My Last Duchess (Browning): V1
My Papa's Waltz (Roethke): V3

N

Not Waving but Drowning (Smith): V3
Nothing Gold Can Stay (Frost): V3
Noyes, Alfred
  The Highwayman: V4

O

O Captain! My Captain! (Whitman): V2
Ode on a Grecian Urn (Keats): V1
Ode to a Nightingale (Keats): V3
Ode to the West Wind (Shelley): V2
old age sticks (cummings): V3
[On His Blindness] Sonnet 16 (Milton): V3
On the Pulse of Morning (Angelou): V3
Ortiz, Simon
  Hunger in New York City: V4
Oysters (Sexton): V4

P

Paul Revere's Ride (Longfellow): V2
Plath, Sylvia
  Mirror: V1
Poe, Edgar Allan
  The Bells: V3
  The Raven: V1

Pound, Ezra
  In a Station of the Metro: V2
Psalm 23 (King James Bible): V4

R

The Raven (Poe): V1
The Red Wheelbarrow (Williams): V1
Richard Cory (Robinson): V4
The Rime of the Ancient Mariner (Coleridge): V4
The Road Not Taken (Frost): V2
Robinson, E. A.
  Richard Cory: V4
Roethke, Theodore
  My Papa's Waltz: V3

S

Sailing to Byzantium (Yeats): V2
Sandburg, Carl
  Chicago: V3
Sexton, Anne
  Oysters: V4
Shakespeare, William
  Sonnet 18: V2
  Sonnet 30: V4
  Sonnet 116: V3
  Sonnet 130: V1
Shapiro, Karl
  Auto Wreck: V3
Shelley, Percy Bysshe
  Ode to the West Wind: V2
Shine, Perishing Republic (Jeffers): V4
Sir Patrick Spens (Anonymous): V4
Smith, Stevie
  Not Waving but Drowning: V3
Sonnet 16 [On His Blindness] (Milton): V3
Sonnet 18 (Shakespeare): V2
Sonnet 43 (Browning): V2
Sonnet 30 (Shakespeare): V4
Sonnet 116 (Shakespeare): V3
Sonnet 130 (Shakespeare): V1
The Sonnet-Ballad (Brooks): V1
The Soul Selects Her Own Society (Dickinson): V1
Stafford, William
  Fifteen: V2
Stopping by Woods on a Snowy Evening (Frost): V1
Strong Men, Riding Horses (Brooks): V4
Swing Low Sweet Chariot (Anonymous): V1

T

Tears, Idle Tears (Tennyson): V4
Tennyson, Alfred, Lord
  The Charge of the Light Brigade: V1

Tears, Idle Tears: V4
Ulysses: V2
This Life (Dove): V1
Thomas, Dylan
    Do Not Go Gentle into that Good
      Night: V1
    Fern Hill: V3
Those Winter Sundays (Hayden): V1
Tintern Abbey (Wordsworth): V2
Toads (Larkin): V4
The Tropics in New York (McKay):
    V4
The Tyger (Blake): V2

U

Ulysses (Tennyson): V2
The Unknown Citizen (Auden): V3

W

When I Have Fears that I May Cease
    to Be (Keats): V2
When I Was One-and-Twenty
    (Housman): V4
Whitman, Walt
    I Hear America Singing: V3

    O Captain! My Captain!: V2
Williams, William Carlos
    The Red Wheelbarrow: V1
Wordsworth, William
    Lines Composed a Few Miles
      above Tintern Abbey: V2

Y

Yeats, William Butler
    An Irish Airman Foresees His
      Death: V1
    Sailing to Byzantium: V2

Cumulative Author/Title Index

Cumulative
Nationality/Ethnicity Index

Acoma Pueblo

Ortiz, Simon
   Hunger in New York City: V4

African American

Angelou, Maya
   Harlem Hopscotch: V2
   On the Pulse of Morning: V3
Brooks, Gwendolyn
   The Bean Eaters: V2
   The Sonnet-Ballad: V1
   Strong Men, Riding Horses: V4
Clifton, Lucille
   Miss Rosie: V1
Cullen, Countee
   Any Human to Another: V3
Dove, Rita
   This Life: V1
Hayden, Robert
   Those Winter Sundays: V1
Hughes, Langston
   Harlem: V1
   Mother to Son: V3
Johnson, James Weldon
   The Creation: V1
McElroy, Colleen
   A Pièd: V3

American

Angelou, Maya
   Harlem Hopscotch: V2
   On the Pulse of Morning: V3
Auden, W. H.
   As I Walked Out One Evening: V4

Musée des Beaux Arts: V1
The Unknown Citizen: V3
Brooks, Gwendolyn
   The Bean Eaters: V2
   The Sonnet-Ballad: V1
   Strong Men, Riding Horses: V4
Clifton, Lucille
   Miss Rosie: V1
Cullen, Countee
   Any Human to Another: V3
cummings, e. e.
   l(a: V1
   old age sticks: V3
Dickinson, Emily
   Because I Could Not Stop for Death: V2
   "Hope" Is the Thing with Feathers: V3
   The Soul Selects Her Own Society: V1
   This Is My Letter to the World: V4
Dove, Rita
   This Life: V1
Eliot, T. S.
   The Love Song of J. Alfred Prufrock: V1
Emerson, Ralph Waldo
   Concord Hymn: V4
Frost, Robert
   The Death of the Hired Man: V4
   Nothing Gold Can Stay: V3
   The Road Not Taken: V2
   Stopping by Woods on a Snowy Evening: V1
Hayden, Robert
   Those Winter Sundays: V1
Hughes, Langston
   Harlem: V1

Mother to Son: V3
Jarrell, Randall
   The Death of the Ball Turret Gunner: V2
Jeffers, Robinson
   Hurt Hawks: V3
   Shine, Perishing Republic: V4
Johnson, James Weldon
   The Creation: V1
Longfellow, Henry Wadsworth
   Paul Revere's Ride: V2
McElroy, Colleen
   A Pièd: V3
McKay, Claude
   The Tropics in New York: V4
Millay, Edna St. Vincent
   The Courage that My Mother Had: V3
Momaday, N. Scott
   Angle of Geese: V2
Ortiz, Simon
   Hunger in New York City: V4
Plath, Sylvia
   Mirror: V1
Poe, Edgar Allan
   The Bells: V3
   The Raven: V1
Pound, Ezra
   In a Station of the Metro: V2
Robinson, E. A.
   Richard Cory: V4
Roethke, Theodore
   My Papa's Waltz: V3
Sandburg, Carl
   Chicago: V3
Sexton, Anne
   Oysters: V4

Shapiro, Karl
Auto Wreck: V3
Stafford, William
Fifteen: V2
Whitman, Walt
I Hear America Singing: V3
O Captain! My Captain!: V2
Williams, William Carlos
The Red Wheelbarrow: V1

Cherokee

Momaday, N. Scott
Angle of Geese: V2

English

Arnold, Matthew
Dover Beach: V2
Auden, W. H.
As I Walked Out One Evening: V4
Musée des Beaux Arts: V1
The Unknown Citizen: V3
Blake, William
The Tyger: V2
Browning, Elizabeth Barrett
Sonnet 43: V2
Browning, Robert
My Last Duchess: V1
Byron, Lord
The Destruction of Sennacherib:
V1
Coleridge, Samuel Taylor
The Rime of the Ancient Mariner:
V4
Donne, John
Holy Sonnet 10: V2
Eliot, T. S.
*The Love Song of J. Alfred
Prufrock*: V1
Hardy, Thomas
*Ah, Are You Digging on My
Grave?*: V4
The Man He Killed: V3
Housman, A. E.
When I Was One-and-Twenty: V4
Hughes, Ted
Hawk Roosting: V4
Keats, John
Ode on a Grecian Urn: V1
Ode to a Nightingale: V3

*When I Have Fears that I May
Cease to Be*: V2
Larkin, Philip
High Windows: V3
Toads: V4
Milton, John
*[On His Blindness]
Sonnet 16*: V3
Noyes, Alfred
The Highwayman: V4
Shakespeare, William
Sonnet 18: V2
Sonnet 30: V4
Sonnet 116: V3
Sonnet 130: V1
Shelley, Percy Bysshe
Ode to the West Wind: V2
Smith, Stevie
Not Waving but Drowning: V3
Tennyson, Alfred, Lord
*The Charge of the Light
Brigade*: V1
Tears, Idle Tears: V4
Ulysses: V2
Williams, William Carlos
The Red Wheelbarrow: V1
Wordsworth, William
*Lines Composed a Few Miles
above Tintern Abbey*: V2

German

Roethke, Theodore
My Papa's Waltz: V3

Irish

Heaney, Seamus
Midnight: V2
Yeats, William Butler
*An Irish Airman Foresees His
Death*: V1
Sailing to Byzantium: V2

Jamaican

McKay, Claude
The Tropics in New York: V4

Japanese

Bashō, Matsuo
Falling Upon Earth: V2

Jewish

Shapiro, Karl
Auto Wreck: V3

Kiowa

Momaday, N. Scott
Angle of Geese: V2

Native American

Momaday, N. Scott
Angle of Geese: V2
Ortiz, Simon
Hunger in New York City: V4

Russian

Shapiro, Karl
Auto Wreck: V3

Scottish

Byron, Lord
*The Destruction of
Sennacherib*: V1

Spanish

Williams, William Carlos
The Red Wheelbarrow: V1

Swedish

Sandburg, Carl
Chicago: V3

Welsh

Thomas, Dylan
*Do Not Go Gentle into that Good
Night*: V1
Fern Hill: V3

Subject/Theme Index

*Boldface denotes dicussion in *Themes* section.

A

Abandonment
   Ah, Are You Digging on My Grave?: 11
Alienation and Loneliness
   The Rime of the Ancient Mariner: 144
   This Is My Letter to the World: 234
   The Tropics in New York: 256
Allegory
   As I Walked Out One Evening: 14, 16, 18
Alliteration
   The Rime of the Ancient Mariner: 135, 140
American Dream
   Strong Men, Riding Horses: 211
American Northeast
   Richard Cory: 116
American West
   Shine Perishing Republic: 161
Angels
   The Rime of the Ancient Mariner: 140
Art and Experience
   This Is My Letter to the World: 234
Atonement
   The Rime of the Ancient Mariner: 125–126, 142, 147

B

Beauty
   The Rime of the Ancient Mariner: 136–39, 142–43

C

Change and Transformation
   Oysters: 93
Christianity
   The Rime of the Ancient Mariner: 134–35, 137, 139, 144
Courage and Cowardice
   Strong Men, Riding Horses: 211
The Covenant
   Psalm 23: 105
Creativity
   This Is My Letter to the World: 233–34
Crime and Criminals
   The Highwayman: 65, 69–72
   The Rime of the Ancient Mariner: 125, 138, 141–42, 147
Cruelty
   The Highwayman: 70–71
   The Rime of the Ancient Mariner: 142
Culture Clash
   The Tropics in New York: 256
Custom and Tradition
   Hunger in New York City: 81
Cycle of Life
   As I Walked Out One Evening: 18
   Shine, Perishing Republic: 164

D

Death
   Ah, Are You Digging on My Grave?: 11–13
   As I Walked Out One Evening: 16–18, 20
   Hawk Roosting: 56
   The Highwayman: 70–72
   Psalm 23: 102–05
   The Rime of the Ancient Mariner: 133, 135–44, 147
   Sir Patrick Spens: 180
   Tears, Idle Tears: 222
Dialogue
   As I Walked Out One Evening: 16–18
Drama
   Sonnet 30: 192
Dreams and Visions
   The Rime of the Ancient Mariner: 136, 138, 140–42, 147
Duty and Responsibility
   The Death of the Hired Man: 46
   Toads: 246

E

Emotions
   The Highwayman: 72
   The Rime of the Ancient Mariner: 134
   This Is My Letter to the World: 35
Eternity
   As I Walked Out One Evening: 14, 16–18
   The Highwayman: 71

Europe
    As I Walked Out One Evening:
        14–16, 19–20
    The Highwayman: 69, 73
    The Rime of the Ancient Mariner:
        126, 145–46
Evil
    The Rime of the Ancient Mariner:
        134
Exile
    Psalm 23: 106–107

F

Fall From Grace
    The Rime of the Ancient Mariner:
        134, 147
Farm and Rural Life
    This Is My Letter to the World: 36
Fate and Chance
    The Rime of the Ancient Mariner:
        125, 141
Fear and Terror
    Psalm 23: 103–04
    The Rime of the Ancient Mariner:
        136–38, 140–42, 145
Foreshadowing
    The Highwayman: 69, 71
    The Rime of the Ancient Mariner:
        138–39
Forgiveness
    The Rime of the Ancient Mariner:
        141–42
Freedom
    When I Was One-and-Twenty: 269
Friendship
    Sonnet 30: 194

G

Ghost
    The Rime of the Ancient Mariner:
        133, 135–36, 138–40, 142, 147
God
    Psalm 23: 102–05, 107
    The Rime of the Ancient Mariner:
        134, 140–42, 144, 147
God and Religion
    Shine, Perishing Republic: 164
Goodness
    Psalm 23: 103–05, 107
Gothicism
    The Rime of the Ancient Mariner:
        125, 133, 135–36, 138–39, 141
Guilt
    The Rime of the Ancient Mariner:
        135, 142

H

Happiness and Gaiety
    The Rime of the Ancient Mariner:
        133, 134, 140, 143

Hatred
    Psalm 23: 104
Hope
    The Rime of the Ancient Mariner:
        135–36, 140–41
The Human Condition
    *Ah, Are You Digging on My
        Grave?:* 4
Humor
    *Ah, Are You Digging on My
        Grave?:* 11, 13

I

Identity
    Hunger in New York City: 81
Imagery and Symbolism
    As I Walked Out One Evening:
        16–18
    The Highwayman: 69, 71–73
    Psalm 23: 102–04
    The Rime of the Ancient Mariner:
        125, 133–35, 138–39, 147
    This Is My Letter to the World:
        234–35
Imagination
    The Rime of the Ancient Mariner:
        142–43
Ireland
    The Rime of the Ancient Mariner:
        145
Irony
    The Rime of the Ancient Mariner:
        134–35, 138

J

Japan
    The Highwayman: 73–74
Judaism
    Psalm 23: 102–07

K

Killers and Killing
    The Highwayman: 65, 70–71
    The Rime of the Ancient Mariner:
        134, 142, 145
Knowledge and Ignorance
    When I Was One-and-Twenty:
        269

L

Landscape
    As I Walked Out One Evening:
        14, 16–19, 21
    Psalm 23: 103, 107
Law and Order
    The Highwayman: 72
Literary Criticism
    *Ah, Are You Digging on My
        Grave?:* 12

Loneliness
    *Ah, Are You Digging on My
        Grave?:* 12
    The Rime of the Ancient Mariner:
        137–38, 144
    This Is My Letter to the World:
        233, 234, 237
Love
    Tears, Idle Tears: 222
Love and Passion
    As I Walked Out One Evening:
        14, 16–20
    The Highwayman: 65, 68–73
    The Rime of the Ancient Mariner:
        126, 138, 141–42, 144, 146
Loyalty
    As I Walked Out One Evening:
        14, 16, 18

M

Marriage
    *Ah, Are You Digging on My
        Grave?:* 11–12
    The Rime of the Ancient Mariner:
        132–33
Memory and Reminiscence
    Sonnet 30: 194
Middle East
    Psalm 23: 103, 105–07
Modernism
    The Highwayman: 65–66, 73
Monarchy
    Psalm 23: 105
Morals and Morality
    The Rime of the Ancient Mariner:
        141–45, 147
Murder
    The Rime of the Ancient Mariner:
        134, 139, 141–44
Music
    As I Walked Out One Evening:
        17–20
    Psalm 23: 102, 106
    The Rime of the Ancient Mariner:
        133, 139, 144
Mystery and Intrigue
    The Highwayman: 65, 68, 70–71

N

Narration
    The Highwayman: 65–66, 68–69, 74
Natural Law
    Hawk Roosting: 57
Nature
    Concord Hymn: 32
    Psalm 23: 103
    The Rime of the Ancient Mariner:
        133, 135–37, 139–40, 142,
        146–47
    This Is My Letter to the World:
        234–37

Nature and Its Meaning
    Hunger in New York City: 81

O

The Outlaw
    The Highwayman: 71

P

Patriotism
    Concord Hymn: 32
    Shine, Perishing Republic: 163
Perception
    The Rime of the Ancient Mariner:
      134, 136, 138, 142–44,
      146–47
Permanence
    Concord Hymn: 32
    The Highwayman: 69–70
    Tears, Idle Tears: 223
Philosophical Ideas
    The Rime of the Ancient Mariner:
      145–46
Politics
    The Highwayman: 74
    The Rime of the Ancient Mariner:
      145–46
Power and Authority
    Sir Patrick Spens: 179
Protection and Security
    Psalm 23: 104
Public vs. Private Life
    Richard Cory: 118
Punishment
    The Rime of the Ancient Mariner:
      125, 135, 139, 141–42, 147

R

Religion and Religious Thought
    Psalm 23: 104, 106–07

The Rime of the Ancient Mariner:
    139, 142, 145
Religious Works
    Psalm 23: 103, 106–07
Reminiscence and Memory
    The Tropics in New York: 256
Rites of Passage
    Oysters: 93
    Psalm 23: 105
    When I Was One-and-Twenty:
      270

S

Sea and Sea Adventures
    The Rime of the Ancient Mariner:
      126, 132, 134–35, 137–40,
      142–45
Search for Self
    Toads: 246
Sentimentality
    Ah, Are You Digging on My
      Grave?: 5
Setting
    The Rime of the Ancient Mariner:
      133
Sex
    Oysters: 93
Sex and Sexuality
    The Highwayman: 66, 68–70,
      71–72
Sin
    As I Walked Out One Evening: 17
    The Rime of the Ancient Mariner:
      134–36, 139–42, 147
Soul
    The Rime of the Ancient Mariner:
      134, 137–38, 142, 144
Spirituality
    Psalm 23: 102–06
    The Rime of the Ancient Mariner:
      134, 138, 140–41

Storms and Weather Conditions
    The Highwayman: 68, 71
    The Rime of the Ancient Mariner:
      133, 135, 138–40, 142–45
Strength and Weakness
    Strong Men, Riding Horses: 211
Success and Failure
    Richard Cory: 118
Supernatural
    The Rime of the Ancient Mariner:
      125, 133, 135–38, 140–41

T

Time
    As I Walked Out One Evening: 18
Time and Change
    As I Walked Out One Evening: 18
Trust
    Psalm 23: 102–04

U

Understanding
    The Rime of the Ancient Mariner:
      126

V

Violence and Cruelty
    Hawk Roosting: 57

W

War, the Military, and Soldier Life
    The Highwayman: 65, 69–73
Wealth and Poverty
    Richard Cory: 118
Wildlife
    The Rime of the Ancient Mariner:
      125, 134–35, 137–38, 141–44,
      147

Subject/Theme Index